THE WORLD BIBLIOGRAPHICAL SERIES

This series, which is principally designed for the English speaker, will eventually cover every country in the world, each in a separate volume comprising annotated entries on works dealing with its history, geography, economy and politics; and with its people, their culture, customs, religion and social organization. Attention will also be paid to current living conditions – housing, education, newspapers, clothing, etc.– that are all too often ignored in standard bibliographies; and to those particular aspects relevant to individual countries. Each volume seeks to achieve, by use of careful selectivity and critical assessment of the literature, an expression of the country and an appreciation of its nature and national aspirations, to guide the reader towards an understanding of its importance. The keynote of the series is to provide, in a uniform format, an interpretation of each country that will express its culture, its place in the world, and the qualities and background that make it unique. The views expressed in individual volumes, however, are not necessarily those of the publisher.

VOLUMES IN THE SERIES

1 *Yugoslavia*, John J. Horton
2 *Lebanon*, Shereen Khairallah
3 *Lesotho*, Shelagh M. Willet and David Ambrose
4 *Rhodesia/Zimbabwe*, Oliver B. Pollack and Karen Pollack
5 *Saudi Arabia*, Frank A. Clements
6 *USSR*, Anthony Thompson
7 *South Africa*, Reuben Musiker
8 *Malawi*, Robert B. Boeder
9 *Guatemala*, Woodman B. Franklin
10 *Pakistan*, David Taylor
11 *Uganda*, Robert L. Collison
12 *Malaysia*, Ian Brown and Rajeswary Ampalavanar
13 *France*, Frances Chambers
14 *Panama*, Eleanor DeSelms Langstaff
15 *Hungary*, Thomas Kabdebo
16 *USA*, Sheila R. Herstein and Naomi Robbins
17 *Greece*, Richard Clogg and Mary Jo Clogg
18 *New Zealand*, R. F. Grover
19 *Algeria*, Richard I. Lawless
20 *Sri Lanka*, Vijaya Samaraweera
21 *Belize*, Ralph Lee Woodward, Jr.
23 *Luxembourg*, Carlo Hury and Jul Christophory
24 *Swaziland*, Balam Nyeko
25 *Kenya*, Robert L. Collison
26 *India*, Brijen K. Gupta and Datta S. Kharbas
27 *Turkey*, Merel Güçlü
28 *Cyprus*, P. M. Kitromilides and M. L. Evriviades
29 *Oman*, Frank A. Clements
31 *Finland*, J. E. O. Screen
32 *Poland*, Richard C. Lewański
33 *Tunisia*, Allan M. Findlay, Anne M. Findlay and Richard I. Lawless
34 *Scotland*, Eric G. Grant
35 *China*, Peter Cheng
36 *Qatar*, P. T. H. Unwin
37 *Iceland*, John J. Horton
38 *Nepal*, John Whelpton
39 *Haiti*, Frances Chambers
40 *Sudan*, M. W. Daly
41 *Vatican City State*, Michael J. Walsh
42 *Iraq*, A. J. Abdulrahman
43 *United Arab Emirates*, Frank A. Clements
44 *Nicaragua*, Ralph Lee Woodward, Jr.
45 *Jamaica*, K. E. Ingram
46 *Australia*, I. Kepars

47 *Morocco*, Anne M. Findlay, Allan M. Findlay and Richard I. Lawless
48 *Mexico*, Naomi Robbins
49 *Bahrain*, P. T. H. Unwin
50 *The Yemens*, G. Rex Smith
51 *Zambia*, Anne M. Bliss and J. A. Rigg
52 *Puerto Rico*, Elena E. Cevallos
53 *Namibia*, Stanley Schoeman and Elna Schoeman
54 *Tanzania*, Colin Darch
55 *Jordan*, Ian J. Seccombe
56 *Kuwait*, Frank A. Clements
57 *Brazil*, Solena V. Bryant
58 *Israel*, Esther M. Snyder (preliminary compilation E. Kreiner)
59 *Romania*, Andrea Deletant and Dennis Deletant
60 *Spain*, Graham J. Shields
61 *Atlantic Ocean*, H. G. R. King
63 *Cameroon*, Mark W. DeLancey and Peter J. Schraeder
64 *Malta*, John Richard Thackrah
65 *Thailand*, Michael Watts
66 *Austria*, Denys Salt with the assistance of Arthur Farrand Radley
67 *Norway*, Leland B. Sather
68 *Czechoslovakia*, David Short
69 *Irish Republic*, Michael Owen Shannon
70 *Pacific Basin and Oceania*, Gerald W. Fry and Rufino Mauricio
71 *Portugal*, P. T. H. Unwin
72 *West Germany*, Donald S. Detwiler and Ilse E. Detwiler
73 *Syria*, Ian J. Seccombe
74 *Trinidad and Tobago*, Frances Chambers
76 *Barbados*, Robert B. Potter and Graham M. S. Dann
77 *East Germany*, Ian Wallace
78 *Mozambique*, Colin Darch
79 *Libya*, Richard I. Lawless
80 *Sweden*, Leland B. Sather and Alan Swanson
81 *Iran*, Reza Navabpour
82 *Dominica*, Robert A. Myers
83 *Denmark*, Kenneth E. Miller
84 *Paraguay*, R. Andrew Nickson
85 *Indian Ocean*, Julia J. Gotthold with the assistance of Donald W. Gotthold
86 *Egypt*, Ragai, N. Makar
87 *Gibraltar*, Graham J. Shields
88 *The Netherlands*, Peter King and Michael Wintle
89 *Bolivia*, Gertrude M. Yeager
90 *Papua New Guinea*, Fraiser McConnell
91 *The Gambia*, David P. Gamble
92 *Somalia*, Mark W. DeLancey, Sheila L. Elliott, December Green, Kenneth J. Menkhaus, Mohammad Haji Moqtar and Peter J. Schraeder
93 *Brunei*, Sylvia C. Engelen Krausse and Gerald H. Krausse
94 *Albania*, William B. Bland
95 *Singapore*, Stella R. Quah and Jon S. T. Quah
96 *Guyana*, Frances Chambers
97 *Chile*, Harold Blakemore
98 *El Salvador*, Ralph Lee Woodward, Jr.
99 *The Arctic*, H.G.R. King
100 *Nigeria*, Robert A. Myers
101 *Ecuador*, David Corkhill
102 *Uruguay*, Henry Finch with the assistance of Alicia Casas de Barrán
103 *Japan*, Frank Joseph Shulman
104 *Belgium*, R.C. Riley
105 *Macau*, Richard Louis Edmonds
106 *Philippines*, Jim Richardson
107 *Bulgaria*, Richard J. Crampton
108 *The Bahamas*, Paul G. Boultbee
109 *Peru*, John Robert Fisher
110 *Venezuela*, D. a. G. Waddell
111 *Dominican Republic* Kai Schoenhals
112 *Colombia*, Robert H. Davis
113 *Taiwan*, Wei-chin Lee
114 *Switzerland*, Heinz K. Meier and Regula A. Meier

To Heinz
who had the courage to start this book
but not the joy of seeing it published.

Contents

Contents

Contents

Introduction

Switzerland is perhaps unique in the world in that it has mastered most of the problems created by cultural pluralism. Indeed, it may well serve as an example to other countries and regions of how diverse groups of people can be integrated into a well-functioning nation. No other country peacefully accommodates such ethnically, linguistically and religiously diverse people within such a small geographical area: Switzerland is a country of 15,941 square miles with a population of 6,500,000.

Travelling on the national highways, a visitor can cross Switzerland from north to south in about two hours and from east to west in three. Of course, by doing so, he would miss almost everything that makes Switzerland interesting. A more leisurely traveller, alert to his surroundings, soon notices curious things on his journey. Villages and towns change their character every few dozen miles; farmhouses are built using different materials and in distinctly different styles. In the northern, eastern and central parts of the country the traveller would hear the people speak a language that sounds like German but is so different from the German spoken north of Lake Constance and the Rhine that a person who speaks high German can hardly understand it. What is more, the dialects change from place to place and from valley to valley: rather than encountering one Alemannic dialect, Schwyzerdütsch, he would find people in Zurich speaking slightly, but distinctly, differently from those in Basel, Bern, Luzern, or any other place within the German-speaking regions.

Just a few miles west of the nation's capital, Bern, the traveller who crosses the small Saane river would suddenly find himself among French-speaking people. South of the mighty St. Gotthard Pass he would need Italian to converse with the native population of Canton Ticino, and in the mountain valleys of Canton Graubünden he would hear Romansh, a romance language which is spoken nowhere else in the world. That this language survives in at least three distinct forms, which are used by less than one per cent of the entire Swiss population, would add to his amazement. An attentive traveller would also notice that the churches he sees everywhere belong either to the Catholic or to the Reformed Protestant religion, with no clearly distinct pattern across the country and with most larger communities having places of worship for both faiths. Despite Zwingli and Calvin, or perhaps because of them, the Swiss have no need for the notion of separation of Church and State: these churches are supported by income taxes levied by the communities.

Statistics from 1988 provide the following information about the Swiss populace: forty-eight per cent are Catholic, forty-four per cent Protestant, eight per cent other; the language distribution is sixty-five per cent German, eighteen per cent French, ten per cent Italian, one per cent Romansh, six per cent other; and politically, there are twenty-three cantons (states) three of which are themselves subdivided. How did the Swiss transform the potentially overwhelming problems of cultural and political pluralism into the distinct asset that it has become?

The reasons for Switzerland's success are to be found largely in the past of a country which was founded in 1291 and which takes pride in its 700-year history. The Swiss Confederation, despite its many constituent parts, is an organically grown entity. It has evolved over centuries as a result of an often violent quest to gain and maintain independence. It is the spirit of this quest which Friedrich Schiller captures in *Wilhelm Tell*. The Thirteen Old Cantons struggled for over three hundred years, but complete independence from the Hapsburg rulers of the Holy Roman Empire did not become a reality until 1648, one hundred years after the Reformation. The old confederacy came to an end with the French Revolution and the Vienna Congress of 1815 which produced the country's present boundaries and which required Switzerland to adopt the perpetual neutrality that has served it so well to this day. Modern Switzerland came into existence in 1848 with a federal constitution that was modelled in part after the Constitution of the United States. Only then did the cantons cede enough of their power to allow the federal government in Bern to take over the functions typical of a modern government. The drafters of the constitution ensured that each of the cantons and the different minorities were treated fairly and were unhampered in their adherence to their cultural identity. The cantons jealously safeguarded their rights, especially in the fields of education, religion and taxation.

The bicameral Federal Assembly consists of a *Ständerat* (Council of States), which has two representatives from each canton regardless of size or population, and the *Nationalrat* (National Council) which has 200 members, chosen from election districts based on population. The executive branch is the *Bundesrat* (Federal Council) and consists of seven members who are elected according to an unwritten convention so as to represent all constituencies. The presidency of the Federal Council rotates among the seven members annually in order of seniority in office. The Federal Tribunal, the highest court, was placed in French-speaking Lausanne, while Zurich as the largest city received the only federal university, the Swiss Institute of Technology founded in 1855.

Excellent education and solid professional training are of prime importance for a country that has practically no natural resources. Switzerland has one of the oldest state school systems, dating back to the early 1800 s when elementary schooling became both free and compulsory. Vocational training which had once been the privilege of the guilds, is supervised by the government and conforms to high standards. Swiss watchmaking is a prime example of what quality workmanship through training can accomplish. Switzerland also participated in the industrialization of Europe as the success of its chemical, machine and textile industries indicates. The giant Swiss pharmaceutical companies are international household names.

Foodstuffs such as chocolate and cheese are, of course, synonymous with Switzerland. The natural beauty of the country and its folkloric traditions have lured many famous foreign visitors to its shores and mountains, even before the advent of modern tourism. The development of a first-rate hotel industry has solidified Switzerland's position as a prime tourist destination. Its super-efficient railroads, highways and world-renowned airline provide quick access to Switzerland's cultural centres, shops and ski slopes.

Switzerland's neutrality and stability have historically provided a safe haven for foreign moneys and together with its industriousness and thriftiness have made it a world leader in the field of banking and insurance. Per capita income is among the highest in the world while unemployment is among the lowest of the industrialized countries. However, Switzerland must face economic challenges in the light of the development of the European Community, an organization which it chose not to join.

Public support of the arts together with the contributions of Swiss artists and writers of international renown have softened the stereotype of the tight-fisted, workaholic, somewhat parochial Swiss. Indeed, the enlightened accomplishments of Switzerland's citizens in industry, science and humanitarian endeavours have been widely acclaimed. Notwithstanding this, the Swiss would, of course, rather forget that women only gained the right to vote in national elections in 1971.

Nevertheless, the peaceful, if not placid, waters of Swiss domestic tranquillity have been troubled at times and doubtless will be again.

During World War I, for example, a deep and dangerous rift separated the German and the French Swiss. Most of the former ardently supported Germany and its cause, while the latter gave their sympathies to France. Tensions repeatedly reached frightening heights but were allayed through deft political manoeuvres. Differences lingered into the inter-war period when a majority of German Swiss voted against joining the League of Nations, but the pro-League vote cast in French Switzerland overrode the opposition. World War II found the country much more united in its resistance to Nazi Germany. The question of whether Switzerland, birthplace of the Red Cross, had lived up to its reputation as a refuge for the persecuted and oppressed troubled the nation only in retrospect.

More recently, new problems have emerged concerning Switzerland's policies toward foreign workers. The workers were desperately needed to ensure the continued expansion of Switzerland's booming economy but, at the same time, the new arrivals were often resented. The government has controlled the considerable influx of 'guest workers' by initiating restrictions and those already resident in the country have slowly found acceptance, and have contributed in many ways to the host country. Then there are the many asylants for whom a permanent residence must be found. The separatist movement in the Jura mountains at one time posed a threat to Switzerland's harmonious existence, but the Jura problem was largely resolved in 1978 when a new canton was carved out of the canton of Bern along religious lines.

Domestic political tranquillity has also been disturbed by the young, some of whom deride the materialism of their elders and express their feelings in demonstrations. In addition, drug addiction amongst the young is a serious problem and claims its grim toll. Moreover, a significant portion of the population is also seeking the abolition of the Swiss army and furthermore there is much concern for the environment which tends to pit the 'greens' against economic growth.

Switzerland's attitude toward cultural differences and minority demands are part and parcel of a strong national fabric in which the identity of the country, and its component groups and individuals, is rooted. Swiss federalism in all its many facets presents one of the most encouraging examples in our time of how creative solutions and cautious compromise can accommodate internal differences. Open discourse, an extensive social welfare system, and Switzerland's unique reliance on the national referendum are just some of the tools with which the Swiss will confront their problems as the nation moves towards the 21st century.

The bibliography

It goes without saying that a bibliography of this size, covering so many areas, can neither be comprehensive nor exhaustive. Our aim was to provide a representative sample of works available in each of the subject areas, with titles that would make it possible for interested readers to dig deeper wherever they desire to do so. We believe that our annotations are of a substantive nature and will help readers to get a good idea about the content of the work in question. Taken as a whole, they provide a storehouse of information about Switzerland found in few other places.

In the spirit of the Clio *World Bibliographical Series*, first priority in the selection of titles was given to English-language works. In many countries where only one language is spoken, the first foreign language for translation is English. This is not so in the case of Switzerland, where the three official languages German, French and Italian, clearly have precedence over English despite the fact that only a relatively small readership has access to the work in question. Thus, we were obliged to include a good number of German-, French- and Italian-language titles, either because no English sources could be found on a specific topic, or because we felt a particular area could not otherwise be covered, or because the work in question was of special importance.

Because they have become fixed in common English-language usage, the names of Zürich and Genève are consistently used in their Anglicized forms of Zurich and Geneva, except when they appear in titles in their local language form. All other place names are given in the prevailing language of their locality, i.e., Basel, not Basle, Bern, not Berne, Luzern, not Lucerne, etc., expect where their Anglicized form is used in an English-language title. The same rules are applied to the names of the cantons.

In most sections of this bibliography entries are listed alphabetically by author or editor, or, where there is neither author nor editor, sponsoring organization. In a few instances, entries are listed alphabetically by title (i.e., journals), by names of subjects (i.e., famous visitors), or chronologically (i.e., individual writers, architects and artists).

In the 'Periodicals' chapter we have included a selective list of some of the most important publications. However, the catalogue *Schweizer Zeitschriftenverzeichnis* (q.v.) published every five years, contains some 4,200 titles of periodicals current during the period of coverage. The complete inventory of all journals, magazines, newspapers, yearbooks, and serials ever published in Switzerland together with their publication history can be found on the cards of the periodicals catalogue of the Swiss National Library in Bern. The page numbers given for periodicals are approximate ones, taken from recent issues (1988) of the journals concerned. Circulation figures, where given, are from the 1989 issue of the *Swiss PR & media directory* (q.v.).

Newspapers are listed alphabetically by place of publication. The circulation figures, rounded off, are from the *Swiss PR and media directory* (q.v.) as are the indications of the political leanings of the papers. Only papers with a circulation of at least 50,000 are included.

Acknowledgements
I would like to express our gratitude for the assistance we were given in the course of compiling this bibliography. The staff of the Landesbibliothek in Bern, where we spent two summers, were most helpful in tracking down material. The Swiss cultural foundation 'Pro Helvetia' donated a good number of books and also provided some financial support. From that office, I would like to single out the services of Hanne Zweifel. Our son Peter read the entire manuscript and his critical comments were of enormous help, as was the encouragement we received from our other children Barbara, Christina and Markus. Dr. Lukas Burckhardt in Bern assisted me in the final stages by checking some citations in the Landesbibliothek. The Department of History at Old Dominion University granted my husband research leave that permitted him to devote himself full-time to this project, and I received a grant from the University's Arts & Letters Committee for the Support of Research and Scholarly Activities for printing and mailing needs.

Finally, my deepest thanks go to my husband who fully aware of his approaching death kept on making entries on the computer at his bedside and encouraged me to do the same. This truly was a labour of love.

Regula A. Meier
Norfolk, Virginia, USA
May 1990

The Country and its People

Short accounts

1 **Focus on Switzerland: the historical evolution; political institutions.**
Pierre Cordey, Pier Felice Brachi. Lausanne: Swiss Office for the Development of Trade, 1982. 2nd ed. 152p.

The first part of this clear and concise publication provides an overview of Swiss history from the time of the Helvetians to the World Wars of the 20th century. The second part deals with the country's political institutions and describes the workings of the federal, cantonal, and local governments, the make-up of the political parties, the structure of the legal system, and discusses Switzerland's foreign affairs. This richly illustrated booklet is a good, convenient introduction to the topics addressed.

2 **Ticking along with the Swiss.**
Edited by Dianne Dicks. Waterford, Republic of Ireland: Friendly Press, 1988. 214p.

Dicks has assembled a collection of personal and entertaining stories about living in Switzerland told by English-speaking writers, interpreters, teachers, and journalists who have become well acquainted with the country and its inhabitants. Her book is not a travel guide, nor the product of scientific study; it contains no propaganda and is not written to teach anything. Its aim is to entertain the reader and this objective is achieved in a pleasant and humorous way.

3 **Switzerland: land, people, economy.**
Aubrey Diem. Kitchener, Ontario: Aljon, 1986. 2nd ed., 1988. 162p. maps. bibliog.

Diem is the author of several articles in *The Geographical Magazine* including: 'Valley renaissance in the High Alps: Val d'Anniviers' (April 1980, p. 492-97); 'Swiss tame the alpine snows' (December 1982, p. 682-89); and 'The Alps' (August 1984, p. 414-20). This book is filled with factual information on the history of Switzerland, its population, economy, transport system, and the 'physiographic divisions'. There are some statistical tables and diagrams and numerous black-and-white photographs. Geographical names are consistently given in the language of the region (Genève and Lac Léman, for example), something the editors of this bibliography have not dared to do.

4 **Once upon an alp.**

Eugene V. Epstein. Zurich; Freiburg, FRG: Atlantis, 1968. 165p.

Epstein is an astute observer of little things in the daily routine of Swiss life which, while quite natural to the Swiss, seem peculiar to the foreigner. The love of *Fondue*, *Schüblig* sausage and *Kirsch*, the universal excuse the *Föhn* wind provides for laziness and headaches, the popularity of newspapers in a land where nothing much happens, the experience of learning how to ski or to play the Swiss national card game *Jass*, the variety of dialects and the impossibility for a non-native to learn them are all topics that provide the fabric for Epstein's funny stories. Epstein has written four more books with further humorous vignettes about the idiosyncracies of the Swiss, namely *Lend me your alphorn* (1977), *Take me to your chalet* (1982), *Malice in wonderland: titillating tales of life in Switzerland* (1985), and *Who put the* **wit** *in Switzerland?* (1988), all published by Benteli, Bern.

5 **Switzerland.**

Dominique Fabre, translated from the French by Jean Lloyd. London; New York: Viking Vista Books, 1961. 192p.

This richly illustrated booklet provides to a considerable extent a caricature of Switzerland. Intended to be humorous according to the Gallic wit of a French journalist, it offers a sometimes distorted view of Switzerland and its inhabitants. Fabre speaks of a deep-seated hostility and hatred between French- and German-speaking Swiss. 'Resentment rages, both ways, between Geneva and Zürich, contaminating everything in its path', he exaggerates. The Swiss woman, Fabre says, reigns supreme in the home: 'the banner which she brandishes in the name of the sacred family virtues is a duster!' The Swiss male, on the other hand, 'is practically a cipher in his own home'. When he comes home, 'every triumphant male . . . immediately falls under the sway of his wife, and makes his first gesture of abdication on the threshold when he puts on the slippers'. Similarly outrageous (or funny?) statements can be found elsewhere in the book. The example of the French-Swiss writer Ramuz shows that 'in spite of himself, the native of Switzerland, the Swiss artist, is condemned to the average in everything, and is barred, by the cruel twist of fate, from being exceptional', which is simply nonsense. To be fair, other parts of the booklet, the chapter on Swiss neutrality, for example, contain more valid and useful information and observations.

6 **On top of the world. Switzerland: a survey.**

Nicholas Harman. *The Economist* (30 October 1982), 20p. maps.

The reporter for *The Economist* went to Switzerland, 'the richest country in the industrial world', 'to admire sound money, small government and direct democracy'. To his surprise he learned that not only do these things actually exist, but that they also work reasonably well. As a matter of fact, 'he found the Swiss much more interesting, and much less complacent, than their reputation leads foreigners to expect'. This brief survey, half the space of which is taken up by full-page advertisements by Swiss firms, succeeds in presenting in a lively and positive manner the characteristics and problems of Switzerland in the 1980s. The captions to some of the photographs are indicative of the topics covered and the journalese of *The Economist* and its reporter: 'The citizen takes the initiative: but what if nobody votes?' 'Drop out of the army, and the landing is hard.' 'These trains climb hills: so do deficits.' 'The seats are hard, but the tourists' franc is getting harder.' 'Switzerland moves on predestinate grooves' and so forth. Harman concludes that the degree of personal frugality which the Swiss, against all temptation, have preserved 'could be their best of all assets'.

7 **Tell me a Swiss joke! Humour from Switzerland. Believe it or not, it exists!**
Edited by René Hildbrand, translated by Birgit Rommel. Bern: Benteli, 1987. 95p.

The booklet opens with a quote by Friedrich Dürrenmatt: 'Wilhelm Tell is still the only Swiss the whole world knows.' Thus, one of Switzerland's leading writers makes a biting yet funny statement about the reputed mediocrity of his people. It is difficult to characterize Swiss humour because of the varied cultures and idioms of Switzerland. Many believe that there is no such thing as Swiss humour because the Swiss are not known to laugh often, but this collection of jokes shows that they have ample reason to laugh about one another, even if the so-called virtues such as hard work, thrift, political 'savvy', and efficiency are the target. The foreigners laugh about the same qualities. They especially like to poke fun at the bankers, brokers, and the supposed money-making skills of all Swiss. Some jokes depict the Swiss as slightly dumb, uncultured, or naive. Many are centred around eating and drinking in public places. This is an entertaining and appealing little book.

8 **Pearls of Switzerland.**
Edmond van Hoorick, Evelyn Baetes, translated from the German by P. A. Blackburn. Fredeburg, FRG: Grobbel, 1983. 96p.

This little book features sayings about Switzerland and the Swiss, mostly by famous people, such as writers and politicians, some from Switzerland, some from foreign countries. Not all of the quotes are flattering. Full-page pictures in colour depict mostly Alpine and rural scenes.

9 **Nationalism and liberty: the Swiss example.**
Hans Kohn. London: Allen & Unwin, 1956. 133p.

This essay by the German-American historian Kohn 'inquires into the character and meaning of Swiss nationalism. It may help to answer the question how far the Swiss experience can set an example for the compatibility of nationalism and liberty and for the peaceful and productive co-existence of various ethnic groups in one common state.' He surveys Swiss history and the contributions of outstanding individuals such as Pestalozzi, and also evaluates a few Swiss writers with this question in mind. The Swiss succeeded in their efforts 'to unite in the defence, and for the strengthening, of their liberties and to develop this defensive alliance into an ever-closer union'. They thus were able to withstand the difficult times of the two World Wars of the 20th century. Their example is of significance.

10 **Switzerland 1989: people, state, economy, culture.**
Bern: Kümmerly & Frey. 96p. maps.

Published in six languages, this short booklet is an excellent introduction to Switzerland. Its pages are packed with information on the Swiss people, their land, history, state, economy, and culture. Numerous maps, statistical tables, and colour photographs make this a most attractive, as well as a useful, pocket-sized booklet for anyone seeking easy access to factual information about the country. It is updated and reissued annually.

11 **Switzerland.**

Herbert Kubly and the editors of *Life*. New York: Time Incorporated, 1964. 160p. (Life World Library).

Kubly, the author of the interpretive text for this volume, is a native of New Glarus, Wisconsin, a place which has many ties with the country of his ancestors. His intimate knowledge of Switzerland is reflected in a text that is fresh and lively as well as brimming with useful information and provocative observations. Each of the ten chapters is followed by a picture-essay, the hallmark of the Life World Library series. The superb photo-essays succeed in capturing much of the essence of Switzerland, modern and traditional, countryside and city, at work and at leisure.

12 **Switzerland for beginners.**

George Mikes, illustrated by Godi Hofmann. London: André Deutsch, 1975. 92p.

This is an amusing little book about things considered 'typically Swiss'; but do the Swiss really put Kirsch in everything they eat, particularly soup? Is it fair to compare the lot of the *Gastarbeiter* with that of the Jews in Nazi Germany? The sixteen essays will entertain the seasoned traveller or Swiss native far more than they would a 'beginner' who might not quite grasp the often biting humour. The drawings, or rather caricatures, by Hofmann are original and funny. This revised and enlarged version of the original 1962 edition was already in its seventh printing in 1987.

13 **Switzerland: the clockwork country.**

John J. Putnam, photographs by Cotton Coulson. *National Geographic Magazine*, Washington, DC, vol. 169, no. 1 (January 1986), p. 96-127. maps.

National Geographic periodically publishes long articles on Switzerland. Since World War II they have appeared under the titles 'Switzerland guards the roof of Europe' (August 1950), 'Surprising Switzerland' (October 1956), 'Switzerland: Europe's high-rise republic' (July 1969), and the one cited here. These articles, though written by different authors, follow a similar pattern. They are lavishly illustrated, primarily with colour photographs of mountain and lake scenery, action photos of parades, folk festivals, and people engaged in sports, shots of people at work show mostly peasants in native costumes, but also a few industrial labourers and bank employees. The text of the early articles resembles the prose of travel brochures. One of the writers makes fun of a customs inspector who is supposed to have told her: 'If you have to Switzerland come for your Magazine an article to write, I hope you else than cuckoo clocks, the yodels, and the alphorns tell.' In the end the joke is on her, because that is what her article is mainly about. To be fair, the articles also present some information about Swiss history, politics, and culture. 'Switzerland: the clockwork country' has slightly more depth inasmuch as Putnam describes in some detail such phenomena as Swiss military preparedness, a political system that works surprisingly well in view of the diversity of the country, and the world of banking, with a glimpse at the private life of one of the so-called 'gnomes of Zurich'.

14 **Why Switzerland?**

Jonathan Steinberg. Cambridge, England: Cambridge University Press, 1976. Reprinted with corrections, 1978. 214p.

In this short book Steinberg touches upon the history, politics, languages, economy, and problems of modern Switzerland. He addresses the question of what makes Switzerland unique and worthy of examination and admiration. The author paints a lively panorama of Swiss peculiarities and succeeds in whetting the appetite of the interested reader. Reflecting the manifestations of recession and youth unrest of the early 1970s, he raises questions as to the viability of the historical concept of Swiss identity. Swiss identity is also the subject of George Steiner's clever little essay 'What is 'Swiss'?' in the *Times Literary Supplement* (7 December 1984, p. 399-400). After reviewing the complexity and tensions of the Swiss situation with its interwoven and many-layered loyalties, Steiner concludes: 'It may be what is *most* Swiss is not to ask the question.'

15 **Imitation of Switzerland: historical reflections.**

Jonathan Steinberg. *Government and Opposition: a Journal of Comparative Politics*, vol. 23, no. 1 (Winter 1988), p. 13-30.

This article appears in a special issue of the London School of Economics and Political Science journal *Government and Opposition* and is devoted to the topic of 'Can the Confederatio Helvetica be imitated?' Steinberg lists four features that 'distinguish the Swiss body politic' and form the 'central characteristics of Swiss history', namely neutrality, federalism, democracy, and wealth. He describes each of the four briefly and points out how each contributed to the uniqueness of Switzerland and in which way each would be worthy of imitation.

16 **Switzerland: image of a people.**

Edited by Alfred Vetter. Bern: Benteli, 1971. 144p. map.

This is a selection of fifteen articles taken from the *Swissair Gazette*. Each features an aspect of Switzerland such as neutrality and foreign policy, industry, banking, humanitarian causes, literature, folk art and yodelling. Numerous black-and-white photographs with captions accompany the text. The authors are experts in their field, and their essays, though condensed, provide a good introduction to the great diversity of the small country. A fold-out mountain panorama in colour features a 360-degree vista from 'the roof of Switzerland', the Dufour Spitze, the country's highest mountain.

17 **What makes Switzerland tick?**

Richard Wildblood. Lewes, England: Book Guild, 1988. 103p.

Wildblood aims to discover the forces which motivate the Swiss and the result of that motivation. His emphasis is on political institutions and processes. His material is presented in a sequence of brief chapters (sometimes less than a page in length), on Swiss neutrality, humanitarian activities, the tax system, education – including vocational training and apprenticeship programmes – trade and industry, tourism, agriculture, banking, insurance, research, patents, transport, and so on. Much of the information is too general and abbreviated to be of much use to a person really interested in finding out what makes Switzerland tick.

Longer works

18 **26 mal die Schweiz: Panorama einer Konföderation.** (Twenty-six times Switzerland: panorama of a confederation.)

Fritz René Allemann. Munich; Zurich: Piper, 1985. 4th ed. 603p. maps. (Piper Panoramen der Welt).

Allemann, a Swiss journalist and writer, provides in this substantial book a picture of the twenty-six mini-states or cantons that make up the Swiss Confederation. Each one of these cantons has a character and a history of its own, and Allemann succeeds in bringing out the individuality of each of them in fascinating detail. Central Switzerland (Urschweiz), where the country's history began, retains many of the old traditions. Zurich, Bern, and Luzern, the leading states in the Old Confederation, are centres of different kinds of power, with metropolitan Zurich being the undisputed financial and economic leader in the country. French Switzerland (Welschland, Romandie) is the land of grain and wine production and of watchmaking, where cosmopolitan elegance is combined with puritan discipline. There is no more informative, reliable, and at the same time enjoyable guide to the cantonal diversity of Switzerland than Allemann's book.

19 **Die Schweiz vom Bau der Alpen bis zur Frage nach der Zukunft.** (Switzerland from the creation of the Alps to the question of the future.)

Edited by Niklaus Flüeler, Roland Gfeller-Corthésy. [Zurich]: Ex Libris, 1975. 703p. maps. bibliog.

Subtitled 'an encyclopedia and reader which gives information on the geography, history, present times, and future of a country', this book contains a wealth of information on all aspects of Switzerland, its people and their way of life. The chapters are written by some seventy experts in their respective fields. Numerous illustrations and photographs, many maps, graphs and tables, and résumés and bibliographies on the margins of most pages give the work its encyclopaedic character. Two indexes allow the reader easy access to any item of interest. Conceived and executed as a gift to the members of the Migros-Genossenschafts-Bund, the alliance of Migros cooperatives, the largest food retailer in the country, this fine work has also been published in French and Italian.

20 **Living and working in Switzerland.**

David Hampshire. Dietikon, Switzerland: Trade Fair Services, 1988. 363p. bibliog.

Hampshire's book is a comprehensive source of practical information on a wide range of everyday subjects. It is not a tourist guide, but a work designed 'to help the newcomer [to Switzerland] make informed decisions instead of costly mistakes'. The material is presented in a highly readable style, sprinkled with (often humorous) asides and cartoons. The book is a mine of carefully verified information on how to find a job in Switzerland, obtain permits and visas, overcome arrival problems, find suitable accommodation, use post office and telephone services, find good schools for one's children, survive motoring in Switzerland, enjoy one's leisure time – doing sports, especially skiing – find shopping bargains, handle bank accounts and taxes, and many other 'how tos'. A number of appendices with useful addresses, a bibliography of works in English, clubs and organizations, subscriptions, weights and measures, and a glossary of English words and their German and French equivalents further enhance the value of this book which rightfully has been praised as 'the best English-language guide for a foreigner in this country'. Similar books with practical advice and hints have been published by the American Women's Clubs of Zurich, Basel, Geneva, and Lausanne. *Living in Geneva*, edited by Mary Guerry of the American Women's Club of Geneva, came out in its 9th edition in 1988.

21 **The Swiss without halos.**

J. Christopher Herold. Westport, Connecticut: Greenwood, 1979. 271p. bibliog.

This book was first published in 1948 by Columbia University Press, when Switzerland, in the aftermath of World War II, stood out as an island of peace and prosperity. Herold wants to dispel the myth of Switzerland as a shining example for all nations on earth, and he does it tongue in cheek, as titles of individual chapters, such as 'War for Export', referring to Swiss mercenaries that used to serve foreign monarchs, or 'Animal Oeconomicum', examining the Swiss businessman, reveal. The Federal Councillors he calls 'members of a board of directors of the Swiss holding company'. The book is a tale of historical and cultural events from Switzerland's beginning up to the present day; it lays bare human imperfections, an exercise that may be troubling to those who are intent on preserving the image of a perfect country. Adhering to the *status quo* has proved so advantageous to the country in its long history that many Swiss patriots believe that Switzerland indeed enjoys God's special blessing.

22 **Switzerland.**

Christopher Hughes. London: Benn, 1975. 303p. maps. bibliog.

Hughes, professor emeritus of the University of Leicester, is an authority on Swiss political institutions. He conceived of this book as a kind of guide 'for the traveller who wishes to understand with his mind what he sees with his eyes'. He has produced an account of a wide range of topics and issues concerning Switzerland which are of interest to him. His lively style brings to life the history of the Swiss cantons and their characteristics. With wit and at times somewhat malicious irreverence, he analyses the many peculiarities of the land which he describes as 'a problem not a solution'. Hughes's volume is an excellent introduction to Switzerland, for it has the attributes of a definitive work on the subject: breadth, reliability, and readability, based on careful research and documentation.

23 **Modern Switzerland.**

Edited by J. Murray Luck. Palo Alto, California: Society for the Promotion of Science and Scholarship, 1978. 515p.

This book consists of twenty-six self-contained articles by individual Swiss authors that aim 'to describe present day Switzerland to the English-speaking world'. The topics covered include demography, geography, energy resources, agriculture, banking, research, technology, public health, labour relations, social security. education, religion, sports, tourism, federalism, the judicial system, politics, national defence, the status of women, the constitution, Swiss relations with the European Community and the United Nations, the International Committee of the Red Cross, Swiss neutrality, and modern art. Each article ends with a brief bibliography, and most of them can be found as separate entries in this bibliography.

24 **La Suisse dans tous ses états. Portrait des 26 cantons.** (Switzerland with all its states: portrait of the 26 cantons.)

Alain Pichard. Lausanne: 24 heures, 1987. 287p. maps. bibliog.

In this fine book Pichard re-examines the cantons of Switzerland with which he dealt in his two earlier books *Vingt Suisses à découvrir. Portrait des cantons alémaniques, des Grisons et du Tessin* (Twenty Switzerlands to be discovered: portrait of the Alemannic cantons, Graubünden, and Ticino), 1975, and *La Romandie n'existe pas. Six portraits politiques* (Romandie [French-speaking Switzerland] doesn't exist: six political portraits), 1978. He describes the struggle between the weight of tradition and the forces of change, with emphasis on the political life of the cantons. The historical and economic factors that make up their personality are not neglected, however. There are relief maps for all cantons and forty full-page photographs. The bibliography, organized by region and canton, provides a convenient introduction to the literature on the Swiss cantons for persons able to read French and German.

25 **The heart of Europe.**

Denis de Rougemont, Charlotte Muret. New York: Duell, Sloan and Pearce, 1941. 274p.

The authors believe that federalism is the system that best guarantees freedom and assures adherence to democratic principles while permitting diversity and individualism. Switzerland, the authors contend, is the prototype for this form of government. They examine Switzerland's long history, its landscape and people, its government and army, and its culture all of which have made its 'federal way of life' possible and have brought peace and prosperity to the nation.

26 **Switzerland in perspective.**

George Soloveytchik. Westport, Connecticut: Greenwood, 1982. 306p. maps. bibliog. (Reprint. Originally published: London; New York: Oxford University Press, 1954).

Parts of this book, especially the introductory chapter 'Switzerland in the world of to-day', are out of date. Other parts have lost none of their pertinence and can still be read with profit and enjoyment. A native of St Petersburg, Soloveytchik stayed in contact with Switzerland from his childhood through two World Wars. His book is written as a testimony of friendship in which he desires 'to give an account of the kind of men and women they [the Swiss] are and how they got to be that way; the complex processes that shaped their destinies, and of the many political and economic problems facing them now'. The book is divided into three major parts, dealing with domestic affairs, economic affairs, and foreign relations. Each part is subdivided into chapters focusing on specific topics such as press and information, banking and insurance, the League of Nations, and Swiss foreign policy under Federal Councillor Giuseppe Motta and his successors. Soloveytchik profiles personalities little known outside Switzerland, yet vital for the country's growth and direction. The author is well read in just about every field of human endeavour and deals critically and in a personal manner with his subject. He steers away from the usual stereotypes, exposes myths, and urges that the Swiss be less concerned 'about Tell and more about the component parts of the Confederation' which he believes to be in danger if educational reforms are not forthcoming and a new idealism cannot be instilled.

27 **The Swiss: a cultural panorama of Switzerland.**
Walter Sorell. New York; Indianapolis, Indiana: Bobbs-Merrill, 1972. 303p. bibliog.

Conceived as a 'cultural Baedeker through Switzerland', this book wrestles valiantly with the characteristics and complexities of this small country of four different languages and varying ethnic, economic, cultural, and folkloric qualities. 'The creative spirit of the Swiss' is exemplified in the field of religion by Protestant leaders from Ulrich Zwingli to Karl Barth, and in education by pedagogic innovators from Jean-Jacques Rousseau and Johann Heinrich Pestalozzi to Karl Jaspers and Rudolf Steiner. In science, technology, and medicine the prominent names include those of the Basel mathematician Leonhard Euler, the enigmatic Paracelsus, and the pioneers in the field of psychology, Carl Gustav Jung and Jean Piaget. Many important figures from literature and the creative and performing arts are presented in short biographical sketches. A second part of the book, 'The creative atmosphere of Switzerland', describes the phenomenon of the attractiveness of Switzerland to foreign visitors, from Goethe to Lenin, and to exiles who found refuge and sanctuary there, from Voltaire to Thomas Mann and Vladimir Nabokov. Raphael E. G. Armattoe's *The Swiss contribution to Western civilisation* (Dundalk, UK: Dundalgan Press, 1944. 91p.) covered much the same ground some thirty years earlier.

28 **An account of Switzerland written in the year 1714.**
Abraham Stanyan. London: Printed for Jacob Tonson at Shakespear's Head over-against Catherine-street in the Strand, 1714. 247p.

Stanyan (1669-1732) was British envoy to Switzerland 1705-14 and to Graubünden 1707-14. In this book he provides a delightful account of the Swiss Confederation of his day. Of the Swiss land he writes that the earth 'treats the inhabitants like a hard step-mother; they earn hard what they get out of her, and seem rather to owe it to their own labour and industry, than to her bounty' – a perennial theme of Swiss accounts of themselves. The Pays de Vaud is not only the most fertile but the most beautiful part of all Switzerland, and 'Bazil' is 'without dispute the finest city in Switzerland'. He describes the political division of the country into seven cantons with an aristocratic kind of government and six country cantons whose democratic government is 'so plain and artless, that it will be easy to give an idea of it in few words'. He provides a long, detailed description of the government of Bern. He tries to dispel 'the widespread notion that the Swiss traffick with men whom they sell to those who will pay most for them'. Foreign service keeps the country from becoming overpopulated. Stanyan also treats religion, the militia system, and trade. Of revenues he says that 'though they may be small, they are greater than expenses; the cantons lay up a little sum every year which grows to a considerable treasure'. An appendix contains a description of the allies of the 'Switzers': Graubünden, Neuchâtel, St Gallen, Geneva, Biel, and Mülhausen.

Picture books

29 **Switzerland past and present.**
Franz Auf der Maur, Markus Niederhauser, translated from the German by Rosamund Bandi. Bern: Kümmerly & Frey, 1983. 192p. map.

This large picture book of well-chosen contrasts succeeds in impressing upon the reader what enormous changes have taken place in the country in the last 100 to 150 years. Colour photographs recently taken of buildings of all kinds and of the countryside are shown side by side with drawings or etchings of the same subject from times past. The photographer has taken great care to position himself at the same angle from which the old pictures were made. The result is striking, and the text further underlines the physical changes that cities, villages, and the landscape have undergone during the last century. The high quality of the colour photography deserves special mention.

30 **Schaffhausen. Stadt und Landschaft = Schaffhausen: city and canton.**
Max Baumann, translated from the German by George N. Zwez. Schaffhausen, Switzerland: Meili, 1975. 157p. map.

This is a picture book of the northernmost canton of Switzerland. The text, in four languages, describes the old city of Schaffhausen near the Rhine Falls and also the country districts that form the canton. The photographs bring out the rural character of this canton: Alemannic villages with their typical wooden-beam construction houses dot the countryside; their inhabitants farm, fish, and grow wine, and very little is shown of the industries that employ most Schaffhausers. The book presents an idyllic and somewhat idealized picture of an unspoiled corner of the world.

31 **Wallis: Erbe und Zukunft.** (Valais: heritage and future.)
Karl Biffiger, Oswald Ruppen. Bern: Haupt, 1975. 117p. maps. (Die grossen Heimatbücher, 5).

The *grossen Heimatbücher* is a series of large-format picture books featuring selected Swiss regions. This one takes the reader to a valley that reaches from the Furka pass in central Switzerland to Lake Geneva. Named Wallis in the upper, German-speaking part, and Valais in the lower, French-speaking part, the valley is dominated by the River Rhône. The Rhône, which is fed by numerous mountain rivers coming down the side valleys, has created a large delta which has been transformed into a vast vegetable garden and orchard, dotted with industrial zones. To the north and south, the valley is framed by high mountain ranges that shield it from the winds, thus allowing fine wines to be produced on its sunny slopes. Irrigation systems, some of them centuries old, and hydro-electric power plants make use of the abundant supply of water. The Wallis was already used by the Romans as an access route to western and northern Europe. Nowadays it is much sought after by tourists, the main attractions being Zermatt and the Matterhorn. The 166 photographs by Ruppen, sixteen of which are in colour, give an impressive pictorial record of this unique Swiss mountain canton.

32 **Wooden bridges in Switzerland.**
Werner Blaser, translated from the German by D. Q. Stephenson. Basel [etc.]: Birkhäuser, 1982. 184p. maps. bibliog.

The greater part of this book consists of photographs, some in colour, of thirty-two roofed wooden bridges, out of about 150 that are still in use in Switzerland. The bridges featured, almost all of which are found in German-speaking Switzerland, are photographed in their natural setting and from close up so that the construction work and the craftsmanship of the carpenters can be appreciated. For many of the bridges, design plans with longitudinal and cross-sections are provided. An introductory text in three languages describes the history of bridge building, with special attention to the carpenters' trade, the different types of bridges, with reproductions of old designs, and the work of bridge building, with photographs of old carpenters' tools.

33 **Fountains: mirrors of Switzerland.**
Pierre Bouffard, René Creux. Geneva: Bonvent & Fontainemore, 1973. 335p.

This is not an inventory of Switzerland's thousands of fountains from the Middle Ages to the present, but an attempt to bring before the reader fountains that are representative of a period, of a style, or as a type. The fountains depicted range from simple village fountains to elaborate architectural masterpieces. As medieval paintings prove, architects designed fountains with great care. Frequently erected at the centre of towns, fountains were not only important as suppliers of water but also as centres of the social interaction of the community. The shapes, building materials, and decorations of these structures are often characteristic of a certain region in Switzerland. Dates cut into the stones proudly tell their age, and we see that some date back hundreds of years; a few are now kept in museums where they are protected from the elements. This beautiful picture book has over 200 full-page photographs, taken by René Creux. They are captioned with brief texts that help to make the visual experience a sheer delight.

34 **Historische Gärten der Schweiz. Die Entwicklung vom Mittelalter bis zur Gegenwart.** (Historical gardens in Switzerland: the development from the Middle Ages to the present.)
Hans-Rudolf Heyer. Bern: Benteli, 1980. 272p. bibliog.

This beautifully illustrated volume provides an instructive and exciting survey of the art of garden building and landscape beautification in the geographical area of Switzerland from Roman times to the present. Monastery gardens are described and illustrated as well as peasants' gardens. The historical creations of the Renaissance, the Baroque, and the 18th century are treated, as are the romantic and English-inspired parks. Chapters on public promenades and lake-shore and spa-garden architecture are interspersed with others on zoological gardens, cemeteries and monuments, and the public green spaces of the 20th century.

35 **Das Engadin.** (The Engadine.)
Toni Hiebeler. Zurich: Silva, 1985. 144p. map. bibliog.

This book is about the mountain world of the valleys of the young Inn river and its people. The Putèr-speaking Upper Engadine with its lakes and the world-famous resort town of St Moritz, as well as the Vallader-speaking Lower Engadine with Scuol-Tarasp and its spas are presented in words and colour photographs. There are chapters on sports and leisure activities in summer and winter, as well as a chronicle of historical events in the Engadine from 3000 BC to 1984. A lexicon of Engadine villages, side valleys, mountains, lakes, touristic installations, folk customs, rail- and motorways, and cultural events is also included.

36 **The Swiss Alps.**

Edmond van Hoorick, Jean Christian Spahni, Erwin Heimann. Thalwil, Switzerland: Sigloch; Zurich: Ex Libris, 1979. 251p.

In the first, textual part (seventy-nine pages in length) of this large-sized book Spahni gives a wide-ranging account of the history of Switzerland, the history of the Alps, the Alps and their inhabitants, and the role of the Alps in the Swiss economy. The second part, 'The scenery of Switzerland', consists of full-page or even larger, fold-out, colour photographs by Hoorick with accompanying text by Heimann. The sequence of pictures begins on the eastern end of Lake Geneva and crosses Switzerland eastward to the mountains of Canton Graubünden, and then northward to the Säntis, the dominant mountain massif of northeastern Switzerland. Of the many picture books about the Alps, this may well be the most beautiful.

37 **The city and canton of Zurich.**

Martin Hürlimann, translated by Max Wildi. Zurich: Atlantis, 1953. 195p.

Master photographer Hürlimann presents with this third revision a virtually new picture book of Switzerland's largest city and the canton of Zurich. Some red-letter dates in the city's historical, cultural, and economic development precede the illustrated text. The narrative sets the photographs in the appropriate time-frame, beginning with 'the ecclesiastical Zurich of the Middle Ages' and ending with modern times or, pictorially, from the Fraumünster church, founded 31 July 853, to the Centre Le Corbusier. The canton is divided into four parts: the lake region, the mountainous Oberland, Northern Zurich with Winterthur and the Zurich Rhine, and the Knonauer Amt. Each part is rich in historical sites, lovely villages, and distinct landscapes. Some aerial photos add yet another perspective.

38 **The Swiss chalet.**

Pierre Jacquet, translated from the French by A. M. Schofield. Zurich: Orell Füssli, 1963. 176p.

This picture book sings the praise of the mountain chalet which 'it can be said without exaggeration . . . ranks equally with the monuments bequeathed to us by Rome, France or Italy. . . .' (!) Not all farm houses and rural dwellings in Switzerland are chalets – the areas richest in typical chalets are the Bernese Oberland, the Pays-d'Enhaut of Canton Vaud, and the Valais. The book has a running text that expounds on the characteristics of the chalet, but more informative are the descriptive commentaries that accompany the full-page black-and-white photographs of forty of the most beautiful chalets.

39 **Our leave in Switzerland: a souvenir of the visit of American soldiers to Switzerland in 1945/46.**

Edited by Arnold Kübler, Gottlieb Duttweiler, Werner Bischof, translated from the German by Mary Bancroft. Zurich: Zur Limmat, 1946. 177p. maps.

During 1945 and 1946 almost 300,000 uniformed GIs [US private soldiers (colloquial use): from Government Issue] spent a week's leave in Switzerland. The war was over and the United States military authorities made arrangements with several European countries to host organized tours for American soldiers stationed on the Continent. Switzerland, not touched by war, was a favourite choice of the young men. *Saturday Review* (4 June 1949) reported on this enterprise under the title 'Tip-toeing through the Edelweiss'. The friendly and clean-cut GIs became a familiar sight in the streets of resort towns and Swiss cities and were well liked by the natives. This book grew out of a desire to offer the furloughed soldiers a meaningful souvenir and to educate them about the country. The 200 photographs, some in colour, and the text clearly cater for the intended audience. Scenery from all parts of Switzerland, highlights of the country's history, and samples of folklore and the artistic life alternate with glimpses at the then current state of technology, industry, and the military. The simple citizen is featured, as are some of the country's leading figures, and quite a number of photographs show the soldiers interacting with their hosts. The book served not only as a memento for the GIs but also for the Swiss, many of whom had never before met an American.

40 **Geneva: crossroads of nations.**

Edited by Benjamin Laederer, translated from the French by T. J. Hamilton Black. Geneva: Editions Générales, 1964. 293p. (Swiss cities and landscapes, 28).

This book has 189 pages of text and 104 pages of photographs, but neither index nor bibliography. Twenty-three prominent Genevans or persons living in Geneva have contributed chapters on many aspects of life in that city. Geneva is featured as the headquarters of important international organizations, the city of Jean Calvin and Henry Dunant; a hub of banking, industry and trade; and a home for the arts and music. The photographs capture the cosmopolitanism of this city as well as its charms.

41 **St. Gallen: Stift, Stadt, Landschaft.** (St Gallen: convent, city, countryside.)

Herbert Maeder, Hermann Bauer, Walter Lendi, Peter Ochsenbein. Olten, Switzerland; Freiburg, FRG: Walter, 1987. 207p. bibliog.

This picture book presents St Gallen, the cultural and economic centre of northeastern Switzerland, with colour photographs by Maeder and texts by three prominent St Gallen intellectuals. The Baroque convent church and the convent library (Stiftsbibliothek) with its treasures of medieval manuscripts form the core of the 'monastery quarter'. The city with its cultural attractions, among them the business university, and popular festivals and fairs, offers a pleasant home for its 70,000 inhabitants. It is surrounded by green hills leading up to the Säntis, the highest mountain of the region, and extending down to the shores of the Bodensee (Lake Constance).

42 **Die Schweiz. Eine Annäherung in Bild und Text.** (Switzerland: an approach in pictures and text.)

Edited by Max Mittler. Zurich: Atlantis; Ex Libris, 1983. 320p. map.

Of all the many picture books about Switzerland this is one of the most beautiful and impressive. Five essays by younger Swiss writers (born since 1940) present some of the dilemmas of contemporary Switzerland in an unemotional, incisive, and enlightening manner. These essays are embedded in portfolios of pictures by somewhat older Swiss photographers. Most of the 204 photographs, some in colour, others in black-and-white, and some covering two or even three of the large-sized pages, are of artistic quality: they evoke moods, use perspectives, and show scenes very different from the run-of-the-mill picture calendar. Some eighty reproductions of old engravings and drawings of land- and cityscapes provide a historical perspective to the modern situation.

43 **Jura.**

Max Mittler. Zurich: Orell Füssli, 1987. 221p. maps.

About one-third of this volume is text, the rest consists of many colour and black-and-white photographs of varying sizes, plus maps and graphs. Conceived as a book of factual information on both the French and the Swiss parts of the Jura mountains, the volume provides an instructive tour through the diverse parts of this region and their historical, political, and economic peculiarities. Excellent photographs combine with the text to capture the essence of this region.

44 **Swiss mountain magic.**

Marjorie Parish. Wabern, Switzerland: Büchler, 1965. 176p.

This picture book contains 123 black-and-white photographs of mountain scenes and mountain people. In addition, there are fifty-three colour plates of alpine flowers. Each flower is described in a short paragraph which states its common and its Latin name, when it is in bloom, its physical characteristics and its place of growth. Many of these small and delicate flowers enchant the wanderer in late spring, just after the snow has melted.

45 **Berne: the heart of Switzerland.**

Edited by Franz A. Roedelberger, translated from the German by E. A. Bell. Bern: Verbandsbuchdruckerei, 1967. 280p. (First edition, 1953).

Some fifty Swiss photographers contributed mostly black-and-white photographs to this book, and there is great diversity in the subjects selected, thus doing justice to the large canton and the city of Bern, the nation's capital. Snow-capped mountain ranges contrast with electric power plants, cheesemaking with car-racing, cultivated wheat fields with alpine meadows, stately old farms with modern office buildings and factories. A 'portrait gallery' of great men and women spanning eight centuries is proof of the leadership Bern has exerted in many fields. Some full-size colour plates feature reproductions of works by Bernese artists, and the history and workings of the government are also explained.

46 **Zurich: metropolis on the Limmat.**

Peter Rüfenacht, Martin Müller, translated from the German by Stanley Mason. Zurich; Munich: Artemis, 1979. 216p. bibliog.

This is a splendidly illustrated picture book of Switzerland's largest city. A lively text in three languages touches on many aspects of Zurich's eventful history and its economic, cultural, and intellectual life.

47 **Lucerne: in prose and photography.**

Edited by Xaver Schnieper, translated from the German by Maureen Oberli. Luzern: Bucher, 1972. 78p.

This booklet provides commentaries by fifteen foreign visitors about Luzern, one of Switzerland's most popular tourist spots. Tolstoy was deeply moved by the city's beauty, but would have preferred it without the presence of English tourists. Schopenhauer found it a 'badly built' city, while Mark Twain takes the reader on an entertaining sightseeing tour. These short prose pieces make delightful reading, and their appeal is enhanced by some gorgeous colour photographs.

48 **Swiss panorama.**

Emil Schulthess, Emil Egli. Zurich: Artemis, 1982; New York: Knopf, 1983. 203p. 28 maps.

It took a photographer with Schulthess's experience, technical know-how, and determination to overcome the frustrating problems encountered while trying to perfect the 360° aerial panorama photography employed for the images in this book. A special camera had to be developed and special films were needed; ways had to be found of mounting the contraption on the helicopter; the crew and the photographer had to learn all about positioning themselves and the craft, about dealing with its vibrations, and adjusting to the climatic conditions. Small photographs illustrate some of the technical devices used, while the twenty-eight over-sized panoramic colour photographs of Swiss land- and cityscapes are of exquisite quality. With his camera suspended from the airborne helicopter, Schulthess sought out the peaks and glaciers of the Alps, the mountain chains and ridges of the Jura, and the valleys and plains of the Central Plateau, dotted with cities and villages. The looping panorama of Bern stands out as a human and technical accomplishment. A factually descriptive text in German, French, and English by geographer Egli provides information about the geographical features and characteristics of the landscapes featured in the photographs.

49 **Reizvolle Schweizer Kleinstadt. Die unbekannten Schönheiten unserer Schweizer Städtchen.** (Picturesque Swiss small town: the unknown beauties of our small Swiss towns.)

Willy Zeller. Zofingen, Switzerland: Ringier, 1975. 248p. bibliog.

Every region of Switzerland has its ancient small towns with their medieval character, narrow streets, proud churches and castles, decorated stone buildings, and houses of wooden-beam construction. This volume presents more than fifty of them through photographs and text.

Travel

Travellers' accounts

50 **Early travellers in the Alps.**
Gavin R. de Beer. London: Sidgwick & Jackson, 1966; New York: October House, 1967. 204p. maps. bibliog. (Originally published in 1930).

This is the first of half a dozen books that Sir Gavin de Beer wrote about his great love and hobby: travelling in Switzerland. It recounts the experiences of people who travelled in the Alps from the 16th to the end of the 18th century. De Beer defines travellers as persons 'who wander about for no purpose other than the interest and enjoyment which the region affords them'. He retells the adventures and achievements of the early humanists and scientists attracted to the Alps, of the first Englishmen to venture into the mountain valleys, of poets and writers, and, finally, of 'the greatest Alpine tourist', the Genevan physicist, geologist, and mineralogist Horace Bénédict de Saussure who produced a wealth of scientific reports and materials on his seven trips to the Mont Blanc and Matterhorn regions. The booklet is illustrated with forty plates and thirty-two figures in the text, all woodcuts and engravings from the works of early travellers, depicting personalities and scenery. Books on similar subjects by the author include *Escape to Switzerland* (London; New York: Penguin, 1945) and *Alps and men: pages from forgotten diaries of travellers and tourists in Switzerland* (London: Edward Arnold, 1932).

51 **Die Schweiz in alten Ansichten und Schilderungen.** (Switzerland in old views and descriptions.)
Edited by Marcus Bourquin. Kreuzlingen, Switzerland: Neptun; Konstanz, FRG: Jan Thorbecke, 1968. 358p. bibliog.

This is a rich collection of pictures and descriptions of Switzerland from the end of the 15th to the middle of the 19th century. Among the numerous writers, poets, composers, and diplomats from many parts of Europe and America represented in this book are Balzac, Cooper, Goethe, Mendelssohn, Rousseau, Schumann, and Stendhal.

The pictures and engravings reproduced were done in a variety of techniques and include examples of the works of Bartlett, Cockburn, Turner, Witz, and various schools of Swiss miniaturists. Bourquin's introduction describes the art-historical developments and the changes in the appreciation of nature in the course of the centuries covered by the book. Three bibliographies and the indexes of authors, artists, and place names provide a scientific apparatus for this rich work that covers so much of the travel and picture literature about Switzerland.

52 **Switzerland.**

James Bunting. London: Batsford, 1973. 224p. map.

Bunting visited Switzerland frequently with his parents during the 1920s and 1930s and his fond childhood memories and his interest in the 'unique' country fostered the idea for this book. Bunting takes the reader on a tour of eleven different regions such as the Forest Cantons, and cities such as Zug and Zurich, as well as neighbouring Liechtenstein. All major regions are covered in this book and much historical, geographical and cultural information is given. Bunting's work appeals because it reflects the author's personal experience in and attachment to the country. Twelve black-and-white photographs enhance the work.

53 **The Bern book: a record of a voyage of the mind.**

Vincent O. Carter. New York: John Day, 1973. 297p.

The author is an American Negro writer who travelled in Europe in the 1950s. His journey led him to Bern to visit a friend at a time when few blacks resided in or even toured the country. Intended neither as an autobiography nor as a travelogue, the book recounts the experiences of a dark-skinned man in a white city and land. Carter, while exploring the Swiss capital is conscious at every moment of his being different, and of the reactions his presence elicits. He remained in Bern longer than he originally had planned despite his negative experiences, experiences which he attributed to the racial prejudice of the Swiss.

54 **The charm of Switzerland: an anthology.**

Compiled by Norman G. Brett James. London: Methuen, 1910. 304p.

This book provides a tour through Switzerland with the help of poets, essayists, and travellers. The major tourist attractions from Geneva to Luzern and the mountains and valleys of the Alps are featured. The great writers of the early Victorian period are especially well represented in this anthology, but later 19th-century figures such as Edward Whymper and John Ruskin are also here. Although there are a few pieces by Swiss and French writers, it is above all Englishmen whose writings are featured in this book. They express themselves eloquently on the beauty and charm of the country that they loved so dearly.

55 **Switzerland and the English.**

Arnold Lunn. London: Eyre & Spottiswood, 1944. 258p.

This account of Anglo-Swiss relations is strongly coloured by the author's background and experiences. Lunn spent much of his youth and adult life mountain climbing and skiing in the Bernese Oberland. An avid sportsman, he was instrumental in organizing some of the first downhill ski races in the Alps during the interwar years. His book is about the love affair of the English (he refuses to use the term Britons and apologizes for it to the Scots) with the Swiss Alps from the romantic writers and painters, among whom one misses, however, the name of J. M. W. Turner, to the modern tourists. The chapters on the British contribution to mountaineering and 'the great Victorian institution', the Alpine Club, are informative and entertaining as are those dealing with the pivotal role the English played in making the Alps into the playground of Europe. *The Englishman in the Alps: being a collection of English prose and poetry relating to the Alps*, edited by Lunn (Oxford: Oxford University Press, 1913), includes material taken from diaries, letters, and excerpts from larger works beginning with a 17th-century account of Hannibal's passage of the Alps.

56 **Die russische Entdeckung der Schweiz: Ein Land in dem nur gute und ehrbare Leute leben.** (The Russian discovery of Switzerland: a land in which only good and honest people live.)
Edited by Jewgeni Netscheporuk. Zurich: Limmat, 1989. 368p.

This anthology of reports and illustrations by Russian travellers and émigrés in Switzerland provides a vivid picture of the impression Switzerland made on these East European visitors. Among the more or less famous people assembled by Netscheporuk are Nikolai Gogol, Alexander Turgenev, Michail Glinka, Michail Bakunin, Alexander Suvorov, Vera Figner, Ilya Ehrenburg, and others. They are overwhelmingly complimentary in their remarks about the country and its inhabitants.

57 **Denn es ist kein Land wie dieses. Die Schweiz als Reise- und Asylland grosser Komponisten.** (For there is no land like this one: Switzerland as land of travel and asylum for great composers.)
Kurt Pahlen. [Bern]: Benteli, [1971]. 103p.

Musicologist Pahlen provides brief sketches of the experiences of Mozart, Mendelssohn, Liszt, Wagner, Brahms, Tschaikovsky, Richard Strauss, Stravinsky, and Bartok during their sojourns in Switzerland.

58 **Old-time travel: personal reminiscences of the Continent of forty years ago compared with experiences of the present day.**
Alexander Innes Shand. New York: James Pott, 1904. 426p.

The longest chapter in this book of reminiscences is devoted to 'Swiss touring'. Shand provides an eyewitness report of the profound changes that the advent of mass tourism wrought in the Swiss Alps within forty years of Shand's lifetime. Zermatt, where the first tourists had been put up by the *curé*, was now being built up with Seiler hotels. The Schweitzerhof [*sic*] in Luzern added *dépendance* after *dépendance* but was no longer supreme, only one of the best among many rivals. The railway tunnelled through the Gotthard, and the picturesque coaches that had rushed down the pass with Wild West-like abandonment were gone for ever. Davos was cashing in on the boom by over-extending its sanatorium constructions, and in Mürren the university dons and headmasters had 'taken to flight before the incursions of the barbarians'. Reproductions of watercolours by A. H. Hallam Murray reinforce the nostalgia of the text.

59 **Exilland Schweiz. Dokumentarischer Bericht über den Kampf emigrierter deutscher Kommunisten 1933-1945.** (Exile country Switzerland: documentary report on the struggle of *emigré* German Communists 1933-1945.)

Edited by Hans Teuwner. Berlin, GDR: Dietz; Frankfurt am Main, FRG: Röderberg, 1975. 374p.

Switzerland served as place of refuge and exile for many persecuted persons from various parts of Europe during the 19th and 20th centuries. A first wave of refugees came after the abortive German revolutions of 1848-49. It brought, among others, Richard Wagner and the great architect Gottfried Semper (1803-79) to Zurich. In 1864 nearly 2,000 Poles sought refuge in Switzerland; after the uprising of the Paris Commune of 1871 the French realist painter Gustave Courbet (1819-77) came to Switzerland where he died in exile. Geneva and the shores of Lake Geneva provided refuge to many Russian émigrés, fleeing from the tsars before 1917 and from the Bolsheviks afterwards – Lenin, Vladimir Nabokov (b. 1899), and Alexander Solzhenitsyn (b. 1918) are three of the most famous ones among them. The largest number of political refugees, however, undoubtedly came during the Nazi era from Germany, but Teubner deals with only one segment of that group: the Communist *émigrés*. His account shows that the Swiss government was hostile toward this segment of asylum seekers. Even though permeated by Communist propaganda and verbiage, the documents and illustrations assembled by Teubner provide a vivid picture of the life of his subjects in labour camps, and their attempts to make their voices heard through secretly produced journals and brochures.

60 **Descriptions géographiques et récits de voyages et excursions en Suisse.** (Geographical descriptions and accounts of travels and excursions in Switzerland.)

Adolf Waeber. Bern: K. J. Wyss, 1899. 440p. Supplement 1909, 172p. (Bibliographie nationale suisse, III).

One of the volumes in the *Schweizerische Landeskunde* (q.v.), this comprehensive bibliography of articles and books on the travel literature of Switzerland up to 1908 contains more than 8,000 titles, arranged geographically and chronologically. Most of the English-language titles were given to Waeber by W. A. B. Coolidge who wrote *Swiss travel and Swiss guide-books* (q.v.). The Alpine literature has a choice place in this bibliography, and there are also indexes of authors and places.

61 **Zermatt saga.**

Cicely Williams. Brig, Switzerland: Rotten, 1978. 196p. (First published by Allen & Unwin, London, 1964).

This book about Zermatt is the labour of love of someone who rates Zermatt above any other mountain resort anywhere in the world, as 'the alpine Holy of Holies', to be approached like a shrine. The first part of the book consists of a historical sketch of the evolution of Zermatt and the Matterhorn into the mecca of mountain climbers and a centre of tourism. All the famous names are here – Whymper, the Taugwalders and Seilers, and Lunn among them – with the stories of their exploits. The second part describes the geography of the Matter valley and portrays life among the natives and the profession of the mountain guide. The third and last part discusses the impact of the tourist explosion after World War II: dozens of new hotels and apartment buildings, téléfériques, cable cars, and ski-lifts, and the avalanche of skiers who now invade Zermatt also in winter. Times have changed, but Zermatt is still a jewel.

Famous visitors and exiles

62 **Edward Gibbon: memoirs of my life.**
Edited by Georges A. Bonnard. London: Nelson; New York: Funk & Wagnalls, 1969. 346p.

Gibbon (1737-94) wrote six drafts of his autobiography. Bonnard, using the existing manuscripts, combined the drafts into a continuous narrative. His thirty-page introduction and copious notes attest the rigorous scholarly standards he employed in this new edition of the autobiography of the famous eighteenth-century English historian. Two of the eight parts are entitled 'Lausanne'. In the first part Gibbon describes his stay in Lausanne from 1753 to 1758; he was sent by his father into 'exile' as punishment for his having become Catholic. Under the guidance of the Protestant minister Daniel Pavilliard with whom he lodged, not only was he brought back to the fold but also acquired fluency in French, deepened his knowledge of Latin and the Roman authors, and learned the rudiments of classical Greek. 'Such as I am in Genius or learning or in manners, I owe my creation to Lausanne: it was in that school, that the statue was discovered in the bloc of marble', he later wrote. In 1783 Gibbon returned to Lausanne where 'the country, the people, the manners, the language were congenial to my taste'. He had selected that cosmopolitan and beautiful city on Lake Geneva 'as the most grateful retreat for the decline of my life', and the last part of his autobiography, 'Lausanne (1783-1793)', describes how in these pleasant surroundings, Gibbon completed the last three volumes of his six-volume *History of the Decline and Fall of the Roman Empire*.

63 **Boswell on the grand tour: Germany and Switzerland, 1764.**
Edited by Frederick A. Pottle. New York [etc]: McGraw-Hill, 1953. 357p. maps. (The Yale Edition of the Private Papers of James Boswell).

Twenty-four year old James Boswell (1740-95) visited Rousseau and Voltaire on the way from Germany to Italy in late 1764. He introduced himself to both and was allowed to visit Rousseau at Môtiers in the Neuchâtel Jura, and Voltaire at Ferney, outside Geneva. 'I present myself, Sir, as a man of singular merit, as a man with a feeling heart, a lively but melancholy spirit' is one of the carefully drafted phrases by which he succeeded in gaining access to Rousseau. Boswell recorded several long interviews in his journal in French. His account of the meal he had with Rousseau and Mademoiselle Le Vasseur gives a unique glimpse of the famous Genevan in a domestic setting. Boswell thanked his host with the words: 'You have shown me great goodness. But I deserved it'. His pride knew no bounds when he was not only received by Voltaire but invited to spend the night at Ferney, as he had suggested in a note to Voltaire's niece. The editor of this volume uses the Boswell journal, much of it written in French, and letters to, from, and about him to weave a continuous story from the moment Boswell touched Swiss soil in Basel on 24 November 1764, to the day he left Geneva on 31 December. He rightfully points out how extraordinary the conjunction of the names Boswell, Rousseau, and Voltaire was and what a happy accident that these figures converged as they did, 'with an essential fitness, and, at the same time, an exquisite incongruity'.

64 **Sketches of the natural, civil and political state of Swisserland [sic]; in a series of letters to William Melmouth, Esq. from William Coxe, M.A. Fellow of King's College; and Chaplain to His Grace the Duke of Marlborough**

William Coxe. London: J. Dodsley, Pall Mall, 1779. 533p.

Between 21 July and early November 1776 Archdeacon William Coxe (1747-1828) traversed on foot the whole of Switzerland from Schaffhausen to the Gotthard to Bern, Geneva, and Basel, with side-trips from the major places. The forty-three letters in which he tells about his experiences and observations are cool and detached, but always positive and interspersed with much encyclopaedic information. He gives an especially long description of his stay in Zurich where 'there is more of the original Swiss spirit of independence, than in any of the large towns of this country'. He writes approvingly of Zwingli's reformation and describes his visits with 'the celebrated Gesner' and 'Mr. Lavater'. In the Zurich arsenal he was shown the bow and arrow with which William Tell was said to have shot the apple off the head of his son. Coxe visited Switzerland again in 1779, 1785, and 1786 and published a three-volume account of his experiences *Travels in Switzerland and in the country of the Grisons* in 1789. A French translation by Ramond de Carbonnières, *Voyages en Suisse par M. William Coxe*, was published in Lausanne in 1790 and is frequently cited in works about early travel in Switzerland.

65 **Goethes Erlebnis der Schweiz.** (Goethe's experience of Switzerland.)

Jonas Fränkel. St Gallen, Switzerland: Tschudy, 1949. 58p.

Johann Wolfgang Goethe (1749-1832) visited Switzerland at several stages of his life. He admired the splendour of its landscape, standing in awe before the majestic mountains and basking in the loveliness of its lakes. On his first journey in 1765 he visited the creative spirits in Zurich, while in 1779 he was attracted by the naturalists and scientists in Bern and Geneva. The last trip in the autumn of 1797 led him again to the shores of Lake Zurich and the company of his life-long friend, Heinrich Meyer. Each of these visits found a record in diary entries, letters, and poems of great beauty. Switzerland was important to Goethe, Fränkel says, in two main respects: as a stimulant for his appreciation and understanding of nature and as the home of some of his dearest friends, especially Meyer. See also *Goethes Briefe aus der Schweiz 1779* (Goethe's letters from Switzerland 1779), published by Holbein in Basel in 1949 and taken from volume 16 of Goethe's complete works, as published in 1828 by Cotta in Stuttgart and Tübingen.

66 **Die Reise der Familie Mozart durch die Schweiz.** (The journey of the Mozart family through Switzerland.)

Lucas E. Staehelin. Bern: Francke, 1968. 112p. bibliog.

When travelling abroad, Leopold Mozart usually kept a journal in which he recorded the family's activities in detail. However, for a period of four months after 9 July 1766, when he and his talented children left Paris to go to, among other places, Switzerland, there is no record. It is through letters written by Leopold or admirers of young Wolfgang (1756-91) that the Swiss experience has to be patched together. The Mozarts stayed in the best and centrally located hotels in Geneva, Lausanne, Bern, Zurich, Winterthur, and Schaffhausen from where they visited important people and did their sightseeing. Many prominent Swiss personalities met the nine-year-old *Wunderkind*, who was actually close to eleven, and raved about his composing, performing, improvising, and sightreading skills. The book is nicely illustrated, and a sample of letters provide a flavour of the times.

67 **Journals of Dorothy Wordsworth.**
Edited by Ernest de Selincourt. London: Macmillan, 1952. 2 vols. maps.

About one-third of the second volume (434p.) of this edition contains the part of the 'Journal of a tour on the Continent' by Dorothy Wordsworth (1771-1855) which deals with Switzerland. Wordsworth had been dreaming of travelling to Switzerland since her youth, and in 1820 this dream became reality. With a party of seven people she travelled across Switzerland from Schaffhausen with its Rhine Falls to Lombardy and back to the Valais and Geneva. She kept copious notes which she found difficult to edit for a book. 'It is', she said, 'utterly unsatisfactory to myself as a description of Switzerland; a land where height, depth, bulk, nay immensity, – profusion – silence – solitude make up the grandest of our feelings, – where it is utterly impossible to describe the objects except by the effects on the mind.' Nevertheless, as the editor observes, the journal, as it was finally put together by a person whose identity is unknown, with its many well-observed details and accurate descriptions, is a worthy part of the travel literature that has emanated from England.

68 **Turner in Switzerland.**
John Russell, Andrew Wilton. Dübendorf, Switzerland: De Clivo, 1976. 148p. maps. bibliog.

Joseph Mallord William Turner RA (1775-1851) visited Switzerland six times between 1802 and 1844. From his travels to many parts of the country resulted thousands of drawings, studies, and sketches, many finished watercolours, and a number of oil paintings. Russell, who wrote the introduction to Turner in Switzerland, comments: 'We may wonder . . . whether any other artist, before Turner or after him, has been more ardent, or more all-comprehending, in his devotion to the Swiss scene.' This large-format book contains a selection of ninety reproductions of Turner's renderings of towns, lakes, mountains, alpine passes, gorges, waterfalls, and bridges. Sixty of the reproductions are in colour, twenty-two of them on double-page spreads. They are of superb quality, bringing out Turner's delicate shades with extraordinary fidelity. Wilton has provided for each of the works reproduced an informative and scholarly commentary, as well as several helpful appendices. This book does justice to the genius of Turner who, of all the many visitors of Switzerland, undoubtedly left the most impressive and substantial legacy of his encounter with the land and its people.

69 **Byron et la Suisse: deux études.** (Byron and Switzerland: two studies.)
John Clubbe, Ernest Giddey. Geneva: Droz, 1982. 182p. bibliog. (Publication de la Faculté des Lettres, Université de Lausanne, 24).

The first of the two studies in this book is entitled 'Byron in the Alps: The Journal of Jon Cam Hobhouse, 17-29 September 1816'. Clubbe describes Hobhouse and his relationship with Byron (1788-1824) before transcribing that part of Hobhouse's diary that covers the friends' journey through the Bernese Oberland. Hobhouse's descriptions inform us of the daily activities, eating, walking, and lodging, and mention the places visited and the people encountered. Reference is made to passages in Byron's *Manfred* that bear direct witness to this alpine journey. The second study, by Giddey, is titled 'La renommée de Byron à Genève et dans le Canton de Vaud (1816-1824)' (The reputation of Byron in Geneva and Canton Vaud [1816-1824]). The poet's relations with the people of Geneva and Vaud were rather superficial; he preferred the comparative solitude of the small circle of close friends at his rented villa Diodati. However, the images and impressions from those days found their way into his writing.

The third canto of *Childe Harold's Pilgrimage*, the 'Prisoner of Chillon', and the writings around the theme of Lake Geneva stem from his days in Switzerland. At his death in 1824, Byron's work was translated and imitated and became known in French-speaking Switzerland. Some hundred years later, Byron's 'immorality' was no longer judged as such, and his sojourn in Switzerland, his life at the villa Diodati, his travels, and his work were commemorated widely and became part of the literary heritage of French Switzerland.

70 **Byron and the Romantics in Switzerland 1816.**
Elma Dangerfield. London; Nashville, Tennessee: Ascent, 1978. 93p. bibliog.

Dangerfield chronicles Lord Byron's stay in Switzerland in 1816 where he travelled to forget the scandals he had caused in England. Geneva and the shores of the lake had become a Mecca for English tourists after Napoleon's travel ban was lifted. Welcomed by Genevans and shunned by British guests, he sought privacy in the villa Diodati at Cologny. A chance meeting with the poet Shelley led for a while to a close companionship and mutual inspiration. Leisurely trips in the company of women inspired the writers' works. Byron, after reading Rousseau's *Nouvelle Heloïse*, traced the places mentioned in the novel, and a visit to Voltaire's Ferney followed; visits to Madame de Staël's château tell of the life in that society. After Shelley's return to England, Byron's friend from Trinity College days, Jon Cam Hobhouse, became his travelling companion. It was during a trip to the Bernese Oberland that Byron began his dramatic work *Manfred*. In a letter from Italy in 1821 Byron wrote of his productive four months in Switzerland: 'How I wrote then!' His creativity had been fuelled by the scenery and meeting of minds.

71 **Gleanings in Europe: Switzerland.**
James Fenimore Cooper. Albany, New York: State University of New York Press, 1980. xliii, 361p.

Cooper (1789-1851) spent the summer of 1828 in Switzerland. He travelled widely to many parts of the country and took copious notes, mainly on the scenery. After his return to the United States he transformed his notes into a book, made up of thirty letters. The work was first published in America under the title *Sketches of Switzerland* in 1836, and in England as *Excursions in Switzerland*, also in 1836. Cooper identified the Swiss scenery with the picturesque. He chose subjects for their painterly appeal, attempting to communicate what language probably could not express. This keen sensibility for the majesty of the Alps sets Cooper's work apart from the run-of-the-mill travel book. The didactic side of Cooper is apparent in his observations on the social conditions he found on his trips and in the political opinions he directed against his opponents at home. This volume is meticulously edited by a team of literary scholars who provided an apparatus of notes, appendices, and commentary, in addition to the substantial 'historical introduction'. Engravings of Swiss scenes by William Henry Bartlett (1809-54) taken from a work published in London in 1836 complement Cooper's writings.

72 **Victor Hugo et la Suisse.** (Victor Hugo and Switzerland.)
Lucien Lathion. Neuchâtel, Switzerland: Attinger, 1974. 155p.

Victor Hugo (1802-85) visited Switzerland five times – in 1825, 1839, 1869, 1883, and 1884. On the first three visits he took notes and wrote letters that make it possible to reconstruct his itineraries. On the last he was seriously ill and no longer wrote. Hugo always travelled fast from place to place, preferring the coach to the railway. Unlike his fellow Romantics, he was not especially enamoured with the mountains; on the Rigi, he did not know whether to call the sunrise beautiful or horrible. 'In the presence of this spectacle, inexpressible, one can understand the imbeciles that populate Switzerland and Savoy. The Alps make many idiots. Not all minds can stand such marvels and walk around in them from morning till evening without losing touch and becoming stupefied. . . '. The trip that left the best memory was that of 1839. Hugo's impressions and observations, among them another one of a long series of travellers' accounts of the Rhine Falls near Schaffhausen, were published in his notes *Le Rhin, Alpes et Pyrénées. Voyages et excursions* (The Rhine, Alps, Pyrenees: voyages and excursions).

73 **My past and thoughts: the memoirs of Alexander Herzen.**

Translated by Constance Garnett, revised by Humphrey Higgins, introduced by Isaiah Berlin. London: Chatto & Windus; Toronto: Clarke, Irwin, 1968. 4 vols.

Russian journalist and revolutionary Herzen (1812-70) went into exile from Tsarist Russia in 1847. He travelled with his family all over western Europe, spending much of his time in Switzerland. In the second volume of his memoirs, chapter 5, entitled 'Paris-Italy-Paris', he tells of his acquisition of Swiss citizenship. 'Except for Swiss naturalisation I would not have accepted citizenship in any European country, not even England; I was repelled by the idea of voluntarily becoming anybody's subject. I did not want to change a bad master for a good one, but to escape from serfdom into being a free husbandman. This was possible in only two countries: America and Switzerland'. For various reasons America was out of the question, 'so there was nothing left but to enter into an alliance with the free men of the Helvetian Confederation'. In 1851 he was accepted by majority vote into the community of Châtel, near Murten, Canton Fribourg, an event that was celebrated with speechmaking and much drinking of local wine. 'So that is how I became a free citizen of the Swiss Confederation and got drunk on Châtel wine'. Other experiences were not so lighthearted, but Herzen never lost his admiration for and appreciation of the Swiss republic which provided a refuge, if not a home, for the harassed traveller and his family.

74 **Charles Dickens in Switzerland.**

Paul-Emile Schazmann. Zurich: Swiss National Tourist Office, 1972. 46p.

This small, nicely illustrated, booklet recounts the story of Dickens's trips to Switzerland. Charles Dickens (1812-70) visited Switzerland in 1844, 1846, and 1853. He spent the second half of 1846 with his wife and children in Lausanne where he worked on *Dombey and son* and *The battle of life*. He observed the political stirrings in Switzerland and wrote to a friend: 'Don't be too hard upon the Swiss. They are a thorn in the side of European despots – my hat shall ever be ready to be thrown up, and my glove ever be ready to be thrown down for Switzerland'. In 1853 he returned for a last time when he went to the Simplon pass in search of the scenery for his theatre production *No thoroughfare*.

75 **Richard Wagner in Zürich.** (Richard Wagner in Zurich.)

Hans Erismann. Zurich: Neue Zürcher Zeitung, 1987. 254p. bibliog.

In 1849 Wagner (1813-83) sought political asylum in Zurich after having participated in the Dresden revolt in his native Saxony. The ensuing nine years were among the most creative phases in his life. The lively and spirited Zurich environment inspired the *Ring*, *Tristan und Isolde*, and *Parsifal*. Experiences on hikes through the Alps are reflected in the *Ring*, and the *Meistersinger* mirrors the Zurich spring festival (Sechseläuten). Wagner thought of constructing the festival hall for the *Ring* in Zurich. As conductor of the Allgemeine Musikgesellschaft, the general music society, he guided Zurich's musical life to a unique climax, so that the usually reserved Zurchers gave him a torch parade. The small Saxon also kept the Zurchers breathless with his social life. He was easily irritated and touchy, and jealousies and escapades eventually led to his departure. Among the social protagonists were his wife Minna and the beautiful Mathilde Wesendonck, the wife of one of his main benefactors, while Cosima von Bülow was already waiting in the wings. Erismann's account is interspersed with excerpts from letters and other documents, numerous full-page plates of old photographs of people and places which Wagner frequented, and of manuscript pages of compositions. See also *Richard Wagners Schweizer Zeit* (Richard Wagner's stay in Switzerland) by Max Fehr (Aarau and Leipzig: Sauerländer, 1934-53, 2 vols); the first volume covers the years 1849-55 and the second the years 1855-72.

76 **My life. Richard Wagner.**
Edited by Mary Whittal, translated from the German by Andrew Gray. Cambridge, England [etc.]: Cambridge University Press, 1983. 786p. map.

The story of Wagner's autobiography and Cosima Wagner's diaries is in itself a chain of intrigue. The first complete edition of *Mein Leben* was not published until 1963, eighty years after the composer's death. It covers the first fifty years of his life, and about one-third of the book is taken up with Wagner's account of his activities while living in Zurich, Switzerland. Unceasingly active, he assembled a circle of friends and supporters, foremost among them Jacob Sulzer, the Wesendoncks, and the Willes; worked on *Tristan*, *Das Rheingold*, and *Siegfried*; conducted concerts and put new spirit into the musical life of Zurich; tried to supervise productions of his early operas in Paris and Dresden; and expressed his ideas in a series of theoretical works on the content and scope of the German opera. *Cosima Wagner's diaries*, edited by Martin Gregor-Dellin and Dietrich Mack, and translated by Geoffrey Skelton (London: Collins, 1978, 1119p.) pick up the story in 1869 when Cosima von Bülow, née Liszt (1838-1930), moved in with Wagner permanently in the villa he rented at Tribschen outside Luzern. A person who had early access to the diaries wrote of them that 'when one day this book can be published without cuts, it will be seen as one of the most important pronouncements of our time, for it covers not only Tribschen, Bayreuth, and Wahnfried, but also to some extent the entire intellectual and political world of its time'.

77 **Ruskin und die Schweiz.** (Ruskin and Switzerland.)
Elisabeth Gertrud Koenig. Bern: Francke, 1943. 152p. bibliog. (Swiss Studies in English, 14).

John Ruskin (1819-1900) visited Switzerland throughout his life. As Koenig shows in the four major chapters of this book, Switzerland was fruitful for him in all his endeavours. The chapters deal with the aesthetic-ethical, the religious, the literary, and the historical components of Ruskin's relationship. Ruskin's passionate love for nature found in Switzerland a reality that approached his ideal of the beautiful. His ethical and literary interests led him to the great contemporary Swiss writer Jeremias Gotthelf, whose studies of human character he found comparable to Scott's soundest works. He read Gotthelf in French translation and participated in the translation into English of

Gotthelf's novel *Ulrich the farm servant*. His Victorian puritanism was reinforced by what he thought was the dismal influence of Catholicism on its adherents, as seen by the poor living conditions of the inhabitants of Sion, capital of Canton Valais.

78 **Dostoïevski: l'homme et l'oeuvre.** (Dostoevsky: the man and his work.)
Pierre Pascal. Lausanne: L'Age d'Homme, 1970. 365p.

Dostoevsky (1821-81) spent the years 1867 and 1868 in Europe, almost an entire year of it in Geneva. In Geneva he made the acquaintance of Russian socialist exiles, among them, Herzen, Ogarev, and Bakunin. Dostoevsky was thoroughly turned off by their socialist and anti-Christian rhetoric. 'In my whole life have I not heard such absurdities, nor did I ever think men capable of expressing such stupidities', he wrote to his niece. Even though Dostoevsky disliked Geneva and also Vevey where he stayed during the summer of 1868, he was able to make much progress on his new novel *The Idiot*. He hated practically everything he had observed in the West and had nothing but scathing comments on all West European peoples. Switzerland he labelled that 'innoble republique where the bourgeois spirit has attained its *nec plus ultra*'. However, the Swiss 'have some good qualities which set them infinitely above the Germans'. His overriding criticism and grief was the fact that the 'Europeans' were so dismally ignorant about everything concerning Russia.

79 **Lucerne [from Prince Nekhloyúdov's memoirs].**
Leo Tolstoy. In: *Tolstoy, short stories: selected and introduced by Ernest J. Simmons*. New York: Random House, 1964, p. 306-31. (The Modern Library).

In his story 'Lucerne', Leo Tolstoy (1828-1910) relates through his friend Prince Nekhloyúdov an encounter which took place on his first trip abroad in 1857. It led him through France, Switzerland, northern Italy, and Germany. The foreign visitor arrives at the luxurious hotel Schweizerhof in Luzern with its beautiful view of the lake and the Rigi mountain. Time and again he is irritated by the English guests he observes on the quay and then later at dinner, showing off their great wealth. The songs of a dwarf-like beggar who leaves without being rewarded by these rich foreigners move him deeply, and he expresses his contempt for the Englishmen and his bewilderment that this could happen in Switzerland with the following words 'Why is this inhuman occurrence . . . possible here, where civilization, liberty, and equality have been brought to the highest point, and where the most civilized travellers from the most civilized nations congregate?' The theme of the heartlessness of the civilized world, the contrast of culture and nature are also present in many of Tolstoy's other tales. The Lucerne incident is recorded on page 138 of *Tolstoy's diaries*, vol. 1, 1847-1894 (edited and translated by R. F. Christian. New York: Scribner's, 1985).

80 **Travels in Switzerland. Alexandre Dumas.**
Edited by A. Craig Bell, translated from the French by R. W. Plummer, A. Craig Bell. London: Owen, 1958. 230p.

Bell has pared Dumas' three-volume account *Impressions de voyage: en Suisse* (1833-34) to a third of its size. The translation preserves the characteristics of Dumas' style: 'ironic humour, vivid descriptions, a flair for the dramatic, and shrewd characterization'. The book describes the adventures of Dumas (1802-70) during a holiday in Switzerland which led him to Geneva, the salt mines of Bex, a bear hunt near Martigny, the Bernese Oberland where 'songs of the countryside' followed him everywhere, the Rigi where twenty-seven travellers from eleven nations gathered at the inn to see the sunrise and where he got involved in a deadly duel between an Englishman and a Frenchman, a chamois hunt in the Glarus Alps, and other points in between and beyond. The editor places *En Suisse* not only among Dumas' best books but 'among the best books of travel ever written'.

81 **Mark Twain und die Schweiz.** (Mark Twain and Switzerland.)
August Hüppy. Zurich: Reutimann, 1935. 99p.

Mark Twain (1835-1910) visited Switzerland in 1878, 1891, and 1897. He recorded his experiences in letters and diaries and in the book *A tramp abroad* (1880). He was an inveterate admirer of the country, even though he liked to poke fun at some of the things he observed. Hüppy says that Mark Twain did with his writings as much for Switzerland in the English-speaking world as Schiller did with his *Wilhelm Tell* in Germany. On his last trip, after years of great financial and personal distress, Mark Twain took refuge with his family in private homes in Weggis on Lake Lucerne, 'the charmingest place we have ever lived in for repose and restfulness'. Dorfpresse Gattikon, Langnau am Albis, Switzerland, has published two charming booklets, entitled *Climbing the Rigi* and *Climbing the Riffelberg and across the Bernese Oberland*. They contain the texts of Twain's accounts of these episodes in English with a facing German translation; each is about fifty pages long and is neatly illustrated with contemporary engravings.

82 **A little Swiss sojourn.**
William Dean Howells. New York; London: Harper, 1892.

The American novelist, editor, and critic William Dean Howells (1837-1920) spent some time with his family near the castle of Chillon on Lake Geneva. They had the bad luck of encountering nothing but rainy autumn weather. The grapes were sour and could be bought more cheaply in London, Howells remarked. However, he did not lose his invariably good spirit, for he comments approvingly on the castles of Canton Vaud; the glistening of the snow on the Dent-du-Midi when one could see the mountains; the surprising lushness of the autumn colours; the quality of the air ('One can't speak too well of the Swiss air, whatever one says of the Swiss sun.'), and the loveliness of the voices of the 'Suissesses' 'which are the sweetest and most softly modulated voices in the world, whether they come from the throat of peasant or of lady, and can make a transaction in eggs and butter in the market-place as musical as chanted verse'. This charming little booklet is illustrated with twenty full-page drawings of Vaudois scenes.

83 **Our life in the Swiss highlands.**
John Addington Symonds, Margaret Symonds. London; Edinburgh: Adam & Charles Black, 1892. 366p.

John Addington Symonds (1840-93), prolific historian of the Italian Renaissance and biographer of English writers, spent – from 1878 on – extended periods of time for health reasons in the 'Swiss highlands', the highlands being Davos in Canton Graubünden. In this book he relates his experiences in that mountain village that was rapidly developing into a world-famous centre for the cure of respiratory ailments and tuberculosis and for winter sports. Symonds and his daughter Margaret, who contributed a few chapters to the book, dwell especially on their activities during the winter, when snow and avalanches cut off the Davos valley from the rest of the world.

Symonds overcame boredom by tobogganing and going on long sleigh rides, but mainly by working hard on his books. He was sustained by the awareness that the air and climate were of such invigorating quality as to promise recovery from his ailment. Parts of Symonds's book read like passages from Thomas Mann's *The Magic Mountain*.

84 **Switzerland in the life and work of Henry James.**
Jörg Hasler. Bern: Francke, 1966. 164p. bibliog.

This doctoral dissertation looks at Henry James (1843-1916) during his formative years, which he spent in boarding schools in Geneva and travelling in the Swiss Alps. Many of the experiences from these years found their way into James's work. They influenced his literary expression and are responsible for his 'sense of place'. Almost all his tales take place in a *pension* or hotel, reflecting the many impressions of Genevan private schools and of the different lodgings the cosmopolitan wanderer encountered on his journeys. The letters by Henry James reprinted in the back of the book are addressed to two female friends and are the property of the University of Basel.

85 **Frédéric Nietzsche en Suisse.** (Friedrich Nietzsche in Switzerland.)
Carl Jacob Burckhardt. Monaco: Imprimerie Nationale de Monaco, 1955. 45p.

Burckhardt composed this essay for oral delivery before the Société de Conférences de Monaco. He touches in an artful but somewhat circuitous fashion on all the major elements of Nietzsche's (1844-1900) relationship with Switzerland. Burckhardt begins with an account of Nietzsche's mental breakdown of 1889 and the sad cicrumstances that led to his hospitalization in a Basel insane asylum until his death in 1900. His first arrival in Basel in 1869 as a young professor of Greek language and literature at the University of Basel had been much happier, but his academic career became much too soon, from 1871 on, overshadowed by illness. Nietzsche established friendly relations with two colleagues, the theologian Franz Overbeck (1837-1905) and the cultural historian Jakob Burckhardt (1818-97). His infatuation with Richard and Cosima Wagner whom he visited weekly at their villa in Tribschen near Luzern, and the ensuing disenchantment, fall also in this period. For the next ten years he lived an erratic life, often seeking relief from his suffering in Sils Maria in the Upper Engadin in the company of the young châtelaine of Marschlins, Méta de Salis. When, during his hospitalization, a psychiatrist asked Nietzsche which his fatherland was, Nietzsche replied: 'Basel, the city of the humanists, and Sils Maria, the little village'. Burckhardt stresses the fact that this man who in his work exalted the strength of the powerful and exhorted the superman to destroy the weak was in his personal life an extremely considerate and delicate human being.

86 **Joyce in Zürich.** (Joyce in Zurich.)
Thomas Faerber, Markus Luchsinger. Zurich: Unionsverlag, 1988. 175p. bibliog.

A telegram promising Joyce (1882-1941) a teaching position in Zurich in 1904 brought him from Dublin to Switzerland. There was no job; without this incident, however, the writer might not have returned time and again to Zurich. He found a safe haven there during both World Wars and also underwent a successful eye operation in the city in 1930. While in Zurich, he and his family lived in modest quarters and depended on the assistance of friends. Joyce frequented Zurich's cafés; these served as meeting places for artists and intellectuals and he formed close friendship with some of them. These acquaintances served him as models for characters in *Ulysses* which he wrote during his first extended stay there. In *Finnegan's Wake* also one finds evidence of models and bits of language that Joyce derived from his Zurich experience. Joyce made no secret of the fact that he did not think much of C. G. Jung's psychoanalysis which received much publicity at the time, and when Jung was asked to write the foreword to *Ulysses* he dispensed his critical remarks freely. The writer, although always treated with respect, remained an outsider in Zurich. He died there in 1941 of the complications of a stomach operation, and he is buried there. Faerber and Luchsinger document Joyce's Zurich years with many photographs and a list of chapters and phrases that originated from that time.

87 **Lenin in Zurich.**

Alexander Solzhenitsyn, translated from the Russian by H. T. Willetts. New York: Farrar, Straus & Giroux, 1976. 309p. bibliog.

Solzhenitsyn's literary account of Lenin's sojourn in Switzerland from 1914 to 1917 is based on careful research and study of historical sources, foremost among them Lenin's own writings of that period. Solzhenitsyn succeeds in creating a convincing picture of the private lives of Vladimir Ilyich Ulianov and his wife Nadya Krupskaya in their small rented apartment (Spiegelgasse 14) in Zurich, and of the streets and libraries of that city of exile. He also recreates with great insight and delight Lenin's interactions with the Swiss socialists, which were often stormy and full of reciprocal insults, and his incessant efforts to keep the Bolshevik cause alive in the face of adversity and mounting despair. In a masterstroke of political intrigue Lenin and Radek used the Swiss socialists as intermediaries to arrange for their trip across imperial Germany aboard the famous sealed railroad car in early April 1917. See also *Lenin als Emigrant in der Schweiz* (Lenin as emigrant in Switzerland) by Willi Gautschi (Zurich and Cologne: Benziger, 1973).

88 **Rainer Maria Rilke: the years in Switzerland, a contribution to the biography of Rilke's later life.**

J. R. von Salis, translated from the German by N. K. Cruickshank. Berkeley, California; Los Angeles: University of California Press, 1964. 322p. (Originally published in 1936).

Rilke (1875-1926) spent the last years of his life in Switzerland. In 1919 he took refuge from the 'five impenetrable, sterile years, interrupting all genuine life' of the World War I period in the castle of Muzot near Sierre in the Rhône valley of Canton Valais. The peace he found there, after a life of wandering through Europe, allowed him to finish the long poem *Duino Elegies* and the *Sonnets to Orpheus*. Von Salis knew Rilke as a family guest and frequently visited him at Muzot. In his book he compassionately records his conversations with the great German lyric poet who became ill with leukaemia. In accordance with his wish, Rilke was buried in the graveyard of the castle-church of Raron, situated on a promontory overlooking the Rhône valley.

89 **Chaplin.**

Roger Manvell. Boston, Massachusetts; Toronto: Little, Brown, 1974. 240p. bibliog.

The last of the seven chapters in this book on Charlie Chaplin (1889-1977) is entitled 'Manoir de Ban – The halcyon years'. Manoir de Ban is the name of the estate near Vevey on Lake Geneva where Chaplin spent the last twenty-three years of his life. The quiet life in Switzerland with his young wife Oona and his large family is in contrast to that of the poor little boy from London turned Hollywood star of silent film, from the man who received hysterical adulation from the masses yet was hounded by dubious accusations of political and moral trangressions. When the United States withdrew Chaplin's re-entry permit at the beginning of an extended vacation abroad, Chaplin decided to go into exile. In *My autobiography* (1964) Chaplin cites financial considerations for choosing to make Switzerland his home. While the artist pursued many interests during these later years, the Swiss experience does not evidence itself in his work. During his years in Switzerland, famous visitors from all over the world came to pay their respect to one of the most significant contributors to this century's popular culture.

Travel guides

90 **Berlitz country guide: Switzerland 1988/89 edition.**
Lausanne, Switzerland: Berlitz Guides, 1985. 152p. maps.

This is the smallest of all travel guides in format and size, easily fitting into a pocket. It provides basic information about the country and describes the major regions and cities from Zurich to Geneva. The booklet also has twenty-five pages of 'Berlitz-Info' with practical advice for the traveller, interspersed with brief sections of English phrases with their German, French, and Italian translations. See also *Berlitz travel guide: Switzerland, French-speaking areas* (Lausanne: Berlitz, 1979). This guide covers only the Western and French-speaking part of Switzerland. It also has a section with useful phrases in English–French translation.

91 **Swiss country inns & chalets.**
Karen Brown, Clare Brown, illustrated by Barbara Tapp. San Mateo, California: Travel Press, 1984. 247p. maps.

The title of this travel guide is misleading. Some hotels featured here, such as the Bellevue Palace in Bern or the Seiler Hotel Mont Cervin in Zermatt do not have the cosy atmosphere, the native architecture, and local flavour that one expects to find in a country inn or chalet. Instead, these, like many others praised by the authors, are first-class hotels that cater to an international clientele. The mainstay of the book are the five itineraries that introduce novice Swiss travellers to the country's famous sights and to places they know from postcards; each tour takes about a week. Daily itineraries with scenic and cultural highlights end in one of the hotels researched by the Browns and illustrated with a drawing by Tapp. The tours for those who want to discover the Swiss mountains, and the one that leads to picturesque medieval villages, are well mapped out. The 'best on a budget' tour necessitates a considerably higher budget than one is used to finding in a 'twenty dollars a day' book. 'Switzerland: by train, boat and bus' should be especially helpful to tourists who want to use public and private transport but are unsure how to plan. While the schedules given for arrival and departure times may no longer be accurate, they, nevertheless, give a good idea about the distances and the different means of transport available. The book contains much general travel information and many useful tips that should facilitate getting around in Switzerland.

92 **Swiss travel and Swiss guide-books.**
William Augustus Brevoort Coolidge. London; New York: Longmans, Green, 1889. 336p.

American-born W. A. B. Coolidge (1850-1926) was one of the outstanding members of the group of Alpinists known as the Victorian mountaineers. He undertook more than 1,700 mountaineering expeditions, first in his teens with his aunt Meta Breevort, and later with her and his dog Tschingel, and still later with members of the Almer family of Grindelwald. Parallel to these exploits, he began to develop a career as Alpine historiographer. Eventually he accumulated a library of 16,000 titles, with emphasis on Alpine and Swiss history. His privately printed bibliography of his writings included 220 items: he had become 'the greatest Alpine historian that the world had ever known' (Ronald Clark, *The Victorian mountaineers*, p. 147). *Swiss travel and Swiss guide-books* is an erudite book with much interesting material. A third of it consists of the description of the more important guide-books available in the 1880s to the traveller to Switzerland, among them Gesner, Scheuchzer, Simler, Merian, the early Baedekers, and Murray. This part is followed by a list of 241 titles of major works about the Alpine regions of Switzerland from the 15th century to the 1850s, and by comments on inns and alpine huts. A final chapter traces in great detail the history of Zermatt. Coolidge's collection of books and papers is in the Zurich central library (Zentralbibliothek).

93 **Fodor's 89: Switzerland including Liechtenstein.**
New York; London: Fodor's Travel Publications, 1988. 355p. maps.

The 1989 Switzerland volume reflects Fodor's intention to enhance its guides with a more critical voice. A series of individually signed introductory essays on such things as the history and institutions of Switzerland, and sports and festivals, is followed by a tour of the country, beginning in Zurich and ending in Ticino. Fodor strikes a nice balance between the discussion of hotels and restaurants, and features on the historical and cultural background of particular places.

94 **Switzerland the cheap way: a travellers' handbook.**
Edited by Marianne Glauser, Brigitte Ringger, translated from the German by Edward Robeson, Kevan Keegan. Zurich: Swiss Student Travel Office, 1978. 114p, 47p of maps.

This is a compact guide to Switzerland with the student traveller in mind. A thirty-page general section contains information on such things as climate, food and drink, history and politics, culture, and the economy; practical information is included on money, transport, postal rates, electricity, opening hours of stores and offices, and so on. In section two the reader is led in a meandering way from place to place across Switzerland, and for each of about fifty places the prospective traveller receives information concerning transport (including tips about the best spots from where to hitchhike), cheap accommodation, and eating places – from the cheapest to the more expensive, and including a few speciality restaurants with local dishes. For the larger places, information is provided concerning entertainment, theatre, concerts, films, sports, shopping, museums, sights, special events, and excursions. Useful addresses and telephone numbers complete the offerings of this handy guide. While prices have gone up since it was published in 1978, this is still the best source of information for people on a tight budget.

95 **Switzerland at its best.**

Robert S. Kane. Lincolnwood, Illinois: Passport Books, 1987. 266p. maps.

Kane provides an introduction to nineteen Swiss tourist centres, among which the major cities are included. The organization of the chapters follows a uniform scheme: a 'background briefing' gives a general description of the historical and geographical setting of the place; the section 'on scene' describes the lie of the land, with major attractions and recommended excursions; in the 'daily bread' part the reader is informed about hotels and restaurants from luxury to moderate; the 'sound of music' section lists music festivals, operas, and symphony orchestras; and under the heading 'incidental intelligence' one is given useful addresses such as that of the local tourist office, or tips about shopping. The whole is done in a pleasant, sympathetic way. Kane does not overpower the reader with information; his entries are carefully selected and well commented, and he displays sound judgement throughout. This guide is for those who do not have to count their pennies.

96 **Walking Switzerland the Swiss way: from vacation apartments, hotels, mountain inns, and huts.**

Marcia and Philip Lieberman. Seattle, Washington: Mountaineers, 1987. 273p. maps.

The first part of this interesting book describes day hikes from five tourist centres where vacation apartments are readily available – Zermatt, Saas-Fee, and Val d'Hérens in Canton Valais; Grindelwald in the Bernese Oberland; and the Lower Engadin in Canton Graubünden – with access, trail markings, elevations, distances, times, and technical difficulties. A second part contains the descriptions of longer, more complex walks that require overnight stays in mountain lodgings; these are in the Bernese Oberland, Valais, Upper Engadin, Ticino, and Emmental. This 'guide book with a difference' has rightfully been praised as 'a definitive guide to a most civilized way of hiking a glorious country'.

97 **Michelin green guide: Switzerland.**

Michelin Tourist Services. Harrow, England: Michelin Tyre, 1985. 8th ed. 217p. maps.

This guide, with its typical elongated, narrow form and its signature green colour, is one of the most appealing and trustworthy products in a steadily growing field of guides for tourists to Switzerland. Since it deals neither with restaurants nor hotels or places of entertainment, its pages can focus exclusively on the description of geographical features, historical background, and cultural and scenic attractions. A general section of some forty pages provides as good an introduction to Switzerland as can be found anywhere. The few proposed touring programmes touch upon the major attractions of the country. The main body of the guide consists of an alphabetical treatment of towns, sights, and tourist regions with numerous maps, city plans, and ink drawings. The liberally used asterisks reliably guide tourists to the things that are especially worthwhile to visit, and the informed commentary is useful even to native Swiss. This is an excellent publication.

98 **Murray's handbook for travellers in Switzerland 1838.**
John Murray, William Brockedon, introduced by Jack Simmons. Leicester, England: University Press; New York: Humanities Press, 1970. 367p. (Victorian Library. Reprint of the 1838 edition).

Murray's Switzerland handbook was one of the earliest major modern guidebooks. It was written by John Murray III (1808-92), who in his early twenties had travelled, notebook in hand, to many parts of the Continent, and by William Brockedon (1781-1854) who wrote most of the mountain sections. As Simmons points out, 'the volume on Switzerland was one of the first, and one of the very best, in the distinguished and extensive series' of some thirty Murray's travel books famous in Victorian England. Its last edition, the nineteenth, was published in 1904. This reprint is, above all, of historical interest. The handbook has an elaborate introduction of fifty pages giving information on money, distances, diligences, horses, and mules; the characteristics of the country with its alpine passes, chalets, pastures, glaciers, and avalanches; and some comments on goitre and cretinism observed among the population. Minute descriptions of 136 itineraries through all parts of Switzerland are full of personal commentary.

99 **Frommer's dollarwise guide to Switzerland and Liechtenstein.**
Darwin Porter. New York: Prentice Hall, 1988-89 edition. 503p. maps.

After a brief introduction with general information on the two countries treated in the guide, the author systematically covers all parts of Switzerland in twelve chapters, with a thirteenth reserved for Liechtenstein. The chapters follow a uniform format, beginning with some general remarks about the place or the region presented, followed by a major part given to a description of the accommodation available, always the deluxe establishments first (which is strange, given that this is a 'dollarwise' guide), a section on 'where to dine', and one on 'what to see'. Less visited destinations are the subject of shorter entries in which the guide section actually may be larger than the one on 'food and lodging'. Much useful information on the public transport system, for example, or the location of tourist offices, pharmacies, recreation facilities, and other items that might help the tourist is included in the entries for the larger cities and tourist centres. The lists of lodgings, generally in the range of $20 to $80 for a single room with breakfast, and food seem to be carefully researched.

100 **Baedeker's Allianz travel guide: Switzerland 1985-87.**
Hans Rathgeb, translated from the German by James Hogarth. Stuttgart; Freiburg, FRG: Baedeker, 1985. 336p. maps.

Baedeker, renowned in the field of travel books, continues its proud tradition with this Switzerland guide. The book with its 233 colour photographs, eighty-three maps, plans and sketches, and one large road map is full of every kind of information a tourist might need or want. The 'introduction to Switzerland' section provides a fine overview of many of the interesting aspects of Swiss history, society, economy, and creative life. Practical information is also included, but the bulk of the space is taken up by 'Switzerland from A to Z', an alphabetical listing and description of the Swiss tourist attractions, from 'Aarau' to 'Lake Zurich'. Discreet red asterisks, one or rarely two, are (too) sparingly used to highlight the major attractions found in nature or created by human hands.

101 **Blue guide: Switzerland.**

Ian Robertson. London: A. & C. Black; New York: W. W. Norton, 1987. 4th ed. 352p. maps. bibliog.

This handy guide has many strong points, not least among them the eighty-page introductory part, the core of which is an overview of Swiss history by Clive H. Church. Other essays by separate authors describe the ecology of Switzerland, and skiing and mountaineering in Switzerland, with useful bibliographies. The bulk of the book is taken up by more than fifty itineraries that cover the country, beginning in Geneva and ending south of the Alps, with maps and plans of the major cities and a few well-chosen illustrations. This informative guide is helpful to travellers who prefer the British itinerary style over the place-by-place approach of the Baedeker and Michelin guides.

102 **Switzerland.**

John Russell. London: Batsford, 1962. 192p. map.

The first edition of this book came out in 1950, and it is one of many travel books about Switzerland by Englishmen. Many of these books enjoyed great popularity and necessitated multiple editions. The revised paperback edition of 1962 takes the traveller from Geneva to Neuchâtel and Bern, through the Valais to Central Switzerland and Zurich, then south to the Ticino, from there to Graubünden, and finally from Basel up the River Rhine to north-eastern Switzerland, ending up in St Gallen. Historical facts, architectural notes, cultural pointers, descriptions of scenery, and quotes from famous foreigners who spent time in the country are woven into a seamless and entertaining story that serves as an informative guide even though modern technology has altered some of the scenes described here. Thirty-one full-page photographs are interspersed in the text. A travel guide from the same period by an American tourist is *Footloose in Switzerland* by Horace Sutton (New York; Toronto: Rinehart, 1952). Sutton's travel columns in the *Saturday Review* were enjoyed for many years by a faithful readership.

103 **Downhill walking in Switzerland.**

Richard and Linda Williams. Tulsa, Oklahoma: Old World Travel, 1988. 82p. maps.

Travel agent Linda Williams and her radiologist husband are experienced world travellers. Since so many hilltops and mountains in Switzerland are accessible by a variety of methods of transport, the Williamses conceived the idea of putting a booklet together about walking down from the tops rather than climbing up. This indeed is a splendid idea, especially for the elderly tourist. The paperback begins with thirty-two full-size colour photographs of scenes from the hikes recommended in the text that follows. The traveller will find information about how to prepare for the adventure, about transport and schedules, lodging, and cost. Zurich is the starting point for these downhill walking experiences because of its airport and the two worthwhile, yet easy descents from the Ütliberg and the Zürichberg. The hikes in the Bernese Oberland are in the well-known resort areas of Grindelwald, Wengen, and Mürren. Tours in Canton Appenzell with the Kronberg and Säntis, in central Switzerland around Lake Lucerne, and in the region of Flims in Canton Graubünden are also featured.

104 **Schweiz Reiseführer. Offizieller Führer des Touring Clubs der Schweiz.** (Switzerland travel guide: official guide of the Touring Club of Switzerland.)
Edited by Günther Wöllner. Bern: Kümmerly & Frey, 1986. 287p. maps.

This guide, which is a revised and updated translation of the *Guida d'Europa/Svizzera* of the Touring Club Italiano (Milan, 1984), contains thirty-six descriptions of routes for car travellers, and nineteen city plans. Swiss cities from Aarau to Zurich are presented in detail, with easy-to-read maps. Practical information with a sample of hotels is also provided.

Tourist maps

105 **Das grosse Autoreise- und Freizeitbuch Schweiz-Europa.** (The big road travel and leisure book Switzerland-Europe.)
Touring Club der Schweiz. Bern: Kümmerly & Frey, 1988. 624p.

The first part of this book (228 pages) consists of a Swiss road map at 1:225,000 and the maps of thirty-five Swiss cities, with street indexes. The margins of the map pages contain information on important tourist attractions and cultural sites, as well as the addresses of chambers of commerce and tourist offices. The second part does the same for all of Europe, from Lisbon to Moscow, and Hammerfest to Catánia. These maps are at 1:1,000,000 and 1:2,750,000. There are also forty-five maps of European cities. A similar publication is the *Auto Reisebuch Schweiz Europa* (Road travel book Switzerland Europe) (Zurich: Das Beste aus Reader's Digest, 1980). It is an atlas and an encyclopaedia in one. A specially attractive feature of this guide are the suggestions for thirty automobile trips of less than 100 kilometres in all parts of Switzerland. Many other road maps are available, almost all of them with English text, at a scale of 1:300,000, or thereabouts. The Swiss National Tourist Office makes such a map available free. Michelin, Hallwag, Orell Füssli, and Kümmerly & Frey retail theirs in most Swiss book stores. There is little to choose between them inasmuch as all provide accurate, up-to-date information and cost about the same.

106 **Schweizer Velokarten.** (Swiss bicycling maps.)
Bern: Kümmerly & Frey.

Fifteen maps at 1:50,000, covering Switzerland north of the Alps, with marked routes for bicycle tours. The maps are marked with helpful information for cyclists, such as danger spots and steep stretches where the bicycle may have to be pushed.

Geography

General

107 **Schweiz aus der Vogelschau.** (A bird's eye view of Switzerland.)
F. Bachmann. Zurich [etc.]: Das Beste aus Reader's Digest, 1976. 316p. maps.

This book divides Switzerland into eight geographical regions. The geographical, geological, historical, and cultural characteristics of each region and its component parts are described. The text is accompanied by stunning colour photographs taken from the air, and locational diagrams help to place the scenes of the pictures on maps. This large-format work is a rich and beautiful introduction to the great variety of Swiss landscapes. An appendix with six essays on technical aspects of aerial photography and the role of aerial photography in cartography, archaeology, and forestry adds to the value of the book.

108 **Geographie der Schweiz.** (Geography of Switzerland.)
Oskar Bär. Zurich: Lehrmittelverlag des Kantons Zürich, 1971. 243p. maps. bibliog.

This large-format textbook for Zurich high schools presents geography in a thoroughly modern manner. Geography here includes the description of physical features of Switzerland; the geological forces that shaped the country; the climate; the flora and fauna; the economy from agriculture and alpine farming to industrialization and hydroelectricity; communication and transport; tourism; trade; forms of settlements; and zoning laws. A few selected regions are described in some detail. Every theme and subject of this book is enlivened by excellent coloured graphs, statistical tables and diagrams, drawings, maps, and photographs. One envies the school system that is able to offer its students such outstanding learning tools. *Géographie de la Suisse* (Geography of Switzerland) by Jacques Barbier, Jean-Luc Piveteau, and Michel Roten (Paris: Presses universitaires de France, 1973) gives an elementary and brief overview of Switzerland for anyone able to read French.

109 **Switzerland #3: the Ticino.**

Edited by William C. Bendig. *The ART gallery: The International Magazine of Art and Culture*, vol. 22, no. 3 (March 1979), p. 85-131.

This issue presents nine short and personal glimpses of the Ticino, the Italian-speaking canton in southern Switzerland. The editors believe that their report may be 'possibly the most comprehensive in the English language'. Canton Ticino became a part of the Swiss Confederation in 1803. It lies south of the snow-capped Alps and borders on Italy whose culture and language it shares, the subtropical climate, two beautiful lakes, the rustic stone dwellings, and local wines make it an attractive playground for tourists. Ticino is a canton of great contrasts: its largest city, Lugano, with its shops, hotels, and many banks is only a short distance away from the tiny and often poor villages in the alpine valleys where the soil is still worked in the old ways; the capital, Bellinzona, has retained much of its medieval character. During the 19th century large numbers of Ticinese were forced to emigrate in search of a livelihood. Walter M. Schirra, the American astronaut, tells in a brief personal reminiscence how he was received as a hero when he visited his ancestral home commune of Loco in the Onsernone valley. Illustrations, many in colour, highlight some of the many cultural attractions of Canton Ticino; they include paintings from the privately owned Thyssen-Bornemisza Collection, Romanesque churches with their frescoes, medieval castles, and Renaissance and Baroque palaces and churches.

110 **The bear and the bishop: a geography of the separatist movement in the Berner Jura, Switzerland.**

Patricia T. Caro. PhD dissertation, University of Oregon, 1976. 165p. maps. bibliog.

The Bernese Jura consisted of seven administrative districts that once formed part of the Bishopric of Basel but were given to Canton Bern at the end of the Napoleonic wars. At the time Caro worked on her dissertation, the Jura separatist movement had just about succeeded in splitting the northern part of the territory from Bern, the bear of the dissertation title, and making it into a new canton. The three southern districts and Laufen had opted to stay with Bern. Caro describes the geographical characteristics of the Bernese Jura and the historical background for the separatist movement. She purports to discern distinct 'landscapes of separatism', mainly due to ethnic peculiarities of housing and settlement styles, yet she is unable to explain why the southern part, which geographically has so much more in common with the north Jura than with Bern, did not join the north. Cato speculates at length about the advantages Canton Jura would have enjoyed had Moutier become its capital instead of Delémont. Religion was the element of ethnicity that proved to be of overriding significance, and as a consequence there is a reorganized political unit that 'disturbs a naive sense of organizing space'.

111 **Switzerland: a survey of its land and people.**

Emil Egli, translated from the German by Britta M. Charleston, Paul Swain, Walter Sorell. Bern: Haupt, 1978. 229p. bibliog.

Egli divides his scholarly but very readable book into two parts. The first is entitled 'Nature: origin and aspects of the country'. Since prehistoric times the Alps, the Central Plateau, and the Jura have undergone great changes caused by climatic and glacial shifts, erosion, the flow of water, landslides, etc. so that the topography of present-day Switzerland is totally different from that of thousands of years ago. Tables and sketches illustrate what natural forces were at work and how they affected the landscape. The second part is entitled 'Settlement, economy and population' and shows how man had to adapt to his surroundings and, in turn, how the presence of man has changed the face of the landscape. Because of the geographical contrasts which are so pronounced in Switzerland and the multi-cultural population, settlements are distinct from one region to another. Switzerland has no natural resources and much of its land is unproductive, yet it enjoys a high standard of living, which Egli attributes to the historical and political development of the country, its early adoption of modern industrial technology, and its 'national character' that inspires the trust of others. This is an important book by one of the leading 20th-century Swiss geographers.

112 **Geographie der Schweiz.** (Geography of Switzerland.)
Heinrich Gutersohn. Bern: Kümmerly & Frey, 1958-69. 5 vols. maps. bibliog.

This is the standard work of descriptive Swiss geography by the former director of the Geographic Institute at the Swiss Federal Institute of Technology in Zurich. Gutersohn devoted one volume to the Jura, two to the Alps, and two to the Swiss Plateau, the part of Switzerland that lies between the Alps and the Jura. He proceeds by discussing geographically self-contained areas within the larger political units, giving due attention to demographic and economic factors that have an impact on the patterns of settlement and thereby on the geographical environment. Gutersohn includes many diagrams, tables, maps, and photographs.

113 **Geographisches Lexikon der Schweiz.** (Geographical lexicon of Switzerland.)
Edited by Charles Knapp, Maurice Borel, V. Attinger. Neuchâtel, Switzerland: Attinges, 1902-10. 6 vols. maps.

Many contributors from all parts of Switzerland have cooperated to create this major work of early 20th-century Swiss scholarship. The volumes cover the geographical entities of Switzerland from 'Aa', the name of several small rivers, to 'Zybachsplatte', a terrain feature on the Wetterhorn in the Bernese Oberland. Major entries, such as the cantons and larger cities, receive extensive treatment, with maps and tables of population, agriculture, industry, and the like. Factual details are also furnished for every village and country town, and these are often accompanied by photographs. Geographical features such as rivers, gorges, lakes, mountains, and mountain groups are described at varying length, depending on their significance. Even though quite old by now, this is still an interesting work to browse in.

114 **Geography in Switzerland: a collection of papers offered to the 24th international geographical congress, Tokyo, Japan, August 1980.**
Edited by Fritz Müller, Laurent Bridel, Erich Schwabe. Bern: Kümmerly & Frey, 1980. 183p. bibliog.

This is a collection of twenty papers, five in French, the others in English, on geographical research currently being carried out in Switzerland. Subjects include the climate of Switzerland in the last 450 years; radiocarbon dating of fossil soils and woods from moraines and glaciers in the Alps; earth resources satellite application to land use planning in Switzerland; part-time farming and its ecological impact in the Swiss Alps; contemporary urban geography, and changes and regional differences in the fertility of Swiss women. The range and scope of the papers reflect the diversity of work engaged in by today's Swiss geographers.

115 **La Suisse, essai de géographie politique.** (Switzerland: a study of political geography.)
André-Louis Sanguin. Gap, France: Ophrys, 1983. 365p. maps. bibliog.

Switzerland is a geographical space, an economic entity, a nation encompassing a multitude of particularities and contrasts. These characteristics are more visible than elsewhere because they are concentrated in a small space. The Swiss are well aware of what distinguishes them from other nations: direct democracy, neutrality, relying on themselves during the last two World Wars – factors that reinforce the idea of the *Sonderfall Schweiz* (the special case of Switzerland). On the other hand, however, Switzerland is wide open to the outside world: its multilingual makeup ties the country to the three great cultural areas that surround it, and its economy is closely intertwined with that of the European Community. Thus, Sanguin points out, the margin of manoeuvrability between 'special case' Switzerland and universalist Switzerland is slim. Sanguin concentrates on the spatial dimension as the vital ingredient of the study of Switzerland from the perspective of political geography. He successfully combines traditional humanistic geography and contemporary social science methods, using vast databanks for computerized statistical analysis of geographical and political factors. His book, with its 56 figures, 7 statistical tables, and 637 entries in the bibliography, is one of the most informative and intelligent one-volume works about Switzerland on the market.

116 **Focus on Switzerland: the significance of the landscape; Switzerland – vacationland.**
Hans Weiss, Werner Kämpfen. Lausanne: Swiss Office for the Development of Trade, 1983. 2nd ed. 2 maps. 119p.

The first part of this booklet, sponsored by the Coordinating Committee for the Presence of Switzerland Abroad, deals with the Swiss landscape, a landscape which is chiefly characterized by the great contrasts it contains within the small, compact area of the country, from the glaciers of the Alps to the palm trees on Lago Maggiore, from the river valleys of the Central Plateau (Mittelland) to the green forests of the Jura ranges. People have adjusted to their surroundings, a fact which may be seen in the variety of dwellings they have built and the different styles of life they have chosen. The second part discusses Switzerland as a vacation land that profited immensely from the natural beauty of its landscape and its ever-changing scenery. The country, while preserving its heritage and traditions, is modern and forward-looking. The volume is beautifully illustrated, but there are also fourteen pages filled with data which provide information on geography, agriculture, industry, tourism, and the people.

The Alps

117 **The transformation of Swiss mountain regions: problems of development between self-reliance and dependence in an economic and ecological perspective.**

Edited by Ernst A. Brugger, Gerhard Furrer, Bruno Messerli, Paul Messerli, translated from the German and French by Barbara Stuckey (et al.). Bern: Haupt, 1984. 699p. maps. bibliog.

More than sixty scholarly articles in this book deal with the economic, political, ecological, and cultural problems affecting the mountain regions of contemporary Switzerland. The mountain areas of the Alps and the Jura, which make up two-thirds of the territory of the country but which support only about fourteen percent of its population, have not participated in the economic growth of the lowlands of the Central Plateau. The authors of the articles, representing different scientific disciplines, address three basic questions. First, what ecological, economic, cultural, and political disparities characterize the development of the mountain areas of Switzerland? Second, what are the causes and consequences of these disparities? Third, how have the various actors, including governments, reacted to desirable and undesirable structures and processes? The result of their investigations is an impressive interdisciplinary inventory of issues and possible solutions.

118 **The Alps.**

Ronald W. Clark. New York: Knopf, 1973. 288p. bibliog.

This is a book written in the popular style for the general reader. The author describes the geography, geology, and topography of the mountain ranges that stretch from the Mediterranean Sea in southern France northward to Geneva and thence eastward across Switzerland, northern Italy, southern Germany, and Austria to the outskirts of Vienna. He singles out the most famous peaks such as the Mont Blanc, the Matterhorn, and the Rigi for special mention. Profiles of people such as Whymper and his victory over the Matterhorn, or Geiger, the glacier pilot, are interspersed throughout the book; nor is Tschingel, the famous canine mountaineer of the St Bernard breed, forgotten. The Alps have experienced a spectacular growth of visitors in the last 150 years, and the author expresses his concern about the threat posed to their ecological balance by the avalanche of traffic that nowadays rolls over and through the mountains.

119 **Forum alpinum.**

Edited by Forum alpinum. Zurich: Forum alpinum; Neue Schweizer Bibliothek; Ex Libris; Büchergilde Gutenberg; Schweizer Volks-Buchgemeinde, 1965. 432p. maps.

This is an extremely rich and interesting collective work on the life and culture of the mountain regions of Switzerland. The core of the book (360 pages long) is made up of essays on seven mountain regions of Switzerland written by prominent demographers, geographers, sociologists, ethnologists, economists, psychologists, agronomists, musicologists, folklorists, educators, and journalists. Each regional section has a commentary part in which natives talk about their lives and problems, and there are segments on the arts and customs with the text of legends and songs, and samples of folk music. The text is written in the four languages of Switzerland. A separate booklet contains the entire text in English, translated by Lili Humm-Crawford. *Forum alpinum* is further distinguished by its artistic content. Throughout this large, square-format book one finds reproductions of full-page original woodcuts by Bruno Gentinetta, depicting mountain people at work and play. Master photographer Jakob Tuggener (1904-88) has composed a number of portfolios of black-and-white photographs especially for this volume. With unerring insight Tuggener probes beneath the postcard surface of touristic Switzerland to discover the essence of the mountain landscape and of mountain living on the alps and farms, as well as in the local industries and villages. An anthology of authentic folk music from the Swiss Alps, consisting of eight long-playing records, formed part of the Forum alpinum project.

120 **Avalanches and snow safety.**
Colin Fraser. London: Murray, 1978. 269p. bibliog.

This is an updated version of Fraser's earlier work *The avalanche enigma* (London, 1966). Fraser, who worked for extended periods of time with the Swiss Federal Institute for Snow and Avalanche Research in Davos, Switzerland, and with the *Parsenndienst*, the famous rescue and safety organization, also in Davos, displays his expertise in this book. It combines scientific information about such things as snow metamorphism and the different kinds of avalanches, with historical and anecdotal passages on accidents and miraculous rescues. Fraser also provides advice on how to behave in heavy snow conditions before, during, and after an avalanche.

121 **Histoire et civilisation des Alpes.** (History and civilization of the Alps.)
Edited by Paul Guichonnet. Toulouse, France: Privat; Lausanne, Switzerland: Payot, 1980. 2 vols. maps. bibliog.

This two-volume work (of 420 and 416 pages respectively) treats the Alps from the Mediterranean Sea to the Vienna Woods as a geographical entity. Its chapters, each with its own bibliography, were written by individual authorities. Volume one provides an account of the Alps in history from prehistoric times to the present. One chapter, by Roland Ruffieux (vol. 1, p. 311-68), is devoted to the history of Switzerland, from the formation of the first alliance to the eve of World War I. Switzerland, or its geographical space, turns up, of course, in most of the other chapters. The second volume deals with the economy and traditional life forms, the mentalities, ethnicity and languages, human responses to the Alps as natural phenomena, the impact of industrialization and tourism, and present-day problems and dangers. Richly illustrated, this fine work gives an informative and sober overview of the role and significance of the Alps for European society. Consult also *Histoire des Alpes: perspectives nouvelles* (The history of the Alps: new perspectives), edited by Jean-François Bergier (Basel; Stuttgart, FRG: Schwabe, 1979. 300p. bibliog. Special edition of vol. 29 (1979), no. 1, of the *Schweizerische Zeitschrift für Geschichte*).

122 **Switzerland and her glaciers: from the ice age to the present.**
Edited by Peter Kasser, Wilfried Haeberli, Werner Kämpfen, translated from the German by Robert Kaegy. Zurich: Swiss National Tourist Office; Bern: Kümmerly & Frey, 1981. 191p. maps. bibliog.

This book was the official catalogue for a travelling exhibit on the glaciers of Switzerland organized under the auspices of the Swiss National Tourist Office. It explores the relationship between glaciers, climate, and human beings from prehistoric times to the present. The book is divided into eight chapters, each written by an expert using the results of modern glacier research. A discussion of the Ice Age and the climate experienced after it is followed by an especially beautifully illustrated chapter with 'historical documents', namely the artistic and scientific record of 18th- and 19th-century painters and scholars. The chapters on 'recent fluctuations of glaciers', 'glacier inventory', and 'information stored in ice' provide insights into the use of modern research techniques and technologies in glaciology. The last two chapters discuss the destructive power of glaciers and their role in the production of hydro-electric power. The technical data in the form of figures and tables, together with artistic renderings, parts of old maps, and (above all) numerous large and gorgeous colour photographs make this an outstanding work on the topic.

123 **The Swiss and their mountains: a study of the influence of mountains on men.**
Arnold Lunn. London: Allen & Unwin; Chicago [etc.]: Rand McNally, 1963. 167p.

As its title indicates, this book is intended as a study of the influence of mountains on men. It contains a wealth of historical, political, and social information on the people in the Swiss mountain cantons. Entertaining stories, quotes from writings, accounts of difficult ascents, and a number of illustrations, both in black-and-white and in colour enhance this little volume. An entire chapter is dedicated to the *Kleinmeister*, artists whose engravings and etchings of mountain scenery are small in size. Lunn also talks of the mountains as a fortress in times of war, and describes the way of life of the *Bergler*, the mountain people. In his book *Switzerland: her topographical, historical and literary landmarks* (London: Harrap, 1928), Lunn explores the Swiss mountains above and below the snowline and claims that while technology leaves its traces, the mountains do not change, and their beauty remains. Vivian H. Green in *The Swiss Alps* (London: Batsford, 1961) in the presence of the Valais peaks writes that she is 'reminded once again of the extent to which tourists and visitors are a transitory phenomenon in two thousand years of Alpine history'. One wonders if Lunn and Green would still come to the same conclusion today.

124 **Die Entdeckung der Alpen.** (The discovery of the Alps.)
R. Oppenheim. Frauenfeld, Switzerland; Stuttgart, FRG: Huber, 1974. 296p. bibliog.

Until far into the 18th century the Alps struck human beings as strange and terrifying, but with Albrecht von Haller (1708-77) and Jean-Jacques Rousseau (1712-78) they became attractive to poets, artists, and scientists. The scientific study of the Alps was accompanied by the drive of Englishmen to climb the mountains. Toward the end of the 19th century alpinism became a sport for the masses. The Alps were conquered by technical progress in the form of better roads across the passes, railways through tunnels in the mountains, and a steadily increasing number of rack-and-pinion (cogwheel) railways, the most famous of which was the Jungfraubahn, opened in 1912, funiculars, cableways, gondolas, chair-lifts, and ski-lifts. The conquest of the Alps threatens to destroy the alpine ecology and dislocates the lives of the alpine population. It is one of the important challenges of our time to bring under control the forces that were unleashed by enthusiasm for the Alps. Oppenheim's impressive account is enriched by 202 illustrations, many of them reproductions of old woodcuts, engravings, and paintings.

125 **The crossing of the Alps.**
Gösta E. Sandström. London: Hutchinson, 1972. 160p. maps.

This book describes in nine brief chapters how the mountain barrier of the Alps was tackled and eventually overcome by people who needed or wanted to travel from northern Europe to Italy or vice versa. Sandström tells the story of Hannibal's crossing of the Alps and has a chapter on the routes of the Romans. In the Middle Ages pilgrims, prelates, and emperors were among the people who undertook the tiresome and often dangerous journey, followed by merchants, traders, and mercenaries. Conditions of travel improved only slowly, with the building of hospices and the construction of roadways and bridges, such as the 13th-century Devil's Bridge in the Reuss valley of Canton Uri – the mountain climbers of the High Alps of the 19th century were a special breed of travellers. The second half of the book deals with the assault on the Alps by railway and road builders. The chapters on 'the St. Gotthard disaster' and 'the long and troublesome Simplon' describe 'the heroic railway age' of the costly and bloody construction of the first railway tunnels through the Alps, opened in 1882 and 1906 respectively. In a last chapter Sandström gives an overview of the tunnelling of the Alps for vehicular traffic, with the tunnel through the Mont Blanc between Italy and France, opened in 1965, leading the way. The chapters on Alpine tunnels are based on Sandström's earlier books, *The history of tunnelling* (1963) and *Man the builder* (1970).

126 **In praise of Switzerland: being the Alps in prose and verse.**
Harold Spender. London: Constable, 1912. 291p.

Spender has assembled a rich collection of writings on the Alps, varying in length from less than a page to fifteen pages. Most of the excerpts are by English authors. Fear of the mountains, which prevailed from antiquity to early modern times, changed to admiration which then found its expression in the poetry and prose of the English Romantics. The 19th-century 'literature of admiration' is complemented by an equally important and voluminous 'literature of adventure', the descriptions of mountain expeditions by pioneers and first-ascent heroes. Shorter chapters deal with the Alps in tragedy (accounts of accidents and deaths), in comedy (from Mark Twain and others), in history (from the *White book of Sarnen* and Byron's 'Chillon') and in fiction (from Sir Walter Scott's *Anne of Geierstein*, and Byron's *Manfred*). Spender's compilation provides an entertaining introduction to the literature on the Alps.

Cartography and atlases

127 **Nos cartes nationales.** (Our national maps.)
Club alpin suisse. Bern: Stämpfli, 1979. 76p. bibliog.

The first exact map of Switzerland, the 'topographic map 1:100,000', known after its director General Guillaume Henri Dufour (1778-1875) as 'Dufour map', was created between 1842 and 1864. It consisted of twenty-five sheets, measuring 70 × 48 cm, and represented the country with extraordinary clarity and, thanks to its innovative shading technique, plasticity. Under Dufour's successor as head of the Federal Bureau of Topography, Hermann Siegfried (1819-79), new trigonometric measurements allowed the creation of maps at the scale of 1:25,000. The first twelve sheets of what came to be known as the 'Siegfried map' came out in 1870; by 1926 it had reached the number of

604. In 1937 the Federal Council ordered the creation of new national maps, *Landeskarten der Schweiz*, at various scales using the most modern techniques and in colour, an undertaking that was successfully completed by 1978. Since then these maps are systematically brought up to date every six to seven years by the Bundesamt für Landestopographie (Wabern-Bern). This small booklet with its convenient illustrations in the text and a useful bibliography provides a succinct introduction to modern mapmaking in Switzerland, an achievement of which the Swiss are rightfully proud.

128 **500 Jahre Schweizer Landkarten.** (500 years of Swiss maps.)
Georges Grosjean. Zurich: Orell Füssli, 1970. 56p. bibliog.

This is an impressive and valuable publication issued on the occasion of the 500th anniversary of the Zürcher Papierfabrik an der Sihl (Zurich paper factory on the Sihl river). It consists of twenty-nine facsimile reproductions of old maps, all of them of large size, some of them folded, in a loose-leaf carton case, 59 × 45 centimetres. The accompanying bound text by Grosjean gives an illustrated overview of the history of cartography in Switzerland, with special reference to the maps in this publication.

129 **Cartographic relief presentation.**
Eduard Imhof, translated from the German by H. J. Steward. Berlin; New York: De Gruyter, 1982. 389p. bibliog.

This highly technical work on the making of maps by the foremost Swiss cartographer, Eduard Imhof, is praised by the translator and editor, H. J. Steward of the Graduate School of Geography at Clark University in Worcester, Massachusetts, as destined to become a 'classic' in the discipline of cartography. The 'scientific artistry' of Imhof is unique in its combination of analysis based on cartographic theories, photogrammetry, and computer manipulation, with portrayal through colours, skeletal and contour lines, shading and shadows, and related techniques. There are 221 figures in the text and an extensive bibliography. In the work *Gelände und Karte* (Terrain and map) (Erlenbach-Zurich; Stuttgart: Rentsch, 1968), Imhof, formerly professor at the Swiss Federal Institute of Technology describes how terrain becomes a map. The work, written with the enthusiasm of a committed cartographer is also indicative of the generally high level of mapmaking in Switzerland. According to Steward, *Terrain and map* has been translated into English for internal use at the US Air Technical Intelligence Center and by the US Army Map Service.

130 **Die Schweiz auf alten Karten.** (Switzerland on old maps.)
Leo Weisz, Eduard Imhof. Zurich: Neue Zürcher Zeitung, 1971. 3rd ed. 250p. bibliog.

This beautifully produced book includes many reproductions of maps and parts of maps of Switzerland from the time of the Romans to the cartographic masterworks of Hans Konrad Gyger (1599-1674) and the maps of the 18th century, and was first published in 1945. This new edition was supervised by Imhof who added a bibliography of 133 entries. Among the scholarly interests of Weisz was a special love for Swiss map history. The old maps of Switzerland were political documents teaching the Swiss about their territory and giving them a feeling of belonging. The early mapmakers approached their task above all as artists. The representation of mountains presented special difficulties. Steadily sharpening their observation of the characteristics of their country and improving their drawing skills, they came closer and closer to giving an accurate picture of the terrain. Weisz provides much biographical information on the mapmakers, and Imhof discusses the technical aspects of their works. The fold-out maps in facsimile reproduction are a special attraction of this fine work.

131 **Atlas der Schweiz.** (Atlas of Switzerland.)
Edited by Eduard Imhof and the Redaktionsbüro, ETH-Zürich.
Wabern-Bern, Switzerland: Bundesamt für Landestopographie, 1965- .

The atlas of Switzerland is a comprehensive thematic cartographic work which, when finished, will illustrate in more than 100 plates Switzerland's landscape, population, economy, and traffic. So far eleven parts have been published with 4 folios, 97 plates, 435 maps, 58 diagrams, 9 charts and tables, and 192 pages of text in German, French, and Italian. The plates and maps can be purchased separately. This major cartographic publication provides a complete account of the natural foundations of Switzerland, its topography, geology, hydrography, soils, climate and weather, rivers and lakes, vegetation, fauna; its demographic, economic, and social structures and their historical evolution; its natural resources, industry, business, tourism, and trade; its traffic, communication systems, railway and road traffic; its education, and some of its landscapes. This atlas of Switzerland has become a huge reservoir of scientific work, and one wonders how many people are aware of the treasures it contains and therefore would be inspired to make use of it.

132 **Karte der Kulturgüter.** (Map of cultural heritage.)
Wabern-Bern, Switzerland: Bundesamt für Landestopographie, 1988.
48p.

The map of cultural heritage at 1:300,000 shows some 2,000 objects and groups of objects of importance in Swiss civilization and history from prehistoric times to the present. A booklet, which contains detailed maps of especially rich centres of cultural artefacts, also has complete lists of the objects mapped, grouped by communities and cantons. The map is complementary to the inventory of cultural goods of national importance, and reveals a density and variety of these witnesses to a rich cultural past which is amazing.

Geology

133 **The structure of the Alps.**

Léon William Collet. Huntington, New York: Krieger, 1974. 304p. bibliog. (Original edition, 1927; reprint of second edition, published by Arnold, London, 1935).

Collet (1880-1957), formerly professor of geology at the University of Geneva, first provides a general scientific description of the geology of the Alps, with special emphasis on the regions most often visited by learned British visitors. He then presents a number of detailed itineraries of geological excursions in the surroundings of Zermatt, Lauterbrunnen, Grindelwald, and Geneva, inviting readers to make use of their scientific knowledge on field trips. The work includes eighty-four figures, and ten plates (or photographs).

134 **Geology of the European countries: I: Austria, Federal Republic of Germany, Ireland, The Netherlands, Switzerland, United Kingdom.**

Edited by Comité National Français de Géologie. Paris: Dunod; London: Graham & Trotman, 1980. 433p. maps. bibliog.

The Switzerland section of this work (p. 231-326) was written by Rudolf Trümpy, professor of geology at the Swiss Federal Institute of Technology in Zurich, and several other Swiss geologists who contributed some of the chapters where Trümpy felt his expertise was lacking. He provides an up-to-date review of Swiss geology with a stratigraphical bias and an emphasis on the Alps. Forty-six charts are integrated in the text which leads from the Jura and adjoining platforms across the molasse basin of the Swiss Plateau to the various formations and regional patterns of the Alps.

135 **Geologie der Schweiz.** (Geology of Switzerland.)

Albert Heim. Leipzig, GDR: Tauchnitz, 1919–22. 2 vols. maps. bibliog.

Volume 1 (704p.) covers the Swiss Plateau (Molasseland) and the Jura. Volume 2 (1018p.) is in two parts and deals with the geology of the Alps. This voluminous work, with its scientific text, many graphs, tables, maps, and photographs, is the crowning achievement of the life work of one of the foremost Swiss geologists. Even though modern research has gone beyond Heim and interprets some of the data differently, his is still the acknowledged basic scientific work on the geology of Switzerland. It is an astounding testimony to one man's industry and erudition.

136 **Three stages in the evolution of alpine geology: de Saussure – Studer – Heim.**

Emmannuel de Saussure. *Quarterly Journal of the Geological Society of London*, vol. 102 (1946), p. xcvii-cxiv. bibliog.

Saussure sees three turning points in the long history of the geology of the Alps, marked by three seminal books. The first, Horace Benedict de Saussure's (1740-99) *Voyages dans les Alpes* (4 vols, Neuchâtel, Switzerland, 1779-96), is an account of de Saussure's observations which he made during his numerous ascents in the Alps. 'If he has founded Geology, he is at the same time the founder of Alpinism.' The Genevan de Saussure did not succeed in reaching any unifying conclusions about the geology of the Alps; the only constant element he found was their unending variety. Bernard Studer (1794-1872), for almost fifty years professor of geology in Bern, in his *Geologie der Schweiz* (2 vols, 1851-53) was a proponent of the eruptive or vertical theory which assumed the action of a vertical force that pushed up the mountains from below at several points at the same time. The third key person in a long string of learned naturalists was Albert Heim who did all his work from his home base at the institutions of higher learning in Zurich. Starting from a thoroughly stratigraphical and tectonic examination of mountain districts in east-central Switzerland he conceptualized the formation of the Alps through the powerful forces of folding, and he reasserted the great importance of erosion. Saussure succeeds in providing a short but very instructive overview of the persevering and tenacious efforts of the 19th-century geologists of Switzerland to find explanations for the puzzling reality that confronted them.

137 **Geology of Switzerland: a guide book.**

Edited by the Swiss Geological Commission, Rudolf Trümpy scientific editor. Basel; New York: Wepf, 1980. 334p. maps. bibliog.

This work has two parts. Part A is an outline of the geology of Switzerland by Trümpy and others, which appeared also in the *Geology of Western Europe* volume (q.v.), published simultaneously in Paris. It was prepared 'in haste' for the 26th International Geological Congress held in Paris in 1980. Part B consists of the plans for geological excursions for participants in the congress. They are similar to the excursions described in the *Geologischer Führer der Schweiz* (Geological Guide to Switzerland) edited by Augustin Lombard, Walter Nabholz, and Rudolf Trümpy (Basel: Wepf, 1967). Seven excursions were conducted by Swiss geological experts. They covered the Helvetic Alps of western Switzerland, the geotraverse of western Switzerland, a cross-section from the Rhine Graben to the Po plain, the Alps of eastern Switzerland, *flysch* and *molasse* of western and central Switzerland, Alpine metamorphism of the Central Alps, and Alpine metamorphism in a cross-section between the Rhine and Valtelline valleys. Daily itineraries for nine days on each excursion with up to eighty-one stopping points had been worked out. The text of part B has more than 200 figures and tables. The expertise and care of the Swiss organizers make this a work of lasting value, especially for the English-speaking geologist.

138 **A guide to the minerals of Switzerland.**
Max Weibel. London [etc.]: Wiley, Interscience Publishers, 1966. 123p. maps.

Switzerland is one of the classic countries for collectors of minerals. The Alps have yielded extraordinary crystals encompassing a great variety of minerals. Weibel provides an overview of the general aspects of mineral occurrences in Switzerland, followed by a description of individual minerals and their regional occurrences. He also provides practical hints for the collector about quarries, native rock-crystal seekers (*Strahler*), prices of Swiss minerals, and organizations of Swiss mineral collectors. Twenty-four colour plates present some seventy mineral crystals.

Environment, Ecology, and Nature Protection

139 **Through the Swiss National Park: a scientific guide.**
R. Bach, Committee for Scientific Research in the National Park.
Basel: Schweizerischer Bund für Naturschutz, 1966. 251p. map. bibliog.

This is an excellent work on the Swiss National Park, an area of 170 square kilometres, in the lower Engadin, Canton Graubünden, in eastern Switzerland. The Swiss National Park, which is a mountainous region with deep narrow valleys and snow-covered peaks, was established by an act of the Swiss legislature in 1914 and is considered to be a national treasure. Its plants, animals, geology, history, and climate are treated in this book by many experts and scientists. The bibliography is extensive, and an index lists several hundred plants and animals living in this protected territory with Latin, English, French, and German names. A specially produced map (1:50,000) is tucked in the back cover and indicates authorized paths and parking areas. See also the picture book *Der Schweizerische Nationalpark: Ein Naturerlebnis* (The Swiss National Park: a nature experience) by Robert Schloeth (Aarau, Switzerland: AT Verlag, 1989).

140 **Illustrierte Berner Enzyklopädie. Band 1: Die Natur: Schönheit, Vielfalt, Gefährdung.** (Illustrated Bern encyclopedia. Volume 1: Nature: beauty, variety, endangerment.)
Bern: Büchler/Berner Zeitung, 1981. 200p. maps. bibliog.

Fourteen authors contribute to this beautifully illustrated volume which covers a wide range of topics related to nature, its life and care in Canton Bern. Geology, climate and weather, lakes and rivers, glaciers, plant life, forests, animals in fields and forests, ecology of lakes and rivers, wetlands, birds, hunt and hunters, fish, fishing and limnology, and nature protection are all presented in a narrative text that is liberally sprinkled with encyclopaedic information in tabular form and diagrams. This comprehensive treatment of the natural environment and history of the second-largest Swiss canton provides a representative picture of environmental care that is applicable to most other parts of Switzerland.

Environment, Ecology, and Nature Protection

141 **Schweizer Naturschutz am Werk.** (Swiss nature protection at work.) Edited by Dieter Burckhardt, Erich Schwabe, Willy Zeller. Bern: Haupt, 1960. 192p. map. bibliog. (Schweizer Heimatbücher, 95/96).

This book was published on the fiftieth anniversary of the founding of the Swiss Federation for the Protection of Nature (Schweizerischer Bund für Naturschutz), and consists of twenty-five short chapters by different authors. In the first (general) part the fundamental theoretical and ideological problems of the organized protection of flora, fauna, and topographical environment are discussed. The second part describes the geography, geology, morphology, flora, and fauna of the larger areas of natural beauty under protection, including the Swiss National Park in Canton Graubünden and the virgin forests of the Aletsch glacier and at Derborence, both in Canton Valais. A dozen chapters in the third part introduce the smaller reserves in various parts of the country. The volume is illustrated with sixteen colour plates and 100 black-and-white photographs.

142 **Raumplanung in der Schweiz. Eine Einführung.** (Space planning in Switzerland: an introduction.)
Martin Lendi, Hans Elsasser. Zurich: Verlag der Fachvereine, 1986. 2nd ed. 371p. maps. bibliog.

Space planning is a multidisciplinary undertaking. It is goal-directed, future-oriented, and has a determining influence on political processes with lasting impact on living space, always taking into account the need to allow future generations their own freedom of decisions. Lendi and Elsasser provide a textbook that combines theory with practical issues. They provide a good overview of the state of space planning in Switzerland, stressing the point that planning needs to be improved and confidence in space planning should be built up in order to ensure that the many efforts that are being made become effective.

143 **Are the Swiss forests in peril?**
Christian Mehr. *National Geographic Magazine*, vol. 175, no. 5 (May 1989), p. 637-51. maps.

This is a brief but informative article on the battle the Swiss are waging against the threatened death of their forests. A combination of natural and man-made forces is denuding the steep slopes of the Alpine valleys, depriving the inhabitants of those valleys of their natural protection against avalanches and rockslides and also creating major hazards for road and railway traffic toward the alpine tunnels and passes. Major efforts are under way to attack the causes of this disaster through strict pollution control laws, and to minimize the impact of the deforestation through massive emergency programmes such as the construction of steel barriers and other artificial protective structures (costing billions of francs), and painstaking, laborious, and sometimes futile programmes of reforestation. Excellent colour photographs by the author and Sam Abell give dramatic testimony to the dangers and challenges that the Alpine environment presents to the Swiss and provide an idea of the enormous amount of labour that they invest in the maintenance of the vital forests.

Flora and Fauna

Flora

144 **Mountain flower holidays in Europe.**
Lionel Bacon. Woking, England: Alpine Garden Society, 1979. 293p. maps.

This is a descriptive text with a few drawings of flowers in the text and thirty-two colour and twenty-nine black-and-white photographs of mountain scenes with flowers. A first introductory chapter familiarizes the reader with the 'basic flora' of the Alps, and includes the majority of the plants 'that will catch the eye of the traveller to European mountains', which 'is to a remarkable degree the flora of the Bernese Oberland in Switzerland'. The second introductory chapter provides some general advice for travellers to the mountains, primarily with the motorist in mind. The bulk of the book consists of a country-by-country tour through Europe from Switzerland to Portugal, to the Balkans and Greece, and back north to Scandinavia, ending up in Spitsbergen. In the Switzerland chapter, Bacon concentrates on the Bernese Oberland, the Valais, and the Engadine for his description of rewarding excursions for the lover of mountain flowers. A richly illustrated book on the same topic is *European alpine flowers in colour* by T. P. Barneby (London [etc.]: Nelson, 1967)

145 **Die Schweiz von A–Z: Ein Führer durch Feld, Wald und Flur.**
(Switzerland from A to Z: a guide through fields, woods, and meadows.)
Edited by Jakob Bill. Zurich: Das Beste aus Reader's Digest, 1979. 502p.

Richly illustrated with colour photographs and occasional drawings, this large-format encyclopaedia covers every facet of the flora and fauna of Switzerland as well as a considerable part of its history, geography, and economy. A staff of more than forty natural scientists was assembled to write the articles, about fifty of which treat at some length specific topics, such as forestry, native mushrooms, birds, climate, rocks and minerals, prehistoric Switzerland, wild flowers, and viniculture. This is an enticing, good-looking, and most informative book.

146 **Schul- und Exkursionsflora für die Schweiz mit Berücksichtigung der Grenzgebiete. Bestimmungsbuch für die wildwachsenden Gefässpflanzen.** (School- and excursion flora for Switzerland, including neighbouring border regions: classification book for wildflowers.) August Binz, Christian Heitz, Marilise Rieder. Basel: Schwabe, 1986. 18th ed. 624p.

First published by Binz in 1920, this guide for the classification of wild flowers has been used by countless Swiss students in countless botany courses. In an introductory section the morphological terms of the guide are explained and the tables are given for the classification of plant families according to the natural system and according to Linnaeus. The bulk of the book consists of apparatus for the classification of flowers. The careful user of this guide will be able to determine the name of any flower he or she finds in Switzerland and its border areas by systematically following the trail through the 156 families and 797 genera listed in this guide. Marilise Rieder contributed 860 figure drawings that help greatly to clarify terms and plant characteristics. See also *Flora der Schweiz und angrenzende Gebiete* (Flora of Switzerland and neighbouring areas) by Hans Ernst Hess, Elias Landolt, and Rosmarie Hirzel (Basel; Stuttgart: Birkhäuser, 1976-80. 2nd ed. 3 vols). This monumental work provides a comprehensive and systematic scientific description of the ferns and flowers of Switzerland. It lists 40 families of plants, 800 genera, and almost 3,500 species. Hundreds of drawings are an integral part of this work.

147 **Geschützte Pflanzen der Schweiz.** (Protected plants of Switzerland.) Elias Landolt. Basel: Schweizerischer Bund für Naturschutz, 1975. 2nd ed. 215p.

This book, sponsored by the Swiss Federation for the Protection of Nature, discusses the problems faced by plants in Switzerland due to the incursion of civilization on their natural habitat. The federal law of 1 July 1966, on the protection of nature and the home country contains an important clause that stipulates that sufficiently large spaces have to be maintained to slow the extinction of endangered plants. Seventy-four species were identified as needing federal protection in the whole of Switzerland. The cantons have issued their own somewhat bewildering lists of fully or partially protected flowers and plants. The book is illustrated with 160 colour photographs.

148 **Schröter's coloured vade-mecum to the Alpine flora.** Edited by W. Lüdi. Zurich: Schumann, 1963. 29th ed. 62p.

Illustrated by Ludwig Schröter and provided with a short text in three languages by Carl Schröter, this booklet was first published in the late 1880s. It contains twenty-six plates with 207 coloured and ten plain drawings of alpine shrubs and flowers. This *vade-mecum* has been the preferred and treasured guide to the alpine flora of untold numbers of amateur botanists who wanted to know the names of the beautiful flowers they encountered on their wanderings in the Alps. The plates of this booklet are now on sale in postcard form at kiosks in mountain resorts and in abridged editions under the title *Alpine flowers*.

149 **A guide to the vegetation of Britain and Europe.**
Oleg Polunin, Martin Walters. Oxford [etc.]: Oxford University Press, 1985. 238p. maps. bibliog.

In a brief general introduction the authors explain ecological concepts and terms, describe the types of soils and climates of Europe, and give a history of the development of vegetation in Europe. The second part, by far the longest of the book, describes the plant communities of Europe. Major parts of the sections on 'Central European vegetation' and 'Alpine plant communities' apply to Switzerland. The third part lists the national parks and nature reserves of Europe – Switzerland is represented by its National Park, fifteen nature preserves, and two landscape protection areas. The book has numerous maps and figures. Hundreds of plants, mainly flowers, are illustrated on sixty plates, and 110 colour photographs, not counted in the pagination, show the great variety of vegetation communities in Europe.

Fauna

150 **The mammals of Britain and Europe.**
Gordon Corbet, Denys Ovenden. London: Collins, 1980. 253p. maps. bibliog.

This book deals with all species of mammals living in a wild state west of the Soviet Union. One hundred and eighty-five species are illustrated in colour, with brief factual descriptions of physical characteristics and measurements. Maps depicting the present range of these animals are found on the pages facing the paintings by Ovenden. More detailed information about identification, range, habitat, and habits is provided by Corbet in the second half of the book. A considerable number of species of mammals can be found in Switzerland, but the marmot, the ibex, and the chamois are the three species most typical of the Alpine habitat of Switzerland.

151 **Where to watch birds in Europe.**
John Gooders. New York: Taplinger, 1978. 299p. maps.

This book, originally published in Great Britain in 1970, 'has been designed to cater for the needs of the ornitho-traveller on a European scale'. The guide lists places, by country, where birds can be watched, with a description of the birds and habitats of the area, a summary table of birds, and travel directions. The section on Switzerland is six pages long. Six places for bird watching are described, five of them, Col de Bretolet, Chavorney Clay-pits, eastern Lac Léman, Lac de Neuchâtel, and Mont Tendre are in western Switzerland, and one, Grindelwald, is in the German-speaking part of the country. A study limited to the birds of the Jura region is *Juravögel. Die Brutvögel des schweizerischen Jura* (Birds of the Jura: the nesting birds of the Swiss Jura) by Ulrich Arnold Corti (Chur, Switzerland: Bischofberger, 1962).

152 **A field guide to the butterflies of Britain and Europe.**
Lionel G. Higgins, Norman D. Riley, Brian Hargreaves. Boston, Massachusetts: Houghton Mifflin, 1970. 380p. maps. bibliog.

This book consists of colour plates on which all butterflies found in Europe, some 760 of them, are illustrated in life size. Captions, facing the plates, provide the names of the butterflies and their key characteristics. Full text descriptions give further information on flight periods, habitats, and the food plants of the caterpillars. Miniature maps of Europe west of the Soviet Union show breeding ranges of 371 species.

153 **New generation guide to the birds of Britain and Europe.**
Christopher Perrins. Glasgow, Scotland: Collins; Austin, Texas: University of Texas Press, 1987. 320p. (New Generation Guide).

This book, illustrated with hundreds of colour paintings and drawings, is a field guide on bird identification and also an encyclopaedic treatise dealing with the biology and lives of birds. The first section describes the evolution of birds; part two, which takes up about half the book, is the directory of species, with colour paintings by Norman Arlott of all birds breeding in Europe and descriptive captions with maps of distribution on the facing pages; part three describes the life of a bird; and part four deals with the ecology of birds. The text, full of fascinating information, easily fulfils the aim of the New Generation Guides series to help the interested amateur bird-watchers not only identify birds but also make sense of what they encounter. *A field guide to the birds of Britain and Europe* by Roger Tory Peterson, Guy Montfort, and P. A. D. Hollom (London: Collins; Boston, Massachusetts: Houghton Mifflin, 1983, 4th ed. 344p.) is the more traditional type of straightforward guide for ornithologists and bird-lovers. The quality of its illustrations and helpful descriptions have made this book a bestseller among field guides to birds. See also *Vögel der Heimat. Monatsschrift für Vogelkunde, Vogelschutz, Natur- und Umweltschutz* (Birds of our country: monthly journal for ornithology, bird protection, and the care of nature and the environment), published by Marcel Künzi (Einsideln, Switzerland, 1930-).

154 **Das Wild der Schweiz. Eine Geschichte der jagdbaren Tiere unseres Landes.** (Swiss wildlife: a history of the wild game of our country.)
Philipp Schmidt. Bern; Stuttgart, FRG: Hallwag, 1976. 708p.

This large-format tome is in three parts. The first part (264 pages) consists of eight chapters on wild animals and the psychology of human hunters, the history of hunting and the fate of wild animals throughout history, legislation concerning hunting at the Swiss federal and cantonal levels, and the task of the state to protect nature and free-living animals. In the second part (200 pages) Schmidt describes the fate of individual species of animals that were hunted before they became extinct and of those that are still being hunted. He deplores the striving for self-fulfilment of the 19th-century hunter which was achieved by killing as many animals as possible and makes a strong plea for the care of the remaining wildlife. The third part is made up of black-and-white photographs and illustrations from old hunting magazines which Schmidt uses to describe the life cycle of the animals, mammals and birds, and the ways they used to be trapped and hunted. See also *Feld Wald Wasser. Schweizerische Jagdzeitung* (Field, forest, water: Swiss hunting journal), edited by Walter Keller and Arnold Schawalder

(Schaffhausen, Switzerland: Verlag Feld Wald Wasser/Schweizerische Jagdzeitung. monthly).

155 **The butterflies of Switzerland and the Alps of Central Europe.**
George Wheeler. London: Elliott Strock, 1903. 162p.

This catalogue and index of butterfly species, varieties, and aberrations has been compiled by Wheeler with the help of many other entomologists. Written before the advent of modern bookmaking, it has no illustrations. The author describes butterflies from the Hesperides to the Papilionides in terms of their physical characteristics, diet and habitat, basing his descriptions on an examination of the actual insects themselves. Since Switzerland describes a political, rather than a geographical area, Wheeler extended his research into neighbouring areas. This is an old book, but one still finds references to it in more modern ones on butterflies in Central Europe.

Archaeology and Prehistory

156 **Ur- und frühgeschichtliche Archäologie der Schweiz.** (Prehistoric and early historic archaeology of Switzerland.)

Edited by Walter Drack. Basel: Schweizerische Gesellschaft für Ur- und Frühgeschichte, 1968-79. 6 vols. maps. bibliog.

These six volumes, written by recognized experts in the field of archaeology, anthropology, and history, represent a scientific and scholarly achievement of the highest order. Together with the journals published by the society for pre- and early history and other organizations in the field (q.v.), this work establishes Swiss archaeologists as being among the most advanced practitioners in the field. The six volumes cover the subject matter chronologically as follows: the Older and Middle Stone Age; the Younger Stone Age; the Bronze Age; the Iron Age; the Roman epoch; and the Early Middle Ages. Numerous drawings, photographs, and maps accompany the text.

157 **Die Helvetier. Kulturgeschichte eines Keltenvolkes.** (The Helvetians: cultural history of a Celtic people.)

Andres Furger-Gunti. Zurich: Neue Zürcher Zeitung, 1984. 180p. maps. bibliog.

Furger-Gunti reconstructs the history of the Helvetians in this large-format, beautifully illustrated volume on the basis of the results of archaeological digs, the evaluation of numerous artefacts, and the reports of writers from classical antiquity. The Helvetians, a Celtic people settled in the general area of what is today the Swiss Plateau and southern Germany, they built fortifications, *oppida*, the lay-outs of some of which are reconstructed by Furger-Gunti. The Helvetians appeared in written accounts of the Romans, especially after the battle of Bibracte in 58 BC, when they were defeated by Julius Caesar and forced to return to their settlements in Switzerland. The photographs, many in colour, of the jewellery, pottery, and artistically crafted arms of the Helvetians give testimony to the high level of achievement of this people and their important contributions to the cultural heritage of Switzerland.

158 **The Alps: archaeology and early history.**
Ludwig Pauli, translated from the German by Eric Peters. London: Thames and Hudson, 1984. 305p. maps.

The Alps, stretching from the Mediterranean coast to the outskirts of Vienna, cover a territory that includes two duchies and parts of six countries. This book treats the geographical expanse that constitutes the Alps as a single entity. It provides an early history of the Alpine region from the first appearance of human beings during the Old Stone Age to the age of Charlemagne and beyond. In a first chapter Pauli reviews 'a million years of history'. He then treats his subject matter topically, devoting chapters to how the people lived, from the pile-dwellings of the Stone Age to the Roman manors and the castles and villages of the Middle Ages; forms of burial and conceptions of the after-life; religion and art, from the bear cult in the caves to the Roman gods and the arrival of Christianity; mule-tracks, road-building, passes, and resthouses; and husbandry, mining, and trade. Switzerland, situated as it is in the centre of the Alpine region, was intimately involved in all phases of this early history and has a large number of sites of archaeological interest. It is part of the attractiveness of this book that the Swiss phenomena are treated as part of a larger whole. There are 166 instructively captioned illustrations. While there is no bibliography *per se*, hundreds of endnotes offer access to the literature on the subjects covered by Pauli in his impressive book.

159 **Switzerland: from earliest times to the Roman conquest.**
Marc-R. Sauter. London: Thames & Hudson; Boulder, Colorado: Westview, 1976. 208p. maps. bibliog. (Ancient Peoples and Places, 86).

The varied relief of Switzerland resulted in diverse ethnic and cultural developments already in its pre- and protohistoric past. Sauter, one of the foremost Swiss archaeologists and anthropologists concisely introduces this involved subject matter. His information, written in precise, scholarly language, is based on the most recent evidence and interpretations. Beginning in the distant past of the world of glaciers, mammoths, and rock shelters, the story moves on to the Neolithic farmers and builders of lake dwellings, constructed on the shores of Switzerland's many lakes. During the Bronze Age migrant groups of people wandered into the country across the Alpine passes and began the period of continuous settlement on the Swiss Plateau and the Jura, which culminated in the flourishing La Tène culture of the Second Iron Age found near Lake Neuchâtel. The Celtic tribe of the Helvetii were the first inhabitants of Switzerland who can be identified by name. They entered history in 58 BC when they were defeated by Julius Caesar. Good maps, many illustrations and line drawings, and a comprehensive bibliography enhance the scholarly value and the enjoyment of this fine publication.

160 **Jahrbuch der Schweizerischen Gesellschaft für Ur- und Frühgeschichte.**
(Yearbook of the Swiss society for pre- and early history.)
Schweizerische Gesellschaft für Ur- und Frühgeschichte. Frauenfeld, Switzerland: Huber, 1909- . vol. 68 (1985). 282p.

The yearbook includes substantial scholarly articles with maps, drawings, diagrams, tables, photographs, and bibliographies on artefacts, burial mounds and other records of the prehistory and early history of Switzerland; reports with documentation on new finds and ongoing digs; numerous book reviews, and is another one of the impressive publications by the experts in this field. See also *Archäologie der Schweiz* (Archaeology of Switzerland) (Basel: Schweizerische Gesellschaft für Ur- und

Frühgeschichte, 1978- .). This quarterly contains scholarly articles with maps, drawings and many illustrations describing and interpreting the results of recent digs and discoveries. Another quarterly on the topic is *Helvetia archaeologica* (Archaeological Switzerland), edited by Rudolf Degen (Basel: Schwabe, 1970).

161 **Zeitschrift für schweizerische Archäologie und Kunstgeschichte.**
(Journal for Swiss Archaeology and Art History.)
Schweizerisches Landesmuseum. Zurich: Schwegler, 1939- .
quarterly. ca. 100p.

Published by the directorate of the Swiss National Museum in Zurich, this impressive large-format publication gives scholarly treatment to a wide range of subjects concerning Swiss art and archaeology. The archaeological articles have maps, drawings, and photographs, and the articles on art history are illustrated with black-and-white and colour reproductions.

History

Historiography

162 **Johannes von Müller: the historian in search of a hero.**
Gordon A. Craig. *American Historical Review*, vol. 74, no. 5 (June 1969), p. 1487-1502.

Johann Müller (1752-1809) from Schaffhausen, Switzerland, is famous as the author of a multi-volume history of Switzerland in which 'he succeeded, more than any other person', in creating 'the myth of the Swiss people, so that even today, when we think of Switzerland, we think unwittingly in his terms and his images'. It was the first historical work in German that had any literary distinction, and its subjects, active in the founding of the Swiss Confederation, aroused unprecedented enthusiasm. Friedrich Schiller's *Wilhelm Tell* would be unthinkable without Müller's history. Craig's article describes how Müller, disdaining the career of a university professor, offered his services to King Frederick II of Prussia, some of the smaller princes of the Holy Roman Empire, the Emperor of Austria, who ennobled him in 1791, and finally to Napoleon who passed him on to his brother Jerome, King of Westphalia, to be appointed minister and first secretary of state. Müller's 'pathetic search for a hero' ended in futility, partly because he was ill-equipped for effective participation in politics and partly because the Germany of his time was politically immature and remained so for another two hundred years.

163 **The letters of Jacob Burckhardt.**
Selected, edited and translated by Alexander Dru. London: Allen & Unwin; New York: Pantheon, 1955. 243p. bibliog.

Dru's introduction provides a good sketch of the life of the famous Basel historian Jacob Burckhardt (1818-97) and a helpful introduction to the letters published in this edition. The letters show Burckhardt as his friends knew him. They include many interesting observations concerning fellow academics, the politics of the day, and persons and influences he either admired or detested. Burckhardt had his roots in Basel where he lived as a bachelor, concentrating on his lectures at the university.

When he received a call to fill the chair of professor of history at the University of Berlin vacated by Ranke, he unhesitatingly declined. 'I would not have gone to Berlin at any price; to have left Basel would have brought malediction on me. Nor is my merit in the matter great; there would be no helping a man of fifty-four who did not know where his modest portion of (relatively) good luck lay'. Dru acknowledges his indebtedness to Werner Kaegi whose definitive *Jacob Burckhardt: eine Biographie* (Basel: Schwabe, 1947-82) had reached the first two volumes by the time Dru's work was published.

164 **Geschichtsschreibung der Schweiz. Vom Spätmittelalter zur Neuzeit.** (Historiography of Switzerland: from the late Middle Ages to the modern era.)
Richard Feller, Edgar Bonjour. Basel; Stuttgart, FRG: Schwabe, 1962. 903p. 2 vols. 35 plates.

In this history of the written record of the Swiss past, the works of chroniclers, annalists, and historians are analysed as to their contributions to historical knowledge, their methodology, their significance in the context of their times, and their literary value. The text is organized chronologically. It identifies the sources for the history of the various parts of Switzerland in the Late Middle Ages and it examines the individuals who expressed themselves on the events of the Reformation and the Counter-Reformation; the chapter on the Enlightenment reflects the increased activity of the intellectuals, above all in the city cantons, while the long final part on the 19th century treats the era of 'scientific' history and ends with an appreciation of those historians who have led the way into the 20th century. The text of this work is characterized by the elegance of its style and its evaluation of the many individuals who have made contributions to the writing of Swiss history. Bibliographical information is provided at the end of each of the biographical sketches.

165 **Burckhardt: the poet of truth.**
Peter Gay. In: *Style in history*. New York: Basic Books, 1974, p. 139-82. bibliog.

The influential Basel historian Jacob Burckhardt (1818-97), according to Gay, perceived the past as a great drama. His most famous work, *Kultur der Renaissance in Italien: ein Versuch* (1860) (*The civilization of the Renaissance in Italy: an essay*, trans. in 1878) does full justice to that drama. His craving for organic coherence led him to see the Renaissance as 'a coherent entity pervaded by a common spirit'. Unlike the optimism that characterizes the work of his teacher Leopold von Ranke, however, Burckhardt's historical vision was 'essentially ambivalent', reflecting his 'conviction that civilization is essentially problematic and fearfully fragile'. Gay has also written an essay, entitled 'Burckhardt's *Renaissance*: between responsibilty and power', in *The responsibility of power: historical essays in honor of Hajo Holborn*, edited by Leonard Krieger and Fritz Stern (Garden City, New York: Doubleday, 1967, p. 183-98).

166 **Gehalt und Deutung der Schweizer Geschichte. Zur Historiographie seit Johannes von Müller.** (Content and interpretation of Swiss history: on historiography since Johannes von Müller.)
Hanno Helbling. In: *Handbuch der Schweizer Geschichte*. Zurich: Berichthaus, 1972, vol. 1, p. 3-25.

Johannes von Müller (1752-1809) ushered in modern Swiss historiography. He created the image of the freedom-loving, Helvetic-patriotic burghers of the Swiss Confederation.

Early 19th-century Swiss historians built on this interpretation and added a religious-ethical dimension by tying freedom to religion, Christendom, and God. With Karl Dändliker (1849-1910) and Johannes Dierauer (1842-1920), a new phase of Swiss historiography began, which, according to Helbling has lasted to the present. To these scholars, Swiss history is above all political history; their focus is Switzerland's development since the Constitution of 1848. Swiss history as national history is also the subject of the work of Wilhelm Oechsli (1851-1919) whose work was probably the most popular presentation of Swiss history and, because of its use in schools, the most influential one in modern times. Helbling's essay gives a good overview of the classical phase of Swiss historiography; it does not discuss any historians born after 1894.

General

167 **Historischer Atlas der Schweiz.** (Historical atlas of Switzerland.)
Edited by Hektor Ammann, Karl Schib. Aarau, Switzerland: Sauerländer, 1958. 2nd ed. 95p.

This oversize atlas, the product of a large team of scholars, contains some 150 maps, illuminating the history of Switzerland from prehistoric times to the early 20th century. Each of the pages has a brief descriptive text in German, French, and Italian. The emphasis is clearly on the political history of the country. The division of the territory during the Middle Ages among feudal lords, monasteries and bishoprics is shown, as well as the geographical distribution of towns and the course of the major trade routes. In the section dealing with the growth of the Swiss Confederation, the plans of decisive battles are given. In the second half of the atlas, the territorial changes of individual cantons are presented. The maps, which contain much information, are clearly drawn and, thanks to the use of colours, easy to read.

168 **A short history of Switzerland.**
Karl Dändliker, translated from the German by E. Salisbury. London: Swan Sonnenschein; New York: Macmillan, 1899. 322p. 2 maps.

This volume, by one of the grand old men of 19th-century Swiss historiography, has a certain quaint charm. Dändliker stresses the role that history played in the creation of the Swiss nation. Swiss history 'not only has, like every other history, a scientific interest . . . but it warms every Swiss heart with enthusiasm for the interests and rights of the people, for the tasks and concerns of the whole Confederation'. Due emphasis is given to the so-called 'heroic age' of Swiss history, the two centuries of the wars of liberation and aggrandizement from Morgarten to Marignano. The Reformation is judged kindly; the Catholic Reformation is treated in a section entitled 'the disastrous effects of the Counter-Reformation'. The narrative, which contains occasional references to social and intellectual history, ends with a description of the turbulent events that led to the complete revision of the federal constitution in 1874.

169 **An outline history of Switzerland: from the origins to the present day.**
Dieter Fahrni, translated from the German by Pro Helvetia. Zurich: Pro Helvetia, 1987. 4th ed. 110p. maps. bibliog.

This is an easy-to-read, introductory survey of Swiss history, enlivened by a fine range of illustrations. Like other Pro Helvetia brochures, it is also available in German,

French, Italian, and Spanish, through the Swiss diplomatic missions abroad or directly from Pro Helvetia, Arts Council of Switzerland, CH 8022 Zurich. Two other comprehensive, narrative histories from the Celts and Romans to the World War II period are *The making of Switzerland: from ice age to common market* by B. Bradfield (Zurich: Schweizer Spiegel, 1964) and *A short history of Switzerland* by E. Bonjour, H. S. Offler, G. R. Potter (Oxford: Clarendon Press, 1952).

170 **Schweizer Kriegsgeschichte.** (Swiss war history.)
Edited by M. Feldmann, H. G. Wirz. Bern: Oberkriegskommissariat, 1915-35. 12 parts. maps. bibliog.

The chief of the general staff of the Swiss army during World War I commissioned this collective work by twenty-two Swiss historians. The first parts published were relatively thin volumes of about 100 pages in length, while parts 2 and 3, published last, consist of about 400 and 700 pages respectively. The volumes treat Swiss history from the perspective of the wars the Swiss have fought, and of the role the army has played in its past and are organized chronologically from the first struggles for independence in the early 13th century to the period leading up to World War I. The 'heroic age' of the 15th century, when the Swiss fought successful campaigns against Savoy, Burgundy, the Holy Roman Empire, and in Italy, and established themselves for a short time as a European power, receives special emphasis. Each part contains maps of significant battles and campaigns and a bibliography reflecting the historical knowledge of the time.

171 **Schweizerische Wirtschafts- und Sozialgeschichte. Von den Anfängen bis zur Gegenwart.** (Swiss economic and social history from the beginning to the present.)
Albert Hauser. Erlenbach-Zurich; Stuttgart, FRG: Rentsch, 1961. 400p. bibliog.

This is a comprehensive history of Switzerland from the beginning of the Swiss alliance at the end of the 13th century to the middle of the 20th century seen from the perspective of the economic and social factors that determined life in the growing political entity that came to be called Switzerland. In five major chronological parts, subdivided into almost fifty chapters, Hauser describes the source of sustenance of the people in agriculture with its diversification; the role of trade, exports and imports; the function of the guilds and much later the trade unions; the development of roads and traffic; demographic changes and social position and ethics; the coming and growth of industries; banks; tourism; the arrival of the railways and of aviation; welfare legislation, and many other topics of a related nature. Hauser's work is still highly regarded as having laid the foundations for most social and economic history projects since its appearance.

172 **Handbuch der Schweizer Geschichte.** (Handbook of Swiss history.)
Hanno Helbling, Emil Vogt, Ernst Meyer, Hans Conrad Peyer, Walter Schaufelberger, Leonhard von Muralt, Peter Stadler, Ulrich Im Hof, Andreas Staehelin, Daniel Frei, Jean-Charles Biaudet, Erwin Bucher, Hans von Greyerz, Hans Ulrich Jost. Zurich: Berichthaus, 1980. 2nd ed. 1320p. 2 vols. bibliog.

The first volume begins with an essay on the content and meaning of Swiss history by Helbling and then examines Swiss history from prehistoric times to the age of the

Counter-Reformation. The second volume continues the story from the *ancien régime* to the 1960s. Most of the authors are or were professors at Swiss universities; all are established authorities in their fields, and they have produced a thorough chronological account of Swiss history. As contributors to a handbook they were especially concerned to incorporate the available historical literature into their presentation, and to this end, copious footnotes throughout provide an exhaustive annotated commentary on the scholarly output of Swiss historians. Each chapter also has a listing of source materials in archives and in printed form and, in some cases an extensive bibliography. This handbook will be a valuable resource for years to come.

173 **Geschichte der Schweiz und der Schweizer.** (History of Switzerland and the Swiss.)
Ulrich Im Hof, Pierre Ducrey, Guy P. Marchal, Nicolas Morard, Martin Körner, François de Capitani, Georges Andrey, Roland Ruffieux, Hans Ulrich Jost, Peter Gilg, Peter Hablützel. Basel; Frankfurt am Main, FRG: Helbing & Lichtenhahn, 1986. 1057p. maps. bibliog.

This is the enlarged one-volume 'study edition' of the three-volume work which appeared in 1982-83 in German, French, and Italian editions. This big book with its many illustrations, maps, tables, and various appendices is the most current and authoritative history of Switzerland available. Its contents reflect the new school of historiography, which, while not neglecting the chronological presentation of events, gives major attention to the social, economic, demographic, and cultural forces that shaped Swiss history. Each of the authors of the nine chapters, which lead from prehistory to the 1970s, addresses issues that are controversial and over which historians are divided. Each also contributed an elaborate historiographical essay at the end of his chapter. Of older general Swiss histories the following deserve mention: J. Dierauer, *Geschichte der Schweizerischen Eidgenossenschaft*, 5 vols., 1919-22; E. Gagliardi, *Geschichte der Schweiz von den Anfängen bis zur Gegenwart*, 3rd ed., 3 vols., Zurich, 1938; H. Nabholz, L. von Muralt, R. Feller, E. Dürr, E. Bonjour, *Geschichte der Schweiz*, 2 vols., Zurich 1932-38; and since World War II: E. Bohnenblust, *Geschichte der Schweiz*, Erlenbach-Zurich, 1974; P. Dürrenmatt, *Schweizer Geschichte*, 2nd ed., Zurich, 1976; S. Widmer, *Illustrierte Geschichte der Schweiz*, 4th ed., Munich, 1977.

174 **History of Switzerland. The first hundred thousand years: before the beginnings to the days of the present.**
James Murray Luck. Palo Alto, California: Society for the Promotion of Science and Scholarship, 1985. 887p. maps. bibliog.

A voluminous compilation of a wide variety of information concerning many aspects of Swiss history and life through the centuries, this work represents the labour of love of a California scientist enamoured with Switzerland. Unfortunately, the vast amount of materials is not digested; gathered mainly from secondary works, facts are piled upon facts with little attention to their relative importance. While the book falls short of being a history, it still has value as reference work. This is especially true of the chapter on 'The Twentieth Century' (almost 400 pages in length) which, in twenty-five sub-chapters, treats every subject of modern Swiss life from summer festivals to the status of women, air pollution, and much more.

175 **Switzerland from Roman times to the present.**
William Martin, Pierre Béguin, translated from the French by Jocasta Innes. London: Elek Books, 1971. 335p. map. bibliog.

This history of Switzerland was first published in 1929 and has since gone through six editions in its French version. An 'appendix' of some fifty pages by Béguin, entitled 'Switzerland since 1928' brings the story up to 1970. This 'essay on the formation of a confederation of states' appeals through its level-headed, brief (yet balanced) evaluation of the men and forces that shaped the Swiss Confederation. Martin makes some interesting points: for example, he thinks that Swiss unity after the Reformation was saved almost certainly by the fact that all cantons sent mercenary soldiers into the service of the kings of France, or that the Republic of Bern which controlled the Vaud and much of the Aargau was, with England and Venice, one of the most enlightened states in 18th-century Europe. The bibliography is skimpy.

176 **The rise of the Swiss republic.**
W. D. McCrackan. New York: AMS Press, 1970. 423p. bibliog. (Reprinted from the New York edition of 1901).

The last paragraph of McCrackan's introduction reads: 'The issue constantly at stake, throughout the history of the Swiss Confederation, has been one of the noblest and the most persistent with which human nature has had to grapple – the question of self-government. In these days Switzerland has become the standard-bearer in all reforms which make for direct democracy and pure politics. Her historical development ought, therefore, to be fully known and duly appreciated by American scholars.' The didactic enthusiasm of these sentences permeates the whole book. McCrackan begins his story with the prehistoric lake-dwellers and ends it with a discussion of the Swiss military system at the end of the 19th century. He is well read in the secondary literature available at the time and provides a reliable chronological account of the major stages in the Swiss success story, interrupted only by occasional comparisons of Swiss developments and institutions with similar ones in America.

177 **Schauplätze der Schweizer Geschichte.** (Scenes of Swiss history.)
Max Mittler. Zurich: Ex Libris, 1987. 216p. maps. bibliog.

This book consists of eighteen chapters, half of them written by authors other than Mittler. They describe scenes of Swiss history from the strongholds of the Old Swiss in their mountain valleys to the forests and fortifications of the Ajoie, the north-west corner of Switzerland, where troops guarded the Swiss border against Germany and France during World War I. Other geographical locations treated are the Alpine passes of the Great St Bernard and the Gotthard, the former traversed by Napoleon and the French in 1800, the latter crossed by General Suvorov with his Russian troops in 1799. Many settings for history are the work of humans, as illustrated by the chapters on Luzern and its bridges, the castles of Bellinzona, the baths of Baden, the iron ore mines in the Gonzen mountain in Canton St Gallen, and the town hall of Bern. This book reconstructs the scenes with the help of authentic contemporary reports, diagrams and maps, reproductions of old drawings and prints, and many photographs, old and new, in black-and-white and in colour. Mittler's fresh approach to Swiss history is both stimulating and entertaining.

178 **Wappen und Fahnen der Schweiz.** (Armorials and flags of Switzerland.)
Louis Mühlemann. Luzern: Reich, 1977. 164p. bibliog.

Hardly anywhere else have so many venerable old signs of armorial art been preserved in practically unaltered forms through the centuries. Mühlemann presents in this fabulously illustrated volume a complete overview of Swiss official heraldry. The armorials of the Confederation and the cantons, of all Swiss cities, cantonal capitals, and a selection of other communities, totalling 212 local armorials, are assembled by him – and all in colour. Every canton receives a description of the historical development of its cantonal armorial with reproductions of original documents such as stained glass (*Standesscheiben*), paintings, and woodcuts, as well as a selection of seals and coins. Mühlemann provides a similar heraldic account of the historical development of the national flag from the banners of the old Confederates and the cantonal military flags of the 17th century to the introduction of today's national flag. His work presents Swiss history from an unusual and fascinating angle.

179 **History of Switzerland 1499-1914.**
Wilhelm Oechsli, translated from the German by Eden and Cedar Paul. Cambridge, England: Cambridge University Press, 1922. 480p. maps. bibliog. (Cambridge Historical Series).

Oechsli's history of Switzerland is a product worthy of inclusion in the Cambridge Historical Series. Oechsli (1851-1919), one of the most prominent Swiss historians of his time, wrote this work late in his life, incorporating into it the profound knowledge of the subject which he acquired during his career as a professor in Zurich. It is unusual in that it summarizes only briefly the events of the first two centuries of the Swiss Confederation. The narrative begins in 1499 when the Swiss achieved *de facto* independence from the Holy Roman Empire in the Swabian War and reaches a first climax with the detailed account of the Reformation and Counter-Reformation (1519-1648) which takes up more than one-third of the text. The author devotes a quarter of the book to the age of the aristocracy (1648-1798) and to the 19th century. Oechsli's forte is the political history of the country; economic, cultural, and intellectual developments are treated summarily in somewhat perfunctory listings.

180 **Collective security in Swiss experience 1291-1948.**
William E. Rappard. London: George Allen & Unwin, 1948. 150p.

This booklet is an abbreviated version 'for the English-speaking public' of the author's *Cinq siècles de sécurité collective (1291-1798)* (Five centuries of collective security (1291-1798). Geneva, Paris, 1945. 603p.) The Swiss League of Alpine Cantons was based on treaties in which the contracting parties promised to protect each other 'in the interest of mutual security and peace'. It was in essence this form of security guarantee that united the heterogeneous self-governing cantons. In a first part Rappard charts the historical growth of Switzerland to the present, while a second part analyses the relevant passages in the various treaties of alliance which were the legal bases for the Confederation until 1798. A third part gives examples of instances in which the principles of mutual protection were applied in intercantonal affairs. Rappard finds many parallels between the Swiss Confederation and the League of Nations, both of which 'were constituted primarily for the protection of their members'.

181 **Chronik der Schweiz.** (Chronicle of Switzerland.)
Edited by Christian Schütt, Bernhard Pollmann. Dortmund, FRG: Chronik-Verlag; Zurich: Ex Libris, 1987. 640p. maps.

This huge book covers the history of Switzerland from prehistoric times to 1987 in strictly chronological instalments, centuries at first, then half centuries – from the early Middle Ages – and then, beginning in 1798, year by year. Within this framework there are 1,639 self-contained articles on every important event in Swiss history (and many unimportant ones), 291 calendars with 4,000 precise facts, 1,369 illustrations, graphics, and maps, and an introductory overview for each of the fourteen chapters into which the chronicle is divided. Sport is one of the areas which is treated with special care: every Swiss who ever won a medal in the Olympic Games is listed under the respective year, as are the soccer champions. Politics take up much space, but cultural events are not neglected. An appendix of thirty-two pages, with numerous tables and statistics and an index of all the persons mentioned, rounds off this astounding treasure-house of facts.

182 **Free and Swiss: the story of Switzerland.**
Georg Thürer, adapted and translated from the German by R. P. Heller, E. Long. London: Wolff, 1970. 198p. maps. bibliog.

Thürer sets the scene by dwelling on the diversity of the Swiss people and the regions where they live, facts which, nevertheless, did not prevent them from achieving unity in the course of seven hundred years of history. He divides the book into thirteen chapters and focuses his narrative on historical periods: the origins of the people, their first attempts at an alliance, their struggle for independence, the conflicts caused by the Reformation, the effects of the French Revolution and Napoleon, the emergence of a federal state in 1848, economic developments in the 19th century, the two World Wars, and the period from 1945 to 1969. An appendix details briefly the history of the individual cantons, while twelve photographs depict characteristic Swiss scenes and influential Swiss personalities. This condensed history is easy reading; it draws on broad knowledge of the country's past, and presents it in a favourable light.

183 **Zürich. Eine Kulturgeschichte.** (Zurich: a cultural history.)
Sigmund Widmer. Zurich; Munich: Artemis, 1975-85. 13 vols. bibliog.

Widmer relates Zurich's history from prehistoric times to the present in twelve compact illustrated volumes of about 120 pages each. He emphasizes the cultural aspects of the history of the city of which he was mayor from 1966 to 1982. His training as a teacher and historian is evident in the scholarly presentation of a wide range of intellectual and cultural subjects and in his pedagogic concern to place local history in the context of European history. Volume thirteen contains a general index and an illustrated chronology of the proud history of Zurich, ending with an entry on the election of the first woman, Elisabeth Kopp from Zumikon near Zurich, to the Swiss Federal Council in October 1984.

Ancient and medieval

184 **The journey to martyrdom of Saints Felix and Regula, circa 300 A.D.: a study of sources and significance.**

Marcel Chicoteau. Brisbane, Australia: Watson Ferguson, 1984. 54p. bibliog.

According to legend, Felix and Regula suffered the death of Christian martyrs in pagan Zurich, then the Roman Turicum, shortly after the year 300. The first documents mentioning the event date from the 9th century. Chicoteau, professor emeritus at Waikato University in New Zealand, wrestles with the difficult question of whether the legend does not in fact reflect a true occurrence. He uses isolated fragments of information and considerable speculation to piece together the possible sequence of events by which Felix and Regula travelled from North Africa to Rome and thence across the Alps to Glarus and Zurich. They were pilgrims and fugitives who after an arduous and adventurous trip died for their faith in a distant outpost of the Roman empire; they live on as patron saints of Zurich. Chicoteau's careful study is a stimulating contribution to the early history of Christianity in Switzerland and of Zurich.

185 **A knight of great renown: the careers of Othon de Grandson in a setting of medieval pageantry.**

Esther Rowland Clifford. Chicago, Illinois: University of Chicago Press, 1961. 313p. bibliog.

This is a carefully researched and lucidly written account of the life and career of Othon de Grandson, a scion of a large family of feudal nobles in the Pays de Vaud of what was then Savoy and is today western Switzerland. Othon lived from about 1238 to 1328, and during his many-faceted and colourful career he was diplomat, right-hand man to Edward I of England, administrator of his familial estate, financial negotiator, and always in the centre of the feudal hierarchy. He took part in two Crusades and was in Rome in the year of the Great Jubilee in 1300. A confidant of both the spiritual and temporal rulers, his activities are exceptionally well documented foı that time. Clifford makes the most of her sources and creates a convincing picture of medieval Europe during the century when it reached and passed its crest.

186 **Die Römer in der Schweiz.** (The Romans in Switzerland.)

Walter Drack, Rudolf Fellmann. Stuttgart, FRG; Jona, Switzerland: Roggi, 1988. 646p. maps. bibliog.

Booming construction in Switzerland since 1960 and extensive archaeological digs in the vicinity of former Roman settlements and along the frontier fortifications on the High Rhine uncovered so much new material, that a rewriting of the history of Switzerland in Roman times became mandatory. In the first part of this book, Fellmann treats the history, civilization, culture, and religion of the Roman times from the defeat of the Helvetians by Caesar at Bibracte (58 BC) to the loss of the provinces north of the Alps in the wake of the incursions by the Alemannians in the fourth and fifth centuries AD. The astonishing wealth of remains of Roman culture on Swiss soil is documented in the second part of the book by Drack. He lists all Roman artefacts outside museums, alphabetically and according to site, in more than 200 communities from Aegerten, Bern, to Zurzach, Aargau. The most beautiful finds are reproduced in twenty-four colour plates. In all, 536 illustrations, maps, and reconstruction sketches accompany the text. This impressive work has the character of a definitive handbook on its subject – until new techniques, such as aerial photography, for example, reveal the presence of still more treasures.

187 **Illustrierte Geschichte der Schweiz. Erster Band: Urgeschichte, römische Zeit und Mittelalter.** (Illustrated history of Switzerland. Volume I: prehistory, Roman era, and the Middle Ages.)
Walter Drack, Karl Schib. Einsiedeln, Switzerland [etc.]: Benziger, 1971. 2nd ed. 231p. maps. bibliog.

This large-format, richly illustrated volume with its many maps and extensive bibliography provides an excellent survey of the intricate historical developments in the territories that later came to be Switzerland. Drack covers the long timespan from the Palaeolithic age to the invasions of the Germanic tribes of the decaying Roman empire and their settlement in various parts of Switzerland, Burgundians in western Switzerland, Alemannians in eastern. Switzerland is rich in significant prehistoric sites and also has many remnants of the times of the Romans. Schib continues the story by describing the place of Switzerland in the Frankish kingdom, the emergence of feudalism, the role of the Church in early medieval society, the founding and growth of towns, and the opening of the Gotthard Pass in the early 13th century. Both authors are renowned historians and experts in their fields.

188 **The plan of St Gall in brief.**
Edited by Lorna Price. Berkeley, California; Los Angeles, London: University of California Press, 1982. 100p.

This large-format publication is based on the three-volume work *The Plan of St Gall* by Walter Horn and Ernest Born, published by the University of California Press in 1979. It deals with a unique architectural document created in the early 9th century. The document consists of five pieces of parchment on which the plan of a great church is sketched, together with forty surrounding buildings and several gardens, designed to serve some 270 monks and laymen. The plan was rediscovered in 1844 in its original home, the monastery of St Gallen. Price, from the art department of the University of California, Berkeley, presents the results of 'the most comprehensive scrutiny of the Plan ever undertaken'. Each building of the plan is reproduced in facsimile, and elevations are drawn to show what the buildings might have looked like had they been built – changes in the political and cultural climate of the post-Carolingian decades had prevented the plan's execution. Price's intimate knowledge of this matter is further reflected in the architectural models with which she completes her book. The scholarship is flawless and the whole publication of the highest quality.

The Old Swiss Confederation

189 **Hans Waldmann: Triumph und Niedergang des berühmten Bürgermeisters.** (Hans Waldmann: triumph and downfall of the famous burgomaster.)
Walter Baumann. Zurich: Neue Zürcher Zeitung, 1989. 128p.

Hans Waldmann whose monument stands in front of the Fraumünster church in Zurich was a controversial figure in Zurich's history. He was beheaded for his many bad deeds, his drinking, whoring, shady financial dealings, and fights. He was born around 1435 in Blickensdorf, Zug and came to Zurich to learn the trade of ironmonger. The guilds and craftsmen had gained the leadership of the city and Waldmann became guildmaster and eventually mayor. His bravery in the Burgundian wars, and his marriage into a wealthy family lent him status. He ruled with an iron hand over the moral, domestic and political issues of his people, amidst accusations of his own wrongdoings. A revolt by the farmers led to his downfall. Waldmann, credited with the international esteem Zurich enjoyed at the end of the Middle Ages as a well-organized city state, was considered a leader of the Swiss Confederation.

190 **Basle and France in the sixteenth century: the Basle humanists and printers in their contacts with Francophone culture.**
Peter G. Bietenholz. Toronto, Canada: University of Toronto Press; Geneva: Droz, 1971. 367p. bibliog.

This scholarly monograph describes the many and diverse contacts between the humanists and printers of 16th-century Basel and their French-speaking contemporaries. Basel was imbued with the spirit of Erasmus and continued to foster humanistic values and corporate endeavours long after his death in 1536. This humanistic spirit gave Basel a cosmopolitan flair, most clearly manifested in its flourishing printing and book trade. Francophones were attracted to Basel, or induced to send their manuscripts to be printed there because Basel with its relative freedom represented an alternative to Calvinist Geneva. Bietenholz has divided his work into four major parts, dealing with the book trade with France; Francophone expatriates in Basel; the focal contacts of the Basel printing industry in France; and a bibliography of close to 1,200 entries of books published in Basel from 1470 to 1650 by Francophone authors, editors, translators, and contributors, and theses of French-speaking students at the University of Basel.

191 **Die Schweiz als Mitgestalterin Europas. Die Geschichte der Fremdendienste. Vom Konzil von Basel (1444) bis zum Westfälischen Frieden (1648).** (Switzerland's encounter with Europe: the history of the foreign services, from the Council of Basel (1444) to the Peace of Westphalia (1648).)
Jean-René Bory. Neuchâtel, Switzerland; Paris: Delachaux & Niestlé, 1980. 302p. bibliog.

Bory has divided the narrative part of this book into more than ninety short sections that lead chronologically from one event to the next. With their instructive captions, the numerous illustrations (many in colour) are an important element for the visualization of the lively times Bory describes. Foreign service meant in essence service for the kings of France for negotiated sums of money, but since the French kings were notoriously short of funds, the Swiss advanced them the necessary credit against a stiff rate of interest; most of the accumulated debt, however, was never paid. In the meantime the Swiss soldiers, under their own commanders and their own flags, fought in countless battles against the enemies of France, primarily the Spanish Habsburgs. Foreign service was an important constant in the history of the Old Confederation, and through it the Swiss cantons remained in contact with the rest of Europe. It served as an outlet for the underemployed male population and brought resources and knowledge of the world into the valleys and towns of the country.

192 **Matthäus, Cardinal Schiner: statesman, soldier and humanist.**
Archibald K. Bruce. [London: Queen's Gate 36a, by the author, 1952]. 95p.

Matthäus Schiner (c.1465-1522), 'the Great Priest of the Swiss', rose by the strength of his mind and his personality from a country urchin to a position of influence in the affairs of Europe. Born in Mühlebach in the Upper Valais, he pursued a career in the church, and in 1499 became bishop of Sion. In 1511 he was made cardinal with eight others by Pope Julius II, in whose efforts against the French, Schiner assisted, and there are speculations that, had he lived longer, he might have become pope. Bruce's unscholarly booklet consists of brief chapters on Schiner's life, the conflicts in Sion with his major adversary George Supersaxo, his relations with Erasmus and the reformers, and his role at the Diet of Worms of 1521. Among the lasting achievements of Schiner is his role in helping the Confederates in negotiations held at Arona in 1503 to retain Bellinzona and the Blenio valley, the major part of what, much later, was to become Canton Ticino. Bruce's source was the two-volume biography by Albert Büchi, *Kardinal Matthäus Schiner als Staatsmann und Kirchenfürst* (Cardinal Matthäus Schiner as statesman and prince of the church), published in 1923 and 1937.

193 **Jean-Jacques: the early life and work of Jean-Jacques Rousseau 1712-1754.**
Maurice Cranston. New York; London: Norton, 1983. 382p. map. bibliog.

The formative years of Rousseau (1712-78) are meticulously reconstructed by Cranston on the basis of primary sources available in Rousseau's collected works, dozens of volumes of his complete correspondences, the correspondences of his contemporaries, archival materials, and a range of secondary works. The result is an impressive, eminently readable story of the first part of Rousseau's life, the years when he wandered from Geneva to Savoy, to Turin, to Madame de Warens again at Chambéry in Savoy, to Lyons, Paris, Venice, back to Paris, and back to Geneva. After long stretches of poverty and humiliation, the self-taught Genevan earned a living as a composer and copyist of music and was accepted into the circle of the Paris philosophers who were engaged in the publication of the *Encyclopédie*. Cranston explores the genesis of the early written works of Rousseau, among them the two discourses of 1750 and 1753 (published in 1755). Cranston agrees with other critics that the second, the *Discourse on the origin of inequality*, 'the masterpiece of his early years', was perhaps Rousseau's most influential book, both because of its impact on the leaders of the French Revolution and as the origin of modern social science.

194 **Was für ein Leben: Schweizer Alltag vom 15. bis 18. Jahrhundert.**
(What a life: Swiss daily life from the 15th to the 18th century.)
Albert Hauser. Zurich: Neue Zürcher Zeitung, 1987. 364p. bibliog.

Professor Hauser bases his cultural history of Switzerland from the 15th to the 18th century on chronicles, folk songs, and folk plays, inscriptions on houses, tools and the like. He also draws from his previous studies of *Bauernregeln* (peasant rules) which had introduced him to the wide realm of human experience of bygone days. Accounts of work and leisure, food and clothing, good and bad days, family and community, and religion and customs are woven into a rich continuous history, all of which is illustrated with woodcuts, photographs and paintings, some in colour.

195 **The Swiss Confederation in the Middle Ages.**
Paul E. Martin. In: *The Cambridge medieval history*. Vol. 7: *Decline of empire and papacy*. Cambridge, England: Cambridge University Press, 1932 (reprinted 1964), p. 183-215.

Martin, then professor of history at the University of Geneva, sketches the political history of the young Swiss Confederation fròm the first alliances of the Forest Cantons in the late 13th century through the heroic age of successful battles and wars against various feudal enemies in the 14th and 15th centuries. He describes the growth of the alliances to the Confederation of the Thirteen Cantons and the expansionist policies of the cantons by which they acquired new territory and became involved in the Italian wars of the early 16th century. Martin's account ends with the story of the defeat of the Swiss in the battle of Marignano in 1515, which led to the withdrawal of the Confederates from international politics and the beginning of a policy of neutrality.

196 **Hirsebrei und Hellebarde. Auf den Spuren des mittelalterlichen Lebens in der Schweiz.** (Millet gruel and halberd: on the trail of medieval life in Switzerland.)
Werner Meyer. Olten, Switzerland; Freiburg, FRG: Walter, 1985. 395p. bibliog.

This most informative panorama of medieval life in Switzerland is based on a thorough knowledge of historical sources and is amplified by numerous illustrations. Chapters on the geographical space and its transformation by its inhabitants, and on the history of the region to the founding of the thirteen-member Swiss Confederation in the early 16th century, are followed by parts dealing with medieval society in all its facets: its class division of nobility, clergy, peasants and craftsmen, and those people living on the margins of society such as whores, beggars, cripples, Jews, gypsies, thieves, and robbers; from clothes to food, work, tools, pay, prices, birth, health care, and death; religion, including the influence of the Church in all phases of life and society; festivals and festivities in town and countryside; medieval law and law enforcement; warfare, military organization, and the evolving mercenary system.

197 **The Swiss at war 1300-1500.**
Douglas Miller, G. A. Embleton. London: Osprey, 1979. 40p. map. bibliog. (Osprey Men-at-arms series).

This booklet seeks to reconstruct the costumes and weapons of the lower ranks among the Swiss troops and the armour of the wealthier soldiers of the heroic age of Swiss history. Illustrations of battle scenes from chronicles and of weapons, armour, and banners from museums enliven the text. The eight rather fanciful colour plates by Embleton do not add much to the work. Its value lies in the factual description of the basic organization of the Swiss troops and of the composition of the cantonal contingents in the battles of the Burgundian wars of the 1470s. The annotations of the illustrations are also quite informative.

198 **Calvin's Geneva.**
E. William Monter. New York [etc.]: Wiley, 1967. 250p. maps. bibliog.

This is a history of Geneva in the 16th century, according to Monter its 'heroic age'. A city of slightly more than 10,000 inhabitants, it gained its independence from Savoy in the late 1520s with the help of its allies Bern and Fribourg, members of the Swiss

League. The political revolution was accompanied by a religious one when, influenced by Bern, the city turned to Protestantism. In 1536 Calvin arrived in Geneva for the first time, and found himself in a tumultuous environment. By the time of Calvin's death in 1564, Geneva had become 'a well-run state' with a 'superbly run church'. Monter recounts these events in the first section of his book. In the second section he describes the main institutions and social groups of Calvin's Geneva, giving a chapter each to the Calvinist Church, the civil government, and the foreign refugee communities. A third and final section assesses Calvin's legacy to Geneva and outlines the course of events during the post-Calvin era, ending in the early 17th century with the *Escalade* of 1602, the successful repulse of the Savoyard attempt to reconquer the city, and the death in 1605 of Theodore Beza, Calvin's successor. Thanks to Calvin, Geneva had become a model 'city set on a hill' for Protestants in many parts of Christendom. The Catholic view, equally widespread, was that of the city as a cesspool upon the face of Europe. Geneva's political achievement consisted in gaining and preserving its independence in a century when many other European cities lost theirs.

199 **Witchcraft in Switzerland: the borderlands during the Reformation.**
E. William Monter. Ithaca, New York; London: Cornell University Press, 1976. 232p. bibliog.

Monter chose to investigate witchcraft in the Jura region, the borderland between France and Switzerland, because the region was 'an interesting juncture of several different major themes and questions in the history of European witchcraft'. Witch hunts and trials were conducted in often strikingly different ways by the various political entities that governed the Jura region. Monter's longest chapter deals with 'the gentle Calvinists' of Geneva. He tries to dispel the existing belief that Calvin and his Geneva dealt especially harshly with witches. The worst outbreak of the witch hunt epidemic in Geneva took place in 1571-72. It saw the execution or banishment of nintey-nine people who were punished as *engraisseurs* or 'plague-spreaders'. A register of their names, occupation, marital status, and age shows that not only spinsters but men and women of all ages were among them. Here, as in the small communes of the Jura mountains, the witches were mostly poor, uneducated people and often 'foreigners'. Their *malificia* consisted of causing the death or misfortune of people or animals. It was enough for a surgeon to verify a Devil's Mark on a suspect's leg to bring him or her to trial. Confessions and names of accomplices were extorted through torture. In his thorough and well-documented socio-historical study Monter lists almost a thousand names of persons who were tried as witches in the Jura region between 1527 and 1681. He repeatedly makes the point, however, that, compared with the extent of witch hunts in other parts of Europe, the Jura incidents were only 'small panics'.

200 **Die Schweizer Bilderchroniken des 15./16. Jahrhunderts.** (The Swiss picture chronicles of the 15th and 16th centuries.)
Edited by Walter Muschg, E. A. Gessler. Zurich: Atlantis, 1941. 195p.

This book contains 208 reproductions of chronicle illustrations, mostly in black-and-white. A short text provides the background for the story told in each picture. The pictures stem from the chronicles of six different artists, of whom Diebold Schilling is the best known and most widely represented here with his Bern chronicle, the Luzern chronicle, and that of the Burgundian wars. As Muschg explains, the chronicles, done a generation or two after the events they illustrate, are inspired by the proud tradition that glorified the deeds of the brave forebears. Whether they depict war scenes, and there are many of those, or the delights of life in the prosperous cities and countryside, they reflect the feelings of a time that basked in the memories of a heroic past. These beautifully illustrated chronicles from the 15th and 16th centuries are found in Swiss archives. Historians have been using them as sources in their research; facsimile printing techniques now permit wide access to these national treasures.

201 **The Reformation in the cities: the appeal of Protestantism to sixteenth-century Germany and Switzerland.**
Steven E. Ozment. New Haven, Connecticut; London: Yale University Press, 1975. 237p.

Ozment sees the Reformation in German and Swiss towns and cities as having been 'in the broadest sense of the word a popular movement, by sixteenth-century standards even a democratic revolution'. The laity was attracted to it because it gave them a religious transvaluation of the concepts, practices, and institutions of the late medieval church. They needed little prompting to embrace the teachings of the reformers. The catechisms and church ordinances of the Protestant reformers set the framework within which religious practice at the local levels was revolutionized, religious life simplified, and secular life enhanced. A new social ethic emerged which demanded 'that people, especially the clergy and the powerful institutions they represented, be useful servants within and not burdens upon their communities'. Ozment sides with those Reformation historians who adopt the 'urban perspective' for an understanding of the success of reformers such as Zwingli in Zurich and Martin Bucer in Strasbourg.

202 **Huldrych Zwingli et la Réforme en Suisse d'après les recherches récents.**
(Huldrych Zwingli and the Reformation in Switzerland according to recent research.)
J. V. Pollet. Paris: Presses Universitaires de France, 1963. 123p. bibliog.

This brief monograph is not intended so much to provide a biography of Zwingli as to throw light on the historical context of Zwingli's spiritual growth and the impact of his work in Zurich. Pollet incorporates the findings of some 250 articles, biographies, and monographs published since 1950 into his text which thus assumes the nature of a comprehensive annotated bibliography. Twelve full-page plates and fourteen smaller engravings in the text add to the enjoyment of the volume. Pollet has made similar contributions to the Zwingli literature in his articles 'Zwinglianisme' in volume 15 of the *Dictionnaire de théologie Catholique* (Dictionary of Catholic theology) (Paris: Librairie Letouzey et Ané, 1950), p. 3745-928, and 'Chronique de théologie historique. Seizième siècle (suite et fin). Réforme suisse', in *Revue des sciences religieuses*, 37 (Religious Sciences Review, 37) (1963), p. 34-59. The latter reviews Zwingli and Swiss Reformation research under the headings 'Zwingli and Zwinglianism', 'Bullinger', 'Zurich anabaptism', and 'Reformation and Counter Reformation in Switzerland'. An impressive work on Zwingli's influence across space and time is *Die Zwinglische Reformation im Rahmen der europäischen Kirchengeschichte* (Zwingli's Reformation in the context of European church history) by Gottfried W. Locher (Göttingen, FRG; Zurich: Vandenhoeck & Ruprecht, 1979).

203 **Johann Caspar Lavater. Philosoph – Gottesmann – Schöpfer der Physiognomie.** (Johann Caspar Lavater: philosopher, man of god, creator of physiognomy.)
Anne-Marie Saton, translated from the French by Cornelia Langendorf. Zurich: SV international/Scheizer Verlagshaus, 1988. 158p. bibliog. (Die grossen Schweizer).

Lavater (1741-1801) spent most of his life in his native city of Zurich. He received his schooling there, was ordained into the Reformed clergy, and in 1786 was promoted to the pastorate of the St Peter's church which he held to the end of his life. In the second half of the 18th century Zurich developed into a cosmopolitan centre of culture where the works of Goethe, Rousseau, and Kant were read and discussed. Lavater was also increasingly influenced by the mystics of his time, among them Franz Anton Mesmer with his ideas about animal magnetism. Lavater became a prolific writer on a wide range of topics, his best-known work being *Physiognomische Fragmente* (1775-78, repeatedly revised until 1803). For his protest over the French occupation of Zurich, he was put in prison by the Directorate in 1799; after his release he was shot by a French soldier, and died in 1801. This richly illustrated, large-format book with its chronological table establishes Lavater as a citizen of the world who had attempted to harmonize faith and reason at a time when the ideas of the Enlightenment and the *ancien régime* were in turmoil.

204 **Modern Christianity: the Swiss Reformation.**
Philip Schaff. New York: Scribner's, 1910. 5th ed. 890p. map. bibliog. (*History of the Christian church*, vol. 7. Reprint: Grand Rapids, Michigan: Eerdmans, 1981).

This volume has two parts, entitled 'The Swiss Reformation' and 'The Reformation in French Switzerland'. In the first part Schaff deals with the Reformation in German Switzerland and Graubünden: Zwingli's religious training, his work in Zurich, the spread of Zwinglianism to other parts of Switzerland and Germany, the civil and religious war that cost Zwingli his life, and the period of consolidation under his successor Heinrich Bullinger to the Second Helvetic Confession of 1566. Schaff calls the Helvetic Confession 'the most widely adopted, and hence the most authoritative of all the Continental Reformed symbols, with the exception of the Heidelberg Catechism'. The second part on the Reformation in French Switzerland is more than three times as long. Calvin's life and career, his labours in Geneva, the organization of his church, his theology, and the doctrinal controversies are treated in depth. More than one hundred pages are devoted to Servetus and the problems he created for Calvin, and this part ends with a chapter on Calvin's faithful friend and successor, Theodore Beza. Throughout the book Schaff introduces new subjects with detailed bibliographies, displaying his thorough knowledge of the historical literature available to him in 1892 when the work was first published. Even though old, this account of the Swiss Reformation is still readable and informative.

205 **Jean-Jacques Rousseau. Philosoph – Pädagoge – Zerstörer der alten Ordnung. Eine Bildbiographie.** (Jean-Jacques Rousseau: philosopher, educator, destroyer of the old order; a picture biography.)
Michel Soëtard, translated from the French by Ingrid Altrichter.
Zurich: Schweizer Verlagshaus, 1989. 160p. bibliog. (Die grossen Schweizer).

Based on many years of research, Soëtard's well-written picture biography captures the many sides of Rousseau's achievements. Rousseau, as author of *Emile*, is a pedagogue; on the other hand, the *Social Contract* has established Rousseau's place as a political philosopher of the first order. With the help of rich and carefully selected pictorial material of excellent quality and with informative captions, Soëtard points out that Rousseau was also a successful botanist, musician, composer, and novelist. A chronological table follows Rousseau's life from his birth in Geneva in 1712 to his death in 1778 at Ermenonville, outside Paris, placing his life and works in the heyday of the *ancien régime* and the Enlightenment.

206 **Jean-Jacques Rousseau: transparency and obstruction.**
Jean Starobinski, translated from the French by Arthur Goldhammer.
Chicago, Illinois: University of Chicago Press, 1988. 421p.

Starobinski's work originated as a doctoral dissertation at the University of Geneva in 1957. It has been published and republished in revised and enlarged editions and translated into other languages, and in the process, has become a classic of modern literary criticism. Starobinski establishes the theme of transparency, the desired communication of the heart, as the dominant motif and the key to understanding Rousseau's work. Transparency may be located in an imaginary past (*Discourse on the origin of inequality*), in a utopian future (*Social contract*), in fiction (*La nouvelle Héloïse*), in infancy (*Emile*), in communication with nature (*Reveries of a solitary wanderer*), or in the contemplation of one's own soul (*Confessions*). However, this transparency is continuously obstructed by social and cultural artifices found in civilization as it evolved in history. The manifestations of alienation which are visible in all of Rousseau's work are overcome, according to Starobinski, by the dialectic process of negating the negation. In Rousseau's life, however, alienation prevailed, and in the end he found refuge only in refusing all contact with the outer world and seeking transparency within himself. Seven essays on Rousseau, which Starobinski wrote for various learned journals or as introductions to the publication of works by Rousseau between 1962 and 1970, add further to the value of this outstanding book.

207 **Costume and conduct in the laws of Basel, Bern, and Zurich 1370-1800.**
John Martin Vincent. New York: Greenwood Press, 1969. 170p. bibliog. (Reprint of 1933 edition published by Johns Hopkins Press).

For centuries, city governments all over Western Europe endeavoured to restrict the display of wealth in fashion and on festive occasions. They passed sumptuary laws and set up supervisory bodies to enforce them. Rules concerning Sabbath observance and profanity were also designed to regulate the conduct of the citizens. Vincent found the study of the Swiss cities of Basel, Bern, and Zurich especially rewarding because the archives of these cities also contain records about the violators of the laws and of the actions taken by the city tribunals against them. Vincent uses these archival materials to provide a lively and entertaining account of social life and customs in Swiss cities from the late Middle Ages through the Reformation to the *ancien régime*. The book has numerous illustrations and several statistical appendices and charts.

208 **Illustrierte Geschichte der Schweiz. Zweiter Band: Entstehung, Wachstum und Untergang der Alten Eidgenossenschaft.** (Illustrated history of Switzerland. Volume 2: Founding, growth and decline of the Old Confederation.)
Sigmund Widmer. Einsiedeln, Switzerland [etc.]: Benziger, 1960. 303p. maps. bibliog.

Widmer's volume in this three-volume history of Switzerland covers the centuries from the founding of the Swiss Confederation in the late 13th century to the eve of its overthrow at the end of the 18th. Like the other volumes, it is enriched by a large number of beautiful illustrations with elaborate, instructive captions. Widmer chronicles the political and military developments that led from the first treaty of mutual support among the three forest cantons on the Vierwaldstättersee (Lake Lucerne) in August 1291 to the height of Swiss military power in the second half of the 15th century. The political relationship of the thirteen cantons and their subject areas, as achieved by 1513, remained stable for the next 250 years in spite of religious civil wars. One of the strengths of Widmer's book is his treatment of the social and cultural aspects of Swiss history during those centuries. The confederation may have stagnated politically, but intellectually it was alive with the ideas of the humanists and reformers of the 16th century and the scientists, literati, and educators of the Enlightenment.

209 **The radical reformation.**
George Huntston Williams. London: Weidenfeld & Nicolson, 1962. 924p. map. bibliog.

The radical reformation of the Anabaptists, Spiritualists, Evangelical Rationalists, and others took place concurrently with the Protestant and the Catholic reformations of the 16th century. The radical or left-wing reformers rebelled not only against the Church of Rome but also against the Protestant reformers and as a consequence incurred the enmity of both. Williams, formerly Winn Professor of Ecclesiastical History at Harvard University, provides in this book a detailed history of the radical movement. It began in Switzerland with the organization of the first Anabaptist convention in 1525 and spread to many other parts of Europe. By 1575 the movement had hardened into sects that continue to exert influence in religion and politics to the present. Williams treats the disparate groups synoptically, with due attention to the personalities and fates of the protagonists. Five of the thirty-two chapters deal specifically with the Swiss radicals. See also 'The Swiss reformers and the sects', by E. G. Rupp and Ernest A. Payne in: *The new Cambridge modern history*, edited by G. R. Elton (Cambridge, England: Cambridge University Press, 1958, vol. 2, ch. 4, p. 96-119; 119-33).

210 **La Suisse et la Révolution Française. Images, caricatures, pamphlets.** (Switzerland and the French Revolution: images, caricatures, pamphlets.)
Edited by Sylvie Wuhrman, Pierre Chessex. Lausanne, Switzerland: Editions du Grand-Pont/Jean-Pierre Laubscher, 1989. 232p. maps. bibliog.

This is the catalogue of the exhibition with the same title in Lausanne in summer 1989. It contains 270 numbered exhibits with the description of the object, a commentary, and a bibliography. One hundred and forty of the exhibits are illustrated in the catalogue, twenty-three of them in colour. The exhibits consist of contemporary newspaper articles, brochures, and broadsides for and against the revolution. The original works of precursors such as Rousseau and participants are displayed. Special events, such as the massacre of the Swiss soldiers at the Tuileries on 10 August 1792, are highlighted with letters and dispatches from soldiers and officers in the service of the French king. The topically organized picture sections are connected by brief essays by fifteen contributors on various aspects of Swiss history and society during the decade that led up to the invasion of Switzerland by the French revolutionary armies in 1798.

Nineteenth and early twentieth centuries

211 **Zürich, the 1820's to the 1870's: a study in modernization.**
Frederick S. Allen. Lanham, Maryland [etc.]: University Press of America, 1986. 132p. maps. bibliog.

This brief book is a pedestrian attempt to tell the story of the modernization of Zurich during the middle of the 19th century. Chapter one portrays the city in the early 19th century when it was still basically a medieval town. Of the ensuing four chapters, two chapters examine political developments, one deals with economics, and one with social and cultural phenomena. Chapter six captures the magnitude of change by describing the city at the end of the fifty-year period chosen by Allen, when it had made the transition to a modern city. The author makes a disclaimer in the preface to his monograph: 'This book is really more of an effort to probe one case of urban modernization in Europe than it is to make a contribution to Swiss historiography', he writes, but how it can be the one without the other is a puzzle.

212 **Niklaus von Flüe als nationale Integrationsfigur. Metamorphosen der Bruder Klaus-Mythologie.** (Niklaus von Flüe as national integration figure: metamorphoses of the Brother Klaus mythology.)
Urs Altermatt. *Zeitschrift für schweizerische Kirchengeschichte*, vol. 81 (1987), p. 51-82.

Niklaus von Flüe (1417-87), referred to as 'Brother Klaus', played an important role at a decisive moment in Swiss history when his mediation at the Diet of Stans prevented the break-up of the Swiss Confederation – this contribution secured his place as one of the great figures in Swiss history. He was also a hermit and a mystic who had left his family to live in solitude in his hut near Sachseln, Canton Obwalden. Common people revered him, and in 1947 he was made a saint of the Catholic church. The article by Altermatt describes the changes in the Brother Klaus myth since the creation of the modern Swiss state in 1848. At various times he was used as the patron of the Catholic-conservative opposition to the new state (1847-48), as the symbolic figure for the reconciliation between political Catholicism and the Liberals (1877), as protector of Switzerland in crisis (1917), as a hero of national spiritual defence (1937), and, finally, as crisis manager in the post-modern society of 1987. This is a stimulating overview of 150 years of Swiss history from an unusual angle.

213 **The industrial reolution in Switzerland.**

B. M. Biucchi. In: *The Fontana economic history of Europe*, vol. 4: *The emergence of industrial societies*, part 2. Brighton, England: Harvester; New York: Barnes & Noble, 1976, p. 627-55. maps. bibliog.

In the early 19th century Switzerland's industrial development was on a par with that of Great Britain. The interaction of the economic, social, and political sectors of Swiss society was such that the country was 'prepared to accept at once from Britain the industrial revolution'. Cotton, silk, watchmaking, woollen, and linen industries provided work in villages and towns all across Switzerland even before the end of the 18th century. Biucchi lists the following factors as characteristic of the industrial development of Switzerland: decentralization, which prevented the rise of large urban centres and delayed the appearance of a proletarian class; availability of considerable reserves of capital due to savings from mercenary income and accumulated profits from trade, which allowed industrial expansion to be self-financed; freedom from government and political restrictions, which aided the evolution toward free trade as the basis for the Swiss economy; and the presence of an 'intellectual bourgeoisie', influenced both by the French Enlightenment and by English Utilitarianism, which provided leadership in adapting Swiss manufacturing with remarkable speed and ease to changing conditions and trends in industries and world markets. Biucchi's article is anecdotal and lacks statistical underpinning.

214 **History of the International Committee of the Red Cross. Vol. 1: From Solferino to Tsushima.**

Pierre Boissier, translated from the French by the Henry Dunant Institute. Geneva: Henry Dunant Institute, 1985. 391p.

Boissier tells the story of the first decades of the International Committee of the Red Cross, the Geneva-based organization that was instrumental in launching the Red Cross movement. Part one of this book makes for lively reading, for it deals with the circumstances of Henry Dunant's presence near the battlefield of Solferino at the end of June 1859 and his desperate attempts to help the abandoned wounded and dying soldiers. He eloquently expressed his dismay at what he had seen in *A memory of Solferino*, whose publication led to the formation of a five-person committee composed of influential Genevans to organize international support for his ideas and redress the situation. Surprisingly successful, the committee's work culminated in the adoption by twelve countries of the Convention for the Amelioration of the Wounded in Armies in the Field, 22 August 1864, the famous Geneva Convention. The signatories agreed to treat medical support personnel, whether voluntary or military, as neutral non-combattants and to designate them as such with a white armband with a red cross on it. The other four parts of Boissier's book tell about the spread of the ideals of the Red Cross during the wars of the 1860s and 1870s and the series of conferences where further international agreements expanded upon the basic ideas contained in the Geneva Convention. Unfortunately, this work contains neither footnotes nor a bibliography.

215 **Sozialer und kultureller Wandel in einem ländlichen Industriegebiet (Zürcher Oberland) unter Einwirkung des Maschinen- und Fabrikwesens im 19. und 20. Jahrhundert.** (Social and cultural change in a rural industrial region [Zurich Oberland] under the impact of the machine- and factory-system in the 19th and 20th century.)
Rudolf Braun. Erlenbach-Zurich; Stuttgart, FRG: Rentsch, 1965. 368p. bibliog.

This is the second volume of Braun's authoritative *Industrialisierung und Volksleben* (Industrialization and life of the people; Rentsch, 1960) in which the Zurich professor of sociology describes the changes brought about in the countryside by the spread of industrial modes of production (Braun thinks the term 'industrial revolution' inappropriate in the Swiss context). In the first volume Braun established the fact that the part of Canton Zurich he studied, the Zurich Oberland, was, in a cultural-morphological sense, a true industrial region even before 1800. In this second volume he meticulously describes (in jargon-free language) how the type of employment patterns changed in the course of the 19th century from cottage industry to machine industry to factory work, the three often existing side by side, and how this development influenced the social order of the region. Making excellent use of local archival sources, especially those of Wald, Braun succeeds with his anecdotal presentation in recreating the reality of social change during an important phase of modern history. The results of his study provide a prototype for examining similar developments in other parts of the world.

216 **Die Geschichte des Sonderbundskrieges.** (The history of the war of the *Sonderbund*.)
Erwin Bucher. Zurich: Berichthaus, 1966. 595p. 9 maps. bibliog.

Bucher's massive book provides a detailed account of the turbulent events in 1847 that culminated in a civil war when a majority of Swiss cantons took up arms to prevent seven Catholic cantons from seceding from the Confederation. The seven had formed a separate alliance (*Sonderbund*) in protest against the anticlerical, modernizing reform efforts of the Liberals. The war which broke out in October 1847 lasted barely a month. The centre of the disorganized *Sonderbund* cantons, Luzern, fell before the federal troops, led by General William Henri Dufour from Geneva. Thanks largely to Dufour's military leadership and humanitarianism the war cost few lives and left no lasting scars among the confederates. In 1848, they cooperated in giving the country a new constitution which created the modern Swiss state, 'the most fortunate and most significant deed' in Swiss history. Bucher has made use of all available source materials and has written the definitive political and military history of this important event in Swiss history.

217 **The triumph of liberalism: Zürich in the golden age, 1830-1869.**
Gordon A. Craig. New York: Scribner's, 1988. 314p. bibliog.

Craig, known for his books on Germany, uses his considerable knowledge of the cultural and political history of central Europe in the 19th century to paint an interesting picture of the small, but intellectually and politically lively town of Zurich. Unperturbed by the fact (of which, of course, he is not aware) that he puts half the city on the wrong side of the Limmat river, he tells the story of the impact of classical liberalism on the development of Zurich. Zurich and its leaders were an important force in federal affairs on the side that brought about the creation of the modern Swiss state during the years 1847-48. It became a centre of learning and a city of refuge for liberals from other countries, developed an international character for the first time in its history, and enjoyed an economic and cultural renaissance in the 1850s. Of the many personalities who stride across Craig's pages Richard Wagner, the German architect Gottfried Semper, Gottfried Keller, Jacob Burckhardt, and the enterpreneur and railway magnate Alfred Escher stand out. Toward the end of the 1860s liberalism underwent a crisis, but its achievements left a lasting mark on the city on the Limmat. Craig's book, originally published as *Geld und Geist: Zürich im Zeitalter des Liberalismus, 1830-1869* (Munich: Beck, 1988), received wide critical acclaim by Swiss reviewers.

218 **Henry Dunant. Finanzmann – Phantast – Gründer des Roten Kreuzes. Eine Bildbiographie.** (Henry Dunant: financier, dreamer, founder of the Red Cross. A picture biography.)
Marc Descombes, translated from the French by Reiner Pfleiderer. Zurich: SV international/Schweizer Verlagshaus, 1988. 159p. bibliog. (Die grossen Schweizer).

The Genevan Henry Dunant (1828-1910), a religious man, was one of the founders of the Young Men's Christian Association in Paris in 1852. During the Italian war of 1859 Dunant witnessed the suffering at the battle of Solferino, so he launched an appeal in the *Journal de Genève* for help for wounded soldiers, and soon after published the booklet *Un Souvenir de Solférino* (1860). Dunant's ideas were well received by influential Genevans who encouraged him to rally statesmen and royalty to his cause. As a result of his efforts, a conference of international dignitaries met in Geneva and in August 1864 signed The Geneva Convention for the Amelioration of the Fate of Soldiers Wounded in Battle, the origin of what later became the Red Cross movement. Dunant was for a time showered with international honours but ended up in poverty in an asylum in Heiden, Canton Appenzell-Ausserrhoden. While writing his memoirs there, he was discovered by the journalist Georg Baumberger, who informed the world that the great humanitarian was still alive. In 1901 he was honoured with the first Nobel Peace Prize, which he shared with the French pacifist Frédéric Passy. This is a nicely illustrated picture book with an elaborate chronology and a good bibliography.

219 **Mountain of truth. The counterculture begins: Ascona, 1900-1920.**
Martin Green. Hanover, New Hampshire: University Press of New England, 1986. 287p. bibliog.

The motto 'truth is to be lived, not lectured' sums up the ideas embraced by the disciples of the counterculture of the Mountain of Truth (*Monte verità*) in Ascona, a small town in the southern foothills of the Alps on the shores of Lago Maggiore. The Mountain of Truth symbolized freedom from the political, military, social, and moral shackles of the time. Hoping to realize a new lifestyle, the pilgrims came for many reasons and from different places to this cluster of simple houses on the hillside above Ascona. Green singles out Otto Gross, a prominent Austrian psychoanalyst, who tried to escape his domineering father; Gusto Grässer, a Hungarian rebel, who chose to live the life of a vagabond in the garb of a prophet; and Rudolf Laban, a 'handsome Don Juan', who became the leader of a new dance movement and attracted great dancers such as Mary Wigman. Laban's notations of dance choreography, his pupils, and his dance schools enjoyed a wide reputation. The movement reached its zenith from 1900 to 1920. Its activities were not confined to this centre, however; the network of Asconans spread all over Europe, and the ideas of its proponents live on in literary works, modern dance, psychoanalysis, and in artistic expressions such as Dadaism and Surrealism. Among the many individuals who at one time or another interacted with the Asconans one finds such figures as Hermann Hesse, D. H. Lawrence, Franz Kafka, Carl Gustav Jung, and Isadora Duncan.

220 **Der Weg zur Gegenwart: die Schweiz im neunzehnten Jahrhundert.** (The way to the present: Switzerland in the nineteenth century.)
Georg Kreis. Basel [etc.]: Birkhäuser, 1986. 248p. bibliog.

A by-product of a series of twelve programmes in three languages for Swiss television, this oversize, richly illustrated book provides an excellent introduction to many aspects of 19th-century Swiss history. Based on a large amount of factual, statistical, and pictorial material, the text is authoritative and (in places) provocative. During the 19th century the foundations of the modern Swiss state were laid and important industrial and societal changes took place which continue to shape contemporary life. Traditional interpretations of the forces at work in the growth of tourism, railway construction, emigration, and industrialization and their impact on political life are amplified at the end of each of the twelve chapters by brief comments on trends in contemporary Swiss historiography.

221 **Guillaume-Henri Dufour. General – Kartograph – Humanist. Eine Bildbiographie.** (Guillaume-Henri Dufour: general, cartographer, humanist. A picture biography.)
Jean-Jacques Langendorf, translated from the French by Cornelia Langendorf. Zurich: SV international/Schweizer Verlagshaus, 1987. 159p. maps. bibliog. (Die grossen Schweizer).

Langendorf has divided the story of the Genevan Dufour (1787-1875) into three parts. Part one describes Dufour's military career. He played an important role in the creation of a Swiss federal army, especially as director of the military school in Thun, Canton Bern, where Louis Napoleon, the future Napoleon III, was one of his pupils. In 1847 the Swiss Diet appointed him general of the federal army; he defeated the secessionist cantons in the *Sonderbundskrieg* (civil war) quickly and with little bloodshed. During the Neuchâtel crisis of 1856 with Prussia he again assumed command of the Swiss army. The second part of this picture biography deals with Dufour's civil career as an engineer who built bridges and fortifications in and around Geneva and created the Rhône Quai. He also excelled as a cartographer and directed the design of the first national map, the 'Dufour map'. For this achievement the highest peak in Switzerland was named Pic Dufour or Dufourspitze in 1865. Dufour also had a distinguished career as a politician. Langendorf's book is a fine tribute to a truly great Swiss.

222 **The Swiss national general strike of November 1918.**
Heinz K. Meier. In: *Neutral Europe between war and revolution, 1917-23*. Edited by Hans A. Schmitt. Charlottesville, Virginia: University Press of Virginia, 1988, p. 66-86.

This account of a critical moment in the history of Switzerland in the 20th century is based on printed documents and a vast array of secondary literature. No other event in recent history disturbed the Swiss political landscape as much as the abortive attempt, in November 1918, by a segment of the labour movement to force the federal government to meet its demands by means of a general strike. Fear of Bolshevism led the Federal Council to respond to the call for a general strike by mobilizing the army in and around Zurich, which was perceived to be the hotbed of revolutionary fervour. Meier concludes that the Federal Council over-reacted and that at no time was there a danger of revolution in Switzerland. See also *Der Landesstreik 1918* (The general strike 1918) by Willi Gautschi (Zurich; Köln: Benziger, 1968; 3rd ed., Chronos, 1988) with an afterword by Hans Ulrich Jost. This is a comprehensive account by an authority on the general strike that ended with the trial of its leaders in 1919.

223 **The achievement of Swiss federal unity.**

W. Oechsli. In: *The Cambridge modern history*. Vol. 11: *The growth of nationalism*. Cambridge, England: Cambridge University Press, 1909 (reprinted 1969), p. 234-61.

Oechsli, then professor of history at the University of Zurich, presents a brief sketch of mainly political history from the collapse of the Old Confederation in 1798, in the wake of the French invasion of the country, to the adoption of the revision of the federal constitution in 1874. The major domestic and foreign policy issues of these 76 years are touched on, and economic and cultural achievements of the period are listed. Oechsli reflects the pride of the late 19th-century Liberals over the successful creation of a moderately strong federal government and the economic progress and prosperity visible in many parts of the country.

224 **The Russian Revolution in Switzerland 1914-1917.**

Erich Alfred Senn. Madison, Wisconsin [etc.]: University of Wisconsin Press, 1971. 250p. bibliog.

This scholarly book provides a history of the numerous groups of Russian *émigrés* in Switzerland during World War I. Representing almost all major nationalities of Russia, they were alike in their opposition to the Tsarist régime but otherwise had little in common. Senn plumbs the intrigues of these groups and, inevitably, homes in on Lenin, the figure of overriding world-historical importance among the motley crowd. The story of the Zimmerwald conference (5-9 September 1915) and the Kiental conference (24-30 April 1916), both near Bern, is told, as is that of the ensuing split in the socialist ranks and between Lenin and the dominant Swiss socialist leader Robert Grimm who would not buckle under the pressure from the Zimmerwald Left.

225 **Assassination in Switzerland: the murder of Vatsla Vorovsky.**

Alfred Erich Senn. Madison, Wisconsin [etc.]: University of Wisconsin Press, 1981. 219p. bibliog.

On 10 May 1923, Vatsla Vorovsky, the Soviet trade representative to Italy, was assassinated by Maurice Conradi, an exiled Russian of Swiss ancestry, in a hotel in Lausanne, Switzerland. Senn describes the circumstances leading to this incident, the sequence of events at the hotel, the reactions to the murder in various parts of the world, and the trial of Conradi and his accomplice. The prosecution failed to convince the jury, and the accused were acquitted. The affair further strained an already tense relationship between Switzerland and the Soviet Union.

226 **The League of Nations in retrospect: proceedings of the symposium.**

Organized by The United Nations Library and the Graduate Institute of International Studies, Geneva, 6-9 November 1980. Berlin; New York: de Gruyter, 1983. 427p.

Three of the essays in this collection of scholarly articles are by Swiss historians detailing their experiences with the League of Nations. They are 'La Suisse et la Société des Nations' (p. 182-95), by Roland Ruffieux; 'La Suisse et la Radio-Nations'

(p. 196-220), by Antoine Fleury; and 'William E. Rappard and the League of Nations: A Swiss contribution to international organization' (p. 221-41), by Ania Peter. Ruffieux describes (1) the events leading to Switzerland's becoming a member of the League; (2) Switzerland's role during the gravest crisis of the League, its sanctions against Italy, and the subsequent return of Switzerland to 'integral neutrality'; and (3) the liquidation of the League at the end of World War II. Fleury discusses the problems created for the Swiss government by the desire of the League to build a radiotelegraphic post on Swiss soil. Radio-Nations was inaugurated on 2 February 1932 but after the return to integral neutrality in May 1938 the Swiss government reneged on its obligations toward Radio-Nations by unilateral action, an event of great symbolical significance. Peter traces the role of internationalist W. E. Rappard in bringing the League of Nations to Geneva, and his work with and ardent support of the League.

227 **Frauen. Zur Geschichte weiblicher Arbeits- und Lebensbedingungen in der Schweiz.** (Women: on the history of female working and living conditions in Switzerland.)
Edited by Regina Wecker, Brigitte Schnegg. Basel: Schwabe, 1984. 117p. (vol. 34, no. 3, of the *Schweizerische Zeitschrift für Geschichte*).

This collection of articles by twelve female historians considers various aspects of women in Swiss history and society, with major emphasis on the 19th and early 20th centuries. The female historians address the problems of women as wage-earners; male disregard for the worth of women's work as reflected in the labelling of their jobs; the role of mandatory instruction in home economics for women as a tool for submission; and, among other topics, prostitution and abortion. Their conclusion is incontrovertible: women were discriminated against in every phase of their lives by the male-dominated society. The editors point out that the field of history presents special difficulties for female scholars because traditionally historians have regarded the male as the 'normal case' of human society. A superficially neutral approach to the role of women in history is not good enough; progress will be made only when a change in perspective leads to a rethinking of established norms.

The interwar years and World War II

228 **The Lucy ring.**
Pierre Accoce, Pierre Quet, translated from the French *La guerre a été gagnée en Suisse* (The war was won in Switzerland) by A. M. Sheridan Smith. London: W. H. Allen, 1967; New York: Berkley, 1968, with the title *A man called Lucy*. 224p. bibliog.

This sensationalist account of the espionage activities in Switzerland during World War II, written by two French journalists, focuses on Rudolf Roessler, the creator of the Lucy spy network. The authors unequivocally label Roessler, a German emigrant living in Luzern, 'the greatest spy of World War II'. According to Accoce and Quet, Roessler gathered information of inestimable value concerning German plans and military moves in Russia and passed them on to the Soviets. He is said to have had access to the Viking line of the Swiss counter-intelligence as well as the use of his own strategically placed German sources, known as Werther and Olga. Some of the authors' claims have been exposed by historians either as speculation or fabrication, and the assertion that Roessler's intelligence activities had a decisive influence on the outcome of the war seems to be exaggerated, to say the least.

229 **Facing the holocaust in Budapest: the International Committee of the Red Cross and the Jews in Hungary, 1943-1945.**
Arieh Ben-Tov. Geneva: Henry Dunant Institute; Dordrecht, The Netherlands [etc.]: Nijhoff, 1988. 492p. bibliog.

In the course of 1944 the fate of the Jews in Hungary steadily worsened, and by early summer of that year tens of thousands of them were deported to Auschwitz. The Israeli historian Ben-Tov, himself a survivor of Auschwitz, describes in a dispassionate yet moving manner the events of those months; his special interest is the role that the International Committee of the Red Cross (ICRC) played in them. On the basis of his study of the materials in the ICRC archives in Geneva and the Swiss federal archive in Bern, Ben-Tov concludes that the highest personalities in the ICRC, especially its president, Max Huber, were more concerned about protecting Swiss neutrality than about the impending fate of the Jews in Hungary of which they had been informed in ample time by Jewish sources. As a consequence, the ICRC did much less than it could have done, and much of that very late. The ICRC representatives in Hungary, however, who had been there since autumn 1943, took measures on their own initiative that saved the lives of thousands of Jews. Ben-Tov praises especially Friedrich Born (1903-63), a Swiss citizen who had lived in Budapest and became the ICRC delegate at the beginning of 1944, for his courageous activities of going beyond his sphere of competence in his fight to save lives. It is curious that Ben-Tov barely mentions the Swiss consul in Budapest, Carl Lutz, who, also on his own initiative, succeeded in helping thousands of Hungarian Jews.

230 **Geschichte der schweizerischen Neutralität. Vier Jahrhunderte eidgenössischer Aussenpolitik.** (History of Swiss neutrality: four centuries of Swiss foreign policy.)
Edgar Bonjour. Basel; Stuttgart, FRG: Helbing & Lichtenhahn, 1965-76. 9 vols.

The first two volumes of Bonjour's monumental work treat the four hundred years of Swiss foreign policy from the end of the involvement of the Swiss cantons in foreign wars in the early 16th century to the aftermath of World War I. Volumes 3 to 6 cover the years of the Nazi era from 1930 to 1945, while the last three volumes are made up of the texts of documents from that period. What in its earliest edition of 1946 had been a one-volume work on Swiss neutrality, had grown thirty years later into a nine-volume opus of almost 4,000 pages. This explosion in size was due to the fact that Bonjour had received access to the archives of the federal government and permission to use its records to write his story. As a consequence his work not only grew in length but also in scope, and what had at first been strictly a history of Swiss foreign policy under the guiding principle of neutrality became a detailed history of Switzerland during World War II. The internal and external difficulties the country faced, the conflict between leading personalities in the army and the Federal Council, and the harsh policy toward the refugees – many of whom were denied asylum in Switzerland – are among the many topics that Bonjour discusses in an engaging yet scholarly manner. His work has provoked spirited reviews and discussions and engendered numerous monographs and articles. A one-volume abridgement of Bonjour's history of Swiss neutrality was published by Helbing & Lichtenhahn in 1978.

231 **Geheimer Draht nach Berlin. Die Nachrichtenlinie Masson-Schellenberg und der schweizerische Nachrichtendienst im Zweiten Weltkrieg.** (Secret wire to Berlin: the intelligence contact Masson-Schellenberg and the Swiss intelligence service during World War II.)
Pierre-Th. Braunschweig. Zurich: Neue Zürcher Zeitung, 1989. 528p. bibliog.

This is a scholarly presentation of the story of the Swiss intelligence service in World War II by the young historian Braunschweig (born 1955). His book opens with a 46-page introduction in which he reviews the existing literature on he subject and discusses his sources, some of which are used by him for the first time. Then follow 323 pages of text and 200 pages of notes and a detailed bibliography. Thanks to his access to the private archives of many of the chief figures of the Swiss intelligence community, Braunschweig is able to throw new light on the basically well-known themes of the Swiss intelligence activities during the war. The 'hot connection' between Oberstbrigadier Roger Masson, chief of the Swiss service of intelligence and security, and SS Brigadeführer Walter Schellenberg, German chief of espionage, so prominently mentioned in the title of the book, is only one of the themes, even though an important and most delicate one. Others are the tug of war going on between General Henri Guisan and Swiss army intelligence and the federal government – as represented by the Federal Political Department under Federal Councillor Marcel Pilet-Golaz – and the conflicts within and between the various branches of the Swiss intelligence services. The first printing of the book was sold out by the time its review appeared in the *Neue Zürcher Zeitung*.

232 **The secret surrender.**
Allen Dulles. New York [etc.]: Harper & Row, 1966. 268p. bibliog.

Allen Dulles served in the Office of Strategic Services (OSS), the forerunner of the American Central Intelligence Agency (CIA), during World War II. From his base in Bern, Switzerland, he conducted the negotiations, labelled 'Operation Sunrise', that led to the surrender of the German and fascist Italian forces in Northern Italy in late April 1945. His narrative is a first-hand account of the operation of an intelligence network on Swiss soil. Not only did the Swiss suffer the Americans to engage in espionage activities in their country, but certain highly placed Swiss individuals, such as Colonel Max Waibel, aided Dulles's effort to convince the German generals in Italy to give up further resistance. See also *1945 Kapitulation in Norditalien. Originalbericht des Vermittlers* (1945 capitulation in Northern Italy: original report of the mediator) by Max Waibel (Basel; Frankfurt, FRG: Helbing & Lichtenhahn, 1981). At the end of this book, the military historian Hans Rudolf Kurz discusses in a substantial commentary the ramifications of Waibel's actions in terms of Swiss neutrality and their significance for the countries involved.

233 **From Sarajevo to Hiroshima: history of the International Committee of the Red Cross.**
André Durand, translated from the French by the Henry Dunant Institute. Geneva: Henry Dunant Institute, 1984. 675p.

This is the second volume (for the first volume see P. Boissier, *From Solferino to Tsushima*) of the history of the International Committee of the Red Cross (ICRC), that Geneva-based and Swiss-run organization which since its founding in the 1860s had given impetus and direction to the international Red Cross movement and distinguished itself time and again by the objective nature of and the absence of any political considerations from its activities. The book covers the period from the wars in Eastern Europe preceding World War I to the end of World War II, a period full of civil strife, regional conflicts, revolutions, and international wars. While the ICRC lacked the means to prevent armed conflict, it tried to protect persons no longer able to fight, and Durand describes how the ICRC extended its protection to new categories of victims, and undertook the greatest relief operations in its history. He also tells the story of the evolution of the Red Cross movement into its present structure with the creation of the League of Red Cross Societies, made up of local and regional Red Cross organizations, and the formation of the International Red Cross which was to be the highest decision-making authority of the Red Cross movement, comprising the National Red Cross societies, the ICRC, and the League of Red Cross Societies, with the International Conference as its supreme deliberative body. Like the first volume, this one is well written but suffers from the fact that there is no scholarly apparatus to speak of; it has few footnotes, no bibliography, and only an index of personal names.

234 **The neutrals.**

Denis J. Fodor. Alexandria, Virginia: Time-Life Books, 1982. 208p. maps. bibliog. (Time-Life Books: World War II).

This book focuses in five chapters and seven picture-essays on Switzerland, Sweden, Spain, Portugal, Turkey, and Ireland, and their special situtation as neutrals during World War II. Thirty-five pages of text and black-and-white photographs are dedicated to Switzerland, the country that stayed out of the war, even though it was surrounded by the Axis powers. Fodor mentions Switzerland's insurmountable mountains, a well-trained citizens' army, and strong defences in the alpine redoubt as deterrents to attackers. There were incidents of spying, smuggling, and illegal crossings of the borders; of intrusion of Swiss airspace by the Allies and the Germans; and of bombing raids caused by pilot error; and Switzerland had to deal with food shortages and a stream of refugees who tried to gain entry into the country. Its refusal to accept many of these refugees later caused the country embarrassment. The well-chosen photographs capture the atmosphere of that difficult time. See also *Neutrals and non-belligerent allies: Switzerland* by Constance Howard (In: *Survey of international affairs 1939-1946: the war and the neutrals*), edited by Arnold Toynbee and Veronica M. Toynbee (London [etc.]: Oxford University Press, 1956, p. 199-230). Parts of Howard's article have been reprinted in *The theory and practice of neutrality in the twentieth century*, edited by Roderick Ogley (New York: Barnes & Noble, 1970, p. 143-53).

235 **The Swiss corridor: espionage networks in Switzerland during World War II.**

Józef Garlinski. London [etc.]: Dent, 1981. 222p. bibliog.

Garlinski, a Polish-born historian of World War II, gives an account of the various Axis and Allied intelligence networks operating in Switzerland during World War II. Based primarily on secondary sources and interviews with people who worked in Switzerland during the war, the book is a good introduction to the subject of the ubiquity of foreign intelligence agencies in neutral Switzerland and the role Swiss intelligence played. Its weakness consists of Garlinski's ready acceptance of dubious claims by memoir writers. One of his key points, namely that Rudolf Roessler's 'Lucy' ring was used to feed 'Ultra' information to the Russians, is not substantiated and is contradicted by more reliable sources. See also *Nachrichtenzentrum Schweiz: Die Schweiz im Nachrichtendienst des zweiten Weltkriegs* (Intelligence centre Switzerland: Switzerland in the intelligence operations of World War II) by Hans-Rudolf Fuhrer (Frauenfeld: Huber, 1972). An army officer, he reveals no secrets but provides an elaborate and useful overview of the many groups that were involved in intelligence work in Switzerland during World War II.

236 **Die Nationale Front: Eine Schweizer faschistische Bewegung 1930-1940.** (The National Front: a Swiss fascist movement 1930-1940.)
Beat Glaus. Zurich [etc.]: Benziger, 1969. 504p. bibliog.

Like other fascist-type movements, called 'fronts' in Switzerland, that burst on to the country's political scene in the early 1930s, the National Front began as a political youth movement. Accepted societal values had become suspect; the economic and political system of Europe was disintegrating; the Swiss federal state was looking old and sick. Fascism was the new force in Europe; it promised to lead the way to renewal and rejuvenation of the values of the heroic past. Glaus, sociologist and historian, describes the development of the National Front on the basis of its publications and other source materials. It had considerable initial success thanks to its appeal among bourgeois and petty-bourgeois circles. The vast majority of the Swiss, however, rejected the National Front's attachment to the ideology of Hitler's Germany, and the Front's disastrous defeat in the Zurich communal elections of 1939 removed the movement as a political force from the Swiss scene. Illustrations, many of them cartoons from the contemporary press, recreate the atmosphere of those years. Two other works covering the same topic and period, and published in the 1960s are *Anpassung oder Widerstand. Die Schweiz zur Zeit des deutschen Nazionalsozialismus* (Accommodation or resistance: Switzerland during the time of the German National Socialism) by Alice Meyer (Frauenfeld, Switzerland: Huber, 1965), and *Faschismus in der Schweiz. Die Geschichte der Frontenbewegung in der deutschen Schweiz 1930-1945* (Fascism in Switzerland: the history of the frontist movements in German Switzerland 1930-1945) by Walter Wolf (Zurich: Flamberg, 1969).

237 **Nur das Gewissen. Carl Lutz und seine Budapester Aktion: Geschichte und Porträt.** (Only the conscience. Carl Lutz and his Budapest action: history and portrait.)
Alexander Grossman. Wald, Switzerland: Im Waldgut, 1986. 284p. bibliog.

Carl Lutz (1895-1975) served for forty-four years in the Swiss diplomatic corps. From 1942 to 1944 he was Swiss consul general in Budapest in charge of carrying out the Swiss mandate of representing the interests of most western Allied countries vis-à-vis the Hungarian government, and there he soon became aware of the German programme to destroy the Jews. When his early efforts to help were stymied by uncaring and, in some cases, hostile bureaucrats in Bern, Washington, and London, he took matters into his own hands. Following his conscience, he designed in July 1944 the ingenious scheme of creating a collective Swiss passport and issuing individual protective passports based on it to tens of thousands of Hungarian Jews. Lutz is credited with having saved the lives of more than one hundred thousand people. In Bern, the government reprimanded him for having overstepped his authority. Late in life he was rehabilitated; however, his courageous humanitarian acts found public recognition only after his death. Grossman's book, with many photographs and appendices, tells the story of Lutz's adventurous years in Budapest, but it also has much to say about official Switzerland's regrettable attitude and policies toward the persecuted European Jews. This book should be read together with Arieh Ben-Tov's *Facing the holocaust in Budapest* (q.v.).

238 **The lifeboat is full: Switzerland and the refugees, 1933-1945.**
Alfred A. Häsler, translated from the German by Charles Lam Markmann. New York: Funk & Wagnalls, 1969. 366p.

This is a popularly written work on what is considered to be a dark chapter in recent Swiss history, namely Switzerland's handling of refugees during the Nazi years. The federal government, supported by large segments of the population, saw in the steadily growing number of foreign civilians and military who sought refuge and asylum in Switzerland a threat to the material survival of the country, and the federal councillor in charge of the police and justice department, insensitively coining the phrase 'the boat is full', issued harsh directives, ordering border officials to prevent refugees from entering the country and to send back those who had entered illegally. A number of prominent Swiss opposed this policy and tried to alleviate its impact through private initiatives. The book has several appendices, among them a chronology of events, a small portfolio of photographs, and some statistical information. Statistics show that almost 300,000 refugees found shelter in Switzerland at one time or another during World War II, some 104,000 of them being military internees. Of the 65,000 civilian refugees and *émigrés*, some 28,500 were Jews. Police reports indicate that a total of 9,751 persons were sent back across the border during the war years. See also *Im Schweizer Rettungsboot: Dokumentation* (In the Swiss lifeboat: documentation) by Max Brusto (Munich: Starczewski, 1967). The sad story of Brusto's disappointing experiences in the Swiss lifeboat is amplified with a number of documents that illustrate how the Swiss bureaucrats treated the hapless human beings under their control.

239 **The ruling few or the human background to diplomacy.**
David Kelly. London: Hollis & Carter, 1952. 449p.

Chapter thirteen of the memoirs of Sir David Kelly deal with his mission as British minister to Switzerland during the first two years of World War II. Having been given the choice between Stockholm and Bern, he selected the latter – partly because he had never been in Switzerland (!) – but once there, Kelly displayed a sympathetic understanding for the special situation of little Switzerland in the midst of Nazi-dominated Europe. After a secret meeting with the commander of the Swiss army, General Henri Guisan, he assured his government that Switzerland would resist Nazi aggression at all costs, and on several occasions he pleaded with London to go easy on Switzerland with their economic warfare plans. On the other side, Kelly repeatedly had to answer complaints by Federal Councillor Marcel Pilet-Golaz, head of the department of foreign affairs, about the violation of Swiss air space by RAF pilots who flew across the country on bombing raids to targets in Northern Italy. After two Swiss cities had been bombed in 1941, Kelly was relieved when his government, 'in view of the friendly relations between the two countries', accepted responsibility and promised to pay compensation for the damage done. Another member of the British Foreign Service, John Lomax, gives his account of the period in *The diplomatic smuggler* (London: Barker, 1965).

240 **Spying for peace: General Guisan and Swiss neutrality.**
Jon Kimche. New York: Roy, 1961. 169p.

Kimche was one of the first to write about Switzerland's difficult passage through the events of World War II. His book was serialized in the Swiss press and published in German under the title *General Guisans Zweifrontenkrieg* (General Guisan's war on two fronts), a title which captures the slant of Kimche's work. Henri Guisan, elected general of the Swiss army at the outbreak of the war by the Federal Parliament, is for

Kimche the personification of the Swiss will of resistance against Nazi Germany. The second front is embodied by the Federal Council whom Kimche criticizes for having made Guisan's task difficult due to its alleged willingness to appease Hitler. Guisan pursued an active policy of neutrality which was inspired by his conviction that Swiss independence could not be secure until Hitler's Germany had been defeated – active neutrality meant gathering intelligence about German plans as well as supporting Max Waibel, an officer in the Swiss army, who for humanitarian reasons had risked his career by negotiating the surrender of the German army in northern Italy. Scholarly publications since Kimche's provocative book have strongly modified its major points: the Federal Council was not nearly as defeatist as Kimche painted it, nor was General Guisan as unwavering in resisting German overtures for negotiations as he would have it.

241 **Die Schweiz und der Zweite Weltkrieg: Bilanz und bibliographischer Überblick nach dreissig Jahren.** (Switzerland and World War II: assessment and bibliographical overview after thirty years.)
Georg Kreis. In: *La seconda guerra mondiale nella prospettiva storica a trent'anni dall'epilogo* (World War II in historical perspective thirty years after its end). Como, Italy: Cairoli, 1977.

In this detailed and thorough bibliographical essay Kreis cites more than one hundred works on Switzerland and World War II that have appeared between 1947 and 1976. After a survey of the conditions that influence Swiss history and memoir writing and the characteristics of this literature, Kreis presents his materials topically. He wants to show not so much how Switzerland reacted to world events as what role it played in them: Switzerland as mediator, as a centre for intelligence, as asylum for refugees, as a country of transit of goods and people, as a trading partner, as a territory that remained inviolate, and as an ideological partisan are the thematic topics under which he groups his entries. The footnotes are frequently annotated and contain further valuable leads into the substantial historical literature produced since the war. Kreis wrote a similar article, entitled 'Die schweizerische Neutralität während des Zweiten Weltkrieges in der historischen Forschung' (Swiss neutrality during World War II in historical scholarship), for *Les états neutres européens et la Seconde Guerre mondiale* (q.v.), p. 29-53. The bibliography of this chapter consists of 133 books and articles, listed in chronological order of publication from 1945 to 1985.

242 **Spionage und Landesverrat in der Schweiz.** (Espionage and treason in Switzerland.)
Karl Lüönd. Zurich: Ringier, 1977. 2 vols.

Two large-sized, richly illustrated volumes, totalling 272 pages, give a lively account of the intricate, sometimes mysterious, and sometimes tragic events taking place beneath the surface of Swiss tranquillity during World War II. Lüönd, a journalist by profession, has read the voluminous literature on the subject of espionage and has pursued many leads through digging in the archives and interviewing surviving participants. The story of the various intelligence-gathering networks that used Switzerland in violation of its neutrality is enriched by photographs of the individuals who ran them and the localities from which they operated. How Swiss counter-intelligence went about stopping these activities makes up another major segment of the work. Stark was the fate of those few Swiss who were caught passing military secrets to Nazi Germany; seventeen of them were executed. Lüönd carries his story into the postwar period with its incidents of espionage activities on behalf of the Soviet Union. See also *Landesverräter. 17 Lebensläufe und Todesurteile, 1942-1944* (Traitors:

seventeen lives and death sentences, 1942-1944) by Peter Noll (Frauenfeld, Switzerland; Stuttgart, FRG: Huber, 1980).

243 **Intelligence operations in Switzerland during the Second World War.**
Heinz K. Meier. *Swiss-American Historical Society Newsletter*, vol. 20, no. 1 (February 1984), p. 21-42.

An overview of the voluminous literature on this topic, dealing with Swiss intelligence and counter-intelligence and foreign-run operations in Switzerland, as well as with foreign, mainly German, espionage efforts against Switzerland. The Germans were well informed about Swiss military defences, and the Swiss were forced to reintroduce the death penalty for traitors. The Swiss, on the other hand, had access to highly placed sources within the Third Reich, whose identities are still not known. Some of the information they gathered may have found its way to the Lucy network of Rudolf Roessler who worked for the Soviet Union; opinion as to the significance of Roessler's efforts continues to be divided. Hans-Rudolf Fuhrer, in a similar article, entitled 'Die Schweiz im Nachrichtendienst' (Switzerland in intelligence) in *Schwedische und schweizerische Neutralität im Zweiten Weltkrieg* (Swedish and Swiss neutrality in World War II) (q.v.), p. 405-26, concludes that Swiss intelligence repeatedly was taken in by false reports about impending attacks on Switzerland and that it was able to carry out its task thanks only to a series of fortunate circumstances. Fuhrer has also written two books on the subject, *Nachrichtenzentrum Schweiz. Die Schweiz im Nachrichtendienst des Zweiten Weltkriegs* (Intelligence centre Switzerland: Switzerland in intelligence during World War II. Frauenfeld, Switzerland: Huber, 1972); and *Spionage gegen die Schweiz im Zweiten Weltkrieg* (Espionage against Switzerland in World War II. Frauenfeld, Switzerland: Huber, 1982).

244 **Rescue to Switzerland: the Musy and Saly Mayer affairs.**
Edited by John Mendelsohn, introduction by Sybil Milton. New York; London: Garland, 1982. 219p. (The Holocaust. Selected Documents in Eighteen Volumes, edited by John Mendelsohn and Donald S. Detwiler, vol. 16).

With the imminent demise of the German military in 1944 the policy of 'rescue through victory' changed to a policy of 'rescue through negotiation'. Thus the lives of many Jews, especially from Hungary, were spared from extinction by the Nazis. Two Swiss distinguished themselves in this rescue effort. One was Saly Mayer (1882-1950), a Swiss Jew, formerly in the textile business and member of the St Gallen municipal council who negotiated the release of about three thousand Hungarian Jews to Switzerland from different concentration camps. Mayer was dealing with SS officer Kurt Becher who had a direct line to Himmler. The Germans demanded money and goods in exchange for the release of Jews. Mayer's delaying tactics were designed to keep the dialogue going. The second was Jean-Marie Musy (1876-1952), a conservative Swiss Catholic and former Federal Councillor, who was known for his sympathy for the Nazis. Ironically, it was his negotiations with SS Brigadier-General Walter Schellenberg and the resulting release of 1,200 Jews from Theresienstadt to Switzerland that provided Musy with an alibi after the war. The sixty-six documents in this volume consist of reports, cables and letters that were exchanged between American officials in Allied countries and Mayer and others involved in the different rescue missions. Except for the testimonies at the Nuremberg Trials of Musy (1945) and Becher (1948), the material comes from the 'Dossier on the Saly Mayer Negotiations', in the Franklin D. Roosevelt Library in Hyde Park, New York.

245 **Exil in der Schweiz.** (Exile in Switzerland.)
Werner Mittenzwei. In: *Kunst und Literatur im antifaschistischen Exil 1933-1945*. Leipzig, GDR: Reclam, 1981. 497p. vol. 2. bibliog.

Mittenzwei states that Switzerland's stringent policies toward emigrants before and during World War II has destroyed the illusion of the country as a 'classical land of exile' and those emigrants who did find a safe haven suffered from limited freedom and isolation. The author researched the fate of many a prominent intellectual, artist, politician and Jew, and also studied organizations, publications, and artistic creations that were inspired by emigrants passing through Switzerland or having found asylum there. He examined the interaction between emigrants and private Swiss citizens such as the publishers Carl Seelig or Emil Oprecht. The Büchergilde Gutenberg, an important publishing house in Germany that was destroyed, was re-established in Switzerland and provided an important forum for the emigrants. An entire chapter is taken up tracing Hermann Hesse's and Thomas Mann's relationship with the host country. The cabaret is shown as the ideal platform for political dissent and social criticism. With the outbreak of World War II and the general mobilization of the Swiss army came new laws designed to protect neutrality. These added to the frustration of the emigrants as did the prohibition of the communist party, or the harsh life in camps. A listing of famous emigrants includes those who created the new Zurcher Schauspielhaus that would become Europe's most important theatre of the period. Forty-nine illustrations of people, places, letters, programmes, etc. enhance the book. See also *Die Flüchtlingspolitik der Schweiz seit 1933 bis zur Gegenwart* (1957) (The refugee policy of Switzerland from 1933 to the present [1957]) by Carl Ludwig (Bern: Lang, 1966).

246 **Der Aktivdienst. Die Zeit nationaler Bewährung 1939-45.** (Active military service: the time of national confirmation 1939-45.)
Andri Peer. Zofingen, Switzerland: Ringier, 1976. 2nd ed. 97p. maps.

An oversized picture book with photographs depicting scenes of life in the military as well as of the civilian home front, from the general mobilization of the army in September 1939 to the repatriation of refugees after the German surrender in May 1945. The numerous pictures are captioned with patriotic texts that reflect the feeling of awe and pride still felt by the generation that participated in the maintenance of Swiss independence during World War II. Reminiscences of individuals who served in the army are distributed throughout the book, and they convey a similar mood. See also *Die Schweiz im Zweiten Weltkrieg. Das grosse Erinnerungswerk an die Aktivdienstzeit 1939-45* (Switzerland in World War II: the great work in remembrance of the time of active service 1939-45) by Hans Rudolf Kurz (Thun, Switzerland: Verlags AG, 1967. 4th ed.).

247 **Operation Lucy: most secret spy ring of the second world war.**
Anthony Read, David Fisher. London: Hodder & Stoughton, 1980; New York: Coward, McCann & Geoghegan, 1981. 258p. bibliog.

This book tells the story of the lengths to which British intelligence supposedly went to feed Stalin vital information. Stalin adamantly refused to believe information given to him through direct diplomatic channels, and Churchill did not want to reveal the secret of Ultra, the name given to the deciphering operation of the German Enigma source. The solution to the problem consisted in the elaborate scheme of using British agents in Switzerland, foremost among them Alexander Foote, to feed Ultra information into the elaborate spy network in existence there, at one of the centres of which was Rudolf Roessler, who used the code name Lucy. The smokescreen worked very well, as Stalin unsuspectingly accepted the steady flow of information that came to him from London via Luzern and Geneva, until the Swiss authorities tracked down the transmitters one by one and arrested the operators. The authors acknowledge the help given them by an impressive array of individuals and institutions in Switzerland and England, but they provide no documentation for their story. The bibliography lists only published works.

248 **La Suisse pendant la guerre.** (Switzerland during the war.)
Edited by Louis-Edouard Roulet. Paris: Presses universitaires de France, 1981. 138p. bibliog. (*Revue d'Histoire de la Deuxième Guerre mondiale*, vol. 31, no. 121, January 1981).

The ten contributions to the 121st issue of the *Revue d'Histoire de la Deuxième Guerre mondiale* are by Swiss historians, most of whom belong to the Swiss historical commission of World War II. Their articles are grouped under four headings: (1) military problems, by Hans Rudolf Kurz; (2) economy and neutrality, by Klaus Urner, Heinz K. Meier, and Daniel Bourgeois; (3) domestic politics, by Georg Kreis, Erwin Bucher, and Roland Ruffieux; and (4) refuge and representation of foreign interests, by L. Mysyrowicz and J.-C. Favez, Martin Schärer, and Jacques Meurant. Most of the articles have copious footnotes and reflect the current historical scholarship on the subject. See also *Die Schweiz im Krieg 1933-1945. Ein Bericht* (Switzerland in the war 1933-1945: a report) by Werner Rings (Zurich: Ex Libris, 1974).

249 **La Suisse de l'entre-deux-guerres.** (Interwar Switzerland.)
Roland Ruffieux. Lausanne, Switzerland: Payot, 1974. 448p. maps. bibliog.

This scholarly history covers the years 1914 to 1940. Ruffieux's emphasis is on the political and economic history of Switzerland during that quarter-century, with due consideration of aspects of social history and foreign policy, and his text, interspersed with many illustrations and twenty-nine charts and maps, provides a readable and reliable synthesis of the voluminous historical literature produced on the subject since World War II. A chronological tabulation of events and an excellent bibliography add to the value of the work. A book which grew out of a Swiss television series and which provides additional information on the topic is '*Wach auf, Schweizervolk!' Die Schweiz zwischen Frontismus, Verrat und Selbstbehauptung, 1914-1940* ('Wake up, Swiss people!' Switzerland between frontism, treason, and self-affirmation, 1914-40) by Heinz Bütler (Gümligen, Switzerland: Zytglogge, 1980).

250 **The eye of the hurricane: Switzerland in World War II.**
Urs Schwarz. Boulder, Colorado: Westview, 1980. 169p. bibliog.

An attempt to tell the story of Switzerland's role in World War II to an English-speaking audience. Written by a prominent journalist who served in the Swiss army during the war, the book covers the major aspects of Swiss neutrality and the many problems that confronted the country during those difficult years. Even though the volume lacks solid documentary foundation, it is a useful introduction to the subject. A successful attempt to follow the course of World War II in Switzerland from the perspective of Swiss public opinions and moods is made in *La Suisse des années sombres. Courants d'opinion pendant la Deuxième Guerre mondiale 1939-1945* (Switzerland during the dark years: currents of opinion during World War II 1939-1945) by André Lasserre (Lausanne: Payot, 1989).

251 **Neutralität und Wirtschaftskrieg: Zur schweizerischen Aussenhandelspolitik 1939-1945.** (Neutrality and economic warfare: on the Swiss foreign commerce policy 1939-45.)
Klaus Urner. In: *Schwedische und schweizerische Neutralität im Zweiten Weltkrieg* (Swedish and Swiss neutrality in World War II), edited by Rudolf L. Bindschedler (et al.). Basel, Switzerland: Helbing & Lichtenhahn, 1985, p. 250-92.

A convenient overview of one of the most important aspects of Swiss history during World War II. Switzerland, dependent on foreign trade for the importation of raw materials for its industries and food for its population and the exportation of its manufactured products, had to fight a tough, six-year-long struggle on two fronts, with Germany and the Western Allies. As the war progressed it became increasingly difficult for the Swiss to find understanding for their continuing trade with Germany from Great Britain and the United States. Urner concludes that, whether or not it is entirely correct to claim that Switzerland did not violate any of its obligations as a neutral, the fact that it was able to maintain its economic activities and thus its economic survival in spite of blockade and counter-blockade must be considered an immense achievement. Eighty-seven annotated footnotes provide access to the voluminous literature on this topic.

252 **Who was Werther?**
Nigel West. In: *A thread of deceit; espionage myths of World War II.* New York: Random House, 1985, p. 51-67.

Between September 1942 and June 1944 German *émigré* Rudolf Roessler provided extraordinarily reliable and sensitive German intelligence information, under the code name Lucy, to the Soviet Union from his residence in Luzern. The identity of the source of Roessler's informant inside Germany, Werther, is still not known. Various theories, some ingenious, others merely sensational, do not stand up to scrutiny. Werther seems to have been an invented persona to act as a cover for all of Lucy's sources, which included, probably, the Swiss intelligence network Viking.

Post-1945

253 **Schweizer Geschichte seit 1945.** (Swiss history since 1945.)
Christoph Dejung. Frauenfeld, Switzerland: Huber, 1984. 228p.

This book grew out of an adult education (Volkshochschule) course given by Dejung. Chronological overviews at the beginning of the book and the individual chapters, as well as some tables and graphs, and brief samples of source texts serve to relieve somewhat the need for factual information in this subjectively treated account. There is no bibliography. Dejung covers the creation of the social state after World War II with the enactment of social security and survivors insurance (AHV); the return to direct democracy; the economic boom; the wave of anti-communism; the nonconformist tendencies in literature; the conflicts over the number of 'guest workers'; the recession of the 1970s; the growing ecological awareness; and the youth disturbances of the 1970s. In addition to the AHV, Dejung emphasizes among the achievements of the federal state the introduction of women's suffrage, and the creation of Canton Jura.

Another volume of lectures given at the Volkshochschule is entitled *Die Schweiz seit 1945. Beiträge zur Zeitgeschichte* (Switzerland since 1945: contributions to contemporary history) by Erich Gruner (Bern: Francke, 1971. Helvetia Politica, series B. vol. VI). In his introduction Gruner points out that the short time-span since the end of World War II has not yet allowed the formulation of definitive historical insights.

254 **Die unheimlichen Patrioten. Politische Reaktion in der Schweiz. Ein aktuelles Handbuch.** (The sinister patriots: political reaction in Switzerland, a current handbook.)
Jürg Frischknecht, Peter Haffner, Ueli Haldimann, Peter Niggli. Zurich: Limmat, 1987. 6th ed. 794p.

This is a detailed documentary account of the many right-wing movements that emerged in Switzerland after World War II. Some had their origins in the anti-Fascist organizations of the prewar and wartime era, while others stemmed from the opposite, pro-Nazi, tendencies that also were present in Switzerland during those years. What they all have in common is a fervent opposition to left-of-centre ideas and groups, thereby fermenting the polarization of politics and society. Riding the anti-Communist wave of the Cold War era, these organizations to varying degrees took it upon themselves to monitor the speech of those who differed with them, creating political pressure groups, and using scare tactics against opponents. Hundreds of persons are featured, with photographs and career histories, in this comprehensive compilation of the often unsavoury aspects of contemporary politics in Switzerland. The number of so-called patriotic organizations, including neo-Nazis as well as religious groups such as the Opus Dei, is staggering. The book, which provides unusual insights into Swiss history of recent decades, is well written and reads like a good detective story.

255 **Dreissig Jahre Schweizerische Korea-Mission 1953-1983.** (Thirty years of the Swiss Korea mission 1953-83.)
Erhard Hürsch, Adolf Kaufmann, Peter Niederberger, Fritz Real, Klaus Urner. Zurich: Archiv für Zeitgeschichte, 1983. 151p. map. bibliog.

In July 1953 the Swiss Federal Council reluctantly agreed to take up the mandate as one of the four powers of the Neutral Nations Supervisory Commission (NNSC) for the armistice in Korea. The Swiss, resolved to carry out this mission in the best tradition of their good services as a neutral, sent a delegation of seventy-six officers and soldiers to Korea to help supervise the implementation of the armistice, but it soon became apparent that both sides were violating the agreement and would not allow the NNSC to fulfil its functions, and within three years the neutral delegations were confined to the barracks at Panmunjon. The Swiss repeatedly considered giving up their mandate but decided to stay on, even if only with a much reduced force of six men. On 15 February 1983, the NNSC had its 1694th plenary meeting: the business consisted of a few routine matters, such as the approval of the minutes of the previous meeting, and was adjourned for another week after an eight-minute-long session. This booklet contains descriptions of the activities of the Swiss delegation to the NNSC by persons who had served in Korea and an evaluation of the significance of their work. Marius Schwarb's dissertation *Die Mission der Schweiz in Korea* (The mission of Switzerland in Korea. Bern: Lang, 1986. 336p. bibliog.) covers the same ground in a detailed, scholarly manner.

256 **Jura separatism in Switzerland.**
John R. G. Jenkins. Oxford, England: Clarendon Press, 1986. 221p. maps. bibliog.

This book deals with that part of the Jura region which formerly belonged to the prince-bishops of Basel and was given to Canton Bern at the Congress of Vienna in 1815. The relationship of this French-speaking region with the 'old canton' was, on the whole, not an unhappy one, even though there were periods of unrest in the 19th century and during the World War I era. After World War II, however, separatism became an effective political force. Through the study of the physical, human, and economic geography, and the geography of language and religion of the Jura, Jenkins examines why the separatist movement became so virulent during the 1950s and 1960s – ultimately forcing Canton Bern and the Swiss Confederation to allow the secession of part of the region and the formation of a new Canton Jura in 1979 – and why the people in the southern half of the region preferred to stay with Bern rather than to join the new canton. There are thirty-eight figures, many of them maps, and nineteen tables with statistical data.

257 **Switzerland and the United Nations. Report of the Federal Council to the Federal Assembly concerning Switzerland's relations with the United Nations.**
Swiss Federal Council. Bern, 16 June 1969. 174p.

This report was prepared by the Federal Council in response to a motion by some National Councillors concerning Switzerland's relation with the United Nations. It consists of two parts. The first part provides (in three chapters) information on the United Nations, the Swiss status of neutrality, and the development of Swiss relations with the United Nations. On this last subject, the report describes first the discussions held in 1945 and 1946 concerning Swiss membership in the organization, the installation of the United Nations in Geneva, and the status of observer accorded to Switzerland. It then considers Switzerland's position in relation to certain United Nations decisions, and, finally, analyses Switzerland's interaction with various organs of the United Nations and with specialized agencies. The second part discusses the feasibility of a possible entry into the United Nations, primarily from the perspective of Switzerland's status of neutrality, and weighs the pros and cons of membership. The Federal Council concluded that the time was not ripe for a recommendation in favour of joining the United Nations, but pledged to study ways of strengthening existing ties and increasing financial contributions to the activities of the United Nations and its organs and agencies. This is an excellent introduction to the question of Swiss membership in the United Nations. The issue is not yet solved and periodically reappears on the Swiss political scene.

258 **Innovative Schweiz. Zwischen Risiko und Sicherheit.** (Innovative Switzerland: between risk and security.)
Edited by Walter Wittmann. Zurich: Neue Zürcher Zeitung, 1987. 297p. bibliog.

Experts discuss in separate essays recent trends in their respective fields and assess the kind of new thinking that is causing change. Most of the contributions deal with aspects of the economic life of the country, but there are also articles on the lagging reform of the political institutions, and the problems of innovation in the fields of education, telecommunications, and national defence. If there is a consensus among the learned authors, it is that desirable ideas for change exist – for example in the health delivery system or the production of energy – but that their implementation encounters difficult psychological and political barriers. In fact, the political process itself must undergo change to create an environment where innovative measures have a chance of becoming reality.

259 **'Europa 92' und die Schweiz. Blickpunkt Integration.** ('Europe 92' and Switzerland: focus on integration.)

Edited by Willy Zeller. Zurich: Neue Zürcher Zeitung, 1988. 122p.

A first part of this booklet contains seven articles dealing with the general question of how the programme of the European Community (EC) to establish an internal common market by 1992 affects Europe as a whole, and the countries of the EFTA (European Free Trade Association) in particular. The second part consists of ten articles on the partnership between Switzerland and the EC. The prospect of the abolition of all trade barriers within the EC presents a tremendous challenge to Switzerland: it calls for a strategy that builds upon the many existing ties between Switzerland and the EC, without reaching the level of membership in the EC, which politically is not feasible. The Swiss government must strive to reduce differences in legal and economic matters with the EC member states; the task of Swiss business, on the other hand, is to maintain its competitiveness. See also *Schweiz–EG. Stimmen der Schweizer Wirtschaft zur europäischen Integration* (Switzerland–EC: voices of the Swiss economy in the European integration), edited by Richard Senti (Zurich: Neue Zürcher Zeitung, 1988).

Genealogy

260 **Familiennamenbuch der Schweiz = Register of Swiss surnames.**
Edited by Arbeitsgemeinschaft Schweizer Familiennamen: Emil and Clothilde Meier, Fred D. Hänni, Stephan and Claudia Mohr. Zurich: Schulthess, 1989. 3rd, improved and corrected ed. 3 vols. 2082p.

This register contains the names of every family, in official orthography, who possessed citizenship in Switzerland in 1962. The surname is followed by the name of the canton or cantons where families with the particular name have citizenship, the place(s) of citizenship (= community of origin), and the exact year or period in which citizenship was granted. The register reveals, for example, that the Meier family had citizenship in Bülach since before 1800, but that in the course of the 19th and 20th centuries many Meiers acquired citizenship in other communities of Canton Zurich and in other cantons. The register contains about 48,500 family names. The Workgroup for Swiss Surnames of the Swiss Society for Genealogical Research would have liked to update the inventory from 1962 to 1982, but regulations concerning privacy, and the huge increase in data – and, consequently, the high cost of data collection – made this impossible. However, Canton Jura, which came into existence after 1962, has been acknowledged.

261 **Bibliographie für Familienforscher. Verzeichnis geschichtlicher Handbücher, gedruckter Quellen und Hilfsmttel.** (Bibliography for genealogists: list of historical manuals, printed sources, and auxiliary works.)
Mario von Moos. Zurich: Schweizerische Gesellschaft für Familienforschung, 1984. 214p. (Arbeitshilfen für Familienforscher in der Schweiz, 3).

Published by the Swiss society for genealogical studies, this work has 1,730 entries, divided into thirteen chapters. Von Moos's objective is to help searchers find their way through the maze of publications that provide biographical and genealogical information. He lists manuals, bibliographies and catalogues, reference works, historical handbooks and journals, parish registers, archives, libraries, and books on family names by cantons. Some of the entries date from the Middle Ages, but most were published in the 19th and 20th centuries. Even though items are not annotated, the von Moos bibliography should be useful to serious genealogists. There are three indexes. See also *Bibliographie der schweizerischen Familiengeschichte* (Bibliography of Swiss genealogy), edited by Schweizerische Gesellschaft für Familienforschung (Muttenz, Switzerland 1946- . annual). The 1982-83 volume, published in 1985, has 33 pages with 300 entries of books and articles, Swiss and foreign, relevant to Swiss genealogy.

262 **Swiss genealogical research: an introductory guide.**
Paul Anthon Nielson. Virginia Beach, Virginia: Donning, 1979. 85p.

This booklet is designed as a practical introduction to the intricacies of genealogical research on Swiss ancestry. Nielson emphasizes the importance of the place of origin as the key to Swiss genealogical research and gives advice on finding leads. The major Swiss tools available to them, such as the family names book, the registers of citizens and families, parochial registers, and other kinds of historical records are described briefly, and some practical suggestions complete the useful guide. Consult also: *Archivalische Quellen für den Familienforscher* (Archival sources for the genealogist) by Albert Bruckner (Zurich: Schweizerische Gesellschaft für Familienforschung, 1981. Arbeitshilfen für Familienforscher in der Schweiz, 1).

263 **Repertorium der handschriftlichen Nachlässe in den Bibliotheken und Archiven der Schweiz.** (List of manuscript deposits in Swiss libraries and archives.)
Anne-Marie Schmutz-Pfister. Bern: Benteli, 1967. 200p. (Quellen zur Schweizer Geschichte, Neue Folge, IV Abteilung: Handbücher, VIII).

This book contains 2,308 names of families and of Swiss and foreigners and lists manuscript collections, family archives, scientific or literary manuscripts of individuals, personal papers, correspondences, memoirs, and other documents deposited in some 130 libraries and archives. Archival sources of societies and organizations are not included. This list is neither a catalogue, nor even a summary inventory; it is simply a guide to sources of potential value to researchers. In 1980, the Swiss National Library published a *Zuwachsliste 1968-1978* (Supplementary list 1968-78) which added some 900 names to the list on the basis of information received from various institutions.

264 **Genealogisches Handbuch zur Schweizer Geschichte.** (Genealogical handbook to Swiss history.)
Edited by the Schweizerische Heraldische Gesellschaft. Zurich: Schulthess, 1900-45. vols 1-3; Fribourg, Switzerland: Schweizerische Heraldische Gesellschaft, 1980. vol. 4.

The first three volumes of this voluminous work were published in instalments. Volume 1, 415p., 1900-8, treats the dynastic nobility of Switzerland. It has thirty-one plates with hundreds of seals of noble families and individuals. Volume 2, 348p., 1935-45 treats the high, dynastic, and low, ministerial, nobility. It has twenty-one plates with seals. Volume 3, 418p., 1908-16, treats the ministerials and the patriciate. It has twenty-one plates with seals. Lastly, Volume 4 – with 335 pages and thirteen plates – treats counts, earls (Freiherren), and ministerials. All four volumes consist of genealogical articles by different authors about particular noble families which include very elaborate family trees and sometimes substantial biographical sketches of individual members of the families. The articles in volume four also have elaborate bibliographies, and the volume contains an index of the noble families treated in the handbook. An amazing amount of material has been brought together in this work, making it an essential tool for the writing of Swiss history of the Middle Ages.

265 **Handy guide to Swiss genealogical records.**
Jared H. Suess. Logan, Utah: Everton, 1978. 92p. maps. bibliog.

Suess has compiled a broad assortment of information about Switzerland and the peculiarities of its genealogical records. The major types of records of genealogical value are described, and addresses of Swiss cantonal archives are provided, among many other pieces of information. There is no systematic organization of the material, but persistent searchers will find answers to some of the practical problems they may encounter in trying to track down their Swiss ancestors.

266 **Jahrbuch 1987. Schweizerische Gesellschaft für Familienforschung.**
(Yearbook 1987: Swiss Society for Genealogical Studies.)
Muttenz, Switzerland: Werner Hug, 1987. 318p.

The Swiss Society for Genealogical Studies has published yearbooks since 1974. The 1987 volume contains seven scholarly articles on family histories and other genealogical topics. The society maintains a Genealogical Information Centre at Steinbühlallee 189, CH 4054 Basel, Switzerland.

Population

267 **Démographie et identité nationale (1850-1914). La Suisse et 'La question des étrangers'.** (Demography and national identity (1850-1914): Switzerland and 'the question of foreigners'.)
Gérald Arlettaz. In: *Etudes et Sources*, edited by Oscar Gauye. Bern: Archives fédérales, no. 11 (1985), p. 83-180.

The first population studies in Switzerland were closely tied to the creation of the federal state in 1848 and the accompanying administrative apparatus. A statistical bureau was opened in 1860, and since 1870 this bureau, today the Federal Statistical Office, has conducted regular decennial censuses. In this substantial article Arlettaz first describes the history of national statistics and their influence on the national consciousness. In the second, longer, part he discusses the results of the late-19th-century censuses which reflect a growing number of foreigners who by 1910 made up almost fifteen percent (?) of the population. While the influx of foreigners generated a great deal of debate over the danger of the alienization (*Ueberfremdung*) of the country, the Swiss state retained its liberal practices until World War I. Klaus Urner in his case-study *Die Deutschen in der Schweiz: Von den Anfängen der Kolonienbildung bis zum Ausbruch des Ersten Weltkrieges* (The Germans in Switzerland: From the beginnings of colonization to the outbreak of World War I) investigates the relationship between the two neighbours over a period of 100 years.

268 **Bevölkerungsgeschichte und Bevölkerungspolitik der Schweiz seit dem Ausgang des Mittelalters.** (Population history and population policy of Switzerland since the end of the Middle Ages.)
W. Bickel. Zurich: Büchergilde Gutenberg, 1947. 333p. bibliog.

This is the authoritative scholarly work on the demography of Switzerland from the late Middle Ages to the end of World War II. Bickel begins with a discussion of theoretical and methodological issues in the field of demography, and then presents his materials in three parts: from the end of the Middle Ages to the end of the 18th century, the 19th century to World War I, and since World War I. In the first part he makes judicious use of sources to arrive at careful estimates of population figures and trends. From 1400 to 1800 the population of Switzerland increased slowly but steadily from 600,000 to 1.7 million. The country was always overpopulated, forcing many Swiss to find their livelihood abroad as mercenaries and others to emigrate, and beginning in 1800 Switzerland experienced a population explosion which saw the number of inhabitants grow from 1.7 to 3.9 million in 1914. Bickel discusses the economic factors behind this development, foremost among them rapid industrialization. In the last part he dwells on the worrisome decline of the birth rate, which, however, was reversed during World War II, just in time for him to modify his pessimistic conclusions about the future of the Swiss population. Throughout the book there are numerous statistical tables that illuminate all aspects of this involved subject so masterfully presented by Bickel.

269 **Bevölkerungswandel in der Schweiz. Zur Entwicklung von Heiraten, Geburten, Wanderungen und Sterblichkeit.** (Population change in Switzerland: trends in the rates of marriage, birth, migration, and death.)
François Höpflinger. Grüsch, Switzerland: Rüegger, 1986. 184p. bibliog.

Höpflinger offers the first broad overview of demographical developments in Switzerland since Bickel's work (q.v.) forty years earlier. With the help of a large number of tables and figures he analyses the population phenomena listed in the title. Contemporary demographic trends are seen in long-term perspective, and in the context of economic, social, psychological, and cultural complexities. Markus Mattmüller is in the process of writing the most comprehensive *Bevölkerungsgeschichte der Schweiz* (Population history of Switzerland) yet. The first part of this work – consisting of vol. 1 *Die frühe Neuzeit 1500-1700* (The early modern era 1500-1700) and vol. 2 *Wissenschaftlicher Anhang* (Scientific appendix) with a total of 735 pages – was published by Helbing & Lichtenhahn, Basel and Frankfurt, FRG, in 1987. Predicted population changes are examined in 'Ausblick auf die Zukunft der schweizerischen Bevölkerung: Bevölkerungsperspektiven 1986-2025' (View of the future of the Swiss population: population perspectives 1986-2025) by Werner Haug, *Schweizerische Zeitschrift für Volkswirtschaft und Statistik*, vol. 124, no. 2 (June 1988), p. 193-210.

270 **The population of Switzerland.**
Kurt B. Mayer. New York: Columbia University Press, 1952. 336p. bibliog.

This study proposes 'to enhance the understanding of Swiss social institutions by the English-speaking public through a descriptive analysis of Switzerland's population'. The population grew, at a slower rate than that of most other West European countries, from 1.6 million in 1800 to 4.7 million in 1950. The factors determining growth (births, deaths, and migrations) are described, as well as the demographic, economic, ethnic-linguistic, and religious characteristics of the Swiss population. The dimensions of international migration through emigration and immigration take up another part of the book, as does the topic of internal mobility and urbanization. Nine charts, four maps, and eighty-nine tables help illustrate the points made in the text. The last of the tables estimated the population of Switzerland to be 4.9 million in 1988 – it was actually well above 6 million.

Emigration: the Swiss Abroad

General

271 **L'emigration suisse outre-mer de 1815 à 1920.** (Swiss overseas emigration, 1815-1920.)
Gérald Arlettaz. In: *Etudes et Sources*, edited by Oscar Gauye. Bern: Archives fédérales, no. 1 (1975), p. 31-95. bibliog.

In this first part of his research in the emigration records of the Swiss federal archives in Bern, Arlettaz investigated the conditions that induced emigrants to leave Switzerland and described the evolution of an official response to the phenomenon through legislation. He also provided suggestions for further research and a bibliographical survey of existing literature on the subject.

272 **Zustand und Aufgaben schweizerischer historischer Wanderungsforschung.** (State and tasks of Swiss historical migration research.)
Carsten Goehrke, Hans Werner Tobler, Klaus Anderegg, May B. Broda, Josef Voegeli, Béatrice Ziegler-Witschi. *Schweizerische Zeitschrift für Geschichte*, vol. 37, no. 3 (1987), p. 303-32.

A team of historians from the University of Zurich and the Federal Institute of Technology in Zurich presents findings concerning the state of migration research in Switzerland. Funded by the Swiss National Foundation for the Promotion of Scientific Research, these researchers used their specialized work on Swiss emigration to Russia and to Brazil to discuss methodology and to attempt a typology of Swiss migration abroad on the basis of comparative analyses. Numerous footnotes provide access to the existing literature on the subject. Archival materials from the Swiss consulates in port cities and other cities in the target countries, sent back to Bern, constitute the largest single source of information on Swiss emigrants. Private archives, the press, and oral history materials, though also important, are less rewarding sources, for they all have one weakness in common: they do not lend themselves easily to quantification. Most secondary works are of the descriptive, humanistic type; very few incorporate the cliometric principle of counting. The authors of this informative article also stress that the bulk of the existing literature deals with emigration overseas, primarily to North America, while the numerically much more important emigration to European countries is largely neglected. No scholarly study exists, for example, on the migration and remigration of Swiss to and from Germany.

273 **Schweizer im Ausland. Von ihrem Leben und Wirken in aller Welt.** (Swiss abroad: about their life and work in all parts of the globe.) Edited by A. Lätt. Geneva: Sadag, 1931. 344p. bibliog.

The articles by different contributors that make up this book provide an overview of the scope and diversity of Swiss emigration to foreign countries. In the first part some general aspects, such as the significance of the presence of Swiss in other parts of the world and Swiss diplomatic representation abroad, are discussed. Almost two-thirds of the space is given to the second part, entitled 'pictures from the Swiss colonies'. The chapters on the Swiss in Italy and in Paris are the longest, but also treated, in descending order of length, are the Swiss in England, the United States of America, Egypt, Argentina, Germany, Denmark, Rumania, South Africa, and Hungary. Special sections deal with Ticinese emigration and the work of the Catholic Swiss missions and the Protestant Basel Mission in Africa and Asia. The third part provides brief biographical sketches of five outstanding contemporary representatives of Switzerland abroad. The work, which was published under the auspices of the New Helvetic Society and the Commission for the Swiss Abroad, is richly illustrated throughout with photographs of social and business activities in the various Swiss colonies and dozens of portraits of individual Swiss who achieved fame and success abroad.

274 **Einführung in die schweizerische Auswanderungsgeschichte der Neuzeit.** (Introduction to Swiss emigration history of modern times.) Leo Schelbert. Zurich: Leemann, 1976. 443p. bibliog.

With this work Leo Schelbert confirmed his expertise in the field of migration history in general and Swiss emigration in particular. In the first part he describes the causes of emigration and the process of emigration. A historical survey of Swiss emigration, military and civilian, into all parts of the world forms part two, and Schelbert illustrates his points by means of a collection of some thirty documents, consisting of official statements, travel reports, and letters. Finally, a 'historiographical introduction' leads to the primary and secondary literature, arranged according to topics and geographical areas. From one of the thirty statistical tables we learn that an estimated 347,000 Swiss lived abroad in 1928, the year with the largest number of Swiss abroad, 73 per cent of them in Europe, and 24 per cent in the Americas.

Emigration to the Americas

275 **Emigration et colonisation suisses en Amérique 1815-1918.** (Swiss emigration and colonization in the Americas, 1815-1918.)
Gérald Arlettaz. In: *Etudes et Sources*, edited by Oscar Gauye. Bern: Archives fédérales, no. 5 (1979), 236p.

Several hundred thousand Swiss emigrated to the Americas during the 19th and 20th centuries, most of them by far (some 260,000) to the United States. After an introductory chapter describing the general conditions of travel and the difficulties the emigrants encountered upon arrival in surroundings that were entirely foreign to them, Arlettaz presents the major factual data of the fate and achievements of the emigrants, country by country. The length of the chapters gives an indication of the importance of particular countries as final destinations. The United States covers 57 pages, Canada 7, Argentina 25, Uruguay 19, Chile 14, Brazil 30, 'Indian' America (from Paraguay to Venezuela) 19, Central America, including Mexico, 11. Brazil receives so much attention because the Swiss immigrants encountered even more difficulties there than in other places, essentially being enslaved on the plantations; in fact the Swiss government had to intervene to help its citizens in Brazil. Arlettaz' work is a major contribution to the emigration aspect of Swiss history. There are summaries in Italian and English.

276 **Memoirs of a Swiss officer in the American Civil War.**
Rudolf Aschmann, translated from the German by Hedwig D. Rappolt, introduced and edited by Heinz K. Meier. Bern: Lang, 1972. 183p. map. (Swiss-American Historical Society Publications, 4).

Aschmann's memoirs *Drei Jahre in der Potomac-Armee oder eine Schweizer Schützen-Compagnie im nordamerikanischen Kriege* (Three years in the Army of the Potomac or a Swiss company of sharpshooters in the North American war) was published in 1865 in Richterswil, Switzerland. It is the only substantial account by a Swiss participant in the Civil War and one of a very small number that describe the activities of the special outfit to which Aschmann belonged, Berdan's Sharpshooters. Aschmann (1841-1909), one of a large number of foreigners who fought in the war, saw action with the Army of the Potomac, the major Northern army in this civil war, from August 1861 until August 1864, when he was wounded at the battle of Deep Bottom in Virginia, and returned home to Switzerland a cripple.

277 **The old land and the new: the journals of two Swiss families in America in the 1820's.**
Edited and translated from the German by Robert H. Billigmeier, Fred Altschuler Picard. Minneapolis, Minnesota: University of Minnesota Press, 1965. 281p.

This book contains two journals written by friends who grew up in the Toggenburg, a valley in Canton St Gallen, and emigrated to the United States in the 1820s, a time when the flow of immigrants was still small and the decision to leave one's homeland and face an arduous voyage to a foreign land entailed a great risk. Both men were keen observers and recorded for their families and friends back home their eventful trips down the River Rhine, their long and arduous ocean crossings, and the many impressions and experiences of life in the New World. They reported candidly on what displeased them, such as the shameful slave trade or a lack of manners, and they voiced their praise for the democratic spirit they found or for America's high living standards. They gained their experiences in places where early immigrants commonly settled: New York, Maryland, Pennsylvania, and Ohio. The editors recognized the contributions these two diaries make to emigration history and took care to translate them in such a way as to preserve the tone and spirit in which they were written.

278 **Le Canada et les Suisses.** (Canada and the Swiss.)
Emile Henri Bovay. Fribourg, Switzerland: Editions Universitaires, 1976. 334p. maps. bibliog.

This nicely illustrated volume traces the history of contacts between Canada and Switzerland from the beginnings in 1604 to the present. Bovay was a member of the Swiss foreign service and worked for years as consul in Toronto. He highlights those individuals of Swiss ancestry and background who rose above the crowd to play a significant role in the history of Canada, among them first and foremost the officials and officers who served the English colonial government, such as Frederick Haldimand and George Prevost, who were governors-general of Canada from 1776 to 1786 and 1811 to 1815, respectively. The exploits of the two Swiss regiments de Watteville and de Meuron during the War of 1812 are reconstructed, together with a list of the officers who served in these two regiments. The volume also contains the catalogue of the works of the Bernese painter of Indian life, Peter Rindlisbacher (1806-34), who began his artistic career as a teenager in Winnipeg and is praised as the 'first painter of the [American] West'. Other chapters deal with the immigration of Swiss since 1926, the Swiss clubs in Canada, and the economic and cultural relations between the two countries. A fifty-four page bibliography is an especially valuable component of this book.

279 **Quest: the life of Elisabeth Kübler-Ross.**
Derek Gill. New York: Harper & Row, 1980. 329p.

Derek Gill first interviewed Elisabeth Kübler-Ross (1926-) for this biography during a six-hour ride from her home in Chicago to one of her many speaking engagements. The diminutive but tireless doctor is known for her book *On Death and Dying* (1969) but it was an article in *Life* (1969) that featured her interview with a young dying leukaemia patient which gained her worldwide attention. Gill's story of the triplet born into a typical upper-middle-class German-Swiss family is in many ways that of any Swiss child of the time of similar background: a father who is the undisputed head of the family, a mother who is wholly occupied with house and family, holidays filled with traditions and outdoor activities. Elisabeth lived in her own mystical world and went her own ways – right after World War II, the young woman went to Belgium and Poland to help rebuild war-torn communities; at home again, she took up medicine, enduring years of deprivation; marriage to a fellow medical student, an American Jew, brought her to America which she at first despised. Wherever the Ross family moved, Kübler encountered some colleagues who questioned the validity of her work, while others served her as teachers and gave her opportunities to lecture and to discuss her experiences in hospitals and clinics with mentally disturbed and dying patients. Over the years, Kübler came to love America for it had given her the freedom and the opportunities for her discoveries. The biography ends in 1969, the year she became famous.

280 **The Swiss in Wisconsin.**
Frederick Hale. Madison, Wisconsin: State Historical Society of Wisconsin, 1984. 40p. maps. bibliog.

This is one of a series of booklets on ethnic groups in Wisconsin sponsored by the State Historical Society of Wisconsin. Nicely illustrated with some old photographs, the booklet tells in anecdotal form the story of the Swiss who chose Wisconsin as their destination in the New World. By 1930 some 7,700 first-generation Swiss-Americans were living there, almost two-thirds of them in rural areas and only slightly more than one-third in urban areas. Hale makes use of census data to analyse the geographical distribution of the Swiss among the counties and their occupations. He also discusses the problem of the relatively small and dispersed Swiss community maintaining its identity. New Glarus (see Schelbert, below) is unique as a settlement of cultural retention. The article 'The Wisconsin Swiss: a portrait' in *Swiss-American Historical Society Review*, vol. 25, no. 1 (February 1989), p. 11-35, by Ernest Menolfi and Leo Schelbert, expands on Hale's booklet.

281 **Schweizer in Amerika. Karrieren und Mißerfolge in der Neuen Welt.**
(Swiss in America: careers and failures in the New World.)
Karl Lüönd. Olten, Switzerland: Walter, 1979. 328p. bibliog.

Swiss emigrants have sought their luck in the New World since the early years of its discovery. While most of them quietly merged into the American 'melting pot', some of them follow the quintessential American success story of the rise from rags to riches, gaining prominence in their chosen careers, whether business, medicine, science, manufacturing, politics, or something else. Lüönd tells the stories of twenty-five of these over-achievers. The careful research underlying these biographical sketches is disguised by an easy, journalistic style of presentation. Examples of Swiss who achieved success or fame include Christoph Graffenried, the founder of New Bern, North Carolina; Johann August Sutter, of California gold rush fame; Jean-Louis Rodolphe Agassiz, Harvard professor of geology and zoology and founder of the Harvard Museum for Comparative Zoology; Louis-Joseph Chevrolet, the motor mechanic who gave his name to one of the most successful lines of cars ever manufactured; Othmar H. Ammann, builder of the George Washington and the Verrazano Narrows bridges for the New York Port Authority; and Elisabeth Kübler-Ross, psychiatrist, famous for her work with the fatally ill.

282 **Les colonies tessinoises en Californie.** (The Ticinese colonies in California.)
Maurice Edmont Perret. Lausanne, Switzerland: Rouge, 1950. 304p.

The Italian-speaking Canton Ticino of the 19th and early 20th century was overpopulated. An agrarian canton, the land could not support the growing number of people and industrialization had not yet begun. As a consequence, tens of thousands of Ticinese left their homes to seek their fortune abroad. Many of these penniless but hard-working Italian-Swiss emigrants went to the United States, most of them settling in California. Finding little success in gold mining, which originally had attracted them, they took up farming instead. They were thrifty, saved what they did not send home, and acquired land for dairy farming. They adapted quickly to the American system and formed prosperous colonies where they continued to observe some of their old customs. Although most of these communities were in rural areas, cities such as San Francisco also attracted a considerable number of Ticinese immigrants. Perret's book with its many tables of demographic data is well researched in the archives of

California and Ticino. See also *L'emigrazione ticinese in California: Epistolario* (The emigration from Canton Ticino to California: letters) by Giorgio Cheda (Locarno, Switzerland: Dadò, vol. 2, in two parts, 1981). It contains 898 letters, written by Ticinese emigrants, found in the archives of villages and towns of Italian-speaking Canton Ticino, and also 103 reproductions of documents, letters, and postcards, illustrating the life and activities of the Italian Swiss in California.

283 **An American apprenticeship: the letters of Emil Frey 1860-1865.** Edited and translated from the German by Hedwig Rappolt. New York [etc.]: Lang, 1986. 227p. bibliog.

Emil Frey (1838-1922) went to the United States in late 1860, shortly before the outbreak of the Civil War. A young man in search of an occupation, he joined a German-American regiment and fought for the Union. He saw action against the Confederates in various theatres of the war and advanced to the rank of captain. At the battle of Gettysburg he was taken prisoner, and he spent eighteen months (from July 1863 until December 1864) in Richmond, Virginia's infamous Libby prison. After his release he rejoined his regiment and served until the end of the war. This book contains fifty-two documents, most of them letters written by Frey to his 'dear parents, brothers and sisters' during the five years he spent in America. Frey returned to Switzerland in 1865, after he had become a naturalized American citizen, without having achieved his initial goal of striking it rich in the New World. An afterword by Hans Rudolf Guggisberg puts Frey's years of 'American apprenticeship' in the context of his long, industrious life, which, among other things, included a five-year tour as Switzerland's first diplomatic representative to the United States from 1882 to 1886.

284 **New Glarus 1845-1970: the making of a Swiss American town.** Edited by Leo Schelbert. Glarus, Switzerland: Tschudi, 1970. 239p. bibliog.

New Glarus, Wisconsin, is one of the more famous Swiss settlements in the United States. It was founded in August 1845 by a group of 118 persons from Canton Glarus who had left their homeland because of scarcity of work and hard times. Their exodus was carefully planned, with advance scouts looking for suitable land and trusted leaders holding the group together during the long trip down the Rhine to the sea, the stormy ocean passage, and the difficult trek to the Middle West. Much of the volume is taken up by the text, in German with an English translation, of the diary of the journey by one of the participants, Matthias Dürst. The geographer Dieter Brunnschweiler contributed a scholarly article with maps and tables on the factors, both environmental and human, that led the citizens of New Glarus to preserve and sustain their Swiss traditions for 125 years. The information is based on his Zurich dissertation *New Glarus (Wisconsin). Gründung, Entwicklung und heutiger Zustand einer Schweizerkolonie im amerikanischen Mittelwesten* (New Glarus, Wisconsin: founding, development, and present state of a Swiss colony in the American Midwest. Zurich: Fluntern, 1954). Schelbert's meticulously researched commentary adds welcome information to the various parts of this book.

285 **Swiss.**

Leo Schelbert. In: *Harvard encyclopedia of American ethnic groups*, edited by Stephan Thernstrom. Cambridge, Massachusetts; London: Harvard University Press, 1980, p. 981-87.

Schelbert provides a useful, compact introduction to the subject of Swiss immigration to America. The activities and role of the Swiss in American life from colonial times to the present are reviewed with careful attention to the many groups and individuals who came to the New World in search of a better life.

286 **Louis Chevrolet 1878-1941.**

Hans Rudolf Schmid. In: *Schweizer Pioniere der Wirtschaft und Technik*, 11. Zurich: Verein für wirtschaftshistorische Studien, 1960. p. 47-67.

While the name Chevrolet is known all over the world as one of the most popular lines of automobiles, few people know the story of the pioneer who is behind the great American success story. This illustrated biography begins in La Chaux-de-Fonds in the Neuchâtel Jura, where Chevrolet was born the son of a poor watchmaker who moved his growing family to Beaune, France, when Louis was six years old. Bicycles and motors held the youth's interest, and the advanced motorization in the United States lured him and his brothers to the New World where they became famous as daredevil car racers. After his youngest brother's fatal racing accident, Louis turned his attention to building motors and designing cars. He was unable to develop a model that lived up to his technical and design standards and at the same time could compete with Ford's much cheaper models. Thus, in 1913, he left the Chevrolet Motor Car Company of Michigan in Detroit which he had helped to found just two years earlier. He worked in different capacities, continuing his search for a better and lighter racing car on his own. In 1933 he returned to General Motors which now built 'his' car successfully. He held a leading position in the Chevrolet Motor Division before several strokes forced him into retirement. Although he never carried out a planned visit to Switzerland, he was always proud of his native country.

287 **A portrait of New Switzerland 1831-1900: origin and development of a Swiss settlement in the United States of America (Madison County, Illinois).**

Max Schweizer, translated from the German by Harold and Lynne Schweizer. Zug, Switzerland: Zürcher Books, 1979. 106p. maps. bibliog.

This illustrated booklet traces the story of the settling of the area of New Switzerland in the wilderness of Southern Illinois in the early 1830s by Swiss immigrants from ten different cantons. In 1837, the town of Highland was founded, and this Swiss town with the Scottish name grew into the largest Swiss settlement in the United States. Picture-essays with translations of contemporary documents reflect the social, educational, and religious life of the community and describe the industries and businesses that flourished there by the end of the 19th century.

288 **Prominent Americans of Swiss origin.**

Edited by the Swiss-American Historical Society. New York: White, 1932. 266p.

This book contains brief biographies of more than seventy Americans of Swiss origin, some born in Switzerland and others born in America as the children of immigrants who affirmed that their Swiss heritage had shaped their character and lives. The editors grouped the biographical sketches according to the professions of the subjects: pioneers, theologians, soldiers, statesmen, physicians and surgeons, industrialists, merchants, bankers, scientists, journalists, and engineers. These men were selected because they had rendered important services to the community; wealth and personal accomplishments alone did not qualify anyone for inclusion in this book. At the time of its publication, Albert Gallatin, who served as Secretary of the Treasury under Thomas Jefferson, and Jean-Louis Rodolphe Agassiz, who held a chair of zoology and geology at Harvard University, were the most prominent men of Swiss origin in American history.

289 **Albert Gallatin: Jeffersonian financier and diplomat.**

Raymond Walters, Jr. New York: Macmillan, 1957. 461p. bibliog.

Geneva-born and -educated Gallatin (1761-1849) came to America in 1780. He moved to the frontier in western Pennsylvania, became a member of the Pennsylvania state legislature, and in 1795 was elected to the US House of Representatives, where he became an active supporter of Thomas Jefferson. In 1801 Jefferson appointed Gallatin Secretary of the Treasury, an office he filled with distinction for the next twelve years. The War of 1812, which he opposed, was the undoing of his fiscal policy, and he relinquished his post, but he continued to serve his adopted country as one of the US negotiators of the Treaty of Ghent, which ended the war, and then as US minister to France and to Great Britain. During the last two decades of his long life Gallatin was active as a banker, an ethnologist who founded the American Ethnological Society in 1842, and the author of several books on American Indian tribes. Walters's scholarly biography portrays Gallatin as 'a superbly able and almost completely selfless public servant'. His statue stands in front of the Treasury building in Washington, DC and Gallatin is undoubtedly the most eminent of the many Swiss who went to the United States. Thomas Aitken's *Albert Gallatin: early America's Swiss-born statesman* (New York [etc.]: Vantage, 1985) adds little to our knowledge of Gallatin.

290 **Sutter: the man and his empire.**

J. Peter Zollinger. New York: Oxford University Press, 1939. 374p. bibliog. (Reprinted Gloucester, Massachusetts: Peter Smith, 1967).

Johann August Sutter (1803-80), the famous Swiss pioneer who helped conquer the Pacific coast of North America, was a controversial figure already in his lifetime. He was seen by some as a hero, by others as a scoundrel, and the debate was fuelled by Sutter's quest for glory, and his discovery of gold. Zollinger bases his story mainly on primary source materials. He sheds light on Sutter's youth and the reasons for his sudden departure from Switzerland; he traces Sutter's journey across the United States to California and back to Philadelphia; but the empire-builder, the high-living folk hero, upon whose vast landholdings gold was found, died a broken man, and the precious metal proved to be a bane not a boon. He was also a failure in his private life as a husband and father. The author succeeds in giving an objective portrayal of Sutter's enigmatic personality. Richard Dillon's *Fool's gold: a biography of John Sutter* (New York: Coward-McCann, 1967) is a more recent and more detailed biography. Among its attractions are two portfolios of old photographs and an annotated bibliography that discusses the Sutter literature, both primary and secondary, in an intelligent and reliable manner.

Emigration to the rest of the world

291 **Schweizer im Zarenreich. Zur Geschichte der Auswanderung nach Russland.** (Swiss in the realm of the Tsar: on the history of emigration to Russia.)
Roman Bühler, Heidi Gander-Wolf, Carsten Goehrke, Urs Rauber, Gisela Tschudin, Josef Voegeli. Final edition by Gabriele Scheidegger. Zurich: Rohr, 1985. 517p. maps. bibliog.

Written by a team of historians, associated with Carsten Goehrke, holder of a chair of East European history at the Historisches Seminar of the University of Zurich, this book is an impressive scholarly study of every aspect of Swiss emigration to Russia. Methodologically thorough, the authors establish clear parameters for the scope of their work and discuss the problems that still need to be addressed. Two appendices consist of charts that show in five-year intervals the number of Swiss who went to Russia and those who returned. Between 1701 and 1916 2,077 Swiss went to Russia, and between 1701 and 1951 1,472 returned. Individual chapters deal with all aspects of emigration and examine the significance of this migration within the European context. There are fifty-one illustrations, numerous tables and charts in the text, and seventeen appendices with statistical material. The experiences of a small group of Swiss under the leadership of Fritz Platten who emigrated to Russia in 1924 are traced in *Schweizer Auswanderer in der Sowjetunion. Die Erlebnisse der Schweizer Kommunarden im revolutionären Russland (1924-1930)* (Swiss emigrants in the Soviet Union: the experiences of Swiss communards in revolutionary Russia, 1924-30) by Barbara Schneider (Schaffhausen, Switzerland: Schaffhauser AZ, 1985).

292 **L'emigrazione ticinese in Australia.** (The emigration from Canton Ticino to Australia.)
Giorgio Cheda. Locarno, Switzerland: Dadò, 1976. 2 vols. maps. bibliog.

The Italian-speaking population of Canton Ticino has furnished a large contingent of emigrants to many parts of the world. Many of them enjoyed success but not the more than 2,000 persons who left the canton between 1853 and 1855 to go to Australia in response to news of gold discoveries. Cheda's meticulous research has unearthed a horror story of deception, misery, and tragic failure. Emigration was the last resort for the extremely poor population of the valleys north of Lago Maggiore, and those who decided to leave for Australia were victimized by unscrupulous agents who induced them to incur debt to pay for the passage to a less-than-certain promised land. Once at sea, they were left to fend for themselves, and many died en route. None of those who reached the mines in Victoria struck it rich; on the contrary, they had to work as labourers in the mines for years just to pay off their debts. Cheda's first volume traces the course of this emigration, and lists 2,126 emigrants by locality of origin with their year of birth, their occupation, and other data. The second volume (460p.) is made up of emigrants' letters which Cheda unearthed in the villages of the Locarno and Valle Maggia districts and a few illustrations, mainly souvenir photographs.

293 **History of the Swiss in Southern Africa, 1652-1977.**
Edited by Felix Ernst, Kurt Scheurer. Johannesburg, South Africa: Swiss Chronology, 1979. 2nd ed. 80p. maps.

This work is organized in the form of chronological tables and lists Swiss soldiers and employees of the Dutch East India Company, 1652-1806; settlers of the Cape to 1806; Swiss in the Great Trek and the Boer War; Swiss in various professions; the diplomatic and consular service; and the Swiss clubs in South Africa. Similar data are provided for other countries in Southern Africa. This small booklet gathers materials that might be used for a history on an otherwise neglected aspect of Swiss emigration.

294 **2000 Ans de présence suisse en Angleterre. L'Etonnante épopée des Suisses d'outre-manche. De l'Epoque romaine à la Communauté Européenne.** (Two thousand years of Swiss presence in England: the astonishing epic of the Swiss of the other side of the Channel: from Roman times to the European Community.)
Béat de Fischer, Jean-René Bory. Neuchâtel, Switzerland; Paris: Delachaux et Niestlé, 1980. 214p. (La Suisse à la Rencontre de l'Europe).

The presentation of this large-format book is notable. It is lavishly illustrated with pictures in the text and full-page colour plates of paintings, mostly of Swiss persons who visited England or in some way played a role in its history, from Cardinal Schiner to Hans Holbein, Paracelsus, Rousseau, Mme de Staël, and lesser-known officers and diplomats. The text itself is mainly a listing of Swiss whose accomplishments de Fischer felt warranted mention. From the Middle Ages to the 20th century, Swiss served in the Royal Army and Navy, and in the imperial administration; were members of university faculties, the Royal Society, and the Royal Academy; and established branches of their multinational companies in Britain. Fischer also touches on some of the intellectual influences Swiss exerted on England, from the Reformers of Zurich and Geneva to Rousseau, Pestalozzi, and in more recent times C. G. Jung and Jean Piaget.

295 **Fast ein Volk von Zuckerbäckern? Bündner Konditoren, Cafetiers und Hoteliers in europäischen Landen bis zum Ersten Weltkrieg.** (Practically a nation of confectioners? Pastry-cooks, restaurateurs and innkeepers from Graubünden in European countries until World War I.)
Dolf Kaiser. Zurich: Neue Zürcher Zeitung, 1988. 212p. bibliog.

The presence of confectioners in all corners of Europe during the 18th and 19th centuries hailing from Canton Graubünden led the author to pose the question 'Practically a nation of confectioners?' A chronicler lamented in 1807 that in his home town, Silvaplana, there were no tailors or shoemakers but twenty-eight 'sugar bakers' (*Zuckerbäcker*). As their fame and numbers increased, they began to emigrate, first to Italy, Venice in particular; eventually their shops could be found from Spain to Norway and from England to Russia. The successful confectioners recruited the sons from the Alpine villages at an early age to serve apprenticeships with them in foreign lands. The emigration often caused considerable hardship among the young trainees some of whom later also built their own successful businesses, but the expatriates did not forget their home towns and many who had become wealthy owners of impressive establishments built large villas in their native Graubünden. Pictures of these stately mansions and of elegant coffee shops and their proud owners enhance the first part of this book. The second part contains brief biographical entries of Swiss emigrants in the confectionery business of Europe. Genealogical charts show that often several generations carried on the trade.

296 **Schweizer Industrie in Russland. Ein Beitrag zur Geschichte der industriellen Emigration des Kapitalexportes und des Handels der Schweiz mit dem Zarenreich (1760-1917).** (Swiss industry in Russia: a contribution to the history of the industrial emigration of the export of capital and of the Swiss trade with Tsarist Russia, 1760-1917.)
Urs Rauber. Zurich: Rohr, 1985. 460p. maps. bibliog. (Beiträge zur Geschichte der Russlandschweizer, 2).

This is one monograph in a projected six-volume series on the Russian Swiss, to be produced at the University of Zurich under the editorship of Carsten Goehrke. Rauber's study is full of interesting information about a little-known segment of Swiss and Russian history during the age of industrialization. Swiss industrial activity in Russia, including industrial trading companies, was substantial in relative as well as absolute terms; as late as 1917, 300 Swiss firms were still active in Russia, especially in the areas of textile, machinery, and food processing. Rauber excels in providing a detailed collective biography of Swiss enterpreneurs at work in Tsarist Russia. He stresses that the relationship was a two-way process from which the Swiss profited at least as much in terms of high returns on investments, economic growth and jobs, as did the Russians who received advanced technology, managerial know-how, and much-needed capital. Some three dozen tables and charts present some of the raw materials on which this pioneering study is based.

297 **One hundred years of the Swiss club and Swiss community of Singapore 1871-1971.**
Hans Schweizer-Iten. Singapore: Swiss Club, 1983. 453p.

This history of the Swiss in Singapore consists of a large number of short biographies against the background of Singapore's history. The period of World War II in the Pacific (1941-45) and the position of the Swiss colony during the occupation by the Japanese is treated in meticulous detail. The book also contains the history of all the Swiss firms and their managers and employees – small-scale textile exporters developed into world enterprises; important industrial firms also established themselves in this teeming metropolis of South-East Asia. Schweizer has made an important contribution not only to the history of the 'Fifth Switzerland', the Swiss abroad, but also to the history of what in recent decades has been labelled the 'Sixth Switzerland', that is, the Swiss industrial firms, commercial enterprises, and service delivery corporations operating abroad.

298 **The romance of Madame Tussaud's.**
John Theodore Tussaud. London: Odhams, 1921. 2nd ed. 320p.

John Theodore Tussaud, a great-grandson of Madame Tussaud, tells in fifty brief chapters the story of his forebear's life and achievements and of the growth of the famous Exhibition of Waxworks after her death. Madame Tussaud (1760-1850) was born Marie Grosholtz, of Swiss parents. Her father died in the Seven Years' War before she was born. Mary lived with her mother in Bern until they moved to Paris with her uncle, who was a medical practitioner and had taken to modelling the limbs and organs of the human body in wax. In Paris she married François Tussaud, which gave Mary the name under which she became famous. Madame Tussaud worked in her uncle's wax figures cabinet, modelling nobles at the court of Louis XVI and later leaders of the French Revolution. In 1802 she left France forever, taking her uncle's Exhibition along with her to England. Eventually, most famous Englishmen would be modelled in wax by one of the Tussauds for their museum. The book has some gruesome illustrations of heads modelled in wax of persons who were beheaded during the French Revolution, among them those of Marie Antoinette and Maximilien Robespierre. Leonard Cottrell's *Madame Tussaud* (London: Evans, 1951. 194p.) is a more recent version of the same story with many of the same illustrations and an update on the fate of the Tussaud clan during World War II and of the development of the waxworks to 1950.

299 **The first Swiss in New-Zealand: an essay.**
Irène Weber-de Candolle. Saigon: [Consulate general of Switzerland, by the author], 1967. 25p.

The author derived most of the information for this book from the records of the Turnbell Library in Wellington, New Zealand. The first Swiss to set foot on New Zealand was a John Webber (from Wäber), an artist who accompanied Captain John Hook on his last voyage and whose sketches and paintings are still valued today. Whalers, traders, and settlers with different skills, some lured by the promise of gold or land, came at different times to different parts of the country. The Swiss distinguished themselves by their expertise in various trades and in farming. Some returned to Switzerland only to bring friends and family back. The as yet unconquered mountains attracted Swiss climbers, and British climbers would often enlist the services of Swiss guides for their conquests.

Languages and Dialects

General

300 **Union et division des Suisses. Les relations entre Alémaniques, Romands et Tessinois aux XIXe et XXe siècles.** (Union and division of the Swiss: the relations between German-, French-, and Italian-speaking Swiss in the 19th and 20th centuries.)
Edited by Pierre du Bois. Lausanne: Editions de l'Aire, 1983. 239p.

This book contains the text of twelve scholarly papers on various aspects of the relationship between the ethnic groups of Switzerland presented at a colloquium at the Federal Institute of Technology in Lausanne in November 1980. Half of these articles are historical treatments of specific issues such as the ethnic relations before the founding of the new confederation in 1848 or the tensions between German-speaking and French-speaking Swiss during the two World Wars of the 20th century. The other half of the articles analyse the bilateral relationships between ethnic groups and the impact on the Romandie district of the recent linguistic development in Alemannic Switzerland of increasing use of the dialect even in schools.

301 **Hugo Loetscher: how many languages does man need?**
Edited by Tamara S. Evans. New York: Graduate School and University Center, City University of New York, 1982. 101p. bibliog.

Five of the seven chapters in this book, are based on lectures which Hugo Loetscher, Swiss writer and journalist, gave at the City University of New York. The multilingual situation of Switzerland, with its four cultures united under one political system, creates a range of problems. Loetscher's travels through different Latin American countries intensified his awareness of the situation in his own country. He depicted Latin America in his novels and asks 'how many Latin Americas are there?' While the language in these countries may be the same, the cultures are not. Loetscher also discusses the limits of verbal expression by juxtaposing literature with the creative arts and photography. He is from the German-speaking part and thus converses in a dialect that, while it has a rich vocabulary, lacks experience in expressing abstract ideas.

Loetscher shows what consequences this special language situation has for the German-Swiss author, who is bilingual within his own language.

Swiss-German

302 **Was ist eigentlich Schweizerdeutsch?** (What is Swiss-German, really?)
Arthur Baur. Winterthur, Switzerland: Gemsberg, 1983. 160p. bibliog.

Baur, 'a linguistically trained journalist', wrote this entertaining and instructive book to make a 'political statement', namely that Alemannic is a separate language and should be listed in the Swiss constitution as one of the four national languages, with High German relegated to one of the three official written languages. Aside from this rather unrealistic proposal, he provides a comprehensive and lively discussion of the various issues concerning the Alemannic language, from its historic beginnings in the Early Middle Ages, through its brief use as a written language in the Late Middle Ages, to its remarkable survival as an almost purely spoken language. There are chapters on the linguistic and grammatical characteristics of Swiss-German; on its use in various social, educational, and political environments and as a literary language; on the organizations and movements that have fought for the preservation of the language and their difficulties in formulating an acceptable way of writing it; on the place of High German in Switzerland, including the use of Helveticisms and Helvetic pronunciation of German words; and on the scientific study of Swiss-German.

303 **Schwyzertüütsch. Grüezi mitenand. Praktische Sprachlehre des Schweizerdeutschen.** (Swiss-German. 'Grüezi mitenand': practical grammar for Swiss-German.)
Arthur Baur. Winterthur, Switzerland: Gemsberg, 1985. 215p.

The author maintains that Swiss-German can be learned just like any other language. If the student has a good knowledge of standard German (and this book assumes this), he will soon understand Swiss because of the similarities of the two languages; to learn to speak Swiss, however, he will have to practise the sounds systematically and to absorb the grammar. Swiss-German is not one single language; the cantons, and sometimes regions within them, have their own pronunciation and different vocabularies. Baur's text teaches Zürichdeutsch (Zurich-German), the dialect spoken by the largest group of German-Swiss, but some characteristics of the Bernese dialect are discussed at the end of the book. Since Swiss is not a written language, there are no uniform rules about spelling and notation, and so the author first has to explain the symbols he uses. The materials in the twenty-four chapters are presented in much the same way as in the standard foreign-language textbooks, and an answer key to the exercises makes self-study possible. Examples of the Bernese dialect spoken by the young, can be found in *Hesch a Kiosk a der Eigernordwand? Schülersprache dargestellt am Beispiel Berns* (Do you have a concession stand on the north face of the Eiger? Youth language, using Bern as an example) by Dorothea Gruner (Ostermundingen-Bern, Switzerland: Viktoria, 1977).

304 **Sprachatlas der deutschen Schweiz. (Language atlas of German-speaking Switzerland.)**
Edited by Rudolf Hotzenköcherle, Heinrich Baumgartner, Rudolf Trüeb (et al.). Bern: Francke, 1962- . maps. bibliog.

The five large volumes published to date examine the *Sprachgeographie* (language differences among regions and localities) of German-speaking Switzerland; all occurring language changes are documented with maps of villages and regions. The first two of the five large volumes published to date deal with phonetic changes. While the first volume (1962) focuses on the qualities of vowels, *Umlaute*, and diphthongs, the second (1965) deals with the varieties of sounds and consonants, sound combinations and length. Volume three (1975) documents grammatical differences which includes verb conjugation, declension, and syntax; volume four (1969) looks at individual vocabulary words, grouped around themes such as the human body, and verbs expressing physical or mental activities; volume five (1983) is a continuation of volume four and lists word groups dealing with social life, clothing, and food. A sixth volume is in preparation. The data for this atlas were collected from 1940 to 1958 in a dense network of more than 400 field offices where workers spent forty to eighty hours interviewing 1,500 persons on the basis of a printed questionnaire of some 2,500 questions. The answers were phonetically transcribed and in some cases recorded on tape. The systematic use of symbols to represent the information collected facilitates understanding the maps. Hotzenköcherle has provided a two-volume introduction to the methodology and the use of the atlas in his introduction.

305 **Rudolf Hotzenköcherle: Die Sprachlandschaften der deutschen Schweiz.**
(Rudolf Hotzenköcherle: the language regions of German Switzerland.)
Edited by Niklaus Bigler, Robert Schläpfer. Aarau, Switzerland [etc.]: Sauerländer, 1984. 496p. maps.

The book was compiled following the death of Professor Hotzenköcherle, the undisputed authority on Swiss dialects and creator of the *Sprachatlas der deutschen Schweiz* (q.v.). It contains material from lectures and writings by Hotzenköcherle on sound and form problems of contemporary Swiss-German as manifested in different regions. The historical background and the maps illustrating the geographical location of the examples given make this work on dialectism interesting even for the lay person.

306 **What standard for diglossia? The case of German Switzerland.**
William G. Moulton. In: *Monograph Series on Languages and Linguistics*, no. 15, 1962. Edited by E. D. Woodworth, R. J. Di Pietro. Washington, DC: Georgetown University Press, 1963, p. 133-48.

'Diglossia' is defined as a language situation where primary dialects exist side by side with a superimposed divergent language that is used for written and formal purposes and which must be learned in school. Moulton, well-known linguist and expert on Swiss-German dialects, states that the diglossia of German-speaking Switzerland is extremely stable and that the speakers of this dialect are fully aware of the distinction between dialect and standard language. He tells the story of how the codified phonology of High German, as established in the standard work of Siebs, was studied by the 'Swiss Siebs Committee'. This committee compared the phonemic systems of the two language types and noted the deviations in Swiss pronunciation from so-called standard German. It then decided that no effort should be made to imitate the North German, considered the best German, as a Swiss wants to 'sound like a Swiss' even when he or she speaks High German. Moulton lists these deviations in this article.

307 **Los emol: Schweizerdeutsch verstehen. Comprendre le suisse allemand. Capire lo svizzero tedesco. Chapir tudestg svizzer.** (Listen carefully: understanding Swiss German.)
Martin Müller, Lukas Wertenschlag. Zurich [etc.]: Langenscheidt, 1985. 96p.

This attractive text is for anyone who would like to understand Swiss-German and has some knowledge of standard German. The goal of the authors is to develop listening and comprehension skills. The book is divided into seven chapters that deal with everyday situations such as eating and travelling, or cultural facts that add to a basic understanding of the Swiss character. In addition, it gives valuable tips about the nature and the diversity of the dialects. The text is written in standard German and features a variety of exercises that can be done with the help of two accompanying tapes in *Schwyzertütsch*. The photographs, cartoons, and short and varied exercises make self-study not only possible but inviting.

308 **Schweizerisches Idiotikon. Wörterbuch der schweizerdeutschen Sprache.** (Swiss thesaurus: dictionary of the Swiss-German language.)
Edited by Friedrich Staub, Ludwig Tobler, Albert Bachmann, Otto Gröger, Hans Wanner, Peter Dalcher. Frauenfeld, Switzerland: Huber, 1881- . 14 vols. (1987. A-Strutz).

The dictionary of the Swiss-German language was begun more than one hundred years ago with the goal of preserving the Alemannic vocabulary. Since then the enterprise has expanded in scope into a comprehensive dictionary that contains a listing of all shades of dialect usage, including the most recent neologisms, a historical dictionary with examples of the old Swiss-German written language dating back to 1300, a dictionary of synonyms, a dictionary of quotations, a dictionary of technical terms (*Sachwörterbuch*), an etymological dictionary, and a lexicon of names of persons and places. Every word receives an extensive treatise and as a consequence the completion of the work, which in 1987 had reached volume fourteen, is not in sight yet. The *Idiotikon* has been praised as an incomparable national treasure and an extraordinary scientific achievement. Unfortunately, its organization, which is based on consonant structure rather than alphabetical order, makes the use of the thesaurus difficult. The situation has been somewhat relieved by the alphabetical index that was included in volume twelve. Walter Haas has provided a lively history of this great undertaking in his illustrated book *Das Wörterbuch der schweizerdeutschen Sprache* (Frauenfeld, Switzerland: Huber, 1981).

French, Italian, and Romansh

309 **Glossaire du patois de la Suisse Romande.** (Glossary of the dialect of French-speaking Switzerland.)
Philippe C. Bridel, Louis Favrat. Geneva: Slatkine Reprints, 1970. 547p. (First published in 1866 in Lausanne).

Most of the examples of this glossary of dialect words and phrases come from the Alpine region of Vaud. The work represents the efforts of an untrained hobbyist who wanted to preserve the ancient idioms. The introduction deals with some of the problems of notation but also points to the pleasure the figurative expressions, proverbs, and naive concepts give the reader. Twenty-six different patois renderings of the parable of the Prodigal Son emphasize the great variety of French-Swiss dialects.

310 **Hat Rumantsch Grischun eine Chance?** (Does *Rumantsch Grischun* have a chance?)

Iso Camartin. *Thema, Magazin zur Forschung und Wissenschaft an den Schweizer Hochschulen*, no. 4 (December 1987), p. 19-22.

The 50,000 Romansh-speaking people in Canton Graubünden have enjoyed the luxury of using five different written languages. In the face of the growing threat of losing their patrimony by being swallowed up by the German-speaking fellow-citizens, the Romansh-speakers seem to be willing for the first time to consider seriously the adoption of an artificially created common written language, called *Rumantsch Grischun*. The creators of this language carefully selected elements from the five existing languages and artfully combined them into a workable new language. The first dictionary and grammar in *Rumantsch Grischun* were published in 1985, and now the acceptance of the language in teacher-training institutions and schools is a matter of politics. Since the citizens realize that the alternative to one common Romansh written language may be no Romansh, chances are good that *Rumantsch Grischun* will continue to make progress and become the accepted common language somewhat like High German is used by the German dialect-speaking compatriots.

311 **Romontsch: language and literature: the Sursilvan Raeto-Romance of Switzerland.**

Douglas Bartlett Gregor. Cambridge, England; New York: Oleander, 1982. 388p. maps. bibliog.

The Rhaeto-Romansh language, spoken by less than one per cent of the Swiss population, consists really of five languages, each with its own history, idiom, and literature. They are: Sursilvan, Sutsilvan, Surmiran and the Ladins of the Upper and Lower Engadin valley. The author deals in a lengthy introduction with the geography of the isolated mountain valleys and villages and the history of the Romansh territory that was at one time part of the Roman province Raetia. He then touches on language, literature, and folklore and shows the consequences of the absence of a unified language. Only strong support by the federal government, the media, and linguistic societies working toward the creation of a common written language, can halt the disappearance of Switzerland's fourth national language. A grammar section provides an introduction to the phonology, orthography, morphology, and syntax of the Sursilvan language, spoken in the Vorder Rhine valley of the north-western part of Canton Graubünden. The anthology that follows consists of ninety poems, letters, and prose pieces in Sursilvan, translated by Gregor on the facing pages and accompanied by biographical notes about the different authors.

312 **A sociolinguistic investigation of multilingualism in the Canton of Ticino Switzerland.**

Jürgen B. Heye. The Hague; Paris: Mouton, 1975. 87p. bibliog.

After World War II, Canton Ticino began to attract large numbers of Swiss from other cantons as well as foreigners, the mild climate of the southernmost Swiss canton being one attraction. The influx of non-Italian speakers did not create social friction. Heye examined language performance and language attitudes with the aid of a questionnaire in Italian and German which was randomly distributed in the major population areas of Lugano, Locarno, and Bellinzona. Samples of this questionnaire, the results and their interpretation form the major body of this work. Heye finds that regardless of socio-economic status, the attitude toward the standard languages is more positive than that toward the corresponding dialects.

313 **Italienische Schweiz – wohin? Die grosse Herausforderung.** (Italian Switzerland – where to? The great challenge.)
Ottavio Lurati, translated from the Italian by Beatrice Bissoli.
Schweizer Monatshefte, vol. 69, no. 1 (January 1989), p. 35-52.

Lurati, professor of Italian philology at the University of Basel, paints a bleak picture of the situation of the Ticino and its Italian-speaking minority in present-day Switzerland. The canton is in the midst of fundamental changes in its ecological, social, demographic, and economic structure. It is in danger of losing its identity, becoming not much more than a corridor for the steadily growing deluge of North–South European traffic. Its 280,000 inhabitants, plus the additional few thousand even more neglected Italian-speakers in the valleys of Canton Graubünden, are a small minority who increasingly find the prevailing languages in their urban centres to be *Schwyzertütsch* (Swiss-German) and English. Lurati argues that while Italian is, according to the Swiss constitution, one of the four national languages, in reality it is at most half a language – the discrimination against Italian in favour of English as the second foreign language in the secondary schools of German- and French-speaking Switzerland is just one example of the marginalization of Italian. Lurati calls for concrete measures to halt the creeping Germanization of Canton Ticino. For a study of the dialects in the Italian-speaking regions see *Dialetto & italiano regionale nella Svizzera Italiana* (Dialect and regional Italian in Italian Switzerland) by the same author (Lugano: Banca Solari & Blum, 1976).

314 **Dialect and High German in German-speaking Switzerland.**
Alfred Wyler, translated from the German by Maureen Oberli-Turner. Zurich: Pro Helvetia, 1989. 43p. bibliog.

Swiss-German is not a single language but consists of a number of dialects differing from one another in vocabulary, pronunciation, and intonation. 'Schwyzertütsch' as it is called, is spoken in eastern, central and north-western Switzerland by about 68% of the population. All children from Swiss-German-speaking areas learn standard German in the first years in school. With some training, this standard written form differs little from High German, while the spoken form retains the local colouring of the speaker – the Swiss do not want to sound like Germans. Even though they may feel uncomfortable in the presence of a native German, the Swiss make little effort to hide the characteristic patterns of intonation typical of the dialect when speaking High German. In other cultures use of the dialect may show the social and educational level of the speaker; not so in Switzerland. Only in schools, on official occasions or when speakers from other language areas are present is High German, or what the Swiss call 'Schriftdeutsch' (written German) used in oral communication. The recent trend to increased use of the dialect in schools, church, and the media is welcomed by some and frowned upon by others for various reasons. Wyler gives a brief description of various dialects from different regions, traces some phonetic changes from Middle High German to Swiss-German, and shows differences in inflection and vocabulary between the two languages. He ends with a brief history of the development of the Swiss-German dialects and their limited use in literature.

Religion

General

315 **Swiss churches in the twentieth century.**
Fritz Büsser. In: *Modern Switzerland*, edited by J. Murray Luck. Palo Alto, California: Society for the Promotion of Science and Scholarship, 1978, p. 381-402.

Büsser, professor of church and dogmatic history at the University of Zurich, provides an overview of the religious situation in Switzerland in the 20th century. Three statistical tables provide a numerical breakdown of the confessions in the cantons and major cities. The organization, structure, and activities of the Protestant and Catholic churches are described, as are, more briefly, those of smaller religious groups. In the last part of his compact presentation Büsser dwells on the efforts and the progress that have been made toward ecumenical cooperation between the churches, culminating in 1971 in the creation of a Working Group of Christian Churches in Switzerland (Arbeitsgemeinschaft Christlicher Kirchen in der Schweiz).

316 **Kirchengeschichte der Schweiz.** (Church history of Switzerland.)
Rudolf Pfister. Zurich: Zwingli Verlag vol. 1; Theologischer Verlag vols 2 & 3, 1964-84. 3 vols. bibliog.

The three volumes comprising this substantial church history cover the subject matter as follows: volume 1 (573p.), from about 180 AD to the early 16th century; volume 2 (756p.), 16th and 17th centuries; and volume 3 (499p.), from 1720 to 1950. Volumes 1 and 2 have portfolios of illustrations. Written by a Protestant theologian, this history clearly has as its focal point the development of the Protestant church since Zwingli. Nevertheless, the history of the Catholic church is not neglected, for, as the author points out, the two confessions do not exist apart from, but rather with, one another. Pfister's work demonstrates the importance of religion in Swiss history.

The Catholic tradition

317 **Hans Küng: his work and his way.**
Edited by Hermann Häring, Karl-Josef Kuschel, translated from the German by Robert Nowell. London: Collins Fount Paperbacks, 1979. 252p. bibliog.

Hans Küng was born in 1928 in Sursee, Canton Luzern. After his training for the priesthood in Rome he went to Paris where he earned a doctorate of theology at the Sorbonne with a dissertation on his Protestant compatriot, Karl Barth. Küng went on to become one of the most important and controversial Catholic theologians of the second half of the 20th century. This book is a tribute to Küng by two of his former students and associates at the Institute for Ecumenical Research at the University of Tübingen. A chronological summary provides access to the significant dates in Küng's life and to the sequence of events that led to his conflict with Rome. The bulk of the book consists of a collection of essays by contemporaries of Küng and by Küng himself on key elements of his theology, designed to provide an introduction to his major writings. This section is followed by a fifty-page-long interview of Küng by the two editors in which he is given the opportunity to 'speak on questions connected with his development, on the background to his work, and on how he sees himself both as a theologian and as a member of the Church'. A bibliography of Küng's published works 1955-78, compiled by Margret Gentner, completes the book. The bibliography consists of 219 titles, not counting the many translations of his works (which are also listed), and some sixty published interviews.

318 **Helvetia Sacra.** (Holy Switzerland.)
Published by the Kuratorium of Helvetia Sacra. Bern: Francke; Basel; Frankfurt, FRG: Helbing & Lichtenhahn, 1972- . bibliog.

This is an ongoing historical project of major proportions that makes systematic inventories of the ecclesiastical institutions of Switzerland: bishoprics, abbeys, and monasteries. The work is tentatively organized into nine parts: (1) Swiss cardinals, apostolic envoys in Switzerland, archdioceses, and dioceses; (2) collegiate convents; (3) the Benedictine order and its relatives; (4) the orders of the Augustinian rule; (5) the Franciscan order; (6) the Carmelites; (7) the regular clergy: Jesuits and Somascans; (8) the congregations; (9) order-like associations. Each part has a varying number of volumes of differing lengths, for teams of researchers have sifted all available archival and printed materials to reconstruct the history of their subjects. The bulk of each volume consists of the factual description of the changing composition and organization of the particular religious body through the centuries and of the innumerable biographies of the individuals who had leadership positions in their organizations and institutions. Extensive bibliographies accompany the volumes.

319 **Schweizer Katholizismus. Eine Geschichte der Jahre 1925-1975: Zwischen Ghetto und konziliarer Öffnung.** (Swiss Catholicism. A history of the years 1925-75: between ghetto and conciliar opening.)
Alfred Stoecklin. Zurich [etc.]: Benziger, 1978. 359p. bibliog.

Swiss Catholicism approached World War II within the spiritual and ideological framework of the First Vatican Council (1869-70). It lived in a largely self-constructed ghetto, but Stoecklin emphasizes that, even though a monolithic church was the declared goal of some influential leaders, the reality of the religious-cultural activities of the Catholics showed a strongly federalistic diversity in the twenty-five cantons of the Confederation. After World War II the ideologically fixed posture of the Church began to soften. The Second Vatican Council (1962-65) provided the impetus for a revival of the internal dialogue among the practising Catholics in the Swiss dioceses through the synodal movement and for subsequent increased contacts with the Swiss Protestants as part of the ecumenical movement. The Swiss Catholic Church today is a vastly different institution from what it was fifty years ago.

320 **Zeitschrift für schweizerische Kirchengeschichte.** (Journal for Swiss church history.)
Fribourg, Switzerland: Paulusverlag. annual. ca. 275p.

Published by the Association for Swiss Church History and edited by Urs Altermatt, professor at the University of Fribourg, this journal contains scholarly articles and reviews that represent the Catholic approach to church history.

Protestantism: general

321 **Reformatio: Evangelische Zeitschrift für Kultur, Politik, Kirche.** (Reformatio: evangelical journal for culture, politics, church.)
Bern: Benteli, 1952- . bimonthly. ca. 80p. per issue.

Published by the Reformatio Society, Zurich, this journal contains articles dealing with current public, ethical and human rights issues from a religious, Protestant perspective.

322 **Handbuch der reformierten Schweiz.** (Handbook of Reformed Switzerland.)
Edited by the Schweizerischer Protestantischer Volksbund. Zurich: EVZ, 1962. 573p. bibliog.

This handbook provides factual information on everything concerning evangelical-reformed Switzerland. Written by different authors and often containing bibliographies, the articles treat many subjects, including the cantonal branch churches of the Swiss Evangelical Federation of Churches; the services provided by the church, theological training at the universities and ther institutions; the activities of the church in the fields of mission, care for the sick and elderly, education, youth organizations, and outreach to the modern human being; the role of the church in politics, the arts, the media, and sports; church organizations; and the relationship of the Reformed Church with other religious groups. The volume has a chronology of the history of Reformed Switzerland, a list of all the Protestant church buildings and assembly halls (with their seating capacities), and two indexes.

Protestant reformers and theologians: from Zwingli to Brunner

323 **Zwingli and Bullinger.**
Edited by G. W. Bromiley. London: SCM Press; Philadelphia: Westminster, 1953. 364p. bibliog.

This volume in the Library of Christian Classics contains the English texts of five works by Zwingli (1484-1531) and one by his successor, Heinrich Bullinger (1504-75). In his introduction Bromiley provides a substantial biography of Zwingli and a description and critique of his personality and work, as well as a shorter sketch of Bullinger's life and work. The works included, *Of the clarity and certainty of the word of God*, *Of the education of youth*, *Of baptism*, *On the Lord's supper*, and *An exposition of the faith* by Zwingli and *Of the holy catholic Church* by Bullinger, are the texts of sermons and disputational writings and explain the doctrinal positions of the two Zurich reformers. In some instances old translations have been adopted, but wherever necessary, new ones have been made. Bromiley provides welcome guidance to the treatises by introducing each with a scholarly description of its historical context and an analysis of its major points. Still further information is found in the annotated notes to the texts. Other English translations of Zwingli works are *Selected works of Huldreich Zwingli*, edited by S. M. Jackson (Philadelphia, 1901, reprinted 1972); *The Latin works of Huldreich Zwingli*, edited by S. M. Jackson and others (3 vols., New York, 1912, and Philadelphia, 1922 and 1929; vol. 2 reprinted as *Zwingli on providence and other essays*, Durham, North Carolina, 1983; vol. 3 reprinted as *Commentary on true and false religion*, Durham, North Carolina, 1981).

324 **Zwingli, a reformed theologian.**
Jaques Courvoisier. Richmond, Virginia: John Knox Press, 1963. 101p. bibliog.

The five chapters of this small book contain the text of the Annie Kinkead Warfield Lectures which Courvoisier, then professor of theology at the University of Geneva, delivered at Princeton Theological Seminary in 1961. Entitled 'the word of God', 'the Christological axis', 'the church', 'the sacraments', and 'church and state', they are in effect introductory outlines of various themes and aspects of Zwingli's theology.

325 **Zwingli the reformer: his life and work.**
Oskar Farner, translated from the German by D. G. Sear. Hamden, Connecticut: Archon, 1968. 135p.

Farner paints a short and very readable portrait of the peasant turned reformer, Huldrych Zwingli. Numerous quotes from Zwingli's sermons illustrate the powerful language the preacher commanded to wipe out the evils among the citizenry of Zurich. His reform movement had the backing of the state. The Anabaptists, his most difficult adversaries, spoke against this church–state union and infant baptism. Zwingli's disagreement with Martin Luther revolved around the interpretation of the Lord's Supper which he did not take literally. The Bible was at the heart of his faith and his preaching, and he contributed to its dissemination through his translation, known as the Zurich Bible. A devoted husband and father and a good citizen, Zwingli died aged forty-seven on the battlefield at Kappel.

326 **Huldrych Zwingli im 20. Jahrhundert. Forschungsbericht und annotierte Bibliographie.** (Huldrych Zwingli in the 20th century: research report and annotated bibliography.)
Ulrich Gäbler. Zurich: Theologischer Verlag, 1975. 473p.

In a first part Gäbler provides a critical review of 20th-century Swiss and international Zwingli research. The second part is a descriptive bibliography of the literature by and about Zwingli from 1897 to 1972. The bibliography lists chronologically by year of publication 1,679 titles of editions of Zwingli works, monographs, and journal and newspaper articles. Four indexes facilitate the use of the bibliography.

327 **Huldrych Zwingli: his life and work.**
Ulrich Gäbler, translated from the German by Ruth C. L. Gritsch. Philadelphia: Fortress, 1986. 196p. bibliog.

Gäbler's is an excellent short biography of Zwingli in which a thorough knowledge of the entire range of Zwingli literature is coupled with an easy, readable style and presentation. The book begins with a chapter on the historical environment of the Swiss Confederation at the beginning of the 16th century and ends with one on Zwingli's historical impact. In between Gäbler tells the story of Zwingli's life in eight chapters from his childhood in Wildhaus in Toggenburg to his death in 1531 on the battlefield in Kappel. Zwingli's intellectual and spiritual growth is described through the analysis of his writings and in its interaction with the communities in which he was active, first and foremost among them Zurich. In addition to an annotated 'bibliographical survey' at the end of the book, there are separate bibliographies after each chapter. A bibliography with 1,619 titles can be found in *A Zwingli bibliography* by H. Wayne Pipkin (Pittsburgh, Pennsylvania: Clifford E. Barbour Library, Pittsburgh Theological Seminary, 1972).

328 **Zwingli's thought: new perspectives.**
Gottfried W. Locher, translated from the German by Milton Aylor, Stuart Casson, Duncan Shaw. Leiden, The Netherlands: Brill, 1981. 394p. bibliog. (Studies in the History of Christian Thought, 25).

This is a collection of fifteen articles of varying length which Locher presented as papers and lectures to international audiences between 1952 and 1979. Almost all of them have been previously published in German-language theological journals. They treat a wide spectrum of topics concerning major aspects of the theology of Huldrych Zwingli, the relationship of his thought to that of other 16th-century religious and humanistic figures, and the impact of his life and work in various parts of Europe. The fifteenth paper of this collection, 'Zwingli's influence in England and Scotland' (p. 340-83), is especially noteworthy. In it Locher not only analyses the reasons why Zwingli is a neglected figure in British religious history but offers suggestions – with a preliminary list of findings – as to why the problem should and how it might be remedied. Like all the other articles this one is carefully documented with extensive annotated footnotes, and in addition it has its own substantial bibliography.

329 **Zwingli.**
G. R. Potter. Cambridge, England [etc.]: Cambridge University Press, 1976. 432p.

This is one of the best one-volume biographies on the great Swiss humanist and reformer Huldrych Zwingli. As the extensive footnotes with their comprehensive bibliographical information show, Potter is thoroughly familiar with archival and secondary sources and thus able to write an authoritative account of Zwingli's life and achievements. Zwingli came to his reformist activities in Zurich through his training as a humanist. His evangelical message was not only approved by the Zurich town council, but also convinced the magistrates of Bern and Basel to reform their churches – the peasant cantons of central Switzerland, however, did not deviate from their loyalty to Rome. Zwingli was challenged also from inside his home base by the disruptive movement of the Anabaptists or Swiss Brethren. In his meeting with Martin Luther in Marburg in October 1529, Zwingli disagreed with his German counterpart on the interpretation of the meaning of the Lord's Supper, a fact that had major religio-political consequences, for the Swiss Reformation and the cantons supporting it would remain permanently separate from their northern neighbour. Potter has also published a representative selection from Zwingli's writings in the series 'Documents of Modern History' under the title *Huldrych Zwingli* (London: Arnold; New York: St. Martin's Press, 1977).

330 **The theology of Huldrych Zwingli.**

W. P. Stephens. Oxford: Clarendon Press, 1986. 348p. bibliog.

Zwingli's thought developed in the context of late medieval scholasticism and Erasmian humanism as well as in the context of Swiss life and society, theological conflict, practical reform, and the serious and scholarly study of the scriptures. Stephens takes these and other factors into account in his illuminating study of Zwingli's theology. The Swiss reformer is seen on his own terms; he was a reformer in his own right, not a variant of Luther. Stephens deplores the fact that the modern critical edition of Zwingli's works is still incomplete which, even though he used all of Zwingli's writings, makes his work only 'provisional'. However, in his chapters on the bible, God, Christ, the Holy Spirit, man, salvation, the word, the sacraments, baptism, the eucharist, the church and the ministry, and the state Stephens displays a thorough historical and theological knowledge and understanding of Zwingli and his work. *Zwingli, a reformed theologian*, by Jaques Courvoisier (Richmond, Virginia: John Knox Press, 1963) is also of interest (q.v.).

331 **Heinrich Bullinger and the covenant: the other Reformed tradition.**

J. Wayne Baker. Athens, Ohio: Ohio University Press, 1980. 300p. bibliog.

Heinrich Bullinger (1504-75) ministered to the needs of Zurich as preacher, pastor, teacher, and author for more than forty years after Zwingli's death on the battlefield at Kappel. But he was more than just Zwingli's successor in Zurich . . . a prolific writer who published a total of 119 works and whose extant correspondence numbers more than 12,000 pieces, Bullinger had contacts with prominent ecclesiastical and political leaders in many parts of Europe. He used his renown and influence in the pursuit of his lifelong goal of achieving agreement and cooperation among the Reformed churches, an endeavour which culminated in the acceptance of the Second Helvetic Confession (1566), a comprehensive statement of the Reformed faith, by the Reformed churches of Switzerland, including Geneva, Germany, France, Eastern Europe, England, Scotland, and Holland. However, differences with the Genevans, as well as the Anabaptists and the Lutherans, continued to exist over Bullinger's view of the covenant and Christian society. Baker analyses with scholarly care the involved theological problem of the meaning of the covenant, God's agreement with man and man's obligations toward God, as interpreted by Bullinger. Baker sets off Bullinger's view of a bilateral covenant against Calvin's teaching on predestination and concludes that it constitutes 'the other Reformed tradition' which influenced not only Reformed theology but also political theories in the late 16th and 17th centuries.

332 **Heinrich Bullinger.**

Robert C. Walton. In: *Shapers of religious traditions in Germany, Switzerland, and Poland, 1560-1600*, edited by Jill Raitt. New Haven, Connecticut; London: Yale University Press, 1981, p. 69-87. bibliog.

In a short first part Walton provides a brief biography of Bullinger, but the bulk of the chapter is devoted to a learned disquisition of Bullinger's theology. In an assessment of his role in the church, Walton tries to answer the puzzling question why Bullinger, who 'in his own day was among the most important Protestant theologians in Europe', is not better remembered. He offers as an explanation that Bullinger 'had been unlucky' in that 'like Erasmus, he suffered the fate of moderate men of his day' and was 'eclipsed by more fanatic friends and supporters. . . .'.

333 **John Calvin: a sixteenth-century portrait.**

William J. Bouwsma. New York [etc.]: Oxford University Press, 1988. 310p. bibliog.

Bouwsma's intention is to revive the historical Calvin (1509-64) who, for a number of reasons, is 'now one of the least known among the great figures of his century'. The Calvin known today is 'chiefly an artifact of later Calvinism'. In this book Bouwsma interprets Calvin as a figure of his time: 'a representative French intellectual, an evangelical humanist, and an exile'. Calvin felt isolated in Geneva and was frustrated by the constant resistance to his policies; he was plagued by tensions and conflicts within himself, created by a variety of anxieties; and he was driven by the fear of the imminence of divine punishment for the evils of human wickedness among people of all walks of life. These anxieties influenced his rhetoric and his dogmatics, but they were balanced, Bouwsma finds, by his Erasmian humanism in a flexible, pragmatic mixture of dogmatic reasoning and existential reality. The historical Calvin was both 'medieval' and 'modern', a true son of his century. By the 18th century Calvinism tended 'toward the polar extremes of evangelical pietism and deistic rationalism, both of which . . . can . . . plausibly claim Calvin as spiritual father'.

334 **A bibliography of Calviniana 1959-1974.**

Dionysius Kempff. Leiden, The Netherlands: Brill, 1975. 249p. (Studies in Medieval and Reformation Thought, 15).

This bibliography of works by Calvin and about Calvin and Calvinism lists items published since 1900. It has close to 4,000 titles. It continues and completes Wilhelm Niesel's *Calvin Bibliographie 1901-1959* (Munich, 1961) which contained 1,566 titles.

335 **A history of the Geneva Bible.**

Lewis Lupton. London: The Olive Tree, 1966-73. 5 vols.

Lupton tells the history of the origin of the Geneva Bible, the famous 16th-century Calvinistic French translation of the scriptures, in five volumes, entitled The Quarrel, Reform, Truth, Travail, and Vision. The first volume describes the beginnings of the project in Frankfurt; Geneva is at the centre of the other four. Lupton discusses the cultural and political climate that shaped the interpretation of the translators, most of whom were expatriates, among them John Knox from Scotland. The Genevan reformers were purists who sought to render a Bible text that was not tainted by any interpretation reflecting the thought of the medieval church, but their zeal made them intolerant, as was manifested by the burning of Servetus. Lupton explains how these controversies arose and how Calvin's mission, as he perceived it, led him and his followers to demand such harsh punishment. Lupton quotes numerous passages from the translated work, making a strong case for the extraordinary accomplishment and for the importance of the Geneva Bible.

336 **Calvin and the Reformation.**

James Mackinnon. New York: Russell & Russell, 1962. 302p.

Mackinnon maintains that Calvin cannot be discussed without reference to Erasmus, Luther, and Zwingli and without understanding the political climate of the time, especially in Geneva. Geneva had embraced the new faith and found in Calvin the mastermind who would make it the centre of the Reformation. With the help of the Genevan civil authorities, Calvin established the 'Rule of God' on earth, often in the face of strong opposition from individuals and citizen groups. His teachings on predestination and the election of the believers created controversy, and a critic of the doctrine of the trinity, Servetus, was burned in 1553 for his heresy. Calvin's doctrines eventually spread to many parts of Europe. Mackinnon gives a thorough account and evaluation of the reformer's work and theology.

337 **Calvin: the origins and development of his religious thought.**

François Wendel, translated from the French by Philip Mairet. Durham, North Carolina: Labyrinth, 1987. 383p. bibliog.

This book was originally published in 1950 by Presses Universitaires de France. In the first part Wendel, former dean of the Protestant Faculty of Theology at the University of Strasbourg, provides a biographical outline of Calvin's life in the context of the political and intellectual currents of the era of the Reformation. The second part deals with Calvin's theological teachings. The Christian Church fathers, as well as the French humanists and his predecessors Luther and Zwingli are among the many influences that shaped Calvin's theology. Wendel analyses Calvin's writings, especially his chief work, the *Institutes of the Christian Religion*, as part of the ferment of religious and secular thought which he helped to form. Wendel sums up his high opinion of Calvin by saying: 'It was because he was the founder of a powerfully organized Church and at the same time the author of a body of doctrine which was able to rally around it the intellectual elite as well as the mass of the faithful, that Calvin made such a mark upon his age and, even beyond it, exercises an influence which does not yet seem likely to decline.'

338 **Theodore Beza.**

Jill Raitt. In: *Shapers of religious traditions in Germany, Switzerland, and Poland, 1560-1600*, edited by Jill Raitt. New Haven, Connecticut; London: Yale University Press, 1981, p. 89-104.

Raitt's brief chapter provides a convenient description of the life, theology, and significance of the reformer Theodore Beza (1519-1605). The French-born and -educated humanist and lawyer came to Geneva in 1548 after he had converted to Protestantism. Since there was no employment for him in Geneva at the time, he accepted an invitation to the Academy at Lausanne where he taught Greek and served a turn as rector. He travelled frequently to France and Germany on diplomatic missions on behalf of the French Protestants, and from 1559 on he worked in Geneva, as Calvin's associate and first rector of the newly founded Academy, where he served as the only regular professor of theology till late in his life. Designated by Calvin as his successor, Beza held the post of 'Moderator of the Venerable Company of Pastors' from 1564 to 1580. In that capacity he was involved in continual mediation between city magistrates and pastors. In his theology he adhered basically to Calvin's teachings.

He lent his support to Bullinger's Second Helvetic Confession and thus made an important contribution to the maintenance of harmony among the Reformed and Calvinistic Protestants. The foremost pastor and theologian of Geneva from 1564 to 1599, Beza 'was a primary shaper of the Reformed tradition'.

339 **Christian faith and public choices: the social ethics of Barth, Brunner, and Bonhoeffer.**

Robert W. Lovin. Philadelphia: Fortress, 1984. 183p. bibliog.

Karl Barth (1886-1968) of Basel and Emil Brunner (1889-1966) of Zurich were two of the most influential 20th-century Protestant theologians. Lovin analyses their theology and teaching for their ethical content against the historical background of the crisis years of the 1920s and 1930s. Both believed that the theology and ethics of the preceding generation were inadequate to meet the demands of their time. They set out on a common path toward renewal but soon parted ways and spent some of their energies in the sometimes bitter 'Barth–Brunner debate'. For Barth, the meaning of good can be established only by the will of God, thus preventing humans from deifying their own choices, yet providing no ethical guidance for making choices. Lovin concludes that 'for all its theological integrity, Barth's position is impossible for public ethics'. At a personal level, however, Barth made clear choices, as is exemplified by the Barmen Declaration of the German Confessing Church of May 1934, which, drafted by him, put the church in bold opposition to the totalitarian régime created by Hitler. Here at last, Lovin comments, was 'a working version of the ethic of the Word of God'. Brunner, even though he too believed that the meaning of moral terms is tied to the will of God, maintained that this will had to be interpreted in a way that fits the needs of human choice and action. He was a theological realist whose message of 'critical cooperation' calls for the union of faith and reason.

340 **Politics and Protestant theology: an interpretation of Tillich, Barth, Bonhoeffer, and Brunner.**

René de Visme Williamson. Baton Rouge, Louisiana: Louisiana State University Press, 1976. 180p. bibliog.

Karl Barth and Emil Brunner are two of the leading twentieth-century theologians of Protestantism. In this book Williamson analyses their voluminous writings for their political content. He concludes that Barth defies classification as a conservative or a liberal, either theologically or politically. He takes him to task for what he characterizes as Barth's unrealistic anti-intellectual attitude that has no room for the power of ideas, since 'as men believe, so they will act, whatever circumstances and conditions may have led them to believe what they do'. Williamson labels Brunner's political thought moderate and conservative. It makes it possible for Christians and non-Christians to be partners 'without one's giving up the unique claim of Christianity or getting mired down in religious eclecticism'. Williamson lists the major works of Barth and Brunner, all of which are available in English translations.

341 **Karl Barth: his life from letters and autobiographical texts.**

Eberhard Busch, translated from the German by John Bowden.

London: SCM Press; Philadelphia: Fortress, 1976. 569p. bibliog. maps.

This is an authoritative biography of the great twentieth-century Swiss theologian Karl Barth (1886-1968) by his last assistant. Busch describes Barth's life whenever possible in Barth's own words from his published works and unpublished materials in the Barth archives in Basel and records of conversations with various groups, and so the work reads in many parts like an autobiography. Busch himself contributes the informed commentary that holds the story together and provides summaries of Barth's theological writings. He also uses 103 photographs, many of them previously unpublished, to show Barth's circle of family, friends, and co-workers. Busch's bibliography indicates that most of Barth's many works have been published in English translations, including the monumental *Church dogmatics* (Edinburgh: Clark; New York: Scribner, 1936-69, 1975. 4 vols in 12 parts. German original *Die Kirchliche Dogmatik*, 1932-55). A shorter biography, *Karl Barth* by David L. Mueller, is available in the Makers of the Modern Theological Mind series (Waco, Texas: Word Books, 1972). Interest in Barth and his theology seems to remain unabated, as evidenced by recent books such as *Karl Barth: studies of his theological method*, edited by S. W. Sykes (Oxford, England: Clarendon Press, 1979) and *Karl Barth: a theological legacy* by Eberhard Jüngel (Philadelphia, Pennsylvania: Westminster, 1986).

342 **Portrait of Karl Barth.**

George Casalis, translated from the German and introduced by Robert McAfee Brown. Westport, Connecticut: Greenwood, 1981. 130p. bibliog. (First edition Garden City, New York: Doubleday, 1963).

The book is divided into three parts. Part one is an introduction which, written shortly after Barth's only visit to the United States, addresses criticisms and questions Americans raised concerning Barth's theology. Part two sheds light on the events and personal contacts that shaped Barth's life, especially during his years in Germany – his political involvement and resistance to the Nazis eventually forced him to leave the country. Part three provides an analysis of the work of the person whom Brown calls one of the greatest theologians of all times. For Barth, Christ is the all-important manifestation of God's love and grace, the centre, the beginning, and the end. 'Man is unworthy, nevertheless God elects him.' Barth's multi-volume *Church dogmatics*, as well as his other writings, are based on his reading of the Bible, the word of God, which has priority over everything, including the Church.

343 **The theology of Emil Brunner.**

Edited by Charles W. Kegley. New York: Macmillan, 1962. 395p. bibliog. (Library of Living Theology, 3).

Kegley's introduction to this volume of interpretative essays describes Brunner's life work as 'one of the two or three finest comprehensive theological efforts of our century'. It is characterized by a balance and judiciousness that is free from the right and left extremes of modern theology and philosophy of religion. The volume opens with the 'intellectual autobiography' of Emil Brunner (1889-1966) in which Brunner describes the persons, forces, and ideas that influenced him and his work from early childhood to his years of maturity as professor of systematic and practical theology at the University of Zurich. The bulk of the book is made up of essays of interpretation and criticism of the work of Emil Brunner by seventeen theologians, philosophers, and churchmen. Brunner then offers brief replies to these essays, clarifying and amplifying his position in response to the questions and issues raised by his contemporaries. The volume concludes with a bibliography of Brunner's works, listed chronologically from 1914 to 1962. Ninety-five numbered entries indicate works that have been translated into English. These and the list of 'main publications of Emil Brunner in English' attest to the fact that Brunner was one of the most widely published and thus, presumably, most influential Protestant theologians in the English-speaking world in the 20th century.

Protestantism: the Anabaptists

344 **Conrad Grebel, c.1498-1526: the founder of the Swiss Brethren, sometimes called Anabaptists.**

Harold S. Bender. Goshen College, Goshen, Indiana: Mennonite Historical Society, 1950. 326p. bibliog.

This is a carefully researched scholarly study of Conrad Grebel's life, thought, and influence. Grebel lived less than thirty years and left few writings, except for some seventy letters, most of which were addressed to Vadian (Joachim von Watt), Grebel's brother-in-law and reformer of St Gallen. From this scant historical record, Bender reconstructs Grebel's life as the son of a Zurich patrician family, a student in Basel, Vienna, and Paris, and a young adult who under the influence of Zwingli in Zurich became a convert to the new, reformed faith. Bender then shows how Grebel almost immediately moved beyond Zwingli's reforms and became the centre of a small group of 'brethren' whose belief in adult baptism and pacifism attracted the wrath of the authorities and led to his and his fellow-believers' persecution. Grebel's early death away from Zurich, the date and cause of which are not known, saved him from the fate of having to suffer a martyr's death, as happened to his brother-in-Christ, Felix Manz, who was drowned in the Limmat river in January 1527. Bender sees Grebel's historical significance in the fact that he was instrumental in creating the movement of evangelical discipleship, the Swiss Brethren, which, under various names and in different guises, spread to many other parts of Europe and, eventually, to North America.

345 **History of the Anabaptists in Switzerland.**

Henry Sweetser Burrage. Philadelphia: American Baptist Publication Society, 1882. 231p.

Anabaptism originated in Switzerland and spread through many parts of Germany and the Netherlands. The Anabaptists refused to acknowledge the union of state and church advocated by the Protestant Reformers and practised the re-baptism of believing adults. Burrage describes the vilifications and persecutions of the Swiss Anabaptists during the 1520s: most disciples were persecuted to differing degrees by local governments, while one of the harshest punishments was the drowning of leader Felix Manz in Zwinglian Zurich. The imperial edict of 1529 decreed that Anabaptists be put to death, and together with other repressive measures, this edict subdued the movement in the Holy Roman Empire. The brethren dispersed, upholding their beliefs and continuing their struggle and heroic suffering in other parts of Europe. Research on the Anabaptists has burgeoned in recent decades, especially in the United States. William R. Estep's *The Anabaptist story* (Grand Rapids, Michigan: Eerdmans, revised edition, 1975) and Claus-Peter Clasen's *Anabaptism, a social history, 1525-1618: Switzerland, Austria, Moravia, South and Central Germany* (Ithaca, New York; London: Cornell University Press, 1972) are examples of scholarly works based on research in the archival sources and use of secondary materials that put the Swiss Anabaptist movement in the wider context of European religious history of the 16th century. Both books have detailed bibliographies.

346 **The Radical reformation.**
George Huntston Williams. London: Weidenfeld and Nicolson, 1962. 924p. map. bibliog.

The Radical reformation of the Anabaptists, Spritualists, Evangelical Rationalists, and others took place concurrently with the Protestant and the Catholic reformations of the 16th century. The Radical or left-wing reformers rebelled not only against the Church of Rome but also against the Protestant reformers and as a consequence incurred the enmity of both. Williams, formerly Winn Professor of Ecclesiastical History at Harvard University, provides a detailed history of the Radical movement. It began in Switzerland with the organization of the first Anabaptist convention in 1525 and spread to many other parts of Europe. By 1575 the movement had hardened into sects that continue to exert strong influence in religion and politics to the present day. Williams treats the disparate groups synoptically, with due attention to the personalities and the fate of the protagonists. Five of the thirty-two chapters deal specifically with the Swiss Radicals.

The Jews in Switzerland

347 **Juden in der Schweiz: Glaube, Geschichte, Gegenwart.** (Jews in Switzerland: faith, history, present.)
Florence Guggenheim-Grünberg, Ralph Weingarten, Willy Guggenheim, Jakob Teichmann. Küsnacht, Switzerland: edition kürz, 1983. 2nd ed. 160p. maps. bibliog.

The first three chapters of this book provide a historical background of the lives of the Jews in Switzerland from the 6th century to the end of World War II. They tell of rampant discrimination in all domains of life, wherever Jews were allowed to settle, and of the struggle to hold on to the old values and customs while fighting for emancipation and equal rights. The number of Jews living in Switzerland grew to 20,000 by 1914 and has remained stable since. Their emancipation finally came in 1866, but there were still residues of discrimination, such as federal laws about the slaughter of animals which did not conform to Jewish laws, and the persistent anti-semitism of some individuals and groups. Nevertheless, the Jews prospered in the relatively free environment of Switzerland after 1866. The arrival of persecuted Jews from the East and the anti-semitic wave that swept through Europe during World War II burdened the small Swiss Jewish community with new and difficult problems. Most recently the Jewish community in the diaspora has been put on the defensive by the creation of the Jewish state and its policies toward the Palestinians. A last chapter explains some Jewish rituals and symbols, the Jewish calendar, and the significance of the role of the Hebrew language in the Jewish faith.

348 **Geschichte der Juden in der Schweiz. Vom 16. Jahrhundert bis nach der Emanzipation.** (History of the Jews in Switzerland: from the 16th century until after the emancipation.)
Augusta Weldler-Steinberg, Florence Guggenheim-Grünberg.
Zurich: Schweizerischer Israelitischer Gemeindebund, 1966-70. 2 vols. bibliog.

During the Middle Ages numerous Jews lived in the towns of what is today Switzerland. Driven away in the course of the 15th century, Jewish families survived only in the countryside, and almost exclusively in a few villages of the Aargau. The first volume of this work picks up the story in the middle of the 17th century when, after the Thirty Years' War, the 'Jewish villages' of Lengnau and Endingen came into existence – they were for two centuries the ghetto and sole location of Jewish community life in Switzerland. Elsewhere in the Confederation individual Jews were admitted or ejected on the whim of the authorities. The second volume describes the struggle for emancipation under the constitution of 1848, at times with the support of representatives of foreign powers in Switzerland, and the tortuous path in the various cantons toward equal rights and respect for Jewish customs. Both volumes are illustrated.

Society

General

349 **The status of women in society and law.**
Margrit Baumann, Marlies Näf-Hofmann. In: *Modern Switzerland*, edited by J. Murray Luck. Palo Alto, California: Society for the Promotion of Science and Scholarship, 1978, p. 361-79. bibliog.

This is a two-part article. The first part, written by Baumann, deals with the status of women in Swiss society and the second, by Näf-Hofmann, with the status of women according to Swiss civil law. Both authors stress the fact that recent years have brought many changes in the status of women and that 'social conventions are subject to a fast-paced transition'. The concern of Baumann that her sketch, which attempted to describe the situation as it existed in the middle 1970s, 'might no longer be valid tomorrow' was indeed justified, as major changes in recent years in the Swiss civil code have modified the laws on marriage and divorce in important respects. See also the article by Vreni Spoerry-Toneatti.

350 **Wohlstand und Armut in der Schweiz. Eine empirische Analyse für 1982.** (Wealth and poverty in Switzerland: an empirical analysis for 1982.)
Brigitte I. Buhmann. Grüsch, Switzerland: Rüegger, 1988. 328p. bibliog. (Basler sozialökonomische Studien, 32).

This dissertation has many tables and diagrams, and much of it deals with methodology, terminology, and the description of tools for measuring and collecting data. The definition of poverty is a threshold problem, and Buhmann rightfully says that it is basically a political decision. The Swiss conference on public welfare, for example, recommended that 8,936 Swiss francs of personal income constitute the lower limit, while the law for the regulation for supplementary payments from the old-age and invalid insurance (AHV/IV) sets it at 13,900 Swiss francs. Depending on the measure, either 3.2% or 11.4% of Switzerland's population live in poverty, i.e. 200,000 or 750,000 people, not counting students and seasonal workers. Other results of the multi-faceted study show that fully employed women earn 7.2% less than men, but only about 6 to 7% of the salary differential can be attributed to discrimination. Private households in Switzerland enjoy a very high level of wealth in comparison with other developed countries; but the wealth is unevenly distributed. The results of Buhmann's investigation are based on a sample of 6,055 Swiss and 981 foreigners living in Switzerland in 1982. Practically no differences in income and wealth were found between Swiss and foreign residents.

351 **Cities with little crime: the case of Switzerland.**
Marshall B. Clinard. Cambridge, England [etc.]: Cambridge University Press, 1978. 208p. bibliog.

Clinard's comparative study finds that cities in Switzerland have a considerably lower crime rate than many cities in other highly urbanized, affluent countries such as Sweden, the United States, and the Federal Republic of Germany. Clinard studied trends in official crime statistics; Swiss police and crime reporting; victimization in Switzerland's largest city, Zurich, measured by theft insurance; white-collar crime and tax violations; political decentralization and the criminal justice system; youth and Swiss society; and crime and the foreign worker. He presents his conclusions in the final chapter on cross-cultural implications of the low Swiss crime rate. Eleven tables in the text and ten appendices provide the statistical data relied on by Clinard.

352 **Die Stellung der Frau in der Schweiz.** (The position of women in Switzerland.)
Eidgenössische Kommission für Frauenfragen. Bern: Bundeskanzlei. First series of reports in four parts, 1979-84. Additional reports 1985, 1987, and 1988. bibliog.

This is a series of book-length reports by different authors produced under the direction of the Federal Commission on Women's Issues. Part I of the first series is entitled *Gesellschaft und Wirtschaft* (Society and economy, 1979). Part II, as its title indicates, deals with *Biographien und Rollennorm* (Biographies and role models, 1982). Part III, *Recht* (Law, 1980) describes the discrepancies in the treatment of men and women under Swiss federal law. Part IV is entitled *Frauenpolitik* (Women's politics, 1984). Two of the additional reports *Die Sonderschutzvorschriften für weibliche Arbeitnehmer in der Schweiz* (The special protective regulations for female workers in Switzerland, 1985) and *Auswirkungen neuer Techniken auf Frauenarbeitsplätze im Buero- und Verwaltungsbetrieb* (Effects of new technologies on women's office and administrative jobs, 1988) are more of a technical nature. The report *Frauen und Männer: Fakten, Perspektiven, Utopien* (Women and men: facts, perspectives, utopias, 1987) with its many tables, figures, and charts provides a convenient overview of the whole complex of issues addressed in these reports. The reports can be purchased individually from the EDMZ in Bern. They all have bibliographies.

353 **Values, trends and alternatives in Swiss society: a prospective analysis.**
Armin Gretler, Pierre-Emeric Mandl. New York [etc.]: Praeger, 1973. 241p. bibliog.

This book was undertaken at the Swiss Federal Institute of Technology in Zurich in order to develop an example (*Leitbild*) for town and country planning in Switzerland. Successful planning 'will be related to ethical, cultural, social, political, administrative, economic, aesthetic, and other factors', and 'the identification and comprehension of all these factors' is a 'prerequisite for a valid overall conception'. Gretler and Mandl present the results of that portion of the study (*Teilleitbild*) that deals with Swiss society. The subject area of society was divided into the sub-categories of demography; the labour force; the condition of women; the family; work and leisure; standards of living; property ownership; urbanization; types of housing and social relations; cantonal party systems and political participation; and external influences on the development of Switzerland, and worldwide interdependence. Each of these topics is given a chapter in which possible developments in the last decades of the 20th century are outlined. Seventy-eight tables provide statistical data of existing conditions, trends, and forecasts to, in some cases, the year 2040. This brief and interesting book manages to present a wealth of information about most aspects of Swiss society and digests many of the results of the vast literature generated by futurologists.

354 **Un modèle en crise: la Suisse.** (Switzerland: a model in crisis.)
Blaise Lempen. Lausanne: Payot, 1985. 175p.

Lempen, a journalist for the Lausanne daily newspaper *Le Matin*, analyses the profound changes he feels Swiss society has undergone in the last two decades, changes which have created a crisis that shakes the foundations of the Swiss system. Materialism is destroying the environment and the quality of life; democracy is being undermined by the growing complexities of social life which leads large numbers of citizens to withdraw from the political process thereby leaving decision-making in the hands of a small élite. A pervasive xenophobia is only one of several social ills; federalism is threatened by political and economic centralization. The catalogue goes on. Lempen knows that similar problems beset other industrialized societies, but he is hopeful that a new mentality will emerge to help the Swiss create a new societal model, for their own sake as well as for the well-being of other nations.

355 **The social structure of Switzerland: outline of a society.**
René Levy, translated from the German by R. Bandi. Zurich: Pro Helvetia, 1986. 3rd ed. 136p. bibliog.

This brief study deals with some of the most important aspects of the social structure of Switzerland. After a description of Switzerland's position and role in the international scene, Levy, who is senior lecturer in sociology at the University of Lausanne, provides an analysis of life and living conditions in Switzerland with attention to such factors as the material and spiritual standard of living, life patterns from childhood to old age, including family and work roles of both sexes, education, economic conditions, politics, and decision-making across the spectrum of society. Levy also describes 'the organisation of living conditions at the local, cantonal, and national levels', stressing differences that exist between urban and rural communities and rich and poor cantons. Finally, he assesses strengths and weaknesses of the system and what might be done to improve it. This panorama of the social and cultural diversity of Switzerland and the everyday problems of its inhabitants is an excellent, sober introduction to the complexity of Swiss society. The booklet is illustrated and has a number of charts, tables, and graphs, as well as a good bibliography of mainly German-language titles.

356 **Value change in the Swiss population.**
Ruth Meyer. *International Review of Sociology*, 2nd series, vol. 17, no. 1 (April 1981), p. 48-64.

This article is based on data collected through questionnaires in 1976. Meyer herself points out that her work can say only little about *changes* in values, and the result is that her presentation of perceived trends in Swiss social and political values is vague, at best. Some of the responses reflect interesting views on such matters as the Swiss democratic system and the military sub-system. Meyer concludes that value changes that have occurred in Switzerland are not the result of an 'erosion of bourgeois values' nor of a 'silent revolution', but rather are typical of the modernization of Western societies.

357 **Neue Lebensinhalte – neue Gesetze. Die Schweizerin heute.** (New life contents – new laws: the Swiss woman today.)
Vreni Spoerry-Toneatti. *Schweizer Monatshefte für Politik, Wirtschaft, Kultur* (Zurich), vol. 69, no. 5 (May 1989), p. 373-81.

In many respects Swiss society has changed fundamentally during the last century. This is even more true for women than for men. Major breakthroughs in the social and political position of women have occurred since the 1960s. The level of education of Swiss women has approached that of Swiss men, and a much higher percentage of women are trained for white-collar jobs than ever before. In 1971 Swiss women received the right to vote and to hold office at the federal level, and in 1981 the Swiss electorate approved an equal rights amendment to the constitution. In 1986 a new marriage law was adopted which established the principle of partnership between husband and wife. The role of mother and housewife has been given equal standing in law to that of breadwinner. Spoerry-Toneatti emphasizes that these changes were introduced through the slow and laborious system of Swiss participatory democracy. Needless to say, the mere enactment of these laws did not solve all the problems of the relationship between men and women in Swiss society. Nevertheless, under the law, the lot of women has improved dramatically.

358 **Geschichte der Frauenarbeit in Zürich.** (History of women in the workforce in Zurich.)
Emma Steiger. Zurich: Statistisches Amt der Stadt Zürich, 1964. 585p.

This is a documentation of the part women played in the workforce of Zurich in the first half of the twentieth century when the contributions of women began to gain recognition. The book is based mainly on studies released by the office of statistics of the city and on a questionnaire for mothers in Zurich 1957-58. Equal educational opportunities for all women, the shift from work on the family farms to salaried jobs, increased industrialization and specialization, changes in family structure and society led to the emergence of the modern woman. She is shown to fill every possible position, often holding down jobs formerly judged as not suited for females. Women who have distinguished themselves in a certain area, such as in the sciences or the arts, are portrayed in depth, together with a photograph. The author has an incredible wealth of information and the study is representative not only for the role of women in Zurich's labour force but that of the country as a whole. An index makes it simple to find information on any type of job filled by women or on contributions of individuals.

359 **Peasant wisdom: cultural adaptation in a Swiss village (Bruson).**
Daniela Weinberg. Berkeley, California; Los Angeles; London: University of California Press, 1975. 214p. map. bibliog.

This cultural-anthropological study examines the Swiss community of Bruson in Canton Valais. Bruson has a population of 250 people. Its economic base is dairy farming, fruit and vegetable production, and some tourism income from winter sports. Weinberg lived in the community for nineteen months, participated actively in its life, conducted interviews, and researched archives. In her detailed report, she compares the 'peasant wisdom' of its inhabitants, described as a common sense or traditional approach to life, favourably to the societal, economic, and cultural forces that are bringing change to Bruson.

Social problems

360 **Sozio-kulturelle Probleme der Eingliederung italienischer Arbeitskräfte in der Schweiz.** (Socio-cultural problems of the integration of Italian workers in Switzerland.)
Rudolf Braun. Zurich-Erlenbach: Eugen Rentsch, 1970. 589p. bibliog.

During the 1960s Italians constituted about two-thirds of the almost 700,000 foreign workers living in Switzerland. Braun studies the assimilation of Italian workers into the Swiss economy and society, and he has produced a masterpiece of sociological research and interpretation. In-depth interviews with Italians and Swiss living in four carefully selected Swiss communities furnish human-interest data on subjects such as the reasons for the emigration of the Italians; the working conditions and professional experiences they find in Switzerland; professional contacts and experiences of Swiss with Italian immigrants; living conditions and eating and consumer habits; adjustments to being away from home and to Swiss ways of socializing; and finally the efforts to learn each other's language to gain acceptance. The Italian workers and their families appear as real persons who express themselves freely and articulately on every conceivable aspect of their situation. Seventy-three tables and eight diagrams amplify and illustrate numerically the findings of the text. To avoid over-simplification, Braun refuses to condense the multi-faceted results of his careful and involved study. He stresses that the assimilation of the Italians is as much a problem of the Swiss as of the immigrants and admonishes his Swiss readers to think of their country as something that is 'becoming' rather than something that is finished.

361 **Kippel: a changing village in the Alps.**
John Friedl. New York: Holt, Rinehart and Winston, 1974. 129p. bibliog.

Kippel, the alpine village chosen for this study in cultural anthropology is located in the Lötschental, a side valley to the Rhône valley in the Upper Valais. In 1970, the village had 472 German-speaking and mostly Catholic residents, and Friedl investigated the social changes the community had undergone during the thirty years since World War II. Interviews, statistics, old photographs, and archival sources helped him to understand how this agrarian, isolated, and poor village slowly changed its character. The practices of the community regarding religion, marriage, inheritance, and communal governance had undergone little change for hundreds of years. After World War II, however, the men began to venture into the main valley in search of work – they became worker peasants, for tending the land became increasingly less attractive despite government subsidies which sought to encourage farming. Social security benefits, the building of hydroelectric plants, work in the new industries in the main valley, and the advent of tourism brought cash to the village and with it a change of lifestyle. Yet, traditions remain strong, prompting the villagers to tend their gardens, keep some animals, and hold on to their land. Consequently, Kippel retains some of its old charm while slowly embracing a more modern lifestyle.

362 **Im Schatten des Wohlstandes. Das ungelöste Altersproblem in der Schweiz.** (In the shadow of prosperity: the unsolved problem of old age in Switzerland.)

Alfred A. Häsler. Zurich: Ex Libris, 1971. 151p.

At the end of the 1960s 700,000 men and women in Switzerland were older than sixty-five, and 110,000 older than eighty. Häsler provides numbers and documentary reports which describe the way Swiss society cares for its senior citizens. He claims that tens of thousands live in dire poverty, dependent on the support of welfare institutions. Their housing is substandard and inadequate for people with physical disabilities, and many in need of care can find no place in old people's homes. Terrible loneliness is the fate of many, and Häsler advocates the integration of senior citizens into the community through the dispersal of their housing among the rest of the population. The State has to improve its services for the old people, but the key element for the betterment of the fate of the elderly is the concern of their fellow-citizens.

363 **'. . . und es kamen Menschen'. Ausländerpolitik und Fremdarbeit in der Schweiz 1914-1980.** ('. . . and people came': policies concerning foreigners and foreign workers in Switzerland 1914-80.)

Werner Haug. Basel: Z-Verlag, 1980. 138p.

Haug provides a critical appraisal of Swiss policies toward foreign workers, inspired by a feeling of solidarity with them. Foreign workers were an important component of the Swiss labour force long before World War I, but the war and the fear of international socialism led to the first discriminatory legislation during the interwar years. After World War II the Swiss labour market absorbed large numbers of foreign workers, now called 'guest' workers. The presence of more than one million aliens, 17.2 per cent of the total population of Switzerland in 1970, led to a popular nativist movement whose goal was to reduce this number drastically. An initiative to that effect was defeated in a national referendum by only a narrow margin. The economic crisis of 1974-76 eased the tension – within three years 35 per cent of the 551,000 employed aliens left the country, thereby relieving unemployment in Switzerland. Switzerland had exported the problem to the home countries of the guest workers. Haug predicts that world economic developments and political and social changes in Europe will force Switzerland to modify its foreign worker policies.

364 **Youth disturbances in Switzerland.**

Edited by the Swiss Cultural Foundation Pro Helvetia. Zurich: Pro Helvetia, 1981. 52p. bibliog.

This booklet presents the text of the 'Theses on the 1980 youth disturbances', drawn up by the Swiss Federal Advisory Commission for Youth Affairs in November 1980, and a commentary on these theses by Hans-Peter Fricker, a member of the commission. A fact-finding phase that included extensive conversations with young people who had been involved in the disturbances at the opera house in Zurich and in other places, was followed by a careful analysis of the collected materials. Based on its analysis, the commission recommended that conflicting interests be brought into the open. Furthermore, the commission concluded that while order was needed, the show of force for its own sake was counter-productive, that the young should be taken seriously and not patronized, and that existing policies were inconsistent and needed to be reappraised. The commission called for a forward-looking, flexible, and non-violent policy to deal with the grievances of the young. The theses found a surprisingly large number of readers; many more copies were sold than had been expected. See also *Der*

Aufstand der Söhne: Die Schweiz und ihre Unruhigen. Eine Untersuchung (The revolt of the sons: Switzerland and its restless ones, a study) by Alfred A. Häsler (Zurich: Ex Libris, 1969).

365 **Communalism and conflict in the Swiss Alps.**
Ellen Burdette Wiegandt. PhD dissertation, University of Michigan, 1977. 291p. maps. bibliog.

This dissertation in anthropology deals with the small community of Mase (population 249 in 1970) in the Val d'Hérens in Canton Valais. Data from local and cantonal archives and participant observations were tested against hypotheses about the linkages between demographic trends, economic status, and political power. The result of the careful statistical evaluation of available data was that the interrelation of historical and environmental factors produced a socio-political group characterized by stability and a lack of stratification at the village level.

Social welfare and public health

366 **The story of the International Red Cross.**
Beryl and Sam Epstein. New York [etc]: Nelson, 1963. 183p. bibliog.

This book recounts the success story of a movement that began with one man who was touched by the suffering of the wounded on a battlefield and which eventually grew into a complex network of international organizations that have come to be called International Red Cross. Today, this organization is so visible and so generally accepted that its existence is taken for granted. The Epsteins highlight the path-breaking activities of the founder of the movement, the Swiss visionary Henry Dunant, and the contributions of Clara Barton, the American philanthropist who was instrumental in convincing the United States to ratify the Geneva Convention. The authors also describe the challenges the organization faced during the two World Wars of the 20th century and they provide an account of the projects the Red Cross carries out all over the world.

367 **A la rencontre de Henry Dunant.** (An encounter with Henry Dunant.)
Edited by Bernard Gagnebin. Geneva: Georg, 1963. 118p. map.

It was a coincidence that Henry Dunant (1828-1910) was near the battlefield of Solferino on a June morning in 1859. The suffering of the abandoned wounded soldiers which he witnessed on that day led him to write *Un souvenir de Solférino* (A memory of Solferino, 1862) and thus began the Red Cross movement. Dunant enlisted the support of governments and individuals to found an organization that would assist the victims of war and natural catastrophes, regardless of their nationality, and he spent his life in the pursuit of this humanitarian effort. This book tells the story with excerpts from his letters and memoirs. It also includes important letters and documents from many corners of the world that give an idea how the founders sought support for their organization. Eighty-eight small photographs of charitable acts carried out by the International Red Cross all over the globe give evidence of a dream come true for Dunant. In 1901, Dunant shared the first Nobel Prize for Peace.

368 **The evolution of social insurance 1881-1981: studies of Germany, France, Great Britain, Austria and Switzerland.**

Edited by Peter A. Köhler, Hans F. Zacher, Martin Partington. London: Pinter; New York: St. Martin's Press, 1982. 453p. bibliog. (Published on behalf of the Max-Planck Institut für ausländisches und internationales Sozialrecht).

The five countries in this study are faced with similar problems in their efforts to establish broadly based social insurance systems. They have to weigh the pros and cons of each system, the scope of benefits and the type of administration that are available in order to best meet their particular needs. Alfred Maurer in his essay on 'Switzerland', pages 384-453, describes the protective systems as regulated by public law and shows the extent of this regulation. He then traces the emergence and development of social insurance from the foundation of the modern Swiss state in 1848 to the present, including all the revisions that were necessitated by social, economic and political changes. The existence of many different types of insurances at many different levels, private and public, make for a great diversity in Swiss social insurance and hamper attempts at coordinating the insurance options available to the citizenry. An extensive 'Systematic Index' at the back of the book provides comparative data for the five countries.

369 **Early child care in Switzerland.**

Kurt K. Lüscher, Verna Ritter, Peter Gross. London [etc.]: Gordon and Breach, 1973. 122p. bibliog.

This is the fourth monograph in a series on child care sponsored by the International Study Group for Early Child Care, established in 1969. The authors show that despite the minute size of Switzerland and its small population (6,269,000 in 1970), an accurate appraisal of child care in Switzerland is impeded by the diversity of its people, the lack of statistics in many areas, the varying regional and cantonal practices, and the many different categories into which workers and their families fall. The traditional philosophy that the family is the basic social unit and that the mother raises the small child still holds true generally; the laws foster this situation. Institutionalized child care is sought only in special circumstances; the environment of the foster home is preferred. Switzerland's strong economy helped the health and welfare of children, but it also attracted an influx of foreign workers and with it, new problems. Most early child care centres are privately sponsored, while *Kindergärten*, if available, are usually public; they are seen as play schools, teaching mainly social and manual skills. The Pro Juventute Foundation is the most comprehensive institution focusing on the affairs of family and child; it provides services in all facets of a child's life. Thirty-one tables from the 1973 *Statistical Yearbook of Switzerland* provide extensive information about family life, economy, leisure, and health issues.

370 **Social rights or responsibilities?**

Walter Rüegg. In: *The Welfare State and its aftermath*, edited by S. N. Eisenstadt and Ora Ahimer. Totowa, New Jersey: Barnes & Noble, 1985, p. 182-99.

Rüegg claims that the high degree of governmental and political decentralization that makes each community responsible for itself is the reason that Swiss social insurance and welfare are so effective. The schools inculcate civic and social responsibility, while compulsory military service reinforces the principle of citizens' duty toward their community, canton, and country. Social responsibility is rooted in primary institutions;

only the local community can effectively manage welfare in a manner that promotes social responsibility and individual autonomy.

371 **Social security in Switzerland.**
Arnold Saxer. Bern: Haupt, 1965. 132p. bibliog.

The author of this well-written and comprehensive work is the former director of the federal insurance office. The structure of Swiss social security is complicated by the fact that there are federal, cantonal, and local arrangements, in addition to private institutions that support the many types of insurance schemes. The different branches of social security include old-age and survivors insurance; disability insurance; health insurance and maternity benefits; accident insurance; family allowance; and unemployment and military insurance. Saxer also discusses migrant workers' benefits and international agreements and laws that impinge on social security. Numerous tables and figures illustrate the requirements for the different entitlements.

372 **Public health in Switzerland.**
Meinrad Schär. In: *Modern Switzerland*, edited by J. Murray Luck. Palo Alto, California: Society for the Promotion of Science and Scholarship, 1978, p. 213-26. bibliog.

Public health care in Switzerland reflects the federalistic nature of the country. There are few areas in which the Federal Constitution confers legislative powers to the Confederation, most important among them, perhaps, the training and certification of doctors, dentists, pharmacists, and veterinarians. Training schools for nurses and other medical personnel are supervised by the Swiss Red Cross, and the diplomas of successful students are considered valid in all cantons by 'intercantonal convention'. Schär discusses the various forms of sickness and invalids' insurance available and the system by which every Swiss is taken care of even if he or she cannot afford health insurance. Various types of hospitals with their specialties are also briefly mentioned, and the general health of the Swiss population is described with the help of a table showing loss of man-years due to accidents and illnesses. The greatest loss of man-years is due to motor vehicle accidents, but drug abuse poses a new and quite serious health problem in Switzerland.

373 **The Swiss way of welfare: lessons for the western world.**
Ralph Segalman. New York: Praeger, 1986. 205p. bibliog.

Most Western nations struggle with the problem of transmitted poverty and intergenerational welfare dependency. Only in Switzerland did Segalman find no transmitted welfare dependency, because 'Switzerland has put its energies and resources into prevention of poverty, into the building of self-support incentives, and into preparation for employability and work competence in its population'. Where poverty exists and aid is needed, it is provided locally with close attention to its impact on the recipients; the goal is to eliminate not only poverty but the causes of it as well. The Swiss system of social insurance, with its three pillars of old-age and survivors entitlements, compulsory occupational retirement scheme, and personal wealth, provides a high degree of security to the Swiss at a much smaller cost than the welfare programmes of other countries. A number of 'indirect controls of welfarization' such as family and community, schooling, vocational preparation, employment, military service, and so on, together with the efficient local welfare programmes, 'add up to effective prevention and control of welfare dependency and a host of associated ills'. Switzerland has demonstrated that the problem is solvable.

374 **Gesundheitswesen in der Schweiz: Aufbau, Daten, Strukturen.** (The health care system in Switzerland: organization, data, structure.) Nils Undritz. Zurich: Neue Zürcher Zeitung, 1987. 142p.

Decentralization in a federal state leads to a multi-levelled governance system in areas such as health care. The government promulgates basic laws regarding problems like AIDS or dangers from environmental disasters and enforces them through regulations, but individual cantons carry the main burden for administering the health services and they in turn rely on insurance companies, agencies and hospitals in both the public and the private sector. Individual communes regulate care for the elderly and the poor and provide home care. While decentralization permits a more personalized service, the quality and scope of services can differ greatly from place to place. Undritz examines the current state of Swiss health care through factors such as mortality rates, societal changes, institutions and health care professionals, and patient needs. An entire chapter deals with the financing of the different health services and provides a wealth of statistics. A listing of Switzerland's most important health services, various tables and graphs showing new demand arising from demographic changes, and information about health care in other industrialized nations make this a comprehensive study. Another informative study on all aspects of Swiss health care is *Das schweizerische Gesundheitswesen. Aufwand, Struktur und Preisbildung im Pflegebereich* (The Swiss public health service: cost, structure, and allocation of cost in health care) by Pierre Gygi and Heiner Henny (Bern: Huber, 1976).

Politics

General

375 **So funktioniert die Schweiz: dargestellt anhand einiger konkreter Beispiele.** (Thus functions Switzerland: illustrated with some concrete examples.)
Jean-François Aubert, translated from the French by Marianne Rohr. Muri bei Bern, Switzerland: Cosmos, 1987. 5th ed. 307p.

Aubert, professor of constitutional law at the University of Neuchâtel, uses the case-study approach to demonstrate how the political institutions of Switzerland function. First, the tortuous path of the Swiss economic stabilization programme through parliament and two popular votes is described – designed to defuse the inflation of the 1960s, it was defeated by the voters. A second chapter deals with the even more involved Jura question. The third chapter has as its subject 'the greatest Swiss enterprise', the old-age and survivors insurance (AHV), approved by the people and the cantons in a referendum on 6 July 1947. Frequently modified, the law not only gave the federal state the new task of participating in the social welfare of its citizens but also created huge sums of money that needed to be administered prudently and fairly. Chapter four deals with the controversial issue of nuclear power plants and challenges presented by the opposition to them by the environmentalists, the Greens, and the pacifists. The fifth chapter contains 'automobile stories', controversies surrounding the introduction of a mandatory seat-belt law, the prohibition of the use of spiked tyres, and the effort made by certain groups to mandate car-free Sundays. This is a stimulating and instructive book.

376 **Participation and Swiss democracy.**
Benjamin Barber. *Government and Opposition*, vol. 23, no. 1 (Winter 1988), p. 31-50.

This is one of a group of articles in a special issue of *Government and Opposition* devoted to the question of whether the Swiss example could be imitated. According to Barber, Switzerland's political features have little in common with American- or

British-style democracy. They are the product of a unique confluence of three guiding ideas namely 'participatory democracy, neutrality and radical federalism (localism)'. 'The sovereignty of the political' is a product of the eminently civic character of the Swiss state. Swiss citizenship conveys to the individual the right to participate at the local, cantonal, and federal levels of government. At all levels the consensus prevails over competition as the favoured approach to problem solving. Barber concludes with the hope that the Swiss model may serve Europe as an example of how 'to retain the ideals of democracy in a modern world that can be fearfully inhospitable to them'.

377 **A crisis in Swiss pluralism: the Romansh and their relations with the German- and Italian-Swiss in the perspective of a millennium.**
Robert Henry Billigmeier. The Hague, The Netherlands [etc.]: Mouton, 1979. 450p. bibliog.

Canton Graubünden is a Switzerland in miniature in its geographical, ethnic, and linguistic diversity. It has three language communities, German, Romansh, and Italian, in order of size. Billigmeier's focus is the fate of the Romansh people and their language. They constitute less than one per cent of the entire Swiss population and are in danger of losing their identity in the wake of the powerful economic and social forces that engulf them. Billigmeier describes the evolution of the Romansh language through the centuries and its division into seven distinct dialects in the various mountain valleys. This division makes the creation of a common written language very difficult. The revivalist movement that began in the 1830s has had some success, but has been hampered by constant internal bickering. The expansion of Swiss-German enterprises into the Romansh areas since World War II and the impact of tourism, among other things, present real dangers for this unique component of Swiss pluralism.

378 **Federalism in Switzerland.**
Vernon Bogdanor. *Government and Opposition*, vol. 23, no. 1 (Winter 1988), p. 69-90.

This is one of a group of papers of a special issue of *Government and Politics* devoted to whether the example of Switzerland can be imitated. Bogdanor affirms that complexity is the most striking feature of federal government in Switzerland. He then proceeds to explain why the system is so complex and provides a description of how it works. Sharing of power, one of the basic principles of federalism, is carried to an extreme in Switzerland. There is a high degree of interdependence among the component parts of the Swiss system; however, the distribution of responsibilities among the levels of government, especially between the Confederation and the cantons, 'seems less the result of political choice than of piecemeal and unplanned development'. There is no unifying factor in national political life; the direction of political parties is decentralized to the cantonal level, creating a large number of arenas for political conflict, which in turn makes it 'possible for all groups, even those in a permanent national minority, to have access to influence and power'. Bogdanor's interesting analysis is summarized in the statement: 'The essence of citizenship, as it is understood in Switzerland, is the search for agreement, with decisions made, not by majority rule, but through different pluralities.' He concludes that while Swiss institutions do not lend themselves to imitation, 'the strategy which has made Switzerland an exemplar of a peaceful plural society' definitely does.

379 **Referendums: a comparative study of practice and theory.**
Edited by David Butler, Austin Ranney. Washington, DC: American Enterprise Institute for Public Policy Research, 1978. 250p. bibliog.

The book includes descriptive chapters on the role of referendums in Switzerland, the United States of America, California, Australia, France, Scandinavia, Ireland, and the United Kingdom. The chapter on Switzerland (pages 39-66), was written by Jean-François Aubert. He discusses the origins of the referendum, the federal constitutional and legal regulations that govern its application, and the role it plays in the political life of the nation. Between 1848 and 31 August 1978, Swiss voters have gone to the polls 297 times to decide issues according to the Swiss system of direct democracy, and all 297 instances are listed. Aubert concludes that Switzerland has shown that, 'at least in a small, sophisticated country, direct democracy can work with almost none of the ill consequences which have been ascribed to it in political argument elsewhere'. The editors in their introductory chapters and the conclusion refer to Switzerland as 'the one truly addicted country'. Excluding Switzerland and to a lesser extent Australia, 'the well established democracies of the world have averaged a total of less than four [referendums] a piece'. See also 'Initiatives, referenda and socialism in Switzerland', by Kenneth R. Libbey in *Government and Opposition*, vol. 5, no. 3 (Summer 1970), p. 307-26.

380 **Interest groups in Swiss politics.**
Bobby M. Gierisch. Zurich: Soziologisches Institut der Universität Zürich, 1974. 160p. bibliog.

Financed by the Swiss National Fund for Promotion of Scientific Research, Gierisch's project was designed to study the national voluntary associations and their interactions with the political and para-political institutions of the country. Much of the space is taken up by the discussion of the methodological problems encountered in the course of the research. Gierisch found thirty organizations with regular political activities at the federal level. Not quite half of them are 'peak organizations' (*Dachverbände*) such as the Swiss trade union alliance (*Gewerkschaftsbund*) representing numerous member associations. Peak organizations concentrate not so much on the forum, such as the Federal Council, but rather on specific issues, which they follow with interest throughout the legislative process. They are well represented on the standing commissions of the federal government, they are invited to participate in federal consultations (*Vernehmlassungen*) and they are directly represented in parliament. Policy decisions within and among the interest groups are generally made through private negotiations and result in compromise.

381 **The political system of Switzerland.**
Erich Gruner. In: *Modern Switzerland*, edited by J. Murray Luck. Palo Alto, California: Society for the Promotion of Science and Scholarship, 1978, p. 339-59.

Gruner, formerly professor of political science and director of the Research Centre for Swiss Politics at the University of Bern, displays his thorough knowledge of the Swiss political system in this concentrated article full of insights. One of the characteristics of the Swiss governmental system is the fact that the government does not depend on the confidence of parliament. The plebiscitary rights of referendum and initiative are 'quasi substitutes for parliamentary votes of no confidence'. The decision-making process is geared toward consensus and is therefore time-consuming. Political parties are only one of the voices in the country's policy debates. According to Gruner interest groups 'carry greater weight in the development of political objectives'. In addition, there are the direct-democracy instruments which since 1970 have increasingly been used by small groups for their nuisance value, posing the threat that Switzerland's decision mechanisms will grind to a halt.

382 **Année politique suisse = Schweizerische Politik 1987.** (Swiss politics 1987.)

Edited by Hans Hirter. Bern: Forschungszentrum für schweizerische Politik, 1988. 334p.

This is the 23rd volume in a series that has been published annually since 1965. Written by teams of academics connected with the Research Centre for Swiss Politics at the University of Bern, the series began with the intention of providing 'a first overview' of the events that happened in Switzerland during the year, but recent volumes have grown in substance and organization into veritable compendia of Swiss political life. The volumes are divided into sections and chapters in either French or German with brief résumés in the other language. The content is based primarily on information gathered from Swiss newspapers as collected and analysed in the documentation archive of the centre. Government and business publications are also screened. The section entitled 'general chronicle' covers everything from foreign relations to social and cultural developments and ends with tables on the results of the federal plebiscites of the year. A second section provides a review of legislation in the cantons, while a third (brief) part deals with political parties, trade organizations (*Verbände*), and other interest groups. Statements are provided with footnotes with a range of references, and bibliographical comments at the end of every chapter provide the most up-to-date access to the literature on the subjects treated. Two indexes complete this informative publication.

383 **Can the *Confederatio Helvetica* be imitated?**

Edited by Ghita Ionescu. Special issue of *Government and Opposition*, vol. 23, no. 1 (Winter 1988), London, 1988. 126p.

This special issue of the London School of Economics and Political Science journal *Government and Opposition* consists of an introduction by Ionescu, six papers presented at a conference on the subject 'Can the *Confederatio Helvetica* be imitated?' held in Geneva in July 1987, and extracts from the personal reminiscences of Denis de Rougemont on 'The campaign of the European congresses'. Relevance, as described by Ionescu, consists of Switzerland's reaction to the changing international surroundings, especially Western Europe, its role in this new environment, and Switzerland's use as a model by the European Community when the latter reaches federative stages, since the Swiss may 'have already solved some of the problems of the new macrocosm in their microcosm'. The papers by Steinberg, Barber, Jean Freymond, Bogdanor, and Klöti have separate entries in this bibliography (q.v.).

384 **Political ideals, financial interests and intergovernmental relations: new aspects of Swiss federalism.**

Ulrich Klöti. *Government and Opposition*, vol. 23, no. 1 (Winter 1988), p. 91-102.

This is one of a group of papers in a special issue of *Government and Opposition* devoted to the question of whether the example of Switzerland can be imitated. Switzerland's federal system is of 'extraordinary complexity'. Even though the basic constitutional order remains unaltered since 1848, the cultural, social, and economic context has changed drastically, creating growing tension between the legal order and social developments. Geographical disparities in wealth, especially between the urban centres and some mountain regions, have created a new cleavage. The struggle over regional interests takes place at the federal level; the cantons try to maintain as much jurisdiction as possible but would like the federal government to foot the bill. The outcome of this struggle may be harmonization, but it may also be a stalemate. In any case, Klöti maintains, neither the classical constitutional model which had been designed for a particular historical situation nor the political culture of the new Swiss federalism lends itself to imitation.

385 **Governments and politics of the German-speaking countries.**
Walter S. G. Kohn. Chicago, Illinois: Nelson-Hall, 1980. 291p. maps.

This is a comparative study of the five German-speaking countries: Switzerland, Liechtenstein, Austria, the Federal Republic of Germany, and the German Democratic Republic. In the nature of an introductory text to Central European governments, the book proceeds topically from an account of the geography, national identity, and constitutional development of each of the countries to a description of their political parties, divided into Communist, Social-Democratic, Christian-oriented, and others. Kohn also describes the legislatures, the executive branches and heads of state, and the administrative systems. Switzerland receives its fair share of attention in a text that is fact-laden and, on the whole, accurate.

386 **Conflict and compromise in multilingual societies: Switzerland.**
Kenneth D. McRae. Waterloo, Ontario: Wilfrid Laurier University Press, 1983. 274p. maps. bibliog.

Switzerland is made up of German-, French-, Italian-, and Romansh-speaking people living in different geographical areas of the country who are characterized by distinctive cultures and lifestyles. Despite these differences, Switzerland is an example of peaceful coexistence and remarkable social and political stability. McRae gives a historical overview of how this came about and how the social and political institutionalization of the linguistic cleavages was achieved. Political parties, federal and cantonal institutions, the media, and educational and cultural policies are analysed in turn, with special attention given to the attitudes and behaviour of the members of the four language groups toward one another. A few maps and many tables and figures are part of the scholarly apparatus of this impressive monograph.

387 **Switzerland at the polls: the national elections of 1979.**
Edited by Howard R. Penniman. Washington, DC; London: American Institute for Public Policy Research, 1979. 198p.

This volume, one in the 'At the Polls' series of the American Enterprise Institute, contains six chapters written by scholars who have established reputations in the field of Swiss political science. George A. Codding, Jr. wrote on 'the Swiss political system and the management of diversity', Erich Gruner (misspelled 'Grüner') with Kenneth J. Pitterle on 'Switzerland's political parties', Henry H. Kerr on 'Swiss electoral politics', Dusan Sidjanski on 'turnout, stability, and the left–right dimension', and Margaret Inglehart on 'sex role, historical heritage, and political participation in Switzerland'. Jürg Steiner contributed 'conclusion: reflections on the consociational theme'. The analysis of the humdrum national elections, with elaborate tables and figures, gives the writers an opportunity to traverse once again the well-ploughed field of Switzerland's unique history and political system.

388 **Handbuch Politisches System der Schweiz = Manuel Système politique de la Suisse.** (Handbook: political system of Switzerland.)
Edited by Alois Riklin, Ulrich Klöti, Raimund E. Germann, Ernest Weibel. Bern; Stuttgart, FRG: Haupt, 1983-86. 3 vols. bibliog.

This is a collaborative work of major dimensions by Swiss political scientists. Each volume is 350 or more pages long, and a fourth one is planned. The work, which addresses the interested public as well as the specialist, is intended to give an up-to-date comprehensive view of the Swiss political system. Volume 1, entitled *Grundlagen = Le context* (foundations), analyses the underlying values of the Swiss political system in the context of its constitutional development, its adaptation to changing social and economic forces, and its reaction to the international environment. Volume 2, *Strukturen und Prozesse = Structures et processus* (structures and processes), looks at the institutions and forces involved in the political process, among them the branches of the federal government and administration, intermediary organizations such as political parties, economic interest groups (*Verbände*), and the media, and, finally, the public and its role in the Swiss democracy. Volume 3, *Föderalismus = Fédéralisme* (federalism), describes first the historical evolution of federalism in Switzerland and its legal foundations, then deals with the territorial components of the Confederation, the cantons and the communes, and finally addresses the dynamic aspects of the relationships between the component parts, including language groups, at the regional and federal levels. Articles are written in either German or French. Chapter summaries are given in the other language and in Italian and, beginning with volume 2, also in English.

389 **Conflict and consensus in Switzerland.**
Carol L. Schmid. Berkeley, California [etc.]: University of California Press, 1981. 198p. bibliog.

Starting from the premise that existing models are deficient in explaining the 'Swiss enigma' of cultural coexistence of diverse ethnic groups, Schmid proposes to solve the problem by looking at 'values and attitudes of the different cultural groups, as well as the political and social underpinnings of Swiss pluralism'. Political factors that help to prevent numerical minorities from becoming sociological minorities are analysed as well as socializing agents such as the schools and their curricula. The results of questionnaires distributed among young people indicate that Swiss of diverse backgrounds are united by a common socio-political foundation, a 'civic culture'. In spite of the 'blemish' of two contemporary problems, the Jura question and the status of foreign workers in Switzerland, the 'predominant pattern . . . seems to be one of cultural diversity rather than subcultural segmentation'. The success of Switzerland contains theoretical and practical implications for other countries. See also *Amicable agreement versus majority rule: conflict resolution in Switzerland* by Jürg Steiner (Chapel Hill, North Carolina: University of North Carolina Press, 1974).

390 **Switzerland's political institutions.**
Oswald Sigg, translated from the German by F. M. Blackwell, D. N. Roscoe, M. Mettler. Zurich: Pro Helvetia, 1987. 2nd ed. 61p. bibliog.

This slim booklet gives a compact overview of Swiss political institutions. Sigg treats the subject in seven brief chapters entitled 'historical aspects of political rights in Switzerland', 'federalism', 'communes and cantons', 'elections and voting', 'intiative and referendum', 'Federal Assembly, Federal Council and Federal Supreme Court', and 'political parties and interest groups'. The text is factually descriptive, and there are a few full-page photographs. A straightforward, descriptive account in eleven brief chapters on the topic is *The political institutions of Switzerland* by Georg Sauser-Hall (Zurich; New York: Swiss National Tourist Office, 1946). The French version *Guide politique suisse* was reissued in 1965 by Payot, Lausanne.

391 **Amicable agreement versus majority rule: conflict resolution in Switzerland.**
Jürg Steiner. Chapel Hill, North Carolina: University of North Carolina Press, 1974. 312p. bibliog.

Steiner sees majority rule and amicable agreement as the two basic models of democratic decision-making. In the amicable agreement model 'discussion goes on until a solution is found that is acceptable to all participants in the decision-making process'. He posits a numbr of hypotheses against which to test the national system of Switzerland. The key hypothesis stipulates that in a political system such as the Swiss with its strong sub-cultural segmentation 'the more often political decisions are made by amicable agreement, the more probable is a low level of intersubcultural hostility'. After a careful methodological introduction Steiner analyses the input function of political parties and of economic interest groups and their role in the formal decision-making process. The description of the output of authoritative decisions takes up another long chapter. Findings are summarized in a large number of 'propositions' spread throughout the book. Not surprisingly, the key hypothesis is confirmed by the Swiss example.

392 **Switzerland exposed.**
Jean Ziegler, translated from the French by Rosemary Sheed Middleton. London: Allison & Busby, 1978. 173p.

This is a polemical tirade against traditional Swiss institutions and values by a Marxist, the Geneva professor of political science and member of the federal parliament, Jean Ziegler. Switzerland, ruled by an oligarchy forming part of 'the hegemonic capital' of the world, is said to be closely tied into the 'secondary imperialism' that is destroying untold lives in the Third World. Secrecy, as exemplified by the Swiss bank secrecy laws which protect tons of 'dirty money' flowing through the Swiss banks, is one of the hallmarks of how the country operates. The 'visible government', which, on paper, has some good democratic aspects, is 'colonized' by the oligarchy. That oligarchy also dominates the army, which among its functions has 'the maintenance of the military–industrial complex'. Swiss neutrality is 'an end in itself' and therefore 'purely negative'. 'The death industry' of the arms manufacturers and dealers proves the 'farce of Swiss pseudo-neutrality'. Ziegler's book has also come out in an American edition with the title *Switzerland: the awful truth* (New York: Harper & Row, 1979).

Political parties

393 **Die Parteien in der Schweiz.** (The political parties in Switzerland.)
Erich Gruner. Bern: Francke, 1977. 2nd rev. ed. 351p. bibliog. (Helvetia Politica. Series B, no. 4).

A detailed, analytical study of the political parties in Switzerland by the authority in this field. About half of the text deals with the historical evolution of the party system and the individual parties that play a role in the contemporary political life of the country: liberals in their various shadings, conservatives and Christian socialists, social democrats and communists, the peasant-bourgeois party, the independents, and other, smaller, parties. The other half of the book is given to the description of the internal workings of these parties and to an account of the changes in their roles in recent decades. Gruner's discussion of the problems of methodology and his analytical approach to the scientific study of parties form the framework of this impressive work.

394 **The Swiss party system: steadfast and changing.**
Henry H. Kerr. In: *Party systems in Denmark, Austria, Switzerland, the Netherlands and Belgium*, edited by Hans Daalder. London: Pinter, 1987. p. 107-92. bibliog.

Kerr left a draft text when he died in 1982. Daniel Seiler of the University of Lausanne edited it slightly to reflect the developments since 1982. In practice, Swiss politics transforms opposition into coalition, conflict into consensus, and diversity into unity. Sources of the Swiss system extend far beyond the reaches of the party system. Among the themes Kerr treats in his instructive article are: parties and politics; the Swiss multi-party system; the parliamentary arena; referendum and initiative: the people in parliament; the electoral arena; the internal arenas of the parties; linkages: parties and other institutions; and the *malaise hélvétique*: prospects for reform. The principal challenge to the Swiss form of representation lies in the fact that in large sectors of public authority it is the special interest groups, and not the citizens, that form the basis of the régime. Kerr reiterates the point made by Gruner and others that Swiss parties are very much confederations of more or less decentralized cantonal parties.

395 **Solidarität, Widerspruch, Bewegung: 100 Jahre Sozialdemokratische Partei der Schweiz.** (Solidarity, opposition, movement: 100 years of the Social Democratic Party of Switzerland.)
Edited by Karl Lang, Peter Hablützel, Markus Mattmüller, Heidi Witzig. Zurich: Limmat, 1988. 408p.

This volume was published for the centenary of the Swiss Social Democratic Party. It contains articles on the philosophical changes in the party platform over the years, the beginnings of the party and its relationship to the Second International, communal socialism in the socialist-dominated city of Biel, the emancipation of women, and the question of party participation in the Federal Council. The Social Democratic Party was founded at a time when industrialization inspired a utopian belief in a just world without oppression and war. Not even the depression of the 1930s could shake the belief in the inevitability of progress, and the boom years of the 1950s and 1960s reinforced the expectations of success. Today the belief in steadily growing prosperity and happiness is shaken. The old ideology is passé. It should not be replaced with fear of an impending political or ecological catastrophe but with a serious attempt to build the foundation for a better future.

396 **The Socialist party of Switzerland: a minority party and its political system.**
Kenneth Richard Libbey. Ann Arbor, Michigan: University Microfilms, 1969. 300p. bibliog. (PhD dissertation in Political Science, Syracuse University, Syracuse, New York).

This study focuses on the Swiss Socialist Party and its activities. The Socialist or Social Democratic Party represents about one-fourth of the Swiss electorate. It asserts that its members are a progressive minority facing a conservative, if loosely organized, majority. Libbey examines the way the party must manoeuvre to get itself heard and to have its reform proposals succeed. The Socialist Party, like everything else in Switzerland, is affected by the variety of cantonal situations due to Swiss federalism. Even though it is, according to Libbey, the most nationally oriented of all parties, it sponsors no less than sixteen daily or weekly newspapers, each primarily devoted to the politics of its own canton or region. Since it is largely isolated within the Swiss system, the Socialist party is dependent on the pragmatic principle of working for limited goals.

397 **Schweizerisches Jahrbuch für Politische Wissenschaft 26, 1986: Politische Parteien und neue Bewegungen.** (Swiss political science yearbook 26, 1986: political parties and new movements.)
Edited by Wolf Linder. Bern: Haupt, 1986. 350p.

The 1986 edition of the yearbook of the Swiss Society of Political Scientists contains seventeen articles addressing developments in the structure of Switzerland's political parties. The articles are grouped under the three headings 'parties in transformation', 'new movements', and 'institutional change'. They give an up-to-date account of the forces that are changing the Swiss political landscape, among them the weakening of party loyalty within the established parties, new movements such as feminism, pacifism, populism, and ecological groups, and the general reduction of the significance of the parties as forces in Swiss political life.

398 **A theory of political decision models: intraparty decision making in Switzerland.**
Jürg Steiner, Robert H. Dorff. Chapel Hill, North Carolina: University of North Carolina Press, 1980. 239p. bibliog.

Steiner studied decision-making within the Free Democratic Party of Canton Bern in 1969-70. From the materials he collected in 111 meetings of various party committees, he identified 466 conflicts. Twelve per cent of these were decided by majority decision, twenty-one per cent by amicable agreement, thirty per cent by non-decision, and thirty-seven by interpretation. This last mode represents an addition to the analysis of decision-making introduced into the political science literature by the authors: it consists of interpretation of the sense of discussion by either the chairman or the writer of the minutes, in the absence of a vote or general agreement. The authors describe in detail the method used in information gathering, the typology of decision models, and the statistical methods of computational analysis, and conclude that their study has certain implications for normative democratic theory. In the case of Switzerland, their study indicates that lack of innovation is the country's greatest problem in implementing new policies. The scope of innovation might best be increased by more frequent use of majority decisions.

Constitution and Legal System

Constitution

399 **Kommentar zur Bundesverfassung der Schweizerischen Eidgenossenschaft vom 29. Mai 1874.** (Commentary on the constitution of the Swiss Confederation of 29 May 1874.)
Edited by Jean-François Aubert, Kurt Eichenberger, Jörg Paul Müller, René A. Rhinow, Dietrich Schindler. Basel: Helbing & Lichtenhahn; Zurich: Schulthess; Bern: Stämpfli, 1987- .

The last commentary on the Swiss federal constitution, published in 1931, was the work of one person, Walter Burckhardt. Since 1931 more than seventy partial revisions of the constitution have been made and four unwritten fundamental rights have been introduced through judicial interpretation by the Federal Tribunal. This new commentary, whose publication is still in progress, will be the collective work of twenty-six authors, almost all of them professors of law at Swiss universities. Their contributions appear in large-format loose-leaf form and will be assembled in three binders in a German and a French version. Each of the 123 articles of the Swiss constitution, including the many amendments will be commented upon in detail by one of the authors. The first contributions in print indicate that this will become a comprehensive and monumental work of Swiss constitutional scholarship.

400 **Petite histoire constitutionnelle de la Suisse.** (Brief constitutional history of Switzerland.)
Jean-François Aubert. Bern: Francke, 1974. 119p. bibliog.

In the first part Aubert gives an overview of the history of constitutional developments in Switzerland, divided into three chronological chapters, 1798 to 1848, 1848 to 1918, and 1918 to 1974. In the second part he describes the institutions of the Swiss Confederation. This part also has three chapters dealing with the structure of the state, the organization of the state, and the role of the state.

401 **The federal constitution of Switzerland: with German text.**
Christopher Hughes. Westport, Connecticut: Greenwood Press, 1970. 223p. bibliog. (Originally published in 1954 by The Clarendon Press, Oxford).

The book contains a translation of the federal constitution with commentary by Christopher Hughes. The commentary on every article and sub-article of the Swiss constitution is elaborate, incisive, and provocative. It contains much useful information on the history and significance of the issues the author considers. Hughes's critical intellect is evident.

Legal system

402 **Swiss company law: translation of the official text with an introduction, synoptic tables, annotations and appendices.**
Bruno Becchio, Allan D. M. Phillips, Urs Wehinger. Chichester, Sussex: Barry Rose, 1984. 184p. bibliog.

The Code of Obligations, which constitutes the fifth part of the Civil Code, codifies the law of Swiss business organizations from partnerships and corporations to cooperatives. The pertinent provisions of the Code of Obligations are translated in this work and carefully annotated, indicating that the translation can be only an approximation, since the historical background and principles involved make the meaning of concepts and terms differ as between Swiss and English law. The authors worked from the German text of the code, but in cases of vagueness they had recourse to the French and Italian texts, which, written in the other two of the three official languages, have equal standing with the German text, one of the many peculiar features of Swiss law. This is an impressive, informative, and enjoyable work.

403 **Amtliche Sammlung der Entscheidungen des Schweizerischen Bundesgerichtes.** (Official collection of the decisions by the Swiss Federal Tribunal.)
Bundesgericht. Lausanne: Arrêts du Tribunal fédéral, 1875- .

The twenty to thirty issues of decisions published annually are divided into five parts as follows: part 1a, constitutional law, about four times a year; 1b, administrative law and international public law, about four times a year; 2, civil law, about five times a year; 3, law concerning bankruptcy and debts, three to four times a year; 4, penal law and implementation (*Strafvollzug*), three to four times a year; 5, social insurance law, about five times a year. Annual and decennial indices allow one to find one's way through the maze of legal matters.

404 **Amtliche Sammlung der eidgenössischen Gesetze.** (Official collection of the laws of the Swiss Confederation.)
Bundeskanzlei. Bern: Eidgenössische Drucksachen- und Materialienzentrale, 1848- .

Known as *Amtliche Sammlung*, or *Recueil officiel* in French, this collection contains all federal laws, executive orders, decrees, and regulations of the Federal Council, and to some extent also of the departments (ministries) of the federal government. It appears about weekly, and is collected into two or more annual volumes.

405 **Nouveau guide juridique suisse.** (New Swiss juridical guide.)
Hans Hiestand, Arthur Bannwart, Claude Schmidt. Lausanne: Librairie Marguerat, 1974. 511p.

This reliable and easy-to-understand book treats all areas of Swiss law of interest to individuals and business. Examples are used to explain fine points of the law, and practical advice on such problems as how to proceed in court cases and how to draft contracts, petitions, and wills is also given. This guide, first published in 1935 in German as *Der schweizerische Rechtsberater* (The Swiss legal adviser), has proved to be a popular reference tool in many Swiss households and offices.

406 **A tale of two courts: judicial settlement between the states of the Swiss and American federations.**
William Gorham Rice. Madison, Wisconsin [etc.]: University of Wisconsin Press, 1967. 133p.

This is a brief account of how the Supreme Court of the United States in Washington, DC and the Federal Tribunal of Switzerland in Lausanne handle disputes that arise among the constitutent parts of their respective countries, the states in the case of the US and the cantons in the case of Switzerland. Rice's emphasis is not so much on an in-depth exploration of substantive rules of law as on the function of each court in the adjudication of inter-state conflicts. Substantive law is described chronologically and topically. Most of the early litigation in both countries arose over boundary disputes. Switzerland also had much inter-cantonal litigation concerning public assistance to the indigent and in the 20th century over water use and the power to tax and prosecute. In general, Rice concludes, the cases before the Swiss Federal Tribunal were more numerous and varied than those before the US Supreme Court, and the plaintiff had a better chance of success before the Swiss than the American court. In both countries the systems have been highly successful in contributing to the preservation of harmony among the states and cantons. There are several appendices with excerpts from the respective constitutions and tables of cases adjudicated in the courts of the two countries. In 1959 Rice published the book *Law among states in federacy: a survey of decisions of the Swiss Federal Tribunal in international controversies* (Appleton, Wisconsin: Nelson, 1959) which focuses on cases brought before the Swiss Federal Tribunal during the years 1919-59.

407 **Swiss corporation law: English translation of official text.**
Swiss-American Chamber of Commerce. Zurich: Swiss-American Chamber of Commerce, 1984. 4th enlarged ed. 75p.

A team of Swiss and American lawyers produced this straightforward translation, without introduction or annotations, of major sections of the Swiss Code of Obligations, and smaller excerpts of the Swiss Civil Code and the Ordinance on the Commercial Register. Much of this work is a duplication of *Swiss company law* (q.v.), even though the translations differ considerably, as is evident simply from the two titles. The purpose of this publication is not so much to guide the reader through the maze of the Swiss law as to present him with a ready-made text and let him fend for himself. In a similar vein, the Swiss-American Chamber of Commerce of Zurich has published a translation of major sections of the Swiss Code of Obligations under the title *Swiss contract law: English translation of official texts* (Zurich, 2nd enlarged ed., 1984. 143p.).

408 **Der Auslandschweizer und die schweizerische internationale Zuständigkeit im Personen-, Familien- und Erbrecht nach NAG Art.28 ff.** (Swiss living abroad and the Swiss international jurisdiction relating to the law of persons, family law, and the law of inheritance according to NAG art.28 ff.)
Mark Eugen Villiger. Zurich: Schulthess, 1978. 244p. bibliog. (Studien zum Verfassungsrecht).

Villiger's dissertation is based on the NAG or *Niederlassungs- und Aufenthaltsgesetz*, 25 June 1891 (Federal civil statute relating to permits for permanent or temporary residence). The work fills a gap in the literature on the rights and jurisdiction of the Swiss abroad. The language is technical and the cases examined are complicated, but nevertheless, the layperson will find answers to questions concerning Swiss citizenship and foreign residence. Jurisdiction is examined in claims for a name change or an inheritance, in questions regarding marital status, and rights and duties among members of a family. Federal policies based on bilateral or multilateral treaties are also considered. Villiger's study is concerned only with the legal situation of holders of permits for permanent or temporary residence in a foreign country from the Swiss point of view.

409 **Ihre Rechte als Frau.** (Your rights as woman.)
Simone Walder-de Montmollin, translated from the French by Edith Ryter. Muri, Bern: Cosmos, 1987. 175p.

A subject index number refers the user of this reference work on women's rights to the paragraph where the particular legal problem is treated and illustrated with examples, and solutions are often offered. The problems are grouped according to topics such as professional training, work, marriage and divorce, children, inheritance, violence against females, and insurance. Selected addresses of organizations in all regions of Switzerland that provide specific assistance are listed. The original French version is *Vos droits de femme* (Lausanne: Payot, 1984).

410 **The Swiss judicial system.**
Luzius Wildhaber. In: *Modern Switzerland*, edited by J. Murray Luck. Palo Alto, California: Society for the Promotion of Science and Scholarship, 1978, p. 311-21.

Wildhaber, professor of law at the University of Basel, provides an excellent introduction to the major characteristics of the Swiss judicial system. Federalism has put its stamp on the judicial system as on everything else in Switzerland. The cantons implement the federal statutes, and the civil, criminal and administrative courts of first and second instance are cantonal. The Swiss Federal Tribunal is, above all, the court of last instance; it is not allowed to review the constitutionality of federal statutes. That function is exercised by the Federal Assembly. Wildhaber describes the proceedings before the various cantonal courts and the federal courts and points out the most important aspects of substantive and procedural law and of the relationship between codified, written, and case law. He emphasizes that much of the law in Switzerland is judge-made. The article is accompanied by a bibliography.

Government and Administration

Federal government and administration

411 **Amtliches Bulletin der Bundesversammlung.** (Official bulletin of the Federal Assembly.)
Bern: Protokollierungsdienst der Bundesversammlung, 1891- .

The official bulletin, formerly called *Stenographisches Bulletin = Bulletin sténographique*, reports the debates in the National Council and the Council of States, primarily those on laws and executive orders of general importance, but occasionally other debates are also included. The bulletin appears four times a year, at the end of every session of parliament. The French speeches made in French appear in French, the German ones in German. The bulletin for the spring session 1988 has 489 pages for the National Council and 124 pages for the Council of States.

412 **Bundesblatt.** (Federal gazette.)
Bern: Stämpfli, 1848- .

The *Bundesblatt = Feuille fédérale* is published weekly and is bound into three or more annual volumes, numbered by year and volume. The chief contents are the messages and reports of the Federal Council on proposed laws and treaties, the texts of laws and regulations, the results of federal votations and elections, and administrative notices. It is the Federal Council's primary vehicle for explaining its policies and is a treasure-house of information on all aspects of Swiss political life.

413 **Responsible bureaucracy: a study of the Swiss civil service.**
Carl Joachim Friedrich, Taylor Cole. New York: Russell & Russell, 1967. 95p. bibliog. (Reprint of 1932 edition, published by Harvard University Press).

Friedrich and Cole provide a spirited discussion of bureaucracy in general and in Switzerland in particular. They describe the functions and the personnel of the Swiss civil service at the federal, cantonal, and municipal levels, and conclude that the Swiss civil service is a fairly highly organized bureaucracy with a distinctly hierarchical structure, limited by legislation and ordinances, and interpreted by the court. In spite of the opposition of democratic sentiment against bureaucratization, the civil service developed since 1848, in response to the technical necessities of the modern industrial system and the need for the maintenance of public safety and order. Friedrich and Cole end their brief study, which in spite of its age is still relevant and readable, with a sustained argument in favour of giving the civil servants not only the right to organize, which they always had, but also the right to strike, which was denied them in Article 23 of the Federal Law on Civil Servants of 1925.

414 **A visit to the Swiss houses of parliament.**
Walo von Greyerz. Bern: Haupt, 1961. 47p.

This small, illustrated booklet gives a pleasant guided tour through the Federal Palace (Bundeshaus) in Bern. Built between 1857 and 1901, it houses the two branches of the Swiss parliament as well as administrative offices of the executive branch of the federal government. Greyerz combines a description of the building and its major assembly rooms with an introductory course on Swiss civics.

415 **Die schweizerische Bundesversammlung 1848-1920.** (The Swiss Federal Assembly 1848-1920.)
Erich Gruner, Karl Frei. Bern: Francke, 1966. 2 vols. 1021p., 253p. bibliog. (Helvetia Politica. Series A. Vols I/II).

The first volume of this substantial work consists of the biographies of 1,467 parliamentarians who were elected or appointed to the Federal Assembly between 1848, when the modern constitution was adopted, and 1919, when the proportional election system was introduced. Each member of the National Council, the lower house of the assembly, and of the Council of States, the upper house, is written up in his native language with all significant personal data, from family background and religious and political affiliation to education, professional, political, and military career, as well as achievements, hobbies, and connections. In the second volume the authors digest the information from volume one and present their findings in elaborate tables and graphs. The commentaries that accompany the tables take on the nature of veritable essays on the sociological and statistical significance of these materials.

416 **Die Wahlen in den schweizerischen Nationalrat 1848-1919. Wahlrecht, Wahlsystem, Verhalten von Wählern und Parteien, Wahlthemen und Wahlkämpfe.** (The elections to the Swiss National Council 1848-1919: right to vote, system of voting, behaviour of voters and parties, election themes, and election campaigns.)
Erich Gruner, with Georges Andrey, Paul Ehinger, Ernst Frischknecht (et al.). Bern: Francke, 1978. 3 vols. 1189p. (in two parts), 300p., 540p. bibliog. (Helvetia Politica. Series A. Vol. VI, 1-3).

The first volume of this monumental work is divided into two separately bound parts. It provides a historical description of the twenty-four elections to the National Council held in the twenty-five cantons of the Swiss Confederation between the founding of the modern Swiss state in 1848 and the introduction of the proportional election system in 1919. It also contains an analysis according to social science principles of the underlying issues and forces at work. The second volume consists only of notes, while the oversized third volume has hundreds of tables, charts, graphs, and maps. The work is a detailed history of the first seven decades of the modern Swiss Confederation, as well as a thorough methodological study of the workings of a system of representative democracy. The elections to the National Council are seen as having been a means for the established Swiss political system to adapt itself to changing economic and social circumstances and thus to soften the impact of painful conflicts.

417 **How Switzerland is governed.**

Hans Huber, translated from the German by Mary Hottinger. Zurich: Schweizer Spiegel, 1968. 63p.

This is a concise, factual introduction to the major elements of the Swiss system of government. Brief chapters contain essential information on the Swiss constitution, federalism, the political rights of the Swiss, the parties, the federal government in its legislative, executive, and judicial components, foreign policy, education, and the army. An old stand-by on the topic is *The government of Switzerland* by William E. Rappard (New York: Van Nostrand, 1936).

418 **The parliament of Switzerland.**

Christopher Hughes. London: Cassell, 1962. 204p. bibliog. (Published for the Hansard Society for Parliamentary Government).

The Swiss parliament is a complex institution. Hughes, political scientist and expert on the Swiss political system, presents in this book the results of his investigations into the intricacies of that system. Going beyond a purely objective examination of parliamentary procedure, he examines also the actual working of the bicameral legislature in terms of personalities and specific incidents. Extraparliamentary interest groups which play a major role especially in the preparatory phases of new legislation are carefully described and analysed. Hughes writes that he originally intended to use the subtitle 'A Study of a Weak Parliament' for his book, but that he finished his 'investigation with a high respect for both the parliament of Switzerland and its members'. Hughes's study in turn demands the respect of its readers because of its learnedness and its penetrating observations. See also *Parlement et société en Suisse* by Henry H. Kerr (Saint-Saphorin, Switzerland: Georgi, 1981) and the freely translated German version of the same *Unser Parlament* (Neuallschwil/Basel, Switzerland: Heuwinkel, 2nd ed., 1985-87). The translation from the French is by Joseph Hanhart.

419 **Der Bund – kurz erklärt 1989.** (The federal government briefly explained, 1989.)

Bern: Schweizerische Bundeskanzlei, 1989. 11th ed. [n.p.].

This brochure, distributed gratis by the EDMZ, 3000 Bern, provides a large amount of factual information in telegram style, with tabulations, a few charts, and photographs of government leaders. It lists the political rights of Swiss citizens and describes the process by which new laws and constitutional amendments come into existence. For the Federal Assembly there are seating charts of the 200 members of the National Council (*Nationalrat*) and the forty-six members of the Council of States (*Ständerat*). Information on the party make-up of these two legislative chambers and their procedures is also provided. The executive branch of the government, the Federal Council (*Bundesrat*), receives considerable attention. All members of the Federal Council since 1848 are listed, as are the presidents of the Swiss Confederation and the federal chancellors. A chart showing the seven departments of the federal administration and their many branch offices and subdivisions is followed by brief paragraphs on the functions of each of these. A last part deals with the judicial branch of the government, the Federal Tribunal (*Bundesgericht*) in Lausanne and the Insurance Court (*Versicherungsgericht*) in Luzern. The names of the judges are provided, and the organization and tasks of the courts and their subdivisions are explained. This sympathetic, useful publication is also available in French, Italian, and Romansh.

Cantonal and communal governments

420 **The death of communal liberty: a history of freedom in a Swiss mountain canton.**
Benjamin R. Barber. Princeton, New Jersey: Princeton University Press, 1974. 302p. bibliog.

Mountainous Graubünden in the south-eastern part of Switzerland is the largest canton in the country. Even though thinly populated, it is characterized by the presence of a variety of ethnic groups and languages, among them the various Romansh sub-languages. Graubünden did not belong to the old Swiss Confederation; it had its own colourful and involved history, and much of this book is taken up by a retelling of this history. Barber finds that in olden times the communities exercised direct self-government, unhampered by ideas of centralized representational government. He deplores the 'eclipse of communalism' that he feels is taking place at the present because of the modern 'growth mania' and warns that this development in Graubünden may mean 'the eclipse of political man as an autonomous participant in the self-governing of his collective life' for Switzerland as a whole.

421 **Fiscal federalism in Switzerland.**
Stephan Bieri. Canberra: Australian National University, Centre for Research on Federal Financial Relations, 1979. 101p. bibliog.

Federalism, the chief characteristic of the Swiss state, also extends into the realm of fiscal management, budgets, taxation and other forms of revenue raising, and financial planning. Bieri shows with the help of numerous tables how federal, cantonal, and communal budgets have grown between 1960 and 1974 and how the vertical task distribution between these political entities works. He concludes that the system is in need of reform if it is to continue to facilitate fiscal equalization between cantons and regions and ensure an effective and equitable financial public sector. The extent and nature of such a reform, however, are open to debate.

422 **Governing the commune of Veyrier: politics in Swiss local government.**
George A. Codding, Jr. Boulder, Colorado: University of Colorado Bureau of Governmental Research, 1967. 98p. bibliog.

Veyrier is one of the almost 3,100 communes that form the smallest political subdivision in the Swiss system; it is situated a few kilometres south of Geneva at the foot of Mount Salève. Codding's booklet was conceived as a contribution to comparative public administration. After two introductory chapters that set the geographical and historical stage, Codding describes the politics of the commune, its government and how it is administered. The solid, reliable collection of data and their presentation in a style unencumbered by social science jargon make this a useful introduction to the study of Swiss communes in general.

423 **Local government in Switzerland: some contrasts with the United Kingdom with special reference to Kanton Graubünden.**
Ioan Bowen Rees. *Public Administration* (London), vol. 47 (Winter 1969), p. 421-49.

An immense contrast exists between the English and the Swiss conceptions of the role of the local government unit. The Swiss example directly contradicts the prevailing official and academic view in the United Kingdom that the amalgamation of smaller units into larger authorities is desirable. Rees uses the example of Canton Graubünden with its 221 self-governing communes to illustrate his contention that direct participation and communal pride give local government an importance far greater than it enjoys in the United Kingdom. He shows how local government works in the areas of planning, schooling, finances, and welfare. Rees concludes that in Switzerland the principal object of local government 'is still to enable a locality to retain as much freedom as possible', and that 'the essential factor is not size, but identity'.

Taxes

424 **Taxation in Switzerland.**
Boleslaw Adam Boczek. Chicago: Commerce Clearing House, 1976. 1310p. bibliog. (World tax series. Harvard Law School, International Tax Program).

A systematic and detailed study of the entire tax structure of Switzerland. The income taxes levied by the (then) twenty-five cantons and more than 3,000 communes occupy a central place in this extensive treatise. The first four chapters provide a general background of the Swiss tax system. Part II (Chapters 5 to 13) is devoted to the analysis of the individual and corporate income taxes. Part III deals with other taxes. Appendices give tables of decisions by the Federal Tribunal and cantonal courts, statutes, administrative materials, and treaties.

425 **Taxation in Switzerland.**
Deloitte Haskins & Sells. New York: Deloitte Haskins & Sells, 1982. 70p. (International tax and business service).

This booklet provides information about taxation in Switzerland in brief, factually descriptive chapters. The first part provides general information about the Swiss tax system. Taxes are levied by the federal government, the cantons and the municipalities. True to the federalism of the country, there are marked differences between cantons and municipalities. A second part deals with income taxes for individuals and corporations, giving rates and describing tax returns, and assessments. Part three consists of a list of other taxes, among them taxes on sales, transactions, commodities, and property, employment, and estate and gift taxes. Rate tables and appendices make up the fourth part of this concise and informative guide through the involved subject of taxation in Switzerland.

426 **The taxation of corporations in Switzerland: profit and capital taxes of the confederation, cantons and municipality.**
André Margairaz, Roger Merkli. Deventer, The Netherlands [etc.]: Kluwer, 1983. 139p. maps.

Margairaz and Merkli explain how taxes on corporations are calculated in Switzerland, a country that levies direct federal, cantonal, and municipal taxes. A 'formal harmonization' of direct cantonal and federal taxes was requested by the people in 1977 but has not yet been carried out. Thus, there are as many cantonal tax laws as there are cantons, and within the cantons communities use different formulas to levy taxes. Anyone wishing to found a corporation or set up an office in Switzerland needs to consider carefully the tax structure of the prospective location. Examples worked out in accordance with the tax laws of different cantons and communities demonstrate how greatly taxes can vary from place to place in a federal state.

Foreign Policy and Foreign Relations

General

427 **Notes de lecture. Notice bibliographiqe sur les publications récentes concernant les relations internationales de la Suisse de 1848 à nos jours.** (Lecture notes: bibliographical review of recent publications on the international relations of Switzerland from 1848 to the present.) Daniel Bourgeois. *Relations internationales*, no. 30 (Summer 1982), p. 231-48.

Intended to provide an introduction to recent literature on the international relations of Switzerland, this article is in fact an almost comprehensive overview of the vast output of articles and monographs in this field. Bourgeois presents his annotated bibliography in topically organized sub-chapters within a general chronological framework from 1848, the year of the founding of the modern Swiss state, through the 19th century, to the war, interwar, and postwar years of the 20th century. A fine, useful tool for anyone interested in the foreign relations of Switzerland during the last one and a half centuries.

428 **Einblick in die schweizerische Aussenpolitik. Festschrift für Staatssekretär Raymond Probst.** (Insight into Swiss foreign policy. A tribute to Secretary of State Raymond Probst.) Edited by Edouard Brunner, Franz E. Muheim, Rolf Stücheli, Paul Widmer. Zurich: Neue Zürcher Zeitung, 1984. 469p. bibliog.

The essays in this *Festschrift* in honour of Raymond Probst, a prominent and successful Swiss diplomat of the post-World War II era, reflect the themes of that time. They pay tribute to the honoree who retired in 1984 after more than forty years of service, and contain reminiscences by friends, but beyond that the essays deal with the perennial issue of Swiss neutrality in a time of economic multilateralism and integration, and the problems created by the influx of refugees to Switzerland in an era of decolonization and worldwide political unrest. A number of contributions focus on American-Swiss problems – Probst was ambassador to Washington during the Carter presidency – arising from trade restrictions on Swiss watch exports, Swiss bank secrecy, and the attempts by the United States to force Switzerland to accept the extraterritorial application of the United States' laws.

429 **Swiss foreign policy.**
Daniel Frei, translated from the German by F. M. Blackwell. Zurich: Pro Helvetia, Arts Council of Switzerland, 1987. 2nd ed. 47p.

This slim booklet provides an introduction into the elements of Swiss foreign policy. Swiss foreign policy is shaped by Switzerland's strategic position, its shortage of raw materials which forces the country to establish economic ties with other countries, and by the linkage between foreign relations and domestic affairs. Out of these formative forces have evolved Switzerland's policy of permanent neutrality and its consistent advocacy of the abolition of trade barriers. The influence of domestic policy is evident in Swiss defence policy and in the approach to current foreign relations problems such as the policy on refugees and Switzerland's position on West European integration and membership in international organizations.

430 **La Suisse et la diplomatie multilatérale.** (Switzerland and multilateral diplomacy.)
Edited by Jacques Freymond. Geneva: Institut Universitaire de Hautes Etudes Internationales, 1976. 302p.

This is a collection of sixteen papers, mostly by senior career officials of the Swiss civil service, on the range of problems that have emerged since World War II due to the growth, in number and in importance, of international organizations. Issues such as the economic relations of Switzerland with developing countries, Swiss technical cooperation with those countries, Swiss energy policy, Switzerland's relationship to the International Monetary Fund (IMF) and the United Nations (UNO), and its role in GATT (General Agreement on Tariffs and Trade) negotiations are among those discussed in this publication by the Geneva Graduate Institute of International Studies.

431 **Migration, cultural tensions, and foreign relations: Switzerland.**
Kurt B. Mayer. *Journal of Conflict Resolution*, vol. 11, no. 2 (June 1967), p. 139-52.

Mayer provides a brief description of one of the major problems in post-World War II Switzerland: the large and sustained influx of foreign, mainly Italian, workers. Work permits increased from 50,000 in 1946 to 721,000 at the seasonal peak in 1946 (in a population of 5.75 million). Due to the unexpected and prolonged economic boom, the need for large numbers of foreign workers was becoming permanent, and to encourage good workers to settle in Switzerland, the Swiss government allowed them to bring their families, with the result that the proportion of Italian speakers increased from 5.2 per cent in 1941 to 9.5 per cent in 1960. The migrants, or at any rate their children, tend to adopt the language of the area in which they have settled. The effects on the religious equilibrium of the country are more profound – Catholics, who had traditionally accounted for about 40 per cent of the population rose to 45.9 per cent in 1960 and even higher since. A wave of xenophobia resulted in the founding of a People's Movement against Foreign Invasion. This nativist organization demanded an immediate end to foreign immigration and a reduction by 30 per cent of the aliens already in the country. Its activities were denounced by the Italian press and created difficulties for the Swiss government in its relations with Italy.

432 **Diplomatische Dokumente der Schweiz 1848-1945.** (Swiss diplomatic documents 1848-1945.)
Nationale Kommission für die Veröffentlichung diplomatischer Dokumente der Schweiz. Bern: Benteli, 1979- . 15 vols.

By 1989, volumes 2, 3, 5, 6, 7-1, 7-2, 8, 9, and 10 were published, but none of the volumes covering the Hitler era and World War II (11-15) were yet available. Each volume contains 400 to 500 documents and is about 1,000 pages long. This is a large-scale undertaking by Swiss professional historians. Specific time-spans have been assigned to teams at the various Swiss institutions of higher learning. Documents, such as dispatches to and from Swiss representatives abroad, correspondences between foreign representatives in Switzerland and the Federal Council, texts of the deliberations and decisions of the Federal Council, treaties, and agreements, are printed in chronological order. An elaborate thematic tabulation provides access to the issues. Lists of offices and officials of the federal government that have to do with foreign affairs, and the Swiss diplomatic and consular representatives abroad and those of the foreign powers in Switzerland, as well as name and place indexes complete the elaborate apparatus of each volume. This mammoth work fulfils the national commission's goal of providing the sources needed for the reconstruction and understanding of the history of the foreign policy of Switzerland, a neutral country which to a high degree is part of the international political system.

433 **Handbuch der schweizerischen Aussenpolitik.** (Handbook of Swiss foreign policy.)
Edited by Alois Riklin, Hans Haug, Hans Christoph Binswanger. Bern; Stuttgart, FRG: Haupt, 1975. 1052p. bibliog.

This hefty volume was written by a team of thirty-seven authors, each an expert in his or her field. Most of the authors are connected with Swiss institutions of higher learning or serve as high officials in the federal government. As is expected of a handbook, the work covers almost every aspect of Swiss foreign policy. (The absence of any section about the United States or the Third World is puzzling.) The first parts are given to the historical, philosophical, and administrative principles underlying Swiss foreign relations. The others deal with Switzerland's human rights activities and good services, its relationship to Europe and to the United Nations, and economic and trade issues and their very considerable impact on Swiss foreign policy. The concept of neutrality as the guiding principle of Swiss foreign policy is acknowledged throughout. The active neutrality pursued by the Swiss has stood them in good stead, but the contemporary problems created by the existence of the United Nations and the growth of the European Community demand a rethinking of the concept. The bibliographies which accompany each chapter are comprehensive, and a number of tables, graphs, and two thorough indexes complete this high-quality product.

Neutrality

434 **Continuity and change in Swiss neutrality from 1815 to 1980: an analysis.**
Frederick William Dame. Saarbrücken, FRG: University of the Saarland, 1981. 331p. bibliog.

This political science dissertation examines continuity and change in Swiss neutrality since the Vienna Congress of 1815, where a 'permanent' neutrality was imposed on the country. The author examines the influence neutrality had – and still has – on the Swiss people, their society, economy, and political system and how it affects foreign relations. Switzerland has not been involved in a war since 1815 and has been able to preserve its security and national interest while adapting to changing situations. In the years following World War II, the conflict between the capitalist and communist systems and between highly industrialized and underdeveloped countries has put Swiss neutrality to new tests. A book that examines Swiss neutrality during the same period as Dame's is *Neutralität – Ideal oder Kalkül? Zweihundert Jahre außenpolitisches Denken in der Schweiz* (Neutrality – ideal or calculation? 200 years of thought on foreign policy in Switzerland) by Daniel Frei (Frauenfeld, Switzerland; Stuttgart, FRG: Huber, 1967).

435 **Neutrality and security policy as components of the Swiss model.**
Jean Freymond. *Government and Opposition*, vol. 23, no. 1 (Winter 1988), p. 51-68.

Freymond identifies the historical factors that have led Switzerland to adopt neutrality as an essential part of its foreign policy. He then analyses the meaning of Swiss neutrality in the context of the 20th century. He distinguishes between the status of neutrality with legal obligations that are valid only in time of war and a policy of neutrality in an everyday, ever-changing world. Swiss neutrality is armed neutrality whose aim is to maintain peace with independence. Even though the army is only one part of Swiss defence policy, it is still the principal factor of dissuasion and will remain so as long as the Swiss retain their will to fight. In recent decades the Federal Council has begun a new policy of openness toward the rest of the world, based on the principles of solidarity, universality, and availability. The economic and political challenge presented by the European Community will put this policy of openness to a difficult test. Freymond concludes with the question: 'what form will the policy of neutrality and the function of defence take then?' A short historical account of Swiss foreign policy under the guiding principle of neutrality is *Swiss neutrality: its history and meaning* by Edgar Bonjour (London: Allen & Unwin, 1946).

436 **Waging peace: the Swiss experience.**
William Bross Lloyd, Jr. Westport, Connecticut: Greenwood, 1980. 101p. (Originally published Washington, DC: Public Affairs Press, 1958).

Modern Swiss neutrality is no accident of history. Centuries of developing and using internal mechanisms to mediate conflicts and avoid war among the Swiss cantons laid the foundation. At various times changing groups of cantons assumed the task of ironing out differences among their confederates. As the history of the war between Zurich and Schwyz in the 15th century and of the religious wars of the 16th century show, these efforts were not always successful, but even in these instances, damaging consequences were prevented by submitting remaining issues to the counsel of peacemakers in the Diet of the Confederation. Some members, among them Appenzell, joined the Confederation with the express stipulation that they be permitted to abstain from any participation in internal conflicts and actively attempt to mediate between disputing parties. Lloyd lists some forty instances of successful mediation during the last two decades of the 15th century alone. He feels strongly that the Swiss example of how to maintain peace contains valuable lessons for the United Nations.

437 **The defense of small states in the nuclear age: the case of Sweden and Switzerland.**
Jerry Wilson Ralston. Geneva: University of Geneva. Graduate Institute of International Studies, 1968. 255p. bibliog.

This thesis explores security problems in a nuclear context as they manifest themselves in the two small (and in many ways similar) neutral countries, Sweden and Switzerland. Both nations have the ability to produce nuclear weapons but would never be a match for either of the superpowers. Switzerland's male population spends many hours performing its duties as citizen soldiers and the country expends vast resources on its conventional weapons system – Switzerland considers its military policy to be a deterrent to potential aggressions and also an obligation for a neutral. Ralston examines basically two questions: what are the theoretical and philosophical implications for a small country, and with what practical problems is an independent nation faced in providing security in a nuclear age? The author traces the public debate and legal aspects concerning the acquisition and production of nuclear arms during the 1950s and 1960s in the two neutrals. Two other books on the topic are *Schwedische und schweizerische Neutralität im Zweiten Weltkrieg* (Swedish and Swiss neutrality in World War II), edited by Rudolf L. Bindschedler (et al.) (Basel: Helbing & Lichtenhahn, 1985) and *Les états neutres européens et la Seconde Guerre mondiale* (The neutral European states and World War II), edited by Louis-Edouard Roulet and Roland Blättler (Neuchâtel, Switzerland: La Baconnière, 1985).

438 **Dokumente zur schweizerischen Neutralität seit 1945. Bericht und Stellungnahme der schweizerischen Bundesbehörden zur Frage der Neutralität 1945-1983.** (Documents on Swiss neutrality since 1945; reports and commentaries of the Swiss federal authorities on neutrality issues 1945-83.)
Edited by Dieter Schindler. Bern: Stuttgart, FRG: Haupt, 1984. 481p. (Schriftenreihe der Schweizerischen Gesellschaft für Aussenpolitik, 9).

This is a collection of statements on Swiss neutrality by members of the federal government and parliament. All documents have been published before in a variety of places and are reproduced in their original form by photomechanical means. Much of the space in this book is taken up by debates over the relationship to the United Nations, the European Community, and the Council of Europe. Issues concerning contractual obligations predominate; the problematical aspects of Swiss neutrality and the question of its value for the community of nations are barely touched upon.

439 **Die guten Dienste der Schweiz. Aktive Neutralitätspolitik zwischen Tradition, Diskussion und Integration.** (The good services of Switzerland: active neutrality policy between tradition, debate, and integration.)
Konrad Walter Stamm. Bern: Herbert Lang; Frankfurt am Main, FRG: Peter Lang, 1974. 266p. bibliog.

'Good services' is defined as measures undertaken by states or individuals to contribute to the settlement of conflicts between other states. Stamm's dissertation describes the activities of Switzerland in this field through mediation of conflicts; the assumption of international mandates in areas of conflict; the protection of foreign interests; the hosting of international organizations and conferences dedicated to the cause of peace; the carrying out of tasks for international organizations in crisis situations; and the assumption of arbitration duties. The institution of good services in the context of Swiss history dates back to the Old Confederation. During World War I the debate raged whether or not to try to play the role of mediator. The interwar years were a period of high activity in arbitration matters and peace initiatives, and membership in the League of Nations, once approved by the voters, led to a series of successful conflict resolutions by prominent Swiss citizens. World War II was the high-water mark of Swiss humanitarian and diplomatic good services, but immediately after the war the neutrality policy of Switzerland found little recognition. This changed in 1955 when Switzerland became a member of the Korean armistice team and Austria received its peace treaty with the expressed obligation to pursue a policy of neutrality on the Swiss example.

Relations with other countries

440 **Switzerland – Third World: repertory of institutions.**
Edited by René Barbey. Geneva: Institut Universitaire d'Etudes du Développement, 1985. 180p. bibliog.

This address book lists agencies and organizations located in Switzerland and engaged in activities in the Third World. The institutions are listed alphabetically according to the name of the organization and by canton. The editor devised a system of twenty-three symbols grouping the organizations according to the type of service they provide and the nature of the organization; for instance, IFD stands for 'federal institutions', and ATM stands for 'cultural associations'. These symbols are entered in the margin of the address list. An index at the back, consisting of the hundreds of organizations across Switzerland (also with their abbreviations) makes for quick reference. The same editor and publisher brought out a somewhat differently organized work as *Suppléments à l'Annuaire Suisse-Tiers Monde*, no. 1, 4th ed., 1987.

441 **Le Troisième Reich et la Suisse 1933-1941.** (The Third Reich and Switzerland 1933-1941.)
Daniel Bourgeois. Neuchâtel: La Baconnière, 1974. 463p. bibliog.

This history of German–Swiss relations during most of the first decade of the Hitler régime is based on documentary materials in German archives. During the 1930s Germany made a determined effort to detach Switzerland from the European system established at the Paris Peace Conference of 1919 and to use frontist political groups to weaken the government, the army, and the press. The German diplomatic representatives in Bern played an active role in these endeavours. After the fall of France the situation became critical for Switzerland: the Nazis drew up plans for an invasion of the country, increased economic pressure, and attempted to lure Swiss sympathizers into open support of the victorious Reich. Switzerland's steps in response to the new situation, such as the special order of the Swiss general, Henri Guisan, to the high officers of the army on the Rütli, the 'cradle' of the Swiss Confederation on Lake Lucerne, and the revised plan for a defensive redoubt (*réduit*) in the Alps, were received very negatively by the Germans. The subversive plans of the Nazi organizations in Switzerland became known in the autumn of 1941, and the frontist leaders were arrested. In this sense German policy toward Switzerland was a complete fiasco. Bourgeois does not deal with the economic aspects of the relationship between the two countries.

442 **Schweizer Kreuz und Sowjetstern. Die Beziehungen zweier ungleicher Partner seit 1917.** (Swiss cross and Soviet star: the relations between two unequal partners since 1917.)
Dietrich Dreier. Zurich: Neue Zürcher Zeitung, 1989. 255p. bibliog.

This is a welcome study, based on Swiss sources, about the relationship between the Soviet Union and Switzerland. Switzerland was one of the few countries to admit representatives of the Soviet government immediately after the October Revolution. The first Soviet mission, however, lasted only six months. Already in November 1918, the Federal Council terminated diplomatic relations, accusing the Soviets of having participated actively in the Swiss General Strike, and for almost three decades the two countries were without diplomatic relations, as an assortment of incidents kept relations less than cordial. Toward the end of World War II, when the Allied victory was assured, the Federal Council, under pressure from business, made attempts to normalize relations, but were snubbed repeatedly by Stalin. The forced retirement of Federal Councillor Marcel Pilet-Golaz, the head of the Swiss foreign ministry, and the repatriation of the Soviet soldiers interned in Switzerland permitted the normalization of relations in 1946. Dreyer finds that Switzerland on the whole navigated successfully between the two power blocs of the Cold War.

443 **Swiss–American economic relations: their evolution in an era of crises.**
Paul Erdman. Basel: Kyklos; Tübingen, FRG: J. C. B. Mohr (Paul Siebeck), 1959. 173p. bibliog.

The United States is less dependent on foreign trade to sell its manufactured products than Switzerland and therefore is able to tailor its trade policies to domestic political needs. These basic factors form the framework for US–Swiss economic relations. The Great Depression, with the enactment of the Hawley-Smoot tariff of 1930 and the abrupt decline in American imports of Swiss goods, strained these relations; the huge amount of capital that was moved from Switzerland to America also reflected the unsettled times. Tensions during World War II revolved around the Allied blockade of the export of raw materials and foodstuffs and the counter-blockade of the Axis powers, which decimated the volume of trade between America and Switzerland. The economic conflicts dragged on into the postwar years, and included matters such as US tariffs on watches, German assets in Switzerland, and the Interhandel affair, involving the wrangle over the ownership of IG Farben shares. See also *Die schweizerisch–amerikanischen Finanzbeziehungen im Zweiten Weltkrieg. Von der Blockierung der schweizerischen Guthaben in den USA über die 'Safehaven'-Politik zum Washingtoner*

Abkommen (1941-1946) (Swiss–American financial relations in World War II: from the blocking of Swiss assets in the USA through the 'Safehaven' policy to the Washington accord (1941-46) by Marco Durrer (Bern; Stuttgart, FRG: Haupt, 1984). This is a broadly conceived and carefully researched monograph on the topic.

444 **Britain and Switzerland 1845-60: a study of Anglo–Swiss relations during some critical years for Swiss neutrality.**

Ann G. Imlah. London: Longmans, 1966. 208p. map. bibliog.

This book represents one of the first attempts to trace the middle years of nineteenth-century Switzerland (1845-60) in the English language and to make use of materials from British archives. Britain's tireless diplomatic intervention was vital for Swiss independence, as the Acts of 1815 that had guaranteed Swiss neutrality were soon endangered. Reactionary European monarchs attempted to use the internal struggles that resulted in a civil war, the *Sonderbundskrieg* of 1847, to expand their influence and to intervene in Switzerland's internal affairs. In 1856 the crisis over the question of Neuchâtel's independence from Prussia created a particular threat to Swiss neutrality. The reader gains insight from the British perspective into Switzerland's foreign, political, and economic relations during these critical years. See also 'Great Britain and neutral Switzerland' by Anthony Adamthwaite, in *Les états neutres européens et la Seconde Guerre mondiale*, edited by L.-E. Roulet and R. Blättler (Neuchâtel: La Baconnière, 1985, p. 257-65).

445 **The United States and Switzerland in the nineteenth century.**

Heinz K. Meier. The Hague: Mouton, 1963. 208p. bibliog.

This study examines the diplomatic relationship between the two countries; it also touches upon cultural and economic aspects of the relationship, as well as immigration. In 1850 the two countries signed a treaty of friendship which remained the firm basis for their dealings with each other for the rest of the century. The early American representatives in Switzerland stressed the uniqueness of Switzerland among the monarchies of Europe and made much of the ideological ties between the Alpine and the American republics. Switzerland sent its first diplomatic representative to Washington only in 1882, reflecting the growing importance of the United States for Swiss exports. Up to that time it had relied on the services of honorary consuls who, situated in the larger cities, watched over the interests of Swiss exporters and immigrants alike. The book is still the basic monograph on its subject.

446 **Friendship under stress: U.S.–Swiss relations 1900-1950.**

Heinz K. Meier. Bern: Lang, 1970. 423p. bibliog.

The two World Wars of the 20th century affected US–Swiss relations in important respects. During World War I Switzerland came to depend on American raw materials and food supplies, and both were hard to come by once the United States had joined the war. During the interwar years American tariff laws stirred up negative reaction in Switzerland. In the second half of World War II Switzerland was subjected to intense pressure by the United States and Great Britain to change its economic policies toward Germany; the after-effects of the tensions created were felt into the early 1950s. Meier points out that in spite of such difficulties, feelings of respect and friendship provided the underlying continuity in the relationship. This book is the only large-scale and detailed scholarly study of 20th-century relations between Switzerland and any other country. An account that follows Meier's work closely in organization and documentation, but without acknowledging it, is 'American wartime relations with neutral European states: the case of the United States and Switzerland' by Arthur L.

Funk, in *Les états neutres européens et la Seconde Guerre mondiale*, edited by L.-E. Roulet and R. Blättler (Neuchâtel, Switzerland: La Baconnière, 1985 p. 283-302).

447 **Liechtenstein und die Schweiz: eine völkerrechtliche Untersuchung.**
(Liechtenstein and Switzerland: a study in international law.)
Dieter J. Niedermann. Vaduz: Liechtensteinische Akademische Gesellschaft, 1976. 174p. bibliog.

The foundation for Liechtenstein's close relations with Switzerland as documented in their bilateral treaties was laid after World War I. It covers all aspects of interaction between the two countries: political, military, customs, monetary, postal, economic, social, and educational. On the international scene, Switzerland represents its tiny neighbour in many countries and organizations, and these arrangements have proved flexible enough to withstand politically troubled times. The author shows that Liechtenstein, however small and dependent on Switzerland, is a sovereign nation. He proposes a course of action for the prinicipality to consider, such as greater interaction with the European Community and a strengthening of ties with Switzerland while assuring participatory rights that it does not currently enjoy.

448 **Swiss relations with the United Kingdom in the formation and development of EFTA until 1976.**
Curt Truninger. Aberdeen, Scotland: Aberdeen University, Department of Politics, PhD thesis, 1976. 456p.

The European Free Trade Association (EFTA) provided a politically acceptable means for Switzerland and the United Kingdom to participate in the process of European cooperation – they worked together closely in the drafting of the Stockholm convention which established EFTA in 1959. However, when in October the British government violated the agreement by imposing a 15% surcharge on all imports from its EFTA partners the organization began to weaken. Switzerland objected strongly to the British measure but desisted from invoking the convention, since no measures existed to force Great Britain to change its policy. Truninger concludes that Britain 'never wholeheartedly supported the EFTA institutions but rather tried to use them for its own means'. One of the appendices consists of copies of two letters by former Federal Councillor Hans Schaffner – who had been instrumental in starting EFTA – in which Schaffner expresses himself very undiplomatically, even though undoubtedly correctly, about 'the worthless British and American guys' (*Gesellen*) who hurt the solidarity of those outside the European Economic Community.

449 **Switzerland and Europe: essays and reflections.**
Jean-Rodolphe de Salis, translated from the German by Alexander and Elizabeth Henderson, introduction by C. J. Hughes. London: Wolff, 1971. 319p.

This book contains selections from two volumes of essays by the Swiss historian and editorialist J.-R. de Salis. As Christopher Hughes points out in his introduction, Salis was an intellectual of many interests who became famous beyond the borders of Switzerland because of his weekly radio broadcasts during World War II, heard and appreciated in many parts of Europe. The essays selected for this volume are organized into three groups entitled 'concerning Switzerland', which contains the essay that gave the title to the book, 'historical essays', two of which describe his trips to Prague and Vienna just after World War II and his triumphal reception there, while the third, 'Sismondi and other essays', displays his skill in interpreting the literary works of Swiss writers.

450 **The Swiss and the British.**

John Wraight. Salisbury, England: Russell, 1987. 474p. map. bibliog.

Wraight, British ambassador to Switzerland from 1973 to 1976, has created an impressive work of love and erudition. The beautifully illustrated volume has three parts. In the first part, Wraight gives a narrative overview of British–Swiss relations and their military and diplomatic, cultural, educational and scientific, and economic aspects. The second part is a chronology from the early Middle Ages, when the Irish monks came to Christianize the Alemannic inhabitants of the Swiss plateau, through the 16th century with its intensive religious contacts between the Zurich reformers Zwingli and Bullinger and their Scottish counterparts, and John Knox and the British exiles who found asylum and received schooling in the Geneva of Calvin, to 1984. From 1580 on there is an entry for almost every year, recording an amazing range of interaction between individuals and organizations of the two countries. The last part consists of a most valuable, exhaustive bibliography of about 1,500 titles. It is divided into four sections, entitled 'historical, political, diplomatic and military', 'geographical, descriptive, travellers, visitors, mountaineering and winter sports', 'cultural, artistic, scientific and religious', and 'economic, commercial, industrial and financial'. A full index completes this interesting and welcome addition to the literature on Swiss relations with other countries.

Army

451 **The Swiss model of national defense.**
Gustav Däniker. *Armed Forces Journal International*, July 1984, p. 33-43.

Having renounced nuclear weapons and a policy of deterrence, Switzerland adheres to the 'much more modest objective [of] the building up of a war and survival potential sufficiently strong to convince any adversary that an attack on Switzerland does not pay'. The Swiss have constructed a comprehensive defence (*Gesamtverteidigung*) with a combat force of some 625,000 well-trained militia that can be mobilized within hours and a fully developed civil defence with 400,000 personnel, shelter space for well over seventy per cent of the population, and an economic war stock programme permitting the survival of the country even during extended periods of import interruptions. The army is, as Däniker shows in his article, well equipped with some of the most modern weapons systems. Its combat doctrine is known as the concept of 'repulse' (*Abwehr*), with the military units taking advantage of the terrain through the use of existing permanent combat installations. Among other relevant and interesting information that Däniker successfully packs into this short article one might single out the fact that every military aeroplane 'is stationed in a network of caverns deep in the mountains where they are not only able to survive even the most massive enemy air attacks, but where they can also be serviced and repaired'. Däniker's conclusion is that the Swiss militia system is worthy of imitation elsewhere in Europe.

452 **The women and the army in Switzerland: a general survey.**
Karl Haltiner, Ruth Meyer. Bern: Institut für Soziologie der Universität Bern, 1980. 130p. bibliog. (Arbeitsbericht aus dem Institut für Soziologie der Universität Bern, 4)

The authors chart the paths of the different women's groups engaged in national defence that came into being since World War II: the Women's Auxiliary Service (FHD) patterned after the army but not equipped with weapons, the Red Cross service, and the Civil Defence. The historical and social developments that prevented these volunteer groups from becoming fully accepted or integrated into the armed forces are explained. Data from questionnaires show that military matters have always been a male prerogative in Switzerland and that the support for the army remains strong. Despite the introduction of women's suffrage in 1971, a change in attitudes and values of women themselves is partly responsible for the current low levels of participation in these groups.

453 **Die Schweizer Armee heute.** (The Swiss army today.)
Edited by Hans Rudolf Kurz. Thun, Switzerland: Ott, 1988. 11th ed. 691p.

Kurz, chief of the office for information and documentation of the Federal Military Department, has assembled forty-eight military men who provide up-to-date information on their field of expertise. In a first part every branch of the Swiss army, from the infantry and air force to the military judiciary and the music bands, receives a chapter. Another section has chapters describing the ideological and constitutional bases of the army, the role of the army in the democratic state, the training of the army, modern equipment and weaponry, the financial and social aspects of national defence, and other topics. The large-format book is illustrated with many black-and-white and colour photographs. In *Hundert Jahre Schweizer Armee* (One hundred years of the Swiss army) by Hans Rudolf Kurz (Thun, Switzerland: Ott, 1978) there are 280 illustrations and several appendices with tables and data that give valuable information on Switzerland's national defence.

454 **La Place de la Concorde suisse.** (The Swiss 'Place de la Concorde'.)
John McPhee. New York: Farrar, Straus, Giroux, 1984. 150p.

Consisting of 650,000 citizens who can be fully mobilized in forty-eight hours, the Swiss army is one of the world's largest as a percentage of population. This delightful booklet gives insights into the working of this army that one does not find in much heavier tomes on the subject. McPhee participated as a guest of the Swiss army in one of the annual refresher courses of mountain troops in the Valais Alps near the confluence of a number of glaciers known as Place de la Concorde. His observations of the manoeuvres of the units in the rugged mountains and his discussions with the citizen soldiers that make up the units reveal the broader role of the army in Swiss life. McPhee succeeds in showing how thoroughly intertwined the relationship is between the army and the society it serves. His book has accurately been described as 'a portrait of Switzerland within the frame of its militia'.

455 **The defence forces of Switzerland.**
Edited by C. H. Stainforth. Tavistock, Devon, England: West of England Press, 1974. 40p. (Armies of the World series of *The Army Quarterly and Defence Journal*).

This slim, illustrated booklet contains eight brief statements by high-ranking Swiss officers on various aspects of the Swiss army, from defence policy and the history of the Swiss army to descriptions of its organization, its disposition and equipment, procurement and deployment of armaments, and training. The information is factual and militarily precise.

456 **The citizen army: key to defense in the atomic age.**
Frederick Martin Stern. New York: St Martin's Press, 1957. 373p.

Since armies serve diverse purposes, different types of armies have evolved. The most important types are, according to Stern, the citizen army and the standing army. In this book Stern is concerned with the citizen army. Its basic characteristics are that it comprises virtually the entire citizenry of a country, is organized in peacetime by universal obligation, and trained on a part-time basis. Stern devotes two chapters to the two most successful precedents, the Swiss and the Australian citizen armies. The 'Swiss model' is presented in some detail, within its historical background and constitutional framework. He stresses the fact that 'military training forms a natural part of the citizen's life' and describes the process by which Swiss males become soldiers and officers and maintain preparedness until they are mustered out of the army at age fifty, or fifty-five for officers. The Swiss army is very economical: 'the Swiss buy for each dollar – or franc – very much more military preparedness than any other country'. It is also technically current. The Swiss system demonstrates 'how a democracy can keep itself strong, and avert war, without ruining either its economy or its liberty'. It can be applied, Stern maintains, in modified form to armies, *and* air forces and navies, of other countries.

Economy

457 **Focus on Switzerland: economic life and the export industries.**
Edited by François Gross, translated from the French by Roger Glémet. Lausanne, Switzerland: Swiss Office for the Development of Trade, 1982. 2nd ed. 115p.

This richly illustrated booklet provides an excellent overview of the character of the Swiss economy. The Swiss economy is intimately tied to the economy of the world and depends on successfully marketing its products abroad. The historical roots of this development are sketched, as are the major industries from the dairy and food industry to the chemical and pharmaceutical, watchmaking, engineering, hydro-electric and nuclear power, machine tool, and textile industries. The role which scientific research, consulting, customer service training, banks, insurance companies, the merchant marine, and the 'sixth Switzerland' of Swiss companies abroad play in maintaining Switzerland's competitive position in the world market is also outlined. The Swiss are able to sell their products abroad thanks to the quality of those products and of their services and the stability of the Swiss franc. The booklet with its many striking photographs is in itself a quality product and as such the best possible propaganda instrument for the subject it describes. The *Focus on Switzerland* series has also been published in German, French, Italian, and Spanish. It is available from the publisher or Pro Helvetia, Swiss Council for Culture, in Zurich.

458 **Die schweizerische Volkswirtschaft. Eine problemorientierte Einführung in die Volkswirtschaftslehre.** (The Swiss economy: a problem-oriented introduction to the science of economics.)
Henner Kleinewefers, Regula Pfister. Frauenfeld, Switzerland: Huber, 1978. 677p.

The two authors have written an economics textbook that covers the subject in five major parts: (1) the history of Swiss economy in five epochs from the pre-technical era to the boom decades of the 1950s and 1960s; (2) the constitutional and ideological framework of Swiss economy; (3) the production factors, such as property, energy, capital, labour, and knowledge; (4) the production results in terms of gross domestic product, foreign trade, public finances, and social security; and (5) current and future problems of the Swiss economy. The parts are divided into chapters and sub-chapters that receive a uniform didactic treatment. The starting point is in each case the presentation of pertinent facts and of concrete problems as revealed by these facts followed by a discussion of the theories that can be derived, ending every time with a precise set of conclusions. The book with its 84 tables and 93 diagrams is well written and provides a comprehensive introduction to Swiss political economy. The latest economic developments are discussed in *Die Volkswirtschaft* (The public economy) by the Schweizerisches Department für Volkswirtschaft (Münsingen, Switzerland: Fischer Druck, 1928- . monthly).

459 **OECD economic surveys 1988/1989: Switzerland.**
Organization for Economic Co-operation and Development. Paris: OECD, May 1989. 121p.

Published annually since 1961 for each of the by now twenty-four member countries of the OECD, these economic surveys provide a detailed analysis of recent economic developments in demand, production, employment, prices and wages, conditions in the money and capital markets, and developments in the balance of payments. Short-term forecasts, as well as analyses of medium-term problems with conclusions for economic policy constitute part of the annual review. The case of Switzerland is summed up in the conclusion that 'Switzerland's economic performance has remained excellent'. Twenty-four tables and twenty-one diagrams help to underline the points made in the text. A statistical annexe with nine tables of data on a wide range of economic indicators and a calendar of main economic events January 1987-April 1989 complete the materials in this fact-filled publication.

460 **Switzerland 1920-1970.**
Hansjörg Siegenthaler. In: *The Fontana economic history of Europe*, vol. 6: *Contemporary economies*, part 2, edited by Carlo M. Cipolla. Brighton, England: Harvester; New York: Barnes & Noble, 1977, p. 530-76.

In this substantial article Siegenthaler concentrates on economic growth in Switzerland during the 20th century up to the early 1970s. Swiss national product per capita increased in real terms 160 per cent between 1910 and 1970, paralleling similar growth patterns in other industrialized countries. Most of the growth came in the quarter century after World War II when 'total product and population advanced on reciprocally dependent courses'. Siegenthaler analyses the factors that are the basis of Swiss economic growth and describes the contributions made by the major segments of the Swiss economy: agriculture, industry, and the service sector. Behind the widely held anachronistic picture of a little country with a quaint domestic industry, typified in the false stereotype of the craftsman turning out his clocks and watches, lies 'a country with a large-scale economy of world standing'. In the last part Siegenthaler evaluates the impact of this economic growth on living conditions in Switzerland which are approaching 'the standards set at the beginning of the century by the lavish consumer habits of the upper classes'. The question of how Switzerland will deal with the less welcome consequences of economic growth in the future must remain open. Twelve tables and figures provide statistical data. Siegenthaler is also the author of 'Switzerland in the twentieth century: the economy', in *Modern Switzerland*, edited by J. Murray Luck (Palo Alto, California: Society for the Promotion of Science and Scholarship, 1978, p. 91-111).

461 **Wirtschaftsbuch Schweiz. Das moderne Grundwissen über Ökonomie und Ökologie in der Schweiz. Ein Arbeitsbuch mit 90 Schaubildern und Kommentaren.** (Swiss economy: modern basic knowledge about economy and ecology in Switzerland; a workbook with 90 graphs and commentaries.)

Rudolf H. Strahm. Zurich: Ex Libris, 1987. 301p. bibliog.

This is a careful analysis of the major elements of a nation's economy in the contemporary world, using the the example of Switzerland. From the various economic theories available, Strahm chooses the holistic socio-ecological approach that sees the economy as an integral part of a larger system which includes human beings, as individuals, families, and societies, as well as nature and the environment with which they interact. The chapter on economic growth, for example, measures the characteristics of the welfare economy against the usually hidden follow-up costs. Simple graphs, based on the latest figures available, impressively demonstrate the points made by the author. They play an important didactic role also in chapters on labour and employment policies; the distribution of the national wealth; the role of the state; agriculture between agrarian industry and nature; energy policy; traffic policy; Switzerland in the world economy; and consumers and renters. In the last chapter on perspectives for the future Strahm develops a possible scenario for Switzerland in the 21st century when private enterprise capitalism is tempered and to some extent replaced by an economy based on solidarity, and where 'hard' technologies, such as nuclear power, have made room for 'soft' technologies, such as solar energy.

462 **The Swiss economy 1946-1986: data, facts, analyses.**

Union Bank of Switzerland, Department of Economic Research. Zurich: Union Bank of Switzerland, 1987. 264p. bibliog.

Switzerland's economy has undergone major changes during the forty years since World War II. This volume presents in summary form and with the help of many charts and tables some important aspects of these changes. It is divided into four parts. The first part deals with the development of the national economy, treating topics such as economic growth and inflation, structural changes and the labour market, and foreign trade. The second part is devoted to Switzerland as a financial centre, providing in brief space a discussion of the factors that have helped Switzerland achieve its status and a description of its structure, with emphasis on the development of the banking system. The third part deals with Swiss economic policy and includes chapters on the country's budget, its tax system and tax burden, its monetary and currency policy, and its structural policy. It ends with a chronicle that lists the important economic and social measures taken at the national level in Switzerland from 1946 to 1986, grouped within each chronological period according to monetary and exchange policy, financial policy, foreign trade policy, structural economic policy, and social policy. The fourth part provides information on economic and business training in Switzerland. Published on the occasion of the 125th anniversary of the Union Bank of Switzerland, this informative and valuable work is available from the bank headquarters in Zurich.

Banking and Finance

463 **Le secret bancaire suisse: étendue et limites en droit privé, pénal, administratif, fiscal, judiciaire, dans le cadre des conventions internationales et selon la jurisprudence des tribunaux des Etats-Unis.**
(The Swiss bank secret: extent and limits in private, penal, administrative, fiscal, and judicial law, in the framework of the international conventions and according to the jurisprudence of the courts of the United States.)
Maurice Aubert, Jean-Philippe Kernen, Herbert Schönle. Bern: Staempfli, 1982. 2nd rev. ed., 503p. bibliog.

This learned treatise discusses all aspects of law concerning the Swiss bank secret. The Swiss bank secret is not a fictitious institution, designed to protect privileges or, worse, to make possible the hiding of assets of dubious origin; it is an essential, if sometimes controversial, part of a system of law that protects the individual against third parties or even the state. The bank secret can be lifted if there is legitimate cause. The authors demonstrate the care and concern with which the public interest has been enabled through legislation, jurisprudence, and practical law to stop abuses. A long chapter that deals with the difficulties Switzerland has experienced with the United States over this issue illustrates that solutions acceptable to both sides can be reached without violating the important principles at stake. Another book on the topic is *Tatsachen über das schweizerische Bankgeheimnis* (Facts about the Swiss bank secret) by Christoph Büchenbacher (Zurich [etc]: Nova, 1977).

464 **Complete guide to Swiss banks.**
Harry Browne. New York: McGraw-Hill, 1976. 534p. bibliog.

At the time this work was published, Browne had been involved for nine years with a dozen Swiss banks on behalf of hundreds of clients. His extensive hands-on experience translates into much practical advice, guarding the investor against pitfalls and suggesting ways of communicating with carefully selected banks. He covers matters of security, services, types of investments, privacy, and taxes, and warns of possible risks.

The paragraphs are short; subheadings clearly define the various subject areas. Browne highlights differences between American and Swiss banking practices. The appendix provides a glossary of banking terms in English and short German–English and French–English lists of pertinent words. Browne also includes his version 'in plain English' of the 'Treaty between the U.S.A. and the Swiss Confederation on Mutual Assistance in Criminal Matters'. Factual information and practical ways of dealing with Swiss banks is also provided in *What the prudent investor should know about Switzerland and other foreign money havens* by Harry D. Schultz (New Rochelle, New York: Arlington House, 1970).

465 **Safety in numbers: the mysterious world of Swiss banking.**
Nicholas Faith. London: Hamilton, 1982. 368p. bibliog.

Faith, a finance journalist, claims to lift the veil of mystery that shrouds the Swiss banking institutions. Historically, information on the inner workings of the 'gnomes of Zurich', that is, the Swiss bankers who allegedly amass piles of dirty money, protect crooks, and manipulate the financial markets of the world, was hard to come by. Swiss banking scandals of the 1970s, however, brought a great deal of information to light. Faith tells many stories, rumoured and factual, and uses press information and archival materials to present the situation as accurately as possible. He sees Swiss banks as becoming more and more like their counterparts around the world.

466 **The Swiss banks.**
T. R. Fehrenbach. New York [etc.]: McGraw-Hill, 1966. 280p.

This sensationalist work purports to expose how Swiss banks protect dictators and gangsters through the bank secret and numbered accounts. The author provides no documentation, nor does he reveal his sources, and the names of many persons he mentions are disguised. Much of the story turns around the famous Swiss bank secret and the, according to Fehrenbach, pivotal role it plays in the country's economy. The bank secret, together with Switzerland's geographical and political advantages, its basically unregulated markets, stable currency, and low taxes account for the phenomenal growth of Switzerland as a financial centre. Chapters on the big banks and the world of the private banker, on the hoarding of money and gold in Switzerland by wealthy and often shady characters from many parts of the world, and on the difficulties the Swiss have had periodically with American authorities since the end of World War II are blended together into a strange mix of journalistic debunking and secret admiration. See also *Those Swiss money men* by Ray Vicker (New York: Scribner's, 1973). This book consists of mostly entertaining tales about Swiss banks and money men without any documentation whatsoever.

467 **Finanz und Wirtschaft.** (Finance and economy.)
Zurich: Finanz und Wirtschaft, 1928- . twice weekly; circulation 27,000; ca. 30p.

A substantial paper with news and articles on monetary, financial, and economic developments on national and international markets. It also publishes journalistic analyses of corporations, industries, banks, and stock markets.

468 **Switzerland: an international banking and finance center.**
Max Iklé, translated from the German by Erich Schiff. Stroudsburg, Pennsylvania: Dowden, Hutchinson & Ross, 1972. 156p.

Iklé, a prominent Swiss banker and former high official in the Swiss finance department, provides a sober, straightforward account of Switzerland's role in international banking and finance. A historical sketch describes the evolution of Geneva, Zurich, and Basel into centres of banking from the 18th century to the 1940s. He then tells how after World War II the Swiss government took an active role in the areas of currency, finance, and business cycles to ensure high employment and low inflation. The major part of the book is devoted to a discussion of Switzerland as a financial centre with sections on the different kinds of banks, international business banking, exchange and currency valuation, and, inevitably, the bank secret. The author also covers a range of other financial institutions, including finance and holding companies, fiduciaries, and insurance companies. They, as well as the big industrial conglomerates with their international interlocking of capital, constitute important elements of the Swiss economy.

469 **Swiss securities law: English translation of official texts.**
Swiss-American Chamber of Commerce, translated from the German by the Legal Committee of the Swiss-American Chamber of Commerce. Zurich: Swiss-American Chamber of Commerce, 1982. 139p.

This book consists of translations of sections pertinent to securities law from various Swiss law texts such as the Swiss code of obligations, the federal law on investment funds, the Zurich law on professional trading of securities, the law on the national bank, and the Swiss criminal code.

470 **The Swiss paradox: rock-solid social and economic fundamentals – rock-bottom equity prices, a longer-term view.**
Lombard, Odier & Cie. Geneva: Lombard Odier, [1988?]. 117p.

This slick publication by one of the leading Swiss private banks elaborates on the theme announced in its title. Numerous coloured charts and diagrams underline the point that Switzerland's social and economic fundamentals, among them political and social stability, a balanced and healthy economic performance with modest economic growth, low inflation, practically no unemployment, and a secure current account, as well as low government profile, stable economic policy, and a strong currency, are superior to those of most other industrialized countries. Despite these excellent fundamentals the Swiss stock market has performed disappointingly during the period 1982-87. It rose less than other major markets during the bull market of these five years and it was severely affected by the crash of world equity prices in October 1987. The Lombard Odier bank analyses the reasons for this poor performance and concludes that, given the economic and social fundamentals, the longer-term view on Swiss stocks and bonds has to be positive. In a last section the bank spells out why investors should consider doing business with and through it. Also written with their clients in mind is *Banking in Switzerland* by Peat, Marwick, Mitchell & Co. (Zurich; Geneva: Peat, Marwick, Mitchell & Co., 1982).

471 **The Swiss equity market: a guide for investors.**
Edited by Henri B. Meier. London: Woodhead-Faulkner; Westport, Connecticut: Quorum Books, 1985. 210p. bibliog.

Eight financial experts and investment bankers associated with HandelsBank NW, wrote this technical treatise with numerous charts and tables on all aspects of securities trading on and through Swiss stock exchanges by Zurich. Chapters one and two are introductory, providing a history of the equity market and its performance. Chapters three to nine describe the various stock exchanges of Switzerland; the types and forms of shares and other securities traded on the Swiss capital market; the procedures involved in the issue of new shares; the actual trading at a Swiss stock exchange; how to list a share on a Swiss stock exchange; the tax situation of foreign investors and the implications of Swiss bank secrecy; and Swiss accounting principles and the reading of Swiss accounts. A first appendix provides an analysis of fourteen important corporations from different sectors in Switzerland with charts of the short- and long-term development of their share prices, and a second appendix contains the text of the 'Agreement on the observance of care by the banks in accepting funds and on the practice of banking secrecy (ACB) with executive regulations of the Swiss National Bank Zurich, and the Swiss Bankers' Association, Basel, of 1st July, 1982'. On related topics, Henri B. Meier has also written *Swiss capital markets* (London: Euromoney, 1983), and HandelsBank NW has published *Swiss banking secrecy, science and fiction* (Zurich, 1982).

472 **Geschichte der Schweizer Banken.** (History of the Swiss banks.)
Edited by Louis H. Mottet. Zurich: Neue Zürcher Zeitung, 1987. 262p.

This is a history of Swiss banking and the prominent bankers that guided its development. These ingenious and courageous men established over hundreds of years a Swiss banking tradition that has gained the trust of the world and has assured Switzerland a place as one of the financial centres with New York, London, and Tokyo. Economic shifts and political upheavals presented constantly new challenges. Johann Jakob Leu (1689-1768), treasurer and later mayor of Zurich was one of the early pioneers; his name lives on in one of the five major Swiss banks. From the 19th century, Christoph Merian Burckhardt from Basel is remembered as banker and patron of the city, and Alfred Escher of Zurich as politician and the founder of the Swiss Credit Bank. Many rose from the ranks of industry and business. Financier Jacques Necker was in the service of France, and Albert Gallatin became United States Treasurer. Switzerland's present viable economy is largely the result of the healthy credit system that has emerged over time and made banking an industry of prime importance for the country. Over two hundred illustrations feature the bankers and the splendid edifices they built, mostly in the urban centres of Geneva, Basel, Bern, Zurich, St Gallen and Lugano. The French version, *Les grandes heures des banquiers suisses* (Neuchâtel; Paris: Delachaux & Niestlé S.A.), appeared in 1986.

473 **The Swiss solution: privacy, tax minimization and wealth building for Americans today.**
Edited by Lawrence C. Oakley. Boca Raton, Florida: Seminars International Incorporated, 1987. 201p.

This is a book for 'people who have only a vague idea about Swiss banking and financial opportunities and want to know more'. It consists of 118 pages of text and about 100 pages of appendices. The text provides information about Switzerland's banking climate, its security and privacy attributes, investment opportunities, and how best to use its banking facilities. The appendices include copies of documents required in such transactions as opening a bank account and various statistics about the Swiss economy, freely copied from available sources.

474 **Banking establishments in Switzerland.**
Publications bancaires. Petit-Lancy, Switzerland: Publications bancaires, 1960- . annual. ca. 200p.

A handy directory of all banking establishments in Switzerland, listed alphabetically by name of the locality. It also gives the names and addresses of banks established in Switzerland having branches, branch offices, representative offices, or affiliated banks abroad, of representatives of foreign banks in Switzerland, and of the members of SWIFT, the Society for Worldwide Interbank Financial Communication, with their international telex numbers.

475 **Raubgold aus Deutschland. Die 'Golddrehscheibe' Schweiz im Zweiten Weltkrieg.** (Stolen gold from Germany: Switzerland as a 'gold turntable' in World War II.)
Werner Rings. Zurich; Munich: Artemis, 1985. 232p. bibliog.

Switzerland played an important role during World War II as a financial centre used by both camps of belligerents for transactions that otherwise would not have been possible. Both sides needed credits in Swiss francs to make purchases of manufactured goods and pay for certain services. Germany profited most from the availability of Swiss credits, even though they were furnished strictly in return for raw materials needed by Swiss industry. When the supply of those raw materials began to ebb, Swiss credits were harder to come by. The Germans had, however, still another means to get valuable Swiss francs: its assets of gold stolen in the countries conquered by their army, especially Belgium and the Netherlands. While other neutrals refused to accept gold payments from Germany, the Swiss National Bank agreed to launder the gold into freely convertible Swiss francs. Rings, a journalist known for his books about various aspects of Swiss history during World War II, describes how the laundering was done and furnishes a calculation as to the value of the services rendered by Switzerland to the two sides. He estimates that the value of Swiss gold transactions with the Allies amounted to about 400 million Swiss francs, while Germany received more than 3 billion Swiss francs through gold transactions and franc credits.

476 **Geschichte des Schweizer Frankens.** (History of the Swiss franc.)
Werner Schmid. Bern: Haupt, 1975. 3rd ed. 232p.

The author begins his story of the Swiss franc with an account of the founding of the Swiss National Bank in 1907 and follows it into the 1970s. The material is presented in chronological order based mostly on official documents. The minor and major crises, measures imposed by governments and banks, inflation and devaluation, revisions and initiatives that influenced the ups and downs of the Swiss franc are treated with clarity and in detail. The study is one in the series of 'Building stones for a future Switzerland' and advocates that informed citizenry must learn from past errors in formulating currency policy.

477 **Swiss stock guide 1988/89.**
Union Bank of Switzerland. Zurich: Union Bank of Switzerland, 1988. 231p.

This handy paperback describes in compact form the major Swiss corporations whose shares are traded on the stock market or over the counter. The reports on the individual companies supply information concerning their business activity, earnings trend, balance sheet, and future prospects. They take into account the latest developments and are accompanied by charts and statistical tables. Nine banks, six insurance companies, some seventy financial and industrial companies, and three investment trusts are listed. Tables at the end provide information on yields of all stocks and their market value at the end of October 1988. This free guide is a valuable service to the investor interested in Swiss corporations.

Business and Industry

478 **Die Wirtschaftsgeschichte der Schweiz. Von den Anfängen bis zur Gegenwart.** (The economic history of Switzerland: from the beginnings to the present.)

Jean-François Bergier. Zurich; Cologne, FRG: Benziger, 1983; Zurich: Ex Libris, 1985. 394p. maps. bibliog.

Bergier, professor of history at the Federal Institute of Technology in Zurich, gives a well-balanced introduction to the many facets of the economic history of Switzerland. The first part describes the impact of geography on the demography and agriculture of the country, while the second part covers the birth and growth of industrial Switzerland, and a third part deals with Switzerland's position as a crossroads for trade, tourism, transportation, and banking. The volume is richly illustrated and contains numerous helpful tables, graphs, and maps, a thirty-three-page chronological table from about 5000 BC to 1980, and a detailed bibliography. This fine work builds on Bergier's earlier monographs *Problèmes de l'histoire économique de la Suisse. Population, vie rurale, échanges et trafics* (Problems of the economic history of Switzerland: population, rural life, exchange, and trade) and *Naissance and croissance de la Suisse industrielle* (Birth and growth of industrial Switzerland), published in 1968 and 1974 respectively by Francke in Bern.

479 **How the Migros system of distribution is affecting economic and politic life in Europe.**

Gottlieb Duttweiler. In: *The Tobé lectures in retail distribution at the Harvard Business School.* Boston, Massachusetts: Harvard University Graduate School of Business Administration, 1960, p. 79-98.

Gottlieb Duttweiler (1888-1962), a giant in Swiss retail, was invited to give a Tobé lecture at Harvard the content of which is reprinted here. Duttweiler founded Migros, a grocery business that began with 'stores-on-wheels'. These trucks stopped at street corners and sold staple goods directly purchased from the producer. Regular stores were added, and the housewives' appreciation of the low-priced, high-quality products led to a rapid growth of the business. Migros kept operating costs to a minimum, and passed on the profits to the customers in the form of lower prices and additional services. It branched out into many food and non-food areas, often forced to do so by belligerent suppliers who would not sell to it. In 1940, Duttweiler transferred the entire concern with its manufacturing facilities and affiliated operations to the then 100,000 registered customers, who thereby became cooperative members. The very existence of Migros affected the business practices, ethics, prices, and quality of service of all food retailers in Switzerland and was a direct cause of the country's outstanding distributive system. See also *Das Abenteuer Migros: Die 60 Jahre junge Idee* (The Migros adventure: the 60-year-young idea) by Alfred A. Häsler ([Zurich]: Migros-Genossenschafts-Bund, 1985).

480 **The Basel marriage: history of the Ciba-Geigy merger.**
Paul Erni, adapted from the German by Stanley Hubbard. Zurich: Neue Zürcher Zeitung, 1979. 419p.

In 1970 the two Basel chemical firms Geigy, then more than 200 years old, and Ciba, eighty-six years old, merged to form the international giant conglomerate of Ciba-Geigy. This book, written by Paul Erni, a highly placed official in the Ciba hierarchy, and illustrated with allegorical drawings by his brother, the well-known artist Hans Erni, describes first how the fusion came about. The second part gives a chronology of the course of events that led towards the merger from World War II to 1978, and the third (longest) part consists of a review of the history of the merger with the help of documents in the form of photographs of many of the actors involved, newspaper articles, letters and memoranda, and financial statements and organizational charts. Because of its antitrust concerns, the United States Justice Department was a major obstacle in implementing their plans. The book provides remarkably candid insights into the 'marriage' that created one of the larger international chemical conglomerates. *The story of chemical industry in Basle*, issued by CIBA Limited on the occasion of its 75th anniversary (Olten, Switzerland: Urs Graf, 1959), begins with the drug trade of the late Middle Ages and ends with the many breakthroughs of the Basel firms in modern times.

481 **A short history of Swiss industry.**
Albert Hauser. In: *Beiträge zur Geschichte der Schweizerischen Industrie und des Gewerbes*, edited by Albert Hauser, Willy Dolf. Zollikon, Switzerland: Bosch, 1949, p. 41-71.

Hauser's history of Swiss industry opens with the 14th and 15th centuries and ends with the year 1948. The powerful guilds which flourished without competition or regulations lost their influence in the 16th and 17th centuries when religious emigrants, trained in new manufacturing and trading skills, came to Switzerland. Watchmaking was brought to Geneva by the Huguenots. The 18th century witnessed growth and diversification of products. The mechanization of factories of the 19th century was seen as a threat to home industries but Switzerland's dependence on export left the country no choice. New industries such as embroidery and hosiery, paper and flower milling, boot- and shoemaking, machine and engineering works shot up. The founding of the Federal Institute of Technology in 1855 added impetus to these developments. The economic and political turmoil of the 20th century (the strike of 1918, the two World Wars, the Great Depression) caused extreme fluctuations in the market and prompted extraordinary measures by the government and private individuals to safeguard against extreme shifts that cause inflation, recession, and unemployment.

482 **World events 1866-1966: the first hundred years of Nestlé.**
Jean Heer. Vevey, Switzerland: Nestlé Alimentana, 1966. 312p. maps. bibliog.

This is the story of one of the largest international food conglomerates, the Swiss-based Nestlé Alimentana. In 1866, enterprising Americans, the Page brothers, founded a condensed milk factory in Cham on Lake Zug, and at the same time Henri Nestlé started to manufacture milk products for babies in Vevey on Lake Geneva. The Cham firm, the Anglo-Swiss Condensed Milk Co., was engaged in sharp competition with the Nestlé Company until the two enterprises merged in 1905 on the basis of parity. By that time Nestlé had gone into the manufacture of milk chocolates through its affiliation with the chocolate firms of Peter and Kohler and (later) also Cailler. In spite of the turbulence of two World Wars and a series of economic depressions, the Nestlé enterprises continued to expand by building manufacturing centres across the globe, adding new products to their line, such as 'Nescafé' instant coffee, invented in 1937, and absorbing other food producers, such as Maggi in 1947. In 1966 the company was poised to engage in what was to become the most explosive phase of growth yet in its successful history. There are fine illustrations in the text, and the second part of the book consists of a portfolio of colour photographs that document the range and diversity of the Nestlé enterprises and the people who work in and are served by them. The first picture shows young birds in a small nest, a *Nestli* in German dialect, the name and trademark of the founder.

483 **Made in Switzerland: Industriereportagen.** (Made in Switzerland: industry reports.)
Markus Mäder, photography by Verena Eggmann. Zurich: Fretz, 1988. 165p.

Mäder who is known for his documentary films paints eleven vignettes of representative Swiss export enterprises. Among them are the headquarters of the Swiss Credit Bank (SKA) in Zurich, the Ciba-Geigy chemical concern in Basel, the cheese-producing dairies in the Bernese Emmental, the Oberhasli power plant, the high-tech AGIE, and Swissair. Mäder acts as a curious outsider, inspects the buildings, penetrates the office and production areas, and observes the worker and his/her specific task in the organization and in relation to the hierarchy. Mäder concludes that accomplishments in the sphere of economy, or 'material culture' (*materielle Kultur*) resemble those in the arts. Eggmann, a well-known photo-journalist, meanwhile captures the wide range of activities of each firm with her camera. The fifty to sixty pounds of pralines produced by Lindt-Sprüngli daily are symbolized by a full-page photograph of hundreds of these round little delicacies, all of the same kind. Coarse burlap bags with cocoa beans, cleaning women in sparkling white uniforms, a smiling director with his heir who will represent the fifth generation of the company round out the picture of the famous Swiss chocolate factory. The two journalists proceed in the same fashion when reporting on the workings of the other ten well-known Swiss concerns and enterprises included in this report.

484 **Technique and history of the Swiss watch.**
Eugène Jaquet, Alfred Chapuis, G. Albert Berner, Samuel Guye, translated from the French by D. S. Torrens, C. Jenkins, Raymond Rudorff. London [etc.]: Hamlyn Spring Books, 1970. 272p.

The authors draw from their combined historical and technical knowledge to trace the development of the Swiss watch industry from its beginnings in Geneva in the 16th century up to 1968. Illustrations are interspersed throughout the large book. The authors relate the amazing development of the watches from the first exquisitely decorated timepieces, now in museums and private collections, to the wrist-chronometer that is automatic, water-tight, anti-shock, and anti-magnetic, with a calendar, to boot. From Geneva the watch industry literally invaded the towns and villages of the nearby Jura mountains, where watchmaking skills were passed on from generation to generation. High-quality workmanship and constant technical advances, together with the aesthetic appeal that adapted to prevailing tastes, made watches a prime export product. A chapter, added for this edition, provides information about watchmaking schools, professional training, the Swiss Laboratory for Horological Research (Laboratoire suisse de recherches horlogères) in Neuchâtel, and the industrial organization of this world-famous Swiss industry. This book was published just before the Swiss watch industry confronted its gravest crisis.

485 **Corporatism and change: Austria, Switzerland, and the politics of industry.**

Peter J. Katzenstein. Ithaca, New York; London: Cornell University Press, 1984. 331p. bibliog. (Cornell Studies in Political Economy).

Political scientists ascribe the stability which the small countries of Western Europe have achieved to their corporate arrangements. Economists, on the other hand, view the same countries as models of economic flexibility and market competition. Katzenstein argues that political stability and economic flexibility are not contrary, but complementary. Switzerland is considered a paradigm of liberal capitalism, Austria of democratic socialism. Both express political conflict over economic choices in the language of social partnership rather than in terms of class conflict. Through their policy networks political actors harness differences in an unending process of small-scale political adjustments. The core of Katzenstein's book consists of the case-studies of the recent history of four industries in trouble: watchmaking in Switzerland, steel in Austria, and textiles in Austria and Switzerland. He asserts that whether the political orientation of a nation is conservative (Switzerland) or liberal (Austria), whether national policy favours centralization (Austria) or decentralization (Switzerland), the integration of state and society in democratic corporatism can facilitate political responsiveness to economic change.

486 **Revolution in time: clocks and the making of the modern world.**

David S. Landes. Cambridge, Massachusetts; London: Belknap Press of Harvard University Press, 1983. 481p.

David Landes, Coolidge Professor of History and Professor of Economics at Harvard University, has written a delightfully informative and richly detailed and illustrated book on the history of timekeeping. About one-third of the text deals with the role that the Swiss watchmaking industry has played in that history. The early beginnings – in the 18th century – of watchmaking in Geneva and some of the Jura villages of what is today western Switzerland, as well as the stupendous successes and crippling crises of the watch industry in the 19th and 20th centuries, are put in the context of worldwide developments. The Swiss, with their unequalled pool of skilled labour and their innovative design and marketing techniques, were able to dominate the world market into the 1970s, when, due to their delay in the assessment of the significance of the 'quartz revolution', their treasured industry faced bankruptcy.

487 **75 years Brown Boveri 1891-1966.**
Edited by Peter Rinderknecht, historical chapter by Otto Mittler, translated from the German by Kenneth M. Evans. Baden, Switzerland: Brown, Boveri & Co., 1966. 289p.

This book commemorates the founding of a small factory in Baden, Canton Aargau, by the brilliant engineer Charles Brown and the skilled businessman Walter Boveri in 1891. Brown pioneered the transmission of power of high voltage over considerable distances, and seventy-five years later, Brown Boveri had become the largest engineering firm in Switzerland and one of the internationally recognized leaders in electrical and thermal engineering. Many photographs of Brown Boveri divisions, subsidiaries, sales offices, testing laboratories, research centres, training facilities for the workforce, housing developments, and leisure facilities for employees in Switzerland and abroad attest to the enormous growth the company has experienced. The text is accessible even to the non-technically inclined reader, while the large photographs of complicated and sleek generators, circuit breakers, turbines, rotors, transformers, and other engines of all kinds are certain to interest the expert. Economic, political, and social problems, such as the depression of the 1930s and the two World Wars, caused setbacks, but the company has been able to maintain its position in a fiercely competitive market thanks to constant adjustment and strong leadership. The firm is now known as ASEA Brown Boveri AG.

488 **Escher Wyss 1805-1955: 150 years of development.**
Edited by H. Sitterding, translated from the German by A. G. C. Wedekind. Zurich: Escher Wyss, 1955. 246p.

Hans Caspar Escher (1775-1859), founder of the Escher Wyss engineering firm, was the son of a prosperous Zurich silk manufacturer. When Hans Caspar saw his first spinning machine, he knew he would some day build his own mechanical spinning mill. On trips to France and England he acquired knowledge about the machines and had no difficulty financing his project in the Neumühle on the Limmat river in Zurich. The banker Salomon Wyss offered legal advice, hence the name Wyss in the style of the firm. A brief history of the company, its leaders, successes, crises, products, and expansion into many parts of the world precedes the technical sections on hydraulic installations, thermal machines, apparatus and plants, research, and materials testing facilities. The detailed descriptions are illustrated with photographs, diagrams, and graphs that trace the technical developments of the firm. However, the layperson will not be able to appreciate fully the highly technical material. The last two chapters deal with the sites of the home company, the Neumühle and the new factory built in the Hard section of Zurich in 1891, and with the company's personnel management and social facilities. The firm is now known as Sulzer-Escher Wyss AG.

489 **The secret empire: the success story of Switzerland.**
Lorenz Stucki, translated from the German by Herder and Herder and Litpress. New York: Herder and Herder, 1971. 342p.

During the 19th century the Swiss built up a 'world empire' through the colossal economic effort of transforming cheaply imported raw materials into highly priced commodities and exporting them for a profit. Native industry and foreign trade fed upon each other in creating an economic empire over which no Swiss flag would wave and which was unprotected by Swiss warships, for, unlike other global economic powers, the Swiss state played almost no part in this private economic imperialism. Dedication to the quality of workmanship, together with a readiness for adventure and risk, as well as frugality and thrift were some of the ingredients that made possible the successes of Swiss businesses and industries, whether in the export of watches and high-fashion textiles, or the selling of banking and insurance services, or the global expansion of the food, chemical, and machine tool industries.

490 **Switzerland – textile machinery land.**
Swiss Association of Machinery Manufacturers (VSM), Textile Machinery Group. Schlieren, Switzerland: Union Druck und Verlags AG, 1983. 64p.

Switzerland can look back on generations of textile machinery makers. This booklet features in colour the sophisticated textile machinery in use today. Spinning, yarn treatment, weaving, knitting, textile finishing, embroidering, final 'making-up' and packing, and textile air engineering require specialized, efficient, and safe machinery. Short captions tell what each piece of equipment is capable of producing. The fifty or so firms that build these machines are also presented briefly. Tear out labels in the back make it easy to obtain specific information from any of these firms, not only about the machines themselves, but also about installation, data systems and other production items. For a free copy of the booklet write to: Textile Machinery Group, VSM, Kirchenweg 4, CH-8032 Zurich, Switzerland.

491 **The Swiss watchmaking industry.**
Union Bank of Switzerland, Economic Research Department. Zurich: Union Bank, 1986. 64p.

The Swiss watch industry has undergone considerable structural changes in the last two decades. Figures show a significant decrease in production units and employment from 1970 to 1985. To remain competitive in a strong world market, the industry would have to adjust to the latest technological advances and marketing strategies. This booklet gives an account of how the downward trend was reversed, the place of the Swiss watch in the international market, and the role of the banks in reorganization and refinancing efforts. A questionnaire distributed to 170 companies involved in watchmaking produced a generally favourable forecast for the future of the Swiss watch industry. With the production of higher-scale watches rather than medium-priced ones, and adaptability to changes in the global market and fashion demands, the future appears promising. A 'Watch Industry Glossary' in the back of the book defines some technical terms. There are also handsome illustrations in colour and many informative data.

Trade

492 **Die Sechste Schweiz: Ueberleben auf dem Weltmarkt.** (The sixth Switzerland: survival on the world market.)
Silvio Borner. Zurich; Schwäbisch Hall, FRG: Orell Füssli, 1984. 228p.

Borner, a widely published economist with expertise in the problems caused by growth and changes in structure and society, is eminently qualified to investigate Switzerland's ability to compete in an ever-changing world market. In the first part of his book he describes the structural changes that have occurred globally in society and technology since the mid-1970s. The second part focuses on the consequences of the politicization of economic relations on industry, business, professional organizations and government and how these institutions respond to the new challenges, while in the third part the author investigates ways for Swiss firms to remain competitive. The term 'sixth Switzerland' used in the title of this book is a take-off of the term 'fifth Switzerland' which is commonly used for Swiss living in foreign countries. The sixth Switzerland consists of the foreign branches of Swiss industrial and commercial enterprises.

493 **Switzerland and Liechtenstein: hints to business men.**
British Overseas Trade Board. London: British Overseas Trade Board, 1975. 64p. (Hints to business men booklets).

The general information in this booklet serves any traveller to Switzerland and Liechtenstein well and covers such topics as climate, weights and measures, electric current, official public holidays, accommodation, transport, and communications such as the telephone system. The businessman will find valuable information on the Swiss economy, import and exchange control regulations and suggestions on how to be successful in making a business deal. Many addresses are listed that can provide additional, current information.

494 **Jahresstatistik des Aussenhandels der Schweiz.** (Annual statistics of Swiss foreign trade.)
Eidgenössische Oberzolldirektion. Bern: Eidgenössische Oberzolldirektion, 1885- . 3 vols per year.

The three large-format volumes of the 1988 edition of this statistical compilation total 1,669 pages. The work lists every kind of goods and materials that crossed the Swiss borders in its export–import trade with the whole world. Volume 1 lists the goods, first according to the numbers assigned to them in the ninety-six chapters of the customs tariff, and then by country, giving balances of trade with each and with groups such as EC, EFTA, and the continents. In 1988 Switzerland imported goods worth 82,398 billion francs and exported 74,063 billion francs' worth, leaving a trade deficit of 8,335 billions. With every continent except Europe the trade balance was positive – the trade deficit with the Federal Republic of Germany alone amounted to 12,574 billion francs. Volume 2 lists items of trade by number of the customs tariff with every country. Volume 3 provides a number of other statistics, such as the means of transport used by each category of merchandise (i.e., cereals by rail, road, water, and air), foreign trade by point of border crossing, by region of origin or destination (cantons), and by country of origin or destination. The largest part, however, is taken up by a minute accounting of customs revenues, raised by levies on imports and duties on exports. The total revenue amounted to 6,377 billion francs in 1988. The Federal Customs Office also issues monthly statistics of Swiss foreign trade.

495 **Mosse Swiss adress [sic]: directory of Swiss industry, trade, commerce and export.**
Zurich: Mosse, 1921- .

The 83rd edition (1988) of this directory consists of two heavy volumes with more than 3,000 pages. It is designed to give access to any firm doing business in Switzerland. Volume 1 lists the firms alphabetically by cantons, locations within the cantons, and in the various communities. Volume 2 lists the firms by commercial and industrial sectors. There are 297,136 addresses in this directory, including also those of trade fairs and exhibitions, business associations, chambers of commerce, and cantonal and federal authorities.

496 **Swiss export products and services directory.**
Swiss Office for the Development of Trade. Zurich: Schweizerische Zentrale für Handelsförderung, 1982. 920p.

Published about every five years, the 1982 issue of the directory contains the names of some 8,500 Swiss manufacturers and suppliers of services engaged in some aspect of export trade. It provides company information and the addresses of official government and trade representatives. Products and services are listed by industrial classification, from agriculture and food to hotel management and schools. The alphabetical index lists some 6,000 terms in four languages (English, German, French, and Spanish). There is also an alphabetical register of about 2,000 trademarks and trade names.

497 **Switzerland your partner.**
Swiss Office for the Development of Trade. Zurich; Lausanne: Schweizerische Zentrale für Handelsförderung.

Under the general title *Switzerland your partner*, the Swiss Office for the Development of Trade publishes at irregular intervals promotional booklets on special sectors of

Trade

Swiss exports. In 1988 there were brochures on *Auxiliary supplies from Switzerland* (104p.) and *Food specialties from Switzerland* (80p.) featuring products such as soups, mineral waters, chocolates, cheeses, wines, pasta, and health and dietetic food. The 1989 title *Production automation from Switzerland* (92p.) examines industrial automation in Switzerland, the Swiss robotic scene, automation in the class room, and numerical machine tool control. Like all the other booklets in the series, it has numerous full-colour illustrations, advertising the products of the participating firms and associations.

Agriculture

498 **Swiss agriculture and food production.**

J. von Ah. In: *Modern Switzerland*, edited by J. Murray Luck. Palo Alto, California: Society for the Promotion of Science and Scholarship, 1978, p. 71-90.

In 1975 6.2 per cent of the workforce of Switzerland was employed in agriculture. Swiss farms are in the middle of European farms as far as average size is concerned, and while larger enterprises are clearly on the increase, the basic unit is still the family farm. The federal government is heavily involved in helping farmers to rationalize production and encourage structural change, and thanks to various support programmes, farm income has kept pace with the increase in industrial wages in the last two decades. Special measures are in place to maintain mountain farming, which is essential for the ecological balance of the mountain regions of the country. Ah, an official in the Swiss Federal Office of Agriculture, sums up his article by saying 'Swiss agriculture can produce top quality products and top yields. Its past performance has been remarkable. Future performance can still be better.'

499 **Die schweizerische Landwirtschaft 1850 bis 1914.** (Swiss agriculture 1850-1914.)

Hans Brugger. Frauenfeld, Switzerland: Huber, 1979. 423p. bibliog.

This is the continuation of the volume by the same author on Swiss agriculture in the first half of the 19th century (Frauenfeld, 1956). Using quantitative methods of research and analysis, Brugger, director of the statistical bureau of the Swiss Farmers' Secretariat in Brugg, Canton Aargau, provides numerous tables and graphs on all aspects of agriculture and its changing nature during the decades before World War I. Chapters on the general situation of the rural population, including demographics, transport, diet, technological support, and insurance for farming in all its diversity, and on animal husbandry are followed by chapters on the export of agricultural products, prices of agricultural products and the economic situation of the peasantry, agricultural organizations, schools, experimental stations, and, finally, the agricultural policies of the federal government and the cantons.

500 **Sectoral policy in an open economy: the case of Swiss agriculture.**
René Brugger. Geneva: University of Geneva. Thèse science politique, 1980. 245p. bibliog.

This doctoral dissertation is a case-study based on theoretical literature and statistical materials that presupposes a good background in policy analysis and agriculture. Brugger first stipulates the existing state of Swiss agriculture, pointing out where desired targets have not been achieved and presenting various measures that would bring about the desired results. He then argues for what he considers to be the best of these policies.

501 **Swiss agriculture: illustrations, figures, comments.**
Werner Kipfer, translated from the German by H. Ossent. Zollikofen, Switzerland: Centre for agricultural educational material of the Swiss Association of Agricultural Engineers, 1972. 80p. maps.

The first part deals with the physical features of Switzerland, agricultural laws, management, plant cultivation, animal production, capital investment, economic output, marketing, training of farmers, and research. Then follow a series of charts, many in colour, illustrating with figures and graphs data such as precipitation, composition of soil, farm size and distribution, crops, animal production and meat consumption, and agricultural exports.

502 **Schweizer Landwirtschaft. Ein bäuerlicher und agrarpolitischer Jahreskreis.** (Swiss agriculture: a farmer's and agripolitical year cycle.)
Leo Meyer, Heinz Baumann. Zurich: Fretz, 1986; Ex Libris, 1988. 137p. bibliog.

The twelve chapters of this book describe in words and pictures the work of farmers from January to December. The traditional or seasonal work associated with a particular month is highlighted and provides a lead-in to a discussion of related agricultural, political, and economic issues. For example, January is traditionally the month when pigs were butchered on the farms in many parts of Switzerland, but today this is a rare occurrence, for meat production has become modernized, and the chapter discusses the problems of mechanized mass animal breeding and the state control of the meat market. The month of May highlights dairy farming, the most important branch of Swiss agriculture, and here photographs show both the old-fashioned way of milking cows in the alp huts and the supermodern sheds with their milking machines and the giant plants in which the milk is prepared for consumption in liquid or dry form or transformed into butter and cheese. The politics of establishing a fair price for milk for producers and consumers alike are also elucidated in this chapter. This innovative book provides an informative picture of agriculture in Switzerland.

503 **Swiss dairy industry.**
Swiss Milk Committee. Liebefeld-Bern, Switzerland: Schweizerische Milchkommission, 1979. 20p.

This brief over-sized brochure provides a great deal of information on the Swiss dairy industry. A historical sketch of dairy farming in Switzerland is followed by figures for actual milk production and a description of the various dairy products produced. The next two sections describe the institutions involved in dairy research and testing – among them the Federal Institute of Technology in Zurich, and the Federal Dairy Research Institute (Eidgenössische Forschungsanstalt für Milchwirtschaft) in Liebefeld-

Bern – and the professional education programmes available. The last part describes the structure of the Swiss dairy industry with its interlocking bodies that exercise supervisory functions. The basic purpose of these organizations is to regulate the 77,500 milk producers, organized into 4,325 cheese and dairy cooperatives, to assure them a base income comparable to that of an industrial worker, through price guarantees and output limits. The Federal Council and the federal parliament have passed a series of laws intended to balance fairly the interests of the producers and processors with those of the consumers, and at the same time advance the national interest in a stable, productive agricultural sector. The text of this informative brochure is in German, English, and French.

Tourism

504 **Rush to the Alps: the evolution of vacationing in Switzerland.**
Paul P. Bernard. New York: Columbia University Press, 1978. 228p. bibliog.

As Bernard points out, 'vacationing in the Alps is a relatively recent phenomenon'. In Switzerland it began less than two hundred years ago, and it became an economically significant factor only during the last century. Bernard traces this development from the early stirrings of interest in the mountains during the Renaissance to the transformation of Alpine Switzerland during the tourism boom of the pre-World War I era. The evolution of concepts such as 'leisure', 'free time', and 'vacation' are historically delineated; the difficulties of travel and the changing modes of lodging and transportation are graphically described; a presentation of the history of taking the waters ('balneology') is as much part of this book as is the characterization of the psychology of hotel-keeping; the sociological and economic analysis of life in the mountain valleys before and after the advent of tourism is balanced by the description of the no less important changes brought about in the vacationer. Bernard puts appropriate stress on the role that the English played in the rush to the Alps. His last two chapters give an entertaining detailed account of how the 'little Upper Engadine village of St. Moritz' became 'the platinum melting pot' that illustrated like no other place the variety and complexity the Swiss vacation had achieved by 1914. This is a gem of a book.

505 **Zürcher Hotellerie: Heute und damals. Bett und Tisch im Kanton Zürich.** (Zurich hotel industry: now and then. Bed and board in Canton Zurich.)
Edi Bohli. Zurich: Rigiblick, 1985. 399p. bibliog.

The beginnings of the Zurich hotel industry date back to the Middle Ages. The hotel Storchen, a four-star establishment today, already housed guests in 1477. A number of hotels in the heart of town also have a long tradition. Some of these may have changed their name, and modernization has altered their appearance to varying degrees, but others were able to protect their well-known and distinct appearance while incorporating the most modern conveniences. Individual hotels in and around Zurich are listed. For each, there are entries about its history, owners (often the same family for generations), clientele (with some famous visitors singled out), structure and special features. Information is given about many aspects of the hotel industry: professional organizations, training, the latest modern conveniences, public relations efforts, special offerings in the area of health or sports, and the *Frauenverein* establishments with their 'no alcohol' policy. Pictures of hotels, their rooms, menus, and advertisements, and various statistics bring the 500-year history of the Zurich hotel industry to life.

506 **Le tourisme suisse en chiffres, édition 1988.** (Swiss tourism in numbers, 1988 edition.)
Bundesamt für Statistik. Bern: Bundesamt für Statistik, 1988. 20p.

This slim booklet packs a great amount of information into its twenty pages. Tables and diagrams with statistics from a variety of sources provide information on the economic significance of tourism, availability of hotel and para-hotel facilities and rates of occupancy. More tourists visit the mountain regions in general than the lake zones and the big cities; the summer season attracts more guests than the winter season. The section on restaurants reveals that there are about 26,800 food service establishments in Switzerland, or one per 240 inhabitants. The chapter on transport contains information on the range of public and private transport available to the tourist, from the extensive Swiss railway network and the postal bus service to the 1,750 installations intended for the tourist, including cogwheel trains, funiculars, téléfériques, and chairlifts. The booklet has two pages of addresses of organizations involved in tourism. It is available in German or French from the Federal Statistical Office in Bern, or the Swiss National Tourist Office in Zurich. Additional statistics can be found in *Tourismus in der Schweiz 1987. Statistischer Bericht* (Tourism in Switzerland 1987: statistical report) by the Bundesamt für Statistik (Bern: Bundesamt für Statistik, 1988. Amtliche Statistik der Schweiz, Nr. 183).

507 **Gastronomie & Tourisme. Revue professionnelle de l'Hôtellerie, de la Gastronomie et du Tourisme en Suisse.** (Gastronomy and tourism: professional journal of the Swiss hotel industry, gastronomy, and tourism.)
Gastronomie & Tourisme. Lugano, Switzerland: Gastronomie & Tourisme, 1972- . bimonthly. ca. 100p.

This is a slick, illustrated magazine with numerous brief articles on hotels, hotel managers, chefs, wines, special dishes, drinks and other such things that interest the members of the many gastronomic, hoteliers', and restaurateurs' organizations that are listed as sponsors of this journal.

508 **Swiss hotel pioneers.**
Louis Gaulis, René Creux, foreword by Werner Kämpfen. Paudex, Switzerland: Fontainemore; [Zurich]: Swiss National Tourist Office, 1976. 223p. bibliog.

This is the story of the men and women who, with drive and talent, became the pioneers of the Swiss hotel industry. They were born between 1800 and 1840 and became active in their profession when Europe witnessed the dramatic changes ushered in by such developments as electricity and the railway. From simple hostels, these innovators created elaborate hotel 'palaces'. Minute attention to food preparation and service and to individual wishes of guests became the hallmark of a good hotelier. To keep the clientele entertained, leisure activities of all kinds were offered. The stories of César Ritz, and entire families such as the Badrutts, the Baurs, Bons, and Seilers are presented here in some detail, and short biographies of over one hundred other hoteliers who were active between the beginning of the 19th century and 1920 are found at the back of the book. The introductory chapters tell of the hazards and inconveniences of early travel, of the rising interest in nature and in the exploration of the Alps, and of the type of accommodation the traveller of those days could expect. The contrast with the situation of the later 19th century inspires respect for the accomplishments of those who founded an industry for which Switzerland is known the world over. The many illustrations of the 'good old days' of the rich and famous may leave one with nostalgia.

509 **Tourism in twentieth century Switzerland.**
Jost Krippendorf. In: *Modern Switzerland*, edited by J. Murray Luck. Palo Alto, California: Society for the Promotion of Science and Scholarship, 1978, p. 275-95. bibliog.

Switzerland enjoys one of the most intensive tourist industries. Krippendorf provides, in concentrated form, a convenient overview of the various aspects of tourism and its meaning for Switzerland. The development of the tourist trade over the course of the 19th and 20th centuries is illustrated with statistical tables, and there are sections on tourist facilities, the economic and social importance of tourism, tourist trade policy, and research and training.

510 **Alpsegen, Alptraum. Für eine Tourismus-Entwicklung im Einklang mit Mensch und Natur.** (Alp blessing, alp nightmare: toward the development of tourism in harmony with human beings and nature.)
Jost Krippendorf. Bern: Kümmerly & Frey, 1986. 88p. bibliog.

This publication is part of a national research project that studies socio-economic developments and ecology in the Swiss mountains. Krippendorf and his fact-gathering teams concentrated their attention on tourism, using as case-studies Grindelwald (Bernese Oberland), Aletsch (Valais), Davos (Graubünden), and Pays-d'Enhaut (Vaud). He groups the findings into seven benefits of tourism and seven dangers. The decisive issue is how to balance costs and benefits. Krippendorf describes the ideals, which he labels qualitative growth, or the development of tourism in harmony with human beings and nature, in ten theses. His text is clearly presented, with diagrams and photographs derived from the fieldwork undertaken by the researchers in the four mountain areas.

511 **Tourism policy and international tourism in OECD member countries.**
Organization for Economic Co-operation and Development. Paris: OECD, 1988. 176p.

Tourism is an increasingly important component of the economies of most countries. The first eighty-six pages of this OECD publication contain data and interpretative text concerning the labour market in the hotel industries of the member countries with case-studies of nine countries, among them Switzerland, the international tourist flows, and the economic importance of international tourism in member countries. The rest of the booklet consists of a statistical annexe with tables on every conceivable aspect of international tourism, including figures for the individual member states.

512 **Swiss hotel guide.**
Swiss Hotel Association (SHA). Bern: Swiss Hotel Association, 1989. 128p.

This guide has been issued annually since 1911 and provides full details on the hotels in Switzerland. The hotel association also publishes special brochures on accommodation for senior citizens, the handicapped, country inns, and family hotels. The hotel guide lists all SHA member hotels alphabetically by and within locality, and the hotels are classified in seven categories in accordance with clearly defined SHA standards. The guide provides addresses and telephone numbers, and lists the prices, in Swiss francs, of hotel rooms for one and two persons, in low season and high season, and, with a battery of symbols, identifies special features of the hotel and the locality. It also lists a few restaurants, the Swiss hotel management schools and their programmes, and hotels abroad under Swiss managament. All explanations are given in German, French, English, and Italian. The guide is available for a nominal fee from the SHA, Monbijoustrasse 130, CH-3001 Bern.

513 **Swiss spa guide 1989.**
Swiss Spa Association. Baden, Switzerland: Swiss Spa Association, 1989. 66p.

Published annually since 1986, this guide in German, French, and English is available from the Swiss National Tourist Office, Bellariastr. 38, CH-8027 Zurich and SNTO branches abroad. It lists twenty-two recognized therapeutic and medicinal Swiss resorts from Andeer, Graubünden, to Zurzach, Aargau. The booklet describes the thermal and mineral springs, the ailments for which the waters are recommended, and their curative effects. The guide also provides information on prices and the special sport and fitness offerings of individual resorts. Colour advertisement for the various spas, showing the hotels, the baths, and their beautiful environments, enhance the attractiveness of this informative booklet.

Public and Private Transport

514 **Swiss travel wonderland.**

Cecil J. Allen. London: Allan, 1972. 168p. maps.

Allen's intimate knowledge of railway planning and construction is demonstrated in this book on Switzerland's 'amazing railways'. The country's high mountains present a special challenge to its transport system. While some routes serve as passageways for international traffic, others make the Alps accessible to the wanderer and winter sports fan. Funiculars, chairlifts, and cable-cars take over where ordinary trains cannot overcome the differences in height. Ships of all kinds ply the waterways. Mountain passes, bold viaducts, narrow-gauge railroads, spiral tunnels, hydro-electric power plants, all are proof of an advanced transport technology. The 190 black-and-white photographs illustrate these accomplishments vividly, and appendices provide data relating to railways and other means of transport. An earlier version of this book was published under the title *Switzerland's amazing railways* (London: Nelson, 1953).

515 **Der Glacier-Express: Zermatt – St. Moritz.** (The Glacier-Express: Zermatt – St. Moritz.)

Paul Caminada. Disentis, Switzerland: Desertina, 1982. 196p. maps. bibliog.

The Glacier-Express connects by rail two of the most famous vacation resorts of the Alps, Zermatt in Canton Valais and St Moritz in Canton Graubünden. Caminada's book has three parts. In the first, which covers half the book, he takes the reader for a ride on the Glacier-Express, with a description of the features of the seven geographical segments that make up the course of the track, providing historical, cultural, and touristic information about the places through which the traveller passes. The second part consists of an account of the history of the difficult and often dangerous construction of the narrow-gauge tracks by the participating private railway companies, the Brig-Visp-Zermatt, the Furka-Oberalp, and the Rhaetian railways. In a short third part Caminada describes some of the additional means of transport available to tourists in the St Moritz and Zermatt regions to enable them to ascend to even greater heights without having to exert themselves, except for pulling the money out of their wallets. The book is beautifully and instructively illustrated.

516 **Handbook of Swiss traffic regulations.**
Federal Department of Justice and Police. Bern: Eidgenössische Drucksachen- und Materialzentrale, 1989. 161p.

This little handbook belongs in the glove compartment of any motorized tourist in Switzerland. An illustrated text gives information about existing traffic regulations, explains signals, and lists legal provisions. The material also prepares for the driving test which is considered demanding. Information on licensing, and advice as to what to do in case of an accident, are also provided. Switzerland has special regulations for cyclists, moped riders, and for driving on steep narrow mountain roads. The dos and don'ts are highlighted in red in 176 short entries.

517 **The Gotthard Railway.**
Franz Marti, Walter Trüb, translated from the German by Kay Gillioz-Pettigrew. Zurich: Orell Füssli, 1976. 3rd ed. 174p.

A short introduction provides data concerning the Gotthard Railway, its history, capacity, and significance. No other transit route through the Alps carries such a large volume of traffic. Even a hundred years after completion, the traveller is in awe of how tracks were laid and how helicoid tunnels, bridges, and viaducts were built. Three hundred and eight captioned photographs of different trains and sections of tracks provide evidence of this great technical accomplishment.

518 **The Rhaetian Railway (RhB).**
Franz Marti, Walter Trüb, translated from the German by Dieter W. Portmann. Lausanne: 24 Heures, 1982. 189p. map.

This picture book has 317 photographs, some in colour, with explanatory text in three languages. The Rhaetian Railway (RhB) is a narrow-gauge system, 394 kilometres in length and built between 1889 and 1914 by enterpreneurs in the mountain valleys of Canton Graubünden. The various railways, among them the Chur-Arosa Railway and the Bernina Railway, merged into the RhB during World War II. The RhB is a marvel in an economic sense, since its elaborate network profitably serves a region that is only thinly populated, and in an engineering sense, since the builders had to overcome numerous natural obstacles. The photographs in this book vividly illustrate this latter point.

519 **Swissair: a portrait of the airline of Switzerland.**
Lorenz Stucki. Frauenfeld, Switzerland; Stuttgart, FRG: Huber, 1981. 227p. maps.

Stucki, a Swiss journalist and writer, provides a lively account of the success story of Swissair, 'the astonishing airline'. From shaky beginnings in the early 1930s, the company has, with government support, evolved into one of the world's most efficient and most highly regarded carrier. Stucki analyses the elements that explain Swissair's success: imaginative leadership, top-notch management, meticulous attention to every detail in the service of the passengers, rigorous training of the personnel at every level and in all parts of the world, and adherence to the principles of courtesy, quality, punctuality, and personal involvement.

Public and Private Transport

520 **Das Verkehrshaus der Schweiz.** (The Swiss Transport Museum.) Alfred Waldis, photography by Michael Wolgensinger. Zurich: Silva-Verlag, 1974. 120p. bibliog.

Waldis was the first director of the Swiss Transport Museum in Luzern, which, since its founding in 1959, has become one of Switzerland's most visited and internationally famous museums. Keeping in step with the latest technological advances, the museum expands its displays as developments necessitate; thus, an astronautics section, complete with an original Mercury space capsule and spacesuit, was added in 1972. The section on navigation shows originals and models of early lake and Rhine ships; the road transport section attracts visitors with some legendary Swiss-built automobiles; the main feature of the large rail transport division is a scale model of the North ramp of the Gotthard Railway; aviation features the Dufaux bi-plane of 1910; and the postal service and telecommunications sections show how time and space were conquered. In addition, there is a planetarium and an archive that contains documentation of all kinds. In most sections visitors are invited to get hands-on experience in an effort to help them understand the marvels of human inventiveness that created the technological achievements before their eyes. Waldis's text is appealing to laypersons and experts alike. The many colour photographs make this an instructive and entertaining picture book.

521 **The Gotthard, Switzerland's lifeline.** Arthur Wyss-Niederer, translated from the German by Kay Gillioz-Pettigrew. Lausanne: Ovaphil, 1979. 263p. maps. bibliog.

The Gotthard has been of great significance throughout Swiss history. In this large-format book with its many illustrations, Wyss describes first the role the St Gotthard pass played in the founding of the Swiss Confederation and its early history. He then tells the colourful story of travel across the St Gotthard in pre-rail times. A final part examines the Gotthard, with its railway and road tunnels, as the 'backbone of modern European communications'. There are six appendices with colour plates of postage stamps, postal seals, old post-marked letters, postal motor coaches, and steam and electric locomotives used on the Gotthard line.

Labour and Trade Unions

522 **Schweizerische Arbeiterbewegung. Dokumente zu Lage, Organisation und Kämpfen der Arbeiter von der Frühindustrialisierung bis zur Gegenwart.** (Swiss labour movement: documents on the condition, organization, and struggles of the workers from early industrialization to the present.)

Edited by Arbeitsgruppe für Geschichte der Arbeiterbewegung Zürich. Zurich: Limmat, 1975. 411p. bibliog.

This paperback by 'the working team for the history of the labour movement of Zurich' consists of seven chapters which treat the subject matter chronologically from the formation of the working class in the early 19th century to the integration of the labour movement into the bourgeois state during the economic boom following World War II. Each chapter has an introduction of between six and twelve pages in length, and these introductions not only explain the context of the documents reproduced but constitute in themselves a concise history of the Swiss labour movement to the early 1970s. Two hundred and nineteen documents, some of them reproductions of posters and campaign materials, are grouped in topics and distributed through the chapters. A statistical appendix provides data concerning the development of the occupation structure in Switzerland since 1800, the membership of the unions from 1881 to 1973, the number of strikes and lock-outs in the last one hundred years, and the membership and success of the political parties of the Swiss working class. This is a very interesting reader with, not surprisingly, a clear leftist slant.

523 **Industry–labor relations: industrial peace.**

Lukas F. Burckhardt. In: *Modern Switzerland*, edited by J. Murray Luck. Palo Alto, California: Society for the Promotion of Science and Scholarship, 1978, p. 173-89.

Arbeitsfrieden (industrial peace) is a key characteristic of labour–management relations in Switzerland. Labour demands have been peacefully negotiated in an unbroken, honest relationship based on mutual esteem between two partners ever since the late

1930s. Burckhardt traces the beginnings of this tradition to the Peace Agreement in the Swiss Engineering and Metalworking Industry of 19 July 1937. Five trade unions involved in metalworking and watchmaking agreed with the employers' association to find solutions to outstanding problems through the adoption of collective agreements through the peaceful consideration of the interests of all participants. The agreement has been periodically renewed and has been used as a model by other industries, for Switzerland has almost complete industrial peace. Collective actions such as strikes and lock-outs, are practically absent from the Swiss labour scene; their place is taken by a thorough system of mediation and arbitration financed by both sides from a so-called partnership fund. Burckhardt has tables with strike statistics from 1927 to 1976 – in 1961 and 1973 not a single working day was lost to strikes – and the results of polls that show that more than eighty per cent of Swiss workers think the system makes sense.

524 **Die Gewerkschaften in der Schweiz.** (The trade unions in Switzerland.)
Edited by Ezio Canonica. Bern: Schweizerischer Gewerkschaftsbund, 1975. 169p.

Nineteen brief chapters, each written by a different author, give an introduction to the world of organized labour in Switzerland. The Swiss trade union movement, which began in the 1830s, is characterized by strong factionalism. The white-collar employee organizations refuse to merge with the blue-collar worker organizations, and ideologically and confessionally inspired groups also go their own ways. Even within the central Swiss Labour Union Alliance (Schweizerischer Gewerkschaftsbund, SGB), which was founded in 1880, the individual unions bargain separately. The SGB with its sixteen unions and some 450,000 members (1974) has the function of an umbrella organization that represents labour in the political process of the Swiss system. Each of the unions belonging to the SGB is described in a separate chapter, with information on its history, structure, problems, and goals.

525 **Die Arbeiter in der Schweiz im 19. Jahrhundert. Soziale Lage, Organisation, Verhältnis zu Arbeitgeber und Staat.** (Workers in Switzerland in the 19th century: social status, organization, relationship to employer and state.)
Erich Gruner. Bern: Francke Verlag, 1968. 1136p. bibliog. (Helvetia Politica. Series A. vol. III).

This large volume offers a panoramic view of the complicated organizational manifestations of the labour movement in Switzerland in the 19th century. The early history of the trade unions and the cooperatives is largely based on formerly unused source materials. Swiss developments are placed in the general framework of the growth of the European labour movement, and the importance of Switzerland as a home for German worker organizations and the League of Communists during the 1840s and in the founding of the First International is analysed. During much of the 19th century misery and destitution were the lot of industrial workers, as the state moved only slowly to solve the worst problems. The workers themselves were slow to organize and become active in the class struggle. The activities of the employers who engaged in social welfare programmes at a relatively early stage complemented the self-help efforts of the unions and cooperatives, without, however, alleviating sufficiently the conflicts that led to the general strike of November 1918.

526 **The peace agreement of July 19th, 1937, in the Swiss engineering and metalworking industries: Konrad Ilg (1877-1954); Ernst Dübi (1884-1947).**

Hermann Häberlin, Walter Ingold, Rudolf Wüthrich, Hans Rudolf Schmid, translated from the German by the English Institute R. A. Langford, Zurich. Zurich: Association for Historical Research in Economics, 1967. 115p. bibliog. (Swiss Pioneers of Economics and Technology, 2).

This illustrated booklet provides a brief history of the collective agreement between labour and management in the Swiss engineering and metalworking industries of 1937, known as the peace agreement. The monograph emphasizes the role of the two key persons involved in the negotiations leading to the agreement: Konrad Ilg, president of the Swiss Metal Workers' and Watchmakers' Union, and Ernst Dübi, president of the the Swiss Engineering and Metalworking Industrialists. Their path-breaking achievement of solving labour conflicts through renunciation of strikes and peaceful mediation became a model for all Swiss industries and is still in place.

Statistics

527 **Bevölkerungsbewegung in der Schweiz 1986. Statistische Resultate.** (Population movement in Switzerland 1986: statistical results.) Bern: Bundesamt für Statistik, 1988. 70p. (Amtliche Statistik der Schweiz, Nr. 147).

'Statistical results' of demographic data have been issued by the Swiss Federal Office for Statistics since 1867. The 1986 volume shows changes in population in Switzerland by month since 1971, with numbers for marriages, divorces, births, and deaths. Progressive statistics allow, among other things, the tracing of changes over time in the composition of the population and help us to understand demographic phenomena such as mortality rate differences between adult persons, depending on whether they were married, divorced, or single. This issue, for example, shows that of 10,000 women studied during the time-span covered, 127 women between the ages of 40 and 66 died and of these, 31 were married, 47 were divorced, and 49 were single.

528 **Das Bundesamt für Statistik kurz erklärt.** (The Swiss Federal Statistical Office briefly explained.) Bern: Bundesamt für Statistik, [1989]. 47p.

The Federal Statistical Office has four major branches: population and employment, public economy and prices, space utilization (*Raumwirtschaft*), and society and education. Each of these branches has a number of sections. This instructive publication describes briefly the tasks of each of the branches and their sections. It lists the statistics and publications that each of them produces and provides their addresses and telephone numbers. The booklet also contains information about two databanks with statistical materials, that are directly accessible to users. The publication succeeds admirably in providing an introduction to and guide through the wealth – and the maze – of statistical information available to the interested public.

529 **Der öffentliche Verkehr 1986. Statistische Resultate.** (Swiss public transport 1986: statistical results.)
Bundesamt für Statistik. Bern: Bundesamt für Statistik, 1987. 210p. (Amtliche Statistik der Schweiz, Nr. 143).

Contains technical information on the 59 railways, 14 cogwheel railways, 151 funiculars, and 436 cable-cars in Switzerland with figures about use, receipts, and expenditure, etc. Streetcars, trolley buses, buses, bus companies, river and lake navigation, and air traffic are other components of public transport covered in this volume. A companion volume, *Schweizerische Verkehrsstatistik 1986* (Swiss transportation statistics, 1986. Bern: Bundesamt für Statistik, 1987. 106p.), presents in the form of chronological series the major facts about public and private transport of persons and goods.

530 **Graphisch-statistischer Atlas der Schweiz.** (Graphic-statistical atlas of Switzerland.)
Statistisches Büro, Department des Innern. Bern: Kümmerly & Frey, 1914.

This atlas, produced by the Statistical Bureau of the Federal Department of the Interior, the forerunner of today's Swiss Federal Statistical Office, is a historical document of great charm and interest to the bibliophile. It has fifty-one tables of cartograms and diagrams in colour. The tables are explained and interpreted in a separate booklet with the title *Erklärungen zum graphisch-statistischen Atlas der Schweiz 1914* (Explanations on the graphic-statistical atlas of Switzerland 1914), published by Stämpfli, Bern, in 1915. The atlas is a masterpiece of advanced graphical presentation of statistical data. The tables cover every aspect of Swiss life before World War I. A map illustrating the proportion of horses in relation to the population, and diagrams showing the number of pigs, cattle, goats, sheep, and horses per 1,000 inhabitants in each of the cantons vividly demonstrate the fact that the work belongs to a bygone era.

531 **Hochschul- und Bildungsstatistischer Überblick. Statistischer Bericht 1985.** (Universities and education: a statistical overview. Statistical report 1985.)
Bern: Bundesamt für Statistik, 1985. 92p.

'Statistical reports' issued by the Swiss Federal Statistical Office provide detailed statistical analyses, in this case of the institutions of higher education in Switzerland. In addition to information about the number of students entering and their level of education, university expenditures, the make-up of the academic and non-academic staffs and the like, we are also told about the number of graduates without jobs in their fields and the percentage of women in the student body of the Swiss universities, which for 1981 was near the bottom of the developed countries with 34 per cent, and compares unfavourably with 49 per cent for the USA and 55 per cent for Norway. The tables and charts are accompanied by explanatory and interpretative texts.

532 **Jahresstatistik des Aussenhandels der Schweiz.** (Annual statistics of the foreign trade of Switzerland.)
Bern: Eidgenössische Oberzolldirektion, 1885- . 3 vols per year.

Published by the Federal Office of Customs, three volumes of about 1,300 pages each in 1987 list every kind of goods and materials that crossed the Swiss borders in its global export–import trade. The Office of Customs also issues monthly statistics of Swiss foreign trade. See also *Statistisches Jahrbuch der Schweiz*. (Statistical yearbook of Switzerland) (Bundesamt für Statistik. Basel: Birkhäuser, 1891-).

533 **Materialien zur Statistik: Verzeichnis der Neuerscheinungen Januar 1986-Dezember 1988.** (Materials on statistics: list of new publications, January 1986 to December 1988.)
Bern: Bundesamt für Statistik, 1989. 43p. (Amtliche Statistik der Schweiz, Nr. 196).

This publication continues the *Verzeichnis der Veröffentlichungen 1860-1985* (List of publications 1860-1985) issued by the Swiss Federal Statistical Office in 1985. It lists the publications generated by that office from 1986 to 1988 in the areas of demography, employment, public economy, prices, enterprises and places of employment, agriculture and forestry, construction and lodgings, tourism, transport and communication, health, education and science, culture and quality of life, political life, public finance, and law and jurisprudence. The fact that in a three-year span some two hundred publications were produced by this office, gives an indication of the wealth and variety of data collected by the busy statisticians of the federal government and made available to the public. The list provides information as to the content of every item, number of pages, and price. Some of the publications, including this list, are available free from the Bundesamt für Statistik, Publikationsdienst, Hallwylstr. 15, 3003 Bern, Switzerland.

534 **Schweizerische Bibliotheken 1986. Statistische Resultate.** (Swiss libraries 1986: statistical results.)
Bern: Bundesamt für Statistik, 1987. 18p. (Amtliche Statistik der Schweiz, Nr. 137).

This publication analyses only forty-six of the more than 6,000 libraries in Switzerland. It contains tables about personnel, appropriations and expenditures, holdings, acquisitions and growth, rate of use, and the interlibrary loans with foreign countries of these libraries.

535 **Schweizerische Verkehrsstatistik 1986. Statistische Resultate.** (Swiss traffic statistics 1986: statistical results.)
Bern: Bundesamt für Statistik, 1988. 106p. (Amtliche Statistik der Schweiz, Nr. 152).

This volume presents data concerning the transportation of persons and goods on rail roads, waterways, by air and by pipe conduits within the borders of Switzerland in 1960 and from 1970 to 1986. Traffic on roads has greatly increased, since the number of private cars has multiplied eighteen times and that of trucks and delivery vans by more than five times since 1960. The number of persons carried by railways increased by only twenty-four per cent since 1960, while motorized private transport grew 355 per cent in the same time span. In 1986 private vehicles made up eighty per cent of all traffic. There are sixty-nine tables, which analyse the topic from every possible angle. This is only one of about a dozen statistical publications by the Swiss Federal Statistical Office dealing with transport and communications.

536 **Statistical data on Switzerland 1988.**
Bern: Swiss Federal Statistical Office, 1988. 26p.

This pocket-size brochure, available free and printed in several languages, contains a sampling of statistical tables and charts from the nineteen subject areas of official statistics handled by the Swiss Federal Statistical Office in Bern. Population, environment, employment, economy, prices, businesses and places of employment, agriculture and forestry, energy, construction and housing, tourism, transport and communication, money, credit and currency, insurance and social security, health, education and science, culture and living conditions, political life, public finance, and law enforcement are the subjects of official statistics. Each is represented with a few highlights that give an indication of the scope and range of statistical information available in the Swiss Federal Statistical Office.

537 **Statistik der Schweizer Städte. Statistisches Jahrbuch des Schweizerischen Städteverbandes.** (Statistics of the Swiss cities: yearbook of the organization of Swiss cities.)
Bern: Schweizerischer Städteverband, 1931- . annual.

Volume 49 (1987) of this publication has 84 pages, and contains information on 128 Swiss cities; statistical tables set forth their size, utilization rate of available space, population trends from 1910 to 1986, marriages, births, deaths, newcomers in absolute numbers and per 1,000 inhabitants, foreigners, schooling, employment, municipal workforce, unemployed, vehicles, tourism, construction, rooms for rent, average cost of rents, water supply, electricity, garbage disposal, income categories, tax levels, revenues and expenditures, and political make-up.

538 **Statistische Erhebungen und Schätzungen über Landwirtschaft und Ernährung.** (Statistical studies and estimates concerning agriculture and nutrition.)
Brugg, Switzerland: Schweizerisches Bauernsekretariat, 1922- . annual.

Volume 64 (1987) of this publication by the Swiss Farmers' Secretariat in Brugg has 190 pages. Like its predecessors, it gives information about every imaginable aspect of farming, among them agricultural production and productivity, fertilizers and use of the land, crop production from grains and vegetables to fruits, and wine, animal husbandry, imports and exports of agricultural products, prices and price indexes, salaries of people employed in agriculture, agricultural credit and insurance, support measures by the Confederation and the cantons, estimated production costs of certain products, the place of agriculture in the Swiss economy, profitability, farming population, agrarian associations, and the professional training of farmers.

539 **Statistisches Jahrbuch der Schweiz. Herausgegeben vom Bundesamt für Statistik.** (Statistical yearbook of Switzerland: published by the Federal Office for Statistics.)
Basel: Birkhäuser, 1891- .

With the 607-page double-volume 1987/88, the long-standing relationship between the Federal Office for Statistics and the Birkhäuser publishing house in Basel has come to an end. The 1989 volume will leave the traditional book format and be produced by computerized publication methods. The statistical yearbook is the basic comprehensive source of information on every aspect of Swiss life. The scope and detail of information are staggering.

540 **Strukturatlas Schweiz.** (Structural atlas of Switzerland.)
Kurt Brassel, Ernst Brugger, Martin Schuler, Matthias Bopp. Zurich: Ex Libris, 1985. 296p. maps.

This splendid work represents the efforts of a sizeable team of young researchers who combined the use of available data with a novel approach of presentation and interpretation to demonstrate the diversity and yet unity of Switzerland. They selected nearly one hundred themes, such as suicide, traffic accidents, and the quality of life in both material and non-material terms describing each of them in words and with maps. For purposes of analysis, they divided the country into 106 regions, 26 cantons, 16 large regions, and 12 types of space of structural similarity. The maps excel in their graphic presentation capturing even the most subtle nuances. Some of the issues included in the themes have never before been researched.

541 **Tourismus in der Schweiz 1986. Statistischer Bericht.** (Tourism in Switzerland 1986: statistical report.)
Bern: Bundesamt für Statistik, 1987. (Amtliche Statistik der Schweiz, Nr. 130).

This is one of several publications on tourism by the Federal Office for Statistics. They include monthly, seasonal, and annual overviews, as well as specialized analyses of such things as Swiss travelling abroad, the balance sheet of tourism for Switzerland, and tourism in some of the cantons. The publications have tables and charts with interpretative texts on such things as numbers of hotel guests and lodgings by region, canton, and individual resort, and the places of origin of the guests. The 1985 annual volume has 130 pages, sixteen tables presenting data for 1985 and 1986, and seventeen tables of retrospective overview going back, in some instances, as far as 1934.

Education

542 **Educational innovations in Switzerland: traits and trends.**
Emile Blanc, Eugène Egger. Paris: Unesco, 1978. 98p. (Experiments and innovations in education, no. 33: an International Bureau of Education series).

The Swiss educational system is characterized by complexity, due to the division of responsibility between the Confederation, the cantons, and local authorities. However, the decade 1965-75 witnessed a growing readiness and flexibility of the cantons to increase coordination. Blanc and Egger make an inventory of these innovations and analyse some of them. Concerted action has been taken under the leadership of the Conference of Cantonal Directors of Education and has sometimes been stimulated by international organizations, such as Unesco and the Council of Europe. Change comes slowly. All major innovations have to pass the hurdle of the popular ballot by the electorate, but once adopted they are rarely subject to reversals. The authors list the educational opportunities available to the eleven- to fifteen-year-old pupils. These are judged to be innovative since they cater to many different abilities. Compulsory schooling ends at age fifteen. Education of the sixteen to nineteen age group has been diversified to establish a balance between the vocational, diploma, and *maturité* tracks. There are eleven types of *maturité* certificates, any one of which permits the holder to enter any of the Swiss universities or technical institutes without further examination. Finally, the public and private sectors work closely together in the fields of pre-school education, vocational training, and adult education.

543 **Recurrent education: policy and development in OECD member countries: Switzerland.**
Norbert Bottani, Ueli Egger, Judith König, Christoph Rauh, Michael Huberman, translated from the French by the authors. Paris: Organization for Economic Co-operation and Development (OECD), 1976. 144p. bibliog.

Similar reports for the status of recurring education in several OECD countries preceded this study. 'Recurrent education' is defined as a strategy that distributes education over the lifespan of a person, or, an alternation of work and education and is necessitated by the rapid expansion of science and technology. The authors cite three cases where such programmes are in place in Switzerland; all accept only adults with work experience. One is at the University of Geneva and trains mostly teachers; another is sponsored by the Fédération Suisse pour l'éducation des adultes (FSEA; Swiss Federation for the Education of Adults) that specializes in designing courses for new professions, and the third is a well-established continuing education programme for the workers of the Federal Post Office. The authors wonder how a 'comprehensive and coherent system' can be developed when regions, cantons, the Federal Government, and trade associations all have a hand in different phases of education, elementary, secondary, apprenticeships, vocational, and graduate education, when there are so many types of schools and when cultural diversity is not willingly sacrificed. All constituents, including political parties will have to cooperate in planning if an up-to-date recurrent education system in Switzerland is to become a reality.

544 **Switzerland: a study of the educational system of Switzerland and a guide to the academic placement of students from Switzerland in educational institutions of the United States.**

Karlene N. Dickey. Washington, DC: American Association of Collegiate Registrars and Admissions Officers, 1981. 129p. map. (World Education series).

Switzerland has a complicated system of education. There is no ministry of education. Cantons until recently had widely different systems that make pupil transfer from one to another difficult. The Concordat, an agreement to streamline public education, has existed since 1970 but is not yet accepted by all cantons. Dickey traces the numerous educational routes available, including the important vocational training, with clarity and depth. This is a handbook for anyone wishing information about the prerequisites for a specific career in Switzerland or about placing a Swiss-educated person in a foreign school system.

545 **Education in Switzerland.**

Eugène Egger. In: *Modern Switzerland*, edited by J. Murray Luck. Palo Alto, California: Society for Promotion of Science and Scholarship, 1978, p. 227-54.

Egger, secretary general of the Swiss Conference of Cantonal Directors of Education, provides an informative introduction to the complex Swiss system of education. The federal government's role in education is limited; the cantons are in charge of financing, directing, and controlling education from kindergarten to the universities. While the cantonal education directors have signed a Concordat on School Coordination, progress toward unifying the twenty-six systems is slow. Egger describes the multiplicity of curricula and education tracks which include post-public school training through vocational and professional schools, a very important aspect of education in Switzerland. He also explains how teachers are trained for all school levels and what efforts are made to bring about reforms at the various levels. Some further factual information on educational research, school buildings, textbooks, teaching aids, statistics, and information centres completes this brief yet comprehensive account of the Swiss school system. Egger has published a similar overview with a considerably enlarged data section with diagrams and statistics, entitled *L'Enseignement en Suisse* (Education in Switzerland) (Bern: Conférence suisse des directeurs cantonaux de l'instruction publique, 1984. 60p.).

546 **Private schools in Switzerland.**

Geneva: Fédération suisse des écoles privées, 1988. 99p. map.

Switzerland has a long tradition of offering private school education to its own people as well as to, usually wealthy, foreigners from all over the world. This guide to private schools lists twenty-three different types of institutions from elementary to professional educational establishments. These are located in all regions of the country, and the text is written in the language region in which the school described is located. Each school is pictured, complete with address and pertinent information, such as the current tuition and, if applicable, the cost for room and board. Schools offering curricula approved by certain foreign countries are noted.

547 **The essential Steiner: basic writings of Rudolf Steiner.**

Edited and introduced by Robert A. McDermott. San Francisco [etc.]: Harper & Row, 1984. 450p. bibliog.

Rudolf Steiner (1861-1925) was born on Marr Island, then in the Hungarian part of the Habsburg empire, now belonging to Yugoslavia, and died in Dornach, Canton Basel-Land, at the centre of his anthroposophic movement. McDermott provides a concise account of Steiner's life and work. He also introduces each of the five sections of readings, which make up the bulk of this book, with helpful comments. His annotated bibliography of Steiner's works in English and of works about Steiner is a model of its kind. Steiner is the founder of Anthroposophy, or Spiritual Science, whose aim it is 'to bring to humanity an entirely new capability – knowledge of the spiritual world by conscious sense-free thinking'. The essential meaning of one's life exists only at the spiritual level. For his followers he created the Goetheanum at Dornach, Switzerland. Designed and built after his plans, the Goetheanum was opened in 1920 with performances of Goethe's entire *Faust*. While Steiner's ideas on philosophy, religion, art, culture, and occultism are largely ignored, he had a considerable impact on education through the schools he founded. Known as Rudolf Steiner schools or Waldorf schools, of which there are several hundreds in many parts of the world, they are inspired by his belief that children should be allowed to develop their creative and spiritual powers in an inspiring environment, free from the straightjacket of the public school curricula and teaching methods.

548 **Sex differences in education: a comparative study of Ireland and Switzerland.**

Barbara Murray. Bern [etc.]: Peter Lang, 1985. 295p. bibliog. (European University Studies: Ser. 22, Sociology; vol. 116).

This is a PhD dissertation in sociology submitted at the University of Zurich. In the first part Murray examines sex-role ideologies and models in modern societies in general and in Ireland and Switzerland in particular. In the second part she outlines the main structural and process characteristics of the Irish and Swiss educational systems with special attention to the extent to which gender is used as a criterion for differentiation between pupils in school organization and curricular planning. Part three contains the findings of Irish and Swiss pupil surveys concerning perceived sex differences in second-level curricula and in educational and occupational aspirations. To the extent that such differences exist, the role of the school in producing them is contrasted with that of individual and social-background factors. Murray finds that the Irish and Swiss situations are similar in many respects, most importantly so in that in both countries a conflict still exists between conscious policies of equal opportunity and freedom of choice for girls and boys and the reality of schools continuing to prepare their pupils for sex-specific adult roles. Murray handles her materials with great methodological care. She alerts the reader that her findings concerning Switzerland are exploratory, since they are based on surveys in the schools of only three Catholic cantons of central Switzerland.

549 **Adult education in Switzerland.**
Monica Nestler, translated from the German by F. M. Blackwell. Zurich: Pro Helvetia, 1983. 66p. bibliog.

There is no comprehensive study of adult education in Switzerland and the author pleads that the education of adults should be a part of educational and social policy. The study shows, with figures from the year 1979, that many more men avail themselves of the existing opportunities than women. The ratios differ between rural and urban areas and also between various cantons. Eighteen institutions that coordinate continuing education programmes, both non-profit and profit-making, are listed. Their different objectives and offerings depend on the clientele they want to serve, be it the elderly, foreigners, hobbyists, workers, or young adults. Employer-sponsored adult education and specialized training are not considered here.

550 **Swiss schools and ours: why theirs are better.**
H. G. Rickover. [Boston]: Little, Brown, 1962. 219p.

Admiral Hyman G. Rickover, known as the father of the atomic navy, studied the school system of Switzerland under the sponsorship of the Council for Basic Education, a private organization dedicated to the improvement of American education. He felt that the Swiss achieved better results with their educational system and wanted to find out why this was so. He also felt that in spite of the many differences between the two countries there were enough similarities to make a comparison valid. Following a fact-finding mission, Rickover concluded that the Swiss success in the schooling of their youth could be attributed, among other things, to better teacher training, the longer school day and school year in Switzerland, standardized curricula and performance levels, and the fact that families are expected to take an active part in the education of their children. Examples of test questions administered in Swiss schools in foreign languages and mathematics are provided at the back of the book.

551 **Schweizerische Lehrerzeitung.** (Swiss teachers' journal.)
Stäfa, Switzerland: Zeitschriftenverlag Stäfa, 1856- . bi-weekly. ca. 35p.

The organ of the Swiss Teachers' Association, this well-made educational journal includes a mixture of scholarly articles, practical teaching tips for use in the classroom, education-political news, and a calendar of events.

552 **Pestalozzi: the man and his work.**
Kate Silber. London: Routledge and Kegan Paul, 1960. 335p. bibliog.

Kate Silber has divided the life and work of the Swiss educator Johann Heinrich Pestalozzi into seven chronological periods, from his birth in Zurich in 1746 to his death among the poor in Neuhof near Brugg in 1827. She mentions his work with the orphans of Stans at the time of the French invasion of Switzerland in 1799 and dwells somewhat longer on Pestalozzi's educational experiments in his institutes at Burgdorf and Münchenbuchsee in Canton Bern and Yverdon in Canton Vaud. Pestalozzi wrote prolifically and established himself as a social critic and reformer as well as a political philosopher and pedagogue whose views were ahead of his time. He saw education and the healthy family as guarantees for the welfare of the society and the nation in the coming industrial age. Silber, thoroughly familiar with Pestalozzi's often difficult writings, judges that his example as a dedicated educator and helper of the poor was of greater merit than his writings. The Verlag Neue Zürcher Zeitung in Zurich published in 1988 the first volume of an announced two-volume biography of Pestalozzi with the title *Pestalozzi: geschichtliche Biographie. von der alten Ordnung zur Revolution (1746-1787)* (Pestalozzi: historical biography. from the old order to the revolution [1746-87]). Written by Peter Stadler, professor of history at the University of Zurich, this new biography promises to be the definitive work on Pestalozzi for years to come.

553 **Johann Heinrich Pestalozzi. Sozialreformer – Erzieher – Schöpfer der modernen Volksschule. Eine Bildbiographie.** (Johann Heinrich Pestalozzi: social reformer, educator, creator of the modern public school; a picture biography.)
Michel Soëtard, translated from the French by Ingrid Altrichter. Zurich: SV international/Schweizer Verlagshaus, 1987. 149p. bibliog. (Die grossen Schweizer).

Soëtard has divided his picture biography of the great Swiss educator Pestalozzi into three parts. In the first part he describes Pestalozzi's upbringing in Zurich as a half-orphan, his schooling, his marriage to Anna Schulthess, his early humanitarian effort as founder of an orphanage on the Neuhof, near Brugg, Canton Aargau, inspired by a burning, but often impractical, idealism of eradicating poverty and bringing freedom to all human beings in a reformed community, and his early literary efforts, culminating in his literary masterwork *Lienhard and Gertrud* (first part published in 1781 by George Decker, Berlin). Part two deals with Pestalozzi's efforts to form a new human being. In war-devastated Stans, Canton Nidwalden, his pedagogy took shape in his work with the war orphans. In Burgdorf and Münchenbuchsee, Canton Bern, he developed with the help of a few devoted collaborators the structure and principles of his method which attracted the attention of educators in many parts of Europe. In Yverdon, Canton Vaud, from 1804 to 1825, he finally perfected his educational method, the core of which was his belief that children's hearts and hands needed as much attention as their heads. In the third part Soëtard provides an account of Pestalozzi's final struggles and his retirement.

554 **The Swiss universities.**
Swiss National Tourist Office. Zurich: Swiss National Tourist Office, 1981. 44p.

This slim booklet provides basic information about the ten university-level institutions of higher learning that exist in Switzerland. They are the universities of Basel, Bern, and Zurich, the Swiss Federal Institute of Technology, Zurich (ETHZ), and the St Gallen Graduate School of Economics, Business and Public Administration in German-speaking Switzerland, and the universities of Geneva, Lausanne, Neuchâtel, and Fribourg (actually bilingual, German and French), and the Swiss Federal Institute of Technology, Lausanne (EPFL) in French-speaking Switzerland. After an introduction with general information about such things as university regulations, degrees, fees, living costs, and scholarships, each university is briefly described with a listing of university seminars and institutes. A tabulation at the end of the booklet lists all the fields of study available at the Swiss universities in which a university degree can be earned. Addresses and phone numbers are given for these institutions and for agencies abroad.

555 **Die Entwicklung der Berufsbildung in der Schweiz.** (The development of occupational education in Switzerland.)
Emil Wettstein. Aarau, Switzerland; Frankfurt am Main, FRG: Sauerländer, 1987. 135p. bibliog.

In the first part of this book, Wettstein (of the Institut für Bildungsforschung und Berufspädagogik des Kantonalen Amtes für Berufsbildung, Zurich) gives an overview of the development of occupational education in Switzerland from the Middle Ages to the late 20th century. He begins with the 13th century when the towns with their guilds regulated the training of the young apprentices and ends on 1 January 1980, when a new federal law regulating occupational education came into force. The study concentrates on education in the crafts and in business, and touches only briefly on the training for professions in agriculture and health, and for women. When Switzerland entered the technological age, more specialized and continuing education was needed and it required the training and certifying of instructors to teach these new courses. The unemployment wave of the thirties made programmes for mainstreaming the unskilled a priority. As practical and theoretical education became more and more specialized, the government increasingly set standards which traditionally had been set by different agencies and professional groups. The chronicle in the second part of the study give a year-by-year account of the development of occupational training, with the section on the years 1751-1980 being especially informative since it records the founding of all types of schools. Practically no information is given about the life of the apprentice or learner.

Science and Technology

General

556 **Research.**

Hugo E. Aebi. In: *Modern Switzerland*, edited by J. Murray Luck. Palo Alto, California: Society for the Promotion and Science and Scholarship, 1978, p. 129-56. bibliog.

Basic research takes place mainly at the universities and their affiliated institutions, but in certain fields, such as chemistry and engineering, a considerable effort is also made in the laboratories of industrial companies. Aebi estimates that in the late 1970s some 10,000 scientists were actively engaged in research in Switzerland. He lists the institutions that are active in such research with their major achievements, and describes the tendency toward the creation of large national research centres. In a section entitled 'research projects', Aebi outlines some examples of current efforts in the fields of psychology, physics, chemistry, virology, and immunology. He concludes his informative article with a discussion of research policy, i.e. 'the sum of activities that promote research and exploit research results', in Switzerland and the problems of setting priorities.

557 **Science in Switzerland.**

Steven Dickman, John Maddox. *Nature. International Weekly Journal of Science* (London), vol. 336, no. 6197 (24 November 1988), p. 323-40.

The authors provide a brief yet informative account of scientific institutions and developments in Switzerland, and their survey 'has mostly nothing but admiration to report'. The overall strength and prosperity of the country derives from success in research and education and the intelligent exploitation of technology and business acumen. Dickman and Maddox describe the academic scientific work done at the various Swiss institutions of higher learning as well as at the specialized federal institutes such as the one for snow and avalanche research in Davos-Weissfluhjoch,

Canton Graubünden, and for high-altitude research on the Jungfraujoch, Canton Bern. They note that the practitioners of academic life are very well paid, and they also illustrate the contributions of industry to scientific research, citing by way of example the chemical giant Ciba-Geigy, which represents the synergy of chemists and biologists, and Hoffmann-La Roche, with its path-breaking work in biotechnology. If there is one blemish in this otherwise rosy picture it is that the Swiss system does not produce enough trained engineers to meet the ever-increasing demands, especially in the information sciences.

558 **Grosse Schweizer Forscher.** (Great Swiss scholars and scientists.)
Edited by Eduard Fueter. Zurich: Atlantis, 1941. 2nd enlarged ed. 340p.

Fueter has enlisted the cooperation of more than one hundred experts to write the entries for the 124 Swiss scholars and scientists featured in this book. The uniform presentation consists of a portrait of each individual, a condensed biographical sketch, a slightly longer evaluation of the significance of his work, and a brief bibliography. Included in the book are persons who have written at least one major work of European significance in their respective fields of learning and who died before 1920. They are listed chronologically, from the humanists of the 15th and 16th centuries to the scientists and philologists of the late 19th century. One of the indexes lists the learned men according to fields of scholarship. The largest group is that of mathematicians, natural scientists, and geographers, while other groups are physicians; lawyers, economists, and sociologists; historians; philologists; theologians; philosophers and pedagogues; and engineers and architects. This book is an eye-opener as to the depth and variety of the achievements of Swiss scholars through the centuries.

559 **Science in Switzerland.**
James Murray Luck. New York; London: Columbia University Press, 1967. 419p.

James Murray Luck, Science Officer in the US Embassy in Bern from 1962 to 1964, reports on the status of science in Switzerland in the 1960s. Part one of the book discusses the different types of secondary schools and graduate institutions which prepare for careers in the sciences. 'Science' as defined by Luck refers to all scholarly work done in Switzerland that adds to human knowledge, e.g. science includes the social sciences. The administration of the two federal institutes of technology in Zurich and Lausanne are in the hands of a federally constituted body, while the seven public universities of Basel, Bern, Fribourg, Geneva, Lausanne, Neuchâtel and the Graduate School of Economics, Business and Public Administration in St Gallen are under cantonal control. Part two deals with many organizations, bureaux, institutes and publications that advance science, and it reports on current research activities in several areas, such as nuclear and space science. A wide range of data support the text.

560 **Swiss contributions to science.**
Joachim Schroeter. New York: American Society for Friendship with Switzerland, 1960. 28p.

This slim brochure provides brief biographical sketches (with photographs) of thirty men who were born in Switzerland or spent their adult careers in Switzerland and made significant contributions to their field of science. Schroeter divided them into four groups according to areas of endeavour, namely architecture and civil engineering with six individuals, mathematics and physics, also with six, chemistry with seven, and medicine and biology with eleven. From the 16th century on, every century is represented by some outstanding scientists, with a slight preponderance of 20th-century representatives, among them several Nobel prize winners.

561 **Politiques nationales de la science. Suisse.** (National science policies: Switzerland.)
Edited by La Direction des Affaires Scientifiques, OCDE. Paris: OECD, 1971. ca. 270p.

This report by the Organization for Economic Co-operation and Development (OECD) consists of two parts. The first, longer part is a review of the characteristics of Swiss science policies. Written by Swiss science experts, it provides a thorough description of the institutional and structural make-up of the Swiss science establishment in the late 1960s. Some eighty tables, charts, and organigrams are distributed through the text. The second part consists of the report of the OECD examiners and the results of their discussions with their Swiss counterparts. This publication is of special interest because it provides an in-depth view of the science situation in Switzerland at the moment when the federal government began to take on a more active role in national science policies than it had had up to that time.

562 **Technology.**
A. P. Speiser. In: *Modern Switzerland*, edited by J. Murray Luck. Palo Alto, California: Society for the Promotion of Science and Scholarship, 1978, p. 157-71. bibliog.

High-technology products constitute a large proportion of Swiss industrial output. Speiser thinks that Switzerland ranks at the top in per capita expenditures for research and development (R&D) in terms of gross national product of all industrialized countries. The government share of R&D in Switzerland is much smaller than in most other countries, less than one-fourth of all R&D expenditures in 1976, for example, as compared with 53 per cent in the USA. The cost of most of the industrial R&D is borne by the chemical and machine industries, which also happen to be Switzerland's major exporters. Speiser describes the major innovations in recent years in these two important branches of Swiss industry and the watch industry. Swiss technological achievements are the results of striving for excellence in a limited range of areas.

563 **Wissenschaftspolitik. Mitteilungsblatt der schweizerischen wissenschaftspolitischen Instanzen.** (The politics of science: information bulletin of the Swiss organs of the politics of science.)
Bern: Schweizerischer Wissenschaftsrat, 1972- . quarterly. ca. 70p.

This publication contains information about the Swiss Science Council (Wissenschaftsrat), the Swiss National Foundation for the Promotion of Scientific Research, the Swiss University and University Rectors' Conference and other bodies involved in the formulation and implementation of science policies. Also included are articles about educational and scientific research policies and politics.

Scientists, social scientists, and engineers

564 **Paracelsus: selected writings.**

Edited with an introduction by Jolande Jacobi, translated from the German by Norbert Guterman. Princeton, New Jersey: Princeton University Press, 1951. 2nd ed., 1958; 3rd printing, 1973. 290p. bibliog. (Bollingen Series, vol. 28).

Jacobi provides a concise introduction to the life and work of Paracelsus (1493-1541). Born Theophrastus Bombastus von Hohenheim in the Swiss pilgrimage site of Einsiedeln, Paracelsus began his wanderings when he was only nine years old. After studying at various European universities he earned a doctor of medicine degree from Ferrara in Italy. Travelling tirelessly across Europe, he increased his knowledge and acquired a reputation as a revolutionary figure in medicine, 'the Luther of the physicians'. His often controversial views went against the grain of accepted teaching, and the irascible and arrogant way with which he defended them brought him many enemies. In 1528 he lost his position as a professor at the University of Basel, after only two semesters there. Paracelsus spent the rest of his life in search of a safe haven from his detractors. He died and was buried in Salzburg. Jacobi has selected excerpts from Paracelsus' voluminous writings on medicine, therapeutics, and medication, cosmosophic philosophy, alchemy, astronomy and astrology, anthropology, and religion and grouped them into nine topical sections. Her fine book is greatly enhanced by 148 woodcuts by 15th- and 16th-century artists, and a twenty-two-page glossary provides access to the arcane vocabulary of this fascinating Renaissance figure.

565 **Magic into science: the story of Paracelsus.**

Henry M. Pachter. New York: Henry Schuman, 1951. 360p. bibliog.

Pachter translated his fascination with the Swiss Renaissance figure Paracelsus into a readable, appealing biography. For him the controversial physicist and philosopher revealed undercurrents of the times which usually remain unexplored in the run-of-the-mill presentations of the brilliancy of the age. Paracelsus, whom his contemporaries identified with the legendary Dr Faustus, personified for Pachter the shaker and mover who, living astride the past and the future, the medieval and the modern, engulfed himself in the study of the philosophy of man; in his work one can trace the intricate ways in which science developed out of the magic conceptions of nature. A necromancer, who wrote a veritable encyclopaedia of occult sciences, Paracelsus praised reasoning and experiment as the true source of knowledge, and Pachter concludes that Paracelsus is best understood 'in terms of his own rebellion against the system which provoked it'. In all the fields where he pioneered, he 'contributed more intuition than observation, more ideas than knowledge'. See also *Paracelsus. Alchimist – Chemiker – Erneuerer der Heilkunde. Eine Bildbiographie* (Paracelsus: alchemist, chemist, innovator of the art of healing: a picture biography) by Lucien Braun, translated from the French by Katharina Biegger (Die grossen Schweizer. Zurich: Schweizer Verlagshaus, 1988. 158p. bibliog.)

566 **Paracelsus: an introduction to philosophical medicine in the era of the Renaissance.**

Walter Pagel. Basel; New York: Karger, 1958. 368p.

The Renaissance physician Paracelsus was born near Einsiedeln, Switzerland, where his father, a chemist and also a physician, was his first teacher. Paracelsus' biography takes up the first part of this voluminous book, while the second part deals with 'philosophical medicine', a new approach to medicine which emerged in the 16th century. Paracelsus became its leading exponent. Man's body and soul were to be seen and treated as one. Paracelsus searched for natural drugs and introduced chemotherapeutic methods into the practice of medicine. His criticism of the teachings of the ancients and his innovative ideas provoked enmity among the professional physicians of his time and forced him to move from place to place. Pagel assesses the originality of Paracelsus' work and discusses its significance for the history and science of medicine.

567 **Leonhard Euler 1707-1783. Beiträge zu Leben und Werk. Gedenkband des Kantons Basel-Stadt.** (Leonhard Euler: contributions to his life and work; memorial volume of Canton Basel-Stadt.)

Edited by J. J. Burckhardt, E. A. Fellmann, W. Habicht. Basel [etc.]: Birkhäuser, 1983. 555p. bibliog.

This substantial book consists of articles by an international cast of academics and scientists, including eight from the Soviet Union, about the 18th-century Basel polymath, Leonhard Euler. The illustrated volume begins with an essay about Euler's life and work. Endowed with a unique memory that seemingly helped him to retain everything he ever heard, read, or wrote, the gift of absolute concentration, and the habit of steady, quiet work Euler produced more than 700 publications, 270 of them during the last decade of his life alone. Nine contributions to this two-hundredth anniversary of his birth year volume deal with his work in the fields of numbers theory, algebra, and analysis; the next six are about his work in physics, and they are followed by three essays on Euler's astronomy and by six contributions to his relationship to academies and important personalities. Three essays deal with Euler's philosophy, theology, and biography, respectively, and three others, finally, describe the editorial history of Euler's *Opera omnia*, a project that is not completed yet, and an annotated bibliography on the *Euleriana*, the literature about him. Each of the essays stands on its own; together, they provide an impressive overview of the scope and breadth of Euler's genius and of the continuing effect of his scientific work on contemporary science and scientists.

568 **Leonhard Euler.**

Rüdiger Thiele. Leipzig, GDR: Teubner, 1982. 192p. bibliog. (Biographien hervorragender Naturwissenschaftler, Techniker und Mediziner).

Leonhard Euler, citizen of Basel, was a mathematician and physicist. Young Euler's restless search to find answers to mathematical problems was aided by his acquaintance with the Bernoullis, the prominent Basel family of mathematicians and by a new interest in the sciences that led to the founding of learned academies in many centres of Europe. Early fame came to Euler as a member of the St Petersburg Academy where he published an important text on mechanics and also the work *Scientia navalis* (*Schiffswesen*, navigation science). His research included many other areas such as optics, cartography, astronomy, statistics, finance, and navigation. He contributed new ideas in the calculus, geometry, algebra, numbers theory, and probability, and he tested the works of Newton, Leibniz, de Fermat and did much of his work after he became totally blind in 1766. Thiele makes use of the biographical materials that the old Euler dictated to his son; it gives insight into the personal and professional struggles of the genius.

569 **Louis Agassiz: a life in science.**

Edward Lurie. Chicago, Illinois: University of Chicago Press, 1960. 449p. bibliog.

Agassiz (1807-73), born Jean-Louis Rodolphe Agassiz in Môtier, Canton Neuchâtel, Switzerland, showed already as a fifteen-year-old 'an insatiable curiosity about nature, a good knowledge of languages, and an intense desire to succeed'. The natural sciences would consume all his energies and bring him great fame. He studied at the universities of Zurich, Heidelberg, and Munich where the young genius was recognized by the leading scientists of the time. Agassiz's work on fossil fishes and his glacier studies brought him invitations to lecture all over Europe where he was noted for his ability to translate complicated findings into popular terms. Alexander von Humboldt secured him a grant from Frederick Wilhelm III of Prussia to study the natural history of the New World. Agassiz arrived in Boston in 1846 and never considered returning permanently to Europe; in 1848 he became professor of zoology and geology at Harvard University; he collected and studied all kinds of animals, and published his findings; and in 1860 he achieved his dream of founding a museum with the opening of the Museum of Comparative Zoology at Harvard. He rejected Charles Darwin's theories on evolution and refused to examine his findings. Not perturbed by critics, he travelled extensively, searching constantly for new specimens and insights. Glimpses of his first unhappy marriage and his second happy one and accounts of the careers of his three children add a human touch to this detailed and scholarly biography of the great Swiss-American scientist.

570 **Robert Maillart: bridges and constructions.**

Max Bill. English version by W. P. M. Keatinge Clay. New York; Washington, DC: Praeger, 1969. 184p.

This is the third edition of a book originally published in Zurich in 1949. Every word in it appears in German, French, and English. Much of the text in this monograph is made up of original writings by Maillart (1872-1940) on various aspects of his work as a pioneer in the use of reinforced concrete in the construction of bridges and mushroom-column structures with beamless floors and ceilings. Bill, in a foreword and two brief interpretative essays, emphasizes that Maillart's constructions were not only technical masterpieces but aesthetic achievements in space. 'One is repeatedly surprised by their novelty, and his originality and rich imagination.' The bulk of the book consists of a portfolio of more than 200 captioned photographs and diagrams of elevations, ground plans, and sections of the most important bridges of Maillart. Essential technical data are provided for each bridge, but Bill's goal throughout was to illustrate 'the most essential factors, the creative and imaginative aspects of his [Maillart's] mind'.

571 **Robert Maillart's bridges: the art of engineering.**

David P. Billington. Princeton, New Jersey: Princeton University Press, 1979. 146p. map. bibliog.

In this splendid book, with its many photographs and diagrams, Billington traces the evolution of the engineer and bridge-builder Robert Maillart from his student days at the Federal Institute of Technology in Zurich to the most creative phase of his career during the last decade of his life. During the forty years of his professional life Maillart advanced from the design and construction of masonry-like bridges such as the Lorraine bridge over the Aare river in Bern, completed in 1930, to the building of thoroughly concrete bridges, the first of which, also in 1930, was the Salginatobel bridge in the mountain wilderness of Canton Graubünden. This bridge was perceived almost immediately by laymen and engineers alike as something new and 'prototypical of the twentieth century'. 'This bridge exemplifies the ideal that in the modern structuring of an environment, efficiency and elegance are merely aspects of the same design seen from the perspectives of science and of art; and that the essence of engineering lies in the integration of the two by the connecting link of economy.' Billington presents in ten chapters a sampling of Maillart's significant works and of his central ideas. Extensive notes refer to the sources and provide some of the technical data and calculations.

572 **Jung: his life and work: a biographical memoir.**
Barbara Hannah. New York: Putnam, 1976. 376p. bibliog.

After becoming intrigued with Jung's work, Hannah moved from England to Zurich where she became a lecturer and training analyst at the Jung Institute. Thus began a thirty-year association with the important Swiss psychologist. Hannah is able to shed some light on issues that have caused controversy, such as Jung's relationship with his close associate Toni Wolff, and she provides evidence of the master's aversion to Nazism. These and her many other first-hand and everyday experiences give this biographical memoir its special place among the many works on Jung. See also *Jung and the story of our time*, Laurens van der Post (New York: Pantheon Books, Random House, 1975). Van der Post, an author of novels and travel books about South Africa, had a long-standing friendship with C. G. Jung. This friendship provided the impetus for this book and a film van der Post did for the BBC: *The Story of Carl Gustav Jung*. The material for this work was gathered in many hours of interviews. Van der Post not only describes the man but attempts to place Jung's personal experiences in the context of those of humanity in general.

573 **C. G. Jung: memories, dreams, reflections.**
Edited by Aniela Jaffé, translated from the German by Richard and Clara Winston. London: Collins and Routledge & Kegan Paul, 1963. 383p.

Jung refused to write his autobiography but provided his long-time assistant and friend Aniela Jaffé with the material for such a work. The project eventually fascinated Jung, so that he wrote major parts himself. We learn of his formative years, his psychiatric work at the Burghölzli Mental Hospital in Zurich, his contacts with Sigmund Freud, his travels devoted to the study of the minds of primitive peoples, his meditations upon Christian mysteries, his dreams and their interpretation, all of which are essential elements of 'Jungian psychology'. Jung's theories differ from those of his erstwhile mentor Sigmund Freud, as his writings, which comprise some twenty volumes, demonstrate.

574 **C. G. Jung: word and image.**
Edited by Aniela Jaffé. Princeton, New Jersey: Princeton University Press, 1979. 238p. bibliog. (Bollingen Series 47:2).

This large-format, richly illustrated book performs the function of a family album for Jungians. Word and picture tell them about the master's youth and schooling in Basel, his work at the Burghölzli in Zurich and the Salpetrière in Paris, and his early scientific publications and relationship with Freud and other leaders in the psychoanalytic movement. In 1909 Jung moved to Küsnacht near Zurich to devote himself to private practice. The book gives an impressive presentation of Jung's 'confrontation with the unconscious' with beautiful illustrations from the 'Red Book', in which Jung transcribed and illustrated his inner experiences; of a variety of mandalas which were for Jung the symbol of human wholeness; from alchemistic manuscripts; and of psychotherapeutic pictures done by patients. Jung's family life and his travels to America, Africa, and Asia are covered, as are his personal relations with friends and disciples. Toward the end of the book much space is given to Jung's work on the 'Tower' at Bollingen on the upper Lake Zurich, where from 1923 on Jung built and sculpted an elaborate structure in which he communed with the archetypal emanations of his surroundings. Jaffé provides a convenient chronology of Jung's life with the titles of his major works, and a glossary of technical terms.

575 **Jung the philosopher: essays in Jungian thought.**
Marian L. Pauson. New York [etc.]: Lang, 1988. 235p. bibliog.

Pauson's book fills a gap in the vast literature on Jung by analysing his ideas and concepts from a philosophical viewpoint. Jung's voluminous and multi-faceted works are studied for answers to speculative questions in contemporary philosophy. Pauson finds that the great Swiss psychotherapist made important contributions to speculative thought in the areas of epistemology, metaphysics, aesthetics, education, religion, the problem of evil, and the question of life after death.

576 **The collected works of C. G. Jung.**
Edited by Herbert Read, Michael Fordham, Gerhard Adler, translated by R. F. C. Hull. London: Routledge & Kegan Paul; Princeton, New Jersey: Bollingen Foundation and Princeton University Press, 1953-79. 20 vols. (American edition: Bollingen Series, 20 vols).

This is the definitive edition of Jung's works in English. Jung supervised the textual revision until his death in 1961. Virtually all his works were newly translated for this edition. Volume 19 consists of a bibliography of Jung's writings, and volume 20 is the general index to the *Collected Works*.

577 **Portrait of Jung: an illustrated biography.**
Gerhard Wehr, translated from the German by W. A. Hargreaves. New York: Herder and Herder, 1971. 173p. bibliog.

In a small booklet with relatively few black-and-white illustrations, Wehr describes and analyses Jung's large body of work in topical fashion: psychological types, psychology and religion, alchemy and the study of the psyche, Jung and Eastern thought, psychotherapy, all set within the biographical and contemporary environment. He succeeds in giving access to Jung and his work through a text that is easy to understand and expressed in relatively clear and simple language. Wehr also wrote the text of the large-sized picture biography *C. G. Jung. Arzt – Tiefenpsychologe – Visionär. Eine Bildbiographie* (C. G. Jung: physician, depth psychologist, visionary; a picture biography) which was published as a volume in the series *Die grossen Schweizer* (The great Swiss) (Zurich: SV international/Schweizer Verlagshaus, 1989. 160p. bibliog.). Lavishly illustrated with some two hundred images, forty-eight of them full-page colour plates, this book emphasizes the fact that Jung's work is of increasing relevance to a world which, becoming sceptical about the quantitive, materialistic approach to life, is searching for a holistic understanding of reality.

578 **Albert Einstein in Bern: Eine dokumentarische Skizze über das Ringen um ein neues Weltbild.** (Albert Einstein in Bern: a documentary sketch about the search for a new world picture.)
Max Flückiger. Bern: Haupt, 1962. 144p.

Einstein (1879-1955) graduated in 1900 in mathematics and physics from the Swiss Federal Institute of Technology in Zurich. In 1902 he arrived in Bern with little more than a violin and pages of a manuscript, but his work as patent examiner allowed him enough free time to pursue his scientific investigations, and in 1905 he advanced his theory of relativity that changed the course of modern physical science. That same year, he became a Swiss citizen, a citizenship he retained to the end of his life. Flückiger uncovers many details and events from Einstein's daily and personal life during the seven years he spent in the Swiss capital, a time that was marked by growing world-wide recognition of his genius. Photographs, letters, and documents from Einstein's Bern years make up the special value of this book.

579 **Albert Einstein und die Schweiz.** (Albert Einstein and Switzerland.)
Carl Seelig. Zurich [etc.]: Europa, 1952. 254p. bibliog.

Einstein had many and strong ties to Switzerland throughout his life, but the major phase of his relationship with Switzerland fell into the years 1895 to 1914 which he spent almost entirely on Swiss soil. During those years he finished his secondary schooling at the Kantonsschule Aarau, Canton Aargau; studied for a diploma for instructor of mathematics and physics at the Swiss Federal Institute of Technology in Zurich; became, in 1901, a citizen of Zurich, a citizenship he would keep for the rest of his life; worked for seven years as a technical expert at the Federal Patent Office in Bern; earned a doctorate in physics from the University of Zurich; received, in 1909, his first honorary doctor's degree from the University of Geneva; was appointed to professorships at the University of Zurich and the Swiss Federal Institute of Technology; and, of course, did some of his most important scientific work. Seelig provides a lively documentary history based on letters and autobiographical statements by Einstein, recollections of friends, colleagues, and students, and records from the archives of the institutions at which Einstein studied and taught. The Swiss years were among the most fruitful and productive of Einstein's life, and Seelig succeeds in conveying the scientific import of Einstein's creative work. A somewhat enlarged version of this book, covering Einstein's entire life, was published in 1955 as *Albert Einstein. Eine dokumentarische Biographie* (Albert Einstein: a documentary biography). It contains a bibliography of 313 entries of Einstein's scientific papers.

580 **Othmar H. Ammann 1879-1965: 60 Jahre Brückenbau.** (Othmar H. Ammann 1879-1965: 60 years of bridge building.)
Urs Widmer. Winterthur, Switzerland: Technorama, 1979. 104p. bibliog.

Othmar H. Ammann's memory was honoured with this publication on the occasion of his 100th birthday. Ammann emigrated to America at the age of twenty-five 'to gain experience'. He took up work with the New York Port Authority where he eventually rose to the top position of chief engineer. After retirement he continued to be productive in his own firm. The book features the many bridges he designed or in the construction of which he had a major hand. Drawings and technical data accompany the photographs. Ammann's suspension bridges were praised not only as superior technical achievements but also for their beauty. The George Washington bridge across the Hudson River and the Verrazano Narrows bridge at the entrance to New York harbour are the best-known examples of his work, but there are fourteen other bridges in the New York area alone that bear his mark. His consulting work and influence are manifest in many other bridge constructions throughout the United States. A list of Ammann's many awards, his publications on technical aspects of bridge building, and articles and books about him testify to the contributions this great Swiss engineer has made to his adopted country.

581 **Plays, dreams and imitation in childhood.**
Jean Piaget, translated from the French by C. Gattegno and F. H. Hodgson. London: Routledge & Kegan Paul; New York: Norton, 1962. 296p.

Piaget (1896-1980), one of the founders of modern child psychology, takes us through six stages of development in an infant's imitation of movement and sound. He then observes the evolution of game playing in a young child which at first is a sensory-motor assimilation and later becomes symbolic play. Piaget's numerous clinical observations are classified and illustrate the theories put forward about a child's path to logical or adult thought processes. This is the third volume in a series of works devoted to the first years of the child's development, the other two being concerned with the beginnings of intelligence and the child's construction of reality.

582 **The language and thought of the child.**
Jean Piaget, translated from the French by Marjorie and Ruth Gabain. London: Routledge & Kegan Paul, 1959. New York: Humanities Press, 1967. 3rd ed. 288p. (International Library of Psychology, Philosophy and Scientific Method).

Piaget, the noted Geneva psychologist, investigated the fundamental structure and different phases in the development of a child's intelligence or logic. Piaget and his associates worked with infants and children in carefully monitored sessions. The resulting case-studies from this 'clinical method' formed the basis for an elaborate system of classification that reveals how children think at different stages of their early years.

Culture and the Arts

General

583 **Focus on Switzerland: intellectual and literary life; the fine arts; music.**
Alfred Berchtold, André Kuenzi, Kurt von Fischer. Lausanne: Swiss Office for the Development of Trade, 1982. 2nd ed. 175p.

This book provides a fine introduction to the intellectual, cultural, and artistic life of Switzerland. Excellent illustrations of individual personalities and their creations give an idea of the richness and the variety of the forces that shaped modern Switzerland. The illuminated manuscript page from the monastery of St Gallen is part of the rich cultural heritage, as is the animated machine sculpture by Jean Tinguely; Arthur Honegger's 'Jeanne d'Arc au bûcher' (Joan of Arc at the stake) is an expression of the twentieth century, as is the Swiss Jazz School in Bern; a play by Dürrenmatt belongs to the literary scene, as does a Romansh poem. Scientists, psychologists, theologians, educators, inventors, and architects have left their marks. The cities lend their support to cultural organizations and the performing arts and provide a meeting ground of the minds not only for the country's citizens but also for the foreign visitors.

584 **Tapisseries Suisses, artistes d'aujourd'hui = Schweizerische Tapisserien, Künstler von heute = Swiss tapestries, artists of today.**
Edited by Cyril Bourquin-Walfard, Marie-Lise Disch-Brack, Claude Frossard, translated from the French by Silvia Gozdzieska. Lausanne: Genoud, 1977. 73p.

This is a catalogue that was assembled for an exhibition of Swiss tapestries that travelled to many European countries between 1977 and 1980. The pieces assembled and the artists represented were chosen in a national contest. The twenty-seven winners are represented with thirty-four works. A short sketch and photograph of each artist and up to three of his or her works, are featured in black-and-white. The Swiss weavers have played a part not only in the national but also in the international renewal of this old art.

585 **Karte der Kulturgüter.** (Map of the cultural treasures.)
Bundesamt für Landestopographie. Bern: Bundesamt für Landestopographie, 1988.

This map on the scale of 1:300,000 shows artistic, cultural, and historical treasures of Switzerland. It is based on a complete inventory of objects of national and regional significance established between 1969 and 1987. A booklet that comes with the map lists all objects, alphabetically, and by canton and within the canton by place. Included are whole settlements, parts of settlements, religious buildings, profane structures, rural dwellings, castles, ruins, industrial complexes, railway stations, roadways and bridges, monuments, fountains, archaeological sites, museums, libraries, and archives. There are seventy-four maps on the scale of 1:10,000 and 1:50,000. The map is an inexhaustible source of information and amazement about the variety and wealth of cultural objects that can be found in Switzerland.

586 **Beiträge für eine Kulturpolitik der Schweiz.** (Contributions to a cultural policy of Switzerland.)
Gaston Clottu, president of the Eidgenössische Expertenkommission für Fragen einer Schweizer Kulturpolitik. Bern: EDMZ, 1975. 506p.

This report by a commission of experts on issues concerning Swiss cultural policies originated in a desire of the Swiss parliament and the Federal Council to (re-)consider the role of government in cultural matters. About two-thirds of the bulky tome consists of a thorough, inclusive inventory of cultural efforts in Switzerland at all political levels from the communities to the federal government. All persons involved in the arts, literature, theatre, music, and film, whether in a creative or interpretative function were catalogued, and their working conditions and relationship to society analysed. Then follows a similarly thorough review of institutions that transmit culture or provide cultural impulses such as libraries, publishers, bookstores, theatres, museums, art galleries, radio and television, the press, youth centres, and adult education. It is these inventories with many tables and diagrams that give this report its value; they give a uniquely precise picture of the cultural life and scene in Switzerland at the beginning of the last quarter of the 20th century. The major conclusion and recommendation derived from the general cultural-political analysis in the second part of the report was that the federal government should play a more active role in cultural affairs and spend substantially more funds on them. A bill to implement these recommendations was voted down by Swiss voters in a national referendum in 1986.

587 **Ars Helvetica. Die visuelle Kultur der Schweiz.** (Ars Helvetica: the visual culture of Switzerland.)
Edited by Florens Deuchler. Disentis, Switzerland: Pro Helvetia/Desertina, 1987- .

The sales prospectus for the *Ars Helvetica* enterprise boasts that it will be a new writing of the history of Swiss art and culture. Sponsored by the Swiss cultural foundation Pro Helvetia and the Federal Office for the Care of Culture (Bundesamt für Kulturpflege). Deuchler has enlisted the collaboration of a team of prominent established and promising younger art historians to author the twelve volumes planned for this project. By the end of 1989 six volumes had been published: *Kunstgeographie* (Geography of art) by Dario Gamboni, *Kunstbetrieb* (The enterprise of art) by Florens Deuchler, *Sakrale Bauten* (Religious structures) by Heinz Horat (q.v.), *Profane Bauten* (Profane edifices) by André Meyer (q.v.), *Malerei des Mittelalters* (Painting of the Middle Ages) by Christoph and Dorothee Eggenberger, and *Malerei der Neuzeit* (Painting of modern times) by Oskar Bätschmann. The volumes are richly illustrated and produced according to the highest scholarly and technical standards. The project was scheduled to be completed by the 700th anniversary of the founding of the Swiss Confederation in 1991. This target date will be missed by several years, partly because the volumes are published simultaneously in all four national languages, German, French, Italian, and Romansh, but the product is well worth waiting for.

588 **Die Kunstdenkmäler der Schweiz.** (The art and historical monuments of Switzerland.)
Gesellschaft für Schweizerische Kunstgeschichte. Basel: Birkhäuser, 1927- .

This is a huge and ongoing project aimed at making an inventory of the artistic patrimony of Switzerland. By 1986 seventy-one substantial volumes of up to 700 pages each had been published. Each canton, including the Principality of Liechtenstein, has one or more volumes, covering the territory district by district and locality by locality. Each volume has maps with symbols and situational plans showing the location of the objects described. Numerous black-and-white illustrations and elevations and plans accompany the history and the description, and detailed bibliographies provide thorough documentation. While eastern and central Switzerland and Canton Ticino are on the whole well covered by the project so far, Canton Bern and western Switzerland, with the exception of Canton Neuchâtel, are lagging far behind. Every volume is written in the language of its part of the country. A similar project, entitled *Das Bürgerhaus in der Schweiz* (The burgher house in Switzerland), was sponsored by the Swiss Society of Engineers and Architects (Schweizerischer Ingenieur und Architekten-verein). It produced a thirty-volume inventory of town dwellings (1907-37). Still another undertaking of this kind, sponsored by the Swiss Society for Folklore (Schweizerische Gesellschaft für Volkskunde), aims at cataloguing the farmhouses in Switzerland (*Die Bauernhäuser der Schweiz*, Basel, 1965-).

589 **Switzerland: a Phaidon cultural guide.**
Edited by Niklaus Flüeler, Lukas Gloor, Isabella Rucki, translation of *Knaur's Kulturführer in Farbe: Schweiz* by Babel Translation, London. Oxford: Phaidon Press; Englewood Cliffs, New Jersey: Prentice-Hall, 1985.

This richly illustrated comprehensive guide is essentially an inventory of the many cultural treasures of Switzerland such as archaeological sites, churches, chapels, monasteries, fortresses, castles, ruins, mansions, townhouses and other dwellings, as well as the most important museums. The entries are listed in alphabetical order according to the places where the objects are located, from Aadorf, Canton Thurgau, to Zwingen, Canton Bern. A map of Switzerland in nineteen sections shows the places covered in the guide, and most cultural objects were photographed in colour specifically for this publication. The introduction gives a useful overview of the interaction of geography, history, and human ingenuity in the creation of Switzerland's cultural heritage.

590 **Kunstgeschichte der Schweiz. Von den Anfängen bis zum Beginn des 20. Jahrhunderts.** (Art history of Switzerland: from the origins to the beginning of the 20th century.)
Joseph Gantner, Adolf Reinle. Frauenfeld, Switzerland: Huber, 1936-68. 4 vols. bibliog.

These four oversized volumes, each with several hundred black-and-white illustrations and plans, comprehensively cover Swiss art history. Volume one deals with the art created on the territory of the later Swiss Confederation 'from the Helvetian-Roman beginnings to the end of the Romanesque style'. It is 554 pages long and describes mainly religious art, manifested above all in architecture, but also in illuminated manuscripts and cult utensils. The entire second volume of 388 pages is devoted to 'The Gothic art', divided into two equal parts, 'architecture' and 'sculpture and painting'. The Gothic still dominates the patrimony of monuments in Switzerland, as it permeated the entire country with its uniform formal and religiously inspired artistic language. The third volume of 435 pages covers the Renaissance, the Baroque, and the Rococo and Classicism of the 18th and early 19th centuries. The fourth volume of 364 pages carries the story through the 19th century to Ferdinand Hodler, with special attention to the technical, economic, and social conditions that influenced the architecture as well as painting and sculpture of this period.

591 **Kunstschätze in der Schweiz. Hundert Meisterwerke der Malerei, der Skulptur und des Kunstgewerbes in öffentlichen, kirchlichen und privaten Sammlungen der Schweiz.** (Art treasures in Switzerland: one hundred masterworks of painting, sculpture, and applied art in Swiss public, ecclesiastical, and private collections.)
Manuel Gasser, Willy Rotzler, Christoph Bernoulli. Zurich: Manesse, 1964. 243p.

This large-format, beautifully produced volume achieves the goal of its editors – to give an idea of the variety and the quality of the art treasures housed in museums and collections in all parts of Switzerland. Each of the one hundred masterpieces is accompanied by an informative art-historical text and description of its dimensions, origin and present location. The whole range of Western art is represented in this volume, from the sculpture of classical Greece and the religious art of the Middle Ages to the Italian, German, Dutch, Spanish, French, and Swiss schools of painting and the 20th-century art of Pablo Picasso, Paul Klee, and Marino Marini. Switzerland, often decried as barren soil for the arts, surprises by the wealth of treasures collected through the centuries by enlightened individuals in public and private positions.

592 **Nation, politics, and art.**
Hans Ulrich Jost. In: *From Liotard to Le Corbusier: 200 years of Swiss painting, 1730-1930*. Edited by the Swiss Institute for Art Research on behalf of the Coordinating Commission for the Presence of Switzerland Abroad. Einsiedeln, Switzerland: Benzinger, 1988, p. 13-21.

In this short essay, Jost, professor of modern Swiss history at the University of Lausanne, seeks to demonstrate that the Swiss state officially recognized and embraced art only when it served the social and political needs of its bourgeoisie. In three parts he shows how this approach to and use of art is reflected in (1) the cultural policy of the state, (2) the social life of the cities, and (3) 'the wholesale appropriation of the land and the mountains of Switzerland'. Nineteenth-century Switzerland saw the development of a cultural policy designed to provide the foundation of a national art tradition, the emergence of the cities where in the name of public interest private circles strove for the promotion of art and science, and the transformation of landscape painting into an instrument of commercial tourism and patriotic discourse. In paintings such as Ferdinand Hodler's *Wilhelm Tell*, 1896-97, 'the quality of a "Swiss" art blends seamlessly and beyond all critical reflection with the mythologized genuineness of the political system of bourgeois society'. Sixteen black-and-white illustrations and fifty notes accompany the essay.

593 **Modern art in Switzerland.**
Hans A. Lüthy. In: *Modern Switzerland*, edited by J. Murray Luck. Palo Alto, California: Society for the Promotion of Science and Scholarship, 1978, p. 489-502.

According to Lüthy, director of the Swiss Institute for Art Research in Zurich, modern art in Switzerland begins with the work of Ferdinand Hodler. Lüthy's article pursues the major trends in Swiss painting and sculpture from Hodler's avant-garde symbolistic paintings of the 1890s to the massive and sometimes even gargantuan sculptures of Jean Tinguely and Bernhard Luginbühl of the 1960s and 1970s. Lüthy notes that 'the arts in Switzerland have definitely enjoyed a golden age in past decades' which helped the development of an unusual number of talented young artists. These artists have established international reputations for themselves and for contemporary Swiss art.

594 **Art in Switzerland: from the earliest times to the present day.**
Peter Meyer, translated from the German by Mary Hottinger. Zurich: Swiss National Tourist Office and Schweizer Spiegel, 1946. 104p.

This booklet – Meyer calls it a pamphlet – touches on many aspects of the arts in Switzerland in twenty-eight brief chapters. Meyer claims that the country produced a variety of artistic creation out of all proportion to its size and finds that even though there is no lack of works of art of the first rank in Switzerland, the peculiar quality of Swiss culture is to be seen less in the isolated work of art than in the high cultural level of the whole, in the dwelling houses and farmhouses, villages and towns, furniture and utensils for daily use. The booklet is enriched by a considerable number of full-page black-and-white and colour photographs of representative works of art of all kinds, from the interior of a Gothic cathedral to a carved wooden milking pail.

595 **Situation Schweiz.** (Situation Switzerland.)
Edited by Annelie Pohlen. *Kunstforum International*, vol. 63/64 (July/August 1983), 380p.

This richly illustrated issue of the journal *Kunstforum* is dedicated to contemporary Swiss art, and especially to painting. Several essays shed light on the difficulty of defining Swiss art because of Switzerland's multi-lingual and multi-cultural society. The 1970s were marked by unrest among the young and rebellious artists against the prevailing materialism. In the 1980s abstract art has made room for content-related art: there are still-lifes, and self-portraits, there is humour and irony, some painters make reference to literature, they tell stories, fantasies and remembrances, the human figure is a recurring theme. The French-Swiss artists show a preference for video and film; all want to induce reflection and provoke thought. Many colour photographs illustrate these statements. The so-called *Zürcher Bewegung* (Zurich movement) of the 1980s attracted the artists to the big urban centre. The work of the 'sprayer of Zurich' who left his witty graffiti on public buildings and freshly restored villas was symbolic of the new spirit. Eight Swiss artists are the subject of an in-depth presentation; best known among them are Meret Oppenheim and Jean Tinguely. Twenty other artists are also briefly introduced with reproductions of their work. In addition, there is a listing of exhibits in public and private Swiss galleries for 1983.

596 **Die Kultur der Schweiz.** (The culture of Switzerland.)
Dietrich W. H. Schwarz. Zurich: Berichthaus, 1967. 408p. maps. bibliog.

Schwarz set himself the monumental task of writing a one-volume cultural history of Switzerland. The multi-lingual, multi-cultural society with a history dating back hundreds of years, and the geographical and climatic differences that seem extreme in a country this small are among the factors that had to be considered; the abundance of text and pictorial material demanded that difficult choices be made. The result is a veritable *vade mecum* that seems to have succeeded in every way. The chronological account follows historical epochs and covers the broad scope of human endeavour, stressing significant events that characterize the particular era. There are 254 photographs, four colour plates, and four maps. The photographs are of men and women, of nature and human dwellings, of artistic and scientific accomplishments, of sad and proud moments, of the old and the new. One of the first photographs shows a harpoon found near Schaffhausen that attests to the presence of humans already in prehistoric times and the last picture is an aerial view of the Swiss National Exhibition in Zurich in 1939 that gave the Swiss a sense of national pride and unity probably never experienced before.

597 **Lexikon der zeitgenössischen Schweizer Künstler – Dictionnaire des artistes suisses contemporains – Catalogo degli artisti svizzeri contemporari.** (Dictionary of contemporary Swiss artists.)
Schweizerisches Institut für Kunstwissenschaft. Frauenfeld, Switzerland; Stuttgart, FRG: Huber, 1981. 539p.

This dictionary lists 2,182 contemporary Swiss artists, and foreign artists who live in Switzerland. This is the third artists' dictionary of the 20th century. It follows the *Schweizerisches Künstler-Lexikon* (Frauenfeld: Huber, 1902-17. 4 vols) and the *Künstlerlexikon der Schweiz, XX. Jahrhundert* (Frauenfeld: Huber, 1958-67. 2 vols) which covered the earlier decades of the century. The major part of the dictionary consists of entries for the artists written in the mother-tongue of the subject. They are in alphabetical order and provide demographic and biographical information, as well as listings of exhibits and publications. An index of more than 100 pages contains, among other things, a list of the artists who have died since 1967, of artists by domicile, home community, and specialization, and of the most important exhibitions of Swiss art at home and abroad since 1945.

598 **Old stained glass in Switzerland.**
Michael Stettler, adapted from the German by D. Q. Stephenson. Zurich: Swiss National Tourist Office, 1953. 48p. bibliog.

This booklet contains twenty colour plates of choice examples of stained glass from various parts of Switzerland. Each plate is accompanied by a descriptive text on the facing page with pertinent data about location, date of origin, and measurements. The objects depicted span more than three centuries, from the late 12th to the early 16th, illustrating the development of glass. The height of glass-making in Switzerland was probably achieved in the beautiful windows from about 1325 of the former Abbey Church of Königsfelden near Brugg, Canton Aargau. Other examples show that impressive religious art was also created in other parts of Switzerland. In the late Middle Ages the emphasis shifted from religious to secular stained glass in the form of coloured glass windows and coats-of-arms in town halls, inns, and the houses of well-to-do burghers. After two centuries, stained glass went out of fashion, and the art of glass-making almost fell into oblivion. It had a renaissance in Switzerland in recent decades, but Stettler has no examples of that development, since it happened after he had published his well-written and illuminating booklet.

599 **Königsfelden: Geschichte, Bauten, Glasgemälde, Kunstschätze.**
(Königsfelden: history, buildings, stained glass, art treasures.)
Michael Stettler, Marcel Beck, Peter Felder, Emil Maurer, Dietrich W. H. Schwarz. Walter, Switzerland: Olten, 1970. 193p. bibliog.

Königsfelden near Brugg, Canton Aargau, houses one of the most important Gothic art treasures in Switzerland: the beautiful stained-glass windows of its monastery church, dating back to the 1320s. The abbey building and many religious objects formerly housed there, fell into decay or were destroyed during the Reformation. The abbey of Königsfelden was endowed by Queen Elisabeth in 1310 in memory of her husband King Albrecht of Austria who had been murdered nearby. She put the administration of the convent into the hands of Queen Agnes, granddaughter of Rudolf of Habsburg. Agnes oversaw the execution of the plans with great personal interest and talent, and left an inventory of the religious treasures that later enabled art historians to identify some objects in the Bern historical museum as stemming from Königsfelden. It is a miracle that the exquisite stained-glass windows have survived. They can be admired in the restored church. Many black-and-white and a few colour photographs by Gerhard Howald and an expertly written text allow a detailed reading of the windows.

600 **Dada: monograph of a movement.**
Edited by Willy Verkauf. London; New York: St. Martin's Press, 1975. 109p. bibliog. (First published in Switzerland, 1957).

Zurich was host to many refugees from all over Europe during World War I. Some of these – mainly artists – evolved into a group that spoke out against war and outdated artistic expressions. On stage, as in the 'Cabaret Voltaire' founded by Hugo Ball, or in art exhibits and writings, they found a forum for the new movement that had emerged and came to be known as Dada. They also published an international periodical by this name. Verkauf's richly illustrated work gives evidence of the style that characterized the literature, graphics, painting, sculpture and cabaret of Dadaism, a movement that had its beginning in Zurich but quickly spread to many other parts of Europe. *The documents of 20th-century art: flight out of time* by Robert Motherwell, Bernard Karpel, Arthur A. Cohen and John Elderfield (New York: Viking, 1974. bibliog.) contains Ball's diaries from 1910 to 1921, translated from the German by Ann Raimes; some other texts from this period are also included. The substantial introduction by John Elderfield is essential for the understanding of Ball's writings and establishes Ball as a major figure in the Dada movement.

Painting and sculpture: general

601 **Swiss painting: from the middle ages to the dawn of the twentieth century.**

Florens Deuchler, Marcel Roethlisberger, Hans Lüthy. New York: Rizzoli; Geneva: Skira, 1976. 198p. bibliog.

The authors of this large-sized, beautifully printed volume distinguish four phases in the history of Swiss painting. The beginnings of painting in Switzerland date back to the time of Charlemagne and run through the Middle Ages, and works of art from this phase consist of illuminated manuscripts, frescoes, and stained-glass windows, while Late Gothic and Renaissance art produced altarpieces, illustrated chronicles, and middle-class portraiture. Unfortunately, much of the art of the first two phases was destroyed during the Reformation. During the Baroque era and the Enlightenment Swiss art reached its nadir, but it recovered during the 19th century thanks to a growing awareness of a common Swiss heritage. By the early 20th century a Swiss school of art began to take shape under the leadership of Ferdinand Hodler. Swiss painters discovered their own country and used its manifold features as a new dimension in their works and as an agent of cohesion among themselves. Sixty-five of the 211 reproductions are in colour.

602 **Painting in America and Switzerland 1770-1870: preliminaries for a comparative study.**

Brandon Brame Fortune. In: *From Liotard to Le Corbusier: 200 years of Swiss painting, 1730-1930.* Edited by the Swiss Institute for Art Research on behalf of the Coordinating Commission for the Presence of Switzerland Abroad. Einsiedeln, Switzerland: Benzinger, 1988, p. 23-33.

Between roughly 1770 and 1870 art traditions evolved in Switzerland and the United States that seemed to reflect specifically national characteristics of genre pictures, portraiture, and landscape painting. Yet neither American nor Swiss works of art of this period were unique inasmuch as they were within the larger context of general nineteenth-century European prototypes and trends. Fortune illustrates his points with twenty-four black-and-white small-scale reproductions of paintings by American and Swiss artists.

603 **The Swiss artist and the European context: some notes on cross-cultural politics.**

William Hauptman. In: *From Liotard to Le Corbusier: 200 years of Swiss painting, 1730-1930.* Edited by the Swiss Institute for Art Research on behalf of the Coordinating Commission for the Presence of Switzerland Abroad. Einsiedeln, Switzerland: Benzinger, 1988, p. 35-46.

According to Hauptman, 'one of the chief problems of Swiss art and the cultural politics surrounding it' is that 'the popular image of Switzerland . . . renders almost no role at all for artistic achievement'. Few Swiss artists have found their way into art-historical surveys of any period. Hauptman traces the slow and tortuous path of Swiss art and artists toward public recognition at home and in international art circles. He describes the pivotal role that Charles Gleyre (1806-74) played in that process and wonders whether artists such as Ferdinand Hodler, Paul Klee, and Alberto Giacometti achieved international fame because of their 'Swiss-ness', or because in their pictorial iconography they transcended it. The article is accompanied by eighteen black-and-white reproductions of paintings by the artists discussed and by ninety-one notes.

604 **Swiss drawings: masterpieces of five centuries.**
Walter Hugelshofer. Washington DC: Smithsonian Institution Press, 1967. 176p. bibliog.

This catalogue accompanied the exhibition of five centuries of Swiss drawings from Holbein to Giacometti which was displayed at the National Gallery of Art in Washington, DC and three other major American museums in 1967-68. The Basel art historian Walter Hugelshofer assembled the works of art from Swiss public and private collections with the support of the Pro Helvetia Foundation and wrote the introduction and notes to the catalogue. The catalogue contains 126 reproductions of drawings, sketches, etchings, woodcuts, and watercolours of some forty artists – of the works featured, thirteen are by Hans Holbein. Hugelshofer points out that the drawings must be seen against the historical setting and trends of their time; they are part of a European tradition. The twentieth century marks the beginning of modern art and what can be called Swiss art in particular under the influence of the independent and strong-willed artist Ferdinand Hodler.

605 **The painted Romanesque ceiling of St. Martin in Zillis.**
Ernst Murbach, Peter Heman, translated from the German by Janet Seligman. New York: Washington: Praeger; London: Percy Lund, Humphries, 1967. 125p. bibliog.

This large-sized book consists of forty-eight pages of text, six pages of black-and-white photographs, and eighty colour plates, all dealing with the village church of St Martin in Zillis, Canton Graubünden. Inside this inconspicuous edifice is a singular work of art, the oldest surviving painted church ceiling extant in Europe. The ceiling was painted around 1140. It consists of 153 panels painted with lively decorative motifs and scenes from the life of Christ and the legend of St Martin. The survival of this work through the centuries is a fortunate accident. The text by Murbach puts St Martin and its treasure within the cultural, historical, and architectural context of its Romanesque origin and explains the iconographic plan of the unknown artist who created the work. The plates by Heman depict eighty of the best-preserved quadrangular panels. Diether Rudloff's *Zillis. Die romanische Bilderdecke der Kirche St. Martin* (Zillis: the Romanesque picture ceiling of St. Martin's church) (Basel: Heman, 1988. 176p.) is a somewhat larger and more elaborate work on the same subject. Again, Heman has contributed the illustrations in the form of 136 photographs, ninety-eight of which are colour plates.

606 **Die Alpen in der Schweizer Malerei – Les Alpes dans la peinture suisse – The Alps in Swiss painting.**
Edited by Marcel Roethlisberger, Hans Hartmann. Zurich: Pro Helvetia, 1977. 338p. bibliog.

This beautiful book served as catalogue to art exhibitions in Tokyo in spring 1977 and Chur, Canton Graubünden, in summer 1977. It contains the reproductions of 150 works of art, mostly paintings, that have been inspired by the mountain world of the Alps. The artist of each work is given a brief biographical sketch, the art work is discussed in detail, and bibliographical information is provided. The introductory text points out that mountains made a late entry into the history of Swiss painting. Caspar Wolf (1735-83) struck the first important note with his oil paintings of the Bernese Oberland, all done in the 1770s. The 19th century is represented by, among others, Alexandre Calame (1810-64) and Giovanni Segantini (1858-99) who, though Italian by birth, did much of his painting in the Engadin valley of Canton Graubünden and infused his mountain scenes with mythical symbolism. In the towering figure of Ferdinand Hodler (1853-1918) Swiss painting and Swiss identity blend together. He grasped the monumentality of the mountains with a style of forceful simplification. From him the way leads via the work of Giovanni Giacometti (1868-1933) to the expressionist paintings of Ludwig Kirchner (1880-1938) and to the representatives of the contemporary art scene.

607 **From Liotard to Le Corbusier: 200 years of Swiss painting, 1730-1930.**
Edited by the Swiss Institute for Art Research on behalf of the Coordinating Commission for the Presence of Switzerland Abroad. Einsiedeln, Switzerland: Benziger, 1988. 191p. bibliog.

This magnificent large-format book was published on the occasion of the exhibition with the same title at the High Museum of Art, Atlanta, Georgia, from 9 February to 10 April 1988. It contains sixty-five full-page colour reproductions of the paintings exhibited. Each work of art is accompanied by a text giving the historical setting and describing the artistic mood of the painting, as well as by a precise description of its dimensions and a scholarly apparatus with notes and bibliographies. In short, the book is a scientific catalogue of the highest scholarly standards. Artists represented by three or more of their works are Giuseppe Antonio Petrini (1677-c.1758/59), Johann Heinrich Füssli (1741-1825), Louis Ducros (1748-1810), Charles Gleyre (1806-74), Frank Buchser (1828-90), Ferdinand Hodler (1853-1918), Félix Vallotton (1865-1925), Giovanni Giacometti (1868-1933), Cuno Amiet (1868-1961), and Paul Klee (1879-1940). For each of the thirty-two painters represented at the exhibition there is a brief biographical sketch at the end of the volume. The introductory essays by H. U. Jost, B. B. Fortune, and W. Hauptman have separate entries in this bibliography.

608 **Ein Jahrhundert Schweizer Kunst. Malerei und Plastik: Von Böcklin bis Alberto Giacometti.** (A century of Swiss art: painting and sculpture; from Böcklin to Alberto Giacometti.)
Hans Christoph von Tavel. Bern: Schweizerische Volksbank, 1969. 241p. (Editions d'Art Albert Skira, Geneva).

The Swiss Volksbank in Bern celebrated its one hundredth anniversary by publishing this beautiful volume. The Bernese art historian von Tavel chose eighty-nine works of Swiss artists for reproduction in black-and-white and colour in consultation with the renowned Skira publishing house and wrote the accompanying text. The first generation of artists included was born between 1827 and 1831 and is represented by such painters as Arnold Böcklin, Frank Buchser, and Albert Anker. The group of painters born between 1857 and 1865 was the last to uphold the traditional treatment of form and light. It includes the gifted painter Ferdinand Hodler as its most famous member, the sculptor Carl Burckhardt who broke with the conventions of the 19th century for good, and artists such as Alberto Giacometti and Paul Klee. In his 'postscript' von Tavel tries to establish what is typically Swiss in his country's art and points to the tension between the world abroad and the homeland in the lives and art of many Swiss artists.

Painters and sculptors

609 **Urs Graf.**
Emil Major, Erwin Gradmann. London: Home & Van Thal, 1950. 151p.

This is a picture book of Urs Graf's graphic works and a few stained-glass windows. Urs Graf (c.1485-1527) was born in Solothurn and learned the goldsmith's trade, but 'merry Basel' is where he lived when not fighting as a mercenary in foreign wars. His loose lifestyle, his foul mouth, and his drinking and whoring were the source of numerous altercations with the law. However, his artistry, style, and choice of subjects were inspired by this free and daring spirit. His depictions of maidens and warriors valiant in the face of death witness a great vitality. The book contains 151 illustrations with captions.

610 **The paintings of Hans Holbein: first complete edition.**
Paul Ganz. London: Phaidon, 1953. 297p.

Germany, Switzerland, and England each claim Holbein the Younger (1497?-1543) as their own. The Swiss base it on the fact that he perfected his art in Basel, where he lived and worked from 1515 to 1532, and acquired citizenship. This comprehensive survey of the painter's pictorial oeuvre is divided into four sections: religious works, portraits, miniatures, and decorative works. There are 218 full-size plates, mostly in black-and-white. A catalogue at the back provides informed comments and additional illustrations. This work is a classic written by a renowned art historian.

611 **Holbein's dance of death and bible woodcuts.**
Edited by Lewis F. White. New York: Sylvan, 1947. 150p.

Holbein's dance of death was first published in 1538 and has since been of interest to many people for a variety of reasons: the researcher tries to establish the authenticity of various woodcuts, the art lover appreciates their high quality, the historian gains through them an understanding of how the Renaissance perceived death, what clothes were worn and what buildings were erected, and the musician studies the old instruments and the dances depicted in them. This then is a unique documentation of the spirit of a period as perceived by one of the greatest masters of that time. The second half of the book consists of woodcuts illustrating stories from the Old Testament.

612 **The drawings of Henry Fuseli.**
Paul Ganz, translated from the German by F. B. Aikin-Sneath. London: Max Parrish, 1952. 106p.

This is a picture book presenting the life and work of Henry Fuseli (also Füssli) of Zurich who was an important master of the Royal Academy in London. England and the cultural climate of the time suited his romantic nature and kept him there until his death. Fuseli's close association with Blake and his knowledge of the writings of the great poets provided themes for his work, while his experiences in Rome influenced his depiction of the human body. Over one hundred illustrations in black-and-white show spirits and ghosts, some portraits, and scenes from literary works and mythology.

613 **The life and art of Henry Fuseli.**

Peter Tomory. New York; Washington, DC: Praeger; London: Thames and Hudson, 1972. 255p. bibliog.

Zurich-born artist Johann Heinrich Füssli (1741-1825) went to England in 1779. He lived and worked in London for the rest of his life, becoming a member of and then a professor of painting at the Royal Academy. He anglicized his name to Henry Fuseli. Tomory treats Fuseli in the context of English art. A chapter on the evolution of his art and the sources of his inspiration takes up almost half the space of the text. Two somewhat shorter chapters on 'themes and symbols' and 'Fuseli's influence' provide further analysis of the artist's creative inspiration and significance in his lifetime and thereafter. Tomory's text is closely referenced to the 254 monochrome plates and the thirteen colour plates in the book. These illustrations show the many ties from earlier art to Fuseli and his influence on Blake and other contemporaries.

614 **Charles Gleyre 1806-1874.**

William Hauptman, Nancy Scott Newhouse. Grey Art Gallery and Study Center, New York University; University of Maryland Art Gallery, 1980. 143p.

This is the catalogue of an exhibition of 114 works of the Swiss artist Gleyre shown at New York University and the University of Maryland in winter and spring 1980. Most of the works exhibited were done in pencil, crayon, and watercolour, but there were also a number of oil paintings. Gleyre belongs to the relatively unknown 19th-century artists whose works have been only recently unearthed and newly appreciated. The catalogue describes him as 'for the most part a solitary, independent artist, choosing a mode of life not attuned to the established pattern of the successful nineteenth-century painter'. He was born near Lausanne, Switzerland, and spent most of his life working in Paris, but a trip to the Near East and Egypt during the 1830s formed one of the most colourful and vivid experiences in his life. The catalogue has two longish essays, one by Hauptman on 'Tradition and innovation' in Gleyre's work, and the other by Newhouse on Gleyre's trip 'From Rome to Khartoum', both with extensive notes. It is illustrated throughout with reproductions of Gleyre's works.

615 **Karl Bodmer's America.**

William H. Goetzmann, David C. Hunt, Marsha V. Gallagher, William J. Orr. Omaha, Nebraska: Joslyn Art Museum & University of Nebraska Press, 1984. 376p. map. bibliog.

This heavy, large-sized, lavishly illustrated book concentrates on the highlight of Karl Bodmer's life and career, the North American journey he made in his early twenties as artist in the expedition of Prince Maximilian of Wied, a well-to-do, aristocratic German explorer of South and North America. As Orr relates in his biography of Bodmer (1809-93), the artist received his early training in his native Zurich and was hired by Prince Maximilian when he was still an obscure Swiss draughtsman. As it turned out, the watercolours and drawings of the people and places of frontier America, especially its Indians, which he did between 1832 and 1834, have never been surpassed in their quality with regard to both the accuracy and the sensitivity to the nuances of their subjects. During his later career in Germany and France, Bodmer produced nothing of comparable significance. The high-quality colour reproductions of Bodmer's sketches and watercolours of life on the upper Missouri country are from the originals which are on permanent loan to the Joslyn Museum in Omaha, Nebraska, and they make it clear why Bodmer ranks among the foremost artists of the western frontier. The copious annotations by Hunt and Gallagher to the 359 works reproduced further enhance the value of this beautiful book.

616 **Böcklin.**
Edited by Hans Dollinger, English version by Thomas Bourke. Munich: Bruckmann, 1975. 97p.

The full-page illustrations in colour and black-and-white chosen for this book on Arnold Böcklin (1827-1901) are representative of the painter's entire work. The pictures are not captioned but they are accompanied by a text in German, French, and English consisting of short quotes selected from Böcklin's memoirs and his wife's diary and from writings of contemporaries and critics that shed light on the painter's ideas and artistic expression. Böcklin's vast landscapes, replete with various kinds of trees, rocks, and waters, are rendered in rich colour. He did not intend to imitate nature but to harmonize the colours for his work the way he saw fit. 'If a painter can't paint how he feels about things, then he may as well give up', he exclaimed. His landscapes are populated with classical, mythological, and fairy-tale figures and creatures – alluring, graceful sirens, nymphs, and mermaids are juxtaposed with strong, frightening centaurs and pans. The plague, war, and death are personified by haunted figures; nearness and distance, the sensual and the spiritual, the masculine and feminine, the tender and the forceful complement each other. The artist is seen as a link between Romanticism and German Expressionsm. One of his most famous works, *The Island of the Dead* (first version), hangs in the Kunstmuseum of the city of Basel where he was born and to which he returned time and again during his life. A brief biography lists important dates and places in Böcklin's life.

617 **Ferdinand Hodler: Selbstbildnisse als Selbstbiographie.** (Ferdinand Hodler: self-portraits as autobiography.)
Jura Brüschweiler. Bern: Benteli, 1979. 188p.

This picture book was published to coincide with the opening of a Hodler exhibit in the Kunstmuseum Basel in 1979. Jura Brüschweiler, a Hodler expert, suggested that the artist's many self-portraits from all phases of his life could be seen as his autobiography, and this then became the theme of the exhibit. There are 115 known self-portraits by Hodler (1853-1918), forty-seven in oil and sixty-eight drawings. The book reproduces 110 of these, the oils full-page and in colour. The self-portraits attest to Hodler's search for identity; some express protest, others are questioning. His dramatic style and iridescent colours brought him recognition beyond the borders of Switzerland, where he is recognized today as one of the country's foremost painters and its earliest representative of modern art. The author also included self-portraits of other painters and paintings and sketches by Hodler of his acquaintances, historical figures, landscapes and caricatures – these shed light on his style and place him in the context of his time.

618 **Ferdinand Hodler.**

Sharon L. Hirsh. New York: George Braziller, 1982. 144p. bibliog.

An 'introduction', forty-eight pages in length and illustrated by sixty black-and-white reproductions of works by Hodler and a few of his contemporaries, provides a concise and informative overview of the artist's life and achievements. Born in Bern in 1853, Hodler moved to Geneva in 1872, where he attracted the attention of Barthélemy Menn who became his sponsor and teacher. With his base in Geneva, he exhibited his works in Paris, Brussels, Vienna, Germany, and Switzerland and received commissions for murals in Jena, Zurich, and Hannover. During the last decade of his life he was showered with honours, culminating in the award of an honorary professorship at the Ecole des Beaux-Arts, his alma mater in Geneva. He died in 1918. The bulk of the book consists of forty-one colour plates which reproduce Hodler's most significant oil paintings, each accompanied by a full-page commentary.

619 **Félix Vallotton: Leben und Werk.** (Félix Vallotton: life and work.)

Günther Busch, Bernard Dorival, Doris Jakubec. Frauenfeld, Switzerland: Huber, 1982. 240p. bibliog.

Félix Vallotton (1865-1925), a painter born in Lausanne, is also known for his literary work that includes plays, prose works, and criticism. This book, however, concentrates on his work as painter and graphic artist. The young Swiss arrived in Paris at the age of seventeen and was soon accepted in the circle of artists which included Bonnard, Denis, and Vuillard. He wrote articles for journals, he made woodcuts, painted portraits, interiors, landscapes, and still-lifes and showed his work in numerous exhibits. Some of his symbolic canvasses are reminiscent of Hodler. In 1900 he became a French citizen. His work met with mixed criticism. He chose few models that were beautiful because he had wanted to show the society of his day, in all its laziness, stupidity, deceipt and hatred. Irony often turned into pessimism, but his tormented soul was soothed by painting nature, particularly the landscape of Lake Geneva and the port town of Honfleur in France. There are 237 full-page illustrations, several in colour. Some autobiographical excerpts from Vallotton's novel *The murderous life* (1927) are dispersed in the text.

620 **Amiet, Cuno, 1868-1961.**

Selection and catalogue by George Mauner. In: *Cuno Amiet, Giovanni Giacometti, Augusto Giacometti: three Swiss painters: an exhibition organized by the Museum of Art, the Pennsylvania State University*. Basel: Ciba-Geigy, 1973. 163p. bibliog.

This catalogue was prepared for an exhibition of works by the three important Swiss painters Augusto and Giovanni Giacometti, and Cuno Amiet. The collection was on tour in America in 1973-74. The varied oeuvre of the important Swiss avant-garde painter Cuno Amiet is less well known than that of the Giacomettis and is often difficult to classify. From the post-impressionism school of Pont-Aven he moved directly to the German expressionist group of the *Brücke*, but not beyond. Even though he recognized the artistic value of abstraction, he did not want to abandon the forms of nature. Influenced by his great contemporaries Hodler, Kirchner, Klee, and Giovanni Giacometti, his work was of the highest quality. He exhibited in Germany, England, Spain, Paris, and the Biennale in Venice (1934). Mauner's short introduction is followed by a chronology, a selected bibliography, a list of exhibitions of Amiet's works, and sixty-three full-page plates, some in colour.

621 **Paul Klee.**

Will Grohmann. New York: Abrams, [1954]. 448p. bibliog.

Will Grohmann presents in this voluminous work one of the most important artists of the twentieth century. The biography is based on ample documentation for all phases of Klee's life and on Grohmann's personal recollections. Klee, a German citizen, had been born and raised in his beloved Bern. The young artist established contacts with members of the *Blaue Reiter*, a German avant-garde group, that led to an appointment as a teacher of painting at the Bauhaus in Weimar and Dessau. The ideas and theories he formulated in his *Pädagogisches Skizzenbuch* (1925, published in English as *Pedagogical Sketchbook*, 1944) contributed greatly to the leadership that this centre of contemporary artistic expression assumed. Graphic art was especially suited to Klee's preference for lines, spatial elements and symbols as it 'tends of its own accord to abstraction'. He returned when Hitler's régime made working in Germany impossible for him, and shortly before his death he wrote 'I have been a resident here [of Switzerland] ever since. My one remaining wish is to become a citizen as well.' However, his application for citizenship was not processed in time for his last wish to become true. More than 500 of Klee's over 9,000 works are reproduced in this splendid book. They consist of drawings, graphics, watercolours, and paintings, beginning with childhood drawings and ending with the angels that he depicted so frequently in his last few months.

622 **Paul Klee.**

Felix Klee, translated from the German by Richard and Clara Winston. New York: George Braziller, 1962. 212p.

Felix Klee, the only son of painter Paul Klee (1879-1940), here provides a personal view of his father, whose *Diaries* he edited in 1956. He quotes extensively from these and from unpublished notebook entries, and he makes use of letters and revives 'household memories'. The text is interspersed with 121 reproductions of drawings and paintings froom Paul Klee's work, and photographs from the family album. Klee's youth in Bern, his extended family, his schooling and later his own family, his artistic development in which music played an important role, his teaching and personal development at the Bauhaus, his trips to foreign countries, his contacts with many artists of the time, and finally his return and last years in his adopted country of Switzerland come to life and provide the foundation for the artist's themes that his son treats in the second part of his book. The third part shows Paul Klee as a teacher of painting at the Bauhaus where he went at the invitation of Walter Gropius. Here he found himself among a group of Europe's most innovative artists, united in the search for a new artistic language. Klee expressed his ideas in writing in his *Pedagogical Sketchbook*. He deemed the graphic arts best suited for his symbolic and abstract figures. In his essay *Schöpferische Konfession* (1920; reprinted here as 'Creative credo') he developed his theories on graphic art as well as his philosophy on the creative process. Three appendices categorize Klee's works according to styles, year and genre, and identify their present location.

623 **Giacometti's code.**

Avigdor Arikha. *New York Review of Books*, vol. 36, no. 8 (18 May 1989), p. 20-24.

Painter and curator Arikha bases this insightful essay on Alberto Giacometti (1901-66) on his personal contacts with the Swiss artist and on recent biographies and essays in exhibition catalogues. Arikha mentions that Giacometti discussed his artistic problems in his writings throughout his life. He was preoccupied with the problem of working from life and of scale. He once said that he 'worked with the model all day from 1935 to 1940'. He wrestled with the paradox that he did not recognize his models any more when he worked with them, and that the sculptures, at one stage in his life, became smaller and smaller the more he worked on them. His drawings consist of line hatchings and blank spaces, which he often made with an eraser. He would start a work from scratch again and again, commenting 'it was no longer the exterior forms that interested me but what I really felt'. The value of Arikha's essay lies in the fact that, unlike James Lord in his massive biography (q.v.), he does not analyse Giacometti's psychology (inundating the reader with intimate and often gossipy details about the artist's life), but concentrates on Giacometti's work itself and indicates how careful use of his writings may deepen the understanding this great 20th-century artist.

624 **Alberto Giacometti and America.**

Edited by Tamara S. Evans. New York: City University of New York, 1984. 152p. bibliog. (Pro Helvetia Swiss Lectureships, 2).

This collection of research papers resulted from a lectureship at the City University of New York Graduate School, held by Swiss art historian Willy Rotzler. Rotzler provides the introduction in which he traces the artistic development of the Swiss painter and sculptor Alberto Giacometti, but most of the booklet consists of contributions by students from Rotzler's seminar. The topics of the individual papers are not specifically connected: one discusses Giacometti's influence on American artists and his relationship with Peggy Guggenheim, another one his first and little-noticed exhibition in New York in 1934-35, and still another one his sculptures and paintings in American museums. Some twenty museums are listed, together with the titles of Giacometti's work they hold. An annotated bibliography of critiques of his work provides good leads for further study. Photographs of the artist's famous attenuated men and women and other works are interspersed throughout the text.

625 **Giacometti: a biography.**

James Lord. New York: Farrar, Straus and Giroux, 1985. 575p. bibliog.

Lord knew Giacometti and his circle of famous friends personally from the years they both lived in Paris. Two previous books on Giacometti and extensive research formed the foundation for Lord's monumental biography. Giacometti was born in the Italian-speaking Bregaglia valley in Canton Graubünden. His father, Giovanni Giacometti, was an accomplished painter, while his mother was the first of many important female figures in his life and work. Alberto's brother Diego became his lifelong assistant. While Paris was the cultural centre that stimulated him (he spent his entire adult life there), the rugged Swiss mountains and the simple life were of lasting influence. Lord has vast knowledge and gives detailed information about Giacometti's extended family, and the leading artists, art dealers, collectors, assorted shady characters, and whores who crossed Giacometti's path. He also speaks with authority about many of Giacometti's works, and he provides his interpretation of the mostly abstract elongated and 'flattened' human figures for which the artist is probably most famous. Notes on Lord's sources, a 307-item bibliography with thirty-eight entries of writings and statements by Giacometti, and fifty-seven of exhibition catalogues, as well as an extensive index make further study inviting. The book is not only an intimate portrait of one of the most important sculptors of the 20th century but also a mirror of the environment and the era which produced him.

626 **Alberto Giacometti: a retrospective exhibition.**
Reinhold Hohl, for Solomon R. Guggenheim Museum. New York: Solomon R. Guggenheim Foundation, 1974. 202p. bibliog.

This is the catalogue of a major Giacometti exhibition at the New York Guggenheim Museum in 1974. Alberto Giacometti was from the Italian-speaking part of Canton Graubünden. He did most of his work in Paris. The influence of cubism and surrealism led to painstaking experimentation with bodies and their abstraction, which in the last two decades of the sculptor's life resulted in the characteristic elongated shapes of his sculptures. The catalogue has 217 captioned illustrations of Giacometti's drawings, paintings, and sculptures. Hohl provides an excellent introduction to the life and art of the man behind this arresting work. The selected bibliography is substantial and lists also several films about the sculptor. A long listing of exhibitions is a further indication of the artist's importance. More recently, the Smithsonian Institution in Washington, DC, published the catalogue *Alberto Giacometti: 1901-1966* of the Giacometti exhibition at the Hirschhorn Museum and Sculpture Garden in 1988. It was edited by Valerie J. Fletcher, with essays by Silvio Berthoud and Reinhold Hohl.

627 **Hans Erni.**
Foreword by Claude Roy. Lausanne: Clairefontaine; Zurich: Ernst Scheidegger, 1964. 168p. bibliog.

This picture book features the contemporary Swiss artist Hans Erni. Roy stresses in his introduction the painter's knowledge of physics and mathematics, of mechanics and chemistry and his interest in machines, sports and crafts. Erni, born in 1909, is an expert draughtsman. His illustrations for books of all kinds, his effective poster and stamp designs, and his large murals and other commissioned works are successful because Erni, while modern, remains realistic. He handles his media with mastery, be it crayon, tempera, or mosaic stones. The large volume gives an especially vivid account of Erni's tempera works. The human figure, usually set against a background of flowing geometric designs, is present in almost every painting. A list of exhibitions of the artist's work from Melbourne to San Francisco, and from Copenhagen to Osaka is found at the back of the book.

628 **Pandämonium – Jean Tinguely.** (Pandemonium – Jean Tinguely.)
Margrit Hahnloser-Ingold, photography by Leonard Bezzola. Zurich: Ex Libris/Kunstkreis; Bern: Benteli, 1988. 324p.

Jean Tinguely was born in Fribourg in 1925. When he was two years old, the family moved to Basel, where he grew up, received his schooling, and did an apprenticeship as a decorator. In 1953 he went to Paris where he worked as an independent artist, developing his speciality, the creation of fantastic machines from scrap metal. One of these machines, Heureka, was one of the main attractions at the Swiss National Exhibition, the 'Expo' of 1964 in Lausanne. Hahnloser begins her book with a brief biographical sketch including photographs of nine self-portraits, and houses and ateliers in which Tinguely lived and worked, followed by an overview of his work, which, in addition to his scrap-metal machines, includes a sizeable output of graphics. The bulk of the book, some two hundred pages, is devoted to what the author calls Tinguely's 'pandemonic' late work. Since 1979 Tinguely has been immersed in a creative eruption of unimaginable power and variety. Bezzola illustrates this creative phase with numerous photographs, both in black-and-white and in colour, of the artist at work, and of his works in a variety of media.

Graphic arts

629 **Offizielle Schweizer Grafik.** (Official Swiss graphic art.)
Walter Bangerter, Armin Tschanen, translated from the German by M. J. Wynne. Zurich: ABC Verlag, 1964. 184p.

This book illustrates a form of applied art in which Swiss artists excel. 'Official Swiss graphic art' refers to posters, catalogues, diplomas, pamphlets, postal stamps, insignias, etc. that are commissioned by an agency of the federal government or by organizations that receive federal support. The federal commission for the arts watches over the quality, aesthetic appeal, and product recognition of the designs submitted. Modern printing equipment developed in Switzerland helped to enhance the professional appearance of the designs and earned Swiss graphic art world-wide recognition. The federal railway and postal systems, Swissair, federally sponsored exhibits, and charitable organizations such as the Red Cross among many others, are represented with several different advertising designs. There are 381 illustrations, a few in colour; some of the designs are from the hands of known artists.

630 **Swiss graphic design & photography '82/83.**
Edited by Karl D. Geissbühler, introduced by Markus Kutter. Zurich: Swiss Graphic Design & Photography, 1982. 152p.

This beautifully illustrated volume is intended to serve two purposes: to make the creative talent of Swiss graphic artists known at home and abroad, and to show prospective customers the wide range of possibilities their products and advertisement can have in the marketplace. Swiss graphic design is a blend of many influences, from the Bauhaus to modern American packaging, from popular magazines to television commercials. The reproductions, many in colour, are grouped according to the message they contain, whether they advertise a product, create a corporate identity, serve as brochures for businesses, or announce exhibitions and shows. The name, address and phone number of each contributing artist, together with samples of his or her work, are provided. The techniques, imagination, humour, and choice of text make for a great variety of visually effective statements.

631 **Schweizer Theaterplakate 1900-1925 = Swiss theatre posters 1900-1925.**
Peter Loeffler. Basel [etc.]: Birkhäuser, 1988. 117p. bibliog.

The core of this book consists of high-quality colour reproductions of twenty-five theatre posters that were designed by Swiss artists during the first quarter of the 20th century. The posters are in the poster collection of the Museum of Applied Arts (Kunstgewerbemuseum) in Zurich. Loeffler, professor of theatre history at the University of British Columbia in Vancouver, Canada, provides an introductory essay on the history of theatre poster art and its development in Switzerland during the 19th century. He describes the threefold purpose of this book as (1) demonstrating that Switzerland also produced cultural posters in addition to the much better known posters advertising tourism; (2) making a contribution to the history of the Swiss theatre; and (3) pleasing 'the visual senses with strong images'. The posters by artists such as Emil Cardinaux and Otto Baumberger announce plays, operas, concerts, ballets, and exhibitions – each is accompanied by a caption that contains information about the subject of the poster. A listing of technical data, giving names of designers, titles, dates, printers, and sizes of the twenty-five posters, is also part of the book. The texts are in German and English. Other recent publications on the Swiss poster include Peter Obermüller, *Kulturelle Plakate der Schweiz* (Cultural posters of Switzerland), Zurich, 1974; Eduard Grosse, *Das neue Schweizer Plakat* (The new Swiss poster), Berlin, 1980; and Bruno Margadant, *Das Schweizer Plakat 1900-1983* (The Swiss poster 1900-83), Basel, 1983.

632 **Idée . . . à jour. Zeitschrift für angewandte Kreativität.** (Idea . . . up-to-date: journal for applied creativity.)
Zürich: Idee . . . à jour, 1959- . monthly. ca. 60p.

This is the official organ of the Association for Commercial Communication and the Federation of Graphic Designers. Its well-made informative issues are devoted to specific themes. The June 1988 issues, for example, has sixteen articles on personnel policy, training and recruitment of persons working in the fields of public relations, advertisement, and graphics. A ten-page tabulation and description of specializations in the field and opportunities for advancement gives a good overview of the graphic and applied public relations professions.

633 **Graphis: international journal of graphic art and applied art.**
Zurich: Graphis Press, 1944- . 96p. bimonthly.

This a slick and beautiful oversized publication that displays the possibilities of artistic design in an unsurpassed manner.

634 **Tourism posters of Switzerland, 1880-1940.**
Edited by Karl Wobman, introduced by Willy Rotzler. Aarau, Switzerland; Stuttgart, FRG: AT Verlag, 1980. 160p.

The Kunstgewerbe Museum in Zurich has over 150,000 posters in its collection. The posters selected for this book are from the years 1880-1940, or, from the beginning of mass tourism and development of the hotel industry to the outbreak of World War II. None advertise a product, all convey the same message: Visit Switzerland! They call attention to a particular region, a spa, a city, and rail, boat or bus travel. But the posters do far more than advertise for one of Switzerland's important industries, they show the artistic taste of an era, for many were commissioned from prominent artists such as Giovanni and Augusto Giacometti. They are cultural documents in that they tell of expectations of the visitors, their pleasure and dreams, and the posters show the fashions of the time, and the popular sports activities, especially winter sports. Colouring and lettering, ornamental designs, allegorical figures and collage-like pictorial inserts characterize the earlier ones, but a new period began with the 1920s, where more vivid colours, a central theme, innovative techniques and individualized presentations became fashionable, and slogans began to appear. The full-page reproductions of these old tourist posters are in colour.

Architecture: general

635 **Architectural guide Switzerland.**
Edited by Florian Adler, Hans Girsberger, Olinde Riege, translated from the German by Florian Adler. Zurich: Artemis, 1978. 2nd ed. 224p.

This is a guide to contemporary architecture in Switzerland. It includes the 218 buildings of the 1969 edition plus 105 new ones. The 323 buildings, drawn from seven distinct regions, are illustrated by photographs and plans in seven geographical regions. A few buildings are from the late 1920s and 1930s, but the vast majority are from the 1960s and 1970s. Most of them are public buildings, such as schools, churches, hospitals, and community centres, but there are also some apartment houses, private dwellings, factories, and public works such as bridges, tunnel entrances, and transmission towers.

636 **Bauen und Wohnen in der Schweiz 1850-1920.** (Building and living in Switzerland 1850-1920.)
Othmar Birkner. Zurich: Artemis, 1975. 261p.

Seventy years of Swiss architecture are covered in this book that features 256 photographs, drawings, and sketches of entire buildings or details. First the materials used for the structures and interiors are discussed. Then a wide variety of buildings are presented, from a tram station to the Swiss Federal Palace. A final chapter examines the trends in architectural styles as an expression of the taste and spirit of the time.

637 **La cathédrale de Lausanne.** (Lausanne cathedral.)
Jean-Charles Biaudet, Henri Meylan, Werner Stöckli, Philippe Jaton, Marcel Grandjean, Claude Lapaire, Ellen J. Beer, Claude Bernard. Bern: Société d'Histoire de l'Art en Suisse, 1975. 264p. bibliog. (Bibliothèque de la Société d'Histoire de l'Art en Suisse, 3).

The cathedral of Lausanne, capital of Canton Vaud, is one of the very great architectural monuments in Switzerland. This meticulously documented and richly illustrated volume does justice to the edifice it describes. Two chapters present the archaeological findings of the scholars and their reconstruction of what the first structure on the site may have looked like. The earliest traces of the crypt date to the second half of the 9th century. Construction on the actual building was begun around 1160 and it was in essence completed in its Gothic splendour by 1250. Grandjean displays his knowledge of the historical sources in a long chapter in which he describes the structure and its component parts. His is a carefully balanced interpretation of the forces that created the perfect blend of traditional elements and creativity that one finds in the cathedral. A chapter on the sculpture which dates to the first half of the 13th century and another one on the grand rose window in the southern façade of the cathedral complete the work.

638 **Burgenkarte der Schweiz. (Map of Swiss castles.)**
Bundesamt für Landestopographie. Wabern-Bern, Switzerland: Bundesamt für Landestopographie, 1976-85.

Four maps on a scale of 1:200,000 in four folders, one each for Northwest, Northeast,

Southwest, and Southeast Switzerland, show the location of hundreds of Swiss castles, country seats, and ruins. Four booklets of between 80 and 100 pages length accompany the maps and include special maps showing the exact location on scales varying from 1:5,000 to 1:50,000, and descriptions of particular points of interest.

639 **Das Schweizer Haus: Wohn-, Wehr- und Gemeinschaftsbau.** (The Swiss house: domestic, defensive, and communal buildings.)
Paul Leonard Ganz. Zurich: Silva, 1963. 148p.

Human habitation in Switzerland, has ranged from the lake dwellings of 2500 BC to the modern cityscape of the 1960s as illustrated in this volume by the ninety-nine pictures. Hundreds of years of Swiss history are reflected in the Roman amphitheatres, forbidding castle towers, medieval towns, Renaissance city halls, Baroque monasteries, and Jugendstil villas. Historically, the building materials for homes, the rooflines, and the window treatment characterized buildings of certain regions. Thus, the wooden chalet of the Bernese Oberland and the stone house from Graubünden with its grafitti are typical only of these specific areas. The design and building materials of modern structures are no longer tied to a region, and they stand side by side with the dwellings from the past.

640 **Das Grossmünster in Zürich. Eine baugeschichtliche Monographie.** (The Grossmünster in Zurich: an architectural-historical monograph.)
Daniel Gutscher. Bern: Gesellschaft für Schweizerische Kunstgeschichte, 1983. 253p. bibliog.

This is a comprehensive and authoritative art-historical monograph on one of the two major churches in Zurich, the Grossmünster. According to legend, the church is the burial place of the Zurich city saints Felix, Regula, and Exuperantius; it is the shrine for relics of its legendary founder, Charlemagne; and it is the place where Huldrych Zwingli began the Swiss Reformation. Architecturally it is Late Romanesque, but the basilica and the towers are in Gothic style, while their polygonal domes are from the 1780s and give the Grossmünster its special character. Art historian and archaeologist Gutscher traces the complex history of this edifice in meticulous detail. He distinguishes six building phases from the inception about 1100 to the completion around 1230. Each of the phases left a number of sculptural works that have never been replaced or restored. The book has 210 illustrations, including reproductions of old engravings and watercolours, that help to visualize the construction history, an illustrated catalogue of 120 sculptural elements that are built into the structure of the church, and seven fold-out measured drawings with elevations to scale.

641 **Sakrale Bauten.** (Religious structures.)
Heinz Horat. Disentis, Switzerland: Pro Helvetia/Desertina, 1988. 280p. maps. bibliog. (Ars Helvetica, III).

This is the third volume in the *Ars Helvetica* (q.v.) series of books on the 'visual culture of Switzerland'. It is concerned with every kind of structural manifestation of the religious spirit to be found in Switzerland. Horat has divided the subject into three major parts. In the first he treats buildings that are used by the community of believers, Christian in general and, until the early modern era, Catholic in particular. The cathedrals of the bishopric seats, town churches, monasteries, hospitals and hospices, and the structures of the various religious orders are presented in word and picture. The second part, 'places along the road', deals with the more commonplace expressions of religious faith, as manifested in crosses and chapels in the countryside, pilgrimage churches, holy mountains, towers, commemorative structures, and burial places. In the third part Horat describes 'the sanctified space', such as the interior of religious buildings, and how this space and its component parts, such as baptistry and baptismal fount, galleries, seating arrangements, screens, choir, crypt, and altar, have been used, remodelled, and adjusted to changing purposes over the centuries. The book has 298 illustrations, many of them plans and elevations of the buildings described.

642 **Schweizer Bauernhaus: Ländliche Bauten und ihre Bewohner.** (The Swiss farmhouse: country dwellings and their inhabitants.)
David Meili. Zurich: Fretz, 1984. 180p. bibliog.

Meili, director of the Ballenberg open-air museum, approaches the topic of rural dwellings more as an anthropologist than as an art historian or architect. An overview of the 'fourth estate', the farmers, shows how much their livelihood depended on the soil and the climate and how these factors dictated the type of farming pursued. Farmers were generally poor, prey to disease and natural disasters and looked down upon by city-dwellers, but the development of cheese and wine production and the rural industries strengthened the rural economic base. Meili then examines how the single farmhouse developed, and shows how the geography largely determined the type of structure and the building materials used. In addition, community councils by the late 18th century had already established standards for the construction of dwellings. The simple alp-hut nestled on a steep slope contrasts with the stately Bernese farmhouse surrounded by rolling green meadows; the farmhouse with its low shingle covered roof of the Jura mountains in the West contrasts with the steep tiled roof of the Toggenburg in the East; and the wooden Bernese chalet contrasts with the stone house of the Ticino.

643 **Profane Bauten.** (Profane structures.)
André Meyer. Disentis, Switzerland: Pro Helvetia/Desertina, 1989. 289p. maps. bibliog. (Ars Helvetica, IV).

Meyer declares in the foreword to this splendid book that his goal was to describe not so much the aesthetic properties of individual buildings as the function of secular architecture as an integral part of settlements and the structure of settlements. In six chapters he traces the development from the founding and subsequent expansion of settlements, to fortifications, rural dwellings and the accompanying seats of the landlords, the village, the town and the cityscape, and, finally, the late-20th-century phenomena of urbanization. In each of these chapters Meyer isolates and describes architectural elements of special importance in their context. In the chapter on the village, for example, he first describes the process of village formation in the course of the Middle Ages and the impact of modern forces on the village structure, and then writes what amount to little essays on specific elements of special importance such as the village square, the village inn, the pastor's mansion, and the schoolhouse. The text is complemented by 251 informatively captioned illustrations. Like the other volumes in the *Ars Helvetica* series, this work is also being published in French, Italian, and Romansh versions.

644 **Schlösser und Landsitze der Schweiz.** (Châteaux and villas of Switzerland.)

Christian Renfer, Eduard Widmer. Zurich: Ex Libris, 1985. 320p.

Castle building ceased in the 15th century. From the 16th century on until the 19th century the country estate became the vehicle for the manifestation of power, money, and taste. Architecture, too, reflected the aristocratization of Switzerland. Renfer, the author of the text, has divided the country into five regions for each of which he has an introductory chapter. He also has written the text to the accompanying photographs that Widmer took for this large-sized and lavishly illustrated picture book. Widmer has worked on a similar project with Meyer, entitled *Das grosse Burgenbuch der Schweiz* (The great castles book of Switzerland) (Zurich: Ex Libris, 1977. 320p. maps. bibliog.). The territory of Switzerland is perhaps the region in Europe richest in castles – archaeologists know of some 3,000 sites. On three hundred of them there are castle ruins or castles; many of the latter are still lived in. The 'Great castles book' presents 127 of them in words and pictures, divided into eight groups according to types and geographical location.

645 **Schweizer Architektur.** (Swiss architecture.)

Pully, Switzerland: Anthony Krafft, 1972- . 5 times per year. ca. 35p.

This large-format journal consists of an editorial section with articles on various facets of the field by leading Swiss architects, and loose leaves in binders of hundreds of architectural projects built in Switzerland – from single-family and apartment houses to farms, garages, sport stadiums, hotels and motels, museums, theatres, educational buildings, and libraries. Each completed project has a double-sided leaf with photographs, drawings, and information concerning location, construction, and, sometimes, cost.

646 **Altes Bern – Neues Bern: Ein Stadtbild im Wandel der Zeit.** (Old Bern – new Bern: a city in the course of time.)

Erdmann Schmocker, Berchtold Weber. Bern: Benteli, 1979. 199p.

One of the oldest existing views of Bern, by the chronicler Diebold Schilling (about 1485), depicts a towering city on a spur above the Aare river. The earliest exact city plan is by Gregorius Sickinger (about 1603). The authors contrast plans and engravings from Bern's past side by side with vistas of the present. The changes are captured both textually and visually. The city grew in four discernible stages still visible by the fortifications, and each part has some noteworthy public buildings lining the narrow streets called 'Gassen'. The tour begins with the newest part of the town, that of the railway station and ends with the oldest that contains the popular bear-pit. Pictures of the clock tower, the minster, the city hall, historic fountains and elegant squares are well known, but these photographs were shot from the same angle captured by chroniclers centuries ago and, therefore, have a novel perspective. The most beautiful private residences are found in the Kramgasse – these townhouses attest to the pride and wealth of their builders. Structural changes and the reasons for these are pointed out. Old and new views from the the tower of the Münster show the growth and modernization that have taken place all around the city and are in stark contrast to medieval Bern which has miraculously been able to preserve its rich heritage.

647 **Häuser und Landschaften der Schweiz.** (Houses and landscapes of Switzerland.)
Richard Weiss. Erlenbach-Zurich; Stuttgart, FRG: Eugen Rentsch, 1959. 368p. 2 maps. bibliog.

The focus of this scholarly work is on Swiss rural dwellings which were built between 1600 and 1850 and which are still inhabited. The house is a mirror of its surroundings, of a landscape that is more than a piece of land, that has a long history which in turn is shaped by man, by his pursuits and needs. Building materials and construction, roof types and fireplaces for heating and cooking, floor plans and land use, the relationship between the individual settler and his community, these are among the topics that are investigated in this book. Good drawings and tables illustrate many of the descriptions given in the text. These are especially helpful to the reader who is not familiar with the great variety of building styles found in Switzerland.

Architects

648 **Borromini.**
Anthony Blunt. London: Allen Lane, 1979. 240p. bibliog.

Borromini's portrait graces one side of the Swiss one-hundred-franc note, while the other shows his architectural masterpiece, St Spivo in Rome. In this way the Swiss honour the man who is considered one of the most important architects born on Swiss soil. Francesco Borromini (1599-1667) left Brissone on Lake Lugano at an early age. He was twenty when he reached Rome, where he eventually became one of the great Baroque architects. The completion of St Peter's was in the hands of the best artists and craftsmen of the time, among them the universal genius Gian Lorenzo Bernini and Carlo Maderno in whose workshop Borromini found employment. Blunt frequently refers to the intense competition between Bernini and Borromini. Each was supported by different factions of the Roman hierarchy, but Bernini generally had the inside track over the irascible Borromini, preventing him from gaining major commissions. Nevertheless, Borromini has a number of masterpieces to his credit, among them the church of St Spivo, the restored and remodelled St John Lateran, and the building of the College of Propaganda Fide. Borromini was inspired by Michelangelo's architectural designs and saw himself as his heir. He too was exposed to the criticism of the conservatives for his innovative and 'willful ingenuity'. The book is illustrated with 150 photographs of drawings and completed major works, as well as of many smaller assignments, such as capitals, lanterns, façades, and balustrades.

649 **Le Corbusier: oeuvres complètes en 8 volumes.** (Le Corbusier: complete works in 8 volumes.)
Edited by W. Boesiger, O. Stonorov, and Max Bill. Zurich: Girsberger, and Verlag für Architektur (Artemis), 1929-70; New York: G. Wittenborn; Praeger; new ed., 1964-70.

The eight large-sized volumes present Le Corbusier's work chronologically from 1910 to his death in 1965. The early volumes are in French, with Le Corbusier's own statements translated into English and German; from volume five on, the complete text is in the three languages. Each volume has about 230 pages, with reproductions of designs and drawings by Le Corbusier, photographs of models and finished works, and detailed captions and descriptions. This is a superb inventory and record of the prolific creativity of this important 20th-century architect and city planner, whose works stand in many parts of the world. The eighth volume, *Last works*, was published in 1970. Many of its illustrations are, for the first time, in colour, and it has a biographical note and tables of contents for all the volumes.

650 **Le Corbusier 1910-65.**
W. Boesiger, H. Girsberger. Zurich: Verlag für Architektur (Artemis), 1960; 1967. 2 vols.

This is a two-volume condensed 'omnibus' edition of Le Corbusier's (né Charles-Edouard Jeanneret, 1887-1965) complete work. The countless photographs, plans and sketches of this famous Swiss architect are accompanied by a text in French, English, and German. The material is divided into five parts: private houses; large projects; museums and religious buildings; paintings, sculptures and tapesteries; and city planning. Corbusier travelled extensively. His buildings and city plans, some never executed, were commissioned by institutions and governments from all over the world. They subscribed to his *esprit nouveau*, his 'new spirit,' which drove him to create architecture for the times he lived in, rather than produce copies of the past. Willy Boesiger has edited a still more condensed, inexpensive pocketbook version, *Le Corbusier*, published by Praeger (New York; Washington, 1972, 260p.). It consists of three parts: sketches, projects and buildings, 1905-39; projects and buildings, 1940-64; and town planning schemes, the *unités d'habitation*, Chandigarh, and museums. The book is supplemented by a biography and a chronological list of projects.

651 **Le Corbusier's sketchbooks.**
Edited by Foundation Le Corbusier and Architectural History Foundation. Boston, Massachusetts: MIT, 1981-82. 3 vols.

Each volume is about 550 pages long and has more than 1,000 illustrations, about one-fifth of them in colour. The three sketchbooks span about fifty years of Le Corbusier's career. The lavishly illustrated volumes provide a unique insight into his art. The *New York Times Magazine* praised them as 'an invaluable repository of Le Corbusier's spontaneous thoughts' and 'one of the most essential bodies of source materials we have on Le Corbusier'.

652 **Le Corbusier in perspective.**
Edited by Peter Serenyi. Englewood Cliffs, New Jersey: Prentice-Hall, 1975. 166p. bibliog.

This volume presents 'a sampling of the writings of the most spirited contemporary critics and selections from significant historical evaluations' of Le Corbusier and his work. The earliest of the more than two dozen critical essays include dates from 1922, the most recent being from 1972; they concentrate on Le Corbusier's activities as architect and city planner. As Serenyi points out in his preface, 'Le Corbusier was also a painter, sculptor, furniture and tapestry designer, and author of over forty books and innumerable articles'. The essays chosen by Serenyi are grouped under seven themes and include both critical voices and admirers. Their quality, range, and diversity make this book an invaluable tool in understanding the content and meaning of Le Corbusier's work and the controversies surrounding it.

653 **The architecture of Mario Botta.**
Christian Norberg-Schulz, Mirko Zardini, Yukio Futagawa. New York: Rizzoli International Publications, 1985. 232p. bibliog.

This oversized volume, splendidly illustrated with 450 architectural drawings and photographs, features the work of the new international architectural celebrity, Mario Botta. Botta was born in 1943 in Mendrisio, Canton Ticino, and began his rise to prominence in the schools and architecture studios of his native Swiss canton and the neighbouring Italian provinces. At the age of forty he was professor of architecture at the Swiss Federal Institute of Technology in Lausanne and an honorary fellow of a number of foreign architectural organizations. Botta's work is strongly influenced by the Ticino with its geographical and cultural characteristics in which regional elements are blended with the classical tradition. He holds the conviction that 'an authentic work of architecture has to belong to its own time. In relating the modern house to archetypal and local memories, however, [the architect] gives it a new profound significance.' The stunning photographs, sixty of them in colour, by the Japanese master photographer Futagawa of Botta's buildings, designs, and sketches give an idea why Botta 'in fact is one of the few architects of the moment who is accepted by "everybody"'.

Photography and film making

654 **Le cinéma suisse.** (The Swiss film.)
Freddy Buache. Lausanne: L'Age de l'Homme, 1974. 314p.

Freddy Buache, director of the Cinémathèque suisse (founded in 1948 in Lausanne), reconstructs the history of Swiss film making from the early beginnings in 1905 with a series of short films on the Vevey grape harvest festival (*Fête des Vignerons*) to the blossoming of the internationally acclaimed creativity of the Swiss film makers after 1968. Buache highlights the successes and setbacks of Swiss film making, and analyses directors and their approaches and the plots of many of their films. Bursts of creativity, during World War II, for example, or in the late 1950s, were interrupted for lack of financial support or the inability to find subject matter. The generation of French-Swiss film makers of the late 1960s, foremost among them Alain Tanner, Claude Goretta, and Michel Soutter, lifted the Swiss film as an art form into the international arena. A number of appendices, the most interesting of which is a 'filmography' in which Buache lists all Swiss films alphabetically by directors, complete the work.

655 **Aspekte des Schweizer Films.** (Aspects of Swiss film.)
Edited by Felix Bucher, Otto Ceresa, Pierre Lachat. Zurich: Stiftung Pro Helvetia, 1979. 81p.

This booklet consists of twelve short articles that provide an overview of film making in Switzerland in 1978, a discussion of the relationship between film and television, and a series of prose portraits of newcomers to the Swiss film scene.

656 **Geschichte des Schweizer Films. Spielfilme 1896-1965.** (The history of Swiss film: feature films 1896-1965.)
Hervé Dumont. Lausanne: Cinémathèque Suisse, 1987. 603p.

This history of Swiss film making is in effect a comprehensive guide to the films produced in Switzerland from 1896 to 1965. It provides an immense amount of information. The first 100 pages are taken up by the descriptions of eighty-four silent films, which is a unique feature of this book. Then follows a catalogue, listing some three hundred sound films. Nearly 1,000 photographs, posters, and stills fill the upper third of the large pages, presenting a continuous pictorial history of Swiss film production. The lower two-thirds contain Dumont's texts of data about the production and showing of the films he catalogues, as well as the summaries of their stories and an evaluation of their artistic value. The ups and downs of Swiss film making, only rarely achieving international recognition, are carefully traced in this book.

657 **L'usage de la liberté: le nouveau cinéma suisse 1964-1984.** (The use of freedom: the new Swiss cinema 1964-1984.)
Martin Schaub, adapted from the German by Eric Jeanneret, Véra Zaslawsky. Zurich: Pro Helvetia; Lausanne: L'Age d'Homme, 1985. 184p.

In the early 1960s Swiss film making was at its nadir by at least one very significant measurement: in 1964 99.8 per cent of the films shown in Swiss cinemas were foreign made. Schaub explains this situation as the residue of the World War II mentality of spiritual national defence that stifled all aspects of cultural life in the country. A new era began in the mid-1960s with the Solothurn Swiss film festivals and the appearance of innovative makers, both French- and German-Swiss. Excellent documentaries, short-subject, and feature-length films that received national and international acclaim made the 1970s the 'golden age' of Swiss cinema. Richard Dindo, Markus Imhoof, Alain Tanner, Claude Goretta, Rolf Lyssy, Michel Soutter, Yves Yersin, Fredi M. Murer, and Daniel Schmid are a few of the artists who gave new vitality to the Swiss film. This book with its sprinkling of black-and-white photographs and its documentary appendix of 'twenty years of Swiss cinema in 110 films' makes an important contribution to the history of this important branch of modern Swiss cultural life.

658 **Vergangenheit und Gegenwart des Schweizer Films (1896-1987). Eine kritische Wertung.** (Past and present of the Swiss film (1896-1987): a critical appraisal.)
Martin Schlappner, Martin Schaub. Zurich: Schweizerisches Filmzentrum, 1987. 203p.

This book has two parts. The first, by Schlappner, deals with the history, themes, and directors of the older Swiss film from 1896 to 1963. It provides interesting glimpses from the beginnings of film making dominated by documentaries and silents with patriotic themes – the fatherland and its army, the citizen and his role as defender of his country, the mountains and the mountain home were featured into the post-World War II era. Among the better products were a series of peasant films by Franz Schnyder, inspired by the novels of Jeremias Gotthelf. The films in general depicted the world of the petty bourgeoisie; the milieu of the workers was not a subject of the film makers. The second part of the book, by Schaub, is the German original version of his book *L'usage de la liberté* (q.v.), extended to 1987 with a chapter entitled 'film landscape in transition'.

Music, Theatre, and Dance

659 **Musical Europe: an illustrated guide to musical life in 18 European countries.**
Edited by Marianne Adelmann. New York; London: Paddington, 1974. 448p.

Adelmann wrote the entry on Switzerland, p. 396-433, one of the longest among the eighteen West European countries treated in this volume. Forty places with some kind of significant musical activity are listed alphabetically, from Adliswil to Zurich. Many have only one entry, while Zurich has the most with eighteen. The venues of musical life are indicated by symbols for concert halls; opera houses; theatres; music festivals; residences, monuments, and portraits of composers and musicians; organs; music archives and libraries; conservatories, master courses, and institutes; research centres and recording studios; instrument makers; music publishers; and record companies. The particular institutions receive descriptions of varying lengths, often with small illustrations on the margin of the pages. Some of the entries are dated, but the overall result reflects the intensity and variety of musical life in all parts of Switzerland.

660 **La Suisse qui chante.** (Switzerland that sings.)
Edited by Paul Budry. Geneva: Slatkine, 1981. 236p.

The natural beauty of Switzerland, cherished tradition and patriotism have always inspired musical expression, and hundreds of choral societies around the country continue the rich musical heritage and specialize in one form of song or another. Seventy-six folk songs in the four national languages with text and music fill over half of the book; the songs come from all regions and population groups and from different centuries. An entire chapter is dedicated to the popular male chorus with four voices (*Männerchor*). The *Festspiel*, a musical performed by laymen in costumes, often combined with dance and commissioned to mark a special occasion such as the commemoration of a historical event, or a local event such as a vintage festival, flourished in the early 20th century. There are 120 illustrations interspersed with the text. The German version, *Die Schweiz, die singt*, was published in 1932 by Rentsch in Erlenbach-Zurich.

661 **The movement therapy.**
Claire-Lise Dutoit, translated from the French by Muriel Anderson (et al.). Surrey, England: Dalcroze Society, 1965. 98p.

This publication appeared in 1965, the centenary year of the birth of the pioneer of music education, Jaques-Dalcroze. He spent most of his professional life in Geneva, first as professor at the conservatory and then for over thirty years, as head of his own institute. Dutoit's book describes Dalcroze's work as a music teacher. His lesson plans focused on a wide range of musical experiences with mind and body working together, and to this end, a sense of 'inner hearing' had to be developed that then could be translated into movement. Dalcroze's system became known as eurhythmics. It proved to have an especially valuable therapeutic effect on physically handicapped and mentally retarded children. Many graduates of the Dalcroze Institute in Geneva have become leaders in music therapy.

662 **Der Jazz in der Schweiz.** (Jazz in Switzerland.)
Hugo Faas. Zurich: Pro Helvetia, 1976. 42p.

The first half of this booklet consists of a brief historical survey of the development of jazz in Switzerland. A form of watered-down jazz music was first played in the winter sports centres of St Moritz, Arosa, and Interlaken with their international clientele. Amateur musicians formed jazz bands in the early 1920s, playing music in imitation of the American bands available on records. Visiting greats, such as Louis Armstrong in 1933 and 1934, gave the movement inpetus, but the 'golden era' of Swiss professional jazz bands came to an end with the outbreak of World War II. During the 1950s and 1960s the annual amateur jazz festival in the Zurich cinema Urban, later Corso, carried Swiss jazz to unprecedented heights. The jazz scene of the early 1970s was characterized by the appearance of the Swiss Jazz School in Bern where professional musicians taught a home-grown style of jazz increasingly more independent of the American example. The second half of the booklet contains brief biographical sketches of outstanding Swiss jazz musicians.

663 **Schoeck, Othmar.**
Kurt von Fischer, Fritz Muggler. In: *The New Grove Dictionary of Music and Musicians*, edited by Stanley Sadie. London: Macmillan, 1980. vol. 16, p. 698-700. bibliog.

Othmar Schoeck (1886-1957) was one of the leading Swiss composers of the 20th century, 'probably the most typical representative of a specifically Swiss art'. His principal achievement was as a composer of lieder, and he may be regarded as the last great figure of the lied tradition. For his nearly 400 songs he chose texts primarily from Romantic poets, covering a wide emotional range suitable to his lyric art. Schoeck was, however, not simply a belated Romantic, for 'alive to contemporary advances in compositional technique, he formed a distinct style from Romantic harmony'. Schoeck also made major contributions to the genre of the opera. *Penthesilea*, after Kleist, and *Das Schloss Dürande*, after Eichendorff, are two of his stage works. He wrote relatively few instrumental works. Schoeck spent most of his adult life in Zurich as composer, conductor, and pianist accompanying lieder singers. The University of Zurich awarded him an honorary doctorate in 1928, and in the 1940s and 1950s he received a number of Swiss and German music prizes and merit awards. The article closes with a substantial bibliography of compositions by Schoeck and works about him.

664 **Great concert artists: Ernest Ansermet.**
Bernard Gavoty, translated from the French by F. E. Richardson, portraits by Jean Mohr. Geneva: Kister, 1961. 34p.

This little volume on the French-Swiss conductor Ernest Ansermet (1883-1969) begins with an essay on the maestro's unique gift of interpretation. Gavoty quotes Swiss composer Arthur Honegger who summarized this almost magical power with the following words: 'Many great men have conducted my works and been my friends. . . . But Ansermet has always seemed to me unique of his kind. Not because he is a mathematician, composer and conductor all in one . . . but because meeting him is an inspiriting [sic] experience. . .'. Ansermet was able to transform inspiration into sound. The essay is followed by a one-page 'life story', numerous portraits, mostly of the older artist with his characteristic white beard, and a discography which lists British and American catalogue numbers for Ansermet's classical and modern recordings. Stravinsky is especially well represented among the latter. As conductor of the *Orchestre de la Suisse Romande* Ansermet's name was for years a household word for Swiss and international radio audiences, and his determination to expose his listeners to contemporary compositions did much to make new works accessible to the general public.

665 **Composer's world: horizons and limitations.**
Paul Hindemith. Cambridge, Massachusetts; Harvard University: 1953. 221p. (Charles Eliot Norton Lectures, 1949-50).

Paul Hindemith's book is intended for the layperson: it treats the world of composers in general. It consists of lectures on perceiving music intellectually and emotionally, on musical inspiration and producing music, on technique and style, on performers and instruments, and makes a case for the training of all-round musicianship. A great contemporary composer here shares his views about all aspects of composing and performing, and he does it with wisdom and modesty.

666 **Rhythm, music & education.**
Emile Jaques-Dalcroze, translated from the French by Harold F. Rubenstein. Surrey, England: Dalcroze Society, 1967. 200p.

This book, first published in 1921, was written by Jaques-Dalcroze (1865-1950), the famous French-Swiss pioneer of music education. Dalcroze spent most of his life in Geneva where he founded an institute dedicated to the training of music teachers and to the composition of songs and musicals for festivals. In this book he describes the response of children to rhythm and shows how the body can be trained to become an instrument to translate the sensation music causes into movement and improvisation. The applications of Dalcroze's theories found their way into dance and choreography, drama and opera. A special branch of eurhythmics was developed for the education of the handicapped and mentally retarded.

667 **Paul Hindemith.**
Ian Kemp. In: *The New Grove Modern Masters: Bartók, Stravinsky, Hindemith*, edited by Stanley Sadie. New York; London: Norton, 1984. p. 227-81. bibliog. (First published in *The New Grove Dictionary of Music and Musicians*, 1980).

Paul Hindemith (1895-1963) was born near Frankfurt and returned there shortly before his death. Kemp provides a short sketch of the composer's life and work. He talks about Hindemith's extraordinary gift as a performer on the violin and other instruments, and his work as conductor, teacher, and composer. When his association with Jewish musicians and his non-traditional compositions offended the Nazis, he left Germany for Switzerland in 1937. He then emigrated to the United States where he held a teaching post at Yale and was in demand as a lecturer. In 1951 he accepted a position at the University of Zurich, and in 1953 he settled permanently in Bolnay near Vevey on Lake Geneva from where he undertook major concert tours as conductor. Kemp divides Hindemith's work into three periods of which the third, 1933-63, comprises the Switzerland years. Among the compositions of these years, Kemp singles out the opera *Mathis der Maler* first performed in Zurich in 1938 – the libretto is based on the life of Matthias Grünewald and shows the painter's search for his and his art's proper role in society during the turbulent times of the Reformation and the German Peasants' Revolt. The story confronted Hindemith with a similar challenge and 'shattered his very soul'. Short musical notations illustrate Kemp's theoretical observations of the composer's style, a style noted for its use of musical forms of the past, the polyphony of its melodies, and its neo-classical integrity.

668 **The Swiss theatre scene: a survey.**
Roland Maurer, translated from the German by Maureen Oberli-Turner. Zurich: Pro Helvetia, 1984. 89p. bibliog.

The Swiss theatre has unique problems in that four different languages are spoken in Switzerland and because the language regions differ greatly in size – the audience for theatrical activities therefore varies greatly. There is no national theatre, but there are several municipal theatres supported with public funds. Of these, only Geneva and Zurich have an international reputation. Maurer provides an overview of the many types of theatrical entities from the professional repertory theatre to the strolling theatre and lists many of the works performed. He points to the strengths of different language areas and the characteristics by which they distinguish themselves. He details the present status of the dramatic theatre, the musical theatre, and the ballet beginning with the 1960s. He points to the efforts companies make to produce modern works only to be met with great resistance by the paying public. Other sections dealing with the influence of radio and television, training possibilities for the stage, organizations that serve the theatre and prospects for the future complete the survey. The illustrations are in black-and-white.

669 **Das Theater – unsere Welt. Das Schweizer Theater 1970-1980.** (The theatre – our world: the Swiss theatre 1970-1980.)
Edited by Hans Mayer. Luzern, Switzerland: Raeber, 1980. 303p.

This comprehensive work on all aspects of the theatre covers far more than the subtitle indicates, both in scope and in time. Some thirty contributors, all experts in their particular area, present the many different facets that make for viable theatre. The dramatist, the actor, the technical, artistic and musical directors, and the critics, all speak out here. Organizations that support and finance theatre and that protect actors and crews and the rights of the writers are discussed in this work, as are the many different types of theatre, the cultural mission and the public relations efforts. The book is richly illustrated with photographs of performances of Swiss works or foreign works on the Swiss stage. It is a worthy commemorative work on the sixtieth anniversary of the Swiss Union of Theatres (Bühnenverband).

670 **Dance and ballet in Switzerland.**
Jean-Pierre Pastori, translated from the German by Jacqueline Gartmann. Zurich: Pro Helvetia, 1988. 97p.

Swiss ballet has little more than a thirty-year history. Interest in this art form was first inspired by foreign performers, choreographers, teachers, and travelling companies. Names such as Rudolf von Laban, Mary Wigman, Harald Kreutzberg, the Sakharoffs, and the *Ballets Russes* stand out. The legacy of the Genevan music educator Emile Jaques-Dalcroze's are the *Festspiele*, musicals performed by laypersons. Eventually six Swiss ballet companies emerged as adjuncts of the publicly supported opera houses – Geneva, Basel and Zurich foremost among them – and the growing popularity of this art form made ballet *soirées* possible. George Balanchine and talented choreographers such as Nicholas Beriozoff, Heinz Spoerli, and Oscar Araiz were instrumental in creating a fast-growing repertory of classical ballets, but also of interpretations of modern music. Individual Swiss dancers and companies have begun to achieve international recognition. The recent founding of the Béjart Ballet Lausanne (1987) did much to revive the enthusiasm for ballet and dance in modern Switzerland. Black-and-white photographs illustrate some of the important productions.

671 **Swiss music on records – classic.**
Schweizer Musik-Archiv. Zurich: Schweizer Musik-Archiv, 1980- .

The 1985-86 edition lists alphabetically some 250 Swiss composers who had works available on record in September 1985. Data are provided on the lifespans of the composers and on their compositions. Notker Balbulus (840-912) is the oldest, Jürg Frey (born 1953) the youngest in the list. Arthur Honegger, Frank Martin, and Othmar Schoeck have most records. The many modern and contemporary composers are represented by only few works on record. Even though the editor emphasizes that this catalogue is by no means a national discography, it is at the very least a source of interesting information about Swiss music life.

672 **Schweizer Komponisten unserer Zeit.** (Swiss composers of our time.)
Edited by Mathes Seidl, Hans Steinbeck. Winterthur, Switzerland: Amadeus, 1983. 247p. bibliog.

This books presents 126 contemporary Swiss composers. Each is allotted two pages which are taken up by a photograph; a short biography, in most cases written by the composer and printed in his or her language; a listing of all compositions, grouped according to type, such as symphonic, vocal, dramatic, and chamber music, records and electronic works; and publications by and about the composer. The works are listed in chronological order or according to opus number. An extensive list of abbreviations makes for a coded and therefore short text. The foreword in French, German, and English was written by the well-known Swiss conductor and composer Paul Sacher. He finds that 'a more appreciative and self-assured attitude towards the arts in general and music in particularly can definitely be noted' among the Swiss public and that 'Swiss achievement in the field of music would now be compared . . . favourably with that of foreign countries'.

673 **Holliger, Heinz.**
Jürg Stenzl. In: *The New Grove Dictionary of Music and Musicians*, edited by Stanley Sadie. London: Macmillan, 1980. vol. 8, p. 650-51.

Heinz Holliger, born 1939 in Langenthal, Canton Bern, has embarked on an international career as one of the foremost oboists of the contemporary music world.

Playing works of the most varied types and periods, he fascinates above all through his extraordinary phrasing technique. Among new effects he introduced on the oboe are harmonies, double trills, glissandos, chords, and sounds derived from a microphone within the instrument. Many contemporary composers have written works for him, and Holliger is himself also a productive composer of both vocal and instrumental music. The *New Grove* article lists his major works and provides a brief bibliography.

674 **Twentieth century composers. Volume II: Germany and Central Europe.**
Hans Heinz Stuckenschmidt. London: Weidenfeld and Nicholson, 1970. 256p.

Switzerland occupies a central place in Europe, both geographically and culturally. Swiss composers reflect that fact in their music, where French and German influences are expressed in a new amalgam. Stuckenschmidt devotes almost one hundred pages of this volume to Swiss composers, giving about ten pages each to the recognized leaders, among them Paul Hindemith (1895-1963), Vladimir Vogel (1896-), Arthur Honegger (1892-1955), Othmar Schoeck (1886-1957), and Frank Martin (1890-1974). Moscow-born Vogel emigrated to Berlin and thence in 1933 to Switzerland where he obtained the right of domicile only in 1940, after marrying a Swiss woman. He lived in Ascona, Canton Ticino. His special contribution to the music of the 20th century were his compositions for spoken choruses. His peculiar *Sprechchor* technique demanded the creation of a chamber choir for choral speech. Ellen Widmann trained and directed the choir in which the human voice was given new forms of utterance. Vogel's oratorio *Tyl Klaas* which extended over four hours in performance was a highly personal protest against dictatorship and the denial of personal liberty. Stuckenschmidt provides similarly interesting and pertinent information for the other composers in his well-written sketch of musical life in 20th-century Switzerland.

Customs, Folklore, and Folk Art

675 **Old inn-signs in Switzerland.**

René Creux. Zurich: Swiss National Tourist Office, 1962. 79p.

Rare is the tourist who does not notice those old inn-signs that are symbols of hospitality inviting him to enjoy food, drink, and rest. The styles the various craftsmen exhibit in the execution of these name-plates are as varied as the themes depicted on them. Lions and horses, Wilhelm Tells and madonnas, trade symbols and mythological figures greet the passer-by. These signs are enjoying a new popularity and the authentic older ones are sought after as antiques. Many are now preserved in museums. The booklet has illustrations of some fifty signs, introduced by a short text.

676 **Yodelling in Switzerland.**

Hans Curjel. Zurich: Pro Helvetia, 1970. 5p.

This is a short essay on the technique and history of yodelling. It serves as an introduction to a musical form that is characteristic of Switzerland and rarely encountered elsewhere.

677 **Fairy tales from Switzerland: the three sneezes and other fairy tales.**

Roger Duvoisin. London: Muller, 1958. 232p.

Many fairy tales and legends told in Switzerland are similar to those of neighbouring countries, while others are specific to a locality or relate to a particular event in the country's long history. Almost every valley, mountain, lake and castle has its own legend. Terrible creatures reign in the mountains and create havoc, instil fear, and cause mischief; others are helpful to the poor and weak. Animals, princes and princesses, dwarfs, children, and old women are endowed with special powers that they use in different ways. Nineteen tales are from French-speaking Switzerland and eighteen are from the German-speaking part. They are retold in simple language for reading aloud. Names of real people and places such as those of the brutal knight of Waldenburg from Basel or of poor Christopher from the Bagnes valley in the Valaisian Alps lend the stories an element of credibility and a local flavour. See also *Märchen und Sagen der Schweiz* (Swiss fairy tales and legends), edited by Hans Peter Treichler

(Zurich; Wiesbaden, FRG: Orell Füssli, 1989). Treichler has assembled five dozen fairy tales and more than one hundred legends from all parts of Switzerland into a large, beautifully illustrated book. The 174 colour and 24 black-and-white illustrations have been taken from rare old books.

678 **Swiss handicrafts: introduction to contemporary folk art.**
Edited by Ambros Eberle, Heimatwerk Zurich. Zurich: Verlag am Wasser, [n.d., n.p.]. maps.

This slim booklet consists of colour photographs with accompanying text. Eberle describes briefly the characteristic regions of Switzerland's cultural landscape and provides examples of their distinct rural architecture, folk art and handicrafts. Some of these, such as traditional pottery, modern ceramics and textiles, embroidery, weaving, wooden masks, cut glass, costumes, paper cut-outs, crafts associated with alpine herdsmen, basketry, and copperware, are illustrated and discussed. The booklet also lists some of the many public museums in all cantons which exhibit Swiss folk art.

679 **Blick in eine Idylle: Schweizer Volkskunst und naive Malerei aus vier Jahrhunderten.** (Look at an idyll: Swiss folk art and naive painting from four centuries.)
Edited by Guy Filippa. Bern: Benteli, 1983. 262p. bibliog.

This colourful large picture book exhibits the work of eighty-seven Swiss folk artists and naive painters of the last four hundred years, ending with artists born before 1910. The artists included in this volume are grouped according to the regions from which they come: Graubünden and Valais, and western, central, and eastern Switzerland. The selection of works is limited to paintings and paper cut-outs and does not cover wood-carvings, embroidery, and other kinds of folk art. The paintings depict religious scenes, scenes from daily life, portraits, and landscapes which are usually populated by little human figures and animals. They painted according to the tradition peculiar to their region and chose motifs well known to them. The captions under the illustrations provide interesting information about the artists. Some of these self-taught folk artists, often village teachers, led very hard lives, but despite deprivation and little reward for their endeavours, they created vibrant pictures and decorative works.

680 **Das Alphorn in der Schweiz.** (The alphorn in Switzerland.)
Brigitte Geiser. Bern: Haupt, 1976. 36p., with 32p. of photographs and musical examples. bibliog. (Schweizer Heimatbücher, 177/178).

The alphorn is the Swiss musical instrument, but little is known about its history. The first description of an alphorn is found in a 1555 edition of a work by Conrad Gesner. The alphorn consists of a long conical tube of wood, curved at the end like a knee; long instruments have low keys, short horns have higher keys. At one time alpine herdsmen used to make their own alphorns; they used them to calm the cows. They can still be heard in valleys of the Alps, but more and more their sounds come out of the cellars of urban dwellings, since alphorns have become hobby instruments, and today the alphorn is played for entertainment and as a tourist attraction. It is never played from sheet music. Players are generally able to find thirteen tones of the harmonic scale through lip vibration into the air column of the horn. The black-and-white photographs show how alphorns are made and present a portrait gallery of twenty-four (semi-)professional alphorn makers. Geiser has also provided summaries of her instructive text in French and English.

Customs, Folklore, and Folk Art

681 **Musical instruments in the Swiss folk tradition.**
Brigitte Geiser. Zurich: Pro Helvetia, 1978. 55p. bibliog.

Switzerland's folk music is as diverse as the country's landscape, and the instruments used for house and dance music differ from those used in the concert halls. They range from the music-box to the alphorn and the wrought-iron cow bell. Geiser organizes Swiss folk instruments into groups: (1) 'instruments the material of which vibrates and produces sounds when struck, rubbed or plucked' (bat, triangle, nutclapper, clapping box, castanets, spoons, broomstick, musical bottles, cow bells, coin rolling; (2) membranophones, instruments where 'a stretched membrane emits a sound of its own when struck or alters the tone of the voice when sung or hummed against' (drums, mirliton = comb and paper); (3) cordophones (zithers, hackbrett); (4) aerophones (whip cracking, whistles, pipes, fifes, flutes, house organs, or simply a blade of grass); and (5) instruments with vibrating tones (harmonica, accordion, animal horn, alphorn). Photographs depict many of these instruments. A good bibliography is included.

682 **Heimatleben.** (Costumes and customs.)
Zurich: Schweizerische Trachtenvereinigung, 1928- . bimonthly. ca. 32p.

Published by the National Federation of Swiss Costumes, this illustrated journal has articles on folk dancing, costume societies, folk customs, folk singing, and historical developments in these areas.

683 **Heimatschutz.** (Protection of the patrimony.)
Zurich: Heimatschutz, 1906- . quarterly. ca. 30p.

The organ of the Swiss League for the Protection of the National Patrimony, this publication contains articles that address issues concerning the ongoing struggle to protect and preserve the national patrimony both in the countryside and in the cities.

684 **Schweizer Trachten = Costumes suisses = Costumi svizzeri = Swiss national costumes.**
Edited by Benjamin Laederer. Geneva: Editions Générales, 1970. [n.p.].

This delightful picture book of costumes from all regions of Switzerland is mostly printed in black-and-white and features the varied national and regional costumes of Switzerland. They are worn mostly on festive occasions such as to traditional games, dances and parades. Some pictures are close-ups of the costume, such as the headdress or the laced bodice, or some embroidery. The brief annotations alert the reader to significant details of the costumes which might otherwise be overlooked. One of the finest books on this topic.

685 **The folk costumes of Switzerland.**
Lucien Louradour, translated from the French by John O'Brien. Zurich: Pro Helvetia, Arts Council of Switzerland, 1989. 29p.

Louradour uses only twelve pages to cover the great variety of Swiss costumes (there are over four hundred different ones) and the reason for this wealth in folk costumes. He then makes some remarks about the different parts of a typical dress, from the footwear to the head-dress, from the everyday costume to the festive Sunday costume, from the traditional garb for women to that for men. Eighteen photographs in colour complete this overview. For more information, the author recommends a comprehensive major work on the topic, *Trachten der Schweiz* (Costumes of Switzerland) by Lotti Schürch and Louise Witzig (Basel: Birkhauser, 1984 [German version, 2nd ed.], published by the National Federation of Swiss Costumes). This work contains 400 photographs in colour.

686 **Swiss Alpine folk-tales.**
Fritz Müller-Guggenbühl, translated from the German by Katharine Potts. London: Oxford University Press, 1958. 225p.

The books begins with the story 'Wilhelm Tell and the founding of the Swiss Confederation' and is followed by a series of legends from the Swiss Alps. These tell of the fate of the herdsmen and their cattle. Historical events have inspired tales of adventure and are placed in familiar localities, such as Zurich or Hallwil. A group of fairy tales and legends of Swiss saints complete this book which attests to Switzerland's rich traditions.

687 **Appenzell peasant art: the native art of the Appenzellers from 1850 to today.**
Arthur Niggli, Ida Niggli, translated from the German by D. Q. Stephenson. Teufen, Switzerland: Niggli, 1975. 128p. bibliog.

The authors photographed about fifty pictures for this book from a travelling exhibition of Appenzell peasant art that was sent to the USA in 1957-58. The earliest of the painted wooden panels included here is from 1893 and the latest from 1955. Collecting these primitive depictions of life in Appenzell is fashionable today and souvenir manufacturers compete with cheap 'Appenzelliana'. The hilly Appenzell countryside, the typical house with its many rows of small windows and attached barn and stable, the annual procession of cattle being led to the mountain pastures by costumed cowherds, the changing of seasons and related activities are rendered over and over in much detail and with vivid colours. Seventeen of the best-known painters are represented with a short biography and selected works. Among them are Johannes Müller, J. B. Waldburger and Alfred Manser. Information regarding the size of the rather small panels, the media used (mostly oil), and the material on which it is produced (wood, canvas, paper) is listed next to each reproduction. Some wood-carvings of New Year mummers, cowherds, cattle and interiors by the more recent Appenzell artist Konrad Zülle complete the booklet. An earlier book on the topic is *Appenzeller Bauernmalerei* (Appenzell peasant painting) by Rudolf Hanhart and Christoph Bernoulli (Teufen, Switzerland: Niggli, 1959).

688 **Schweizer Volksbräuche.** (Swiss folk customs.)
Erich Schwabe. Zurich: Silva, 1969. 139p. bibliog.

The excellent colour photographs of this volume were taken by Michael Wolgensinger. He succeeds superbly in capturing the often curious traditions in the various regions and localities of Switzerland, some dating back centuries, such as the 'Vogel Gryff' of Kleinbasel, a man dressed as a giant bird whose appearance was recorded as early as 1392. Religious customs find expression in colourful festivals and parades, and the variety of masks and traditional costumes is astounding. Schwabe's text is essential to understand the symbolism of the traditions and elaborate costumes.

689 **Schweizer Volksmusik. Die Zeitschrift mit der volkstümlichen Note.** (Swiss folk music: the journal with the popular note.)
Altdorf, Switzerland: Schweizer Volksmusik, 1964- . bimonthly. ca. 50p.

The official organ of the Federation of Swiss Friends of Popular Music, this illustrated magazine features folk musicians, bands, and singing and yodelling groups. It also reports on past events, announces upcoming ones, and gives the news of local societies that belong to the federation.

690 **Schweizer Trachten: in Bild und Tradition.** (Swiss costumes: in pictures and tradition.)
Edited and published by Slatkine, Geneva, 1986. 192p.

With the advent of tourism in the first half of the 19th century, engravings and woodcuts became popular souvenirs, and Swiss costumes were a favourite object of interest of the foreign visitors. Every canton has a variety of different costumes to be worn on different occasions. Some of the most beautiful renderings of traditional dresses from different collections of engravings were chosen for inclusion in this book. Each costumed figure is seen against the native setting and is accompanied by the text the artist wrote at the time he created the work; his peculiar style and orthography were left unchanged to catch the spirit of the time, and his words express enthusiasm for the subject, and love of the country. Edgings of cities and countrysides by Johann Jakob Bidermann, or Biedermann, (1763-1830) who is considered the foremost artist of Swiss cantonal capitals and landscapes of the Romantic period, are also featured. The illustrations are in colour.

691 **Tell. Werden und Wandern eines Mythos.** (Tell: growth and wandering of a myth.)
Edited by Lilly Stunzi. Bern: Hallwag, 1973. 344p. bibliog.

Five authors analyse various aspects of the history of the myth of William Tell, the most important figure in Swiss folklore. Tell was not always regarded as a legendary character. At various times of danger to Switzerland his struggle against tyranny was used to uplift the morale of the people. The story of his life has inspired a long tradition of literary, artistic, and folkloric representations, not only in Switzerland but in many other parts of the world, not least the United States of America. Stunzi has assembled a rich collection of carefully captioned illustrations; the oldest, a woodcut showing Tell shooting the apple from the head of his son, dates from the early 16th century.

692 **Popular customs and festivals in Switzerland.**
Zurich: Swiss National Tourist Office, 1986. 47p. map.

This appealing and informative booklet provides access to Switzerland through its popular customs and festivals and explains their meaning. Descriptions of events, frequently accompanied by a photograph, demonstrate that all parts of the country have their traditions, often dating far back into history and reflecting the variety in culture, religion, and climate of the various regions. Festivals are especially numerous during the winter months, from St Nicholas day to carnival. The other seasons, however, also have their share of festivities. These year-round rituals provide the continuity of a precious heritage in the midst of a fast-changing world.

693 **Volkskunde der Schweiz: Grundriss.** (Folklore of Switzerland: outline.) Richard Weiss. Erlenbach-Zurich: Rentsch, 1946. 436p. 5 maps. bibliog.

This well-documented work by a leading Swiss folklorist presents subject matter that was relatively new when the book was written, but the content of the book is not outdated. Scientific research in folklore attempts to collect and interpret objects and visible expressions of the imagination of the common people, the folk (*Volk*). Weiss carefully investigates such expressions of human endeavour as they are manifested in Switzerland. The number and variety of customs and traditions in the cantons and regions of this small country are truly astounding. Weiss points out that the task of protecting these customs and traditions is in the hands of the special interest groups who practise them. There are 314 photographs, depicting old houses, artefacts of all kinds made from all sorts of materials, scenes from religious and folk festivals, and local customs.

694 **Swiss folk art.** Edited by Robert Wildhaber. Zurich: Pro Helvetia, 1971. 68p. bibliog.

This little paperback does not pretend to give an overview of folk art in Switzerland but rather examines assorted representative objects and summarizes the folk art scene in specific regions of Switzerland. Wildhaber defines in his foreword what folk art is, and what in particular is Swiss folk art. Various branches of folk art are described in sixteen brief chapters by different experts. Chapters are devoted to votive pictures, peasant painting in Appenzell and in Gruyère, religious and other textiles, embroidery, straw craft, jewellery, pottery, the development of tiled stoves, and objects produced for special festivals, such as carnival masks. Italian-speaking Switzerland is covered in one short chapter. Twenty-eight plates illustrate the text.

695 **Dances in Switzerland.** Louise Witzig. London: Parrish, 1949. 40p. map. bibliog.

Witzig, formerly general secretary of the Swiss National Costume Society, has published a number of books on Switzerland's songs and dances in an effort to preserve a heritage that has enriched Swiss folk life for hundreds of years. She defines the different types of dances, such as the typical Swiss *Ländler*; she describes the steps, the body movements, and hand grasps; and then she chooses four typical dances and gives clear directions how they are to be performed. Illustrations in colour show the traditional dress for each of the dancing couples.

696 **Schweizer Trachtenbuch.** (Swiss book of costumes.) Louise Witzig. Zurich: Schweizerische Trachtenvereinigung, 1954. 280p. bibliog.

Two hundred years ago simple costumes were the everyday dress of peasants. With increased prosperity, however, elaborate festive costumes came into use. Different regions in Switzerland developed their own characteristic dresses to be worn on different occasions. The fashion of the time dictated the shape of hats and bodice. The materials used, such as linens, wools, silks, and embroidery, were manufactured in Switzerland. After World War I, traditional Swiss costumes appeared to be heading for extinction, but the dangers of the Nazi era rekindled interest in Swiss heritage and culture. Societies were formed to ensure that designs and materials remained as authentic as possible and that new generations would have access to this important part of Swiss tradition. Witzig travelled from region to region with her camera, researching her topic, and she selected 200 black-and-white pictures for this volume.

Food and Drink

697 **Tante Heidi's Swiss kitchen.**

Eva Maria Borer, translated from the German by Hilda Morris. Tadworth, England: Kaye & Ward, 1985. 148p. bibliog.

This is the most recent of an unending trickle of Swiss cookbooks in English. Its German title, *Die echte Schweizer Küche* (The genuine Swiss kitchen), is more descriptive, even though perhaps not quite as cute as 'Tante Heidi'. The book contains the usual range of recipes of Swiss dishes. Special features are the twenty pages of 'modern health cookery', devoted mainly to the movement of 'reform' cooking connected with the name of Dr Bircher of *Bircher Müesli* fame, and the two appendices with lists of Swiss sausages and Swiss breads. Trudi Christiansen-Bär has written a booklet just on *Swiss cookies* (Salt Lake City, Utah: Edelweiss Publications, 1983. 87p.). Her recipes evoke mouthwatering memories from childhood.

698 **The Swiss cookbook.**

Nika Standen Hazelton. New York: Atheneum, 1973. 371p.

Hazelton is well known for her many cookbooks. Her book on Swiss cooking profits from the fact that she spent her childhood in Switzerland and visited the country many times thereafter. The first part of the book is a personal 'cook's tour' in which Ms Hazelton tells us of festive meals and such things as eating habits in the Emmental valley, hospitality on Swiss trains, and Swiss wines and cheeses. Hazelton includes only authentically Swiss dishes. The Swiss do eat sauerbraten and pizzas but these dishes are native to neighbouring countries and, therefore, not included. The second part of the book contains 250 recipes. Tested in American kitchens, each serves four to six persons. They include regional and local dishes and German-, French-, and Italian-Swiss specialities, from appetizers to desserts. This book is a must for those wanting to learn about Swiss cuisine

Food and Drink

699 **Cooking in Switzerland.**

Marianne Kaltenbach. Münster, FRG: Wolfgang Hölker, 1984. 160p.

Kaltenbach, a Swiss author of cookbooks and gastronomic journalist, has her own restaurant 'Zum Raben' in Luzern. After a brief 'gastronomic tour through Switzerland' follow twelve chapters with recipes on groups of dishes, from soups and stews to fish, meat, offal, poultry and game, potato dishes, vegetables, cheese and egg dishes, sweet main meals, cereals and pasta, as well as spicy pies and pastries, desserts, cakes and pies, cookies, and holiday and deep-fried pastries. The recipes are announced as 'collected, recorded and tested by Marianne Kaltenbach'. The book is decorated with old-style drawings.

700 **Swiss cooking.**

Anne Mason. London: Deutsch, 1964. 154p.

In gathering the recipes for this Swiss cookbook, Mason was careful to choose only recipes that have a tradition and could be duplicated in the kitchen of an English housewife. Thus, recipes that call for cheeses unavailable outside the country, call for exotic ingredients or require modern gadgets are not included. There are specialities from all four language areas, from different cantons and regions. Mason has a short chapter each on Swiss wines, the making of preserves and on such well-known Swiss fare as the *Birchermüsli* or the Swiss dumpling called *Spätzli*. From soups to entrées and desserts, there is a nice variety that permits anyone to put together a genuine Swiss meal far away from the native kitchen. The instructions are easy to follow and titbits about the origin and history of some of the recipes enhance this cookbook.

701 **A toast to Swiss wine.**

Doug Sager. *Swiss Scene: News and Views on Switzerland*, vol. 7, no. 9 (September 1989), p. 10-21.

This chatty little article provides about as much information on Swiss wines and wine-growing in Switzerland as can be found anywhere in English. Sager's emphasis is on the wines grown in French Switzerland, understandably so, since this is the part of the country that produces by far the largest quantity of Swiss wines. The other regions are mentioned briefly with their major products, the Merlot from Canton Ticino, and the Pinot Noir from the St Gallen Rhine valley. The light country wines from Cantons Zurich and Schaffhausen are not found worthy of any comments by Sager. Sager describes the main types of grapes used to produce the wines and the conditions under which they are grown. The difficult terrain in Canton Valais and along Lake Geneva makes wine production expensive. The illustrated article is rounded out by comments about wine tasting, the what, where, when and how of wine drinking, and wines in Swiss gastronomy, and by a vintage chart of the 1980s. Swiss wine, in general, should be drunk young. A calendar of wine festivals in all parts of the country is also included in this informative article.

702 **Guide fromage suisse 1989.** (Swiss cheese guide 1989.)

Edited by the Swiss Cheese Union. Bern: Swiss Cheese Union, 1988. 132p. maps.

Two-thirds of this guide in four languages (French, German, Italian, and English) are taken up by a list of restaurants where people can enjoy cheeses from Switzerland 'in the most pleasant surroundings'. The specialities of the houses are indicated by symbols. The guide then lists 'sights to see' in all parts of Switzerland, i.e. places that are associated with Swiss cheeses, folk customs, and agriculture. Some two dozen entries refer the reader to agricultural museums and dairies where visitors may see how cheese is made. The section on 'famous cheeses from Switzerland' reveals the fact that Switzerland produces cheeses other than Emmental ('Switzerland Swiss' in the USA) and Gruyère. The pleasant booklet with its colour illustrations of cheese dishes is available free from Swiss Cheese Union, Inc., P.O. Box 8273, CH-3001 Bern.

703 **Culinary excursions through Switzerland.**

Peter Widmer. Künzelsau, FRG; Männedorf, Switzerland: Sigloch, 1985. 213p.

This cookbook is so beautifully appointed, the glossy paper so elegant, that few will use it in their kitchen. The author, after sketching Switzerland's past, introduces the reader to the country's cheese- and wine-making traditions, to its many festivals and customs, and to its alpine and urban regions, with an eye on the culinary delights they feature. Widmer raises the question: What is Swiss cuisine? The answer is not easily found. While some see the Swiss cuisine as a 'mosaic of the cuisines of neighbouring Germany, France, Italy, and Austria', others are quick to mention *Rösti* and *fondue* but little else. Widmer looked for dishes from the native and 'home-grown' cuisine which consist of simple and hardy fare. His recipes have been handed down from generation to generation, are native to a certain area, and were not altered to reflect modern ingredients. Of the approximately seventy recipes, eleven are potato dishes; soups and casseroles are also prominently featured. Each recipe is preceded by some interesting fact about its origin and takes up just one fourth of the double page, while the rest is one glorious photograph of the prepared dish, complete with tablecloth, china, silver, a bottle of wine, and an appropriate garnish. The many ways in which the simple dishes are presented reveal a table culture that will inspire any cook to look for more varied and attractive ways to serve foods.

Sports and Recreation

Sports

704 **Portrait of a pioneer: Sir Arnold Lunn, 1888-1974: the Arnold Lunn memorial lecture held under the auspices of the Ski Club of Great Britain and the Alpine Ski Club, London, May 10th, 1979.**
Walter Amstutz. Dübendorf, Switzerland: De Clivo, 1979. 20p.

This is a eulogy of Sir Alfred Lunn filled with personal reminiscences and anecdotes by one of his close Swiss friends. Lunn, who received an honorary DPhil degree in 1954 from the University of Zurich, is praised as the inventor of Alpine downhill and slalom racing and a great friend of Switzerland, as reflected in his many publications.

705 **Leisure-time activities: sports, games and hiking.**
Hans Brunner. In: *Modern Switzerland*, edited by J. Murray Luck. Palo Alto, California: Society for the Promotion of Science and Scholarship, 1978, p. 255-74.

Brunner, professor at the Swiss School for Physical Education and Sports in Magglingen in the Bernese Jura, provides an informative overview of the role of sport in Swiss life and of the major sports organizations of the country. He stresses that sport is primarily the domain of non-governmental sports clubs and, as a leisure-time activity, must not interfere with education or the job. The state, however, plays a role in the area of physical fitness – it has mandated three hours of instruction in physical education and sports per week for boys and girls in all Swiss schools, and for teenagers the federal government provides opportunities for instruction in many kinds of sports. Annual rifle or pistol shooting practice is compulsory for all Swiss males of military age. Switzerland with its many lakes, forests, and mountains provides many opportunities for sports such as hiking, mountaineering, orienteering, cycling, swimming, and sailing in summer, and skiing, cross-country skiing, skating, ice hockey, sledging, and curling, among others, in winter. Excellent means of communication and transport ease the accessibility of the arenas for sports activities.

706 **Swiss handguns: Swiss pistols and revolvers from 1817 to the present day in words and illustrations.**
Fritz Häusler. Frauenfeld, Switzerland: Häusler, 1975. 140p.

Printed in German, French, and English, this book covers all ordinance handguns issued by the Swiss army since 1817, as well as the development of civilian handguns during the last few decades. The 112 illustrations, captioned in three languages, show the weapons, often with details of interest to the collector. The English-language text is on pages 119-40. This book should delight gun fanciers.

707 **The story of ski-ing.**
Arnold Lunn. London: Eyre & Spottiswoode, 1952. 224p.

This is for the most part the history of British skiing, one of mankind's oldest sports, dating back to c.2500 BC. The range of experiences and competitions described in this book are predominantly taken from the Swiss scene. The development of skiing equipment and techniques, the founding and activities of clubs, the popularity and kinds of competitions are traced up to the close of World War II. A table at the back records the results of championships and winter Olympic Games in skiing from 1925 to 1951.

708 **Foot-loose in the Swiss Alps.**
William E. Reifsnyder, Rachel Burbank. San Francisco: Sierra Club, 1974. 444p. 32 maps. bibliog. (A Sierra Club Totebook).

The first six chapters of this pocket-sized guide give general information useful to the understanding and enjoyment of hiking in the Swiss Alps. They describe geological and geographical aspects of the Alps, provide a helpful vocabulary for talking with German- and French-speaking people, give valuable tips about transport, communication, and clothing needs, and inform about special lodging arrangements provided by the Swiss Alpine Club (SAC). In the seven chapters that follow, extended and worthwhile hiking trips through many parts of the Swiss Alps are described. Maps set out distances and elevations along the different trails.

709 **The Cresta Run: history of the St. Moritz Tobogganing Club.**
Michael Seth-Smith, foreword by Prince Philip, Duke of Edinburgh. London [etc.]: Foulsham, 1976. 272p.

This book deals with a very small chapter of the history of winter sports and tourism in Switzerland. In 1884 a few Englishmen sojourning in St Moritz employed the services of a young Swiss geometrician to design a tobogganing track from St Moritz to the village of Cresta which would include curves and banks and could be iced. No sooner was the course built than the tobogganing enthusiasts organized a race, dubbed the Grand National. It was held on 18 February 1885, and was lost by the St Moritzers to a team that had come over from Davos. The book, with its many illustrations, describes the evolution of the sport through the decades of the 20th century, the ups and downs of the St Moritz Tobogganing Club, and the modifications to the great Cresta Run, the hero of the book. As Prince Philip points out in his foreword, the goings-on and some of the characters involved 'are in the best traditions of British eccentricity'. Roger Gibbs's *The Cresta Run 1885-1985* (London: Melland, 1985. 64p. bibliog.) is an enticing picture book that succeeds in capturing the flavour of the changing nature of the sport from the early, 'primitive', sledging to today's racing with ultra-modern streamlined super sledges. In the process we are given a lively impression of winter sports in St Moritz through the decades.

Sports journals

710 **Naturfreund.** (Friend of nature.)
Zurich: Landesverband Naturfreunde Schweiz, 1920- . bimonthly. ca. 30p.

This illustrated magazine contains articles, news, and advertisements for hikers, cross-country skiers, birdwatchers, environmentalists, and other friends of nature.

711 **Petri-Heil. Schweizerische Fischereizeitung.** (St Peter's luck: Swiss fishing newspaper.)
Zurich: Graf & Neuhaus, 1942- . monthly. ca. 16p.

Promoted as 'the independent, illustrated sportsfishermen newspaper', this publication is all about fish and fishing in Swiss lakes and rivers, with much information about the numerous fishermen's organizations that exist in many parts of the country.

712 **Rad und Motor Sport. Das aktuelle Rad- und Motorsport-Magazin.** (Bicycle and motorcycle sport: the up-to-date bicycle and motorcycle sports magazine.)
Zurich: Schweizerischer Rad- und Motorfahrer-Bund, 1901- . weekly. ca. 30p.

Articles in this publication are mainly about bicycle racing, with reports about and results of races. The journal also includes a current calendar of coming events, as well as news from the many clubs that belong to the Swiss Bicycle and Motorcycle Federation.

713 **Schweizerjäger.** (Swiss hunter.)
Bern: 1969- . bimonthly. ca. 60p.

This publication is the official organ of the Swiss licensed hunters and wildlife protection federation. It includes articles with an emphasis on the preparation of hunters to receive the hunting permit and reports on coming hunts and other events, with news from member clubs throughout the country.

714 **Ski. Schweizer Skisport.** (Ski: Swiss ski sport.)
Derendingen, Switzerland: Habegger, 1968- . 8 times per year. ca. 45p.

The official organ of the Swiss Ski Federation, this publication gives most of its space to the exploits of the Swiss Alpine men's and women's skiing teams and their individual members. Nordic skiing also receives some attention, as does ski jumping.

715 **Sport.**
Zurich: Sport, 1920- . 3 times per week. ca. 20p.

The leading Swiss sports newspaper with a circulation of 84,000, *Sport* covers all competitive sports in which Swiss participate. It also includes investigative reports and editorials. The major French-language sports newspaper is *Semaine sportive*; it appears twice weekly, with a circulation of 19,700.

716 **Sport aktiv. Zeitschrift für Turnen und Leichtathletik.** (Active sport: journal for gymnastics and track and field events.)
Solothurn, Switzerland: Vogt-Schild, 1858- . 25 times per year. ca. 40p.

This is the official organ of the Federal Associations of Gymnasts (*Kunstturner*) and National Games Athletes (*Nationalturner*), and of the Swiss Track and Field Federation. It contains short, illustrated articles on the sports of the participating organizations and their successful members and reports about national and international competitions. There are also articles on exercise and news from the clubs affiliated with the national organizations.

Mountaineering

717 **The Alpine journal: a record of mountain adventure and scientific observation.**
Alpine Club. London: Alpine Club, 1864- .

The first volume, 1863-64, of this venerable journal was published in London in 1864, containing accounts of ascents and excursions in various parts of the Alps, with maps, woodcuts and lithographs. Founded by John Ball, the Alpine Club's first president, this journal was to be 'a record of mountain adventure and scientific observation'. It served the Victorian mountaineers and succeeding generations of nature lovers as an outlet for describing their experiences in the Alps and other mountainous regions of the world. The frequency of its publication varied over the years. Volume 92 for the year 1987 has very little about the Alps in its 327 pages, and almost all articles, illustrated with full-page black-and-white photographs, describe climbing high mountains in other parts of the world. The substantial book review section is valuable for its leads to publications about all aspects of mountaineering.

718 **The early Alpine guides.**
Ronald Clark. London: Phoenix House, 1949. 208p. maps. bibliog.

The early guides had to find their way without maps, paths at higher altitudes, or huts for shelter. They had to develop the techniques of mountaineering, while serving as pack-animals and toilers in the rock and ice for the amateur climbers whom they served. This book tells the story of some of the 'exceptional men whose ability made them the friends of many eminent Victorians'. Among them are the Valaisans Andermatten and Bennen, the Oberländer Lauener, Almer, and Anderegg, and the Chamonix men Balmat and Croz – they and others are featured in this book, together with the Englishmen who hired them. Photographs of a considerable number of these pioneers and a table of the principal ascents between 1842 and 1882 illustrate this work. A special place is reserved for white-bearded Christian Almer of Grindelwald and his petite wife, who climbed the Wetterhorn in 1896 on their golden wedding anniversary.

719 **The Victorian mountaineers.**

Ronald Clark. London: Batsford, 1953. 232p.

Clark describes the nascent sense of reverence which arose from man's contemplation of the Alps, how the new-found interest in the world above the snow-line was popularized, and how the sport of mountain-climbing was created from scratch. It was during the second half of the 19th century that British barristers, scientists, clergymen, and gentlemen of leisure 'strode, half conquerors, half pilgrims, into the remote world of the high Alps'. One chapter is given to a brief history of the Alpine Club, founded in London in 1857, while others deal with Edward Whymper, the conqueror of the Matterhorn, W. A. B. Coolidge, 'the Boswell of the Alps', women climbers, and mountaineering in Britain.

720 **A history of mountaineering in the Alps.**

Claire Eliane Engel. Westport, Connecticut: Greenwood, 1977. 296p. bibiog. (Originally published in 1950 by Scribner's, New York.)

The 17th century is the historical epoch that marks the beginning of mountain climbing. In the early days, fear of or disinterest in the unknown 'horned summits' prevailed, and legends of dragons and ghastly mountain stories made the rounds. Scientists were the first to penetrate these unknown fortresses in the pursuit of their scientific studies, but later they were joined by passionate climbers, explorers, and, finally, tourists. Many of the experiences of the early lovers of the Alps found their way into journal articles, literary works, and monographs – the press featured those who were first to reach a peak or to ascend an old peak by a new and more dangerous route. Improved climbing methods came to their aid, and the Alpine Club did much in making access to the Alps easier and safer. A chapter on 'Mountains in War-Time' shows both the dangers the Alps presented and the protection they afforded. Some black-and-white illustrations are included.

721 **The white spider: the story of the north face of the Eiger.**

Heinrich Harrer, Kurt Maix, translated from the German by Hugh Merrick. London: Hart-Davis, MacGibbon, 1976. 2nd rev. ed. 312p. map.

Illustrations in black-and-white give a good idea of what an incredible challenge the conquest of the north face of the Eiger mountain presented to even an experienced mountain climber. The Eiger is one of three peaks belonging to the Jungfrau group. During the 1930s it became an obsession for climbers from many nationalities to reach the Eiger by way of the exceedingly steep *Nordwand*. A list at the back of the book informs the reader of about fifty such attempts. The first attempt, in 1935, was fatal. The first successful ascent took place in 1938; Heinrich Harrer was a member of the party.

722 **A century of mountaineering 1857-1957.**

Arnold Lunn. London: Allen & Unwin, 1956. 263p.

This book was produced for the centenary of the Swiss Alpine Club. Sir Arnold Lunn, who from boyhood days shared his love and knowledge of the Swiss mountains with a large English readership, was eminently qualified to trace the different phases of mountaineering. He tells of the early days of mountain exploration, how men from different corners of the world and for many reasons were drawn to the mountains and how their reactions ran the spectrum from utter contempt to fetishism. He singles out great explorers and shows how new climbing techniques made mountaineering safer and easier. There are a number of illustrations, some in colour.

723 **Matterhorn centenary.**

Sir Arnold Lunn. London: George Allen & Unwin, 1965. 144p.

Sir Arnold Lunn, an authority on Swiss mountaineering, wrote this book on the history of the Matterhorn to coincide with the centenary of its first successful ascent by Edward Whymper in 1865. Other ascents described, some of them fatal, give a good idea of the fascination this famous mountain has exerted over many alpine climbers from near and far. A few photographs of mountaineers and of the proud Matterhorn are included.

724 **The Matterhorn.**

Guido Rey, translated from the Italian by J. E. C. Eaton; revised with two additional chapters by R. L. G. Irving. Oxford: Blackwell, 1946. 278p.

This book is the 'product of a great passion and of long experience, the intellectual offspring of a man's whole life'. The man in question is Guido Rey. His passion was the Matterhorn, and the book he wrote is one of the more colourful and passionate in Alpine literature. Rey, born on the Italian side of the fascinating mountain, belongs to the second generation of Matterhorn climbers, following the 'pioneers' and 'conquerors' whose exploits he describes in the first three chapters of his book. He himself put his skills and enthusiasm into attempts to ascend the mountain by new routes via the Z'Mutt ridge and the Furggen ridge at the very end of the 19th century. The qualities of the great mountaineer and guide come through in the descriptions of his successes as well as failures, namely confidence and daring, foresight and prudence, indomitable perseverance, and an iron will. Irving's additions consist of some forty photographs of Matterhorn scenes and climbers, a number of endnotes, and two chapters in which Rey's story is mundanely carried through the period of World War I and beyond.

725 **Eiger: wall of death.**

Arthur Roth. London: Gollancz, 1982. 351p.

The face of the Eiger mountain in the Bernese Oberland, the *Nordwand* (north face), was denounced earlier in this century by the president of the Alpine Club as 'an obsession of the mentally deranged'. The unclimbable wall was conquered at last in 1938. Roth retells the story of the many men, all highly experienced mountaineers, who attacked the Eiger *Nordwand*, for a long time unsuccessfully; for some the price of failure was death, by falling off the face of the mountain or being swept off by snowslides, by having their heads smashed by plummeting rocks, by freezing to the wall in slabs of ice, trapped by their own gear, by dying of cold and hunger, or by being strangled to death by their ropes. The heroic deeds of rescue teams are also described. The words are reinforced by dramatic photographs that give a good impression of the difficulties of this mountain. Modern extreme alpinism has led to ascents in winter, by direct routes, and solo, but not yet to success in 'clean' or 'free' climbing, that is, climbing without any kind of supportive equipment. This is a fascinating book.

726 **Die Alpen. Zeitschrift des Schweizer Alpen-Clubs.** (The Alps: Journal of the Swiss Alpine Club.)

Schweizer Alpen-Club. Bern: Stämpfli, 1925- . quarterly journals; monthly bulletins.

An illustrated magazine, about 70 pages in length, with popular articles on subjects related to mountaineering and the Alps.

727 **The playground of Europe.**

Leslie Stephen. London: Longmans, Green, 1871. 321p.

This is a collection of articles that Stephen (1832-1904) wrote for various British magazines. An Anglican clergyman who achieved notoriety when he relinquished Holy Orders and wrote about his experiences in *An agnostic's apology*, Stephen was an enthusiastic mountaineer and faithful member of the Alpine Club over which he also presided. In *The playground of Europe*, one of the best-written books on Alpine climbing, he claims that 'whilst all good and wise men necessarily love the mountains, those love them best who have wandered longest in their recesses, and have most endangered their own lives and those of their guides in the attempt to open out routes amongst them'. Stephen's stories of ascents of peaks and crossings of glacier passes, or *Jochs*, in the Bernese and Valais Alps during the 1860s are lively and often humorous. With refreshing understatement he 'utterly repudiate[s] the doctrine that Alpine travellers are or ought to be the heroes of Alpine adventures'. Whatever credit there is must go to the guides, and this holds true even of one Michel about whom he advises 'see that [he] is in his normal state of sobriety when you take him for a guide, and carry the brandy-flask in your own pocket'. Stephen's excursions also extended to the Dolomites and the Carpathian mountains, but he invariably returned to the Swiss Alps, which he had in mind when he gave his book the catchy and now famous title 'the playground of Europe'.

728 **A survey of early American ascents in the Alps in the nineteenth century.**

J. Monroe Thorington. American Alpine Club, 1943. 83p. bibliog.

Americans were among the early travellers to the Alps. The earliest description of the crossing of an Alpine pass by an American dates from September 1763 when Philadelphians John Morgan and Samuel Powel had themselves carried in chairs across the Mont Cenis pass. Thorington, president of the American Alpine Club, gathered his material from written and oral reports, diaries, press notices, and *Führerbücher*, books which the guides kept. Most of the booklet is devoted to ascents of Mont Blanc, but it also lists some 100 individual Americans with brief biographical sketches and, in some instances, photographs. The whole of the rest of the Alps is dealt with in fewer than twenty pages.

729 **Hours of exercise in the Alps.**

John Tyndall. Ann Arbor, Michigan [etc.]: University Microfilm International, 1978. 473p. (Reprint of the 1897 edition published by D. Appleton, New York).

This is a collection of twenty-six essays written by Tyndall (1820-93) to save 'the memory of strong and joyous hours' spent in the Alps and to please mountain-lovers. Tyndall achieved a pre-eminent position as a scientist during the 1860s thanks to his work in the Alps on glaciers and the properties of air, light, and sound at high altitudes. In the pursuit of his scientific studies he began to enjoy mountaineering for its own sake. He wrote: 'Herein consisted the fascination of the Alps for me; they appealed at once to thought and feeling, offering their problems to one and their grandeur to the other, while conferring upon the body the soundness and the purity necessary to the healthful exercise of both'. He describes mountaineering expeditions in the Alps, from Mont Blanc in the west to Piz Morteratsch in the east. He stresses that 'the perils in the High Alps are terribly real' and illustrates this point with lively accounts of accidents and near-accidents.

730 **Scrambles amongst the Alps in the years 1860-1869.**
Edward Whymper. London [etc.]: Nelson, 1900. 5th ed. 480p. (Originally published in 1871).

Whymper's famous book tells the story of his assaults on the Matterhorn which culminated in the first successful ascent of 13-15 July 1865. His triumph occurred only five years after Whymper (1840-1911) first set eyes on a mountain. Sent to the Continent to sketch some of the great Alpine peaks for a London publisher, he caught the mountaineering fever. He practised mountain climbing in the French and Valais Alps, getting closer and closer to the Matterhorn, the mountain that held an irresistible attraction for him, mainly because it had never been climbed. He and three other Englishmen conquered it with the help of their Chamonix and Zermatt guides, narrowly beating a team that ascended from the Italian side. On the way down an accident cost the lives of four of the members of the party of seven. Whymper's *Scrambles* describes other exploits of his, most of them 'new excursions', in other words, climbs never before made by others. He succeeds well in capturing the flavour of the pioneering days of alpinism. But it was the story of the tragic end of the first ascent of the Matterhorn that made Whymper into a international figure. This book has become a classic of Alpine literature and is still being published (London: Century; Toronto: Lester & Orpen Deneau, 1985. 412p. map). Introduced by Ronald W. Clark, and illustrated with Whymper's own drawings, the work is praised as 'the world's leading story of mountain adventure since it was published in 1871'.

731 **Women on the rope: the feminine share in mountain adventure.**
Cicely Williams. London: Allen & Unwin, 1973. 240p. bibliog.

Williams, an experienced mountaineer herself, relates the story of 'the feminine share in mountain adventure'. It had its beginning in 1808 when a young Chamonix woman let herself be dragged and carried by guides to the top of Mont Blanc. She afterwards used the tales of her mountain prowess to attract customers to her tea stall. The first woman to climb Mont Blanc, rather than being hauled, was Henriette d'Angeville, whom contemporaries came to call the bride of Mont Blanc – she achieved her feat in 1838. From these beginnings more 'petticoat pioneers' slowly began to climb in the Valais Alps and the Bernese Oberland. In 1907 the Ladies' Alpine Club was founded, and before long there were 'ladies only' ascents. In recent years women teams, *cordées féminines* (roped parties of women climbers), have climbed peaks in the Himalayas, and the 1971 International Expedition to Mount Everest included a woman for the first time. Williams's story, supported by photographs, is entertaining and informative; she displays exact and detailed knowledge of a little-known chapter of human enterprise.

Leisure

732 **Camping Führer '89 Schweiz.** (Camping guide '89 Switzerland.)
Edited by Abteilung Publikationen des TCS. Geneva: Touring Club der Schweiz, 1989. 40th ed. 442p.

This guide lists all Swiss camping places in eleven regions of Switzerland and 300 of the most beautiful camping sites in other parts of Europe. It provides much detail on each camping place, with colour photos of the larger ones and location maps. It also contains a wide range of general cultural and practical information.

733 **Leisure time in Switzerland: Switzerland for leisure.**
Edited by Kümmerly & Frey. Bern: Kümmerly & Frey, 1975. 128p. 12 maps.

This is a handy atlas in four languages, created by Kümmerly & Frey, the leading publisher of maps and geographical materials in Switzerland, which informs its readers of the many possibilities of spending one's leisure time in Switzerland. The atlas is divided into sections on sports, spas and health centres, nature and environment, cultural and historical monuments, museums, libraries and adult education centres, music, theatre and film, festivals and congresses, and fairs. Each section contains pertinent information in abbreviated style, such as addresses of local tourist offices, or the opening times of museums. A series of twelve schematic maps gives a visual image of the geographical location of the various leisure-time activities. A map of Switzerland on the scale of 1:300,000, with a wealth of graphically represented facts, is part of this smartly packaged publication.

734 **Das grosse Freizeit- und Ferienreisebuch Schweiz.** (The big leisure- and vacation travel book Switzerland.)
Edited by Kümmerly & Frey. Bern: Kümmerly & Frey; Geneva: Touring Club der Schweiz (TCS), 1989. 528p. maps.

This is, among other things, a beautiful and very rich picture book on Switzerland. With its suggestions for one hundred hiking trips, fifty bicycle tours, and twelve adventures on Swiss rivers it is an almost inexhaustible source of ideas for meaningful leisure activities. Each recommended route is described in detail and accompanied by a panoramic map. Among the book's other features are a nature section with illustrated descriptions of flowers, animals, minerals, and fossils; a section on weather and climate; an overview of the history of settlement of the country; lists of the TCS-controlled camping places and of youth hostels; addresses of zoos and nature parks, botanical gardens, and tourist offices.

735 **Schweizer Jassbuch.** (Swiss jass book.)
Edwin J. Nigg. Niederteufen, Switzerland: Schellen Verlag, 1977. 120p.

This is an entertaining little book about Switzerland's favourite game called *Jass*. *Jass* is played everywhere, in the family, around the *Stammtisch* in restaurants, during a break at work, or on television shows. The booklet tells about the origin and long tradition of the card game and explains the rules of more than seventy different versions of the game. As a special feature it provides a short history of playing-cards, enriched by illustrations of cards from many parts of Europe. The author received the materials for his booklet from the archives of the Schaffhausen firm of AG Müller which has provided Swiss *Jass* players with cards for more than 150 years.

736 **Schweizerische Schachzeitung. Obligatorisches Organ des Schweizerischen Schachverbandes.** (Swiss chess review. Mandatory organ of the Swiss chess federation.)
Schweizerischer Schachverband. Zug, Switzerland: Zürcher, 1900- . monthly. ca. 30p.

This publication contains reports about chess tournaments and club competitions with numerous matches and diagrams, and also some instructional material, such as opening strategies, and chess problems. There is also news from member clubs and a calendar of coming events. News about Swiss national and international chess tournaments with move-by-move recapitulations of many matches are contained in *Die Schachwoche. Aktuelle Schachnachrichten aus aller Welt* (The chess week: current chess news from all over the world) (Schachagentur Caissa. Sarmenstorf, Switzerland: Schachagentur Caissa, 1980- . 50 times per year. ca. 30p.)

737 **Walking in Switzerland.**
Brian Spencer. Ashbourne, England: Moorland; Edison, New Jersey: Hunter, 1986. 207p. maps.

Spencer describes a selection of easy-to-follow walks in ten centres across Switzerland, namely, Appenzell, Arosa, St Moritz, Saas Fee, Grindelwald, Kandersteg, Champex, Zermatt, Altdorf, and Münster (Obergoms). He advises users of his guide on how to reach these places and which maps to use for the walks.

738 **Camping 89 in Switzerland.**
Edited by Verband Schweizerischer Campings. Zurich: Verband Schweizerischer Campings, 1989. maps.

Written in five languages (German, French, Dutch, English, and Spanish) this guide covers Switzerland in eleven regions, each individually paginated. Swiss camping sites are very popular because they are generally well run and well kept and situated in areas of scenic beauty. The Society of Swiss Camping Site Owners has classified the sites according to location, amenities, management, and sanitary installations.

Coin and stamp collecting

739 **The coinage of Switzerland, 1850 to date: an up-to-date pricing guide.**
Robert L. Clarke. Chicago: Argonaut Publishers, 1969. 64p.

In the first part of this book, the author gives some historical background of coins beginning with pre-Roman times. He talks about Swiss coinage in general and sets 1850 as the date for modern coinage. Each Swiss coin is then briefly discussed with information on the metal composition and dates of issue. Commemorative and shooting festival coins are included. The second part of the book pictures each type of coin and provides data for the collector; the pricing guide distinguishes five grades (four for gold) and lists dealers' asking prices in the United States at the time this book was published.

740 **Schweizer Münzen und Banknoten. Der Katalog für Sammler.** (Swiss coins and banknotes: the catalogue for collectors.)
Herbert Rittmann. Zurich: Ex Libris, 1980. 176p. bibliog.

The substantial introduction (64 pages, double columns) to this volume provides an informative history of money in Switzerland from the striking and circulation of coins at the time of the Old Confederation to the development of the modern monetary system. During the 19th century a plethora of coins of foreign and cantonal origin, with widely varying gold and silver contents, hampered trade and commerce. Notwithstanding the negative effect on business which the lack of standardization had, the federal government was unable to assume the sole right to coin and issue money, especially banknotes, until the outbreak of World War I, when the Federal Council declared that the notes issued by the Swiss National Bank were the only legal tender in the country. At the same time the 'Swiss' franc with its own distinct value was established. The catalogue has illustrations of all coins issued in Switzerland from the time of the Helvetic Republic in 1799 to the present, including those of the cantons, together with price notations. Illustrations of the banknotes are reproduced in colour.

741 **Helvetische Münzenzeitung.** (Swiss numismatic journal.)
Zurich: Helvetische Münzenzeitung, 1966- . monthly. ca. 50p.

This is basically a price and sales catalogue for Swiss coins, with one or two informative articles on numismatic subjects and many announcements of meetings and auctions.

742 **The postage stamps of Switzerland 1843-1862.**
Paul Mirabaud, Alex de Reuterskiöld. Lawrence, Massschusetts: Quarterman Publications, 1975. 286p. bibliog.

Originally published in Paris in 1899, this book has much information on the early postal history of Switzerland. The first part describes the cantonal stamp issues that preceded the federal assumption of postal service; these include the Zurich 4 and 6, the various Geneva Eagles and the Basel Dove. A number of transitional stamps were followed by the first official federal issues, the Poste local or Ortspost, Rayon, and 'Silk Threads' stamps. One hundred pages of the book are devoted to early cancellations, here called 'obliterations', with hundreds of dated facsimiles, probably the most valuable section of the book for the collector of classic Swiss stamps. The plates at the back are of poor quality; black-and-white images have been substituted for the original colour plates.

743 **Schweizer Briefmarken-Zeitung.** (Swiss philatelic journal.)
Bern: Buri Druck, 1889- . monthly. ca. 70p.

This is the official organ of the union of the association of Swiss philatelic societies, with short articles on stamps and the collection of stamps from all over the world. Half the space is taken up with advertisements by stamp dealers and auctioneers. A relatively recent addition to the field of specialized philatelic journals, reflecting a newly emphasized trend in stamp collecting (the collecting of complete sets) is the *Postgeschichte Internationale Fach-Zeitschrift für den Brief- und Stempelsammler* (Postal history: international specialized journal for the collector of letters and cancellations) (Zürich: Postgeschichte-Verlag, 1980- . quarterly. ca. 40p.)

744 **Schweizerische numismatische Rundschau.** (Swiss numismatic review.)
Schweizerische Numismatische Gesellschaft. Lausanne: Anita Schwartz, 1891- . annual. ca. 160p.

This review is published by the Swiss Numismatic Association. Since 1949 the society also issues a quarterly gazette of about thirty pages in length, *Schweizer Münzblätter*, which, like the yearbook, contains scholarly articles, with illustrations, on coins from other epochs of history and book reviews in German or French.

745 **Zumstein-Schweiz/Liechtenstein-Katalog.**
(Zumstein-Switzerland/Liechtenstein stamp catalogue.)
Bern: Zumstein, 1935- . annual. ca. 450p.

Of the several catalogues of Swiss stamps, this is the most widely used. It is handy, nicely printed, informative, with every stamp design depicted in full colour. For every stamp, prices are given for mint condition, unused, cancelled, and on cover. As a new feature, the 1989 edition has an arrow next to the stamp pointing upward or downward indicating the market trend.

Literature

Anthologies

746 **Grenzgänge: Literatur aus der Schweiz 1933-45. Ein Lesebuch.** (Border walks: literature from Switzerland 1933-45; a reader.)
Edited by Hans Rudolf Hilty. Zurich: Unionsverlag, [n.d.]. 552p.

This voluminous anthology is a forum for writers, Swiss and other nationalities, *émigrés*, and refugees who were living and working in Switzerland during the Hitler years. It begins with selections that reflect the challenges and dangers of the 1930s, a time when unemployment was rampant. Hopes for a new Germany that had been kindled by Hitler's advent to power soon turned into a nightmare, and scores of writers left Germany. Many of these uprooted people experienced economic hardship, and even those who were able to live comfortably in exile could not escape the harsh reality of being away from their homeland. The Swiss did not have to fight in the war that broke out in 1939, but they could not close their eyes to the destruction and suffering just over their borders. This book is a documentation of twelve tragic years in Europe's history. It contains works by some one hundred writers from different countries who in one way or another spoke out against the inhumanity of those years. The book ends with short biographies of the writers included, among whom are such well-known figures as Thomas Mann and Hermann Hesse. More than thirty illustrations, mostly graphics in black-and-white, underline the horror of that time.

747 **Schweizer Lyrik des zwanzigsten Jahrhunderts: Gedichte aus 4 Sprachregionen.** (Twentieth-century Swiss poetry: poems from four language regions.)
Edited by Bernd Jentzsch. Zurich; Cologne: Benziger, 1977. 427p. bibliog.

Jentzsch, the compiler of this substantial book, is a native of the German Democratic Republic. His interest and expertise in German-Swiss poetry predate his move to Switzerland in 1977. He has chosen forty-six German-Swiss writers of this century, some writing in their dialect, for inclusion in his anthology. The selection of poems in French, Italian, and Romansh was done in collaboration with colleagues from those language areas. Each of the latter three languages is represented by about fifteen poets, and the editor includes several poems by each writer. The breadth and depth of the content, combined with the informative bio-bibliographical entries at the end of the book produces a veritable handbook of 20th-century Swiss poetry. Jentzsch discusses in his postscript the difficulties he encountered in the selection process, and how he wrestled with the problem of defining the characteristics that give a work its Swiss identity.

748 **Bestand und Versuch. Schweizer Schrifttum der Gegenwart.** (Inventory and experiment: contemporary Swiss literary production.)
Edited by Bruno Mariacher, Friedrich Witz (et al.). Zurich: Ex Libris, 1964. 923p. bibliog.

This survey of contemporary Swiss literature includes samples from the works of more than 160 Swiss writers. They represent all literary genres and are printed in the languages in which they were written, namely German, French, Italian, or Romansh, as well as some Swiss-German dialects. The editors did not intend to present a history of Swiss literature, nor did they want to interpret, evaluate or classify their selections. The diversity of experiences of the different writers living in such a small country is startling and raises anew the question as to what is 'typically Swiss'. The editors attempt to show that Swiss literature, while undeniably a part of the European scene, can stand on its own and, however diverse, has a national character. A bio-bibliographical register at the end of their large volume gives the reader important information about the writers who are included.

749 **Die schönsten Schweizer Erzählungen.** (The most beautiful Swiss stories.)
Edited by Max Rychner. Basel: Berichthaus, [n.d.]. 511p.

The twenty-nine short stories selected for this anthology are mostly by German-Swiss authors. French-Swiss and Italian-Swiss writers are represented by their strongest voices, Charles Ferdinand Ramuz and Francesco Chiesa respectively, and their stories are translated into German. Jeremias Gotthelf, Gottfried Keller, and Conrad Ferdinand Meyer stand out among the 19th-century writers. These three have a secure place not only in the history of Swiss but also of German literature: the first depicted life among the farmers in the Bernese Emmental; the second built his stories around the problem of the relationship of the citizen and the State; and the third used historical themes for his novellas. Friedrich Dürrenmatt and Max Frisch in the 20th century are best known internationally for their dramas, but they have also novels and short stories to their credit. Rychner's anthology provides hours of enjoyable reading.

750 **CH Ein Lesebuch = Choix de textes = Raccolta di testi = Collecziun da texts.** (CH [Confoederatio Helvetica = Switzerland]: a reader.)
Published by the Swiss Federal Council. Bern: Schweizerische Bundeskanzlei, 1975. 684p.

This book has been put together by a team of culturally active intellectuals under the sponsorship of the Swiss Federal Department of the Interior. It assembles prose pieces by more than eighty persons from all the language areas of Switzerland, and the selections are printed in their original languages, without translation. The texts were chosen to reflect and document the intellectual and political life of Switzerland during the one hundred years since the last major revision of the Swiss constitution in 1874. The first part contains articles that discuss the nature and character of the Swiss Confederation in the context of its history and traditions; the bulk of the work presents contributions to the history and understanding of problems and conflicts that confronted the country from the outbreak of World War I to the early 1970s; while the third part discusses issues which demand the continuing attention of the contemporary Swiss. Among the individuals chosen for representation in this work are writers, politicians, artists, businessmen, scientists, academics, and others, four of them women. For each there is a brief bio-bibliography. This book makes fascinating reading; it assembles in a relatively compact space some of the most significant contributions to and commentaries on Swiss intellectual life in the 20th century.

751 **Anthology of modern Swiss literature.**

Edited by H. M. Waidson. London: Wolff; New York: St Martin's Press, 1984. 228p. bibliog. (International PEN Books Anthologies, 4).

Waidson's anthology consists of poems and short prose pieces by about seventy writers from all four language regions of Switzerland. In his introduction to the volume Waidson talks about Swiss neutrality and the difficulties Swiss writers have to overcome because of the smallness of their country, but correctly concludes that 'the difficulties and professional occupations of writers in Switzerland are no doubt comparable to the position of many authors in Great Britain and many other parts of the world'. He does not reveal what criteria he used in the selection of the entries included in this anthology, and works of established writers are mixed in with those of lesser-known ones; some poems are in traditional verse form, while others represent the style of the avant-garde; the prose pieces are brief excerpts from larger works. The value of this anthology lies in the fact that these samples give English-language readers access to works by Swiss writers that are otherwise unavailable. Waidson, who translated most of the German texts and some of the French himself, achieves his goal of demonstrating that 'Switzerland has at present a lively, varied and often exciting literary landscape'.

Literary history and criticism

752 **Swiss literary culture since 1945: productive antagonisms and conflicting identities.**

Michael Böhler. *German Quarterly*, published by the American Association of Teachers of German, vol. 62, no. 3 (Summer 1989), p. 293-307.

In literature the blending of the four Swiss national languages into a kind of literary unity does not exist. Diversity is the essential cultural basis of Switzerland. Böhler devotes the gist of his perceptive article to the cultural dynamics of German-Swiss literature. As key elements of those dynamics he isolates antagonisms on the cultural, political, and personal level between the writer and his environment and conflicting identities, expressed in a 'wandering point of vision' that makes for shifting perspectives. These forces were at work during the first fifteen years after World War

II, which were 'a kind of Golden Age for Swiss literature'. With Max Frisch and Friedrich Dürrenmatt it rose first to a leadership role in German literature in general, and later even to world prominence. Since then Swiss literature has further evolved – a shift away from social and political criticism toward the subjectivity of a 'new inwardness' indicates that one's identity as a human being in an increasingly dehumanized world is becoming of greater concern to the writer than his identity as a Swiss. Böhler concludes his article with the somewhat startling statement: '. . . Switzerland as a national entity may no longer be a dominant or an explicit theme; implicitly, however, . . . the "Swissness" of Swiss literature is as present as ever'.

753 **Swiss literature.**
In: *Cassell's encyclopaedia of world literature*, J. Buchanan-Brown, general ed. New York: Morrow, 1973, vol. 1, p. 540-42.

Cassell's presents Swiss literature under two subheadings, 'French' and 'German'. The 'French' article was written by Guilbert Guisan, who also wrote eighteen 'Franco-Swiss biographies' in volumes two and three of the encyclopaedia. Hermann Boeschenstein contributed the 'German' article, as well as twenty 'German-Swiss biographies'. The Italian-Swiss writers are summarily dealt with as belonging 'to the main stream of Italian literature', and the only one to have a biographical entry is Chiesa. Romansh literature, on the other hand, has its own separate article on p. 485-86 of volume one, written by Reto Raduolf Bezzola who also contributed eighteen(!) 'Romansh biographies'.

754 **The four literatures of Switzerland.**
Guido Calgari. London: Adam Books, 1963. 29p. bibliog.

This very brief summary in English of Calgari's long work on the four literatures of Switzerland (*Storia delle quattro letterature della Svizzera*. Milano: Nuova Academia Editrice, 1958) takes the reader from the Middle Ages to the 1950s, highlighting events that shaped Swiss life, and singling out the representative works of leading writers. Calgari investigates the effects that the multiplicity of languages have on Swiss letters and tries to define what is typically Swiss in this diverse literature. He finds that 'the intermingling of literature with politics, morals and traditions is a basic characteristic of Swiss literary creation'.

755 **Die vier Literaturen der Schweiz.** (The four literatures of Switzerland.)
Guido Calgari, translated from the Italian by Erika Tobler. Olten, Switzerland; Freiburg, FRG: Walter, 1966. 591p. bibliog.

Calgari, formerly professor of Italian literature at the Federal Institute of Technology in Zurich, divided his book into four parts, one each for the literatures of Alemannic, Rhaeto-Romansh, Italian, and French Switzerland. Within the parts, he follows a chronological outline from the beginnings of each of the respective literatures to the middle of the 20th century. Calgari's narrative, expository style of writing is pleasant to read, and his erudite presentation of the vast subject matter is interspersed with informed personal judgements on schools of writing and individual writers. This work represents a remarkable pioneering achievement; it has become the starting point for anyone dealing with the literatures of Switzerland. A summary version is described above.

756 **Modern Swiss literature: unity and diversity.**
Edited by John L. Flood. London: Wolff; New York: St Martin's Press, 1985. 146p.

This slim volume is made up of eleven papers which were presented at a symposium on Swiss literature in London in March 1984. Four papers of a general nature analyse the forces that shape the works of Swiss writers. Despite the existence of three major cultural and language entities, each with special ties to its neighbour across the border, there is a national responsibility and a sense of loyalty to the fatherland. But pride about the country's history and its democratic political system is mixed with criticism of, among other things, the materialism that seems to dominate Swiss life and of the country's disregard for the preservation of nature. The Romance-language literatures of Switzerland are treated in four essays: a paper on the emergence of a distinct French-Swiss literary culture during the first half of the 20th century is followed by an account of the development of the French-Swiss novel after 1945; the smallest of the Swiss languages, Romansh, receives a brief review of its limitations and perspectives; and the paper on Italian-Swiss writers shows how closely tied their work is to the soil and the history of their native Ticino. Even though the body of their writings is small, they form an important part in the diversity of Swiss literature. Three papers deal with German-Swiss literature: one essay on the *Künstlerroman* from Gottfried Keller to Max Frisch; one on aspects of the contemporary German-Swiss theatre; and one on contemporary Swiss poets writing in German.

757 **Die zeitgenössischen Literaturen der Schweiz.** (The contemporary literatures of Switzerland.)
Edited by Manfred Gsteiger. Zurich; Munich: Kindler 1974. 752p. maps. bibliog. (Kindlers Literaturgeschichte der Gegenwart).

This hefty, richly illustrated volume consists of a lengthy introduction and four chapters by different authors on the four literatures of Switzerland. In his introduction 'Contemporary Switzerland and its literatures', Gsteiger paints a panorama of the interaction between the historical situation of Switzerland during the three decades since the end of World War II and its literary activities. He provides the usual catalogue of factors that contribute to the peculiarity of the Swiss literary scene: linguistic and cultural diversity, difficulties of writers in finding a public sufficiently large to support them, the (presumed) absence of a national consciousness, the conflict between supranational and regional forces, the love–hate relationship of writers with their society, the polarities of smallness and greatness, narrowness and openness, centre and periphery. All these aspects are illustrated with copious references to the lives and works of contemporary writers and literary critics. All persons mentioned in the book are listed in the bio-bibliographies of the appendix. In 1980 an updated edition of this work was published by Fischer Taschenbuch Verlag in Frankfurt am Main as volumes 7 and 8 in *Kindlers Literaturgeschichte der Gegenwart*. All illustrations and maps, a six-page preface by Gsteiger on Swiss literature in the early 1980s, and a few additional titles in the bibliographies were removed.

758 **Swiss literature.**
In: *Encyclopedia of world literature in the 20th century*, edited by Leonard S. Klein. New York: Frederick Ungar, 1984, rev. ed. vol. 4, p. 381-89. bibliog.

The section on Swiss literature in this four-volume encyclopedia is divided into five parts, namely 'Swiss literature in German', written by Robert Acker, 'Swiss literature in Swiss-German', 'Swiss literature in French', 'Swiss literature in Italian', all written by Augustin Maissen and updated by Rita Stein, and 'Swiss literature in Romansh', by John Van Eerde. The articles give a good overview of the major writers and their significant works, and each part ends with a useful bibliography. The encyclopaedia also has separate entries on Spitteler, Ramuz, Walser, Frisch, Dürrenmatt, and possibly others – it is hard to tell, since there is no index, or any other kind of listing of writers.

759 **Swiss literature.**

Heinz K. Meier. In: *Columbia dictionary of modern European literature*, edited by Jean-Albert Bédé, William B. Edgerton. New York: Columbia University Press, 1980, p. 794-97. bibliog.

This brief entry by the editor of the Swiss section of the 1980 *Columbia dictionary of modern European literature* gives a compact overview of and introduction to modern Swiss literature. It presents Swiss literature as a distinguishable entity, in spite of the fact that Swiss writers express themselves in different languages. The *Columbia dictionary of modern European literature* has separate entries on the following Swiss writers and literary critics: Albert Béguin (1901-57) by Suzanne Nalbantian; Peter Bichsel (born 1935), Jakob Bosshart (1862-1924), Meinrad Inglin (1893-1971), and Otto F. Walter (born 1928) by Regula A. Meier; Erika Burkart (born 1922), Friedrich Dürrenmatt (born 1921), Jürg Federspiel (born 1931), Max Frisch (born 1911), Kurt Marti (born 1921), Adolf Muschg (born 1934), and Albin Zollinger (1895-1949) by Rolf Kieser; Blaise Cendrars (1887-1961), Jacques Chessex (born 1934), and Charles Ferdinand Ramuz (1878-1947) by Ursula Schoeni; Francesco Chiesa (1871-1973) and Giuseppe Zoppi (1896-1952) by Hermann W. Haller; Jakob Schaffner (1875-1944) by Hans Bänziger; Carl Spitteler (1845-1924) and Emil Staiger (born 1908) by Marianne Burkhard; Jean Starobinski (born 1920) by Gerda R. Blumenthal; and Robert Otto Walser (1878-1956) by Herbert L. Kaufman. These articles were published as a group in the June 1982 issue of the *Newsletter of the Swiss-American Historical Society* (vol. 18, no. 2), p. 4-39.

760 **Swiss men of letters.**

Edited by Alex Natan. London: Wolff, 1970. 286p. bibliog.

This book consists of twelve essays which are written by different authors and do not have a common theme or follow a discernible outline. Calgari, author of a standard work on the four literatures of Switzerland, provides a short introduction to the historical and cultural characteristics of Swiss literature. Three of the chapters are devoted to French-Swiss writers, among whom Henri-Frédéric Amiel with his *Journal intime* and Charles Ferdinand Ramuz are singled out. A chapter on Italian-Swiss literature explains how the writers of this small canton south of the Alps look to Italy for inspiration. The Rhaeto-Romansh language and its literature present a special case as is ably demonstrated in another chapter. The chapters on German-speaking writers deal with the life and work of well-known individuals such as Jeremias Gotthelf and Max Frisch.

761 **Schweiz = Suisse = Svizzera = Svizra: Schriftsteller der Gegenwart = Ecrivains d'aujourd'hui = Scrittori d'oggi = Scripturs da nos dis.** (Switzerland: writers of today.)
Edited by Schweizerischer Schriftsteller Verband. Bern: Buchverlag Verbandsdruckerei, 1978. 235p.

This reference work gives short bio-bibliographical sketches of Swiss writers from all four language areas: 773 are from the German, 339 from the French, 73 from the Italian, and 28 from the Romansh part of Switzerland. The entries are in the native language of the particular author and are based on questionnaires that were filled out and returned by each writer.

762 **Contexts of literature: an Anglo-Swiss approach.**
Heinrich Straumann. Bern: Francke, 1973. 170p. map. bibliog. (Swiss Studies in English, vol. 75).

Straumann, formerly professor of English studies at the University of Zurich, chose twelve essays, from over fifty he had written over many years, for this book. Each essay investigates how the contact with Switzerland influenced English and American individuals or institutions or vice versa – the contact may have been made on visits to the country or by reading about it. Switzerland is mostly seen in a positive light in the works of Englishmen such as Lord Byron and Matthew Arnold. Swiss literary critics acknowledge the contributions of individuals such as William Faulkner to Swiss literature. English politics and literature of the 1930s and the appearance of the best-seller in America are seen by Straumann as having had a considerable influence on Swiss writing and thought. He calls the mutual influences of little Switzerland and the large English-speaking countries a 'literary phenomenon'.

German-Swiss literature and writers: general

763 **Frisch und Dürrenmatt.** (Frisch and Dürrenmatt.)
Hans Bänziger. Bern; Munich: Francke, 1971. 6th rev. ed. 312p. bibliog.

The first edition of this book dates from 1960. With the rising interest in the Swiss playwrights and novelists Max Frisch (born 1911) and Friedrich Dürrenmatt (born 1921) six additional editions followed in short succession. Both writers' portraits are on the cover but their life, work and development are told separately. Yet, parallels and contrasts between the two are never far from Bänziger's mind. He draws from ample documentation and quotes from the press, theatre people and programmes, critics, the general public, and from speeches by and about Frisch and Dürrenmatt. The origins of many an idea that found its way into the authors' works are shown to be rooted in their background, their life, and experiences. Their harsh criticism and response to a Switzerland that prided itself for having been spared a terrible war, left them open to personal attacks as did their work, especially their dramatic work that broke with tradition. Their names were soon known not only to a German-speaking but a worldwide audience. The profiles of these two foremost Swiss writers of the postwar German literary scene also reveal much of the cultural and political climate of the times. The materials Bänziger has collected on the two men during the last ten years or so are incorporated in *Frisch und Dürrenmatt: Materialien und Kommentare* (Frisch and Dürrenmatt: materials and commentaries) (Tübingen, FRG: Niemeyer, 1987. 184p. bibliog. [Untersuchungen zur deutschen Literaturgeschichte]).

764 **Bibliographie zur deutschsprachigen Schweizerliteratur.** (Bibliography on German-language Swiss literature.)
Bern: Schweizerische Landesbibliothek, 1977- .

Annual typed volumes compiled by different persons from *Das Schweizer Buch* (q.v.) and some forty Swiss journals and newspapers. Volume 11, covering the year 1986 (Bern, 1988), was compiled by Gaby Rauch. It has 2,118 entries, consisting of the titles of works by and of articles and monographs about German-Swiss authors. The bulk of the entries, however, consists of lists of reviews and commentaries on the works of these authors in the daily newspaper press and in journals. The prefatory remark points out that the bibliography has three parts, but since there is no pagination one is at a loss to find them. There is an index of names, but as yet no cumulative index.

765 **Three Swiss realists: Gotthelf, Keller, and Meyer.**
Edited by Robert Godwin-Jones, Margaret T. Peischl. Lanham, Maryland [etc.]: University Press of America, 1988, 234p. bibliog.

A short assessment of the literary and political tradition in Switzerland precedes the analysis of the three Swiss authors presented in this book: Gotthelf, Keller, and Meyer. Products of the nineteenth century, they are, according to Godwin-Jones and Peischl, representatives of German literary realism and excel in the literary genre of the novella. Each author's life and work is then treated separately and is followed by a novella as an example of the individual's writing. The English translations of these novellas were carefully reviewed by Godwin-Jones and Peischl. Gotthelf suffers most in translation, for his idiosyncratic use of standard German mixed with Bernese dialect words and expressions cannot be rendered satisfactorily. The translation of *Hans Joggeli, the rich cousin* (1848) in this volume provides only a faint idea of the power of the country preacher's sermons on good and evil. Keller is best known for his novel *Green Henry*. This liberal, middle-class citizen of Zurich is represented with two shorter works *Pankraz, the sulker* (1855) and *The forger of his fortune* (1860) both taken from his Seldwyla stories. Meyer is the master of the historical novella and the framework technique as is illustrated here with *The monk's wedding* (1884). The comprehensive and didactical treatment afforded the three writers and their work serves also as a fine introduction to Swiss literature in general.

766 **Zeitgenössische Mundartliteratur der deutschen Schweiz: Ein theoretischer und geschichtlicher Überblick.** (Contemporary dialect literature in German Switzerland: a theoretical and historical survey.)
Walter Haas. *Michigan Germanic Studies*, vol. 6, no. 1, 1980, p. 58-119. bibliog.

Existing stereotypes equate dialect with the spoken and popular language of the 'people', and therefore dialect literature is narrowly tied to the spatial and social circles of lower population strata. These stereotypes, Haas maintains, are disappearing in the Swiss context, in as much as dialect is used more and more frequently in the realm of literature in place of high German. Dialect is not only a functional language variety but a formal language system and as such is being applied to a wide range of literary forms. Haas reviews the forms of modern Swiss-German dialect literature from experimental and abstract poetry, to the leading and most widely known kind of contemporary dialect literature, the *chanson*, to the theatre, including translations of classical theatre works into dialect, radio plays (*Hörspiele*), spoken long-playing records, movies, and prose literature, including translations of works from other languages. According to Haas, these modern developments have made dialect literature a genuine part of general literature. German-speaking Switzerland, with close to 3,000 dialect works in print, has possibly the most voluminous dialect literature in the world; yet, scientific literary studies of this substantial body of works are still scarce.

767 **Literaturszene Zürich. Menschen, Geschichten und Bilder 1914 bis 1945.** (The literary scene of Zurich: people, stories, and images 1914 to 1945.)
Gustav Huonker. Zurich: Unionsverlag, 1985. 191p. bibliog.

In eighteen chapters Huonker tells stories of the literary scene of Zurich from the Dada movement in World War I to the first success of Max Frisch as a playwright at the end of World War II. Zurich, always a centre of Swiss literary life, gained additional stature as the city of refuge and exile for writers and artists from many parts of Europe, Hugo Ball, Hans Arp, James Joyce, Bertold Brecht, and Thomas Mann being among the more famous. Huonker writes lovingly about the many lesser-known native writers and their struggle to make a living and find an audience. The ventures of the Zurich publishers are described, as are the productions of the cabarets and theatres. Richly illustrated, with examples of texts and facsimiles, this volume is an impressive documentation of the intellectual life of Zurich and its important role as the home and city of exile of many creative spirits during the turbulent decades between 1914 and 1945.

768 **Contemporary authors of the German-speaking countries of Europe: a selective bibiliography.**
Margrit B. Krewson. Washington, DC: Library of Congress, 1988. 306p.

Pages 248 to 306 of Krewson's compilation contain 492 entries, complete with Library of Congress call numbers of works by and about thirty living German-Swiss writers. Most titles are in German. Some secondary works, especially about Dürrenmatt and Frisch, are listed, without annotations.

769 **German literature in English translation: a select bibliography.**
Patrick O'Neill. Toronto [etc.]: University of Toronto Press, 1981. 242p.

This bibliography with its 1,894 entries achieves its goal of providing a useful tool for 'establishing the availability of readable English versions of the major works of German literature'. The book is divided into five parts, entitled 'general collections', 'before 1700', 'eighteenth century', 'nineteenth century', and 'twentieth century'. In each part writers are listed alphabetically, with separate entries for individual works and different translations of such works. The listing is enumerative rather than critical, and almost all translations are products of 'the golden age of translation' of the post-World War II era. Swiss writers and their translated works are to be found in all sections, if one knows their names. Teachers, for whom this work seems primarily intended, would have profited from a simple system of indicating the national or geographical origin of the writers included.

770 **Die deutschsprachige Literatur der Schweiz seit 1945.** (The German-language literature of Switzerland since 1945.)
Elsbeth Pulver. In: *Die zeitgenössischen Literaturen der Schweiz*, edited by Manfred Gsteiger. Zurich; Munich: Kindler, 1974, p. 141-406. bibliog.

Pulver's long and richly illustrated chapter on German-Swiss literature since 1945 covers every aspect of the topic: prose, poetry, the theatre, dialect writing, literary criticism, essays. She observes that the year 1945 does not represent a distinct break in the course of German-Swiss literature. The tradition of the writers who had been born in the late 19th century, among them Meinrad Inglin and Robert Walser, held sway to the end of the 1950s. Beginning in 1959, however, a new generation of authors, among them Otto F. Walter, Jörg Steiner, and Peter Bichsel, put their stamp on the contemporary German-language literature. Another, somewhat less pronounced, new literary wave began in 1968, when writers appeared on the literary scene who were born mostly after 1939. While Pulver gives Friedrich Dürrenmatt und Max Frisch their due, she is just as attentive to their many less famous contemporaries. She succeeds in making clear how amazingly diverse and rich the literary production of German-speaking Switzerland has been in the decades since World War II.

German-Swiss writers

771 **Salomon Gessner: his creative achievement and influence.**
John Hibberd. Cambridge, England [etc.] : Cambridge University Press, 1976. 183p. bibliog. (Anglica Germanica Series, 2).

Salomon Gessner (1730-88), son of a well-established Zurich middle-class family, achieved fame in Europe during his lifetime. His success was due to his being in harmony with the climate of opinion of his time. He appealed in his literary work to the feeling for nature and natural simplicity that emerged in the mid-18th century. Aristocrats and intellectuals as well as ordinary citizens responded enthusiastically to the combination of moral sentiment and rococo playfulness in his work. Soon after his death, however, he fell out of favour with the public. Hibberd skilfully assesses Gessner's achievements as writer, engraver, and painter and concludes that his artistry has been underrated by literary critics and deserves greater recognition.

772 **A few words about William Shakespeare's plays: by a poor ignorant citizen of the world who had the good fortune to read him.**
Ulrich Bräker, translated by Derek Bowman. London: Wolff, 1979. 112p.

Bräker (1735-98), an impoverished peasant, avid reader, and self-taught poet from the Toggenburg valley in eastern Switzerland, found Shakespeare's plays in a local library. He read them with abandonment and enthusiasm, writing copious notes and commentaries as he went along. His manuscript on Shakespeare's plays consists of twelve volumes, each covering three plays. Bräker is fully absorbed by the characters of the different plays; he converses with them and addresses them directly. At the end he is at a loss how to thank Shakeaspeare for the gift he has presented him, and the last word Bräker utters is 'Amen!' Another book by the author, *The life story and real adventures of the poor man of Toggenburg*, translated from the German by Derek Bowman (Edinburgh: Edinburgh University Press, 1970) was published anonymously in 1789 in Zurich as *Lebensgeschichte und natürliche Abenteuer des Armen Mannes im Toggenburg*. The work immediately appealed to readers because of its originality and simple beauty and became a 'best-seller'.

773 **Jeremias Gotthelf: Leben, Werk, Zeit.** (Jeremias Gotthelf: life, work, time.)

Hanns Peter Holl. Zurich; Munich: Artemis, 1988. 200p. bibliog.

Jeremias Gotthelf (1797-1854), epic storyteller and country preacher, gave his last novel the title *Zeitgeist und Berner Geist* (*Spirit of the Age and Spirit of Bern*). Gotthelf's ministry in the small farming community of Lützelflüh did not keep him from sensing the political climate of the time. He was aware that the world witnessed the advent of great industrial and scientific inventions and Holl examines the writer and his work in that larger context. Gotthelf's literary career did not begin until 1837 with the publication of the *Bauernspiegel* (*The Farmer's Mirror*). The stories take place within a radius of about fifteen miles of his parsonage, the language is that of the simple men and women whose sins need to be eradicated and whom he warns about the pitfalls of the new ways. The novels and novellas are rooted in the present, provincial on the surface, yet, as Holl documents, the farmhands, grandmothers and schoolteachers who populate the stories speak with the voices of people who know what goes on around the world. Gotthelf's collected works consist of twenty-four volumes of literary works and eighteen volumes of letters, sermons, political writings, and speeches. Holl attempts a new grouping of Gotthelf's work according to themes and to problems that characterize the fermenting period of the early 19th century. The book is richly illustrated and an excellent documentation of the time and of the life and work of one of Switzerland's foremost writers.

774 **Jeremias Gotthelf: an introduction to the Swiss novelist.**

H. M. Waidson. Oxford: Blackwell, 1953. 231p. map. bibliog. (Modern Language Studies).

Waidson provides a brief biographical sketch of Jeremias Gotthelf, pseudonym for Albert Bitzius, who spent his life as a Protestant minister to the small Bernese farming community of Lützelflüh. Through his novels and short stories he achieved fame as one of the great prose writers of the 19th century. More than half of the space of the book is taken up by Waidson's discussion of the literary work of Gotthelf. He distinguishes three types of novels – those of social reform, maturity, and politics – and three types of short stories, namely calendar stories, legendary-historical tales, and tales of contemporary realism. Gotthelf's characters, the circumstances, and the colouring of the language were inspired by his parishioners whose misdeeds, greed, prejudice, and godlessness he was trying to eradicate with his sermons in print. The local flavour, derived from the frequent use of Bernese-German peasant dialect and idioms, makes access to Gotthelf's work at times difficult and prevents it from achieving full international recognition, even though Waidson sees Gotthelf in the same class of writers as Scott, Dickens, and Tolstoy. See also 'Jeremias Gotthelf' by J. R. Foster, in *German men of letters: twelve literary essays*, vol. 5, edited by Alex Natan (London: Wolff, 1969).

775 **The black spider.**

Jeremias Gotthelf, translated by H. M. Waidson. Dallas, Texas: Riverrun, 1980. 135p. (First published in translation London: Calder, 1958).

Jeremias Gotthelf was a Bernese country preacher who tried to educate his flock with novels and tales set in his peasant community. To render his message more accessible to his peasant audience he employed colloquial language and idioms and colourful imagery. The black spider is a symbol for the plague and the ensuing battle between good and evil. This short story, first published in 1842, has become the best-known work by the author.

776 **Gottfried Keller 1819-1890.**

In: *Nineteenth-century literary criticism*, vol. 2, edited by Laurie Lanzen Harris. Detroit, Michigan: Gale Research Company, 1982, p. 410-26. bibliog.

The multi-volume publication *Nineteenth-century literature criticism* contains 'excerpts from criticism of the works of novelists, poets, playwrights, short-story writers, and other creative writers who lived between 1800 and 1900, from the first published critical appraisals to current evaluations'. One of the few Swiss writers included to date in this ongoing publication is the novella and short-story writer, novelist, poet, and essayist Gottfried Keller. (The others are Amiel and Wyss.) A brief biographical sketch is followed by whole essays and lengthy excerpts of literary criticism from books and journal articles that appeared between 1880 and 1977 on many aspects of Keller's achievements as a creative writer. The selections give a good introduction to his major works. Together with the titles listed in the 'additional bibliography' they constitute the essence of Keller criticism in English.

777 **Gottfried Keller: life and work.**

J. M. Lindsay. London: Wolff, 1968. 258p. bibliog. (Dufour Editions).

This book is a good introduction to the life and work of Gottfried Keller, citizen of Zurich, Swiss patriot, and writer. Keller (1819-90), who started out as a painter, spent some of his formative years in Germany. These experiences are reflected in his quasi-autobiographical novel *Der grüne Heinrich* (translated as *Green Henry*), first published in 1854, and edited and modified repeatedly until 1880, when it appeared in its final form. Back in Zurich, he took the post of cantonal secretary. His writings of that period in his life reflect the liberalism of the time and the positive attitudes of the burghers toward life and the fatherland. His *Gesammelte Gedichte* (Collected poems, 1883), draw heavily on his own experiences; they tell of his closeness to nature, his love of women which never led to fulfilment, and of his veneration for his native Switzerland, and they establish Keller as a lyric poet. Keller also proves himself to be a master of the short-story form or the novella, as seen in his Seldwyla stories, Zurich novellas, legends, and epigrams. His last work, *Martin Salander* (1886), reflects a growing disenchantment with the turn that national and local politics took under the influence of materialism and industrial expansion.

778 **Conrad Ferdinand Meyer.**

Marianne Burkhard. Boston, Massachusetts: Twayne, 1978. 175p. bibliog.

The literary career of C. F. Meyer (1825-98) did not really begin until the poet reached the age of forty-five. The bulk of his work was written in the course of a mere two decades. Burkhard calls the first phase of Meyer's life 'the long period of preparation' and tells about his early historical interests, the political climate of Zurich and Europe, his bouts of mental illness, and his travels and circle of friends. History, mostly the period of the Renaissance and Reformation, furnishes the background for most of Meyer's novellas and ballads, but his protagonists do not correspond to the historical hero. Burkhard shows that the world of great men and heroic deeds fulfilled a personal longing and that Meyer's heroes – no matter how powerful and convincing – are 'ambiguous' heroes. The framework technique is used with skill, and the principal character usually narrates the story in the first person. In the verse cycle *Huttens letzte Tage* (Hutten's last days) Meyer's attention to form together with the popularity of the theme results in an artistic climax. The poet's preoccupation with form is further demonstrated in the many *Neufassungen* (revisions) of his early lyric work and underline his search for poetic expression and perfection. The English translations of the poems included here are especially valuable since his mostly symbolic poetic work has not been published in English.

779 **The poetry of Conrad Ferdinand Meyer.**

Heinrich Henel. Madison, Wisconsin: University of Wisconsin Press, 1954. 333p. bibliog.

Henel states that no critical edition of Meyer's poetry exists and that many of his poems have never been published. They can be found in the Central Library (Zentralbibliothek) in Meyer's native Zurich, and Henel received permission to use some of the unpublished poems for his book. They and all other quoted verses and titles are in German only. The collected poems of Meyer appeared in 1882 in a one-volume edition, carefully put together by the author. The poems are arranged according to subject matter, such as travel, love, deities, and others. Henel sees in Meyer 'a pioneer of the symbolist manner in German verse'. Subject matter is only of secondary interest to the author; his overriding concern is to 'make poetry'. Comparing poetry with music, Henel points to the many recurring motifs Meyer uses. They become the symbols that form the basis for his themes and ultimately create the harmony of his poetic work. Henel also emphasizes the importance of cycles for Meyer, illustrated, for example, in the nine-part arrangement of the poetry volume. The book has extensive notes that shed light on the genesis of many of the poems discussed in the text.

780 **The stories of C. F. Meyer.**

W. D. Williams. Oxford: Clarendon Press, 1962. 221p.

Williams opens this critical and thorough analysis of Meyer's seven historical short stories with a discussion of the nature and characteristics of the novella. Each of the seven novellas is then discussed individually. The background of the story is described, and Meyer's technique and style are evaluated. Williams praises Meyer as a master of this genre of literature.

781 **Carl (Friedrich Georg) Spitteler 1845-1924.**
In: *Twentieth-century literary criticism*, vol. 12, edited by Dennis Poupard. Detroit, Michigan: Gale Research Company, 1984, p. 333-53.

The multi-volume *Twentieth-century literary criticism* compilation deals with writers who died between 1900 and 1960. The substantial entry on Spitteler consists of a photograph of the poet, a biographical sketch of his life with a bibliography of his works, and full-length reprints of reviews and critiques of Spitteler's works in literary journals and book chapters. The critiques are by prominent literary personalities from different decades since Spitteler's death, reflecting an ongoing and continuing preoccupation with his work. An 'additional bibliography' of secondary literature about Spitteler concludes what is the best presentation in English of this important early 20th-century Swiss writer. See also 'Carl Spitteler' by Werner Günther, in *German men of letters: twelve literary essays*, vol. 5, edited by Alex Natan (London: Wolff, 1969).

782 **Prometheus and Epimetheus: a prose epic.**
Carl Spitteler, translated from the German by James F. Muirhead. London: Jarrolds, 1931. 318p. (Original title: *Prometheus und Epimetheus*, 1880-81).

Carl Spitteler is best known for his epic *Olympischer Frühling* (Olympian Spring) which brought him the Nobel prize for literature in 1919. *Prometheus and Epimetheus* preceded that work by more than thirty years. It is a poem in prose form. The figure of Prometheus occupied Spitteler throughout his life. It is not patterned after the Greek figure but a creation all his own. Translator Muirhead reveals in his prefatory note what problems the English translation posed and how the resemblance of German and English as they are used in various editions of the Bible aided his effort.

783 **Hermann Hesse.**
Franz Baumer, translated from the German by John Conway. New York: Ungar, 1969. 119p. bibliog.

Baumer begins with a chapter entitled 'Meeting in Montagnola', the last place Hesse (1877-1962) lived and where the lovely colours and pleasant climate of Canton Ticino brought him peace and inspired him to paint and to garden. Although imagined, the meeting is used by Baumer to demonstrate the strong influence the surroundings had on Hesse's personal well-being and his work throughout his life. Baumer states that Hesse never wrote about anything that he had not personally experienced and goes on to document this by chronologically tracing the homes and stations Hesse passed through in his life and the literature from these phases, often supporting his statements with quotes from Hesse's writings. Despite the poet's quest for solitude, he met many famous personalities who shaped his thinking and appeared in his writings under fictitious names.

784 **Hermann Hesse 1877-1962.**
In: *Contemporary literary criticism*, vol. 25, edited by Jean C. Stine. Detroit, Michigan: Gale Research Company, 1983, p. 258-62.

This ongoing multi-volume publication *Contemporary literary criticism* features individual writers by reprinting significant passages from published criticism. Hesse,

'German-born Swiss novelist, poet, short story writer, editor, and critic', appears in volumes 1, 2, 3, 6, 11, 17, and 25. Since no critiques are printed twice, the seven entries of bodies of Hesse criticism provide a thorough and comprehensive overview of and introduction to the work of this important writer. Nowhere else can one find a similar collection of articles from many, sometimes obscure, sources on Hesse, in any language. The reviews in volume twenty-five deal with his *Pictor's metamorphoses and other fantasies* on the occasion of the book's publication in English in 1981. Hesse also has an entry in *Contemporary authors – permanent series* (vol. 2, edited by Christine Nasso. Detroit, Michigan: Gale Research Company, 1978, p. 252-59). The bulk of the entry consists of a detailed listing of everything Hesse wrote: poetry, novels, short fiction, non-fiction, letters, other published work, and collected works, with (where they exist) English-language editions. A biographical sketch, an interpretative essay, and a bibliography on 'biographical/critical sources' complete this thorough and comprehensive treatment of Hesse.

785 **Hermann Hesse: an illustrated biography.**
Bernhard Zeller, translated from the German by Mark Hollebone. New York: Herder and Herder, 1971; London: Peter Owen, 1972. 176p. bibliog.

The life of Hermann Hesse is told here in ten short chapters. The biography draws on letters, entries in diaries, and from Hesse's work in which thinly disguised characters, places and scenes especially from his early years reappear time and again. Hesse wanted to go 'beyond them (the childhood years) into the distant ancestral past' and the first chapter traces that ancestry. Young Hermann's imagination and creative talent were noticed early, as was his stubborness and restlessness. Born in Calw, Württemberg, he left home at a tender age to attend different schools and to serve as an apprentice in various places. Times of depression that were to recur throughout his life and for which he would later seek psychiatric treatment began at this period. One learns of his relationship with his first wife, of his disgust at German militarism, of his visit to India and his divorce. He found relative peace only in his later years with his third wife Ninon in Montagnola, Canton Ticino. Among his many famous acquaintances were Thomas Mann and André Gide. He received the Nobel prize for literature in 1946 but his contemporaries were slow to recognize him as one of the great authors of the 20th century. Hesse's poetic and allusive style, his reflective language, and the conflicts portrayed gained him posthumously world-wide attention from a younger generation that could identify with him. Some of the many photographic illustrations have never been seen in print before. A bibliography and chronology complete this work.

786 **Inquiry and testament: a study of the novels and short prose of Robert Walser.**
George C. Avery. Philadelphia: University of Pennsylvania Press, 1968. 278p. bibliog.

This study analyses the novels and short prose pieces by Robert Walser (1878-1956) whose work, forgotten for a time, was rediscovered shortly after his death in an asylum. The publication of his collected works started in 1966. The heroes in his three novels are all self-seekers, but their experiences are narrated with great sensibility. Avery demonstrates Walser's preoccupation with language and discusses the characteristics of his style and the meaning of his themes. Passages from Walser's works are included in English and German.

787 **Robert Walser 1878-1956.**

In: *Twentieth-century literary criticism*, vol. 18, edited by Dennis Poupard, James E. Person. Detroit, Michigan: Gale Research Company, 1985, p. 414-38.

The entry on Walser in this publication consists of a biographical and critical introduction, a list of Walser's principal works, excerpts of criticism with bibliographical citations, a few photographs, and an additional bibliography for further reading. Walser, novelist, short-story writer, essayist, and poet, was selected for inclusion as 'one of the most important Swiss authors to have written in German'. By some estimates, Walser wrote over a thousand prose pieces and poems but saw only few of them in print, since he was generally neglected by the reading public. Extremely sensitive to criticism, he destroyed the manuscripts of several novels. When he entered a mental institution in Herisau in 1933, he stopped writing, saying 'I am not here to write, but to be mad'. Walser said of his prose pieces that they were 'nothing more nor less than parts of a long, plotless, realistic story. . . The novel I am constantly writing is always the same one, and it might be described as a variously sliced-up or torn-apart book of myself'. The bulk of the entry on Walser consists of a series of major essays of criticism, providing a survey of the historical response to his work, beginning with an essay of 1957 by Christopher Middleton and ending with one by Susan Sontag in 1982. The length of the entry reflects the amount of attention Walser has received in recent decades from critics writing in English. One of Walser's three novels is *Jakob von Gunten*, translated by Christopher Middleton (New York: Random House, 1983. Originally published by the University of Texas Press, 1969).

788 **Max Frisch: three plays.**

Translated from the German by Michael Bullock. London: Methuen, 1962. 254p.

The Fire Raisers (*Biedermann und die Brandstifter*, also translated as *The Firebugs*), *Count Oederland* (*Graf Oederland*), and *Andorra* are the three plays chosen for this book. The *Fire Raisers* carries the subtitle 'a morality without a moral'. At the centre of the play is Herr Biedermann, a modern Everyman who gives lodging to two suspicious characters who openly prepare to set their host's house on fire. In *Count Oederland* a respected judge disappears to lead a terrorist movement against the establishment. *Andorra* lays prejudice and anti-Semitism bare. Bullock's translations are very close to the original and are proof of his familiarity with the great Swiss playwright's language and intentions. In *The Plays of Max Frisch* by Michael Butler (London: Macmillan, 1985), Frisch's plays are discussed by interweaving content and criticism in an easy to read fashion. Nine of Frisch's ten plays were first performed at the Zurich *Schauspielhaus* (theatre) where the high standards that *émigrés* brought during the war years, first inspired him to write plays.

789 **Max (Rudolf) Frisch.**

In: *Contemporary literary criticism*, vol. 4, edited by Sharon K. Hall. Detroit, Michigan: Gale Research Company, 1987, p. 180-207.

This is the sixth time that Frisch (born 1911) is featured in *Contemporary literary criticism*. He is also in volumes 3, 9, 14, 18, and 32. Each time a different set of literary criticism from book review journals, literary periodicals, and books is used to illuminate the many aspects of the writer's work. Passages are quoted at length, and the body of critical assessment accumulated in these entries constitutes a very substantial inventory of works about Frisch. The excerpts in volume 44, published on the occasion of his being awarded the Neustadt International Prize for Literature, deal with the general assessment of the significance of Frisch's oeuvre, whether novels, dramas, diaries, or journalistic writings. *Contemporary authors*, a parallel publication by the same publisher, described as a 'bio-biographical guide', has an extensive bibliography on Frisch on pages 192-94 of volumes 85-88 (1980).

790 **Perspectives on Max Frisch.**

Edited by Gerhard F. Probst, Jay F. Bodine. Lexington, Kentucky: University Press, 1982. 225p. bibliog.

This is a compilation of twelve essays written by ten different authors. Some of the contributions are reprints. They focus on the different genres (drama, prose, and diaries) in which Frisch writes, or on special problems in his works, such as his treatment of women, 'the other sex'. The book is intended as a general introduction to Frisch. However, the serious Frisch scholar will find a bibliography at the back that takes up forty-seven pages. Probst claims that it presents 'the most comprehensive bibliography of primary and secondary literature published in this country [USA]'.

791 **The visit: a tragi-comedy.**

Friedrich Dürrenmatt, translated from the German by Patrick Bowles. London: Cape, 1962. 109p.

The visit (*Der Besuch der alten Dame*) is Dürrenmatt's most frequently performed play. A macabre piece, it is a parody of Western society, greed, and human weakness. The translator took special care to observe English verse tradition and idioms without affecting the intended meaning. For other plays, see *Friedrich Dürrenmatt: four plays 1957-62*, translated from the German by G. Nellhaus, M. Bullock, W. McElwee, J. Kirkup (London: Cape, 1964). The texts of the four plays are prefaced by Dürrenmatt's essay on 'Problems of the theatre', where he writes 'for me the stage is not a battlefield of theories, philosophies and manifestos, but rather an instrument whose possibilities I seek to know by playing with it'. Dürrenmatt's highly individual style, his imagination, his gift for the dramatic, and his love of the stage result in biting comedy and make him one of the century's foremost dramatists. In *Romulus the Great* (*Romulus der Grosse*) a Roman emperor watches indifferently as his empire is coming to an end while everybody around him struggles to save it. In *An angel comes to Babylon* (*Ein Engel kommt nach Babylon*) the king of Babylon changes place with the only surviving beggar in his kingdom. The other two plays are *The marriage of Mr Mississippi* (*Die Ehe des Herrn Mississippi*) and *The physicists* (*Die Physiker*).

792 **Friedrich Dürrenmatt: his five novels.**

(The individual stories were published by different publishers from 1952 to 1959 and were translated by different people). London: Pan Books, 1985. 413p.

Friedrich Dürrenmatt is best known for his dramatic work that gained him a reputation as one of the foremost dramatists of the German language since World War II. But he also had considerable talent as a writer of spellbinding fiction as is revealed by the five prose pieces included in this collection, works which are funny and paradoxical at the same time. The best known is a detective story that bears the unsettling title *The judge and his hangman* (*Der Richter und sein Henker*). The other stories are *The quarry* (*Der Verdacht*), *Once a Greek* (*Grieche sucht Griechin*), and *The pledge* (*Das Versprechen*). Also included is the radio play *Traps* (*Die Panne*).

793 **Friedrich Dürrenmatt.**

In: *Contemporary literary criticism*, vol. 43, edited by Daniel G. Marowski and Roger Matuz. Detroit, Michigan: Gale Research Company, 1987, p. 119-30.

Like his equally famous Swiss compatriot Max Frisch, Dürrenmatt (born 1921) has been featured six times so far in this publication, namely in volumes 1, 4, 8, 11, 15, and 43. Each time a short biographical sketch is followed by a number of lengthy reprints of reviews and critiques of works that caught the attention of literary critics. Among those prominently featured in volume 43 is *The physicists*, one of the more recent plays by Dürrenmatt. The collection of reviews and essays about Dürrenmatt and his literary work represented in these volumes is a very substantial body of criticism on the great playwright and writer. Dürrenmatt also has an entry in volumes 17-20, revised edition, of the bio-biographical parallel publication *Contemporary authors*. The book *Über Friedrich Dürrenmatt* (About Friedrich Dürrenmatt), edited by Daniel Keel (Zurich: Diogenes, 1980), is a collection of some of Dürrenmatt's speeches and writings, and contains contributions by well-known literary critics. This substantial book has a detailed chronology and a long bibliography.

794 **The theatre of Friedrich Dürrenmatt: a study in the possibility of freedom.**

Kenneth S. Whitton. London: Wolff; Atlantic Highlands, New Jersey: Humanities Press, 1980. 242p. bibliog.

Whitton writes in his foreword that he wants to put Dürrenmatt 'firmly in the framework of the comic tradition in the theatre'. He goes on to state that Dürrenmatt uses comedy to expose the ills of modern society but does not become pessimistic since he believes that an individual can attain freedom from that which causes his anguish, hence the subtitle of this book. The first chapter deals with Dürrenmatt's relation to Switzerland and his Swiss-ness, and how his native country and the German-speaking audiences and critics received his work. The second chapter gives a definition of the nature and evolution of the *Komödie* (comedy). The sixteen plays are treated in chronological order against this background. They are arranged in groups according to the similarity of themes, theatrical elements, and philosophical intent of the author. Notes which follow each chapter put statements or quotes in context. The bibliography at the end not only lists Dürrenmatt's complete oeuvre but also furnishes a list of secondary materials, in German and in English, that were published before 1980. This is a personal look at the playwright shaped by Whitton's interviews with the author and extensive research.

795 **J(ürg) F. Federspiel 1931- .**

In: *Contemporary literary criticism*, vol. 42, edited by Daniel G. Marowski, Roger Matuz. Detroit, Michigan: Gale Research Company, 1987, p. 143-46.

This entry presents critical reviews of the two works by Federspiel that have been translated into English, *The ballad of Typhoid Mary* (1982), and *An earthquake in my family* (1985). The biographical introduction presents Federspiel as novelist, short-story writer, poet, dramatist, journalist, scriptwriter, critic, and essayist who 'writes in a terse prose style and occasionally employs black humour to convey his view of the absurd and arbitrary nature of humanity's fate'. The reviews reprinted here speak of 'powerful and enigmatic stories' and use such terms as 'extravagant' and 'grotesque' to describe his style.

796 **The near and the far: the writings of Adolf Muschg.**

H. M. Waidson. *German Life & Letters*, vol.6, no. 1 (1975), p. 426-37.

Waidson looks briefly at Muschg's prose and dramatic work, beginning with *Im Sommer des Hasen* (1965) (In the year of the hare) and ending with Muschg's fourth novel *Albissers Grund* (1974) (Albisser's circumstances). Muschg tries to come to terms with his repulsion of and attraction to his home setting, Switzerland, and Zurich in particular. He examines how the culture of a foreign land has an impact on him and his characters. In *Im Sommer des Hasen* he traces the experiences of a group of Swiss men in Japan. The tensions between the known and the strange or exotic raise questions often left unanswered, but which stimulate the readers to clarify their own position. Muschg thus gives a vivid portrayal of modern men and how they interact, understanding and misunderstanding each other.. His lively style and imagination find a suitable outlet in the dramatic genre, in a play such as *Rumpelstilz* (1968) that centres on a middle-aged hypochondriac in a philistine setting.

797 **And really Frau Blum would very much like to meet the milkman: twenty-one short stories.**

Peter Bichsel, translated from the German by Michael Hamburger. London: Calder and Boyars, 1968. 88p. (Originally published as *Eigentlich möchte Frau Blum den Milchmann kennenlernen*. Olten, Switzerland: Walter, 1964).

The twenty-one miniature prose stories are Peter Bichsel's (born 1935) first literary work and brought him the prestigious prize of the Gruppe 47. The stories do not have much action; they are about everyday people and happenings. Space and time are limited. Nevertheless, these vignettes are masterpieces of simple language that evoke deep emotions. Another well-known book by the author is *There is no such place as America*, translated from the German by Michael Hamburger (New York: Delacorte, 1970. Originally published as *Kindergeschichten* [Children's stories], Neuwied and Berlin: Luchterhand, 1969). The seven short stories published in this book are by no means tales to entertain children only. They lead the reader into a strange world that makes him slightly uneasy: there is the story of the old man who names everything in his room differently and eventually creates a language no one can understand, or the tale about America, a country that may not even exist – have haunting qualities that account for Bichsel's attractiveness and success.

798 **Erich von Däniken 1935- .**

In: *Contemporary literary criticism*, vol. 30, edited by Jean C. Stine, Daniel G. Marowski. Detroit, Michigan: Gale Research Company, 1984, p. 421-28.

Von Däniken is a controversial non-fiction writer, best known for his *Chariots of the Gods? Unsolved mysteries of the past* (*Erinnerungen an die Zukunft*, 1968). With this book and its sequels he became a world-wide celebrity. He claimed that 'scientists are doing yesterday's thinking. I try to see with tomorrow's eyes'. As the series of excerpts from reviews of his numerous books published in English in this entry show, his work and ideas were subjected to strong criticism. He is attacked by scientists and religious critics alike for using unscientific methods and basing his theories on misleading documentation. His work is characterized as fantasy and 'science fiction in reverse'. However, as another critic ruefully writes, there are enough 'credophiles' in the world to make von Däniken's books international best-sellers, selling tens of millions of copies. 'Whether considered as a piece of radical reinterpretation of world history or as a bit of unconvincing comparative hucksterism, von Däniken's [*Pathways to the Gods*] still reads like a daring and exotic adventure story.' A bibliography of von Däniken's works can be found in *Contemporary authors*, vols 37-40. Detroit, Michigan: Gale Research Company, rev. ed. 1979, p. 576-77.

French-Swiss literature and writers: general

799 **La Suisse romande au cap du XXe siècle: portrait littéraire et moral.**
(French-speaking Switzerland at the turn of the 20th century: literary and moral portrait.)
Alfred Berchtold. Lausanne, Switzerland: Payot, 1963. 990p.

This is a substantial intellectual and cultural history of the French-speaking part of Switzerland, the Romandie, from about the 1890s to the 1920s. These decades saw an ouburst of creativity reflected in all areas of the cultural life of the cantons and the region, in philosophy and education, as well as in psychology and history. Poetry flourished, and an autonomous theatre came into existence. In painting the names of Félix Vallotton and above all of Ferdinand Hodler stand out, in music those of Emile Jaques-Dalcroze and the young Ernest Ansermet. Beginning around 1904 the primacy of ethical values in the literary work of French-Swiss writers was replaced by aesthetic values. This development was dominated by Charles Ferdinand Ramuz, whom Berchtold calls the greatest creative writer of the Romandie since Jean-Jacques Rousseau. The book is illustrated, mainly with photographs of the outstanding individuals who made up the rich tapestry of intellectual life of the Romandie at the turn of the century.

800 **Écrivains d'aujourd'hui: la littérature romande en vingt entretiens.**
(Writers of today: French-Swiss literature in twenty interviews.)
David Bevan. Lausanne, Switzerland: Editions 24 heures, 1986. 209p. (Collection Tel fut ce Siècle).

Bevan, professor of French at a Canadian university and biographer of C. F. Ramuz, prepared the questions for his interviews with the French-Canadian literary scene in mind. He wants to know if there is a French-Swiss literature and what its relationship is to that of France. He poses questions concerning the views of the writers on nature, religion, travel, literary genres, and their peers. While the author's answers vary, clearly the literature of France was and is important for the development of French-Swiss literature. Also apparent is that the Swiss writers see their work as being recognized by French literary critics and the French reading public and that it is increasingly assuming an important part in the body of Francophone literature. Ramuz is judged uniformly as being of central importance for 20th-century French-Swiss literature. Other contemporary French-Swiss writers seen as leaders by the interviewees are Chappaz, Chappuis, Chessex, Jaccottet, and Mercanton. A listing of the works written by the twenty authors is found at the back of the book. See also *Écrivains*

Romands 1900-1950 (Writers of French-speaking Switzerland 1900-1950) by [Myrian] Weber-Perret (Lausanne, Switzerland: Imprimerie Centrale, 1951). This critical analysis covers half a century and over one hundred writers.

801 **La littérature de la Suisse romande expliquée en un quart d'heure: suivie d'une anthologie lyrique de poche.** (The literature of French-speaking Switzerland explained in fifteen minutes: followed by a pocket anthology of poems.)
Bertil Galland. Geneva: Zoé, 1986. 136p.

Galland originally wrote the short article on the literature of French-speaking Switzerland that makes up the first quarter of this book for the *Encyclopaedia Universalis* (Paris, 1985). This reprint is supplemented with poems by twenty-five French-Swiss writers. Galland sets out by asking the recurring question 'Is there a French Swiss literature?' and he answers with an emphatic 'yes'. He disagrees with fellow critic and writer Jacques Mercanton who holds that literature is defined by the language in which it is written and since there is no *Romand* language there is no *Romand* literature either. Galland sees the widely varied cultural heritage of the different regions of French-speaking Switzerland as providing the distinguishing mark for the unique Swiss character of its literature. Geneva and Neuchâtel, urban and Protestant; Fribourg and Valais, both Catholic; the Geneva lake area and Canton Vaud; and the new Canton Jura, all are part of the mosaic that is the *Suisse romande*. Galland's quick literary history begins with Calvin and Rousseau, touches on C. F. Ramuz, the voice from the Vaud that put its stamp on the Romand literature of the twentieth century, and ends with contemporary writers. The anthology's earliest poems are by Ramuz (1878-1947) and the latest ones by Pierre-Alain Tâche, born in 1940. Galland shows that there is coherence, despite polyphony, and independence within a common nationality and language in the literary production of the *Suisse romande*.

802 **Die französischsprachige Literatur der Schweiz.** (The French-language literature of Switzerland.)
Manfred Gsteiger. In: *Die zeitgenössischen Literaturen der Schweiz*, edited by Manfred Gsteiger. Zurich; Munich: Kindler, 1974, p. 407-546.

The character of French-speaking Switzerland, the Romandie, has been shaped by two historically caused factors, its participation in the linguistic and literary tradition of the French-language sphere on the one hand, and its political and cultural independence from French centralism on the other. This independence is manifest within the Romandie by a pronounced federalism which breaks up the apparent unity into a colourful patchwork of separate entities and regions. Gsteiger takes this fact as the guiding principle in the organization of this chapter. Fribourg and its writers are moulded by conservatism and Catholicism; Vaud combines peasant values with the urbanity of its city-dwellers; the Valais writer is tied to nature and at the same time influenced by technology; Geneva represents Calvinism and cosmopolitanism; in Neuchâtel intellectualism and revolt have a long tradition; and in the Jura one finds solitude and self-determination as important phenomena. If one characteristic stands out as being typical for many of the French-Swiss writers, it is the fact that they are rooted in the soil of their native region. A slightly revised version of this essay has been published as a separate book with the title *La nouvelle littérature romande: essai* (The new French-Swiss literature: essay) (Vevey, Switzerland: Galland; Lausanne and Zurich: Ex Libris, 1978, 249p.). A bibliographical sketch lists almost 250 French-Swiss writers alphabetically with the titles of their works that have been published since 1945.

French-Swiss writers

803 **Mistress to an age: a life of Madame de Staël.**
J. Christopher Herold. Westport, Connecticut: Greenwood, 1975. 500p. bibliog. (Originally published in 1958 by Bobbs-Merrill).

Herold does not claim this to be a 'definitive biography' of Madame de Staël (1766-1817). His work is intended as a general biography that 'would restore her to life in the public mind'. Madame de Staël, daughter of the Swiss Paris banker Necker, travelled extensively in Germany, Italy, and other countries. Her father's estate near Geneva, the Château of Coppet, served her as a refuge on different occasions when Napoleon exiled her from Paris. She wrote her important work *On Germany* (*De l'Allemagne*, 1810) while there. She also drew a côterie of admirers to the shores of Lake Geneva, among them Benjamin Constant, the eccentric author of *Adolphe*, with whom she had one of her love affairs. Her writings on philosophy, politics, literature, religion, and love influenced Swiss thought of the period and contributed to the growth of romanticism in French literature.

804 **Mme de Staël.**
Renée Winegarten. Leamington Spa, England [etc.]: Berg, 1985. 133p. bibliog. (Berg Women's Series).

Winegarten has written a short, lively, modern biography of Mme de Staël. Born Anne Louise Germaine Necker, the daughter of wealthy Swiss parents living in Paris, she achieved fame in her own time as a society woman and a writer. Winegarten ascribes much of Mme de Staël's quest for happiness and power and her free-spirit liaisons with a succession of lovers to the repressive upbringing by her Calvinist mother. Mme de Staël's social successes during the last years of the *ancien régime* and the revolutionary and Napoleonic periods of French history are described as well as her remarkable success as a writer. Her most successful literary work, the novel *Corinne* (1807), displayed a new spirit in literature, the spirit of liberty, especially for women. With it, Mme de Staël 'invented the richly creative myth of the independent woman of genius'. She asked, with Corinne: 'Should not each woman, like each man, clear a path for herself in accordance with her character and gifts?' Mme de Staël's personality was one of startling contradictions, but in her integrity and her belief in the value of the individual she remained constant. Winegarten sums up her appraisal with the sentence: 'The author of *Corinne* was the first woman of middle-class birth to stun the world with her great talent, to imprint it upon both the literary and the political spheres, and to employ it to alter the mentality of women as well as men.' The booklet has a few illustrations, a helpful chronology, and a select bibliography of Mme. de Staël's works and correspondence and of some secondary works.

805 **Journal intime.** (Intimate journal.)
Henri-Frédéric Amiel, edited by Bernard Gagnebin, Philippe M. Monnier. Lausanne, Switzerland: L'Age d'Homme, 1839-70. 7 vols. Excerpts published in French and English between 1883 and 1970.

Henri-Frédéric Amiel's journal comprises seven large volumes written over thirty years. Orphaned as a child, Amiel (1821-81) always felt different from people around him and became melancholic. He developed a great interest in the sciences and arts and travelled extensively, and his German studies in Berlin prepared him for a coveted professorship at the University of Geneva. His daily journal entries record everything, from the weather to his most personal thoughts about life and death and his own being, and are of interest not only as a personal document but for the light they shed on the life and intellectual climate of 19th-century Geneva. Excerpts from critical essays by fifteen critics, spanning the time from the first publication in English of parts of the journal in 1885 to 1970 are contained in the brief article 'Henri Frédéric Amiel 1821-1881' in *Nineteenth-century literature criticism*, vol. 4, edited by Laurie Lanzer Harris and Sheila Fitzgerald (Detroit, Michigan: Gale Research Company, 1983).

806 **Charles-Ferdinand Ramuz.**

David Bevan. Boston, Massachusetts: Twayne, 1979. 140p. bibliog. (Twayne's World Author Series, 512).

Bevan characterizes Ramuz (1878-1947) as 'a writer whose entire life was devoted to the search for an exact coherence between a vision of the world and the chosen means of expression'. In his mature and best novels Ramuz succeeded in totally integrating subject matter and style in a remarkable narrative technique that situates him firmly among such greats of the European literature of the 1920s as Gide, Woolf, and Joyce. Bevan provides only a minimum of biographical information about Ramuz. A ten-year sojourn in Paris from 1904 to 1914 was important above all for the fact that in the midst of metropolitan culture Ramuz became truly aware of his identity with the people and soil of his homeland, the Pays de Vaud. A winter spent in the village of Lens in the mountains of Canton Valais gave Ramuz 'his most forceful and decisive adult experience', an encounter with the elemental, wild forces of raw nature. Most of Bevan's book is devoted to brief descriptions and analyses of Ramuz' literary works. Bevan, as he demonstrated in his earlier *The art and poetry of C.-F. Ramuz* (Cambridge, England: Oleander, 1976), is especially interested in narrative technique. Since he finds all existing translations of Ramuz' books 'lamentable' and 'an unacceptable impoverishment of the original work', he provides, together with the French original, his own translations of the many passages he quotes to make his points. It is a sad fact that this brief study of the great Swiss novelist Ramuz is the only book-length work on any of the French-Swiss writers currently in existence in Anglophone countries.

807 **C. F. Ramuz.**

Michael H. Parkinson. In: *The rural novel: Jeremias Gotthelf, Thomas Hardy, C. F. Ramuz.* Bern [etc.]: Lang, 1984, p. 205-46. bibliog.

Ramuz, considered the foremost writer of French-speaking Switzerland, is one of three authors examined by Parkinson in the context of the rural novel. Most of Ramuz' novels take place in his native Vaud and show the strong, mystical ties between its inhabitants and their mountainous surroundings. Parkinson agrees with others that the psychological aspects of Ramuz' work outweigh the societal, and that solitude or an exceptional individual seem to interest the author more than the behaviour of a group or community. Yet his peasants often react collectively to a catastrophic event or an unexpected act of an individual. The hero in Ramuz' novels is usually a person who is not integrated into the routine of the settled community, exemplified in the well-known novel *Derborence* (*When the mountain fell*, 1934 [q.v.]), by the protagonist Antoine. Ramuz often contrasts the life of the peasant or wine-grower with that of the city-dweller and clearly decides in favour of the former. But he also shows the limitations, the vulnerability, and the lack of communication that characterize the peasant communities. Parkinson uses many quotes from Ramuz' work to illustrate his observations.

808 **When the mountain fell.**

Charles Ferdinand Ramuz, translated from the French by Sarah Fisher Scott. New York: Pantheon, 1947. 221p.

Ramuz' novel was originally published under the title *Derborence* (Paris: Grasset, 1934). Derborence is the name of a secluded, uninhabited valley high up in the mountains. Only during a few summer months is there life up there when the cattle from the village below are driven to the alp for summer grazing. One day, a devastating landslide covers men and cows and blankets the beautiful pasture with tons of rocks. Ramuz tells how the grief-stricken families in the village wrestle with the tragedy. They are startled when Antoine appears like a ghost, the only, miraculous, survivor of the rock slide. He is obsessed by the belief that his companion is still alive and he returns to the horrible scene of the accident. Ramuz pays homage in this novel to the irresistible power of nature as encountered in the mountains and to the life of hard work and suffering of the people living in these mountains. This being one of his mature works, the style of the narrative and the dialogue is intimately tied to the gripping subject matter. His best-known novel is *Terror in the mountain*, translated from the French by Milton Stansbury (New York: Harcourt, Brace & World, 1968). It was originally published under the title *La Grande Peur dans la montagne* (Paris: Grasset, 1926). An Alpine village owns pastureland high up in the mountains that some twenty years ago had brought misfortune to those who tended the flock. The young villagers vote to make use of the alp again, and again men and cattle experience a terrible fate, 'for the mountain has her own notions. She has her own will'. The author's closeness to nature is reflected in a story filled with mystical qualities and vivid colours.

809 **Selected writings of Blaise Cendrars.**

Edited by Walter Albert, preface by Henry Miller. Westport, Connecticut: Greenwood, 1978. 274p.

Blaise Cendrars (né Frédéric-Louis Sauser) (1887-1961) was born in La Chaux-de-Fonds, Canton Neuchâtel. The author's biography takes up some forty pages and tells of his father's nervous ailment and wanderlust and of the mother's makeshift housekeeping as the family moved from country to country while their son was sent from boarding school to boarding school. At age fifteen, Blaise struck out on his own, travelling as far as Russia, America and Canada, but always returning to Paris where he was part of the cultural scene and the avant-garde movement. While the experiences from these wanderings found their way into Cendrars' prose and poetry, little points to his Swiss origin. In *Les Pâques à New York* (Easter in New York) he uses the Alexandrine verse freely to tell of his Easter 1917 experience in New York where he remembers the Biblical passion story while pondering about present-day life in the metropolis. A varied and rich selection of lyric and prose pieces is included, with individual works printed side by side in French and English, giving a taste of the often violent language and passionate style of this tirelessly active world-traveller and bohemian.

810 **Blaise Cendrars (pseudonym of Frédéric-Louis Sauser-Hall) 1887-1961.**

In: *Contemporary literary criticism*, vol. 18, edited by Sharon R. Gunton. Detroit, Michigan: Gale Research Company, 1981, p. 90-98.

Cendrars is introduced as 'a French-Swiss poet, novelist, autobiographer, essayist, and editor' whose 'efforts to adapt the techniques of musical composition to writing poetry, along with other formal innovations, made him an important figure in French letters'.

The bulk of the entry consists of significant passages from published criticism of Cendrars and his major works. Fellow-writers such as Henry Miller and literary critics such as Walter Albert and Jay Bochner are quoted at length in their assessment of this significant 20th-century French-Swiss writer. There is a short bibliographical entry under 'Sauser-Hall Frederic [sic] (Blaise Cendrars) 1887-1961' in *Contemporary authors*, vols 93-96 (1980).

811 **Les heures de James Joyce.** (The hours with [of] James Joyce.)
Jacques Mercanton. Lausanne, Switzerland: L'Age d'Homme, 1967. 96p.

The French-Swiss writer Mercanton knew James Joyce during the last years of the Irish poet's life and portrays him here as he remembers him from many encounters, during hours of work and hours of leisure. The conversations between him and Joyce, often in the presence of Joyce's wife, provide insights into some very personal spheres of each of the two writers' lives.

812 **A father's love.**
Jacques Chessex, translated from the French by Martin Sokolinsky. New York; Indianapolis, Indiana: Bobbs-Merrill, 1975. 199p. (Originally published as *L'Ogre*. Paris: Grasset & Fasquelle, 1973).

Chessex (born 1934), novelist and poet, received the Prix Concourt for this book, the first Swiss writer ever to win this prestigious French literary prize. Chessex tells the haunting story of the life of Jean Calmet and his love–hate relationship with his father. Even after the powerful old man's death, traumatic scenes from the past recur and eventually lead Calmet to commit suicide. The story is written with great psychological insight and in superb language.

Italian-Swiss literature and writers

813 **Dizionarietto degli scrittori della Svizzera Italiana.** (Little dictionary of Italian-Swiss writers.)
Edited by ASSI (Associazione degli scrittori della Svizzera italiana). Lugano, Switzerland: Cenobio, 1976. 67p.

This bio-bibliographical dictionary acquaints the reader with some sixty contemporary writers of Canton Ticino and the Italian-speaking valleys of Canton Graubünden. They are listed in alphabetical order. Lists of their works are given, but no critical notes are provided. Only ten per cent of the inhabitants of Switzerland speak Italian; consequently the representatives of this language have the usual difficulties minorities experience in finding a broad enough readership among their compatriots. Italy, for some unknown reason, proves not to be receptive either to the Italian-Swiss writers.

814 **Contemporary Swiss-Italian literature: from acquiescence to rebellion.**
Piergiorgio Conti. *Swiss American Review*, January 25, 1989, p. 7-8.

This is the text of a lecture which Conti delivered as holder of the Pro Helvetia chair at the Graduate School of the City of New York. In it he surveys the achievements of the

Italian-Swiss writers of the 20th century. He characterizes them as persons with two souls, one Swiss, the other Italian. Their real home is abroad, on the other side of the Gotthard or beyond Chiasso in Lombardy. They write 'Italian literature of Switzerland'. Conti is quite critical of the old masters Francesco Chiesa (1871-1973) and Giuseppe Zoppi (1896-1952) who produced what he describes as a 'literature of innocence', dealing with 'our garden', 'our alps', and 'our lilies'. A reaction to that kind of writing began to set in in the 1950s and reached the stage of rebellion by the mid-1960s. Writers such as Remo Beretta and Giovanni Orelli (born 1928) refused to use the provincial commonplaces that had been put into the service of sterile folklore – their themes deal with the destruction of the cultural values of the peasant tradition – and they use the irony and sarcasm which also invade contemporary poetry. The works of Plinio Martini (1923-79) express in a violently polemical form the ideas of 'a clear, determined and direct political rebellion', mirroring the profound changes that have occurred in Italian-Swiss society in the last thirty years. Conti provides a bibliography which shows that a number of works by Italian-Swiss writers have been published in German and French translations. Not a single one is available in English.

815 **Die italienischsprachige Literatur der Schweiz seit 1945.** (The Italian-language literature of Switzerland since 1945.)
Alice Vollenweider. In: *Die zeitgenössischen Literaturen der Schweiz*, edited by Manfred Gsteiger. Zurich; Munich: Kindler, 1974, p. 547-608.

At the beginning of her short chapter, Vollenweider points out that the Italian language and culture community in Switzerland amounts to barely three per cent of the Swiss population. Rather than rallying their tiny forces, the 200,000 Italian-Swiss of Canton Ticino and the Italian-speaking valleys of Graubünden engage in particularism to an extreme – they are a fragmented minority. Vollenweider lists other factors of significance for an understanding of the situation in which Italian-Swiss writers find themselves, including the spread of German influence in the canton and a relationship to Italy which is cool and distant. Much more important than the cultural presence of Italy for the literature of Italian Switzerland was the life and work of the patriarch of Ticinese culture, Francesco Chiesa (1871-1973). Vollenweider also points out that Ticino has more poets than prose writers. The small reservoir of materials available to the Italian-Swiss writer hampers the poet less than the prose writers. Many individuals are mentioned with brief biographical data, and radio and television work is also covered.

Rhaeto-Romansh literature and writers

816 **Annalas da la Società Retorumantscha.** (Yearbook of the Rhaeto-Romansh Society.)
Chur, Switzerland: 1886- .

This publication contains, in addition to historical, linguistic, and folkloristic contributions, creative literature by writers from the three main branches of the

Rhaeto-Romansh language area, namely Sursilvan, which is spoken in the Vorder Rhine valley; Sutsilvan/Surmeiran or Grisun central from middle Graubünden; and Ladin with its subdivisions of Engiadin'ota, spoken in the Upper Engadin and Engiadina bassa, from the Lower Engadin.

817 **The curly-horned cow: anthology of Swiss-Romansh literature.**
Edited by Reto R. Bezzola, translated from the Ladin by Elizabeth Maxfield Miller and from the Surselvan by W. W. Kibler. London: Owen, 1971. 215p. bibliog. (UNESCO Collection of Representative Works: European Series).

This is a collection of poems and prose pieces by writers in one or the other of the Romansh languages. The oldest selection is by a person born in 1627, the most recent by one born in 1934. In all, twenty-seven writers are represented. The title of the volume is from a Ladin tale by Schimun Vonmoos (1868-1940). Bezzola contributed a preface in which he sketches the history of Romansh literature and a bibliography, while an appendix includes the Romansh text of a few poems which gives the reader an idea of how they sound in the original.

818 **Raetoromanische Gegenwartsliteratur in Graubünden: Interpretationen; Interviews.** (Rhaeto-Romansh contemporary literature in Graubünden: interpretations, interviews.)
Iso Camartin. Disentis, Switzerland: Desertina, 1976. 298p. bibliog.

Camartin presents twelve living Romansh writers by providing a critical analysis of one or more works of each of the writers, interviewing each of them about aspects of their work, and by providing a bio-bibliography for each. His introduction and a lengthy final chapter dwell upon the special situation of the Romansh-language writer as a representative of a small minority, a minority that is also divided within itself. His intention is not to unearth great unknown treasures, of which he does not think there are any, but to create a mirror in which one is able to catch some glimpses of life among the Rhaeto-Romansh people of Canton Graubünden. For the Romansh-speaking individuals the contemporary literature is a living reminder that their language heritage is still alive and responsive to care and nurture.

819 **The predicament of Romansh literature.**
John van Eerde. *Books abroad: an international literary quarterly*, vol. 50, no. 2 (Spring 1976), p. 341-45.

Romansh is the native language of slightly more than 50,000 Swiss, or 0.8 per cent of the population, and of these, more than 12,000 live outside Canton Graubünden. The key factor for understanding the problems of Romansh is that it is splintered into several Romansh languages and literatures. This lack of uniformity is the chief obstacle to its survival. Van Eerde sees some hope in the activities of the Ligia Romontscha, also called Lia Rumantscha, which, among other things, helps writers to get their works into print. Each of the several Romansh tongues continues to produce literary figures of merit, mainly prose writers, but also playwrights and poets. Their extremely limited audience prevents Romansh writers from attaining more than local fame. Yet, the situation seems brighter than it was only some ten years earlier.

820 **Litteratura. Novas litteraras. Ediu dall' Uniun da scripturs romontschs.**
(Literature: literary news; published by the union of Romansh writers.)
Chur, Switzerland: Gasser, 1978- . twice per year. ca. 150p.

This publication contains articles on the Romansh languages, texts of poems and short prose pieces, and reviews. The second issue of the year usually has a bibliography, mostly of *belles-lettres* in Romansh and articles and books about Romansh writers.

821 **Die rätoromanische Literatur der Schweiz. Ein Überblick bis heute.**
(The Rhaeto-Romansh literature of Switzerland: an overview up to the present day.)
Leza Uffer. In: *Die zeitgenössischen Literaturen der Schweiz*, edited by Manfred Gsteiger. Zurich; Munich: Kindler, 1974, p. 609-78.

There was no generally accepted high Romansh or written language at the time of this publication. The several dialects have evolved into three distinct written languäges, each a product of a historical development in separate valleys of Canton Graubünden. Uffer uses Interromansh, the modern, artificial style of writing for Romansh words and terms. The beginnings of Rhaeto-Romansh literature go back to the 16th century. The Reformation provided a stimulus for the development of the language, especially through translations of various parts of the Bible, as well as other religious writings into Romansh. Oral tradition in the form of passion plays, and also in folk songs, played an important role in the preservation of the language. The breakthrough from a primary concern for the preservation of the language to its use as a tool of literary creativity came in the first half of the 20th century. The contemporary writer, however, lives and works in a precarious situation, since his mother tongue is endangered by the spread of other languages, especially German. G. Mützenberg in his *Destin de la langue et de la littérature rhéto-romanes* (Lausanne, Switzerland: L'Age d'Homme, 1974) treats the subject in a similar manner to Uffer.

Children's literature

822 **Cocoa beans and daisies: how Swiss chocolate is made.**
Pascale Allamand. New York; London: Warne, 1978. 48p.

Allamand tells the story of how the cocoa beans from Africa and the milk from the cows grazing in the Swiss mountains eventually meet and find their way into a Swiss chocolate factory where a number of different machines turn out delicious chocolates in all shapes and sizes. The black-and-white photographs are accompanied by a short and simple text in large letters that succeeds well in explaining what function each machine has in the rather complicated fabrication of this well-known Swiss product. Two chocolate recipes and pictures of youngsters with a 'sweet tooth' complete the book. Allamand is a well-known Swiss illustrator of children's books. Among them are *Wilhelm Tell* (1981)) told by Nina Bawden, and *The little goat in the mountain* (1977), illustrated and written by Allamand and translated into English by Michael Bullock, published by Cape in London. The illustrations are in colour.

823 **Anton the goatherd.**

Alois Carigiet. New York: Henry Z. Walck, 1966. 34p.

Carigiet, who grew up in the mountains of Canton Graubünden, recalls in this illustrated children's book scenes from his childhood. He tells the story of Anton, the goatherd, who tends the villagers' goats during the summer. In the early morning, he takes them high up to the alps and lets them graze. A storm comes up, and Old Stina's three goats get away, but a scary search finally locates the lost animals. In the evening, the villagers, alerted by the soft tinkle of bells, await the returning flock and wonder how Anton sprained his ankle. He will not tell, but Stina's herbal medicine and special verse will soon make it well again. The full-page illustrations by Carigiet render details vividly and in radiant colours. Similar simple and heartwarming mountain stories by the same author are told in *The pear tree, the birchtree and the barberry bush* (1967) and *Anton and Anne* (1969). These books were also published by Walck. Carigiet is the winner of the 1966 Hans Christian Andersen International Children's Book Award for his illustrations.

824 **Mary & the wildcat.**

Jacques Chessex, translated from the French by Victor Gollancz Inc., illustrations by Danièle Bour. London: Gollancz, 1980. 23p. (First published as *Marie et le Chat Sauvage*, Paris: Grasset & Fasquelle, 1979).

This beautifully illustrated tale by French-Swiss author Chessex, about little Mary who would rather play with a wild cat in the forest than go to school, demonstrates in simple language that love of nature and freedom can be reconciled with the duties that are demanded even of a child.

825 **A bell for Ursli.**

Selina Chönz. illustrated by Alois Carigiet. New York: Henry Z. Walck, 1950. 42p.

This is the earliest and most successful of the half dozen or so children's books illustrated by Carigiet. The American audience fell so much in love with it that six printings had to be made between 1950 and 1966. Chönz tells a simple story from the Swiss Engadine mountains in rhymed verses: little Ursli would like to carry a big bell like the older boys in the spring procession held to usher out winter. He remembers a huge cowbell way up in a lonely alpine hut and goes to fetch it. Tired from the long hike, he spends the night on the alp and has everybody in the village worried. But in the procession 'It's little Ursli, ding, dong, dell/ Who has by far the biggest bell.' Carigiet's illustrations take the reader to a faraway mountain world; the details are fascinating and the colours happy and rich. *Florina and the wild bird* (1966) and *The snowstorm* (1958) are two other children's books written by Chönz, illustrated by Carigiet, and published by Walck. They tell of other adventures in the life of Ursli and of his little sister Florina.

826 **My village in Switzerland.**

Sonia and Tim Gidal. New York: Pantheon Books, 1961. 81p. maps.

This is an illustrated book written for children about a Swiss boy, Simon, who is growing up on a farm in the scenic Emmental valley. Simon tells about his life, work, and play as the youngest of five children. The family shares chores in the house, the garden, the stable, and the fields. A school excursion to Bern, the capital, and to the beautiful Jungfrau mountain is a welcome diversion from the hard work on the farm. A Swiss-style wrestling match gives an opportunity for a festival that brings the community together. The cheese known as Swiss cheese all over the world is called Emmentaler in Switzerland because it originates from this valley, and a visit to the cheese dairy in Simon's village tells how this cheese is made. The photographs date the book, but the story could still take place today.

827 **Three centuries of children's books in Europe.**
Bettina Hürlimann, translated from the German and edited by Brian W. Alderson. London: Oxford University Press, 1967. 297p. bibliog.

Hürlimann devotes one of seventeen chapters of her overview of the development of children's books in Europe to Switzerland. Entitled 'Toward a history of children's books in Switzerland', this chapter provides in ten pages a convenient and unique introduction to the subject. Hürlimann gives the year 1645 as the starting point for children's books in German-speaking Switzerland. She shows how a custom in the town of Zurich of giving children a copperplate engraving with a poem underneath on New Year's Day led to the collecting and later publishing of these *Neujahrsblätter*. Moralizing stories with a pronounced didactic slant predominated the content of the *Neujahrsblätter*, but historical, biblical, and symbolical themes were also represented. They appeared until the middle of the 19th century. Educator Pestalozzi and writers Bodmer and Rousseau exerted an influence not only on children's literature but also on writers of works intended for children. Important titles and authors for the nineteenth and twentieth centuries are briefly touched upon, among which Johanna Spyri's *Heidi* (q.v.), written in the 1880s and already translated into English in 1884, is clearly a favourite of all times. *The Swiss family Robinson* (1812) (q.v.) by Johann David Wyss is also internationally known. Sagas with historical associations, fairytales and stories closely modelled on everyday life characterize Swiss children's literature of all periods.

828 **Flower fairy tales.**
Ernst Kreidolf, translated from the German by Elaine Boney, Silke Reavis and the Green Tiger editorial staff. La Jolla, California: Green Tiger Press, 1979. 30p. (A Star & Elephant Book).

The Swiss artist Ernst Kreidolf (1863-1956) has created a series of exquisite picture books for children that have long been admired in Switzerland and Germany. However, the artist's work has been discovered by the English-speaking world only long after his death. In the same year as the *Flower fairy tales* (*Blumen Märchen*), the Green Tiger Press also published the *Dream garden* (*Traumgarten*), and *Servants of the Spring* (*Lenzgesinde*). In Kreidolf's fantasy world flowers, trees, and animals are animated; they speak, walk, and interact. The pictures are delicately drawn and rendered in beautiful colours. Each full-page drawing is accompanied by a text that sets the stage for the lively scenes depicted. Here, a buttercup and her little one are hitched to a butterfly for a ride above the wide wide world; there, glow-worms are providing pulsing light for a dance of the flowers. Kreidolf's imagination and superb artistry have given children's books a new dimension.

829 **Schweizer Bilderbuch-Illustratoren 1900-1980. Lexikon.** (Swiss picture book illustrators 1900-1980: encyclopaedia.)
Edited by Verena Rutschmann. Disentis, Switzerland: Desertina, 1983. 231p.

The Jugendbuch Institut (Institute for Children's Books) in Zurich, founded in 1937, furnished the documentation for this work. Since illustrated Swiss children's books of artistic value did not appear until the turn of this century with Kreidolf's *Blumen Märchen* (Flower fairy tales [q.v.]), the starting date for this study was given. Only the works of Swiss citizens, published in Switzerland were considered for inclusion; additional criteria are stated in the introduction. The book consists of some essays on children's picture books of a general nature, a biographical part portraying a number of prominent illustrators often with a photograph, an encyclopaedia listing some 350 artists and the 1,100 book titles they have to their credit, and eighty full-size reproductions of illustrations in colour that attest to the great versatility, imagination, and humour of their creators. A real treasure-house for all lovers of children's books.

830 **Johanna (Heusser) Spyri 1827-1901.**
In: *Children's literature review*, vol. 13, edited by Gerard J. Senick. Detroit, Michigan: Gale Research Company, 1987, p. 174-86.

Spyri, author of more than forty books, is recognized as Switzerland's most beloved and enduring writer for children. In the standard format of the Gale publications on literature, this article opens with a brief biographical sketch of Spyri. This is followed by excerpts from reviews, criticism, and commentary in English-language publications on Spyri's best known work, *Heidi* (q.v.). *Heidi*, published in 1880 and in an English translation in 1884, is considered a classic of children's literature as well as one of the most popular stories to originate outside the English-language area. Critics praised it as a book that is both realistic and entertaining, a masterpiece of literary craftsmanship, and a tribute to the land and people of Switzerland. More critical voices attacked the strong religious flavour of the book and the submissive acceptance by its characters of outdated social conditions. An example of such a view is provided in the excerpts from Jack Zipes's article 'Down with Heidi, down with Struwwelpeter, three cheers for the revolution: towards a new children's literature in West Germany' in *Children's literature: annual of the Modern Language Association seminar of children's literature and the Children's Literature Association*, vol. 5 (1976), p. 162-80. The prevalent tone of the critics quoted in the Gale volume, however, indicates its inherent human interest and literary value will assure *Heidi* a permanent place among the most treasured children's books in world literature.

831 **Heidi.**
Johanna Spyri, translated from the German by M. Rosenbaum. London [etc.]: Collins, 1986. 176p. (Collins Children's Classics).

This is a recent English edition, one of more than one hundred that have been published since the appearance of the original *Heidi* in 1884. Spyri tells the story of an orphaned little girl who wins the heart of her hardened grandfather with whom she has come to live way up on the alp. Her aunt takes Heidi away from her grandfather and places her with a well-to-do family in Frankfurt to become the playmate of crippled Clara. Heidi becomes homesick and is allowed to bring Clara to her beloved Swiss mountains. The book has become a classic of children's literature, touching the hearts of young and old all over the world.

832 **Johann David Wyss 1743-1818.**

In: *Nineteenth century literature criticism*, vol. 10, edited by Laurie Lanzen Harris, Emily B. Tennyson. Detroit, Michigan: Gale Research Company, 1985, p. 465-73. bibliog.

Like all other presentations in this multi-volume publication, the Wyss entry begins with a biographical sketch combined with a brief interpretative essay. Little is known about the life of Wyss. He was pastor at the Bern minster and became world-famous as the creator of *The Swiss family Robinson*, 'a tale whose immediate popularity was succeeded by enduring renown as a classic of children's literature'. The book originated as a story told by Wyss for the education and enjoyment of his four sons. His second son published the manuscript in 1812-13 under the title *Der Schweizerische Robinson, oder, Der schiffbrüchige Schweizerprediger und seine Familie*. The third son contributed sixty illustrations to the book. It was translated freely and adapted into numerous languages. Most of the hundreds of editions of the book have been based on the French translation and continuation of the story made by the baroness de Montolieu in 1816. The excerpts from nine critical appraisals of Wyss's book reprinted in this entry stem mainly from introductions to various editions from 1837 to 1963. William Dean Howells wrote: 'What I really grieve for, and it is the only thing, is that there is no especial scope given for the imaginations of the girl readers of the book', while Golding summed up her critique with the sentence: 'The great strength of the book lies in Wyss's ability to evoke the spirit of close family life.'

833 **The Swiss family Robinson.**

J. D. Wyss, translated from the German by William H. G. Kingston. Harmondsworth, England: Penguin, 1987. 383p. (Puffin Books).

Wyss's story of the adventures of a shipwrecked family and their ways of responding to the challenges they faced in living on a deserted island amidst strange animals and plants has fascinated generations of readers since its publication in 1812. This translation into English is among the most recent, but it is only a slightly edited version of that of 1814.

Museums, Libraries, and Archives

Museums

834 **Museumskarte der Schweiz.** (Map of Swiss museums.)
Bundesamt für Landestopographie. Wabern-Bern, Switzerland: Bundesamt für Landestopographie, 1982.

This map shows the location of 538 museums of all kinds on a 1:300,000 scale map of Switzerland. A booklet that comes with it has detailed maps in larger scales and brief descriptions of the nature and specialization, address, and opening times of each of the museums. Symbols are used to distinguish the various kinds of museums: museums of art and applied art; local culture (Heimatmuseum) of the village, town, valley, or region; natural science; technology, transport, and communication; history; ethnography, including non-European cultures; popular traditions and folklore; agriculture; and guilds and professional occupations.

835 **Museen der Schweiz.** (Museums of Switzerland.)
Edited by Niklaus Flüeler. Zurich: Ex Libris, 1981. 335p.

This picture book is generously laid out and richly illustrated with over 700 pictures. It provides an overview of the wealth and variety of Swiss museums. Of about 540 museums in Switzerland, ninety-six are presented here with text and illustrations. Many of the buildings that house the collections are also featured, from small local and regional museums to major new museums that incorporate the latest technology in their exhibitions. The book also deals with legal obligations, loan arrangements, and the relationship between the individual collector and the state.

836 **Ballenberg.**
Max Gschwend, David Meili, Rudolf Hunziker. Aarau, Switzerland: AT Verlag, 1988. 207p.

Ballenberg is a large open-air museum on a mountainside of the same name above the village of Brienz, Canton Bern. The museum, devoted to the display of the culture of rural life, opened its doors in 1978. Fifty-five rural dwellings from all parts of Switzerland have so far been relocated to the museum and organized in regional clusters in the natural setting of the mountain. The houses are equipped with authentic peasant furniture, and in the work areas of the buildings various activities appropriate to a particular region are carried out, such as different kinds of husbandry, weaving, charcoal-burning, wine-making, and vegetable- and flower-gardening. This large-sized, richly illustrated book provides a colourful inventory of the impressive progress made by the museum during the first ten years of its existence.

837 **Ancient castles and historic mansions in Switzerland.**
Fritz Hauswirth. Zurich: Swiss National Tourist Office, 1975. 94p. map. bibliog.

This handy guide begins with an alphabetical listing of the ninety-four castles and mansions selected for inclusion in this publication from about 3,000 in existence in all parts of Switzerland. Ancient strongholds, stately mansions, impressive towers, and lovely châteaux, some in ruin, some restored, some sitting atop mountains, some built over water, represent a good cross-section of this national treasure. Half of each page is taken up by a photograph of the dwelling; underneath is a brief text describing the components, the history, and the present use of the place, with visiting hours, where open to the public. A small sketch shows the location of the building with respect to the village or city in which it stands. A fold-out map of Switzerland helps to locate the buildings.

838 **Museen, die nicht jeder kennt.** (Museums that not everybody knows.)
Anne Kunz. Basel: GS Verlag, 1987. 242p.

This guide directs the reader to lesser-known museums that house very specialized collections and are frequently located off the beaten path. It lists names, addresses, telephone numbers and hours of operation of these institutions. A text of about two pages for each museum places the collections in a larger cultural and historical context. The handy guide with its 250 black-and-white photographs is available in German, French and English.

839 **Schweizer Museumsführer: mit Einschluss des Fürstentums Liechtenstein.** (Swiss museums guide: including the principality of Liechtenstein.)
Claude Lapaire, Martin R. Schärer. Bern; Stuttgart, FRG: Haupt, 1980. 3rd ed. 369p.

This handy guide to 538 museums, including four in Liechtenstein, lists public and private collections of every kind, in large cities and small mountain villages. Critical for the institution's inclusion was its accessibility to the public. The entries are organized alphabetically, according to the locality where the museum is found, and every item is entered according to a uniform scheme. The entries provide information about the collections housed in the museums, opening hours, and a short history of and bibliography for each museum. There is also a list of these museums by canton and another one of individuals connected with each collection. The entries are in the language of each museum's respective locality. Some museums are illustrated.

840 **The museums of Basel.**

Annemarie Monteil, translated from the German by Eileen Walliser. Basel: Birkhäuser, 1977. 304p. map. bibliog.

Published by the government of Canton Basel-Stadt, this large-sized book with its more than 100 colour plates provides a beautiful introduction to the wealth that is accumulated in the great museums of Basel. Five major museums are presented, with brief texts describing their histories and collections. They are the Museum of Fine Arts with its collection of paintings and its cabinet of prints and drawings; the Museum of Ancient Art; the Historical Museum; the Museum of Ethnography and Swiss Popular Traditions; and the Museum of Natural History. Each plate is carefully described in German, French, and English. An appendix contains brief texts on thirteen additional Basel museums.

841 **Schatzkammer der Schweiz. Kostbarkeiten des Schweizerischen Landesmuseums = Patrimoine culturel de la Suisse. Joyaux du Musée National Suisse = Patrimonio culturale della Svizzera. Ogetti preziosi del Museo Nazionale Svizzero = Heritage of Switzerland: the cultural treasures of the Swiss National Museum.**

Edited by Jenny Schneider, Fritz Hofer. Zurich; Munich: Artemis, 1980. 223p.

This magnificent book features the most precious objects of the Swiss National Museum in Zurich, each an important component of the 10,000-year-long cultural history of Switzerland. Each of the 110 objects is given its own full-page photograph, most of them in colour. The left-hand page facing the photograph provides a scholarly description of the object's origin, historical background, and cultural and artistic significance. The first object is a small, flat limestone tablet engraved with animals from the Old Stone Age. The chain of interesting and often beautiful artefacts runs from the later prehistoric times to the Roman era and thence to the Middle Ages all the way through to modern times. Religious art and *objets d'art* are well represented, as are secular objects, such as armour, swords, goblets, jewellery, coats of arms, and pieces of furniture. From the 18th and 19th centuries the editors have selected colourful uniforms, silver coffee pots, enamelled glass, a painted wardrobe from Appenzell, a faience tureen, costume jewellery from Nidwalden, and printed *indiennes* cotton textiles from Glarus. The volume ends with a reproduction of Ferdinand Hodler's monumental depiction of the battle of Murten.

842 **Museums discovered: the Oskar Reinhart collections.**

Franz Zelger. Ft. Lauderdale, Florida: Woodbine Books, 1981. 208p. bibliog. (Created by Shorewood Fine Art Books, New York).

To appreciate the two collections that Oskar Reinhart (1885-1965) has given to the public, one must know something about this collector's collecting strategies, and Zelger's introduction to this picture book fulfils that task. The first collection was given by the patron to his home town of Winterthur, the industrial, second largest city of Canton Zurich, in 1951 and is known as the Oskar Reinhart Foundation. It comprises more than 500 works by Swiss, German, and Austrian artists of the 18th, 19th, and 20th centuries. The second collection of some 200 paintings, drawings, and sculptures, 'almost all of them masterpieces of the first rank', includes choice works by Old Masters as well as by French painters and sculptors of the 19th century. For the housing of these pieces Reinhart acquired the beautiful villa of Am Römerholz, above

Winterthur. Painstaking care and some idiosyncratic planning went into the acquisition and hanging of the paintings. The mansion and the collection were given to the Swiss Confederation upon Reinhart's death in 1965. About fifty works from each of the two collections are reproduced in colour in this book, each accompanied by pertinent data about the artist and the painting or sculpture, and a descriptive and interpretative text. Another book, Rudolf Koella's *Sammlung Oskar Reinhart. Am Römerholz, Winterthur* (Zurich: Füssli, 1975), is devoted exclusively to the Am Römerholz collection, and includes 153 plates and a catalogue of all the art works it houses.

Libraries and archives

843 **Archive, Bibliotheken und Dokumentationsstellen der Schweiz.** (Archives, libraries, and documentation centres of Switzerland.) Amt für Wissenschaft und Forschung. Bern: Amt für Wissenschaft und Forschung, 1976. 805p. (4th ed. of the *Führer durch die schweizerische Dokumentation* [Guide through Swiss documentation]).

This hefty guide lists the Swiss archives, libraries, and other repositories for documents that participate in the exchange of scholarly and scientific information and make their holdings available to the general public. There are 668 such institutions. For each institution, the guide provides information as to the year it was founded, the major strengths of its holdings, the organizations and bodies for which it is the depository, the size of its collection by number of monographs, periodicals, manuscripts, maps, and other kinds of documents, its catalogues, the regulations governing its use, and a bibliography. There are two indexes, one alphabetical by institution and the other by subject matter.

844 **Bibliothekstaschenbuch Schweiz.** (Pocket guide to Swiss libraries.) Edited by Rainer Diederich, Hermann Schneider. Aarau, Switzerland [etc.]: Sauerländer, 1988. 158p. bibliog.

This handy guide lists 837 academic and public Swiss libraries, from the Aargau cantonal library in Aarau to the city and cantonal library in Zug. Each entry consists of the address of the institution (with telephone, telex, and telefax numbers), the year of its founding, the size of its collections in numbers or metres. The guide groups books, periodicals, manuscripts, microforms, photographs, slides, maps, and tone- and information carriers. Special catalogues and databanks are also mentioned, as are regulations for users, and the strength of each particular collection.

845 **Das Schweizerische Bundesarchiv von 1798 bis zur Gegenwart.** (The Swiss Federal Archives from 1798 to the present.) Walter Meyrat. Bern: Bundesarchiv, 1972. 172p bibliog.

Meyrat provides a history of the federal archives from the first central national archive founded during the time of the Helvetic Republic (1798-1803) to the modern institution in its stately Italian Renaissance-style building in Bern-Kirchenfeld which was completed in 1899. His is primarily a house chronicle, dealing with the various archivists and their staffs, and their achievements in terms of collecting, classifying, and storing archival materials. A list of federal archives publications and a chronology of events from 1798 to 1972 form part of the book.

846 **Bibliotheken in der Schweiz.** (Libraries in Switzerland.) Vereinigung Schweizerischer Bibliothekare. Bern: Schweizerische Landesbibliothek, 1976. 192p.

This large-format illustrated book contains brief descriptions of the history, purpose, organization, and holdings of forty-nine of the several thousand libraries in Switzerland. All types of libraries are represented: the university libraries, among them those of Zurich and Basel, two of the largest libraries in the country; public libraries, among them the Pestalozzi Society library in Zurich; specialized libraries, such as the Swiss National Library in Bern, the Stiftsbibliothek St Gallen, and the Bibliotheca Bodmeriana in Cologny-Genève; libraries of industrial enterprises and firms, such as the pharmaceutical library of Wander AG in Bern; and, finally, the libraries of international organizations in Geneva, among them the United Nations, formerly League of Nations, library. The introduction in six languages, including English and Russian, by Franz Georg Maier, former director of the Swiss National Library, stresses the fact that the library system of Switzerland is, in its diversity, a reflection of the historical growth and the intensely federal nature of the Swiss state. This is a most enjoyable and instructive book.

Books and Bookmaking

847 **A history of European printing.**

Colin Clair. London [etc.]: Academic Press, 1976. 526p. bibliog.

Two chapters of this historical survey of printing in Europe from Gutenberg to the early 20th century are devoted to Switzerland. In 'Switzerland's first printers', p. 87-93, Colin Clair mentions the printers who produced the Swiss *incunabula*, that is, books printed before 1500 – most of them worked in Basel, among them Johann Amerbach and Johann Froben. In Geneva three printers worked between 1478 and 1509, but the first book printed in Switzerland was produced by a canon of the small abbey of Beromünster near Luzern in November 1470. The chapter 'Swiss printing in the sixteenth century', p. 179-84, brings the other Swiss cities into the picture, especially Zurich with Christoph Froschauer. In Basel Froben continued his output, publishing more than 250 works, mainly in Greek and Latin, before his death in 1527 and making of Basel one of the great centres of the European book trade.

848 **Der Schweizer Buchhandel.** (The Swiss book trade.)

Zurich: Schweizerischer Buchhändler- und Verleger-Verband, 1943- . semi-monthly. ca. 50p.

This journal is published by the Swiss Association of Book Dealers and Publishers and the Association of Swiss Dealers in Second-hand Books and Engravings. It contains some information about trends in the book trade, but much of the space is taken up by news and announcements of an organizational nature, and even more by advertisements by publishers.

849 **Librarium. Zeitschrift der Schweizerischen Bibliophilen-Gesellschaft.**

(Librarium: Journal of the Swiss Society of Bibliophiles.)

Zurich: Werner G. and Mirjam Zimmermann-Liebert, 1958- . three times per year. ca. 80p.

This journal contains exquisitely illustrated scholarly articles on beautiful books and news about the society and international bibliophile conferences.

Books and Bookmaking

850 **The book trade of the world. Volume 1: Europe and international section.**
Edited by Sigfred Taubert. Hamburg: Verlag für Buchmarkt-Forschung; London: André Deutsch; New York: R. R. Bowker, 1972. 543p.

The chapter on Switzerland (p. 436-58) touches in thirty-five numbered sections on all aspects of the book trade in Switzerland. The sections contain precise, factual information with data as of the late 1960s on topics such as retail prices, market research, children's literature, professional training of book-trade employees, taxes, book production, translations, book design, publishing, wholesale and retail trade, book imports and exports, bibliophily, literary prizes, book design, and others. Names and addresses of the major organizations are given, and almost every section has a brief bibliography. The product is a neat and welcome overview.

Mass Media

The press

851 **Leitfaden der Schweizer Presse.** (Repertory of the Swiss press.) Geneva: Annonces suisses, 1985. 2 parts: 446p., 605p.

Part A lists all daily and weekly papers appearing in Switzerland. It gives information on the address, circulation, periodicity, political tendency, and editorial staff of each paper. Papers in nine languages, including Esperanto and Arabic, are listed. The media index has some 450 entries, and some 4,000 members of the editorial staffs are listed in another index. Part B for periodicals is divided into two volumes, the major part in B1 being periodicals in German, and in B2 those in French. For each periodical the title, address, type and speciality, circulation, and name of the chief editor are given.

852 **Structural picture of the Swiss press: trends and prospects.** Ernst Bollinger. *Gazette* (Leiden, The Netherlands), vol. 16, no. 3 (1970), p. 149-69.

Bollinger believes that the success of the popular boulevard newspaper *Blick* is responsible for the new direction the formerly drab and not too readable Swiss newspapers took in the 1970s. The multilingual population and the many political affiliations that are reflected in the great number of dailies make it difficult to present a structural picture of the Swiss press. Figures given for circulation reveal that a significant number of readers reside outside Switzerland. See also *La presse Suisse: structure et diversité* (The Swiss press: structure and diversity) by Ernst Bollinger (Bern: Herbert Lang; Frankfurt am Main: Peter Lang, 1976). Switzerland has the most newspapers per capita in the world – in absolute numbers, its 116 daily newspapers are surpassed only by the 121 of the Federal Republic of Germany – but Bollinger recognizes a trend toward the disappearance of small papers and the financial concentration in the hands of relatively few publishers, and he makes an interesting attempt to gauge the quality and the political influence of various papers.

853 ***Blick*: Immer dabei! Die tägliche Inszenierung des gesunden Volksempfindens.** (*Blick*: always with it: the daily presentation of the people's common sense.)
Jürg Bürgi. Basel: Lenos, 1984. 279p. (Mediaprint, 7).

The tabloid *Blick*, published by Ringier, has become the largest Swiss daily paper in its twenty-five-year history with a circulation of over 350,000 at the time of its 25th anniversary in 1984. Neither political nor private pressure could halt production because of the substantial readership hungry for stories of scandals, murders and crimes, and political controversy. Bürgi gives an account of the growth and development of the paper from its beginning in 1959; he analyses the stories covered, the opposition that had to be overcome, the marks left by the staff and especially the editors who increasingly stressed that their paper served an educational function in exposing existing prejudice. What was once a sensational illustrated paper intended for the 'little man' now represents the conservative stands of a broad spectrum of people from all social groups. Its outward appearance, however, has not changed much. There is an abundance of pictures (with a pin-up girl prominently displayed in every issue), the headlines are in large letters and different founts, the articles are well researched but short as are the sentences and paragraphs. There is usually just one idea expressed per sentence, facts are illustrated with numbers, and direct quotes are common. Many prominent people were asked to contribute to this book by stating their opinion about the paper. Some declined to comment, but the positive and negative responses of those who did answer show that whatever one may think, the *Blick* has become a paper to be reckoned with.

854 **Die Schweiz und das Dritte Reich. Vier deutschschweizerische Zeitungen im Zeitalter des Faschismus 1933-1939.** (Switzerland and the Third Reich: four German-Swiss newspapers in the age of fascism 1933-1939.)
Erich Dreifuß. Frauenfeld, Switzerland; Stuttgart, FRG: Huber, 1971. 251p. bibliog.

Dreifuß analyses the editorial policies and reportage of four prominent Swiss newspapers, the socialist *Volksrecht* (people's right, VR, Zurich), the liberal *Neue Zürcher Zeitung* (new Zurich gazette, NZZ), the Catholic-conservative *Vaterland* (fatherland, VL, Luzern), the *Neue Berner Zeitung* (new Bern gazette, NBZ) of the farmer, small business, and burgher party are the four newspapers during the first half of the Hitler era. The VL distrusted Hitler and his national-socialist party from the start, but did not take a truly firm stand on many issues as long as the Church was not directly affected. The VR, on the other hand, never relented in its condemnation of the events taking place in the land of its neighbour to the north. The NBZ, reflecting the anti-capitalistic orientation of its peasant constituency, for a long time wrote with approval of the progress that Germany made under Hitler. Finally, the NZZ, finally, the most influential paper of the four, was overtly hostile toward everything national-socialism represented, but it did not think it productive to engage in a crusade against the Third Reich.

855 **Ein toter Baum aus dem Bannwald der Demokratie: Das *Volksrecht* 1898 bis 1973.** (A dead tree from the protective forest of the democracy: the *Volksrecht*, 1898-1973.)
Ulrich Frei. Zurich: Chronos, 1987. 405p. bibliog.

The disappearance of the *Volksrecht* (People's Right) in 1973 created a considerable stir in the political scene of the time. Frei traces the history of this once well-known newspaper of the Zurich Social Democrats and analyses the reasons for its demise. From financial records, he proves that the mounting losses, which reached 836,500 Swiss francs in 1973, were not due to advertisers abandoning the paper, as was claimed by management, but to heavily increased personnel costs. Nor were internal bickering and party/management/owner conflicts a major reason for the paper's decline. The paper had begun to lose its readers in the 1950s when it was still outwardly sound and strong. More than coincidentally, television and the appearance of tabloids such as the sensationalist *Blick* (q.v.) heralded a media revolution which deprived the political press in Switzerland of a large part of its readership. The *Volksrecht* was only one, though perhaps the most prominent one, of the victims of this media revolution. Frey's story is well researched and documented with a number of appendices. It is an important contribution to the history of the Swiss press in the last three decades.

856 **The Swiss press and foreign affairs in World War II.**
Frederick H. Hartmann. Gainesville, Florida: University of Florida Press, 1960. 87p. bibliog. (University of Florida Monographs: Social Sciences, no. 5).

Beginning in 1934 the Swiss government enacted a series of laws regulating the press, establishing the framework within which the Swiss press was to operate. For example, through post-publication censorship, the state could penalize editors for perceived poor judgement or irresponsibility. Control of the press, which at first was in the hands of the army, passed to the Federal Council; this control became a tool for coordinating press content and foreign policy. Editors of the newspapers cooperated on the whole quite willingly; their patriotic thinking was not at odds with the goals of the Federal Council, namely to maintain Swiss neutrality in the face of an overpowering and irritable Nazi Germany. A little more than one-third of this booklet is devoted to a description of the way the Swiss press reported and commented on Hitler's war, alternating between boldness and caution. The Swiss public invariably complained that the press was too cautious; the Federal Council, on the other hand, sought to address the constant flow of complaints from the German diplomats in Bern.

857 **Publishing in Switzerland: the press and the book trade.**
Linda S. Kropf. Littleton, Colorado: Libraries Unlimited, 1973. 139p.

In sixty pages of text Kropf gives a profile of Switzerland as a multilingual nation, a discussion of the characteristics of the Swiss press, and an overview of Swiss book publishing. The second half of her book consists of two directories, one of newspapers in Swiss communities of more than 8,000 inhabitants, the other a directory of the country's publishing firms. The book, which evolved from a master's thesis in library science, has been researched and written with care. However, newspaper and book publishing have undergone major changes since Kropf wrote her work, and a considerable part of her information is now outdated.

858 **The mass media of the German-speaking countries.**
John Sandford. London: Wolff, 1976. 235p.

This book has seven chapters, four for 'West Germany' and one each for Austria, Switzerland, and 'East Germany'. The chapter on Switzerland, p. 155-83, provides an excellent introduction to the newspaper press and to broadcasting in Switzerland. The Swiss newspapers, Sandford says, 'especially in the German-speaking areas, are still typically staid, highly localized in distribution, minute in terms of circulation, and party-political in their editorial policy'. The *Blick* (q.v.) and a few of the large dailies, are exceptions to this rule. Sandford has similar trenchant observations for magazines and periodicals. The section on broadcasting describes the complicated regulatory structure of Swiss broadcasting with its semi-official supervisory bodies for television, radio, wired radio service, and short-wave programming and financing.

859 **Die Schweiz im Nervenkrieg. Aufgabe und Haltung der Schweizer Presse in der Krisen- und Kriegszeit 1933-1945.** (Switzerland in the war of nerves: task and attitude of the Swiss press during the years of crises and war 1933-1945.)

Karl Weber. Bern: Lang, 1948. 316p.

Within a few years of Hitler's rise to power in Germany, the relationship between the Swiss federal government and the Swiss press lost its previously placid character and became tense and emotional. The Swiss newspapers reported about events in Germany, beginning with the Reichstag fire, in a manner that was objectionable to the Nazi régime. As Europe drifted toward war, the Federal Council found it necessary to remind the press that its freedom of expression was subject to the overriding foreign policy objectives of the State. With the outbreak of war the federal authorities issued and enforced emergency press laws that restricted the freedom of the press for more than five years. Weber analyses the philosophical issues involved and then describes the sequence of events abroad, reaction to the events in the press, censorship by the authorities, and manifestations of protest by editors of the newspapers. Even though forty years old, this work is still regarded as authoritative on its subject. Max Nef produced an equally important analysis of federal press policies during the war, which was made public as *Bericht des Bundesrates an die Bundesversammlung über die schweizerische Pressepolitik im Zusammenhang mit dem Kriegsgeschehen 1939-1945* (Report of the Federal Council to the Federal Assembly on the Swiss press politics in connection with the war 1939-45. Bern, 1946).

860 **The Swiss press: an outline.**

Karl Weber. Bern: Herbert Lang, 1960. 46p. bibliog.

Weber's short outline of the Swiss press begins with an investigation of the relationship between the State and the press. In 1798 the liberty of the press was mentioned for the first time in the Swiss constitution with the clause 'The liberty of the press is a natural corollary of the right of every citizen to be informed'. But it was not until 1848 and the creation of the modern Swiss Confederation that this liberty became a reality. In the ensuing years amendments were added. Switzerland's precarious political situation during World War II led to an emergency decree which restricted for a time the freedom of the press – articles from the Swiss Criminal Code of 1942 regarding those measures are reprinted here. Weber finds the Swiss press 'extremely decentralized' as evidenced by the large number of newspapers and periodicals it produces, where even communes under 10,000 inhabitants may have their own paper. Statistical information about such things as circulation, foundation dates of newspapers and journals and their political orientation, and organizations and institutions serving the press make this an interesting overview of the Swiss press from its beginning to the year 1960.

861 **A great Swiss newspaper: the story of the *Neue Zürcher Zeitung*.**
Elizabeth Wiskemann. London [etc.]: Oxford University Press, 1959. 90p.

The first issue of the *Zürcher Zeitung*, or Zurich gazette, appeared on Wednesday, 12 January 1780. The paper evolved from a small, twice-weekly sheet into an internationally recognized daily. The British journalist and writer Wiskemann traces the history of this development, giving due regard to the strong personalities that guided the policies and the politics of what came to be the *NZZ*, the New Zurich gazette. The politics of the *NZZ* during the 19th century were those of the Radical or Liberal party that dominated the political life of the country, and during the Nazi era of the 20th century it maintained an unwaveringly critical stance toward Hitler and his ideology. A network of university-trained journalists who report from the centres of political and economic activity in many parts of the world constitutes a large part of the paper's strength. As Wiskemann writes: 'The *Neue Zürcher Zeitung* is rightly proud of the continuity of its policy: precisely this has transformed it from an almost revolutionary radical paper in the mid-nineteenth century into a pillar of enlightened, individualistic conservatism in the mid-twentieth.'

Newspapers

862 **Basler Zeitung.** (Basel newspaper).
Basel, 1977- . Daily, except Sunday. Circulation 113,100. Independent.

Successor to the *National-Zeitung* (1842-1977) and the *Basler Nachrichten* (1845-1977).

863 **Berner Zeitung.** (Bern newspaper.)
Bern, 1979- . Daily, except Sunday. Circulation 61,000; 121,800 with regional editions. Independent.

Successor to the *Berner Nachrichten* and the *Berner Tagblatt*.

864 **Der Bund.** (The alliance.)
Bern, 1850- . Daily, except Sunday. Circulation 62,300. Independent–Liberal.

865 **La Suisse.** (Switzerland.)
Geneva, 1898- . Daily. Circulation 70,000; Sunday 101,500. Independent.

866 **Tribune de Genève.** (Geneva tribune).
Geneva, 1879- . Daily, except Sunday. Circulation 63,700. Independent.

Mass Media.

867 **Le Matin.** (The morning.)
Lausanne, 1862- . Daily. Circulation 53,900; Sunday 126,500. Independent.

868 **24 heures.** (24 hours.)
Lausanne, 1972. Daily, except Sunday. Circulation 96,800. Independent.

869 **Corriere del Ticino.** (Ticino courier.)
Lugano, 1890- . Daily, except Sunday. Circulation 34,100. Independent.

870 **Luzerner Neuste Nachrichten.** (Luzern latest news.)
Luzern, 1897- . Daily, except Sunday. Circulation 57,600. Independent.

871 **St. Galler Tagblatt.** (St Gallen daily.)
St Gallen, 1838- . Daily, except Sunday. Circulation 53,900. Liberal.

872 **Blick.** (Glance.)
Zurich, 1959- . Daily. Circulation 379,800. Independent.

This publication has the largest newspaper circulation in the country. Written in the brash, sensationalist style of the German *Boulevardpresse*, its appearance revolutionized the Swiss newspaper scene, leading to the demise of many of the weaker political party papers and forcing the others to spruce up their presentation of the news and the general lay-out of their papers. Unlike the other German-Swiss newspapers which depend for about ninety per cent of their sales on subscriptions, the *Blick* relies almost entirely on street sales.

873 **Neue Zürcher Zeitung.** (New Zurich gazette.)
Zurich, 1779- . Daily, except Sunday. Circulation 141,500, including 8,800 for the edition abroad. Liberal.

The oldest newspaper in the country, the *NZZ* is also the most prestigious. It still maintains its own network of journalists in many of the important business and political centres of the world. It is read by businessmen and government officials in many parts of the world, and its editorial opinions are often quoted in the world press.

874 **Tages-Anzeiger.** (Daily announcer.)
Zurich, 1893- . Daily, except Sunday. Circulation 256,800. Independent.

A popular family paper with the second highest circulation in the country. Its weekly air mail edition, with a circulation of 8,000, is read by Swiss all over the world.

Radio and television

875 **25 ans ensemble: télévision suisse romande.** (25 years together: television of French Switzerland.)
Nicolas Bouvier. Lausanne, Geneva: Société suisse de radiodiffusion et télévision, 1979. 3 vols.

Three slim, but richly illustrated booklets of sixty pages each tell the success story of French-Swiss television, whose subscribers increased from 4,457 in 1954 to 1,920,689 in 1979. Booklet one provides a documentary history with many photographs of the early days of French-Swiss television in Lausanne during the 1950s. Booklet two contains the chronicle of two decades of mature work during which French-Swiss television made tremendous progress in recording and transmitting televised images – in November 1960 the Federal Council confirmed its decision to locate the Swiss TV studios in Geneva and Zurich. Booklet three deals with the administrative structure and the organization of television and radio services in Switzerland today. La Radio et la Télévision Romande (RTSR – French-Swiss Radio and Television), with headquarters in Lausanne report to the Société suisse de radiodiffusion (SSR – Swiss Radio Corporation); the SSR is not an organ of the State, but a private corporation holding the concession to provide a public service. However, television transmission in Switzerland is the responsibility of PTT (post, telephone, and telegraph) which is a federal agency. Since the installation of the first broadcast station on the Uetliberg in Zurich, the PTT has added 957 broadcast and transmission stations to assure reception of the TV programmes in every nook and cranny of mountainous Switzerland.

876 **1935-1985. 50 Jahre Schweizer Radio International.** (1935-1985: 50 years of Swiss Radio International.)
Edited by Gerd H. Padel, Walter Fankhauser, Benno Bruni, Nicolas D. Lombard, Lance Tschannen. Bern: Schweizer Radio International. Schweizerische Radio- und Fernsehgesellschaft, 1985. 149p.

Swiss Radio International (SRI) in 1985 had 126 full-time and 360 part-time employees. With a budget of 15 million Swiss francs it maintained twelve broadcasting stations (*Sender*) and produced 15,061 hours of programming in nine languages, 8,306 of them for intercontinental emission and 6,755 for Europe. The booklet describes how SRI evolved from its beginnings as a regular short-wave service in 1935. In 1939 a special short-wave centre was built in Schwarzenburg, Canton Bern, and under difficult circumstances the Swiss short-wave service provided news and commentary during World War II eagerly listened to in many parts of Europe, especially the weekly programmes of Jean-Rodolphe von Salis and René Payot. Since the early 1960s the federal government has supported the short-wave service with ever-increasing appropriations, reaching 50% of SRI's operating costs by 1984. The other 50% comes from revenues raised by the Swiss Radio Company from concession fees by Swiss radio owners. SRI's mandate is to establish closer ties between the Swiss abroad and their native country and to promote a positive image of Switzerland worldwide. Opinion polls rate it as among the most trustworthy in the world.

877 **Swiss PR & media directory.**
Zurich: Renteria, 1989. 16th ed. 320p.

Part 1 of this directory lists public relations and press services of some 700 firms, authorities, and organizations, divided into eighty-two categories from 'employers' (*Arbeitgeber*) to 'living' (*Wohnen*). Part 2 provides the addresses of the editorial units of the Swiss news media, including news services, the daily and weekly press, press and picture agencies, freelance journalists, radio, television, videotext services, and TV satellites, and of magazines, professional periodicals, and press associations. This is a most useful publication for finding pertinent information, presented concisely, on any of the public relations, media, and press products of and in Switzerland.

Periodicals

Popular illustrated magazines

878 **Annabelle.**
Zurich: Tages-Anzeiger, 1938- . 24 times per year; circulation 114,200; ca. 120p.

Together with its French-language counterpart *Femina* (circulation 41,000) this is the leading Swiss journal for fashion and other subject matter generally perceived to be of interest to women.

879 **Das gelbe Heft. Schweizer Woche.** (The yellow magazine: Swiss week.)
Zofingen, Switzerland: Ringier, 1884- . weekly; circulation 210,500; ca. 100p.

The oldest and one of the most popular illustrated family magazines of Switzerland, this weekly is read in many farmhouses throughout German-speaking Switzerland.

880 **Illustrazione ticinese. La prima rivista familiare ticinese fondata nel 1931.** (Ticinese illustrations: the leading Ticinese family magazine, founded in 1931.)
Cassarate, Switzerland: Illustrazione ticinese, 1931- . 14 times per year; circulation 87,600; ca. 60p.

Illustrated family magazine, widely read in Canton Ticino and in the Italian-speaking valleys of Canton Graubünden.

881 **Meyers Modeblatt.** (Meyer's fashion journal.)
Zurich: Meyers Erben, 1924- . weekly; circulation 209,400; ca. 90p.

The most popular of the journals targeted to women in Switzerland.

Periodicals. Popular illustrated magazines

882 **Schweizer Familie.** (Swiss family.)

Zurich: Tages-Anzeiger, 1894- . weekly; circulation 303,000; ca. 130p.

Developed out of its predecessor *Das Schweizer Heim* (The Swiss home), this hebdomadal enjoys a larger readership than its Ringier competitor, *Das gelbe Heft* (q.v.), probably because it is of somewhat greater appeal in the urbanized parts of German-speaking Switzerland.

883 **Schweizer Illustrierte.** (Swiss illustrated.)

Zofingen, Switzerland: Ringier, 1911- . weekly; circulation 222,700; ca. 125p.

Together with its French-language counterpart, the weekly *Illustré* (Illustrated), circulation 132,700, is the splashiest of the Swiss popular weekly illustrated magazines, coming closest to the German mass products that also sell well in Switzerland, such as *Quick* and *Der Stern*.

884 **Tele. TV Radio Zeitung.** (Tele: TV-radio journal.)

Zofingen, Switzerland: Ringier, 1967- . weekly; circulation 282,900; ca. 130p.

This publication provides the weekly programmes of the television channels from all over Europe that can be received by Swiss cable subscribers, and also the radio programmes of the Swiss radio stations and some foreign ones. Its French-language counterpart, *Radio-TV-Je vois tout* (Radio-TV-I watch everything) has a circulation of 112,300.

885 **Wir Brückenbauer. Organ des Migros-Genossenschafts-Bundes.** (We bridge builders: organ of the Migros cooperative alliance.)

Zurich: Migros-Genossenschaft, 1942- . weekly; circulation 900,000; ca. 50p.

The French-language edition, *Construire*, has a circulation of 265,000, and the Italian-language edition, *Azione*, 50,000. The journal is sent free to all households that belong to the Migros alliance, Migros being, among other things, the largest retail food distributing chain in Switzerland. The *Brückenbauer* has outgrown its purely commercial function of advertising Migros products and offers a range of illustrated articles of an informative and entertaining nature. It has also lost most of the political missionary zeal of the founder of Migros, Gottlieb Duttweiler, but it is included here as an example of a kind of periodical literature, a sales flyer-cum-magazine, prevalent in Switzerland. A close second in terms of numbers and looks to the *Brückenbauer* is the *Coop-Zeitung* with its French- and Italian-language editions *Coopération* and *Cooperazione*, with circulations of 815,00, 245,000, and 34,700 respectively.

Periodicals dealing with politics, business and the economy, and culture

886 **ASZM Allgemeine schweizerische Militärzeitschrift.** (General Swiss military journal.)
Frauenfeld, Switzerland: Huber, 1834- . monthly; ca. 65p.

Pre-dating the creation of the modern Swiss Confederation in 1848, this old publication is the organ of the Swiss officers' society. A typical issue (June 1988) has articles, in most cases with illustrations, on technical military problems, leadership training, modernization of armaments and equipment, international defence issues, the decriminalization of conscientious objection to military service, reviews of books and foreign journals, and an overview of military developments in other parts of the world.

887 **Der schweizerische Beobachter.** (The Swiss observer.)
Glattbrugg, Switzerland: Beobachter, 1927- . semi-monthly; circulation 467,400; ca. 70p.

This popular journal makes it its business to investigate critically administrators and managers at all levels of public life and in private business in an effort to uncover scandals, minor or major, and to redress injustices inflicted upon the 'little people' by the 'system'. Its investigative reporting has led to lawsuits on some occasions, and to important reforms on others.

888 **Du. Die Zeitschrift der Kultur.** (Thou: the journal of culture.)
Zurich: Conzett & Huber, 1941- . monthly; circulation 17,500; ca. 130p.

An 'upmarket', richly illustrated journal that covers all aspects and all periods of art and a wide range of cultural topics with notes about international art exhibits and reviews of art books. Individual issues usually have a thematic emphasis. Available with English-language summary of its contents.

889 **L'Hebdo.** (The weekly.)
Lausanne, Switzerland: L'Hebdo, 1981- . weekly; circulation 25,400; ca. 70p.

Weekly news and information journal, along the lines of the American news magazines *Time* and *Newsweek*, covering a variety of political and societal subjects. One of the more aggressive and critical journals published in Switzerland, *L'Hebdo* is itself in the news once in a while for its controversial reporting.

890 **Jahrbuch der Neuen Helvetischen Gesellschaft.** (Yearbook of the New Helvetic Society.)
Aarau, Switzerland [etc.]: Sauerländer, 1930- . annual.

Published until 1975 under the title *Die Schweiz* (Switzerland), the annual volumes of varying length are usually devoted to a single subject that is analysed from a number of viewpoints by prominent contributors. The 1987 volume, for example, has as its theme 'Switzerland and the world'.

Periodicals. Periodicals dealing with politics, business and the economy, and culture.

891 **Nebelspalter. Schweizerische humoristisch-satirische Wochenschrift.** (Piercing the fog: Swiss humoristic-satirical weekly.)
Rorschach, Switzerland: E. Löpfe-Benz, 1875- . weekly; circulation 51,200; ca. 60p.

The *Nebelspalter* is an institution in Switzerland. In prose, in verse form, and with drawings and caricatures this weekly magazine satirizes incidents and personalities from Swiss public life and makes fun of Swiss foibles in general. Its courageous stand against the Nazi-type frontist movements during the Hitler era has earned the *Nebelspalter* lasting recognition.

892 **L'oeil. Revue d'art mensuelle.** (The eye: a monthly art review.)
Lausanne: Nouvelle Sedo, 1955- . monthly; ca. 90p.

Large-size, highbrow art magazine, richly illustrated, with articles on all aspects of the arts in Switzerland and France above all, but also some other countries. Also included are news and announcements about auctions, exhibitions in museums and galleries, and new art books.

893 **Politik and Wirtschaft. Das Schweizer Magazin.** (Politics and economy: the Swiss magazine.)
Glattbrugg, Switzerland: Curti Medien, 1986- . monthly; circulation 31,000; ca. 100p.

A new slick, highbrow magazine, it employs up-to-date techniques of presentation with photographs and numerous coloured charts in its articles on current problems and issues in Swiss politics and economy, somewhat along the lines of *The Economist*. This monthly also contains an international section.

894 **Schweizer Monatshefte für Politik, Wirtschaft, Kultur.** (Swiss monthly for politics, economy, and culture.)
Zurich: Schulthess, 1921- . monthly; circulation 2,500; ca. 90p.

This monthly journal includes articles and commentaries on political, economic, and cultural topics of current interest, written by knowledgeable authors who represent a wide spectrum of opinions. Notes and reviews are also featured.

895 **Thema. Magazin zur Forschung und Wissenschaft an den Schweizer Hochschulen.** (Theme: magazine on scholarship and science at the Swiss universities.)
Gemeinschaftsproduktion der Pressestellen der Schweizer Hochschulen und des Schweizerischen Nationalfonds, 1986- . semi-annual; circulation 48,000 German, 25,000 French; ca. 40p.

Each issue of this large-format journal is devoted in its entirety to a single theme. Issue 4, December 1987, for example, has eleven articles by professors from all Swiss universities and the Swiss National Foundation on the topic of language and languages in Switzerland. Together they give an excellent picture of the many facets of language study. Other issues have dealt with nutrition, and Switzerland and outer space. Stimulating and informative, this journal treats involved scientific and scholarly topics in jargon-free language.

896 **Turicum. Vierteljahresschrift für Kultur, Wissenschaft und Wirtschaft.** (Turicum: quarterly for culture, science, and economy.) Zurich: Orell Füssli, 1970- . quarterly; circulation 24,000; ca. 80p.

As the title 'Turicum', the Roman name for Zurich, indicates, this glossy publication focuses on Zurich. Nicely illustrated articles feature various aspects of Zurich's cultural life, its economic activities, and scientific achievements.

897 **Unsere Kunstdenkmäler.** (Our art monuments.) Edited by the Gesellschaft für Schweizerische Kunstgeschichte. Bern: Stämpfli, 1949- . quarterly. ca. 150p.

Three of the quarterly issues of this illustrated journal for the members of the society for Swiss art history are made up of topical articles on selected themes; the fourth contains a detailed and enticing programme of the many papers and guided art excursions available to members at the annual conferences of the society in various Swiss cities. Issue 3 of 1987, for example, is dedicated to a discussion of art history in Switzerland from Johann Caspar Füssli's *Geschichte und Abbildung der besten Künstler in der Schweiz* (History and illustration of the best artists in Switzerland), published in two parts in 1755 and 1757, to the late-20th-century multi-volume art history project *Ars Helvetica* (q.v.). Issue 4 of 1987 deals with new results of Baroque research, while issue 1 of 1988 is concerned with medieval wall-painting in Switzerland. The articles, with copious notes and bibliographies, are in either German, French, or Italian with résumés in the other two languages. With its numerous book reviews, announcements, and calendar of events this is an extremely well-made journal.

898 **Weltwoche.** (World week.) Zurich: Weltwoche-Verlag, 1933- . weekly; circulation 98,500; ca. 48p.

Published on Thursdays in newspaper format, *Weltwoche* is characterized by provocative in-depth articles and commentaries on Swiss and international politics, society, and culture.

Professional journals and yearbooks

899 **Aussenwirtschaft. The Swiss review of international economic relations.** Grüsch, Switzerland: Rüegger, 1946- . quarterly; ca. 120p.

Published by the Swiss Institute for Research into International Economic Relations, Economic Structures, and Regional Science of the Hochschule St Gallen für Wirtschafts- und Sozialwissenschaften. Articles by an international collection of authors on a wide range of topics concerning international economic relations. Most articles are in English.

Periodicals. Professional journals and yearbooks

900 **Botanica Helvetica. Berichte der Schweizerischen Botanischen Gesellschaft.** (Botanica Helvetica: Bulletins of the Swiss Botanical Society.)
Basel: Birkhäuser, 1891- . semi-annual; ca. 200p.

Research papers in the areas of systematics/ecology, morphology, anatomy, histology/cytology, physiology, biochemistry, and mycology/phytopathology, among others. Most articles are in English and have illustrations, charts, graphs, maps, and bibliographies.

901 **Geneva news and international report: the magazine of Switzerland's international life.**
Edited by Padina De Mello. Geneva: Geneva News Publishing Company, 1980- . monthly; ca. 50p.

The publication contains sections on finance, leisure, international trade, travel, personalities, etc. Each issue usually has a somewhat longer feature article. In the May 1989 issue, for example, one finds on p. 22-33 'The Swiss schools guide – a look at private and international education in Switzerland'. Thirty schools in French Switzerland and eight in German Switzerland are described in detail.

902 **Gesnerus. Vierteljahresschrift herausgegeben von der Schweizerischen Gesellschaft für Geschichte der Medizin und der Naturwissenschaften.** (Gesnerus: quarterly journal published by the Swiss Society for the History of Medicine and of the Natural Sciences.)
Aarau, Switzerland: Sauerländer, 1943- . semi-annual; ca. 170p.

Scholarly articles on the history of medicine. Subjects include, among many others, health care through the ages, pharmacological developments, evolution, psychology, and psychiatry. There are numerous book reviews. Few articles are in English, but there are English summaries.

903 **Helvetica Chimica Acta.** (Swiss chemical papers.)
Basel: Helvetica Chimica Acta, 1918- . 8 times per year; ca. 250p.

Published by the Swiss Chemcial Society, this publication consists of scientific papers by researchers in chemistry form all parts of the world. Most papers are in English.

904 **Helvetica Physica Acta. Official Journal of the Swiss Physical Society.**
Basel: Birkhäuser, 1928- . 8 times per year in 1988; ca. 150p.

Lengthy research papers by scientists and scientific teams from many parts of the world are the features of this publication which covers all fields of modern physics, among them quantum mechanics, theoretical and mathematical physics, condensed matter. Most articles are in English.

905 **Journal of Applied Mathematics and Physics.**
Basel: Birkhäuser, 1950- . bimonthly; ca. 150p.

Research papers by mathematicians from all parts of the world. Most of the papers are in English.

906 **Kyklos: international review for social sciences.**
Basel: Helbing & Lichtenhahn, 1947- . quarterly; ca. 170p.

The articles, written by an international cast of scholars, are predominantly in the field of economics.

907 **Mitteilungen der Antiquarischen Gesellschaft in Zürich.** (Bulletin of the antiquarian society of Zurich.)
Zurich: Hans Rohr, 1837- . annually.

This is the oldest of the local history publications in Switzerland. The society also publishes a *Neujahrsblatt* (new year's bulletin). Together, the two publications are a rich source not only of Zurich's history but also of many aspects of Switzerland's history. Volume 55 of the bulletin, the 152nd *Neujahrsblatt* (Zurich, 1988), is a 248-page monograph by Walter P. Schmid on the young Alfred Escher, who became one of the dominant figures of the political and economic life of Zurich and the Swiss Confederation in the second half of the 19th century. The study is based on archival manuscript sources and has twelve illustrations and a bibliography.

908 **Museum Helveticum. Schweizerische Zeitschrift für klassische Altertumswissenschaft.** (Museum Helveticum: Swiss journal for the study of classical antiquity.)
Basel: Schwabe, 1944- . quarterly; ca. 60p.

'Classical' classical scholarship, concerned with fragments of Greek and Latin texts, is the mainstay of this journal.

909 **Oncology: international journal of cancer research and treatment.**
Basel [etc.]: S. Karger, 1948- . bimonthly; ca. 70p.

One of a series of specialized medical journals with research papers by an international cast of medical scientists, published by the international medical publishing firm of Karger. It also features book reviews.

910 **Revue Suisse. Schweiz = Suisse = Svizzera = Svizra = Switzerland.**
Zurich: Swiss National Tourist Office, 1927- . monthly; circulation 23,200; ca. 80p.

This multilingual magazine is sponsored by the Swiss National Tourist Office and several transport and tourism enterprises. Articles, illustrated with magnificent black-and-white photographs, feature Swiss regions and cultural attractions. The July 1988 issue, for example, is devoted to the wanderings, centuries ago, of the Walsers from the Matter valley in Canton Valais across alpine passes to the valleys of Canton Graubünden. Each issue has a monthly calendar of cultural and tourist events in all parts of the country.

911 **Revue suisse de zoologie. Annales de la Société suisse de zoologie et du Musée d'histoire naturelle de Genève.** (Swiss review of zoology. Annals of the Swiss zoological society and the Museum of Natural History in Geneva.)
Geneva: Sro-Kundig, 1893- . quarterly; ca. 290p.

The review contains scientific papers with photographs, drawings, and bibliographies on a wide range of zoological subjects. Most articles are in French, but there is an English table of contents.

912 **Schweizer Archiv für Heraldik.** (Swiss heraldic archive.)
Luzern, Switzerland: Schweizerische Kreditanstalt, 1887- . semi-annual; ca. 80p.

Published as a yearbook by the Swiss Heraldic Society until 1987, in 1989 the yearbook and the quarterly *Archivum heraldicum*, an 'international bulletin' which was also issued by the society, were combined into a semi-annual publication. It contains scholarly articles by Swiss and foreign authors on heraldry, coats of arms, and family escutcheons; and there are also book reviews and bibliographies, as well as communications from the affiliated societies.

913 **Schweizer Ingenieur und Architekt. Schweizerische Bauzeitung.** (Swiss Engineer and Architect: Swiss Journal of Construction.)
Zurich: Verlags-AG der akademischen Vereine, 1883- . weekly; ca. 35p. and ca. 30p. of advertisements, separately numbered.

This is the official organ of the Swiss Association of Engineers and Architects, the Society of Graduates of the Federal Institute of Technology, and of the Swiss Association of Consulting Engineers. It includes technical articles, with photographs, maps, drawings, and figures on subjects related to architecture and construction, and there are announcements of public competitions for architectural projects; organizational news; many employment listings.

914 **Schweizerische Ärztezeitung.** (Bulletin of the Swiss physicians.)
Bern: Huber, 1920- . weekly. 48p. reviews.

Weekly journal with popularly written articles concerning the schooling and postgraduate training of physicians, medical issues such as AIDS and prenatal diagnostic practices, ethical questions confronting physicians, and book reviews and announcements with a calendar of events.

915 **Schweizerische Juristen-Zeitung.** (Swiss journal for lawyers.)
Zurich: Schulthess, 1904- . semi-monthly; ca. 20p.

This is the official organ of the Swiss Bar Association. It contains professional articles on current issues in Swiss jurisprudence, reports on decisions by cantonal courts, book reviews, and announcements.

916 **Schweizerische Zeitschrift für Geschichte.** (Swiss journal of history.)
Basel: Schwabe, 1951- . quarterly; circulation 1,950; ca. 100p.

Published by the Swiss General Society of History, this journal contains scholarly articles in German, French, and occasionally Italian on all epochs of Swiss history; there are also numerous book reviews and notes.

917 **Schweizerische Zeitschrift für Soziologie.** (Swiss journal for sociology.)
Montreux, Switzerland: Imprimerie Corbaz, 1975- . 3 times per year. circulation 800; ca. 200p.

Published by the Swiss Society for Sociology, this journal contains articles in German or French with data on and analysis of Swiss society, reflecting the state of sociological research in Switzerland. The journal is open to all schools of sociology. There is a table of contents in English.

918 **Schweizerische Zeitschrift für Volkswirtschaft und Statistik.** (Swiss journal for political economy and statistics.)
Bern: Stämpfli, 1865- . quarterly; ca. 130p.

Published by the Swiss Society for Statistics and Political Economy, this journal contains scholarly articles and reviews. Summaries of the articles are also given in English.

919 **Schweizerisches Archiv für Volkskunde.** (Swiss archives for popular traditions.)
Basel: Schweizerische Gesellschaft für Volkskunde, 1897- . quarterly; ca. 65p.

Published by the Swiss Society for Folklore, the society which also publishes a bulletin, *Schweizer Volkskunde*, six times a year. Learned articles, often illustrated, on a wide range of subjects in the field of popular traditions and folklore are the main content of the journal.

920 **Schweizerisches Jahrbuch für internationales Recht.** (Swiss yearbook for international law.)
Zurich: Schulthess, 1944- . annual; ca. 380p.

Published by the Swiss Society for International Law, this yearly publication contains scholarly articles on international treaties and conventions, and legal questions concerning international organizations. Much space is taken up by documentation of how international public and private law is interpreted by Swiss jurists and courts. There is an extensive section of book reviews.

921 **Schweizerisches Jahrbuch für politische Wissenschaft.** (Swiss yearbook for political science.)
Bern: Haupt, 1961- . annual; ca. 350p.

The individual volumes in the series are devoted to single themes. Volume 27 (1987), for example, contains thirteen scholarly articles on elections and voting patterns. The yearbooks also contain annual bibliographies of works published in the field. The 1987 volume has 452 titles on pages 315-46.

922 **Swiss-American Historical Society Review.**
Chicago, Illinois: Erdman Schmocker, 1960- . 3 times per year; ca. 50p.

Until no. 1 of vol. 25 (February 1989) this publication carried the title *Swiss-American Historical Society Newsletter*. It features Swiss-Americans and their lives and contributions to American society and carries some reviews and Society news.

923 **Swiss business: international Swiss magazine for trade and investment.**
Zurich: Schweizerische Handelszeitung-Verlag, 1988- . bi-monthly. ca. 70p.

This illustrated magazine provides up-to-date news on Swiss industry and Swiss finance with a strong slant toward the promotion of Swiss firms and their products abroad. It has been called 'Switzerland's first and only business magazine in English'.

924 **Swiss journal of hydrology, hydrobiology, limnology, fisheries science, waste water treatment.**
Basel: Birkhäuser, 1920- . twice per year.

925 **Swiss review of world affairs: a monthly publication of the *Neue Zürcher Zeitung*.**
Zurich: Swiss review of world affairs, 1951- . monthly; circulation 4,500; 32p.

Contains articles on a wide range of topics on foreign affairs and domestic developments in foreign countries, written by correspondents of the *Neue Zürcher Zeitung* specifically for this journal with an occasional editorial from the *NZZ* and with some illustrations from that paper. The review is available worldwide by subscription.

926 **Swiss scene: news and views on Switzerland.**
Zurich: Swiss Scene Verlags AG, 1983- . 10 times per year. 64p.

An illustrated public relations magazine with regular entries such as a financial review, the investment and business scenes, tourist news, what's on in Switzerland, and a number of feature articles. Advertisements take up relatively little space. The June 1989 issue had a lengthy report on Switzerland's private clinics, 'health care à la carte', the July/August 1989 issue featured Liechtenstein in a fourteen-page article, and the September 1989 issue had an even longer segment on Swiss wines. Shorter articles in each issue praise the beauty and attraction of Swiss cities and resorts, describe the cultural life in larger cities, and sell the uniqueness of Swiss specialities.

927 **Swissair Gazette.**
Zurich: A. Vetter for Swissair. monthly; circulation 450,000; ca. 100p.

This large-sized multilingual (English, German, French) magazine is distributed free of charge aboard Swissair planes. Each issue has a theme, i.e. the Eiffel Tower (June 1988), or the port of Hamburg (May 1989), or Visperterminen, Canton Valais (September 1989), with in-depth articles in one or the other of the three languages and unusual illustrations with captions in three languages, especially commissioned for the particular issue. About half of the space is taken up by Swissair destinations and route maps, advertisements, and tips for shopping and lodging. This is one of the classier airline magazines.

928 **Theologische Zeitschrift.** (Theological journal.)
Basel: Friedrich Reinhardt, 1945- . quarterly; ca. 95p.

Published by the theology faculty of the University of Basel, this journal includes scholarly articles on theological subjects from early Christendom to the present. It also features reviews.

929 **Werk, Bauen & Wohnen.** (Production, construction and habitation.) Zurich: Werk, Bauen & Wohnen, 1914- . monthly; ca. 90p.

The official organ of the Federation of Swiss Architects and the Association of Swiss Interior Architects contains articles discussing current issues in the field of architecture, and technical presentations with photographs, diagrams, and architectural drawings on a main theme in each issue. There is also a calendar of events, and announcements of symposia and architectural competitions.

930 **Zeitschrift für Schweizerisches Recht.** (Journal for Swiss law.) Basel: Helbing & Lichtenhahn, 1852- . 10 times per year. 120-150p.

This journal for the public and private law of Switzerland contains scholarly articles on various aspects of the law and reviews of professional publications.

Reference Books

Biographical dictionaries

931 **Schweizerisches Zeitgenossen-Lexikon.** (Swiss lexicon of contemporaries.)
Edited by Hermann Aellen. Bern; Leipzig: Gotthelf, 1932. 2nd ed. 1032p.

The lexicon lists alphabetically about 3,000 Swiss and foreigners who lived in Switzerland in the early 1930s with brief biographical notices in telegram style in the respective mother tongue – entries are based on information furnished by the individuals included, and many have detailed bibliographies. This is a kind of *Who's who in Switzerland*, but dating from twenty years before that publication reached Switzerland.

932 **Neue Schweizer Biographie.** (New Swiss biography.)
Edited by Albert Bruckner. Basel: Berichthaus, 1938-42. 1 vol. and 1 suppl. 723p.

About 5,500 Swiss and Liechtensteiners prominent during 1938 to 1941 are listed. The short biographical entries in the respective mother tongue (and often with a photograph) are based on information provided by the persons included. They also provide summary bibliographical information. The supplement has a complete index.

933 **Die 24 Nobel-Preise der Schweiz.** (Switzerland's 24 Nobel prizes.)
Alexander Dées de Sterio. Rorschach, Switzerland: Nebelspalter, 1982. 135p. bibliog.

This slim book presents the men and organizations in Switzerland who received Nobel prizes from 1901 to 1982. Three Swiss citizens, among them Henry Dunant, and nine international organizations based in Switzerland, among them the International Committee of the Red Cross (three times), received the Nobel peace prize. Two, Carl

Spitteler and Hermann Hesse, received the Nobel prize for literature, and twelve for physics, chemistry, physiology, and medicine. The individual recipients and their achievements are briefly described. Most of the recipients of science Nobel prizes were born abroad, as was Hesse, but did their research and achieved their successes in Switzerland. There are some illustrations.

934 **Persönlichkeiten Europas: Schweiz.** (Personalities of Europe: Switzerland.)
Stansstad, Switzerland; Luzern: Iatas, 1974. [n.p.].

A committee selected the eight hundred persons included in this volume for their achievements, and spanning various areas of general interest. The curriculum vitae of each is provided in a text that is based on personal interviews and careful documentation, and for each there is also a photograph with his or her signature. Male personalities from the political and economic life of the country predominate, while representatives from science and culture are less well represented. The volume offers much interesting information, but still gives the impression of haphazardness in its selection of the subjects. It is certainly dated: the early 1970s seem to be far removed from the late 1980s.

935 **Biographisches Lexikon verstorbener Schweizer. In Memoriam.** (Biographical lexicon of deceased Swiss: in memoriam.)
Zurich: Schweizerische Industriebibliothek, 1947-69 (vols 1-6); Basel: Kirschgarten, 1975-82 (vols 7, 8).

This publication lists close to 4,000 prominent Swiss from many walks of life – officers and businessmen, professors and artists, industrialists and politicians – who died during the years preceding the publication of the respective volume. Volume 1 includes persons who died between 1936 and 1946. Almost only men are listed in these volumes; the occasional woman is a rarity. Individuals are usually given one page, with a photograph and an obituary provided by family members or friends. No criteria are given by the publishers for inclusion, and there is no discernible system in the listing. This publication is useful, but only if one happens to know the year of death of an individual and if persons related to the deceased have made the effort to have him or her included.

936 **Who's who in Switzerland including the Principality of Liechtenstein 1988-1989.**
Geneva: Nagel, 1988/89. 598p.

A biographical dictionary containing about 3,500 biographies of prominent people in and of Switzerland and the Principality of Liechtenstein. It is published biennially.

Directories

937 **Katalog der Schweizer Presse. Zeitungen, Amtsblätter, Anzeiger, Publikums-Zeitschriften.** (Catalogue of the Swiss press: newspapers, official publications, publicity sheets, journals for the public at large.)
Zurich: Verband schweizerischer Werbegesellschaften, 1939- .

The 1987 edition, with 98 pages, lists some 800 publications belonging to the categories mentioned in the title. Designed for potential advertisers, this catalogue provides information on the certified number of copies printed of each paper, its frequency of publication, its size, its volume of advertisements, and the cost of advertisements. A parallel publication does the same for 1,900 professional and technical journals.

938 **Kompass: register of industry and commerce of Switzerland and Liechtenstein.**
Zurich-Gockhausen: Kompass Schweiz, 1947- . annual.

Volume 37 (1987/88) of this publication has two parts. Part 1, with 1,780 pages, lists 32,000 industrial, commercial, financial, and transport enterprises alphabetically by locality and within the localities. Information is provided on such things as management and key personnel, range of products and commercial activity, share capital, and number of employees. Part 2, with 1,944 pages, lists the enterprises by industrial classification. It also provides the names and addresses of the official government and trade representatives of Switzerland abroad and has an index of products and services.

939 **Neues Schweizerisches Ortslexikon.** (New geographical directory of Switzerland.)
Munich; Luzern: C. J. Bucher, 1983. 23rd ed. 347p. map.

The directory lists every community in Switzerland. For localities of 100 or fewer inhabitants the names of the communes to which they belong are given. Each commune is listed with its postal code number and a series of symbols that indicate whether or not the place has a post office, railway connections and other means of public transport, its altitude above sea level, number of inhabitants, number of households, and telephone area code.

940 **Schweizer Musik-Handbuch. Informationen über Struktur und Organisation des Schweizer Musiklebens 1987/88.** (Swiss musical guide: information on the structure and organization of Swiss music life 1987/88.)
Edited by Hans Steinbeck. Zurich: Schweizerisches Musikarchiv, 1987. 226p.

The guide has two parts. The first part lists organizations, societies, and federations that are engaged in the making of serious music; professional schools and training institutions for musicians; prizes, scholarships, and competitions; music festivals; orchestras, ensembles, jazz groups, choral societies, operas, and ballets; radio and television; music publishers; record series featuring Swiss music; periodicals devoted to music; and libraries and archives that have special music collections. The second part consists of a listing of musical organizations in Switzerland by city, from Aarau to Zurich. Since this guide was first published in 1979 similar handbooks have appeared for Swiss folk and *chanson* music, jazz and rock, cabaret, mime, theatre, and puppet theatre, and cultural organizers.

941 **Swiss art guide 1984/85.**
Edited by Christian von Faber-Castell, Peter Walthert. Zurich: Peter Walthert, 1984. 430p.

This directory lists the addresses of 728 museums of all kinds with opening times and names of their directors; 1,912 art dealers, sometimes with their specialities; auctioneers; restorers; art critics; public and private promoters of culture; foundations; information centres; art trade associations; art training institutions; and insurance companies. A very thorough and useful guide to the Swiss art scene.

942 **Swiss atomic yearbook 1985/86.**
Edited by the secretariat of the Swiss Association for Atomic Energy (SVA). Bern: SVA, 1985. 96p.

This is a directory of: Swiss nuclear power plants and their holding companies with addresses and names of directors and public relations officials; federal offices and federal commissions with their staff and chief personnel, with brief explanations of the roles of these authorities; official agencies to contact for information; the federal institutes involved in reactor and nuclear research; the university institutes, hospitals, and engineering schools connected with nuclear research; and the builders, suppliers, and other entities involved in the production of atomic energy.

943 **The Swiss food and beverage industry 1988.**
Zurich: Verlag für Wirtschaftsliteratur, 1988. 98p.

This annual directory lists firms and enterprises engaged in the Swiss food and beverage industry. The enterprises are divided into twenty-four sections, according to the commodity produced: for example, dairy industries, growers of fruits and vegetables, and producers of wine and beer. Within these sections they are listed alphabetically by and within localities. There are various indexes.

Encyclopaedias

944 **Enzyklopädie der aktuellen Schweiz.** (Encyclopaedia of contemporary Switzerland.)
Edited by André Eiselé. Lausanne: Mondo, 1974-75. 4 vols. maps.

Three hundred writers, journalists, lawyers, professors, and specialists have covered every aspect of modern Swiss life in 1,000 articles. Numerous illustrations, maps, charts, and tables complement the text. The articles are written in easy-to-comprehend language. This encyclopaedia, which has also been published in French, is an outstanding source of information about modern Switzerland. Included are a thematic list of contents and an elaborate index.

945 **Encyclopédie illustrée du Pays de Vaud.** (Illustrated encyclopaedia of Canton Vaud.)
Edited by Bertil Galland. Lausanne: 24 heures, 1973-87. 12 vols.

This encyclopaedia covers its subject matter topically. Individual volumes, edited by different experts in their fields, are devoted to nature, geography, economy, history, the arts (2 vols), contemporary economic changes (2 vols), and the daily life of the Vaudois (2 vols). The contents of these volumes are thematically organized and presented in narrative form, with detailed indexes giving easy access to specific information. The twelfth volume (of 400 pages) contains a bibliography with 3,864 titles, topically organized, a subject index, and author indexes for individuals and collective efforts (*anonymes*), as well as a general index for all volumes. The encyclopedia is superbly illustrated throughout, but especially so in the twelfth volume with its numerous full-page colour plates. Similar projects have been undertaken for other Swiss cantons, among them the *Encyclopédie de Genève* (Fribourg, Switzerland: Office du livre, 1982. maps. bibliog.) By 1986 five volumes had been published; four more are planned.

946 **Illustrierte Berner Enzyklopädie: Die gültige Selbstdarstellung von Stadt und Kanton Bern in sechs Bänden.** (Illustrated Bern encyclopaedia: the definitive self-portrait of the city and canton of Bern, in six volumes.)
Edited by Peter Meyer. Bern: Büchler, 1981-87. 4 vols. bibliog.

With the publication of the fourth volume, funds ran out for this project and it was declared to be complete.. Each volume of about 200 pages is made up of self-contained essays by experts in the field. The four volumes cover (1) flora, fauna, and the geographical environment, (2) the history, (3) settlements and architecture, and (4) art and culture in Canton Bern. This work is beautifully illustrated.

947 **Historisch-Biographisches Lexikon der Schweiz.** (Historical-biographical encyclopaedia of Switzerland.)
German edition by H. Tribolet. Neuchâtel, Switzerland: Administration des Historisch-Biographischen Lexikons der Schweiz and Verlagsanstalt Victor Attinger, 1921-34. 8 vols. maps. bibliog. (Published under the patronage of the Allgemeine Geschichtsforschende Gesellschaft der Schweiz).

This dictionary, with its almost 6,000 double-columned pages in small print, and its many maps and illustrations in black-and-white and in colour, is a masterwork of large-scale cooperation among hundreds of amateur and professional historians, archaeologists, genealogists, numismatists, heraldists, economists, art historians, and folklorists. The work comes close to fulfilling its aim of providing a comprehensive inventory of the historical knowledge of its time. More than fifty years old, it still is an inexhaustible source of information on everything connected with Swiss history before 1930, especially in the areas of local history and genealogy. A similar project is being undertaken to reflect the historical knowledge of the late 20th century.

Bibliographies

Guides to bibliographies

948 **Analytische Bibliographie der Gesamtregister schweizerischer Zeitschriften.** (Analytical bibliography of the general indexes of Swiss periodicals.)
Maja Studer. Bern: Schweizerische Landesbibliothek, 1974. 125p.

In compiling this guide to bibliographical materials hidden in periodical literature, Studer analysed the tables of contents, indexes, and registers of 400 Swiss periodicals. The results are divided into twenty-two subject areas, following the organization of the Swiss catalogue of periodicals, *Schweizer Zeitschriftenverzichnis 1981-1985* (q.v.). Some 35,000 titles in the periodical holdings of the Swiss National Library were searched systematically for information pertinent to this analytical bibliography.

949 **Analytische Bibliographie der laufenden schweizerischen Bibliographien.** (Analytical bibliography of the current Swiss bibliographies.)
Régis de Courten, Josef Kamer. Bern: Schweizerische Landesbibliothek, 1972. [n.p.].

This is an inventory of close to 100 bibliographies published periodically in Switzerland, whether as independent publications or found in journals. For each bibliography there is a short description, followed by a year-by-year listing of the number of titles contained in the bibliography from the year of its initial publication to 1968. A detailed table of contents organized on the universal decimal classification system and indexes of subject matter by key words, collective authors and societies, as well as titles of bibliographies and periodicals all facilitate the use of this research tool.

950 **Bibliographies et ouvrages de référence suisses (et plus particulièrement suisses romands). Essai de bibliographie analytique.** (Swiss [and more particularly French-Swiss] bibliographies and reference works: an essay of analytical bibliography.)
Régis de Courten. Neuchâtel, Switzerland: Groupe romand de formation professionnelle de l'Association des bibliothécaires suisses, 1982. 60p.

In a first part of seventeen pages, de Courten, head of the bibliographical information service of the Swiss National Library, lists 'national bibliographies'; a second part of eleven pages presents 'special bibliographies' such as periodicals, official publications, and manuscript collections; and a third part of twenty-five pages consists of a list of 'specialized bibliographies' such as historical, biographical, and genealogical works, cantonal bibliographies of the six French-speaking cantons, and bibliographies in the fields of geography, economics, political science, law, education, popular traditions, the arts, linguistics, literature, and the sciences. There is also a listing of address books, directories, and encyclopaedias. The works are briefly described in telegram style. This typed, hectographed 'bibliographic essay' gives a good idea of and introduction to the great number of bibliographical tools that are available to researchers on Swiss subject matters.

951 **Manuel analytique et critique de bibliographie générale de l'histoire suisse.** (Analytical and critical manual of general bibliography of Swiss history.)
Jean Louis Santschy. Bern: Lang, 1961. 251p.

Bibliographies on Swiss history produced before 1959 list some 160,000 titles, including monographs, periodicals, articles in periodicals, yearbooks, and collections. Santschy describes only the general bibliographies, as distinct from cantonal or special bibliographies, dividing them into several groups and providing an often detailed critical commentary in 506 numbered sections. Among others, he analyses the *Historisch-Biographisches Lexikon der Schweiz* (q.v.), the compilations by Josef Leopold Brandstetter and Hans Barth, the *Bibliographie der Schweizerischen Landeskunde* (q.v.), to which he devotes eighty of his descriptive paragraphs, and the *Schweizer Bücherverzeichnis* (q.v.). This interesting book has a methodical table of contents and several indexes.

952 **Schweizerische Sammelbiographien. Eine annotierte Auswahlbibliographie.** (Swiss collective biographies: an annotated selective bibliography.)
Ralph Schnegg. Bern: Schweizerische Landesbibliothek, 1982. 115p.

Schnegg lists 444 independent works that contain biographical information about more than ten Swiss individuals. The titles are divided into thirteen chapters according to the profession of the subjects such as 'clergy', 'politicians, magistrates, and jurists', 'military', and 'physicians'. For each work listed, Schnegg indicates how many persons are treated and how detailed the information is. An elaborate table of contents and two indexes provide easy access to the information contained in this book.

General bibliographies and catalogues

953 **Bibliographie der Schweizerischen Landeskunde.** (Swiss National Bibliography.)
Commission centrale pour la Bibliographie suisse. Bern, 1892-1945. Reprint: Nendeln, Liechtenstein: KTO Press, 1976.

This was an attempt to compile a comprehensive bibliography of everything published in all fields of knowledge concerning Switzerland from the origins of printing to the early 20th century. Experts in the particular subject areas enlisted the collaboration of many contributors to achieve the goal of creating a bibliographical inventory. Eventually fifty-five works in eighty-two volumes were produced, containing about 300,000 titles. As an example, the volume *Fauna Helvetica* (Swiss fauna) consists of ten fascicules with several hundred pages listing titles dealing with mammals, birds, fishes, insects, etc. Some compilers also listed manuscripts in libraries and archives. The project remained unfinished, but the many parts of this immense undertaking that were completed constitute the basic bibliographies in their respective fields.

954 **Sachregister zur Bibliographie der Schweizerischen Landeskunde. Mit einem Verzeichnis aller erschienenen Faszikel der Bibliographie und dem Hinweis auf die bereits bestehenden Einzelregister.** (Subject index of the Swiss National Bibliography: with a list of all published fascicules and a reference to already existing individual indexes.)
Hugo Aebersold. Nendeln, Liechtenstein: KTO Press, 1976. 37p.

This is a most useful, even indispensable, tool for access to and use of the Swiss national bibliography (*Landeskunde*). Aebersold lists the fascicules in order of publication within their topical classification, and provides a subject matter index.

955 **Das Schweizer Buch. Bibliographisches Bulletin der Schweizerischen Landesbibliothek in Bern.** (The Swiss book: bibliographic bulletin of the Swiss National Library in Bern.)
Bern: Schweizerische Landesbibliothek, 1943- .

This semi-monthly lists in card-catalogue form *Helvetica* ('all things Swiss') received by the Swiss National Library, consisting of bibliographically independent publications in Switzerland, by Swiss, and about Switzerland, publications by Swiss government agencies, international organizations with their seat in Switzerland, and so-called *Ausland Helvetica*, or foreign publications that are related to Switzerland either by author or content. Periodicals are listed only with their first number and when they change titles. Maps form a separate group. Issue sixteen of each year contains music publications, including compositions. Materials are divided into twenty-six subject fields, within which they are listed alphabetically by author. The 15 June 1988 (1988/12), issue has 664 entries. Semi-annual and annual cumulative indexes are published. *Das Schweizer Buch* is the successor to the monthly *Bibliographisches Bulletin der Schweiz* (Bibliographical bulletin of Switzerland) (Bern, 1901-42), and the *Bibliographie und Literarische Chronik der Schweiz* (Bibliography and literary chronicle of Switzerland) (Zurich; Basel, 1871-1901).

956 **Schweizer Bücherverzeichnis.** (Swiss book catalogue.) Zurich: Schweizerischer Buchhändler- und Verleger-Verband, 1951- . (Schweizerische Nationalbibliographie. Katalog der Schweizerischen Landesbibliothek, I).

This catalogue is published at five-year intervals. It lists all books that were published in Switzerland during the time-span covered by the volume. Originally, each volume had two parts, one classified by authors and collective authors (anonyms) with an index of key words, the other by subjects. Since 1975 only the subject part is being published – the most recent issue, 1976-1980 (Zürich, 1983) has 1,262 pages. For the authors and anonyms one has to use the annual indexes provided in *Das Schweizer Buch* (q.v.).

957 **Schweizer Zeitschriftenverzeichnis 1981-1985.** (Catalogue of Swiss periodicals 1981-85.) Zurich: Schweizerischer Buchhändler- und Verleger-Verband, 1986. 248p. (Schweizerische Nationalbibliothek. Katalog der Schweizerischen Landesbiliothek Fünfjahresausgabe 1981-85).

Since 1951-55 this publication appears every five years. It lists every kind of periodical publication – including calendars, catalogues, address books, and official publications – except newspapers. The most recent volume for the years 1981-85 (1986) has 4,631 entries of titles which were published, changed, or discontinued during the time-span covered by the volume. For each title listed information is provided concerning the organization issuing or sponsoring the publication, the frequency of publication, the year it was first published, the number of the current volume, the publisher, the format, the size of the issue, and the call number at the Swiss National Library. The Swiss National Library in Bern carries 2,000 additional periodicals that are not listed in this catalogue. The consecutively numbered titles are divided into twenty-four subject areas, from 'general' (*Allgemeines*) to 'women's journals' and 'diverse', ending with 'erotica'. In between, every aspect of Swiss intellectual, cultural, political, and economic life is covered. The index lists all titles alphabetically; those that are published in several languages or are known under different names are listed several times. Anybody needing or wanting to know anything about Switzerland should find access to his or her subject of interest through this valuable publication.

958 **Bibliographie générale des ouvrages publiés ou illustrés en Suisse et à l'étranger de 1475 à 1914 par des écrivains et des artistes suisses.** (General bibliography of the works published or illustrated in Switzerland or abroad from 1475 to 1914 by Swiss writers and artists.) Frédéric Charles Lonchamp. Paris; Lausanne, Switzerland: Librairie des bibliophiles, 1923. 500p.

Lonchamp lists 3,376 illustrated books, and typographically or textually noteworthy prints. Works were chosen for inclusion because of their illustrations consisting of engravings, lithographs, caricatures, etc. They include incunabula, important proto-typographs, original imprints, and first editions, and are annotated with bibliographical information and descriptions of their illustrations. Twelve synoptic tables, organized alphabetically or chronologically, list the works according to place and date of publication, and categories and types of publication. There are two indexes, by authors and artists, and by titles.

Specialized bibliographies

959 **Bibliographia scientiae naturalis Helvetica. Das Schrifttum zur schweizerischen Landeskunde aus den Bereichen der Naturwissenschaften, der Landbau- und der Forstwirtschaften sowie der Geographie.** (Swiss natural sciences bibliography: publications concerning Switzerland from the fields of the natural, agricultural, and forestry sciences as well as geography.)
Bern: Schweizerische Landesbibliothek, 1927- .

Annual issues begin with coverage for the year 1925. Until 1969 the bibliographies also included the 'exact sciences'. Volume 62, for the year 1986, published in 1987, has 310 pages with 3,399 entries from about 600 Swiss periodicals. There are some titles of independent works and maps, but most of the entries are articles in the fields of the natural sciences, agriculture, forestry, and geography. Geographical, subject, and author indexes are included.

960 **Bibliographie der Schweizer Geschichte.** (Bibliography of Swiss history.)
Bern: Eidgenössische Drucksachen- und Materialzentrale, 1913- .

This bibliography is published annually by the Swiss National Library. The 1985 volume, published in 1987, has 230 pages with 2,326 entries, consisting mostly of articles on Swiss history from some 1,000 Swiss and foreign journals. A relatively brief chronological section is followed by a much longer part organized according to subject matter, for example, local history and economic history.

961 **Bibliographie der Schweizer Presse.** (Bibliography of the Swiss press.)
Edited by Fritz Blaser. Basel: Birkhäuser, 1956-58. 2 vols. 1441p.

This is the basic inventory of Swiss newspapers published up to 1955, but the work also lists periodicals up to 1803. Some 7,000 titles in alphabetical order are carefully described with subtitles, changes in titles, preceding and succeeding publications, dates of publication, publishers, editors, political orientation, bibliography, and libraries where they can be found. Indexes list the titles according to first date of publication (1597[!] to 1958), by canton and locality, and by country for the émigré and foreign press.

962 **Bibliographie der schweizerischen Amtsdruckschriften.** (Bibliography of Swiss government publications.)
Bern: Schweizerische Landesbibliothek, 1946- . annual.

Since 1985 this bibliography is no longer in print, but available only in hectographed, bound volumes. The 1987 volume has 154 pages with 1,438 entries. It lists the official publications of the branches and institutions of the federal government, intercantonal bodies such as the conference of the cantonal directors of education, the cantons, and the communes. There is only one index of place, subject matter, office, and author.

963 **Bibliographie des schweizerischen Rechts.** (Bibliography of Swiss law.) Basel: Helbing & Lichtenhahn, 1946- . annual.

This work is published as a supplement to the *Zeitschrift für Schweizerisches Recht* (q.v.) (Journal for Swiss law). The 1986 issue lists 1,165 books and articles related to legal questions from some forty Swiss periodicals. The detailed table of contents has sections on subjects from history of law to all branches of law, judges and court, law decisions, and periodicals and yearbooks.

964 **Bibliographie zur Schweizer Kunst; Bibliographie zur Denkmalpflege.** (Bibliography on Swiss art; bibliography on the care of cultural assets.) Zurich: Institut für Denkmalpflege, Eidgenössische Technische Hochschule Zurich, 1979- . annual.

Volume 8, 1985/86, has 462 pages with 4,697 entries from almost 800 journals from all over the world. The bibliography on Swiss art covers (in 260 pages) the whole range of artistic endeavours from architecture and the fine arts to applied and decorative arts, archaeology, folk art, museums, and exhibitions. The bibliography on the conservation of Swiss cultural assets has 92 pages and includes sections on gardens, cemeteries, old towns, architecture, industrial architecture, archaeology, painting on glass, books and plastic, applied and decorative arts, furniture, paper, textiles, photography, films, audio tracks, museums, and collections. A combined index gives access to this amazing accumulation of titles.

965 **Bibliography on foreign and comparative law.** Charles Szladits. New York: Columbia University in the City of New York, Parker School Studies in Foreign and Comparative Law, 1955.

Lists all books, articles, and translations in English of works on Swiss law from 1790 to 1953.

966 **Guide to foreign language legal materials: French, German, Swiss.** Charles Szladits. New York: Oceana Publications, 1959. 599p. (Columbia University in the City of New York, Parker School Studies in Foreign and Comparative Law.)

Pages 333 to 507 of this book deal with Swiss law. Szladits provides a thorough introduction to Swiss law with useful translations or explanations of all Swiss terms encountered in the text. In a first part, 'sources of law', he discusses the constitutional bases of the legal system, the organization of the courts, enacted law, customary law, case law, and auxiliary sources of law. The second part, 'repositories of the law', provides access to the vast literature on Swiss law through the analysis of bibliographies, legislative materials and commentaries, and doctrinal writings. The work which is in the form of an annotated bibliography clearly fulfils its objective of providing 'American lawyers with the tools necessary in pursuing the study of comparative and foreign law'.

967 **Jahresverzeichnis der schweizerischen Hochschulschriften.** (Annual list of Swiss university publications.) Basel: Universitätsbibliothek, 1897- .

The 1985 volume, published in 1987, with 251 pages, lists 2,062 dissertations, habilitation monographs, and inaugural lectures generated in the eleven institutions of higher learning of Switzerland. There is a table of contents by university and faculties within the university, and there is an alphabetical index of authors, but a subject index is sorely missing.

968 **Law bibliography.**
Zurich: Studio Verlag, 1977- . annual. 2 vols.

Volume 1 (233 pages) of the 1982 edition of this work deals with Switzerland, while volume 2 (176 pages) deals with Austria and Liechtenstein. The Switzerland volume has 639 entries, all independent works of print and non-print materials, published commercially or not. The entire scope of law is covered in what amounts to a national bibliography. In addition to the bibliographical data, each entry also has a more or less detailed description and annotation in the language of the work listed. An elaborate index contains a detailed key words register in addition to the usual categories.

969 **Schweizerische Bibliographie für Statistik und Volkswirtschaft.** (Swiss bibliography for statistics and public economy.)
Bern: Stämpfli, 1937- . biannual.

Published by the Swiss Society for Statistics and Pubic Economy and the Federal Office for Statistics, this work covers some 500 periodicals from all over the world. The 1983/84 volume, published in 1986, has 421 pages with some 8,000 entries, organized according to the international decimal classification system. Sixty per cent of the entries are journal articles, predominantly from the public economy area. There are author and subject indexes.

970 **Schweizerische Bibliographie zur politischen Wissenschaft.** (Swiss political science bibliography.)
Lausanne; Bern, 1959-72. Since 1972 in *Schweizerisches Jahrbuch für politische Wissenschaft* (q.v.).

Volume 27 (1987), p. 315-46, lists 452 titles of books, chapters of books, and journal articles by Swiss political scientists, about Switzerland, or published in Switzerland. There is no index, only a rudimentary table of contents.

971 **Schweizerische pädagogische Bibliographie.** (Swiss pedagogical bibliography.)
Geneva: Schweizerische Dokumentationsstelle für Schul- und Bildungsfragen, 1968- . annual.

The 1986 volume has 185 pages. It lists monographs, an extensive selection of articles from some 160 Swiss periodicals, mostly pedagogical, as well as the more important federal and cantonal legislation concerning schools and education, and some articles from daily and weekly newspapers. The detailed table of contents is the only avenue of access to the materials in this bibliography, for the index lists only authors.

972 **Switzerland: selected publications about Switzerland written in English: a bibliography.**
Beatrice von Coburg. Bern: Swiss National Library, Information Department, 1972. 58p.

This bibliography consists of 543 titles of works published on Switzerland in English up to 1972. In areas such as travel descriptions, tourism, and writings on Swiss landscape von Coburg readily found titles, but areas such as the natural sciences yielded little in the way of monographs, and therefore some articles were included to fill the gap. The entries are grouped under nine headings: generalities; philosophy; psychology; church; social sciences; nature and natural sciences; art; literature; history. An index of authors and persons at the end of the booklet makes for easy reference. The entries under 'generalities' cover a broad spectrum of Swiss life from topics concerning government to accounts by foreign travellers; albums and maps are also included.

973 **The economies of the German-speaking countries of Europe: a selective bibliography.**
Margrit B. Krewson. Washington, DC: Library of Congress, 1986. 98p.

This selective bibliography lists titles of books dealing with the economies of East and West Germany, Austria, Switzerland, and Liechtenstein that, presumably, can be found in the collections of the Library of Congress in Washington, DC. There are some seventy-five titles for Switzerland under the subheadings 'economic history', 'economic conditions and policy', and 'economic forecasting'. Almost everything listed is in German, and entries are not annotated. Krewson's curious statements in the introduction that 'Switzerland's is the smallest of the economies included in this bibliography, with the exception of Liechtenstein', and that 'Switzerland is less an industrial state than a center of finance and commerce' do not inspire confidence in the rest of her work.

974 **The German-speaking countries of Europe: a selective bibliography.**
Margrit B. Krewson. Washington, DC: Library of Congress, 1985. 121p.

Ninety-one titles in this bibliography 'cover' Switzerland, all with publication dates in the 1970s and 1980s, most of them in German, with a sprinkling in English. The selection of titles seems to be haphazard. One hopes that the holdings of the Library of Congress are stronger than Krewson's compilation indicates.

Indexes

There follow three separate indexes: authors (personal and corporate); titles; and subjects. Title entries are italicized and refer either to the main titles, or to other works cited in the annotations. The numbers refer to bibliographical entry rather than page numbers. Individual index entries are arranged in alphabetical sequence.

Index of Authors

C

D

E

F

I

J

K

L

M

T

U

V

W

Z

Index of Titles

D

E

F

G

I

N

O

P

Q

R

S

T

U

V

W

Y

Z

Index of Subjects

C

D

H

I

J

M

N

Q

R

T

U

V

W

Map of Switzerland

This map shows the more important towns and other features.

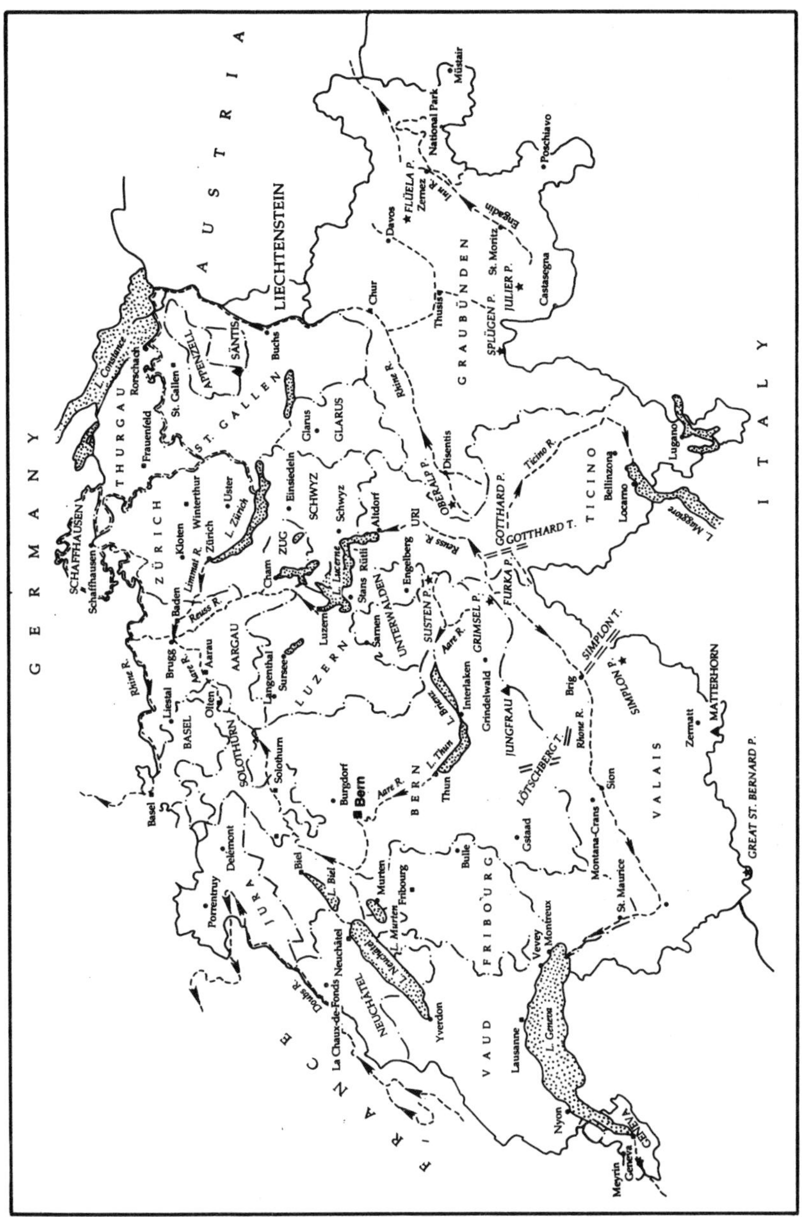